Bangladesh's Macroeconomic Policy

"This book fills in important lacuna in economic research on Bangladesh by bringing together for the first time serious analytical work on macroeconomic issues facing the country. The authors are well-known authorities in their respective fields, and their work is of uniformly high standard, informed by both rigorous theory and cutting-edge empirical methodology. The book should prove an invaluable resource to researchers and policy-makers both in Bangladesh and elsewhere in the developing world."

—Siddiqur Rahman Osmani, *Professor of Economics, Ulster University, UK*

"The book gives ideas on how macro policies in Bangladesh passed through various phases with different challenges. The performance of the economy of Bangladesh has been captured in the array of essays incorporated in the book. The most significant aspect of the book is that the papers are written by independent professionals from outside the realm of policy makers and regulators. The book will, therefore, be useful for all."

—Salehuddin Ahmed, *former Governor, Bangladesh Bank*

Monzur Hossain
Editor

Bangladesh's Macroeconomic Policy

Trends, Determinants and Impact

palgrave
macmillan

Editor
Monzur Hossain
Bangladesh Institute of Development Studies (BIDS)
Dhaka, Bangladesh

ISBN 978-981-15-1243-8 ISBN 978-981-15-1244-5 (eBook)
https://doi.org/10.1007/978-981-15-1244-5

Cover design: eStudio Calamar

This Palgrave Macmillan imprint is published by the registered company Springer Nature Singapore Pte Ltd.
The registered company address is: 152 Beach Road, #21-01/04 Gateway East, Singapore 189721, Singapore

Preface

This book attempts to provide a deeper insight into macroeconomic policies and practices that have been pursued in Bangladesh since her independence in 1971. The book consists of research papers written by reputed researchers on issues, pertaining to current macroeconomic policy debates and challenges in Bangladesh. This book, to the best of my knowledge, is the first of its kind in Bangladesh based on macroeconomic topics researched earnestly and, therefore, is expected to be welcomed by a wide array of readers. The book includes empirical research papers that evaluate various macroeconomic policies and reflect on a future direction under four themes: (i) macroeconomic policy, growth and poverty; (ii) monetary and fiscal policy; (iii) international trade and finance; and (iv) finance and growth. A total of 17 chapters are included in the book that analyze trends, determinants and impact of various macroeconomic indicators in the context of policy shifts.

The book has been organized thematically. Part I of the edited volume consists of four chapters on macroeconomic policies and performances linking with growth and poverty reduction strategies. Chapter 1 of the book, written by Monzur Hossain, provides an overview of the macroeconomic performance of the country, challenges of growth and future growth potential, public expenditures and resource mobilization strategies along with investment and financing requirements for higher growth linking findings of various chapters of the book. It also highlights why macroeconomic policies are important for poverty reduction. The analysis underscored the need for complementarity of monetary and fiscal policies, integrated financing strategy, reforms in institutions and capacity building of revenue mobilizations for embarking into higher growth trajectories.

Chapters 2 and 3 analyze the inflation dynamics in Bangladesh. Chapter 2, written by Monzur Hossain and Mustafa K. Mujeri, and Chap. 3, written by Mustafa K. Mujeri, Monzur Hossain and Tahreen T. Chowdhury, analyze the pattern, nature and consequences of inflation and its interface with wage pattern in Bangladesh. In the backdrop of rising inflation, it is important for the policy makers to know which types of households are more affected by rising inflation and what measures can be adopted to redress their disadvantages, at least partially. The persistence of inflation and inflationary expectations over a sustained period underscores the need for a fresh look at the pattern of inflation faced by various groups of households, particularly to understand how different groups could cope with sustained inflation in terms of their consumption behavior as well as earning strategies. In terms of the nature of recent inflationary episodes in Bangladesh, particularly with a dominant role of food inflation, the effect of rising food prices might differ across households based on the share of food consumption in their consumption baskets. Therefore, Chap. 2 investigates the inflationary impact on two specific groups of households—day labor and fixed income with four categories of each, such as poor, lower-middle income, upper-middle income and high income—as well as shows how these groups can adjust to higher levels of inflation. In addition to estimating consumer price indexes (CPIs) for different household groups, Chap. 3 examines the wage-inflation dynamics of different income groups and assesses how their consumption and welfare are affected by the inflation-wage dynamics.

Chapter 4, written by Monzur Hossain, Mahbubur Rahman and Md. Atiqur Rahman, evaluates the impact of energy price adjustments under an economy-wide macroeconometric model. Considering the increasing burden of subsidies and fiscal imbalances, the government has made several rounds of energy price revisions in recent years. This has led to sharp reactions among various quarters on its possible consequences on the economy. While an upward energy price revision is apparently inflationary from the consumer and producer perspective, allocative efficiency and diminishing fiscal burden could have an offsetting effect on the price level. Therefore, a partial analysis may not be appropriate to gauge the proper impact of energy prices on various economic indicators. From these concerns, this study assesses the impact of energy price adjustments under a macroeconometric modeling framework.

Part II comprises four chapters on fiscal and monetary policy aspects of Bangladesh. Chapter 5, penned by Monzur Hossain and Md. Wahid

Ferdous Ibon, assesses the effectiveness of monetary policy in Bangladesh in the light of its formulation, efficacy in demand management and growth potentials. Chapter 6 reviews the public expenditures in Bangladesh over a reasonable period and highlights the pros and cons of cyclicality of fiscal policies in Bangladesh. In this chapter, Zahid Hussain and Monzur Hossain assess that while Bangladesh is not at risk of debt distress over the medium to long term, there remain some pockets of vulnerability such as contingent liabilities which might exert pressure on the fiscal stance, particularly those from state-owned financial and non-financial enterprises. In Chap. 7, Selim Raihan and Iffat Anjum assess the impact of fiscal policy on private investment and growth. Using Vector Error correction model specifications, they identify that there is a positive and significant long-run causal relationship between real gross domestic product (GDP) growth and government expenditures, as well as between real GDP growth and tax revenue. In Chap. 8, Naoyuki Yoshino and others suggested an innovative idea of spillover revenue-sharing approach to attract private investors in financing public infrastructures. Their proposed method, though needs an implementable modality, is expected to increase rate of return for private investors, which can open up a new window for public-private partnerships.

Part III consists of six chapters related to trade policies and pattern, exchange rate management and financial flows. Chapter 9, written by Monzur Hossain, reviews trade policies, patterns and potentials in Bangladesh since her independence in 1971. This chapter analyzes various trade liberalization policies implemented in Bangladesh in phases and examines how these policies have contributed to overall trade performances. In Chap. 10, Monzur Hossain and Narayan Chandra Nath analyze comparative advantages of Bangladeshi products and evolving markets and, within that context, highlight the issues that may be addressed in the short-to-medium-term period to harness trade potentials.

Chapter 11, penned by Monzur Hossain and Mansur Ahmed, provides an assessment of exchange rate management in Bangladesh in the context of adoption of floating regime in 2003. This study analyzes exchange rate policies in Bangladesh covering pre and post-floating regimes and provides a discussion on alternative policy options. The study examines the *de facto* exchange rate regime and assesses various aspects of the exchange rate management including market interventions and its extent, overvaluation, and so forth. Finally, the chapter draws some pragmatic policy recommendations for exchange rate management in Bangladesh.

Chapter 12, written by Monzur Hossain, identifies the determinants of capital flows to least developed countries. The study analyzes official development assistance (ODA) and foreign direct investment (FDI) flows to 49 least developed countries (LDCs) and assesses the persistency of the different types of flows in different geographic regions. The results indicate that capital flows to the LDCs, particularly FDI and external debt, are associated with various factors, such as macroeconomic stability, financial sector development, trade openness, natural resource abundance and political environment. However, the determinants of capital flows vary significantly across regions. While FDIs are of a natural resource-seeking type in Africa, it is mostly efficiency-seeking type in Asia. The results suggest for appropriate policies aimed at improving macroeconomic and financial environments along with political stability in order to ensure more capital flows to the LDCs.

Chapter 13, written by Sultan Hafeez Rahman and Monzur Hossain, evaluates various aspects related to aid effectiveness in Bangladesh. The chapter assesses the role of aid in Bangladesh in terms of four aspects of the economy: savings and investment, balance of payment support, fiscal stability and social sector development. The overall effectiveness of aid has been evaluated here in terms of the resultant improved economic performance and subsequent declining importance of aid.

In Chap. 14, Shubhasish Barua and Farhana Rafiq examine the macroeconomic determinants of international remittances and its impact on economic growth. Using a panel data of remittance flows from 12 major host countries to Bangladesh over the 2005–2017 period, this chapter examines the role of macroeconomic factors and financial sector development in Bangladesh in determining the flows of remittances. They find that while the effect of income differential between the host countries and Bangladesh is statistically insignificant, financial sector development played a positive role in increasing remittance flows through increasing access to financial services in Bangladesh. They have also found that there is a positive long-run relationship between remittances and GDP, which highlights the importance of remittances for economic development in Bangladesh.

Part IV comprises three chapters that deal with issues related to finance and growth nexus in Bangladesh. Chapter 15, written by Monzur Hossain, provides an overview of the current state of the financial sector, its performance, liberalization policies undertaken so far and its consequences and further development needs.

In Chap. 16, Baqui Khalily highlights the role of microfinance in sustainable development and economic growth in Bangladesh. In Bangladesh, microfinance institutions (MFIs) contributed to around 43 percent of the households' access to financial services, which might have impact on poverty reduction and food security as well as on economic growth. He argues that due to expanded outreach of the MFIs, the credit market is now uniquely divided between banks and MFIs in Bangladesh.

In Chap. 17, Monzur Hossain reviews the current structure of Bangladesh's capital market, and its role in long-term investment financing. This chapter highlights that absence of adequate number of institutional investors and underdeveloped secondary bond market are major impediments to the capital market to meet the long-term financing needs of the country. Therefore, a set of recommendations is made in this chapter to strengthen the capital market in Bangladesh.

Dhaka, Bangladesh Monzur Hossain

Acknowledgments

This book compiles various research works on Bangladesh's macroeconomic policy conducted during the last ten years with fund support from various donor agencies and BIDS research endowment fund. Some of the papers were published as working papers and book chapters, and a few were published as journal articles, particularly in the journal *Bangladesh Development Studies.* These papers are added to this edited volume in order to make this book a comprehensive one in the area of Bangladesh's macroeconomic policy. In this context, I thank the respective institutions, such as Bangladesh Institute of Development Studies, Asian Development Bank Institute and Bangladesh Institute of Bank Management for providing necessary permissions to partially or fully reproduce those articles. It is, therefore, relevant to mention that though some data and results in some papers appear to be somewhat older, the relevance, context and application of methods are still valid and useful for policy analysis. The contributors have tried their best to update the data and issues as much as possible. Though I have contributed in most of the chapters, it would not have been possible to prepare those manuscripts without the contributions from the co-authors. I, therefore, thank all the contributors for their valuable contributions which has made this book a success.

I thank KAS Murshid, Wahiduddin Mahmud, Siddiqur Rahman Osmani, Mohiuddin Alamgir, Salehuddin Ahmed, Naoyuki Yoshino, Atiur Rahman and other colleagues for their inspiration and encouragement for this book. I thank the anonymous referees for their valuable suggestions on the manuscripts of this book. I also thank Sandeep Kaur, the publishing editor of the book, for her continuous support and cooperation. Research assistance provided by Marjan Hossain, M.B. Zaman and others are duly acknowledged. I also thank Md. Mohin Uddin Mizan and Farah Nusrat for their excellent copy-editing service.

Dhaka, Bangladesh Monzur Hossain

Contents

Contributors

Mansur Ahmed The World Bank, Washington, DC, USA

Iffat Anjum South Asian Network on Economic Modeling (SANEM), Dhaka, Bangladesh

M. A. Baqui Khalily Department of Finance, University of Dhaka, Dhaka, Bangladesh
Institute of Inclusive Finance and Development (InM), Dhaka, Bangladesh
Department of Business Administration, University of Asia Pacific, Dhaka, Bangladesh

Shubhasish Barua Department of Development Studies, University of Dhaka, Dhaka, Bangladesh

Tahreen T. Chowdhury Bangladesh Institute of Development Studies (BIDS), Dhaka, Bangladesh

N. Hendriyetty Asian Development Bank Institute (ADBI), Tokyo, Japan

Monzur Hossain Bangladesh Institute of Development Studies (BIDS), Dhaka, Bangladesh

Zahid Hussain The World Bank, Dhaka, Bangladesh

Md. Wahid Ferdous Ibon Department of Economics, University of Dhaka, Dhaka, Bangladesh

Solani Lakhia Asian Development Bank Institute (ADBI), Tokyo, Japan

Mustafa K. Mujeri Institute for Inclusive Finance and Development (InM), Dhaka, Bangladesh

Narayan Chandra Nath Bangladesh Institute of Development Studies (BIDS), Dhaka, Bangladesh

Farhana Rafiq Department of Economics, American International University-Bangladesh, Dhaka, Bangladesh

Sultan Hafeez Rahman BRAC Institute of Governance and Development, BRAC University, Dhaka, Bangladesh

Mahbubur Rahman University of Portsmouth, Portsmouth, UK
Bangladesh Institute of Development Studies (BIDS), Dhaka, Bangladesh

Md. Atiqur Rahman Bangladesh Institute of Development Studies (BIDS), Dhaka, Bangladesh
University of New Mexico, Albuquerque, NM, USA

Selim Raihan Department of Economics, University of Dhaka, Dhaka, Bangladesh
South Asian Network on Economic Modeling (SANEM), Dhaka, Bangladesh

Naoyuki Yoshino Asian Development Bank Institute (ADBI), Tokyo, Japan
Keio University, Tokyo, Japan

Abbreviations

7FYP	Seventh Five-Year Plan
ADB	Asian Development Bank
ADF	Augmented Dickey–Fuller Test
AIC	Akaike Information Criterion
ASEAN	The Association of Southeast Asian Nations
ATM	Automated Teller Machine
BARI	Bangladesh Agriculture Research Institute
BBS	Bangladesh Bureau of Statistics
BCSIR	Bangladesh Council for Scientific and Industrial Research
BEER	Behavioral Equilibrium Exchange Rate
BER	Bangladesh Economic Review
BERC	Bangladesh Energy Regulatory Commission
BICM	Bangladesh Institute of Capital Market
BIDS	Bangladesh Institute of Development Studies
BKB	Bangladesh Krishi Bank
BMET	Bureau of Manpower, Employment and Training
BO	Beneficiary Owner
BOT	Build-Operate-Transfer
BPoA	Brussels Program of Action
BRCA	Balassa Revealed Comparative Advantage
BSEC	Bangladesh Security Exchange Commission
BSTI	Bangladesh Standard and Testing Institution
CAB	Current Account Balance
CAGR	Compound Annual Growth Rate
CBN	Cost of Basic Needs
CBPR	Central Bank Policy Rate
CDF	Credit and Development Forum

CDS	Central Depository System
CGE	Computable General Equilibrium
CMDP 2	Second Capital Market Development Program
CMDP 3	Third Capital Market Development Program
CPI	Consumer Price Index
CRAR	Capital to Risk (Weighted) Asset Ratio
CRR	Cash Reserve Requirement
CRR	Cash Reserve Ratio
CSE	Chittagong Stock Exchange
CSR	Corporate Social Responsibility
CV	Coefficient of Variation
DAC	Development Assistance Committee
DAM	Department of Agricultural Marketing
DGEN	DSE General Index
DOT	Direction of Trade Statistics
DOT	Directly Observed Therapy (see Chap. 13)
DPI	Data on Political Indices
DPP	Development Project Proposal
DSA	Debt Sustainability Analysis
DSE	Dhaka Stock Exchange
DSES	DSE Shariah Index
DSEX	Dhaka Stock Exchange Broad Index
ECF	Extended Credit Facility
ECGS	Export Credit Guarantee Scheme
ECM	Error Correction Model
ECT	Error Correction Term
EIEC	Executive Index of Electoral Competitiveness
EMP	Exchange Market Pressure
EPB	Export Promotion Bureau
EPZ	Export Processing Zone
ERD	Economic Relations Division
ESAF	Enhanced Structural Adjustment Facility
EU	The European Union
EV	Equivalent Variation
FAS	Financial Access Survey
FCB	Foreign Commercial Bank
FDI	Foreign Direct Investment
FEER	Fundamental Equilibrium Exchange Rate
FOB	Freight On Board
FPE	Final Prediction Error
FRA	Financial Reporting Act
FRC	Financial Reporting Council

FSRP	Financial Sector Reform Program
GCC	Gulf Cooperation Council
GCF	Gross Capital Formation
GDP	Gross Domestic Product
GFCF	Gross Fixed Capital Formation
GNP	Gross National Product
GPF	General Provident Fund
GSI	Global Subsidies Initiative
GSI	Geographic Specialization Index
HAI	Human Assets Index
HHI	Herfindahl-Hirschman Index
HIES	Household Income and Expenditure Survey
HIV	Human Immunodeficiency Virus
HQIC	Hannan-Quinn Information Criterion
HS	Harmonized Commodity Description and Coding Systems
IC	Indicator of Crisis
ICT	Information and Communication Technology
IDA	International Development Association
IDCOL	Infrastructure Development Company Ltd
IFI	International Financial Institution
IMF	International Monetary Fund
InM	Institute for Inclusive Finance and Development
IPO	Initial Public Offering
IPoA	Istanbul Program of Action
IRF	Impulse Response Function
IT	Information Technology
LDC	Least Developed Country
LIEC	Legislative Index of Electoral Competitiveness
LPL	Lower Poverty Line
LR	Log Ratio
MDG	Millennium Development Goal
ME	Management Efficiency
MFI	Microfinance Institution
MFN	Most-Favored Nation
MFS	Mobile Financial Service
MoF	Ministry of Finance
MPE	Mean Percentage Error
MPI	Multi-Dimensional Poverty Index
MPS	Monetary Policy Statement
MRA	Microcredit Regulatory Authority
MSME	Micro, Small and Medium Enterprise
MTO	Money Transfer Operator

NBFI	Non-Bank Financial Institution
NBR	National Board of Revenue
NER	Nominal Exchange Rate
NFA	Net Foreign Asset
NPL	Non-performing Loan
NSD	National Savings Directorate
NSDC	National Savings Directorate Certificate
ODA	Official Development Assistance
OE	Operating Efficiency
OECD	Organisation for Economic Co-operation and Development
OTC	Over the Counter
PCB	Private Commercial Bank
PCI	Per Capita Income
PFI	Private Financial Initiative
PFM	Public Financial Management
PKSF	Palli Karma-Sahayak Foundation
PM	Prime Minister
PNAS	Proceedings of the National Academy of Sciences of the United States of America
PP	Phillips-Perron Unit Root Test
PPI	Producer Price Index
PPP	Public-Private Partnerships
PRGF	Poverty Reduction Growth Facility
PRIME	Programmed Initiatives for Monga Eradication
PWT	Penn World Table
QR	Quantitative Restriction
R&D	Research and Development
RAKUB	Rajshahi Krishi Unnayan Bank
RCA	Revealed Comparative Advantage
RCI	Revealed Comparative Indices
RCT	Randomized Controlled Trial
REER	Real Effective Exchange Rate
REOPA	Rural Employment Opportunities for Public Assets
RER	Real Exchange Rate
RMG	Ready-made Garments
RMSPE	Root Mean Square Percentage Error
ROA	Return on Assets
ROE	Return on Equity
SAARC	South Asian Association for Regional Cooperation
SAFTA	South Asian Free Trade Arrangement
SB	Specialized Bank
SBI	Symmetric Balassa Index

SBIC	Schwarz's Bayesian Information Criterion
SD	Supplementary Duty
SDB	Specialized Development Bank
SDG	Sustainable Development Goal
SEC	Securities and Exchange Commission
SENSEX	Stock Exchange Sensitive Index
SHS	Solar Home System
SLR	Statutory Liquidity Requirement
SME	Small and Medium Enterprise
SOCB	State-Owned Commercial Bank
STSI	Standardized Trade Specialization Index
SVAR	Structural Vector Autoregression
TCL	Total Classified Loan
ToT	Terms of Trade
TPI	Trade Potential Index
TPP	Technical Project Proposal
TRI	Trade Restrictive Indices
UAE	United Arab Emirates
UK	United Kingdom
UN	United Nations
UN Comtrade	United Nations International Trade Statistics Database
UNCTAD	United Nations Conference on Trade and Development
UNDP	United Nations Development Programme
UPGP	Union Parishad Governance Project
UPL	Upper Poverty Line
UPPR	Urban Partnerships for Poverty Reduction
USA	The United States of America
VAR	Vector Autoregression
VAT	Value-Added Tax
VECM	Vector Error Correction Model
WDI	World Development Indicator
WITS	World Integrated Trade Solution
WPI	Wholesale Price Index
WRI	Wage Rate Index
WTO	World Trade Organization

List of Figures

List of Tables

List of Boxes

PART I

Macroeconomic Policy, Growth and Poverty

CHAPTER 1

Macroeconomic Policy, Economic Growth and Poverty Reduction in Bangladesh: An Overview

Monzur Hossain

1.1 Introduction

Bangladesh will celebrate her 50 years of independence in 2021. Once termed as a development "basket case", the country has now emerged as a "development surprise" with particular progress in social and development indicators (Asadullah et al. 2014). The economic growth of Bangladesh over the last two decades remains stable, and has been rising at an average rate of over 6 percent. In the last few years, the growth was over 7 percent. Poverty has halved from around 50 percent in 2000 to around 25 percent in 2016. Bangladesh has also made remarkable progress in attaining several Millennium Development Goal (MDG) targets, especially in social indicators in which the country has done markedly better than neighboring countries. Nonetheless, macroeconomic stability is thought to have played a strong role in achieving impressive economic performances. This chapter, thus, attempts to provide an overview of how macroeconomic policies contribute to impressive economic performances and poverty reduction in Bangladesh.

M. Hossain (✉)
Bangladesh Institute of Development Studies (BIDS), Dhaka, Bangladesh

M. Hossain (ed.), *Bangladesh's Macroeconomic Policy*,
https://doi.org/10.1007/978-981-15-1244-5_1

Achieving macroeconomic stability is at the center point of macroeconomic policy making that prompts to better economic performances. Various combinations of levels of key macroeconomic variables, such as growth, inflation, fiscal deficit, current account deficit, and international reserves together could determine macroeconomic stability. As for example, while a large current account deficit, high and rising level of public debt, double-digit inflation rate and stagnant or declining GDP are the sources of instability, current account and fiscal balances consistent with low and declining debt levels, low single digits inflation and rising per capita GDP are the common indicators of macroeconomic stability. Therefore, it is important to analyze the trends and determinants, and to some extent the impact of several macroeconomic indicators on broader economic outcomes to assess the extent of macroeconomic stability a country has achieved over time.

Maintaining macroeconomic stability is crucial for facilitating private sector development that could promote higher economic growth.[1] The absence of macroeconomic stability makes the domestic macroeconomic environment less predictable, and such unpredictability affects resource allocation decisions, investment and, ultimately growth. In that situation, domestic and foreign investors are discouraged and resources are diverted elsewhere (e.g. see Ramey and Ramey 1994). Various cross-country studies confirm that growth, investment and productivity are positively correlated with macroeconomic stability (Easterly and Kraay 2000). From this perspective, analysis of the role of Bangladesh's macroeconomic policy in achieving higher economic growth and poverty reduction is very much relevant in the policy discourse, and therefore, is the context of this chapter.

Though there were waxes and wanes in macroeconomic performances in the 1970s and 1980s, afterwards Bangladesh has been able to maintain reasonable macroeconomic stability without experiencing any crisis. Such a long-term macroeconomic stability has been thought to be the key driver of the recent higher economic growth trajectories. Maintaining a viable balance of payments (BOP), a reasonable balance between fiscal revenues and expenditures, and savings and investment for quite a long time indicates that a good macroeconomic management is in place. Along with that, necessary fiscal, financial and trade liberalization measures undertaken in the 1980s and 1990s have contributed to macroeconomic stability and consequently to positive economic outcomes, though there are still

[1] Macroeconomic instability can generate *volatility* of key macroeconomic variables or predicts future volatility.

scopes for further reforms in many areas. With accelerating speed of growth of the economy, poverty reduction pace has somewhat slowed down in recent times in Bangladesh at the backdrop of rising income inequality. In order to sustain the current episodes of higher economic growth, the sources and quality of growth need to be well understood, and accordingly, measures need to be undertaken to avoid irrational economic exuberance and overheated economic activities.

While macroeconomic stability spurs growth, economic growth influences poverty, given that income inequality is restrained. There has been a strong empirical association between national per capita income and national poverty indicators. Analyzing data of 80 countries over four decades, Dollar and Kraay (2002) found that the income of the bottom one-fifth of the population rises at a similar rate of the overall growth of the economy. Further, they showed that the effect of growth on the income of the poor was indifferent between poor and rich countries. However, another study examining 143 growth episodes found that the "growth effect" dominates over the "distribution effect" (White and Anderson 2001). The findings of these studies indicate somewhat association between growth and poverty reduction, but not the causality between them. Rather, the issue can be seen in the way poverty reduction strategies are aligned with stable macroeconomic policies that are important to achieve higher growth. This is how, macroeconomic policies are related to poverty reduction.

In line with the above discussion, in Sect. 1.2 this chapter highlights the macroeconomic performance of Bangladesh over time in terms of internal and external balance and growth. Section 1.3 discusses the possible sources of the growth highlighting the role of monetary, fiscal and trade policies as well as their responses to real and financial exogenous shocks and Sect. 1.4 highlights the implications of growth on poverty reduction in the context of rising inequality. Finally, Sect. 1.5 concludes the chapter.

1.2 Macroeconomic Performances of Bangladesh

The economy of Bangladesh has been performing quite well for the last two decades with GDP growth rates of over 6 percent. The impressive performance of the economy can be seen as a result of a major shift in policy stance from a nationalized economy in the 1970s to a private-sector-led economy in the 1980s and 1990s with various reforms in the trade and financial sector. The impressive economic performance of Bangladesh is largely attributed to right policies and priorities set for sectoral, social and infrastructure development. Sound public finance remains in the forefront of demand management policies that ensure price stability through minimizing inflationary seigneuries, lower levels of distortions in the taxation structure and positive investment returns despite having relatively lower real interest rates at developing country-standard.[2]

Bangladesh has overcome many challenges since her birth in 1971. Per capita income rose to US$1430 in 2016 from under US$100 in the early 1970s, and the country has achieved food self-sufficiency by now, thanks mainly to agricultural mechanization. From a slow start in the 1970s, GDP growth rate has accelerated to above 7 percent over the decades despite natural calamities, global financial crisis and political unrest at home (Table 1.1). Bangladesh made commendable progress on several Millennium Development Goal (MDG) targets, especially in social indicators in which the country has done markedly better than neighboring comparators. Bangladesh's home-grown economic reform measures aided by foreign assistance and democratic transition are credited with impressive economic performance since the early 1990s. Major trade and financial liberalization programs were implemented as part of the structural adjustment reforms supported by the World Bank and the International Monetary Fund (IMF). Implementing current account convertibility in March 1994 and adoption of floating exchange rate system in June 2003,

Table 1.1 Growth rates of GDP and broad sectors (percent)

Years	*Total GDP*	*Agriculture*	*Industry*	*Service*
1972–1980	3.68	1.86	5.26	5.17
1980–1990	3.90	1.84	3.16	5.43
1990–2000	4.90	3.03	7.37	4.56
2001–2010	6.03	3.66	7.74	7.0
2011–2015	6.32	3.53	9.19	5.95
2016	7.11	2.79	11.09	6.25
2017	7.28	2.97	10.22	6.69

Source: Bangladesh Economic Review, Ministry of Finance, various issues

Note: Compound annual growth rates (CAGR) have been calculated for different decades, until 2015; for the remaining years, annual growth rates are reported

[2] Though interest rate structure in Bangladesh is not considered very competitive, the bank interest rate spread which has been around 5 percent for a long time induces positive investment return. The issue has been discussed elaborately in Chap. 16.

as part of exchange and trade system liberalization agreed with the IMF for its support under Enhanced Structural Adjustment Facility (ESAF) and Poverty Reduction Growth Facility (PRGF) programs respectively, created conditions for improved investments including foreign direct investment (FDI), growth and balance of payment (with both exports and imports facilitation). Besides, in the context of bilateral donor assistance, Bangladesh adopted reform policies in project management, procurement and implementation, which led to various positive development outcomes (UNDP 2010).

Domestic savings and investments were low in the 1970s before they picked up in the 1980s. Notwithstanding the level and rate of savings (domestic and national), aid always played a role in total investments (physical asset accumulation) even in the paradoxical case when national savings exceeded total investments. Without aid, investments especially public investment would have been lower, and so would growth performance (see Chaps. 6 and 13 for details). Policy shift toward privatization and promotion of the public sector started from the late 1970s, and the immediate result of the policy was a short-lived investment boom with investment in both public and private sectors growing at nearly 15 percent annually in real terms during the late 1970s to early 1980s. This was made possible mainly due to an increasing flow of foreign aid and adoption of a privatization strategy coupled with some provisions of other incentives such as highly protected markets for domestic industries.

In the early 1980s, domestic savings and the investment saw a downward trend when the external aid climate deteriorated. As a result of aid decline as well as deterioration of the country's terms of trade, the country had faced an episode of severe macroeconomic imbalances. In order to overcome such macroeconomic imbalances, major reform measures were initiated in the early 1980s. However, the beginning of the 1990s saw a more comprehensive program of macroeconomic reforms. The reforms of the 1980s and 1990s[3] helped reduce fiscal and external deficits to a

[3] The policy reforms in the 1980s included mainly the withdrawal of food and agricultural subsidies, privatization of state-owned enterprises, liberalization of interest rates and other financial obligations and withdrawal of quantitative restrictions. The reforms of the early 1990s were particularly aimed at moving toward an open economy, such as making the current account convertible, reducing import duties and removing virtually all controls on the movements of foreign private capital. In addition, on the fiscal front, value added tax (VAT) was introduced. As indicated earlier, reforms of the early 1990s led to an improvement in macroeconomic indicators. It may be relevant to point out here that the quality of reforms in the two decades may vary as the decade of the 1980s was ruled by a military government while transition to parliamentary democracy happened in the early 1990s.

sustainable level consistent with the level of aid availability. So, even with a declining share of aid as percent of gross national income (GNI), savings and investments increased (see Chap. 13).

Investment and saving rates and the growth performance, consequently, improved. The ratio of investment to GDP, which had stagnated at less than 17 percent in the 1980s, increased to about 23 percent at the end of the 1990s mainly due to increase in private investment, leaving public sector investment rate almost unchanged at around 6–7 percent of GDP. Private investment in recent years has been stagnated at around 21–23 percent of GDP, though public investment has increased to about 8 percent of GDP. Political uncertainty, poor doing business condition and infrastructure bottle-necks are some of the key reasons that restrain higher growth of private investments.

Though the economic indicators in the early 1990s saw a sharp improvement in the backdrop of donor-driven reforms, there has been a lot of criticism of such reforms which had no pre-announced target or timetable. Subsequent trend of key macroeconomic variables suggests that the apprehension about policy reforms was somewhat misplaced. The growth of GDP, which averaged 3.7 percent annually during the 1980s, increased to 4.4 percent in the first half of the 1990s and further to 5.2 percent in the second half of the 1990s. During the 2000s, the country achieved impressive economic growth, about 6 percent on average, which was thought to be the positive outcome of the reforms undertaken in the 1980s and 1990s.

1.2.1 External Sector Performance

The export-GDP ratio increased from less than 6 percent in the latter half of the 1980s to the current level of around 15 percent. With the increase in imports, the trade openness of the economy (the combined ratio of imports and exports to GDP) has increased to about 48 percent in recent years, sustaining a higher growth performance of the economy.

Until 1992, net official development assistance (ODA) was contributing significantly to Bangladesh's foreign exchange reserve buildup as it was higher than the reserve (without grant) of the country. Since 1993, foreign exchange reserve has been surpassing the ODA, with a significant contribution from overseas remittances and export earnings (see Chap. 13). Thus, ODA contributed positively to the BOP in the 1970s, 1980s and 1990s; however, its significance in maintaining a viable BOP has been diminishing since 2000 mainly because of higher remittance receipts and export earnings from the ready-made garments (RMG). Though Bangladeshi taka was made convertible to current account in 1994 under the Article VIII of the IMF Articles of Agreement, capital account has not yet been made convertible. It is now time to rethink about capital account convertibility, albeit partially, to promote foreign investments in the context of LDC graduation. Since exports are highly concentrated on one product (RMG) and remittance income is dependent on host economies, maintaining a viable BOP will be a big challenge in the coming days.

Trade balance gives an idea about dependence on foreign aid or external income other than exports of goods. It is worth noting that proportion of trade balance to GDP hovers around 7 percent in all the periods. However, import coverage ratio (coverage of import payments by export earnings) has increased significantly from about 31 percent in 1981–1985 to about 66 percent in 2006–2010, indicating that foreign aid was an important source of foreign exchange requirement to cover import payments until 1990. Thus, foreign aid has contributed in maintaining viable BOP that contributed to sustained level of economic growth (Chaps. 9 and 10).

Trade liberalization policies coupled with floating exchange rate policies contributed positively to the external sector performance. Sound macroeconomic management with stable inflation has helped Bangladesh reduce its dependency on aid; simultaneously strong foreign exchange reserve position gives a cushion against any external shock. In achieving such good progress in macroeconomic management, not only the amount of aid but also the policy prescriptions supported by multilateral agencies as part of aid package contributed significantly.

1.2.2 *Fiscal Stability*

With substantial dependence on foreign aid, during the 1980s, the fiscal deficit came down from 6.6 percent of GDP to 5.4 percent, and afterwards, in most of the years, fiscal deficit remained within 5 percent of GDP. While total government expenditure has increased from 12.5 percent in 1990 to about 16 percent in 2011, the tax-GDP ratio has increased from 6 percent to over 9 percent during the same period. With an increased level of government expenditure coupled with increased tax revenue, the direct contribution of aid in financing fiscal deficit has declined from 80 percent in 1990 to 40 percent in 2011. Net foreign financing in deficit finance was more than 75 percent before 1990, which indicates the overwhelming importance of aid in maintaining fiscal stability in that period in Bangladesh (Chaps. 6 and 13).

It is important to note here that the tax-GDP ratio in Bangladesh has been the lowest even among the South Asian Association for Regional Cooperation (SAARC) countries for quite a long time. The lower growth of tax revenue over time indicates that there was a possibility of fiscal unsustainability in the absence of foreign assistance. Though the dependence on foreign aid in financing fiscal deficit has decreased over time, the relevance of aid/ODA still remains significant in managing inter-temporal fiscal policy of the government. It is thus imperative to increase tax-GDP ratio to maintain higher growth and reduce dependence of aid/ODA on fiscal balance (Chap. 7).

The Bangladesh government has been historically allocating a large amount of subsidies to different sectors, with the energy sector being the main beneficiary of subsidies in recent times. Considering fiscal burden and distortions in the factor markets, the government needs to reduce the burden of subsidies by upward revision of energy prices, which might have little impact on inflation and growth that could be offset by other complementary measures (see Chap. 4 for details).

The fiscal imbalances always resulted in budget deficit. The financing budget deficit in Bangladesh follows a pattern that relies first on foreign grants, supplemented by non-bank borrowing and then by borrowing from banks to meet these deficits. This pattern has failed to establish a sustainable approach of deficit financing. Borrowing from national savings directorate certificate (NSDC) at a lower rate than market creates distortions in the money market as people tend to save in NSDC at a higher rate than the banks can offer. Tax revenue mobilization efforts are not up to the expected level, which forces the government to finance deficits from costly sources. Therefore, fiscal reforms are needed in the deficit financing sectors—both in borrowing and revenue mobilization contexts. Though there is no immediate risk of fiscal unsustainability as analyzed in Chap. 6, there is no room for complacence.

1.3 Economic Growth and Sources of Growth

It is widely argued that remittances, mechanization of agriculture and growth of RMG sector are the key drivers of growth in Bangladesh. Financial development over time has played a catalytic role in mobilizing remittances (see Chap. 14). Financial development has been impressive in terms of both quantity of institutions and diversity of services that facilitates efficient intermediation of financial resources and promotes growth

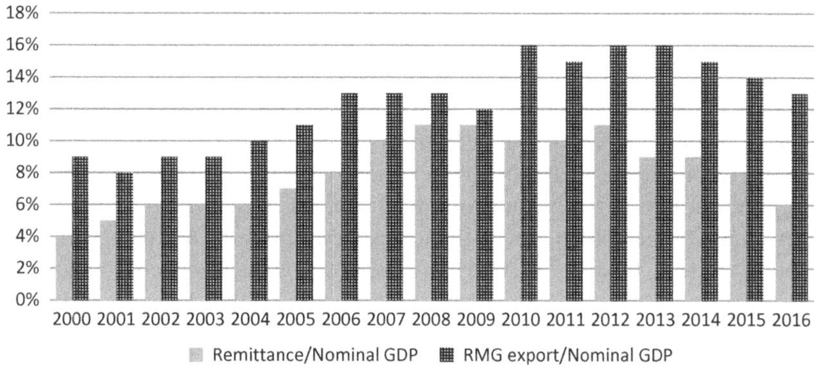

Fig. 1.1 Share of remittance and RMG exports in GDP. (Sources: BBS and Bangladesh Bank)

(Chap. 15). However, in recent years, the share of remittance and RMG export, two important sources of growth, has been declining (Fig. 1.1). A big transformation through the adoption of technologies has taken place in Bangladesh in the last two decades which is thought to be instrumental for embarking on higher growth trajectory through enhancing total factor productivity, and that has been partly making up the declining role of RMG and remittances. Mobile phone adoption is now over 90 percent: this not only facilitates communication, but also increases household welfare and women empowerment (Hossain and Samad 2017). Mobile financial services are now occupying an important place in Bangladesh economy; in 2017, 21.2 percent of the individuals have a mobile money account that facilitates remittances and increases household income and consumption (BIDS Survey 2018). Iqbal and Pabon (2018) similarly argued that the drivers of growth, perhaps, have been changing, and a structural change has occurred in the economy over time.

There is no denying that the key facilitator of higher growth of the economy is the macroeconomic stability that the country has been maintaining for a long time, particularly from 2000 onward (Table 1.2). Monetary policy, which has been accommodative but restrained to some extent, plays a good role in maintaining an acceptable level of inflation over a long period of time (see Chap. 5). A managed exchange rate policy ascertains exchange rate stability over a long time since 2003 after adopting *de jure* freely floating regime, mainly due to restricted domestic demand and lower level of connectivity with international financial and capital market (see Chap. 11). Fiscal policy, though expansionary and pro-cyclical, has been able to maintain a budget deficit within a rule-of-thumb, 5 percent of GDP, and largely fiscal sustainability has been maintained. Though public development expenditures have been increasing every year and now stands at around 8 percent of GDP, the quality of them is a big concern. However, financing development is a cause of concern as tax-to-GDP ratio, which is now at around 10 percent, remains below the international average, which is even the lowest among South Asian neighboring countries (see Chap. 7). Alternative sources of development financing need to be harnessed in the context of lowering ODA volume and tight conditions of receiving foreign loan in the backdrop of graduating from LDCs expected by 2024.

With the vision of achieving middle-income status by 2021, the government sets a target to achieve its GDP growth rate at 8 percent in the terminal year of the Seventh Five Year Plan (SFYP) in FY2020. In addition, to attain SDGs, it is imperative to increase public expenditures to various social sectors. Considering huge financing needs for implementing various development activities as postulated in the SFYP and the Sustainable Development Goals (SDGs), the government needs to intensify resource mobilization efforts both on the domestic and foreign fronts. An integrated financing approach including private, public and foreign sources needs to be adopted along with some market-based solutions for financing public infrastructure by sharing spillover tax revenues and adopting land trust approach (see Chap. 8).

1.4 Growth and Poverty Reduction

A sustainable and stable set of macroeconomic policies is the pre-requisite condition for poverty reduction.[4] A country's poverty reduction strategy should depend on a set of issues including privatization, trade liberalization, banking and financial sector reforms, labor markets, the regulatory environment and the judicial system (Ames et al. 2001). Furthermore, the strategies should aim to enhance efficiency of public investment in health, education and other priority social service sectors. In the context of reasonable macroeconomic stability and necessary reforms undertaken in the 1980s and 1990s, poverty reduction has geared up in subsequent periods (Fig. 1.2a). Access to micro finance to a large section of rural

[4] Higher inflation usually tends to hurt the poor and fixed-salary group people more than others as they cannot adjust quickly to price changes (Chaps. 2 and 3).

A. Growth and Inequality B. Poverty

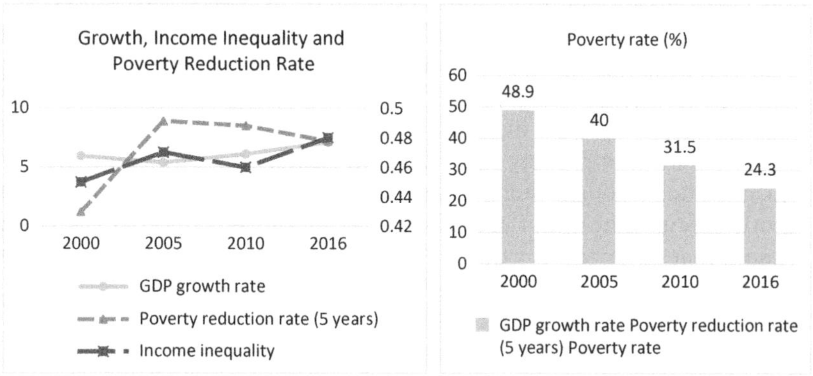

Fig. 1.2 Growth, inequality and poverty reduction. (Source: Household Income and Expenditure Survey, BBS, various years)

population has also played an important role in accelerating economic growth (See Chap. 16).

However, an unbalanced regional economic growth has led to a persistent level of economic inequality. With rising economic growth, inequality has also been rising which has slowed down the poverty reduction rate, leaving a big chunk of people below the poverty line (Fig. 1.2b). Osmani (2018) in a recent study argued that declining real wages of unskilled laborers in the face of massive rural-urban migration, occupational shifts and rising labor productivity have contributed to slowing down the pace of poverty reduction and worsening of income inequality after 2010.

Why macroeconomic stability is important for poverty reduction? Macroeconomic instability can place a heavy toll on the poor. For example, higher inflation imposes greater burden on the poor than on the rich because they tend to hold most of their financial assets in the form of cash which does not allow them to protect the real value of their incomes and assets from inflation (see Chaps. 2 and 3 for details). Moreover, inflation generally erodes the real wages and assets of the poor more than those of the non-poor. Beyond certain thresholds, inflation deters output growth, which also affects the poor who infrequently use money for economic transactions. In addition, instability might cause "hysteresis"—a phenomenon where low output growth might have a lingering negative impact on poverty through shocks to the human capital of the poor (e.g. see Duryea et al. 1999).

The impact of growth on poverty can be determined by the distributional patterns and the sectoral composition of growth. If the poor get the benefits of growth through equitable distribution of income, growth can be termed as pro-poor (Ames et al. 2001). Ravallion (1997) shows that with a more equitable distribution of income, the impact of growth on poverty will be higher. This is also supported by the current situation of Bangladesh, as the poverty reduction rate decelerates with rising income equality rate. Though there is apparent trade-off between growth and equity, a large number of empirical studies, however, rejected the claim arguing that equity in its various dimensions might be growth enhancing (See Alesina and Rodrik 1994; Deininger and Squire 1998; Perotti 1992, 1996; Persson and Tabellini 1994).

The sectoral composition of growth can have an impact on poverty. Growth in labor-intensive sectors of the economy will have a greater impact on reducing poverty than growth in other sectors. For example, various country-specific and cross-country studies showed that growth in the agricultural and tertiary sectors that are more labor-intensive has had a major effect on poverty reduction than the growth in manufacturing sector (See Datt and Ravallion 1992; Thorbecke and Jung 1996; Timmer 1997; Bourguignon and Morrisson 1998). Agricultural mechanization, growth of micro, small and medium enterprises (MSMEs) and labor-intensive RMG are the key sectoral contributors to growth in Bangladesh over time. This reinforces the case for preferential access to industrial country markets for RMG exports from Bangladesh for quite a long period. Bangladesh has been able to make necessary economic transformation by shifting focus from rural agrarian-based growth to private-sector-led growth that reduces the risks of output variability, which, in turn, contributes to decreasing poverty. However, a more diversified economy with a vibrant manufacturing sector might ensure sustainable improvement in living standards in the long run.

1.5 Conclusion

Though Bangladesh, since 2000, maintains a reasonable macroeconomic stability, still there are pockets of vulnerabilities, particularly in fiscal fronts. Having right macroeconomic policy mix in the domain of macroeconomic management allows Bangladesh to achieve a sustained higher growth in recent periods, albeit with slight rising income inequality. Hence, policy makers should strive to maintain macroeconomic stability with efforts to reducing income inequality. The important traits for macroeconomic policy encompassing fiscal, monetary and exchange rate policy would be to follow a set of defined targets of key macroeconomic indicators with broader objectives of achieving higher growth and lower poverty.

Bangladesh, like other developing countries, aims at enhancing the quality of growth by improving income distribution so that the poor get the fruits of such growth. For accelerating poverty reduction, structural and governance reforms must be accompanied with supporting policies, such as land tenure reform, changes in marginal and average tax rates, increases in pro-poor social spending, and so on. Though these issues do not exclusively fall in the domain of macroeconomics, they reinforce the point that macroeconomic policy alone is not sufficient for poverty reduction.

Further, it is necessary to avoid sectoral growth-enhancing policies that are distortionary because they might impede overall growth. Trade policy in Bangladesh, though legally binding, is based on an unpredictable set of tariff and para-tariff structures that needs to be streamlined by bringing in more reforms in tariff structure with a predictable approach. The discredited industrial policies of Bangladesh must be strengthened by incorporating a predictable set of policies and by avoiding duplications and distortions. Such policy reforms should aim to create an enabling environment and level-playing field, conducive to private sector investment and broad-based economic growth. Only then, the country can maximize the beneficial impact of sustained economic growth on poverty reduction.

Finally, a pragmatic and sustained fiscal policy is required that has to be complemented by an accommodative monetary policy. The monetary transmission channels are not responding well. So, more reforms in the financial sector would be required. Institutional reforms would be needed in modernizing financial sectors by developing and establishing futures market, bond market, and hedging options to support increased demand for investments in the backdrop of the country's march toward middle-income countries. Despite the fact that many of the macroeconomic targets of the country under different five-year plans have not been realized, either due to the global recession, domestic political confrontation or lack of proper macroeconomic management, there is a dearth of capacity in the government to properly monitor indicators and provide subsequent policy suggestions. To protect the economy from adverse and unintended consequences of local and global factors, along with fiscal and monetary policy responses, it is imperative for the government to enhance its capacity in macroeconomic management to ensure macroeconomic stability in the medium-to-long run.

Appendix

Table 1.2 Some macroeconomic indicators of Bangladesh

Indicators/Year	*1990*	*2000*	*2005*	*2010*	*2015*	*2017*	*2018*	*2019*
Real GDP Growth Rate (percent)	5.94	5.94	5.38	6.10	6.55	7.28	7.4	7.6
Government Revenue as percent of GDP	6.67	8.87	10.63	11.50	10.78	13.5	14.3	15.1
Tax Revenue as percent of GDP	5.69	6.78	8.67	9.25	9.28	11.5	12.3	13.1
Total Government Expenditure as percent of GDP	12.77	14.98	15.10	15.99	15.81	18.5	19.3	20.1
Government Development Expenditure as percent of GDP	6.32	7.20	6.05	4.12	5.31	6.2	6.5	6.7
Government Revenue Expenditure as percent of GDP	6.64	7.78	9.06	11.16	9.86	12	12.5	13.1
Outstanding External Debt as percent of GDP	34.81	34.40	32.13	21.43	12.3	11.3	12.1	11.7
Workers' Remittance as percent of GDP	2.50	4.14	6.41	10.98	7.84	8.0	7.9	7.8
Export as percent of GDP	5.00	12.23	14.42	16.19	17.34	15.6	15.7	15.9
Imports as percent of GDP	12.33	17.77	21.90	23.72	24.75	21.1	21.2	21.5
Trade as percent of GDP	17.33	30.00	36.32	39.91	42.09	36.7	36.9	37.4
Current Account Balance as percent of GDP	−7.10	−1.10	−0.90	3.70	−0.55	−1.5	−1.8	−2.1
Inflation (percent)	6.13	2.79	6.48	7.31	6.19	5.44	5.78	5.6

Sources: Bangladesh Bureau of Statistics (BBS), Bangladesh Bank

References

Alesina, A., & Rodrik, D. (1994). Distributive politics and economic growth. *The Quarterly Journal of Economics, 109*(2), 465–490.

Ames, B., Brown, W., Devarajan, S., & Izquierdo, A. (2001). *Macroeconomic policy and poverty reduction*. Washington, DC: International Monetary Fund.

Asadullah, M. N., Savoia, A., & Mahmud, W. (2014). Paths to development: Is there a Bangladesh surprise? *World Development, 62*, 138–154.

BIDS. (2018). *How much is mobile money worth? Bkash experience in Bangladesh*. Dhaka: Bangladesh Institute of Development Studies. Unpublished.

Bourguignon, F., & Morrisson, C. (1998). Inequality and development: The role of dualism. *Journal of Development Economics, 57*(2), 233–257.

Datt, G., & Ravallion, M. (1992). Growth and redistribution components of changes in poverty measures: A decomposition with applications to Brazil and India in the 1980s. *Journal of Development Economics, 38*(2), 275–295.

Deininger, K., & Squire, L. (1998). New ways of looking at old issues: Inequality and growth. *Journal of Development Economics, 57*(2), 259–287.

Dollar, D., & Kraay, A. (2002). Growth is good for the poor. *Journal of Economic Growth, 7*(3), 195–225.

Duryea, S., Behrman, J., & Székely, M. (1999). *Schooling investments and macroeconomic conditions: A micro-macro investigation for Latin America and the Caribbean*. Washington, DC: Inter-American Development Bank, Research Department.

Easterly, W., & Kraay, A. (2000). Small states, small problems? Income, growth and volatility in small states. *World Development, 28*(11), 2013–2027.

Hossain, M., & Samad, H. (2017). Mobile phones, household welfare and women's empowerment: Evidence from rural off-grid regions. Presented in *BIDS Research Almanac Seminar*, 2017, Dhaka.

Iqbal, K., & Pabon, N. F. (2018). Quality of growth in Bangladesh: Some new evidence. *Bangladesh Development Studies, XLI*(2), 43–64.

Osmani, S. R. (2018). Aspects of the poverty scenario in Bangladesh during 2010–2016. *Bangladesh Development Studies, XLI*(3), 1–31.

Perotti, R. (1992). Income distribution, politics, and growth. *The American Economic Review, 82*(2), 311–316.

Perotti, R. (1996). Redistribution and non-consumption smoothing in an open economy. *The Review of Economic Studies, 63*(3), 411–433.

Persson, T., & Tabellini, G. (1994). Is inequality harmful for growth? *The American Economic Review, 84*, 600–621.

Ramey, G., & Ramey, V. A. (1994). *Cross-country evidence on the link between volatility and growth* (No. w4959). National Bureau of Economic Research.

Ravallion, M. (1997). Can high-inequality developing countries escape absolute poverty? *Economics Letters, 56*(1), 51–57.

Thorbecke, E., & Jung, H. S. (1996). A multiplier decomposition method to analyze poverty alleviation. *Journal of Development Economics, 48*(2), 279–300.
Timmer, C. P. (1997). *How well do the poor connect to the growth process?* Cambridge, MA: Harvard Institute for International Development.
UNDP. (2010). *Assessment of development results, Bangladesh, 2010.* New York: United Nations Development Program.
White, H., & Anderson, E. (2001). Growth versus distribution: Does the pattern of growth matter? *Development Policy Review, 19*(3), 267–289.

CHAPTER 2

Inflation and Household Welfare: Evidence from Bangladesh

Monzur Hossain and Mustafa K. Mujeri

2.1 Introduction

The Bangladesh economy had experienced a moderate rate of inflation in the 1990s and the first half of the 2000s, at an average rate of less than 4.0 percent, before it moved to a two-digit level in 2007–2008. Bangladesh was worst hit by inflation in 2007–2008 and 2010–2011 when inflation crossed two-digit level with significant upward movements in food inflation. In 2007–2008, the 12-month average inflation rate rose to 12.28 percent (2005–2006 base), which after slowing down in the next two years again reached 10.89 percent in 2010–2011—the highest ever in the recent history of Bangladesh.[1] However, afterwards inflation has been stabilized within a range between 5 percent and 7 percent. One characteristic

[1] Recently Bangladesh changed the base year for estimating inflation to 2005–2006 from its earlier base of 1995–1996. We reported/estimated inflation using 2005–2006 as the base year.

M. Hossain (✉)
Bangladesh Institute of Development Studies (BIDS), Dhaka, Bangladesh

M. K. Mujeri
Institute for Inclusive Finance and Development (InM), Dhaka, Bangladesh

M. Hossain (ed.), *Bangladesh's Macroeconomic Policy*,
https://doi.org/10.1007/978-981-15-1244-5_2

of recent inflation in Bangladesh is that it is mostly led by food inflation. The inflationary episodes in Bangladesh largely follow the trends of high global commodity price volatility, particularly rice prices in domestic and global markets (Hossain and Rafiq 2014). The sources of high inflation were not the same throughout the earlier decades. While inflation was dominated by non-food items in the first half of the 1990s, the opposite was seen in the latter half of the 1990s. Similarly, food inflation dominated the whole decade of 2000s, but an increasing relative importance of non-food inflation is being seen from 2010 onward.

The rising rate of inflation in recent years has raised significant concern regarding its adverse effect on the economy, especially relating to its negative welfare consequences on different socioeconomic groups, particularly the poor. The immediate adverse effects of higher inflation include, among others, reduction of real income of the households. In addition, inefficiencies and inequities may result from inflation-induced changes in relative prices. In Bangladesh, it is important to recognize the high costs of inflation for the poor and disadvantaged groups. The traditional claim is that inflation is costly for the poor, since their purchasing power is eroded, especially for those groups whose earnings are fixed in nominal terms; their assets are devalued more as they hold a larger share of their assets in liquid form compared with the non-poor, and it is difficult for the poor to hedge against inflation due to their limited access to the financial system.

In the backdrop of rising inflation, it is important for the policy makers to know which types of households are more affected by rising inflation and what measures can be adopted to redress their disadvantages, at least partially. The persistence of inflation and inflationary expectations over a sustained period underscores the need for a fresh look at the pattern of inflation faced by various groups of households, particularly to understand how different groups can cope with sustained inflation in terms of their consumption behavior as well as earning strategies.

In terms of the nature of recent inflationary episodes in Bangladesh, particularly with a dominant role of food inflation, the effects of rising food prices might differ across households, based on the share of food consumption in their consumption baskets. It is widely argued that while daily labor households (both farm and non-farm) are able to adjust their wages with rising inflation, at least partly, and fixed income households are in a disadvantageous position as their purchasing power erodes with rising inflation. In addition, among the fixed income groups, relatively poorer households might be able to undertake some inflation-coping strategies by involving with other part-time jobs and income-generating activities. Thus, it is important to investigate the effect of inflation on these two different groups of households—day laborers and monthly salaried (fixed income) households. Moreover, even the nature of inflation might vary depending on income levels of these two types of households. Therefore, the focus of this chapter is to investigate the inflationary impact on two specific groups of households—day laborers and fixed income with four categories of each, such as poor, lower middle income, upper middle income and high income.

To see the effects of inflation, the first step would be to estimate separate consumer price index (CPI) for each of the above groups. In the next step, it is useful to examine how different groups can adjust, if at all, to higher levels of inflation. The redistributive role of inflation through its effect on wages has been widely recognized in the literature. Empirical literature suggests that wages lag behind inflation. When inflation is on a rising trend, price rises tend to run ahead of increases in wages. Therefore, inflation leads to a shift of income away from wage earners, and toward profits. This has led to the claim that inflation increases income inequality as it hurts the poor relatively more than the rich (see Laidler and Parkin 1975; Fischer and Modigliani 1978). However, several empirical studies in the US suggest that inflation has not generated major impact on the distribution of income. More surprisingly, several researchers point out that inflation has redistributed income to the lower income quintiles and toward labor income in the US (Bach and Stephenson 1974; Blinder and Esaki 1978). This shows that inflation may even improve income distribution in specific situations. On the other hand, the study by Cardoso and Urani (1995) provides some evidences on how inflation eroded the poor's income in Brazil during the 1980s. Similar empirical evidence is obtained for Russia, Poland and China, as these countries experienced significant and rapid inflation during their transition to a market economy.

Another important channel of redistribution of income and wealth through inflation is the debtor-creditor channel. The redistribution is from nominal creditors to nominal debtors if interest rates on assets are denominated in terms of money without fully adjusting to the inflation rate. As summarized by Laidler and Parkin (1975), the losers from inflation appear to concentrate on the rich and the poor, because the middle income group, having more nominal debt than those at either extreme of the wealth distribution, is likely to be less affected. But there is evidence that, in adjusting to inflation, the rich react more quickly than the poor. The evidence on these issues is, however, overwhelmingly based on the US data and it is not clear to what extent one may generalize from it to other economies, as no empirical regularity has emerged yet.

This chapter, therefore, aims to identify the major socioeconomic groups who are most affected by the adverse impacts of inflation in Bangladesh and recommends policy measures, so that the vulnerability of these groups to inflationary hardships can be reduced. More specifically, the chapter focuses on the following aspects: (i) pattern and characteristics of recent inflationary episodes in Bangladesh and examining of the underlying sources of inflationary dynamics; (ii) the extent of inflation faced by different household groups, such as poor, middle income and rich in urban and rural areas and within this context, examining how their positions vary across the income/expenditure distribution; and (iii) policy implications including measures for protecting the vulnerable populations from the adverse impact of inflation.

The chapter is organized as follows. After the introductory remarks of the present section, Sect. 2.2 provides a brief review of the relevant literature on inflation and its consequences on household welfare and poverty. Section 2.3 then analyzes the trends and sources of inflation in Bangladesh. Section 2.4 discusses data and methodologies used in the study. Section 2.5 assesses the impact of inflation on different household groups and finally, Sect. 2.6 concludes the chapter with some policy recommendations.

2.2 Inflation and Household Welfare: A Review of Literature

There are numerous studies that have examined the effect of price change on the household's welfare, especially in the context of developing countries. However, these analyses are mostly confined to the explanation of the mechanism of inflationary effect on different households, leaving aside specific conclusions regarding the effects across different income groups.

The World Bank (2010) has assessed the impact of the 2007–2008 food price inflation on poverty in three countries—Bangladesh, Nepal and Pakistan. The study analyzes the welfare effects of food price inflation by categorizing households' net marketing position. Equivalent Variation (EV) measure has been used to estimate the welfare effects of changing food prices. The results show that in Bangladesh, households incur welfare losses by 25 percent as a result of a 50 percent increase in the price of rice. Welfare losses are the smallest in Pakistan, where the maximum loss is about 6 percent. The EV measure is negative for about 80 percent of all households in Bangladesh, which means that there are many more losers than gainers.

Ivanic and Martin (2014) assessed the short-run poverty impacts of the 2010–2011 surges in food prices. The study identifies, in the context of rising food prices, that the adverse welfare impact on net buyers outweighs the benefits to net sellers, resulting in an increase in the number of poor and in the depth of poverty.

A study, conducted by the Asian Development Bank (ADB 2008), evaluates the macroeconomic impacts of high and rising food prices and its impact on households. Applying the Oxford Economics Global Model, the study traces the impacts of fast climbing food and energy prices on developing economies in Asia under two situations—the first supposing that the 57.5 percent increase in world food prices in the first quarter of 2008 continues through the year-end and the second assuming that the 66.5 percent rise in world oil prices is added on top of the food price increase. Simulations are conducted adopting three different scenarios where the increase in food prices is 10 percent, 20 percent and 30 percent. The results of the study show that the increase in food prices in the Philippines by 10 percent, 20 percent and 30 percent threatens creating an additional 2.72 million, 5.65 million and 8.85 million poor people, respectively. The increase in food prices also tends to intensify income inequality in the Philippines. The results show that increases in food prices by 10 percent, 20 percent and 30 percent raise the Gini index by 0.55, 1.10 and 1.65 percentage points respectively. The study also indicates a reduction in the average standard of living of different income groups, specifically a 4.16 percent decline precipitated by 10 percent jump in food prices.

To address the adverse impact of the increase in food prices, the ADB study recommends that export restrictions should be discouraged, domestic markets should be unrestricted, and government controls over prices and resource allocation should be avoided. To alleviate the social impacts of such price shocks, the extremely poor must be provided well-targeted assistance in the form of cash transfers, food-for-work, feeding programs and food stamps; small and marginal farmers must have equal access to credit, fertilizer, improved seeds, pesticides, electricity, and water and should be provided market access across the region and in the global marketplace. It is also recommended that in the long run, improvements be made in land and labor productivity in agriculture through long-term investments and technological advances including upscaling of research and development (R&D), and sustainable land use.

In the context of global commodity price volatility, Hossain and Rafiq (2014) have analyzed the impact of rising inflation on the financial sector. They argued that there exists an inflationary threshold level that exerts an adverse impact on the credit market, which also affects the households. For example, high inflation reduces the rate of return on savings, which discourages people to save, thereby limiting the supply of loanable funds. Mortaza and Hasnayen (2008) have calculated inflation rates for selected household groups using the 2005 Household Income and Expenditure Survey (HIES 2005) data of Bangladesh. They find that recent inflation is mainly driven by higher food prices; and the inflation rate faced by the poor exceeds the corresponding rates for the non-poor groups. The study however does not provide any in-depth analysis on how much adverse impact inflation exerts on different household groups.

The relationship between inflation on the one hand and poverty and income inequality on the other remains a debated issue, although many find that inflation aggravates poverty and worsens income inequality (see Romer and Romer 1998; Easterly and Fischer 2000; Datt and Ravallion 1998). Various channels have also been posited through which inflation hurts the incomes of the poor more than the incomes of the non-poor (see Neri 1995 for some examples from Brazil).

Several other channels between inflation and inequality have also been documented in the literature. For example, Dolmas et al. (2000) relate inflation and income inequality through central bank independence, since pressure for redistributive social programs with rising income inequality in democratic countries may be financed via higher inflation which paradoxically may further worsen inequality when central banks are not independent. Albanesi (2001), while looking at an economy in which government consumption can be financed via taxation or inflation, shows that in the more unequal societies, the poor are more vulnerable to inflation due to their dependence on cash balances, while their negotiating power is further weakened relative to the non-poor by this vulnerability leading to higher inflation. The inclusiveness of economic growth is also affected by inflation. The analysis by Ferreira et al. (2008) in Brazil shows that higher education levels, redistribution programs and convergence across regions are closely correlated with lower income inequality and that inflation has a detrimental effect on inclusion. Cardoso and Urani

(1995) report that inflation increases income inequality and has different effects on various educational groups.

An important strand of inflation analysis is thus the impact of changes in food prices on the poor. Rising food prices in general raise the incomes of the food producers. This could compensate for lower incomes of the non-food producing households in the rural areas provided that the share of such households (e.g. net purchasers of food) is low. Deaton (1989) by analyzing the effect of higher rice prices in Thailand shows that higher food prices can benefit many groups in society although the middle class producers of food benefit the most overall. Ravallion (2000), using data from India, shows that food prices do not have an independent effect on real wages. He observes that, while households may have to bear the immediate burden of rising food prices, rising rural productivity will affect both food producers and wages of rural laborers in the longer term, which would reduce rural income inequality. The effect of higher food prices on income distribution can, thus, be neutral if wages can adjust sufficiently.

In the above context, the prospects of migration may add another dimension to the analysis. In countries where significant potential for rural-urban migration exists (e.g. in Bangladesh), higher rural wages (resulting from higher food prices) relative to urban wages may affect household migration decisions. A shift in relative prices toward food, which constitutes the overwhelmingly large share of the consumption basket of the wage laborers, could have large effect on the migration decision. If the poor urban workers return to their homes due to changing rural-urban wage differentials, the proportion of the poorest segments in the urban areas will decline, ceteris paribus, reducing urban inequality and somewhat mitigating the effects of higher food prices on income distribution. On the other hand, if higher food prices encourage the extreme poor households in rural areas to migrate to urban areas to take advantage of higher urban wages, the net effect in the rural areas will be reverse: it is likely that those households with relatively high and stable incomes would not migrate, indicating that the rural poor who would immigrate are likely to be poorer, and their movement to the urban areas would reduce inequality.[2]

[2] The potential migrants, however, may not include the hard-core and the lowest income rural households including the elderly, disadvantaged, disabled and poor female headed households since these households probably would not have the minimum assets needed and social contacts required for migration to urban areas and big cities.

The analysis by Walsh and Yu (2012) with three samples of data (international, India and China) shows that higher non-food inflation is associated with worsening income inequality across all three samples, supporting the view that income inequality is aggravated by higher levels of inflation. However, they report lower detrimental effect for food inflation. Taking into account the endogeneity of inflation, inequality and growth, the analysis using international and Chinese data shows that higher food inflation is associated with declining income inequality. For the Indian data, the results show that non-food inflation widens income inequality in both urban and rural areas. However, food inflation has different effects. The effect on urban inequality is ambiguous, but food inflation is strongly associated with lower inequality in the rural areas.

The above results, however, need to be interpreted in the context of specific features of the Bangladesh economy. In particular, Bangladesh may be considered as a "closed economy" in the case of its staple food, rice, as most of the product is grown domestically. Moreover, the country faces a very different food price dynamics and income inequalizing process as compared to countries like India and China or countries which import a large share of their food needs. Most of the rural households are also rice growers and they may not be as susceptible to global commodity price shocks as others. In addition, Bangladesh has significant regional variation in terms of surplus or deficit in availability of food from domestic production so that the effect of food inflation could differ across regions.

One study in India on welfare effects at the household level of rising inflation (especially food inflation) shows that, contrary to the conventional wisdom, the main category of poor households, negatively affected by the rise in prices, is overwhelmingly rural (representing 77 percent of all losing poor households), both farmers and non-farmers (De Janvry and Sadoulet 2009). These rural households account for 79 percent of the aggregate welfare loss among the poor. From a policy standpoint, much of the response to high food prices in many countries is focused on the urban poor as they are presumed to be the main losers. This study shows that the urban poor account for only 22.9 percent of the total number of poor losers, and 21.4 percent of total expenditure losses among the poor in India.

Moreover, from the policy perspective, it is important to remember that the urban poor are easier to reach, typically through various targeted distribution and cash transfer programs, and they are politically more organized and vocal, close to the seat of the government and effective in protesting so that their plights are more likely to be addressed. A more pressing reality is that, as results of the above study show, the rural households are the main categories at risk and they are also the more difficult group to reach through available targeting instruments. This indicates how important it is to respond to food inflation by raising the productivity of land and labor in smallholder farming and facilitating access to even tiny plots of land for landless rural households to produce more of their own food needs. In general, insufficient attention seems to have been given to approach the food security issues through improved capacity to produce for home consumption by the poor households.

2.3 Trend and Sources of Inflation in Bangladesh

2.3.1 Trends in Inflation

The estimated inflation rate shows that Bangladesh has been worst hit by two episodes of inflation, one in 2007–2008, partly due to supply chain disruption caused by political turmoils as well as the actions taken by the then caretaker government against hoarders during 2007–2008, and the other one in 2010–2011 partly due to global commodity price volatility in the face of global economic recession in 2010–2011 (Table 2.1). The yearly average inflation is estimated at 12.28 percent in 2007–2008 and 10.89 percent in 2010–2011 with food inflation at 16.69 percent and 14.09 percent, respectively. During the period, rural households are observed to experience much higher inflation, mainly driven by food prices. The average food inflation was 17.7 percent in rural areas and 14.16 percent in urban areas in 2007–2008. After experiencing a high episode of inflation in 2007–2008, Bangladesh experienced somewhat lower inflation in the following two years, ranging between 7 percent and 8 percent when there were relatively low prices of food, particularly rice price playing the key role to drive down inflation. Again, inflation started soaring from 2010 to 2011 with a new phenomenon of rising non-food inflation.

The trends of inflation suggest that food inflation is higher than non-food inflation along with increasing gap between food and non-food inflation until 2011–2012. A non-conventional divergence between food and non-food inflation has long been observed in Bangladesh. Inflation also varies across locations. The reason for this gap is that the weights of the commodities in the consumption bundles vary significantly between rural and urban areas and among various income groups. The average

Table 2.1 Inflation in Bangladesh (percent), 2008–2016

Fiscal year	*National*			*Rural*			*Urban*		
	General	*Food*	*Non-food*	*General*	*Food*	*Non-food*	*General*	*Food*	*Non-food*
2007–08	12.28	16.69	6.35	13.58	17.73	6.73	9.84	14.16	5.84
2008–09	7.68	8.10	7.15	7.96	7.84	8.26	7.16	8.77	5.61
2009–10	6.83	6.33	7.66	5.82	5.00	7.39	8.83	9.66	8.02
2010–11	10.89	14.09	6.21	11.71	15.01	5.70	9.34	11.88	6.71
2011–12	8.76	7.89	10.19	8.78	7.71	10.94	8.72	8.35	9.15
2012–13	6.78	5.22	9.17	6.14	4.64	8.94	8.02	6.64	9.50
2013–14	7.35	8.56	5.55	7.07	8.11	5.21	7.89	9.67	6.01
2014–15	6.41	6.68	5.99	6.20	6.40	5.81	6.80	7.31	6.24
2015–16	5.92	4.90	7.43	5.26	4.20	7.22	7.11	6.55	7.72

Source: Bangladesh Bureau of Statistics (BBS); Bangladesh Economic Review (BER) 2016

Note: Inflation rates refer to FY 2005–06 as the base year

share of food items in the consumption basket is about 58.7 percent in the rural areas, while the share is 48.2 percent in the urban areas (HIES 2010). The share of food items in consumption expenditure, particularly of rice, moreover, remains high for lower deciles groups, declining slowly as one move toward higher deciles. Further, rice accounts for about 40 percent of food expenditure for the poor, while it accounts for 25 percent of food expenditure for the non-poor, of which the share of coarse rice is higher among the day laborer households in rural areas. On the other hand, the medium quality rice expenditure is higher among the fixed income households and day laborers in urban areas.

The pattern of rice expenditure and rice prices indicates that a sharp rise in the price of rice, and food in general, can be expected to wreak havoc among the lower income groups. In particular, it can be expected to increase the misery of those who are already living below the poverty line, and who cannot adjust wages to price changes at least in the short run. The current trend indicates that the impact of food price, especially rice price inflation on the rural people, could be significant in view of the high weights of food (rice) items in their consumption basket. Therefore, the burden for the lower income groups with the increase of food prices largely depends on how these groups could adjust their income and consumption behavior.

2.3.2 Rice Price Movements

Considering food price as an important source of inflation, it is important to examine the trends of rice prices in domestic markets as well as in international markets. The movements of rice prices in the international markets show a rising trend since 2008; a similar trend is also observed in the domestic market (Figs. 2.1a and 2.2). Before 2010, in the domestic market, rice price, both coarse and medium, experienced a drastic growth in 2008. Price of medium and coarse rice grew by 38 percent and 46 percent respectively in 2008. Rice price reached the peak point in 2009 but declined in 2010. However, the trend followed an increasing path from 2010 to 2012 but experienced a sudden fall in 2013 when price of medium and coarse rice decreased by 18 percent and 14 percent respectively. But the trend did not sustain as all rice prices started soaring from 2014. Price of medium rice reached the peak point at 53 Tk per kg while for coarse rice, it was 46 Tk per kg in 2016 (Table 2.2).

The international prices of agricultural commodities have showed increasing pattern during the period under review. According to FAO (2008), international nominal prices of all major food commodities reached their highest levels in nearly 50 years while prices in real terms were highest in 30 years. The FAO food price index increased by 53 percent for the first three months in 2008 compared with the same three months in the previous year. Afterwards, as Fig. 2.2 shows, prices started declining. The upward movements of prices of commodities, particularly rice, were associated with several factors, the most important one being the worsening of the outlook for crops in major rice producing countries in the respective years, particularly 2007–2008 and 2010–2011. The resultant outcome was the drawdown of stocks by key rice producing countries with subsequent imposition of ban on rice export in 2007–2008 by Thailand, Vietnam, India, albeit temporarily. Although the ban on rice export was not imposed in 2010–2011, tighter global supply-demand balances due to drawdown of stocks as well as weakening of US dollar from September 2010 also contributed to rising rice prices in this year. Price of rice and wheat followed a stable trend since 2011, while price of soybean oil shifted to a slightly downward trend in 2014.

Price volatility of different varieties of rice and other commodities, as shown in Table 2.3, indicates intra and inter-year fluctuations of rice prices. Rice price volatility was significantly higher in 2009–2010 and 2010–2011,

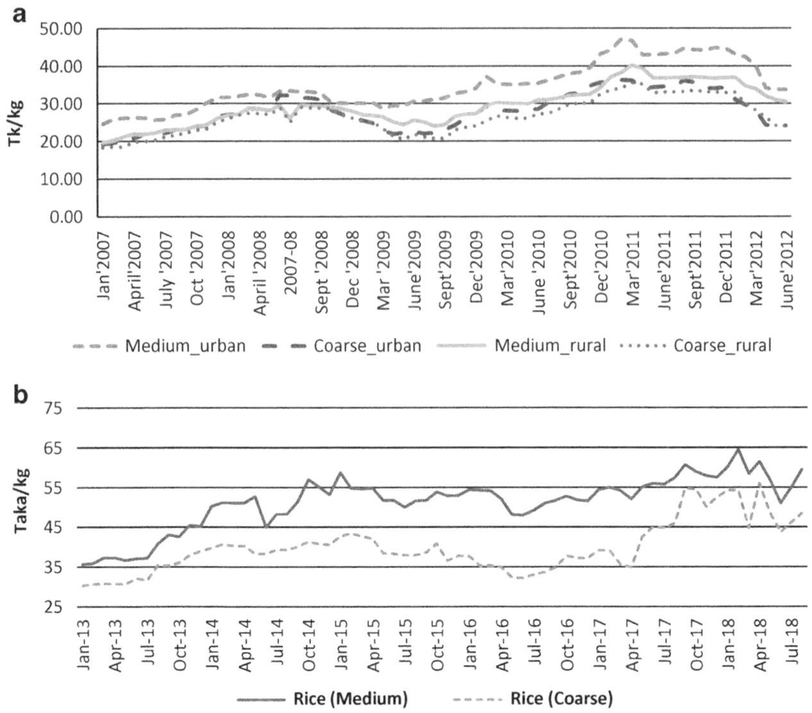

Fig. 2.1 (**a**) Monthly Average Retail Price of Rice. (Source: Bangladesh Bureau of Statistics (BBS); Department of Agricultural Marketing (DAM)). (**b**) Monthly Average Retail Price of Rice at Principal Towns. (Source: Department of Agricultural Marketing (DAM))

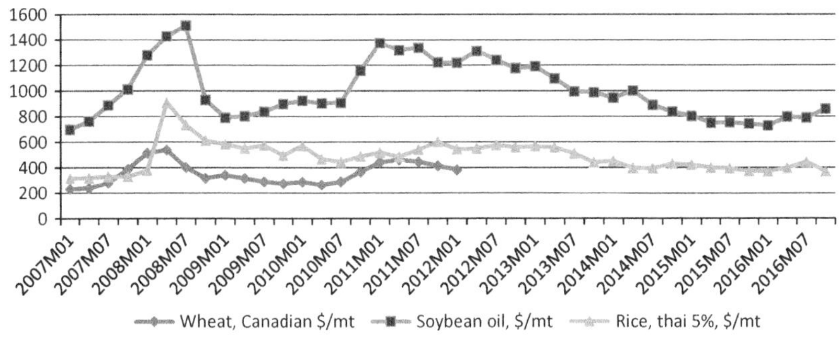

Fig. 2.2 International Price of Selected Commodities (US$ per metric ton). (Source: Pink data set, The World Bank)

Table 2.2 Prices and yearly changes in price of rice (Tk. per kg)

Year	*Price (Tk. per kg) at National Level*		*Percentage Changes (percent) in Rice Price (Tk. per kg)*	
	Medium	*Coarse*	*Medium*	*Coarse*
2006	22.03	17.58		
2007	23.68	19.11	7.49	8.70
2008	32.74	27.87	38.26	45.84
2009	36.25	27.50	10.72	−1.33
2010	33.48	25.74	−7.64	−6.40
2011	41.09	33.48	22.73	30.07
2012	41.72	31.70	1.53	−5.32
2013	34.19	27.19	−18.05	−14.23
2014	45.89	37.23	34.22	36.93
2015	52.57	39.93	14.56	7.25
2016	51.81	46.16	−1.45	15.60
2017	53.13	38.03	2.55	−17.61

Source: Statistical Yearbook, Bangladesh Bureau of Statistics (BBS)

which was about Tk. 3 per kg for coarse and medium rice. Similar pattern of high price volatility was observed for other commodities including soybean (edible) oil in Bangladesh and in the global markets. The volatility of commodity prices in Bangladesh largely follows the trend of global commodity price volatility. Thus, the upward movements of rice prices and its higher volatility could have important implications for domestic inflation.

The above discussion on rice price movements suggests that the upward movement of prices (volatility) of rice in 2007–08 and 2010–11 could have been reflected in food inflation as well as in overall inflation. The relevant question is, therefore, to assess the extent to which the rising and volatile rice prices contribute to household-specific inflation which is investigated in Sect. 2.5.

Several other issues also emerge from the trends and sources of inflation. First, inflation in Bangladesh is seen to be dominated by food inflation. Rice prices, particularly of coarse and medium quality, matter for inflation. International rice and commodity price movements also contribute to inflationary developments in Bangladesh. Second, inflation rates vary with location; particularly there have been significant differences in inflation rates between urban and rural areas, which are also related to rice market situations. Third, food inflation remained higher than non-food inflation for a relatively longer period until 2010–2011

Table 2.3 Commodity-specific price volatility, 2006–2011

A. Bangladesh (Monthly)

Year	*Atap*	*Aman Medium*	*Aman Coarse*	*Boro Medium*	*Boro Coarse*	*Aus Medium*	*Aus Coarse*	*Rice fine(Polao)*	*Wheat (Ata)-Best Quality*	*Soy Bean Oil*
2005	1.15	3.21	10.61	0.58	0.58	0	.	0	1.73	10.12
2006	0.87	1.11	0.52	0.72	0.45	1.50	0.42	1.37	1.31	4.96
2007	2.3	17.6	6.58	2.27	9.00	2.13	2.29	24.93	8.49	17.04
2008	1.44	15.28	2.31	1.96	27.67	1.94	2.56	19.28	6.18	7.83
2009	1.88	2.17	1.60	2.57	2.09	2.83	1.67	9.93	1.96	4.54
2010	1.88	2.02	3.23	2.04	2.62	0.58	3.55	2.39	3.71	6.98
2011	3.58	5.25	2.29	4.09	1.73	3.60	3.30	3.49	1.82	6.40
2012	1.24	1.29	0.75	4.01	1.78	1.41	0.75	11.74	1.88	1.62
2013	3.19	13.22	21.26	15.08	7.99	2.29	0.58	1.93	1.53	6.86
2014	0.88	17.95	14.60	8.41	0.71	.	0.58	4.65	1.72	14.21
2015	0.71	5.32	8.62	0.58	1.00	.	.	3.56	4.84	12.86
2016	2.55	3.39	4.06	1.93	4.23	.	2.08	7.86	0.94	5.56
2017	1.81	3.97	5.18	14.37	15.83	6.56	.	4.87	2.14	29.10
2018	1.49	5.87	2.96	21.28	2.49	2.12	3.58	1.78	1.51	1.03

Source: Department of Agricultural Marketing (DAM)

Note: Prices of all the commodities are retail level prices reported monthly and volatility had been computed from annual values (12-month data points from January to December)

B. Global (Monthly)

Year	*Rice Thai 5 percent*	*Rice Thai 25 percent*	*Soy bean oil*	*Palm oil*	*Triple superphosphate*	*Urea*
2005	286.27	265.38	544.59	450.56	201.48	217.35
2006	304.88	277.12	599.34	508.30	201.63	222.14
2007	326.43	306.50	886.06	816.69	339.05	307.11
2008	650.19	..	1260.81	1042.92	879.38	514.98
2009	554.99	458.07	853.07	741.15	257.42	251.08
2010	488.91	441.51	1000.86	933.02	381.89	288.90
2011	543.03	506.04	1297.66	1193.37	538.26	398.92
2012	562.98	543.80	1225.60	1043.40	462.00	398.60
2013	505.89	472.96	1055.39	870.73	380.75	339.61
2014	422.83	382.17	905.97	837.47	382.00	308.44
2015	386.00	372.58	755.63	663.39	377.67	277.94
2016	396.17	385.33	814.99	735.70	291.08	194.13
2017	398.92	384.67	850.40	750.90	283.33	213.88

Sources: The World Bank Commodity Price Data (The Pink Sheet)

and afterwards, non-food inflation started exceeding food inflation. Finally, since consumption of different varieties of rice matters for inflationary developments, inflation might vary across income levels of households.

2.4 Data and Methodology

For the study, relevant price data are collected from the Bangladesh Bureau of Statistics (BBS) and the group-specific consumption weights have been calculated from the unit level data of the Household Income and Expenditure Survey (HIES) 2010 of BBS.

Historical wage indices from 1970 to 2012 for different groups are taken from various publications of BBS. In addition, wage rate for different professional groups have been collected through a primary survey conducted in November 2012. The survey was conducted in 14 randomly selected districts of seven divisions with emphasis on rice producing areas. A total of 1473 respondents were interviewed to understand their employment history, income pattern, wage earnings and related characteristics. The details of sampling techniques, sampled areas and types of income groups interviewed are given in Tables 2.6, 2.7 and 2.8 in Appendix.

2.4.1 Construction of Consumer Price Indexes

Inflation in Bangladesh is measured by changes in the CPI which is calculated using Laspeyre's index with consumption share as fixed weights. The BBS, as the national statistical agency, has the sole responsibility of estimating the CPI inflation. The current practice is to use the average weights in rural and urban areas to estimate respective CPIs in the two locations.

In the present study, in order to calculate CPIs for different household groups, we first identified different income groups such as poor, lower middle income, upper middle income and higher income categories. The poor households are specified using the per capita income thresholds available from HIES 2010, while other groups have been defined using evidence collected from other studies and definitions available in the relevant literature. The definitions of poor, lower and upper middle income and higher income households are given in Table 2.9 in Appendix.

In the next step, consumption weights have been estimated by using consumption expenditure of these groups from HIES 2010. Price data are taken from BBS which collects the information on a regular basis through price survey from different parts of the country. As noted earlier, the study uses 2005–2006 as the base period for calculating inflation rates of different groups in consistent with the current BBS practice of using 2005–2006 as the base year for estimating the country's inflation rate instead of the period of 1995–1996 as used earlier.

2.5 Impact of Inflation on Different Household Groups

The trends and sources of inflation discussed in Sect. 2.3, pointing to the importance of assessing the varying rates of inflation across different household groups, in both rural and urban areas. In particular, differences seem to exist in inflation rates in terms of different food and non-food consumption patterns of these household groups.

This section examines the extent of variation of inflation faced by different household groups. For this purpose, group-specific CPIs have been constructed by redefining consumption weights for the selected groups in both rural and urban areas as well as food and non-food items using the HIES 2010 data. These have been constructed using 2005–2006 as the base year. The constant weights, derived from the consumption baskets of 2010 (from HIES 2010), have been used to construct the CPIs for the years 2008–2011 by making a conservative assumption that respective households have not significantly diversified their consumption basket during this short period of time. The CPIs and subsequent inflation rates, faced by these groups, have been separately calculated for food and non-food items in terms of rural and urban locations.

2.5.1 Food Inflation

Table 2.4 reports the estimated yearly average inflation rate based on CPI food inflation for day laborers and fixed income households in rural and urban areas for the period 2008–2011. It is observed that different rural households faced low food inflation in 2008–2009 and 2009–2010 due to a sharp decline of rice prices from the level of 2007–2008, while the average food inflation rates remained almost the same ranging between 14 percent and 16 percent in other years. The inflationary trends are largely consistent with rice price trends as shown in Sect. 2.3.2. Interestingly, it appears that while poorer households were in most advantageous position during the lowest level of inflation (2008–2009 and 2009–2010), they

Table 2.4 Estimated food inflation for different household groups (percent)

A. Rural

	Day labor households				*Fixed income households*				*All*			
	2007–08	*2008–09*	*2009–10*	*2010–11*	*2007–08*	*2008–09*	*2009–10*	*2010–11*	*2007–08*	*2008–09*	*2009–10*	*2010–11*
Poor	18.94	5.96	3.82	18.35	20.04	6.56	5.03	19.40	16.89	5.01	6.32	16.44
Lower middle income	17.17	6.26	5.05	17.77	15.85	7.22	6.34	14.49	15.15	5.97	6.91	14.20
Upper middle income	20.41	5.77	4.67	19.93	18.64	7.57	5.36	16.73	15.79	7.02	6.52	14.00
Upper income	20.48	7.02	4.64	19.00	16.08	8.29	6.36	13.78	13.81	8.13	7.36	11.56
All	16.33	4.68	6.36	16.39	14.33	7.66	7.11	12.55	14.86	6.15	6.99	13.82

B. Urban

	Day labor households				*Fixed income households*				*All*			
	2007–08	*2008–9*	*2009–10*	*2010–11*	*2007–08*	*2008–9*	*2009–10*	*2010–11*	*2007–08*	*2008–9*	*2009–10*	*2010–11*
Poor	18.37	6.85	5.24	15.73	16.67	7.53	7.14	13.46	18.06	6.83	6.20	14.77
Lower middle income	17.94	6.69	6.21	14.61	15.96	7.94	8.07	12.42	16.84	7.29	7.50	13.24
Upper middle income	16.79	5.84	8.04	14.07	14.85	9.00	8.66	11.32	15.41	8.50	8.39	11.69
Upper income	13.81	8.13	7.36	11.56	13.94	9.99	9.28	10.01	14.33	9.75	9.18	10.19
All	14.86	6.15	6.99	13.82	14.92	8.99	8.64	11.22	15.81	8.33	8.11	12.01

Source: Authors' calculation

became more vulnerable with gradual spiraling of inflation. Overall food inflation in rural areas was found to be lower than urban areas, as opposed to the recent findings of the BBS. Although the share of rice in food basket does not differ significantly between rural and urban areas, the difference arises due to higher share of medium quality rice in food basket of urban people (Fig. 2.3).[3]

A comparison of the yearly average food inflation for day laborers and fixed income groups in rural areas shows that the relatively poorer fixed income households face higher inflation than those of the day labor households. In contrast, other categories of day labor households face relatively higher inflation than those of fixed income categories. In urban areas, except the upper income group, low income group of day labor households face relatively high inflation indicating that they face more hardship due to higher inflation. The important question is: what explains the difference in inflation rates faced by different household groups? One reason is that these groups (e.g. urban day labor groups) mainly prefer medium quality rice, the price of which was much higher than the coarse rice in urban areas (the difference is more than Tk. 5 per kg). Point-to-point inflation also shows that poor and lower middle income categories of households face relatively higher food inflation than the other income groups in both rural and urban areas (Figs. 2.4, 2.5 and Table 2.4).

2.5.2 Non-food Inflation

Compared to food inflation, non-food inflation continues to remain at a lower level during 2007–2011, which hovers around 5–6 percent. Overall, non-food inflation in urban areas is estimated to be somewhat higher than that of rural areas. From 2010 to 2011, non-food inflation started spiraling and reached its peak at 11 percent in urban and 10 percent in rural areas, and surpassed the food inflation rate (Fig. 2.6 and Table 2.5).

Non-food inflation rates for daily laborers and fixed income households are plotted in Fig. 2.7. One can observe that there is no significant difference in non-food inflation faced by these two groups particularly in rural areas. However, there have been some differences in non-food inflation

[3] The price per kg of medium quality rice varies substantially from the price of coarse rice in urban areas. One possible explanation could be that the medium quality rice available in the rural areas is perhaps inferior to the ones available in the urban areas, and thus the prices may not be strictly comparable.

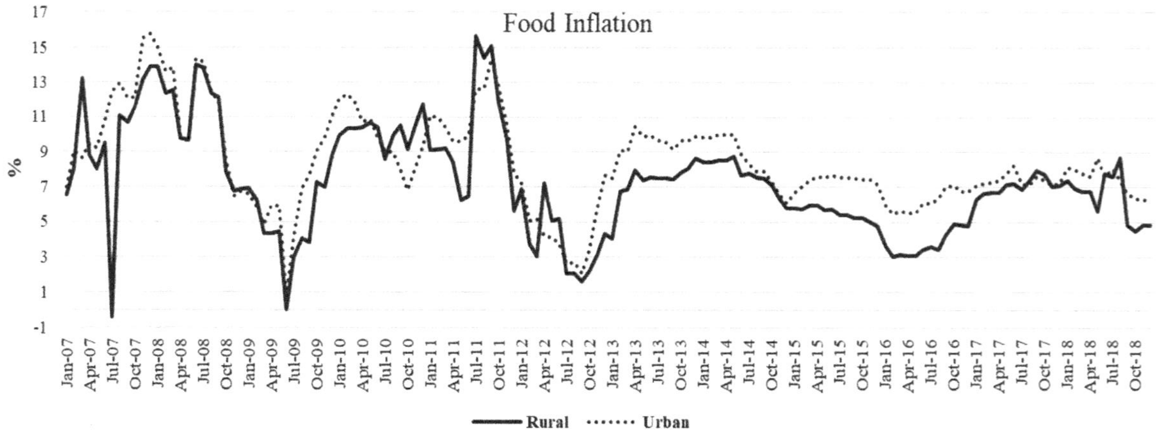

Fig. 2.3 Point-to-point food inflation in Bangladesh (percent). (Source: Bangladesh Bureau of Statistics (BBS))

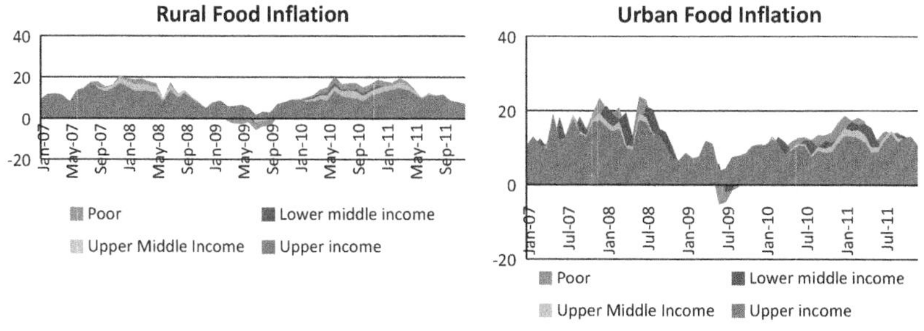

Fig. 2.4 Food inflation (point-to-point: percent) faced by different income groups. (Source: Authors' calculation)

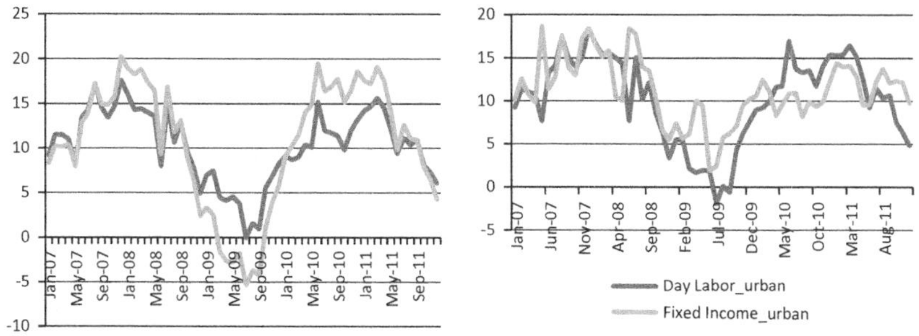

Fig. 2.5 Point-to-point food inflation (percent) faced by day labor and fixed income households. (Source: Authors' calculation)

faced by day labor and fixed income groups in urban areas. While non-food inflation for day laborers has been fluctuating in a sporadic manner, it is mostly stable for fixed income groups in urban areas.

The characteristics of non-food inflation for different household groups are twofold. First, no significant variations are observed among income groups in terms of non-food inflation they face. Second, there exists non-linearity in non-food inflation in terms of income level and spatial distribution. Across income groups, rural poorer households face slightly higher non-food inflation than the other groups. On the other hand, in urban areas, high income groups faced higher non-food inflation than other groups until 2010. However, when non-food inflation crossed the double-digit level, the poorer households started to face higher non-food inflation than others. While rural households seem to be vulnerable to

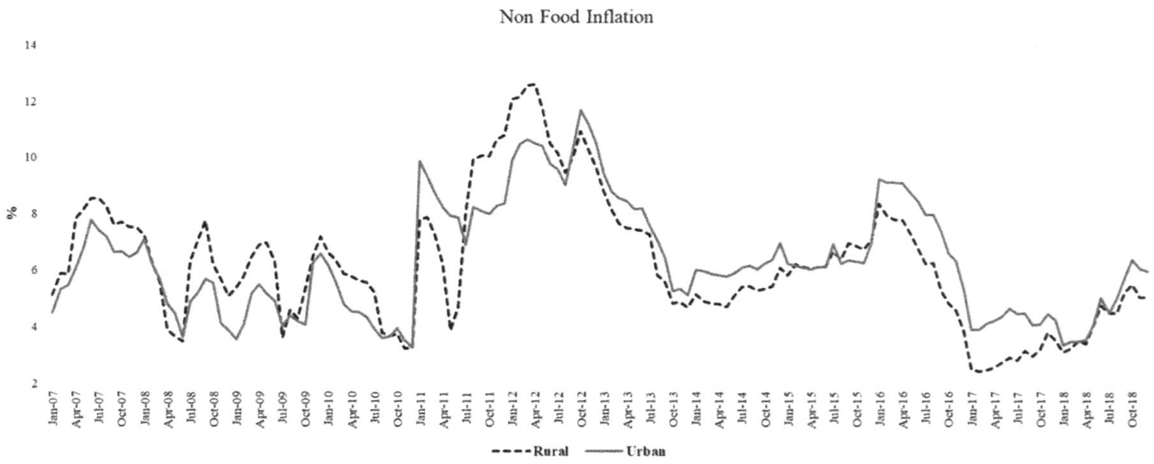

Fig. 2.6 Point-to-point non-food inflation (percent) in rural and urban areas. (Source: Authors' calculation; Bangladesh Bureau of Statistics (BBS))

Table 2.5 Non-food inflation (percent) for different household groups

A. Rural

	Day laborer					*Fixed income*					*All*				
	2007–08	*2008–09*	*2009–10*	*2010–11*	*2011–12*	*2007–08*	*2008–09*	*2009–10*	*2010–11*	*2011–12*	*2007–08*	*2008–09*	*2009–10*	*2010–11*	*2011–12*
Poor	6.60	5.92	5.56	4.54	11.00	6.45	5.82	5.24	4.47	11.00	5.94	5.60	5.40	4.46	10.66
Lower middle	6.60	5.89	5.04	4.46	11.14	5.97	4.91	4.90	4.40	10.33	5.67	5.44	5.02	4.26	10.51
Upper middle	5.22	5.23	5.21	4.37	10.51	6.01	5.01	4.91	4.05	10.25	5.23	5.16	5.38	4.13	10.01
Rich	5.22	5.12	5.10	4.17	10.27	5.66	5.00	5.62	3.89	9.69	4.99	4.98	5.73	3.96	9.77
Total	6.51	5.44	4.93	4.47	11.17	5.67	4.65	5.00	3.99	10.30	5.98	5.06	5.00	4.26	10.66

B. Urban

	Day laborer					*Fixed income*					*All*				
	2007–08	*2008–09*	*2009–10*	*2010–11*	*2011–12*	*2007–08*	*2008–09*	*2009–10*	*2010–11*	*2011–12*	*2007–08*	*2008–09*	*2009–10*	*2010–11*	*2011–12*
Poor	4.96	5.30	3.37	5.52	14.93	3.98	3.52	4.56	4.06	11.72	4.61	4.69	3.50	5.08	14.21
Lower middle	4.83	4.65	3.43	4.77	14.48	4.28	3.45	4.33	4.28	11.99	4.39	4.20	3.84	4.71	13.44
Upper middle	4.44	3.70	3.98	4.10	13.22	4.99	3.41	5.40	4.66	10.18	4.92	3.58	4.67	4.64	11.19
Rich	3.05	3.61	4.30	4.41	12.59	5.39	3.75	5.83	5.61	10.47	4.96	3.94	5.82	5.91	11.39
Total	4.70	4.70	3.52	4.93	14.38	4.93	3.60	5.27	5.00	10.91	4.69	4.11	4.58	5.19	12.56

Source: Authors' calculation

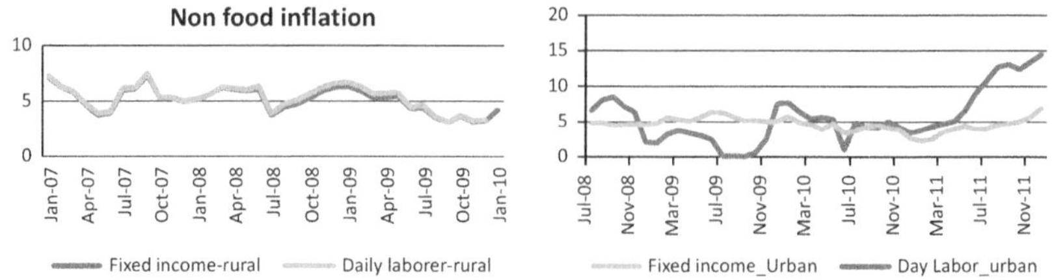

Fig. 2.7 Non-food inflation (percent) faced by fixed income and day labor households in rural and urban areas. (Source: Authors' calculation)

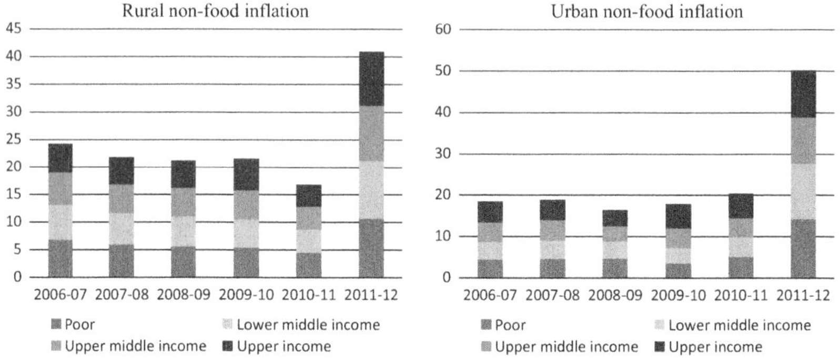

Fig. 2.8 Non-food inflation (percent) faced by different income groups. (Source: Authors' calculation)

single digit moderate non-food inflation, urban poorer households find it tolerable until it goes beyond the double-digit level (Fig. 2.8).

The analysis of inflationary pressure faced by different groups exerts some stylized facts, as follows:

- Both day labor and fixed income household groups have faced higher food inflation than non-food inflation during 2008–2010. In relative terms, the urban household groups face higher food inflation than those in the rural areas.
- In terms of food inflation, relatively poor fixed income household groups faced higher inflation than the daily wage labor households in the rural areas. In contrast, poor and lower middle income day laborers in urban areas faced higher inflation than those of fixed income households. It is observed that the share of medium quality rice in

the consumption basket of the urban day labor households is higher which might have been reflected in their respective inflation rates. In general, poor and lower middle income households face higher inflation in both rural and urban areas than their other counterparts.

- Non-food inflation tended to be lower than food inflation during 2008–2010, and it started crossing food inflation only in 2010–2011. In terms of non-food inflation, there have been no significant differences among rural and urban households. Rural poorer households faced slightly higher non-food inflation than the other groups. On the other hand, in urban areas, high income groups faced higher non-food inflation than others until 2010. However, when non-food inflation crossed the double-digit level, poorer households started facing higher non-food inflation than others. It suggests that there might be non-linearity in non-food inflationary characteristics especially in the urban areas.

2.6 Conclusions and Policy Recommendations

This study makes an in-depth analysis to assess the impact of inflation on different groups of household in Bangladesh in the face of recent inflationary episodes. For the assessment, day laborers and fixed income households are considered, and within these households, various income groups, such as poor, lower middle income, upper middle income and higher income groups are considered. Separate consumer price indexes (CPIs) are constructed for each of the groups to assess the extent of inflation they had faced during 2008–2011.

In the context of recent trends and sources, inflation in Bangladesh is dominated by food inflation. Rice prices, particularly coarse and medium quality rice prices, significantly matter for inflation. International rice and commodity price movements also contribute to the inflationary developments in Bangladesh. It is also observed that inflation rates vary with locations; particularly there have been significant differences in inflation rates between urban and rural areas, which are also related to rice market situations. Food inflation remained higher than non-food inflation for relatively longer period until 2010–2011, and afterwards non-food inflation started to overshoot food inflation. The trends and sources of inflation justify the categorization of households in terms of income levels, as consumption of different varieties of rice matters for inflationary developments across households.

The results based on CPIs suggest that both daily labor and fixed income household groups faced higher food inflation than non-food inflation. Urban household groups faced relatively high food inflation than those in the rural areas. In terms of food inflation, poorer fixed income household groups faced higher inflation than those belonging to daily labor groups in the rural areas, indicating that day laborers are somewhat able to adjust their nominal incomes with rising inflation through keeping track with their real wages. In contrast, poor and lower middle income daily laborers in urban areas face higher inflation than those of fixed income households. It is observed that the share of medium quality rice in the consumption basket of urban daily labor households is higher, which might be reflected in their respective inflation rates. In general, poor and lower middle income households face higher inflation in both rural and urban areas than their other counterparts. Thus, poorer fixed income groups in rural areas and day laborers in urban areas face relatively higher food inflation than the other groups.

Non-food inflation tended to be lower than food inflation during 2008–2010, but it started to cross food inflation in 2010–11. In terms of non-food inflation, there have been no significant differences among rural and urban households. Rural poorer households face slightly higher non-food inflation than the other groups. On the other hand, in urban areas, high income groups faced higher non-food inflation than others until 2010. However, when non-food inflation crossed the double-digit level, poorer households started facing higher non-food inflation than others. It suggests that there exists non-linearity in non-food inflationary characteristics in urban areas.

The analysis in this study suggests that food prices, *inter alia*, remained at the center point in the discussion of inflation during the period. Various income groups including poorer households are found to be highly sensitive to food inflation. The critical question, therefore, relates to finding ways so that these income groups can cope with the inflationary developments. Therefore, appropriate policies in the short to medium run are necessary to mitigate the adverse welfare consequences of inflation on these groups of households.

In view of the existence of significant heterogeneity among different poor groups and the conflicting nature of impact of specific policies on different groups, it is important to devise policies keeping the priority of specific poor sub-group. Such policies need also to consider the group's access to key productive assets and keep its characteristics of livelihood strategies in view rather than anchoring policies on average impact estimates on the poor. Although the issue has not been explicitly addressed in the present study, the net welfare loss of female-headed households is generally higher than that of the male-headed ones, so that special attention is needed on female-headed households within the mitigation programs. At the same time, providing agriculture credit, making input supplies more reliable, and relaxing trade policies may bring consumer gain in the short run, while providing timely market information would assist the producers to take informed decisions.

The distributional consequences of rising prices of domestically produced rice and other agricultural products suggest that it is important to adopt policies that reduce seasonal variability in prices of different commodities, especially rice, and provide a remunerative and fair price for rice to the growers after harvest. For vegetables and other non-rice food crops, the priority should be to strengthen the marketing links both horizontally and vertically, promote market integration, and support processing and high value activities. The thrust of the macroeconomic policies should be on increasing domestic production and stabilizing supply, since it is more likely that the average income of the poor is negatively related to aggregate demand variability in Bangladesh. The monetary policy framework should reflect the above concerns through its support to growth augmenting policies along with ensuring reasonable price stability.

Since a large majority of the poor belongs to the category of landless laborers who subsist on casual agricultural wage employment, it is possible that, in addition to direct transfers, policies that put upward pressure on agricultural wages, can be effective in raising the welfare of these poorest groups. In this context, public works programs, which employ large numbers of unskilled workers from poor households to improve public infrastructure, raise the demand for labor which, if large enough, can push wages up through general equilibrium effects. In such a case, the welfare gains of public works programs would bring benefits even to other households who are not directly employed under these programs.[4]

[4] One may argue that the welfare gain in society as a whole is somewhat ambiguous since a rise in wages would have a negative welfare effect on the employers. It may, however, be argued that the labor-employing households are invariably better off than the labor-supplying households and are fewer in number. Hence, from the social point of view, the trade-off is welfare enhancing and worth accepting.

Appendix

Required sample size for wage rate survey

To decide about a nationally representative sample of wage workers, we apply the following formula:

$$N_c = Z^2\left[P(1-P)/d^2\right]*def$$

Here N_c represents the number of workers to be interviewed, and *def* represents design effect. For household survey, *def* is usually considered to be between 1.5 and 2. Here we assume it 1.5 and consider Z at 10% level of significance, precision $d = 0.1$ at 10% level. Here P is the proportion of households having specific type of workers (see Tables 2.6 and 2.7; Source: HIES 2010 and LFS 2010). Therefore, the required number of workers would be $N = 193$ from each division. As we have decided to conduct the survey in all seven divisions to make the sample representative, thus, ***a total of 1351 respondents (wage workers) were interviewed.***

Table 2.6 Estimated sample size for different groups

	P	Z	d	def	$N = Z^2*P*Q*def/d^2$
Agriculture day laborer/fisheries	0.21	1.68	0.10	1.50	70
Construction worker	0.05	1.68	0.10	1.50	20
Fishermen (culture)	0.02	1.68	0.10	1.50	8
Tailor/garment workers	0.01	1.68	0.10	1.50	4
Home maid	0.012	1.68	0.10	1.50	5
Housekeeper (daroan, aya, gardener)	0.012	1.68	0.10	1.50	5
Rickshaw/van puller	0.07	1.68	0.10	1.50	28
Driver/helper	0.07	1.68	0.10	1.50	28
Carpenter	0.05	1.68	0.10	1.50	20
Weaver	0.013	1.68	0.10	1.50	5
Total (each division)					**193**
For seven divisions					**1351**

Table 2.7 Sample size distribution across regions

Divisions	*Districts*	*Sample*
Dhaka	Dhaka and Tangail	About 100 samples (proportionately) from each of the districts
Chittagong	Chittagong and Comilla	About 100 samples (proportionately) from each of the districts
Rajshahi	Naogaon and Sirajganj	About 100 samples (proportionately) from each of the districts
Khulna	Jessore and Satkhira	About 100 samples (proportionately) from each of the districts
Barisal	Bhola and Patuakhali	About 100 samples (proportionately) from each of the districts
Rangpur	Dinajpur and Gaibandha	About 100 samples (proportionately) from each of the districts
Sylhet	Sylhet and Habiganj	About 100 samples (proportionately) from each of the districts

Table 2.8 Definitions of different household groups

Groups		*Definition for Rural (in terms of per capita monthly income)*	*Definition for Urban (in terms of per capita monthly income)*	*Definition for National (in terms of per capita monthly income)*
Poor households	Daily wage laborer Monthly salaried (fixed income)	>= Tk. 1130 (according to BBS upper pov. Line)	>= Tk. 1200 (according to BBS upper pov. Line)	>= Tk. 1280 (according to BBS upper pov. Line)
Lower middle income	Daily wage laborer Monthly salaried (fixed income)	Tk. 1131–3000	Tk. 1201–3000	Tk. 1281–3000
Upper middle income	Daily wage laborer Monthly salaried (fixed income)	Tk. 3001–4000	Tk. 3001–4000	Tk. 3001–4000
High income	Daily wage laborer Monthly salaried (fixed income)	>Tk. 4000	>Tk. 4000	>Tk. 4000

Note: Different groups are defined in terms of per capita income by adjusting ratio of population under each category (particularly poor) based on HIES 2010

Table 2.9 Weights in food baskets

		Day Laborer Households				*Fixed Income Households*			
		Poor	*Lower middle income*	*Upper middle income*	*Higher income*	*Poor*	*Lower middle income*	*Upper middle income*	*Higher income*
Rural	Rice-fine	0.68	0.83	0.94	1.22	0.77	0.88	0.62	1.37
	Rice medium	6.21	3.85	16.62	11.24	43.80	20.30	44.49	30.36
	Rice-coarse	34.18	28.18	19.26	15.82	18.59	21.28	9.61	10.04
	Total	41.07	32.86	36.82	28.28	63.16	42.46	54.72	41.77
Urban	Rice-fine	0.38	0.43	0.63	0.58	0.74	0.84	1.23	1.73
	Rice medium	15.60	15.13	19.32	16.21	19.87	18.82	17.87	14.93
	Rice-coarse	24.64	18.49	9.82	6.42	13.74	7.82	5.60	2.42
	Total	40.62	34.04	29.77	23.21	34.35	27.48	24.70	19.07

References

ADB. (2008). *Food prices and inflation in Developing Asia: Is poverty reduction coming to an end?* Manila: Asian Development Bank.

Albanesi, S. (2001). *Inflation and inequality* (Luxembourg income study working paper no. 323). Luxembourg.

Bach, G. L., & Stephenson, J. B. (1974). Inflation and the redistribution of wealth. *The Review of Economics and Statistics, 56*, 1–13.

Basu, A. K. (2013). Impact of rural employment guarantee schemes on seasonal labor markets: Optimum compensation and workers' welfare. *The Journal of Economic Inequality, 11*(1), 1–34.

Blinder, A. S., & Esaki, H. Y. (1978). Macroeconomic activity and income distribution in the postwar United States. *The Review of Economics and Statistics, 60*, 604–609.

Cardoso, E., & Urani, A. (1995). Inflation and unemployment as determinants of inequality in Brazil: The 1980s. In *Reform, recovery, and growth: Latin America and the Middle East* (pp. 151–176). Chicago: University of Chicago Press.

Datt, G., & Ravallion, M. (1998). Farm productivity and rural poverty in India. *The Journal of Development Studies, 34*(4), 62–85.

De Janvry, A., & Sadoulet, E. (2009). The impact of rising food prices on household welfare in India. Berkley: Institute of Industrial Relations, UC Berkley.

Deaton, A. (1989). Rice prices and income distribution in Thailand: A nonparametric analysis. *The Economic Journal, 99*(395), 1–37.

Dolmas, J., Huffman, G. W., & Wynne, M. A. (2000). Inequality, inflation, and central bank independence. *Canadian Journal of Economics/Revue canadienne d'économique, 33*(1), 271–287.

Easterly, W., & Fischer S. (2000). *Inflation and the poor* (NBER working paper 2335). National Bureau of Economic Research, USA.

FAO. (2008). *The state of food and agriculture 2008*. Rome: Food & Agriculture Org.

Ferreira, F. H., Leite, P. G., & Litchfield, J. A. (2008). The rise and fall of Brazilian inequality: 1981–2004. *Macroeconomic Dynamics, 12*(S2), 199–230.

Fischer, S., & Modigliani, F. (1978). Towards an understanding of the real effects and costs of inflation. *Review of World Economics, 114*(4), 810–833.

Hossain, M., & Rafiq, F. (2014). Global commodity price volatility and domestic inflation: Impact on the financial sector in Bangladesh. In M. K. Mujeri & W. Mahmud (Eds.), *Adjusting to global economic volatility*. New Delhi: Academic Foundation.

Ivanic, M., & Martin, W. (2014). *Short-and long-run impacts of food price changes on poverty*. Policy Research Working Paper, 7011. Washington, DC: The World Bank.

Laidler, D., & Parkin, M. (1975). Inflation: A survey. *The Economic Journal, 85*(340), 741–809.

Mortaza, M. G., & Hasnayen, S. (2008). Inflation accounting across income groups: Does inflation hurt the poor more in Bangladesh? *Bangladesh Bank Quarterly, 5*(3), 30–41.

Neri, M. (1995). On the measurement of real wages in high inflation. *Research and Economic Planning, 25*(3), 497–525.

Ravallion, M. (2000). Prices, wages and poverty in rural India: What lessons do the time series data hold for policy? *Food Policy, 25*(3), 351–364.

Ravallion, M., & Dutt, G. (1999). *Growth and Poverty in Rural India* (Policy Research Working Paper). The World Bank Group. Available at: http://documents.worldbank.org/curated/en/620321468773982302/Growth-and-poverty-in-rural-India

Romer, C. D., & Romer, D. H. (1998). *Monetary policy and the well-being of the poor* (No. w6793). National Bureau of Economic Research.

Statistics, B.B.O. (2005/2010). *Household income and expenditure survey, 2005 and 2010*. Dhaka: Bangladesh Bureau of Statistics.

Walsh, M. J. P., & Yu, J. (2012). *Inflation and income inequality: Is food inflation different?* (No. 12–147). International Monetary Fund.

World Bank. (2010). *Food price increases in South Asia, national responses and regional dimensions*. Washington, DC: World Bank.

CHAPTER 3

Labor Market Dynamics, Inflation and Wage Adjustments in Bangladesh

Mustafa K. Mujeri, Monzur Hossain, and Tahreen T. Chowdhury

3.1 Introduction

The impact of wage formulation mechanisms on persistence of inflation has received wide attention in recent policy discourse. Downward wage rigidity and its consequences on employment and inflation remain an issue of intense debate in the labor market analysis of developing countries. An analysis conducted by Agenor and Hoffmaister (1997) in four middle-income developing countries (Chile, Korea, Mexico and Turkey) shows that any innovation in the rate of growth of nominal wages generates an increase in inflation along with rise in real wages, creating conflicting demand and supply side effects associated with the rise in wages. This suggests that accounting for wage shocks is important for understanding the inflationary process in developing countries. It also appears that wages react significantly over time to price shocks, probably reflecting the backward indexation of nominal wages.

M. K. Mujeri (✉)
Institute for Inclusive Finance and Development (InM), Dhaka, Bangladesh

M. Hossain • T. T. Chowdhury
Bangladesh Institute of Development Studies (BIDS), Dhaka, Bangladesh
e-mail: tahreen@bids.org.bd

M. Hossain (ed.), *Bangladesh's Macroeconomic Policy*,
https://doi.org/10.1007/978-981-15-1244-5_3

The relationship between agricultural wages and staple food (rice) prices has been a subject of intense empirical analysis, especially in Bangladesh, as agricultural wages influence the welfare of the poorest groups in the rural areas comprising mostly the agricultural laborer households. In particular, rice being the staple, change in rice prices has a significant impact on agricultural wages in Bangladesh. Several past studies find a positive relationship between agricultural wages and rice prices (e.g. Ravallion 1994; Palmer Jones 1993; Palmer Jones and Parikh 1998). These studies hypothesize a positive relationship with partial adjustment in the short run, and complete adjustment in the long run. The causality runs from higher rice price creating better incentives for raising rice production and leading to greater demand for factor inputs including labor which leads to higher wages. On the other hand, a few studies posit no or negative relationship between rice price and agricultural wages. In Philippines, an analysis of the welfare implications of a decrease in rice prices for agricultural households, who are net purchasers of rice and net suppliers of labor, shows that most households benefit in the short run but lose in the long run (Lasco 2005).

Some studies, however, suggest that wages may not be so flexible. Several empirical studies provide evidence in support of the finding that wages do not fully adjust to higher food prices, in which case the poor suffer more given the higher share of food in their consumption basket (Christiaensen and Demery 2007; Rashid 2002; Warr 2005). Overall distributional impact depends, as Wodon and Zaman (2008) point out, on the extent to which households are net producers or consumers of food.

The evidence is thus relatively strong that headline inflation exacerbates income inequality, but there seems to exist some evidence that rising food prices may have a more moderate or even benign impact on inequality. One issue that emerges from the above is: does this indicate that non-food inflation is particularly damaging to the poor? For instance, if higher food prices in rural areas pass through to wages, that is, if rural wages are elastic to food price increases, then food inflation should be less harmful, and could be even beneficial to income inequality in the rural areas. A similar relationship could also hold in the urban areas, but since most of the rural households are engaged in agriculture, the relationship will be stronger in the rural areas. In contrast then, non-food inflation should be detrimental to income inequality in both rural and urban areas. The analysis of agricultural wages and outputs in India shows that there is a strong adverse impact of inflation on real agricultural wages and (hence) on absolute poverty in the short run (Ravallion and Dutt 1999). The adjustments of real wage rates, however, take time so that the short-run gains to poor people of labor-demanding productivity growth are far lower than the long-run impacts.

With a relatively high growth and transitional economy, Bangladesh is more likely to have a complex relationship between food production and rural wages. With higher growth, more productive and remunerative employment opportunities seem to be emerging (despite rising agricultural productivity) in the urban areas which make it more attractive and less difficult to shift from rural to urban unskilled labor market compared to the past. Along with countering the increase in income inequality, this potential provides a "safety valve" for the rural workers relative to a situation where urban employment opportunities are limited, in which condition, food inflation could bring more detrimental effects for the rural consumers.

This chapter examines the dynamics of inflation and wage adjustments in the labor market of Bangladesh, especially keeping in view the rising food inflation in recent years. Section 3.2 discusses rural labor market and agricultural wages and Sect. 3.3 discusses inflation and wage adjustment process over time. Section 3.4 discusses data and methodology and Sect. 3.5 discusses the empirical results. Section 3.6 provides conclusion and policy recommendations.

3.2 Rural Labor Market and Agricultural Wages

Early development theories adopt the view that there exists surplus labor in the rural economy in countries like Bangladesh, so that additional employment would have no effect on the real wage (e.g. see Lewis 1954; Ranis and Fei 1961). By this view, the rural sector has a large labor surplus, and so there is little scope for the poor to gain via real wages. However, alternative views of the rural labor market allow a labor surplus to co-exist along with a process of wage determination in which labor-augmenting technological progress can lead to higher real wages (see, Drèze and Mukherjee 1989; Osmani 1990; Mukherjee and Ray 1991; Datt 1996). In developing countries, labor markets are often found to exhibit short-run stickiness in wages, and there are some evidences that this is also true in agricultural labor markets in similar settings (e.g. for evidence in the context of Bangladesh see Ravallion 1990; Boyce and Ravallion 1991).

3.2.1 *Agricultural Employment: Dynamics of Wage Changes*

Generally, the framework for labor market analysis in developing countries is characterized by the existence of "dualism" and strong entry barriers across different segments of the labor market. The dualism presumes the existence of two distinct segments of economic activity, typically classified as "organized" and "unorganized" sectors. The organized sector offers more regular, stable and higher paid jobs, while the unorganized sector is associated with irregular, unstable and low-paid jobs. In similar tradition, the labor market dualism in Bangladesh is well documented along with varying explanations for the existence of wage differentials across different segments of the labor market, covering demand and supply side factors as well as institutional impediments.

The employment characteristics, especially of the poor households, show that the share of working population having primary employment as agricultural wage laborers is extremely high in the two lowest consumption quintiles. Overall, about 50 percent of all male laborers aged 15 and above were employed as agricultural laborers in 2000 and the share declined to 40 percent in 2010 (BBS 2011). For women, although far fewer are recorded as economically active, the importance of employment as agricultural laborers is even more pronounced. For women, the percentage of laborers engaged in agricultural labor category has increased over time (from 48 percent in 2000 to 65 percent in 2010). Given that the rural population has been growing steadily, this also indicates quite a sizeable increase in the number of agricultural laborers in rural Bangladesh.[1] Moreover, the characteristics of these households show strong correlations between employment as agricultural laborers and low living standards in terms of per capita consumption, education status and other welfare indicators. In addition, these relationships seem to have remained relatively unchanged over the years. In the context of India, similar situations have been explained in terms of increasing "proletarianization" that pushes out smallholder cultivators from agriculture into wage laborers emanating from both push and pull effects, with agricultural labor emerging out as the "last-resort" employment option (see Kijima and Lanjouw 2005).

Several analyses in India show that the expansion of informal non-farm employment is strongly correlated with rise in agricultural wages (see, for

[1] The number of day laborers, who mostly work in agriculture, increased from 8.6 million in 2005–06 to 10.6 million in 2010, an increase of 23 percent. Over the same period, total employed labor in the country rose by 14 percent. See BBS 2011.

instance, Lanjouw and Murgai 2009; Berg et al. 2012). This is consistent with the process of labor market tightening. Although the poor and unskilled agricultural wage laborers may find it difficult to gain access even to the informal non-farm employment, the siphoning off of the better segments of agricultural labor puts pressure on wages across the entire market. These dynamics have significant implications on the changing composition of the agricultural labor force, with the poor and unskilled segment of the market gaining more significance.

There is evidence that real agricultural wages respond positively to higher farm yields, presumably through effects on labor demand, such as due to multiple cropping. There is also a strong link through food prices. While the impact of agricultural growth on food prices is quantitatively small, even small food price changes can have large effects on absolute poverty. Inflation also has adverse effects on the poor, via its short-term effect on real wages and food prices.

Using time series data, several studies have reported that the real agricultural wage experienced a downward trend during the period from 1949–50 to 1980–81 in Bangladesh, although overall agricultural productivity increased (Khan 1984; Ravallion 1990; Boyce and Ravallion 1991; Ravallion 1994). Boyce and Ravallion (1991) further argue that, since the short-run elasticity of wages to rice price is low, an increase in nominal rice price can have adverse effects on the poor, for whom wage is the main source of income and rice occupies a major share of their expenditure.[2]

However, by re-analyzing the data of the above studies, Rashid (2002) reports contrary results using a co-integration framework. His results suggest that agricultural wage and rice price maintained a strong co-integrating relationship during the period under review. He also shows substantially higher long-run elasticities of agricultural wage rate with respect to rice price compared with the earlier estimates (0.72 and 0.69 for Boyce-Ravallion and Palmer Jones data sets relative to 0.46 and 0.47 respectively in the two studies). Further, the study shows that rice price, a variable that maintained strong relationship with agricultural wage until the late 1980s, lost its significance in the later periods while the urban wage rate, proxied by the wage of unskilled construction workers, became the most significant variable in explaining the dynamics of agricultural wage. This is consistent with the long-term trend of falling real rice price and the rising

[2] Available studies suggest that expenditure elasticity of rice for the bottom quartile of the rural population in Bangladesh ranges from 0.68 to 1.01. See Ahmed and Shams 1994, Goletti 1994, Hossain 1988.

urban wage rate relative to agricultural wage rate, explaining the unprecedented growth of urban population in the country.

There seems to be a strong general view that economic growth in Bangladesh has not been inclusive enough, and the poor have mostly been left behind in the process. While the view is supported by many indicators of economic and social development, this does not seem to be backed by recent data that matter the most, for example, trends in the wages of agricultural laborers in rural areas. The available nominal wage rate index from BBS shows that over the period of 30 months from January 2010 to July 2012, the average nominal agricultural wage shot up by 41 percent in Bangladesh. Similar increase in the case of wage for construction worker is 57 percent compared with 17 percent for manufacturing worker and 19 percent for wages of fisheries worker. These are significant improvements even after allowing for inflation during the period.

3.2.2 Agricultural Labor Market: Dominant Features

In Bangladesh, almost all households depend on employment as their primary source of income. This is especially true for the poor households, since the only abundant productive resource that the poor have is their own labor. Another important aspect of the labor market in Bangladesh is the formal-informal divide in employment which has significant consequences for return to labor and security of employment. The concept captures the forms of employment that lack regulatory, legal and/or social protections. Informal employment is defined in terms of the nature of enterprise in which the work takes place (e.g. the informal sector) and the relationships in employment.[3] The vast majority (87 percent) of the total employed laborers in Bangladesh are engaged in informal activities. The gender difference in this respect is wide: of the total female employed laborers, 92 percent are employed in the informal sector while similar share is 85 percent for male laborers.

[3] In practice, enterprises are considered informal in Bangladesh if they are not registered with the relevant authority. Thus, employment in the informal sector comprises all employment in informal enterprises including self-employed/own account workers, unpaid family helpers, day laborers, paid employees in informal enterprises, informal employers and other similar categories. Outside the unregistered and/or small enterprises sector, employment may be considered as informal if it lacks core legal or social protections (e.g. domestic workers). Moreover, *de facto* informal employment may also exist within the formal sector such as for different categories of casual workers.

According to the Labor Force Survey 2010, the total number of day laborers is 10.6 million which constitutes nearly 20 percent of the total employed labor force. Of the total, 5.8 million (55 percent) are categorized as agricultural day laborers. The day laborers predominantly work in the rural areas, with nearly 80 percent of them working in the rural labor market. The share of agricultural day laborers in the rural areas is even higher at 92 percent and is comprised of predominantly male workers (93 percent). The Survey reports the weekly earnings of nearly 44 percent of the male and 29 percent of the female agricultural day laborers in the range of Tk. 501–1000 with not much variation between the rural and urban areas.[4] The shares of male and female agricultural day laborers with weekly wage earnings in the range of Tk. 1001–1500 are 27 percent and 12 percent, respectively.

With the overwhelming dominance of smallholding farms (having land less than 2.50 acres) in Bangladesh, hired agricultural labor is traded mostly in decentralized local markets. The composition of farm employment varies with the size of farms; marginal farms are mostly dependent on family labor while large farms are found to be more dependent on hired labor. Thus, the farm-level employment pattern is often a mix of family and hired laborers mostly engaged in standard crop production activities including plowing, sowing, weeding and harvesting. Under the decentralized setting, the wage setting behavior is mostly non-institutional. In most cases, the contracts are negotiated between the landowners and the laborers bilaterally. It is also important to recognize that wage contracts for casual agricultural laborers are typically of very short durations (often on a daily basis) and hence can easily reflect recent changes in market conditions and/or commodity prices. As such, the agricultural labor market features in Bangladesh are quite flexible and reflect few institutional constraints.

Moreover, since agricultural production exhibits considerable seasonality in work intensity determined by the well-defined time span of major farm activities related to crop production, demand for agricultural laborers in various seasons is significantly affected by the crop calendar of the location.

[4]According to the Household Income and Expenditure Survey (HIES) 2010, nearly 48 percent of the poor workers work in the agriculture sector while 27 percent are in the services sector and the rest in the manufacturing sector. It is also reported that half of the poor workers are concentrated in daily wage employment. See BBS 2011.

3.3 Inflation and Wage Adjustments

3.3.1 A Framework for Analysis

In Bangladesh, rising inflation, especially led by food inflation in recent years, has raised the question as to whether there has been a compensating rise in the incomes of the poor for whom a major chunk of total expenditure is accounted for by food articles. The present section deals primarily with the agricultural laborers, for whom wages constitute the principal source of income and probably the most important determinant of their economic status. In addition, agricultural wage laborers constitute a major segment of the rural poor, and the relative incidence of poverty is also more severe among the agricultural laborers in Bangladesh. According to the Household Income and Expenditure Survey (HIES) data, poverty incidence among the agricultural workers was 37.0 percent in 2010 compared to the national average of 31.5 percent (BBS 2011).

The major goal of economic policy in Bangladesh is to promote rapid economic growth that is both inclusive and sustainable. For ensuring such growth, an important pre-requisite is to maintain a stable macro environment and create conditions for economic and social justice. Since independence, despite rising economic growth which has averaged more than 6.0 percent in recent years, inflation has continuously eroded the purchasing power of the people, especially the poor. For instance, the last four decades since the 1970s have witnessed a 24-fold increase in the nominal price of rice, the staple food, at the retail level. This section provides an analysis of the economic impact of inflation vis-à-vis the income changes of the agricultural labor households using a simple model.

We assume that the total consumption of an agricultural wage earner household i (C_i) is described by a Cobb-Douglas function (which is linearly homogeneous) in nominal income Y_i and price level P_i:

$$C_i = AY_i^{\alpha} P_i^{1-\alpha}. \tag{3.1}$$

Equation (3.1) in turn gives the real consumption C_i of the household as a function of real income (Y_i/P_i or the purchasing power):

$$c_i = \frac{C_i}{P_i} = A\left(\frac{Y_i}{P_i}\right)^{\alpha}. \tag{3.2}$$

Through log differentiating of the function (3.2), one can get the percentage change in the real consumption of the household *i*:

$$\dot{C}_i = \varepsilon_i \left(\dot{Y}_i - \dot{P}_i \right). \tag{3.3}$$

Where, ε_i is the real income elasticity of consumption and a dot above a variable indicates percentage change.

Equation (3.3) shows that a fall in the purchasing power (that is, when $\dot{P}_i > \dot{Y}_i$) is translated proportionally into consumption ($\dot{C}_i < 0$) as ε_i is positive.

For household *i* which is a poor agricultural wage earner, our interest is to assess the effect on its consumption of a price rise due to inflation vis-à-vis wage adjustment as by assumption agricultural wage is the principal source of household income of the wage laborer.

We assume that the post-inflation price is P_1 which is higher than the pre-inflation price by a fraction *k* of price P_1 so that pre-inflation price becomes $P_1(1 - k)$. This gives the inflation rate (which is the percentage increase in price) as:

$$\dot{P}_1 = k/(1-k). \tag{3.4}$$

Now let us assume that the household's wage income, Y_1, in the post-inflation period is higher than that in the pre-inflation period by an amount t so that:

$$\dot{Y}_1 = t. \tag{3.5}$$

Hence, we can write:

$$\dot{C}_1 = \varepsilon_i (t - s). \tag{3.6}$$

Where, $s = \dfrac{k}{1-k}$.

Equation (3.6) shows that the compensation cost for inflation is high in terms of the required income increase, *t*. For instance, if we want to compensate for a 20 percent rise in prices, income has to increase by 25 percent or more for ensuring, $\dot{C}_1 \geq 0$.

For simplicity, we assume that there are two individuals in society; individual 1 is poor and individual 2 is non-poor. Denoting C_1 and C_2 as their respective consumptions, the total national product is:

$$C = C_1 + C_2. \tag{3.7}$$

And the percentage change in national product will be given by:

$$\dot{C} = (1-\delta)\dot{C}_1 + \delta\dot{C}_2. \tag{3.8}$$

Where, $\delta = \frac{C_2}{C}$.

In the short run, $\dot{C} = 0$ and if the policy is to maintain the same percentage change in the consumption of the poor and the non-poor ($\dot{C}_1 = \dot{C}_2$) then

$$\dot{C}_1 = \varepsilon_i (t - s)\dot{C}_2. \tag{3.9}$$

This shows that the wage increase of the poor must fully compensate the loss in purchasing power due to inflation ($t = S$) if the consumption distribution is to be maintained. However, if $S > t$, that is, the inflation rate exceeds wage increases, then the consumption of the poor will fall relative to the non-poor and vice versa. It shows that, in the short run when the total supply is fixed, the process of distribution of consumption among the poor and the non-poor is a zero-sum game: if one gains, the other loses. And, since the gains are determined by changes in the purchasing power, the poor need to be compensated adequately to ensure that their relative position in society is not worsened.

3.3.2 *Wage Change-Inflation Dynamics*

We now examine the wage change-inflation dynamics over time in Bangladesh with agricultural wage laborers as the focal group in order to bring out the implications of inflation on the cost of living of the poor. We start with an analysis of the changes in their purchasing power over time by comparing the increases in agricultural wages and inflation, assuming that the agricultural wages constitute the sole source of income for these workers ($y_1 = w$) and the price level facing them is represented by the consumer price index (CPI). Table 3.1 shows that food price rose faster rela-

Table 3.1 Average inflation and changes in relative price

		Average inflation rate (percent)					*Price relative to general price level (CPI)*				
		1996–00	*2001–05*	*2006–10*	*2010–14*	*2015–18*	*1996–00*	*2001–05*	*2006–10*	*2010–14*	*2015–18*
National	General	6.17	4.29	7.66	8.12	5.89	1.00	1.00	1.00	1.69	2.26
	Food	7.48	4.26	8.80	8.42	6.18	1.06	1.02	1.15	1.81	2.44
	Non-food	4.34	4.40	5.99	7.76	5.44	0.99	0.98	0.92	1.53	2.04
Rural	General	6.31	4.36	7.72	7.90	5.53	1.00	1.00	1.00	1.71	2.26
	Food	7.37	4.24	8.51	8.09	5.76	1.02	1.01	1.04	1.81	2.39
	Non-food	4.50	4.61	6.27	7.64	5.11	0.96	0.99	0.93	1.56	2.06
Urban	General	5.83	4.10	7.49	8.56	6.56	1.00	1.00	1.00	1.65	2.26
	Food	7.76	4.32	9.39	9.24	7.15	1.04	1.05	1.12	1.83	2.56
	Non-food	3.94	3.89	5.27	7.88	5.91	0.96	0.95	0.88	1.49	2.00

Source: Various issues of the monthly report "Consumer Price Index (CPI), Inflation Rate and Wage Rate Index (WRI) in Bangladesh" of BBS

Note: The inflation rates refer to 1995–96 as the base since figures for earlier years are not available with the new base of 2005–06

Table 3.2 Average nominal wage rate index

	General	*Manufacturing*	*Construction*	*Agriculture*	*Fisheries*
1970–75	147	141	161	156	117
1975–80	311	277	371	334	295
1980–85	615	604	674	564	628
1985–90	1179	1232	1263	1023	1145
1990–95	1634	1743	1558	1503	1664
1995–00	2136	2369	2008	1880	2054
2000–05	2891	3430	2570	2429	2560
2005–10	4399	5358	3707	3735	3823
2010–15	7333.8	8046.0	7298.4	7288.8	5989.2

Source: Various issues of the monthly report "Consumer Price Index (CPI), Inflation Rate and Wage Rate Index (WRI) in Bangladesh" of BBS

Note: For the periods 1970–75 to 2010–15, base year 1969–70=100

tive to general price level (as measured by the CPI) in both rural and urban areas since the mid-1990s. The relative price increases are also higher in recent years and in urban areas.

Table 3.2 gives the average nominal wage rate index for four different groups of daily wage workers (manufacturing, construction, agriculture and fisheries). It can be seen that although the manufacturing wage index was nearly 10 percent lower than the agricultural wage index during 1970–75, the situation reversed during 2008–11 and the manufacturing wage index stood at 42 percent higher than the agricultural wage index. It can be seen that the wage indices of construction, agricultural and fisheries workers move rather closely and their absolute values are also quite similar.

For measuring changes in income and cost of living in recent years, the cumulative growth in nominal wages and CPI inflation in each year after 2000 is given in Tables 3.3 and 3.4 respectively. Table 3.3 shows that agricultural wages in Bangladesh on average increased by 9.1 percent per year over the 2000–2010 periods. Similar changes are 9.3 percent for manufacturing workers followed by 8.0 percent for fisheries and 7.5 percent for construction workers. The average growth of nominal wages was 9.22 in the period of 2000–2015 where agriculture wage rate grew by 10.74 percent while manufacturing grew by 8.85 percent (Table 3.3).

The cost of living of the workers, on the other hand, increased at an annual average growth rate of 6.6 percent during the period 2000–2018 (Table 3.4). This, in terms of Eq. (3.3), suggests positive change in real consumption of the laborers who mostly belong to poor households in the country. Table 3.5 provides further information that explains Eq. (3.3) in

Table 3.3 Percentage increase in nominal wage index over 2000

Fiscal Year	*General*	*Manufacturing*	*Construction*	*Agriculture*	*Fisheries*
2000–01	4.14	4.81	3.06	5.11	3.20
2005–06	46.69	58.88	26.38	43.59	41.06
2010–11	141.92	150.94	117.98	161.41	127.16
2014–15	272.34	253.68	293.88	354.30	221.13
2015–16	296.59	–	–	383.38	–
2016–17	322.42	–	–	415.26	–
2017–18	349.68	–	–	448.29	–
Average per year (2000–2015)	9.22	8.85	9.83	10.74	8.17

Source: Various issues of the monthly report "Consumer Price Index (CPI), Inflation Rate and Wage Rate Index (WRI) in Bangladesh" of BBS

Table 3.4 Percentage increase in CPI inflation after 2000

Fiscal Year	*General*	*Food*	*Non-food*
2000–01	1.93	1.38	3.04
2005–06	32.10	32.54	31.96
2010–11	93.89	108.40	72.80
2015–16	190.43	211.20	164.80
2016–17	206.23	229.90	177.02
2017–18	223.93	253.40	187.36
Average per year (2000–2012)	6.59	7.25	5.61
Average per year (2000–2018)	6.54	7.09	5.72

Source: Various issues of the monthly report "Consumer Price Index (CPI), Inflation Rate and Wage Rate Index (WRI) in Bangladesh" of BBS

Table 3.5 Average real wage rate index (1969–70=100)

	General	*Manufacturing*	*Construction*	*Agriculture*	*Fisheries*
1970–75	77	76	81	...	...
1975–80	73	65	87	...	...
1980–85	87	85	96	...	...
1985–90	104	109	111	81	90
1990–95	110	118	105	90	101
1995–00	119	132	112	105	112
2000–05	138	164	123	105	115
2005–10	149	183	123	115	121

Source: Various issues of Statistical Year Book from 1975 to 2010, BBS

terms of the real wage rate of the different group of workers (taking ´y₁= ´w, where w is the wage rate).

As Table 3.5 shows, the real wage rate indices for all categories of workers have shown rising trends since the 1970s. The real wage rate index of manufacturing workers has shown the highest increase followed by the indices of construction and fisheries workers. The index of agricultural workers has shown the least growth. It largely stagnated during the decade beginning since the mid-1990s and has shown some rising trend after 2005.

Table 3.6 interprets Eq. (3.3) in terms of the ratio of the cumulative growth of nominal wage index for different group of laborers to that of CPI inflation $\dot{w}/\dot{p}_1$ where, p_1 is the CPI inflation. From the model described in the previous section, one can conclude that when, $(\dot{w}/\dot{p}_1) < 1$, there would be a fall in the real consumption of the working households $(\dot{q}_1 < 0)$.

The information given in Fig. 3.1 shows that the ratio remained above unity in all years during 2000–01 to 2017–18. This indicates that the consumption of the agricultural workers did not experience any fall in the 2000s despite rises in inflation especially in recent years. As a matter of fact, the absolute value of the ratio was lowest in 2007–08 after which it has been rising steadily. This suggests that on average, the wage rate of the agricultural workers has risen by a margin that has been adequate to neutralize the adverse impact of price hike in recent years.

The annual growth of the wage rate index (both nominal and real) over the decades shows that almost all indices experienced higher growth dur-

Table 3.6 Growth in wage rate index in Bangladesh (percent per year)

	1970–1980	*1980–1990*	*1990–2000*	*2000–2015*
Nominal wage rate index (1969–70=100)				
General	17.50	12.78	5.31	9.01
Fisheries	34.25	12.26	4.63	7.90
Construction	19.92	11.78	4.52	9.57
Manufacturing	15.67	14.69	6.06	8.74
Agriculture	18.50	11.12	5.06	10.35
Real wage rate index (1969–70=100)				
General	−0.77	3.06	1.00	4.27
Fisheries	…	2.51	0.97	0.61
Construction	1.47	2.03	0.35	1.01
Manufacturing	−1.72	4.67	1.82	5.01
Agriculture	…	1.42	1.02	1.98

Source: Various issues of Statistical Year Book from 1975 to 2015, BBS

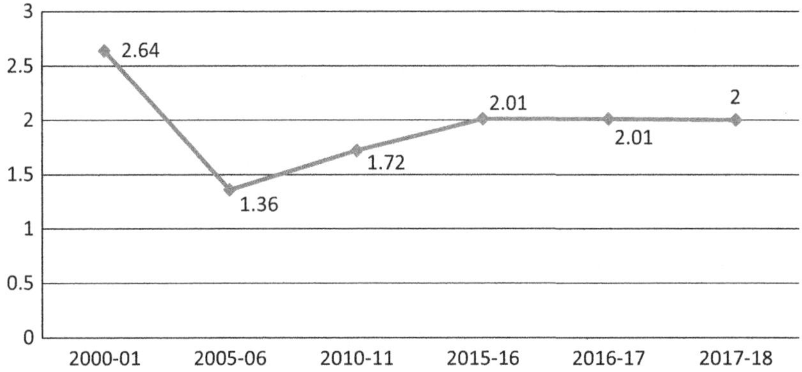

Fig. 3.1 Growth of agricultural wages relative to growth of CPI inflation 2000–2018. (Source: Various issues of the monthly report "Consumer Price Index (CPI), Inflation Rate and Wage Rate Index (WRI) in Bangladesh" of BBS)

ing the period of the 2000s (Table 3.6). In particular, the agricultural wage rate index experienced the highest growth during the decade followed by the growth rate of the manufacturing wage index. The analysis shows that the average return to labor has risen robustly in the past decade contributing positively toward improving the living standards of the working population.

3.3.3 Recent Wage Movements in Agriculture and Non-Agriculture: Survey Results

Since wage adjustment plays an important role in withstanding inflationary impacts, movement of wages of daily wage laborers is a significant aspect of the process. For examining recent wage movements, the present study collected wage data of daily agricultural laborers from 14 districts, during December 2012, covering five regions of the country.[5] From each district, around 100 sample households were selected, covering both rural and urban areas. The total sample size was 1434 daily wage laborers in both agriculture and non-agricultural activities. The agricultural laborers

[5] The five regions are: Northern (Rangpur division), Western (Rajshahi division), Central (Dhaka division), Eastern (Chittagong and Sylhet divisions), and Southern (Barisal and Khulna divisions).

included farm and fisheries workers; while non-agricultural laborers covered unskilled labor from a wide range of occupations such as construction workers, transport workers including rickshaw/van pullers, tailors, hotel/restaurant workers and temporary housekeepers/maids.

In view of a somewhat limited coverage of the above data for certain categories of non-agricultural unskilled workers, for example, helpers in construction sites, carpenters and other daily laborers, the above information was also supplemented by the daily wage data taken from the Monthly Statistical Bulletin of the BBS. Figures 3.2 and 3.3 show the average rural daily nominal and real wages respectively for the period, covering Bangla months of Baishakh to Chaitra (from mid-April of the earlier year to mid-April of the following year) during 2009–10 to 2012–13 (data for the latest year was until December 2012). In nominal terms, one can see a consistent rise in both agricultural and non-agricultural wage rates over the period. In 2009–10, the average nominal wage of agricultural laborers was Tk. 192 per day while the same was Tk. 170 for non-agricultural laborers. The wage rate increased by 14 percent and 7 percent in 2010–11 and 2011–12 respectively for agricultural laborers, while the increase was by 25 percent and 18 percent respectively for non-agricultural laborers. Moreover, the trend in agricultural wages shows fluctuations with distinct seasonal peaks while the non-agricultural wage has a more smooth growth. It can be seen that agricultural wage remained higher than the

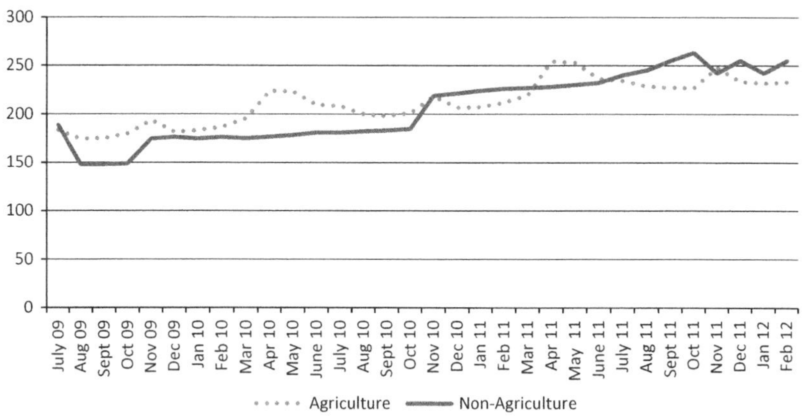

Fig. 3.2 Nominal daily wage rate in agriculture and non-agriculture. (Source: BIDS Survey 2012 and BBS)

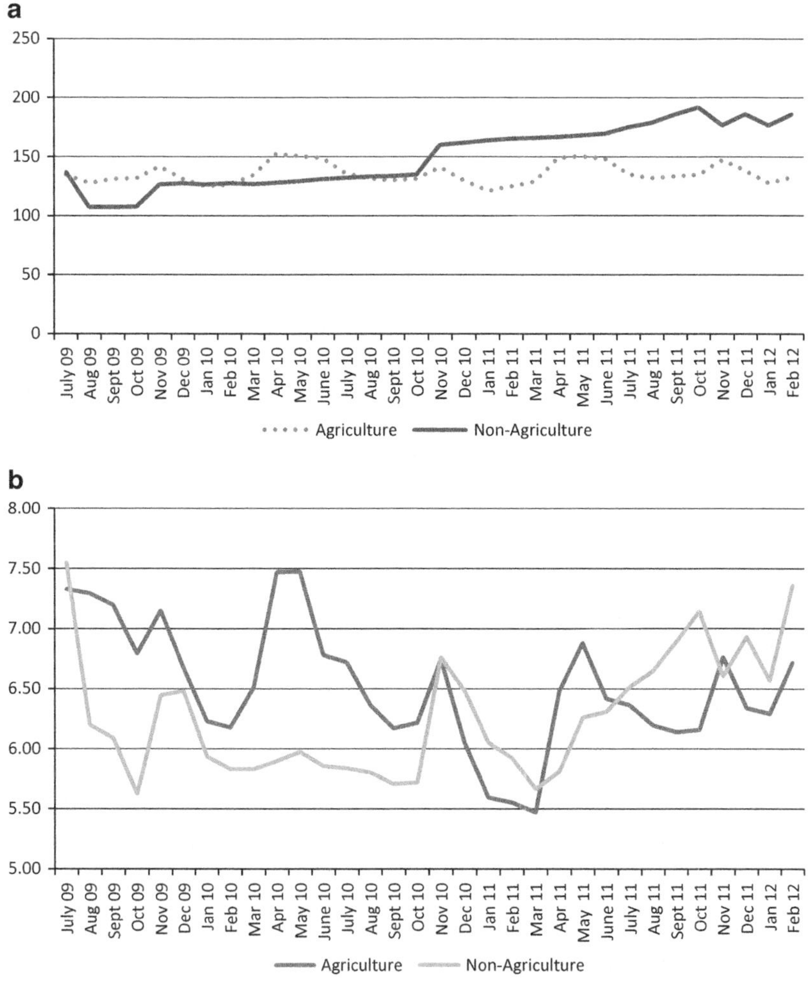

Fig. 3.3 Real daily wage rate in agriculture and non-agriculture. (**a**) Deflated by group-specific CPI. (**b**) Kg of coarse rice equivalent. (Source: BIDS Survey 2012 and BBS)

non-agricultural wage until the end of 2010, probably due to the high response of rural agricultural wage to rice price. The situation was reversed afterward with the average non-agricultural wage rate exceeding the agricultural wage.

In Fig. 3.3a, daily real wage rates are shown by deflating the nominal wages by group-specific CPI deflators calculated in the present study. From this figure, it is evident that the real agricultural wage rate has remained consistently below the non-agricultural wage rate since the middle of 2010, and the gap has widened over time. Moreover, the real agricultural wage has witnessed wider fluctuations relative to non-agricultural wage.

As seen in earlier chapters, food accounts for the largest share of expenditure for most households in Bangladesh and this is especially true for the poor rural households. It is worthwhile, therefore, to examine the trend of real wages in terms of food inflation. In this context, rice is the main staple food with a high share in total household food expenditure and contributes nearly two-thirds of the total per capita caloric intake. Since coarse rice is the staple for the poor households, Fig. 3.3b plots the patterns of real wage in terms of kg of coarse rice equivalence.

From the Figure, it can be seen that, in July 2009, an agricultural laborer on average could buy 7.3 kg of coarse rice with his/her daily wage, while for the non-agricultural laborer the amount was 7.6 kg in July 2010. Agricultural laborers could buy about 6.7 kg of rice using one day's wage, while a non-agricultural laborers daily wage was equivalent to 5.8 kg of rice. In July 2011, the purchasing power of daily wage of an agricultural laborer further eroded to 6.4 kg of rice, while that of a non-agricultural laborer rose to 6.5 kg of rice. In February 2012, it has risen to 6.7 kg of rice for agricultural laborer and 7.4 kg of rice for the non-agricultural laborer. Despite these increases, the real wages of both groups of laborers in 2012 remain lower than their respective rice equivalent values in 2009.

There are also significant variations in the wage rate across different regions of the country. Table 3.7 gives the average rural wages of agricultural laborers for the five regions considered in the study. It also contains peak and lean season wages during the years. Panel A gives the nominal daily wage in taka. As can be seen, the average wage rate is the highest in the Central region and lowest in the Western region; the difference between the two regions was more than three times in 2009–10 which marginally reduced to two-and-a half times in 2012–13. Similar high variation is also observed between the peak and lean season wages in the two regions. There has, however, been a trend of lowering of differences between the peak and the lean season wages among the regions.

Table 3.7 Daily wage rate of agricultural laborers by regions

Region	*2009–10*			*2010–11*			*2011–12*			*2012–13*		
	A	P	L	A	P	L	A	P	L	A	P	L
A. Nominal wages in Tk.												
Northern	142	152	136	158	180	145	177	186	171	187	191	184
Western	98	152	83	109	148	98	132	217	108	136	213	116
Central	320	369	285	330	386	288	344	409	303	361	434	322
Eastern	234	250	224	255	260	254	280	281	270	295	297	290
Southern	183	205	177	211	220	202	241	250	231	240	255	215
CV	0.44	0.40	0.43	0.40	0.39	0.39	0.36	0.32	0.36	0.36	0.35	0.37
B. Real wage (deflated by group-specific CPI)												
Northern	106.10	118.20	98.40	101.70	112.70	94.90	104.90	118.20	98.40	102.90	105.10	101.20
Western	78.10	122.70	62.10	74.90	127.50	57.60	75.80	122.70	62.10	74.80	117.20	63.80
Central	209.50	250.20	172.00	208.00	243.50	178.80	204.30	250.20	171.90	198.60	238.80	177.20
Eastern	169.10	187.20	159.60	159.80	166.30	148.60	163.50	172.00	154.80	162.30	163.40	159.60
Southern	139.30	151.00	125.30	135.30	155.00	121.00	139.10	151.00	125.30	132.10	140.30	118.30
CV	0.37	0.33	0.36	0.38	0.32	0.39	0.36	0.33	0.36	0.32	0.31	0.33
C. Real wage (in terms of kg of coarse rice)												
Northern	5.20	5.90	4.80	4.70	5.00	4.40	4.80	5.30	4.60	5.50	5.60	5.40
Western	3.50	4.70	2.70	3.50	5.50	2.50	3.30	4.90	2.90	4.00	6.20	3.40
Central	10.50	12.60	10.30	9.60	11.20	8.30	8.80	11.00	8.20	10.50	12.70	9.40
Eastern	8.60	10.30	7.80	7.40	8.30	6.40	7.70	8.10	7.30	8.60	8.70	8.50
Southern	6.90	8.40	6.10	6.20	7.10	5.20	6.60	6.70	6.30	7.00	7.40	6.30
CV	0.39	0.38	0.46	0.38	0.33	0.41	0.35	0.35	0.36	0.32	0.31	0.33

Source: BIDS Survey, December 2012; BBS

Note: The years refer to Bangla calendar months (April–March). For 2012–13, the data cover April–December 2012. A is average, P is the peak season and L is lean period reported daily wage. For 2012–13, real wages in Panel B and Panel C are computed by deflating with CPI (general level) and average price of coarse rice respectively. CV is the coefficient of variation. For definition of the regions, see text

The above can probably be taken as a sign of greater integration of the labor markets across the regions and lower fluctuations in the demand for laborer over different times of the year. The coefficients of variation have also shown declining trends.

In Panels B and C, real wage rates are given for the same period.[6] In panel B, the real wage rate is computed by deflating nominal wage by group-specific CPI computed in the present study, while Panel C gives the real wage in terms of kg of coarse rice equivalence of the nominal wage. Both the alternative measures show moderate growth as well as declines in real wage in different regions during the period. In terms of group-specific CPI deflated real wage of the agricultural laborers, the average wage marginally declined in all regions over the three-year period (2009–10 to 2011–12). The peak and the lean period wages remained mostly unchanged in different regions. The trends are similar in terms of the quantity of rice that can be purchased with the daily nominal wage. Although no definite regional pattern can be seen, the declines are more prominent in regions where real wages are relatively high (e.g. Central and Eastern regions) compared with regions with depressed wages (e.g. Southern Western and Northern regions).

The above results indicate that, in the face of inflation, the wage laborers are able to adjust wage rates in order to make up, even if partially, for the loss in real income. Even though a clearly rising trend in the daily wage of agricultural laborers in real terms is not observed in different regions, the figures indicate that the agricultural laborers are at least able to prevent any drastic fall in their purchasing power through nominal wage adjustments. The real wage of unskilled workers (which is relevant to the poor) in non-agriculture sector also follows a similar trend (see Figures in Appendix).

Thus it appears from the above analysis that the daily wage laborers in both agriculture and non-agriculture sectors, who constitute the largest poor group in the country, are usually able to protect the level of their daily real wage in the face of rising inflation through upward adjustment in the nominal wage rate without any substantial time lag.[7] One factor that facilitates such quick indexation of the nominal wage rate to inflation is the

[6] For details on nominal and real wages at regional levels, see figures in Appendix.

[7] This has often been made possible through the pursuit of the widely used traditional practice of setting nominal wage rate in many locations on a daily basis keeping in view the price of rice in the local market. This not only protects the real income of the poor day laborers but also ensures their access to a minimum quantity of the wage good (rice).

prevailing characteristics of the agricultural labor market that ensure flexibility and permit almost daily wage bargaining keeping in view the reservation wage of a minimum quantity of the wage good (rice). A similar behavior is also noticed in the informal labor markets that set the daily wage rates in construction, services, transport (including rickshaw pulling) and other low-paid activities in which the poor are the major participants.

The evidence on wage adjustment thus indicates that the poor day laborers in Bangladesh have some ability to at least partially revise their nominal wage income rather quickly to compensate for the loss in real income due to inflation. This shows that nearly half of the poor in the rural areas and more than one-third in the urban areas (who belong to the daily wage labor households) can negotiate an upward adjustment in their major source of earning, the wage component of household income, in the face of inflation. This group, therefore, can somewhat protect themselves against the onslaught of inflation although the net welfare impact could go either way, since they would probably receive higher prices for some of the commodities that they sell while they would pay higher prices for many of the goods they purchase.

On the other hand, most of the components of income and expenditure of the poor households belonging to the self-employed category, who constitute more than one-third of the poor households in both rural and urban areas, are affected in diverse ways, and so the net impact of inflation is difficult to predict a priori. The welfare of the salaried poor households, though constituting only around 5 percent of the rural poor households but around a fifth of urban poor households, are more likely to be negatively affected since their real income is eroded by rising inflation while they pay higher prices for purchased goods. The remaining major poor group comprising nearly 10 percent of the poor households in both rural and urban areas belongs to unemployed/not working category households and these households, no doubt, become extremely disadvantaged with rising inflation.

3.3.4 Seasonal Labor Migration: A Coping Strategy

Labor migration remains an important component of the traditional livelihood strategies, especially of the agricultural labor households in Bangladesh. While migration to the Middle-East and other global destinations has of late assumed a significant role, seasonal migration (e.g. "labor circulation") across different regions of the country still remains a major feature of the country's labor market. Various studies, especially those focusing on village level dynamics, point out large scale seasonal labor migration, particularly of male labor, from certain parts of the country (e.g. the northern region) to other regions (e.g. the eastern and central regions) in search of temporary livelihood. Such migration contributes to the rural economy of these primarily seasonally dominated crop-employment intensive areas in different ways, for example, by providing access to employment in migration destinations (having somewhat more diversified local economies) at higher wages as job opportunities become scanty in these depressed locations, and by enhancing incomes and food security for these poor households during difficult times.

Despite the decline in the relative importance of agriculture, the seasonal migration patterns, however, are more dominated by agriculture. Sharp contrasts in the composition of economic activities and differences in agro-ecological characteristics create both push factors that provide incentives for laborers to migrate seasonally in search of short-term livelihood opportunities. In addition, there exist pull factors that create migration opportunities in certain locations.

The important issue, however, is: does seasonal migration contribute to reducing wage differential across locations and make a positive contribution to the livelihoods of the migrant labor households? While answer to these questions are beyond the scope of the present study, one may observe that for the seasonal migrants, such migration is, at least in a large part, a component of their coping mechanism although, for some households, temporary migration plays an important contributory role in improving their livelihoods. Obviously, the gains from such migration can be significantly enhanced by making the labor market more efficient through improved information flows and reduced transaction costs.

From the perspective of improving the labor market outcomes, the priority is to reduce the push factors, especially through developing alternative and supplementary livelihood opportunities in employment deficit areas, and strengthen the pull factors that would encourage labor to migrate in response to positive economic opportunities. Right policies based on credible information on the numbers involved in seasonal migration and understanding various flow patterns and their characteristics can make the process more effective and productive from the perspective of the poor.

3.4 Data and Methodology

This chapter provides an analysis of the short-run links between nominal wages and inflation across different daily labor and fixed income group households using vector autoregression (VAR) techniques. The VAR model allows examination of the impulse response of wages to inflationary shocks, and vice versa. Although it has been widely recognized that wage shocks might have led to inflationary developments, the analysis in the Sect. 3.3 suggests that wages follow the pattern of inflation in Bangladesh, at least in the short run. Thus, it seems important to examine econometrically, the impulse response of nominal wages to price (CPI) shock. Since our focus is on the short-run links between nominal wages and prices, we have abstracted from considering explicitly longer run determinants of wages and prices, such as productivity and product market structure.

Although the role of wages in the inflationary process is well recognized in theory, it has been investigated by several empirical studies as well. While Montiel (1989) finds an important role of wages on inflation, some other studies, such as De Haan and Zelhorst (1990), Moser (1994), Loungani and Swagel (2001), find no significant impact of nominal wage on inflation. Similarly, based on structural VARs, Hoffmaister and Roldos (1996) find that, while it is possible to capture indirectly the effect of wage shocks on prices through their impact on aggregate nominal shocks, they could not identify the specific contribution of wages to nominal price fluctuations.

3.4.1 Data

For estimating variance decompositions, we use rural daily wage rate of day laborers and monthly wage rate of non-agricultural laborers obtained through the primary survey conducted under the study. For inflation, estimated CPIs (see Chap. 2) for different income categories of day laborer and fixed income groups are used. The monthly wage data for the time period spanning over 2009–2012 are used.

The Augmented Dickey-Fuller test shows that all the variables are stationary in their logarithmic forms. Therefore, these two variables are used to estimate basic VAR models.

3.5 Empirical Results

3.5.1 *Daily Labor Households*

At a forecast horizon of less than one year (10 months), variance decomposition shows that inflation shocks are a very important source of fluctuations in daily wages, accounting for 40.46 percent shocks in wage after three months in rural areas (Table 3.8, Panel A: II). This shows that the rural daily labor households have been able to quickly adjust 40 percent of inflation shocks into wages within three months of inflation shock, and thereafter with a slow adjustment, they could adjust 54 percent in 10 months of inflation shocks. However, wage itself could not explain price shocks for any of the inflation series (Table 3.8, Panel A: I), mainly due to the short-term nature of the data.

It can be observed that extreme income groups, such as poorer and higher income day labor households could adjust inflation to wages quicker than those of other day labor households. They could adjust 56 percent of inflation shocks through wage adjustment by three months and about 60 percent by 10 months. For other day labor households, adjustment pace remains almost the same (40 percent in three months and 55 percent in 10 months).

The variance decomposition analysis suggests that wage formation does not have any impact on inflation in Bangladesh; rather inflationary pressures exert upward pressure on wage adjustments for daily wage laborers, at least in the short run. The daily labor households could adjust 40 percent of inflationary shocks within three months of inflationary shocks. However, afterwards the rate of adjustment becomes rather slow.

3.5.2 *Fixed Income Households*

The variance decomposition shows that compared with the daily labor households, fixed income households are mostly unable to adjust inflationary shocks into wages. The poorer and lower middle income fixed income groups could adjust only about 10 percent of inflation shocks into wages after five months in urban/semi-urban areas (Table 3.9, Panel A: II). The results show that the non-agricultural poorer fixed income households are able to adjust 25 percent of inflation into wages in 10 months of inflation shock, while the upper income households could adjust about 30 percent to wages in 10 months after the inflationary shocks. However, wage itself could not explain price shocks for any of the inflation series (Table 3.9, Panel A: I).

3.5.3 Impulse Responses

The impulse responses (Fig. 3.4) show that an innovation in the rate of inflation responds positively to the increase of daily wage rate for daily labor households, particularly for the poor. The wage response to inflationary shocks is prominent in three months, and afterwards the response is very minimal for daily labor households irrespective of their income levels. The analysis indicates that the day laborers can adjust a substantial portion of inflation to real wages very quickly, due to which the adverse impact of inflation on them appears to be less. Therefore, although poor daily labor households face relatively high inflation, not much loss in terms of welfare takes place due to flexibility in wage adjustments. However, as Fig. 3.5 shows, fixed income households cannot adjust the inflationary shocks quickly—there exists substantial time lag in wage adjustments. Thus, these groups of households face the most hardship resulting from inflationary shocks.

3.6 Conclusions and Policy Recommendations

This chapter examines the dynamics of inflation and wage adjustments in the labor market of Bangladesh, especially keeping in view the rising food inflation in recent years. The analysis shows that the daily wage laborers in both agriculture and non-agriculture sectors, who constitute the largest poor group in the country, are usually able to protect the level of their daily real wage in the face of rising inflation through upward adjustment in the nominal wage rate without any substantial time lag. A similar behavior is also noticed in the informal labor markets that set the daily wage rates in construction, services, transport (including rickshaw pulling) and other low-paid activities in which the poor are the major participants. The poor day laborers in Bangladesh have some ability to, at least partially, revise their nominal wage income rather quickly to compensate for the loss in real income due to inflation. On the other hand, the self-employed category and salaried poor households are more likely to be negatively affected since their real income is eroded by rising inflation while they pay higher prices for purchased goods. The remaining major poor group comprising nearly

10 percent of the poor households in both rural and urban areas belongs to unemployed/not working category households, and these households, no doubt, become extremely disadvantaged with rising inflation.

In Bangladesh, supply side factors resulting from disruptions in domestic production and supply (e.g. due to floods or natural disasters) and unusually high and rising global prices of food, fuel and other essential commodities usually trigger inflationary pressures in the economy. This highlights the importance of prudent supply management as an important strategy to fight inflation. In a situation when inflation becomes persistent, direct measures are important to reduce inflationary pressures instead of leaving the burden of keeping inflation at low levels on demand management policies alone. With rising food prices, one useful way to dampen the price effects of food supply shocks is to maintain adequate strategic buffer stock of food that could be released when needed through different food transfer programs targeted at the poor and food insecure households.

Keeping in view the financial burden of subsidies in the context of limited fiscal space of the government, targeted safety net programs, feeding programs for school children, food-for-work program, open market sales and guaranteed employment program for the poor and disadvantaged households especially during the lean seasons are some useful measures that can be used in the short run to enhance food entitlements and stabilize prices. Along with mitigating the inflationary impact on the poor through generating short-term employment opportunities and providing access to transfer incomes in the rural areas, it is important to ensure food to the poor at subsidized prices, especially in the urban areas as they do not have any surplus food at home.

Historically there exists a close association between poverty and agricultural wage employment in Bangladesh. Hence, other dimensions of well-being such as education levels and nutrition status are also likely to be strongly and inversely correlated with agricultural wage employment. Different rounds of HIES data show that the probability of being employed in agricultural wage labor falls monotonically, as one moves up the consumption distribution. As such, changes in poverty are likely to be correlated with changes in agricultural wages in the rural areas. The present analysis also notes that real wages have risen over time (continuing a trend that started in the early 1980s) and the rate of increase appears to have accelerated in recent years.

The nature of employment in the regular non-farm category, in general, is characterized by better terms and involves higher skills and wages, and hence can support higher consumption levels. In most cases, however, the poor households do not have access to such employment. In the case of casual non-farm employment, education and other positive elements of quality labor are not particularly relevant, and lower education is not a major hurdle in getting such employment in the non-farm activities as long as such employment opportunities exist. As such, casual non-farm employment can be accessed by the poor, especially those who have some education. On the other hand, self-employment in the non-farm sector is a truly heterogeneous category, comprising productive and remunerative employment at the one end and the "last–resort" option at the lowest end.

In view of these complex dimensions of the rural non-farm employment, the poverty impact of the expansion of the non-farm sector depends more on the nature of activities that drive the expansion of the sector. More importantly, the pro-poor expansion of the non-farm sector is largely determined by activities that are education and skill intensive and provides productive and remunerative employment opportunities.

In the medium term, responses such as improving institutional capacities and governance structures including investments in agricultural research, technology and extension services and in improving trade, marketing and post-harvest facilities are the feasible ways of sustaining positive outcomes. Similarly, investment in education and health in rural areas, infrastructure such as irrigation and rural roads can bring out productivity gains and alleviate the trend of higher rice prices and food prices in general. As the poor have limited income to spend on essential non-food items, priority public expenditures should be reviewed to ensure their access to critical non-food items pertaining to long-term human development such as education and health. At the same time, efforts to stay on inclusive growth path would facilitate policies for addressing the challenges of rising and high food prices facing the poor.

Obviously, efforts to keep inflation within tolerable limits involve a long-term battle with support of prudent policies. In order to ensure high and sustainable growth in domestic output consistent with price stability, Bangladesh requires continuous pursuit of supportive macroeconomic policies; heightened business confidence and growth in private sector led investment; measures to address power, transport and other infrastructure constraints; speedy implementation of ongoing structural, institutional and financial sector reforms; and policy continuity and reasonable socio-political stability over the medium term.

Appendix

Table 3.8 Variance decomposition of daily wages

A. Variance decomposition of daily wages (rural) to food inflation (rural)

I. Variance decomposition of LWAGE_R				*II. Variance decomposition of LCPI_R*			
Period	*S.E.*	*LWAGE_R*	*LCPI_R*	*Period*	*S.E.*	*LWAGE_R*	*LCPI_R*
1	0.0234	100.00	0.00	1	0.044	2.590	97.413
2	0.034	99.27	0.73	2	0.051	2.256	97.744
3	0.040	99.38	0.62	3	0.065	40.460	59.539
7	0.051	99.46	0.54	7	0.074	51.169	48.831
10	0.054	99.47	0.50	10	0.076	54.209	45.791

B. Variance decomposition of daily wages (rural) to food inflation of poor daily labor households (rural)

Variance decomposition of LWAGE_R				*Variance decomposition of LCPI_DLP*			
Period	*S.E.*	*LWAGE_R*	*LCPI_DLP*	*Period*	*S.E.*	*LWAGE_R*	*LCPI_DLP*
1	0.0240	100.000	0.000	1	0.0359	1.603	98.397
2	0.0340	96.578	3.422	2	0.0406	3.712	96.289
3	0.0392	96.059	3.940	3	0.0580	53.226	46.774
7	0.0480	96.344	3.656	7	0.0700	62.630	37.369
10	0.0500	96.345	3.655	10	0.0730	64.878	35.122

C. Variance decomposition of daily wages (rural) to food inflation of lower middle income day labor households (rural)

Variance decomposition of LWAGE_R				*Variance decomposition of LCPI_DLM1*			
Period	*S.E.*	*LWAGE_R*	*LCPI_DLM1*	*Period*	*S.E.*	*LWAGE_R*	*LCPI_DLM1*
1	0.024	100.000	0.000	1	0.0480	0.568	99.431
2	0.035	98.835	1.164	2	0.0510	0.544	99.455
3	0.039	98.375	1.624	3	0.0670	40.274	59.725
7	0.049	98.365	1.634	7	0.0770	53.501	46.498
10	0.052	98.349	1.650	10	0.0803	56.156	43.843

(*continued*)

Table 3.8 (continued)

D. Variance decomposition of daily wages (Rural) to food inflation of upper middle income day labor households (rural)

Variance decomposition of LWAGE_R				*Variance decomposition of LCPI_DLM2*			
Period	*S.E.*	*LWAGE_R*	*LCPI_DLM2*	*Period*	*S.E.*	*LWAGE_R*	*LCPI_DLM2*
1	0.0217	100.000	0.000	1	0.035	6.359	93.64147
2	0.0320	89.912	10.088	2	0.036	12.088	87.91211
3	0.0360	83.348	16.652	3	0.044	39.450	60.55042
7	0.0440	81.831	18.169	7	0.056	52.138	47.86151
10	0.0460	81.383	18.618	10	0.059	55.049	44.95115

E. Variance decomposition of daily wages (rural) to food inflation of higher income day labor households (rural)

Variance decomposition of LWAGE_R				*Variance decomposition of LCPI_DLU*			
Period	*S.E.*	*LWAGE_R*	*LCPI_DLU*	*Period*	*S.E.*	*LWAGE_R*	*LCPI_DLU*
1	0.0220	100.000	0.000	1	0.0344	8.245	91.754
2	0.0327	91.389	8.610	2	0.0360	13.672	86.327
3	0.0368	86.907	13.092	3	0.0458	45.663	54.336
7	0.0447	86.515	13.484	7	0.0570	57.744	42.255
10	0.0474	86.344	13.655	10	0.0610	60.494	39.505

Source: Authors' compilation; income categories are defined in Chap. 2 (Hossain and Mujeri)

Notes: LWAGE_R = log (wage for rural); LCPI_R = log (CPI for rural); LCPI_DLP = log (CPI for poor day labor); LCPI_DLM1 = log (CPI for lower middle income day labor); LCPI_DLM2 = log (CPI for upper middle income day labor); LLCPI_DMU = log (CPI for upper income day labor)

Table 3.9 Variance decomposition of monthly wages

A. Variance decomposition of monthly wages to food inflation (poor)

I. Variance decomposition of LWAGE_FI				*II. Variance decomposition of LCPI_FIP*			
Period	*S.E.*	*LWAGE_FI*	*LCPI_FIP*	*Period*	*S.E.*	*LWAGE_FI*	*LCPI_FIP*
1	0.034	100.00	0.00	1	0.04	0.52	99.47
5	0.070	96.01	3.98	5	0.04	10.15	89.84
8	0.090	94.66	5.33	8	0.04	19.68	80.31
10	0.102	94.18	5.81	10	0.05	25.43	74.56

(continued)

Table 3.9 (continued)

B. Variance decomposition of monthly wages to food inflation (lower middle income)

Variance Decomposition of LWAGE_FI				*Variance Decomposition of LCPI_FIM1*			
Period	*S.E.*	*LWAGE_FI*	*LCPI_FIM1*	*Period*	*S.E.*	*LWAGE_FI*	*LCPI_FIM1*
1	0.0348	100.000	0.000	1	0.0519	0.147	99.85300
5	0.0742	99.574	0.426	5	0.0570	15.527	84.47300
8	0.0967	99.515	0.484	8	0.0610	25.904	74.09500
10	0.1110	99.496	0.504	10	0.0640	32.225	67.77477

C. Variance decomposition of monthly wages to food inflation (upper middle income)

Variance Decomposition of LWAGE_FI				*Variance Decomposition of LCPI_FIM2*			
Period	*S.E.*	*LWAGE_FI*	*LCPI_FIM2*	*Period*	*S.E.*	*LWAGE_FI*	*LCPI_FIM2*
1	0.0340	100.000	0.0000	1	0.0487	0.387	99.612
5	0.0731	98.849	1.1503	5	0.0528	15.229	84.771
8	0.0948	98.643	1.3560	8	0.0567	26.289	73.710
10	0.1083	98.572	1.4270	10	0.0590	32.862	67.138

D. Variance decomposition of monthly wages to food inflation (higher income)

Variance Decomposition of LWAGE_FI				*Variance Decomposition of LCPI_FIU*			
Period	*S.E.*	*LWAGE_FI*	*LCPI_FIU*	*Period*	*S.E.*	*LWAGE_FI*	*LCPI_FIU*
1	0.0349	100.000	0.000	1	0.0523	0.1233	99.876
5	0.0740	99.711	0.288	5	0.0585	18.0300	81.969
8	0.0970	99.674	0.326	8	0.0631	29.5740	70.425
10	0.1110	99.661	0.339	10	0.0660	36.3720	63.627

Source: Authors' compilation from BIDS Survey. Different income groups are defined in Chap. 2 (Hossain and Mujeri)

Notes: LWAGE_FI = log (wage for fixed income group); LCPI_FIP = log (CPI for fixed income poor); LCPI_FIM1 = log (CPI for lower middle fixed income group); and so on

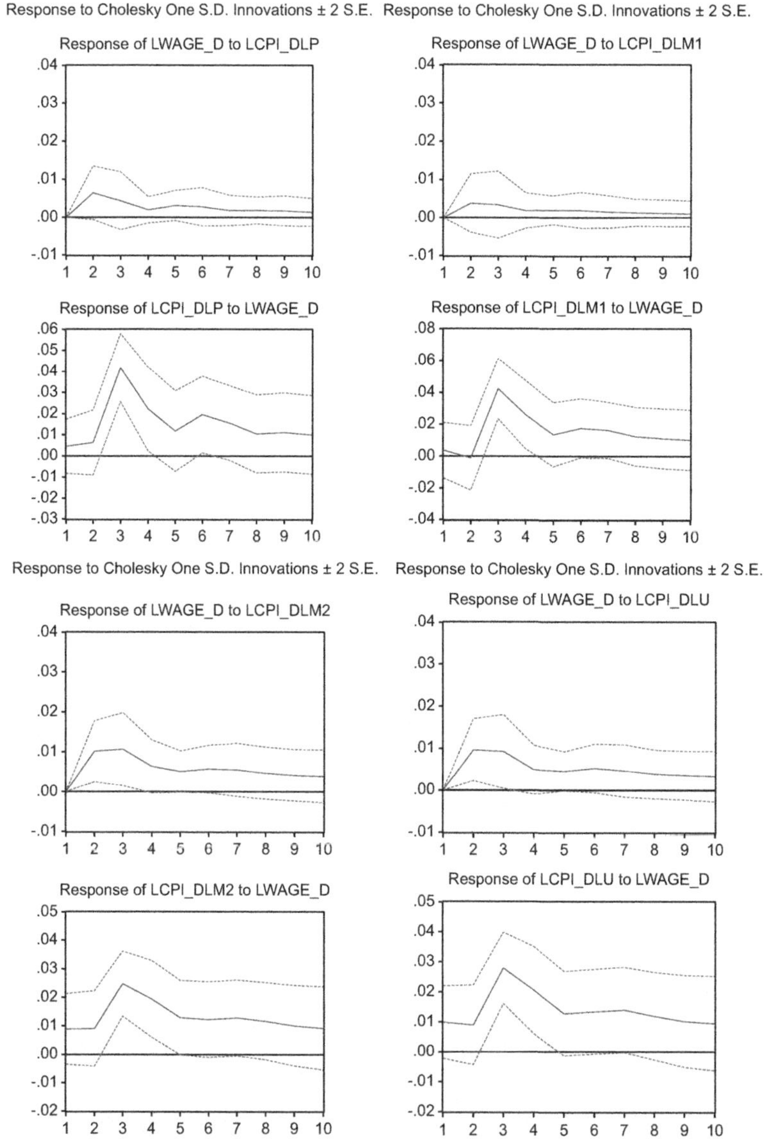

Fig. 3.4 Impulse responses to wages for daily labor household groups

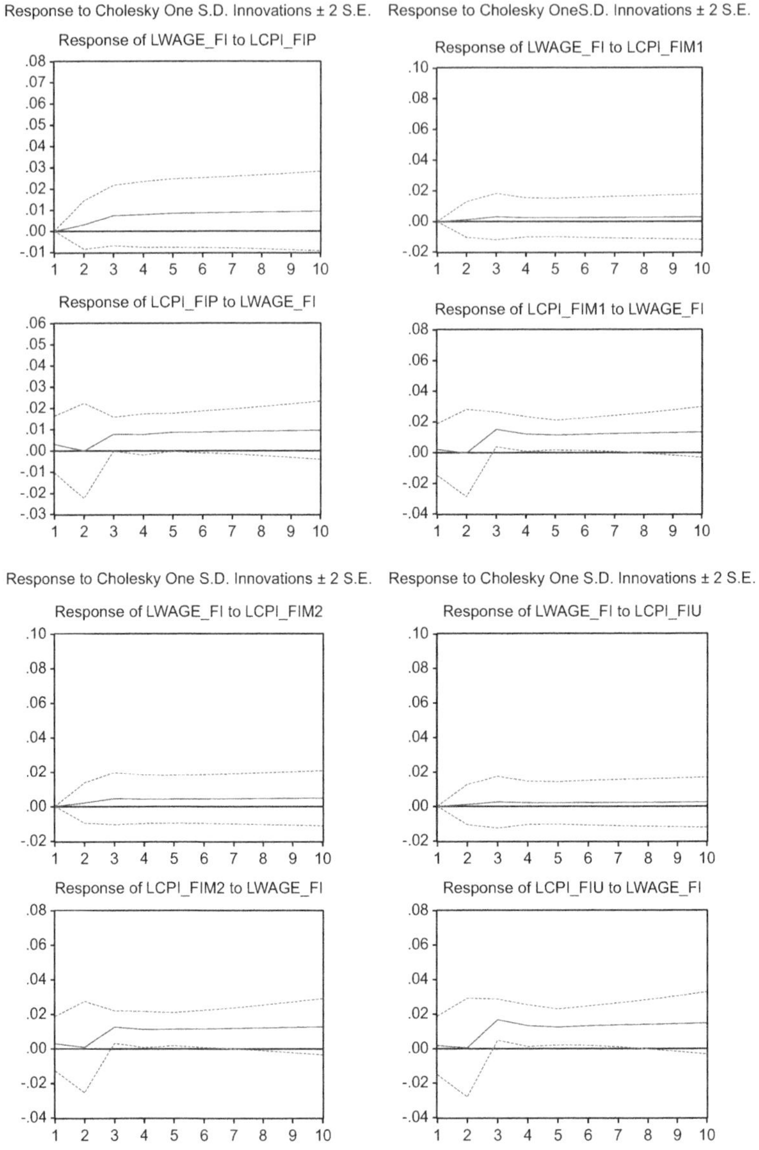

Fig. 3.5 Impulse responses to wages for fixed income household groups

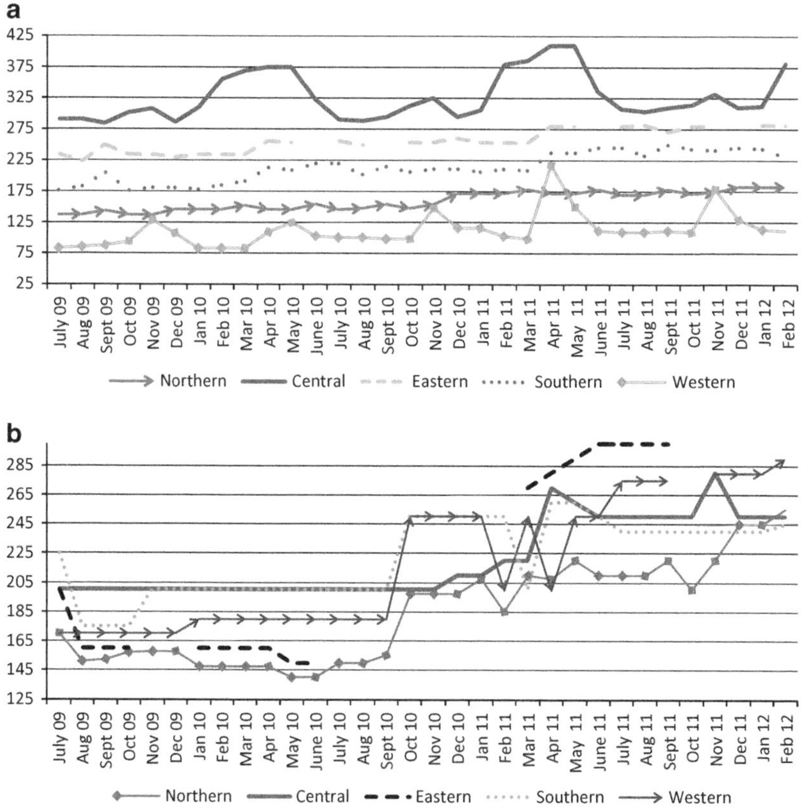

Fig. 3.6 Nominal daily wage of agricultural and non-agricultural labor by region. (a) Agriculture. (b) Non-agriculture

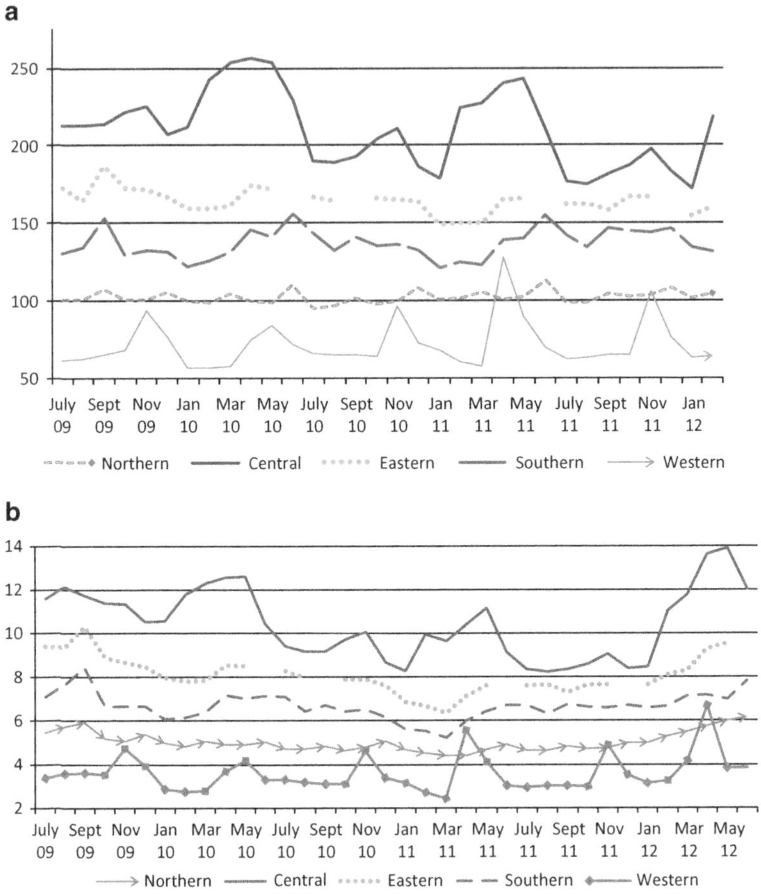

Fig. 3.7 Real daily wage of agricultural labor by region. (**a**) Deflated by group-specific CPI inflation. (**b**) Coarse rice equivalence in Kg

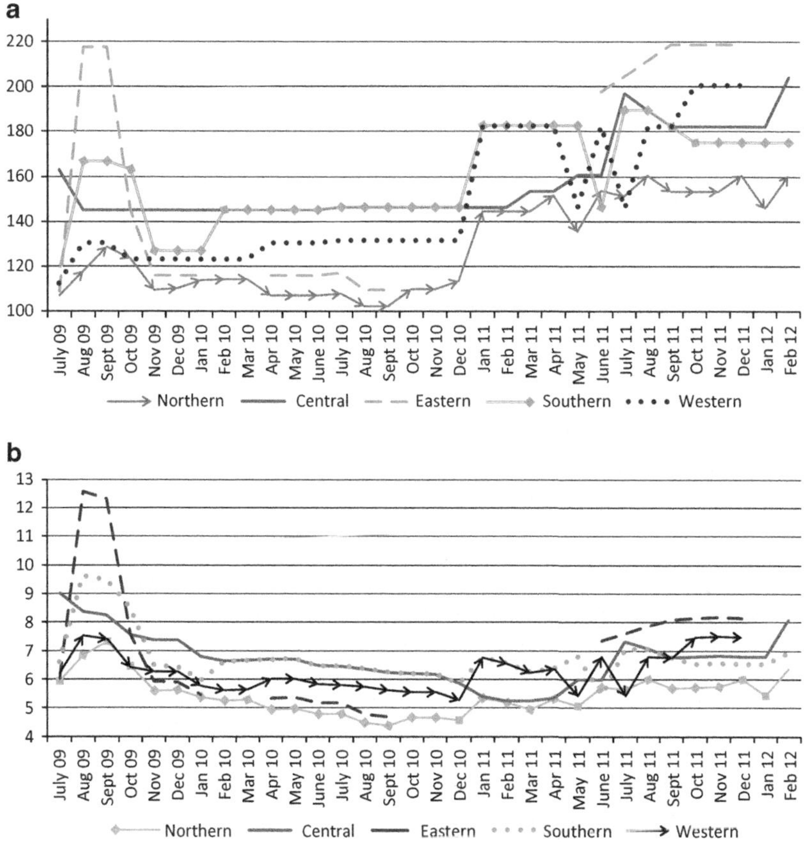

Fig. 3.8 Real daily wage of non-agricultural labor by region. (**a**) Deflated by group-specific CPI inflation. (**b**) Coarse rice equivalence in Kg

References

Agenor, P-R., & Hoffmaister, A.W. (1997). Money, wages and inflation in middle-income developing countries (IMF Working paper). Available at: https://www.imf.org/en/Publications/WP/Issues/2016/12/30/Money-Wages-and-Inflation-in-Middle-Income-Developing-Countries-2444

Ahmed, A. U., & Shams, Y. (1994). Demand elasticities in rural Bangladesh: An application of the AIDS model. *The Bangladesh Development Studies, 22*(1), 1–25.

BBS. (2011). *Report on labor force survey 2010*. Statistics Division, Ministry of Planning, Dhaka, Government of the People's Republic of Bangladesh. Available at: http://www.mccibd.org/images/uploadimg/statistics/Labour%20Force%20Survey%202010.pdf

Berg, E., Bhattacharyya, S., Durgam, R., & Ramachandra, M. (2012). Can rural public works affect agricultural wages? Evidence from India (CSAE Working Paper. WPS/2012–05). Available at: http://conference.iza.org/conference_files/worldb2012/bhattacharyya_s8177.pdf

Boyce, J., & Ravallion, M. (1991). A dynamic econometric model of agricultural wage determination in Bangladesh. *Oxford Bulletin of Economics and Statistics, 53*(4), 361–376.

Christiaensen, L., & Demery, L. (2007). *Down to earth: Agriculture and poverty reduction in Africa*. Washington, DC: The World Bank.

Datt, G. (1996). *Bargaining power, wages and employment: An analysis of agricultural labor markets in India*. New Delhi: Sage.

De Haan, J., & Zelhorst, D. (1990). The impact of government deficits on money growth in developing countries. *Journal of International Money and Finance, 9*(4), 455–469.

Drèze, J. P., & Mukherjee, A. (1989). Labour contracts in rural India: Theories and evidence. In S. Chakravarty (Ed.), *The balance between industry and agriculture in economic development. International Economic Association series*. London: Palgrave Macmillan.

Goletti, F. (1994). *The changing public role in a rice economy approaching self-sufficiency: The case of Bangladesh* (Vol. 98). Intl Food Policy Res Inst.

Hoffmaister, A.W., & Roldos, J. (1996). The sources of macroeconomic fluctuations in developing countries: Brazil and Korea (IMF Working Paper No. 96/20). Available at: https://www.imf.org/en/Publications/WP/Issues/2016/12/30/The-Sources-of-Macroeconomic-Fluctuations-in-Developing-Countries-Brazil-and-Korea-1874

Hossain, M. (1988). *Nature and impact of the green revolution in Bangladesh* (Vol. 67). Intl Food Policy Res Inst.

Khan, A. R. (1984). Real wages of agricultural workers in Bangladesh. *Economic and Political Weekly*, PE40-PE48.

Kijima, Y., & Lanjouw, P. (2005). Economic diversification and poverty in rural India. *Indian Journal of Labour Economics, 48*(2), 349–374.

Lanjouw, P., & Murgai, R. (2009). *Poverty decline, agricultural wages, and non-farm employment in rural India: 1983–2004*. Washington, DC: The World Bank.

Lasco, M. C. D. (2005). *Dynamics of agricultural wages and rice prices in the Philippines*. Doctoral dissertation, Michigan State University. Department of Agricultural Economics.

Lewis, W. A. (1954). Economic development with unlimited supplies of labour. *The Manchester School, 22*(2), 139–191.

Loungani, M. P., & Swagel, M. P. (2001). *Sources of inflation in developing countries* (No. 1–198). International Monetary Fund.

Montiel, P. J. (1989). Empirical analysis of high-inflation episodes in Argentina, Brazil, and Israel. *Staff Papers, 36*(3), 527–549.

Moser, M. G. G. (1994). *The main determinants of inflation in Nigeria*. Washington, DC: International Monetary Fund.

Mukherjee, A., & Ray, D. (1991). Wages and involuntary unemployment in the slack season of a village economy. *Journal of Development Economics, 37*(1–2), 227–264.

Osmani, S. R. (1990). Wage determination in rural labour markets: The theory of implicit co-operation. *Journal of Development Economics, 34*(1–2), 3–23.

Palmer Jones, R. W. (1993). Agricultural wages in Bangladesh: What the figures really show? *The Journal of Development Studies, 29*(2), 277–300.

Palmer Jones, R. W., & Parikh, A. (1998). The determination of agricultural wage rates in Bangladesh. *Journal of Agricultural Economics, 49*(1), 111–133.

Ranis, G., & Fei, J. C. (1961). A theory of economic development. *The American Economic Review*, 533–565.

Rashid, S. (2002). *Dynamics of agricultural wage and rice price in Bangladesh: A re-examination* (No. 595-2016-39976).

Ravallion, M. (1990). Rural welfare effects of food price changes under induced wage responses: Theory and evidence for Bangladesh. *Oxford Economic Papers, 42*(3), 574–585.

Ravallion, M. (1994). Agricultural wages in Bangladesh: What do the figures really show? *The Journal of Development Studies, 31*(2), 334–345.

Ravallion, M., & Dutt, G. (1999). Growth and Poverty in Rural India. Policy Research Working Paper, The World Bank Group. Available at: http://documents.worldbank.org/curated/en/620321468773982302/Growth-and-poverty-in-rural-India

Warr, P. (2005). Food policy and poverty in Indonesia: A general equilibrium analysis. *Australian Journal of Agricultural and Resource Economics, 49*(4), 429–451.

Wodon, Q., & Zaman, H. (2008). *Rising food prices in sub-Saharan Africa: Poverty impact and policy responses*. Washington, DC: The World Bank.

CHAPTER 4

Impact of Energy Price Adjustments on Bangladesh Economy: A Macro-Econometric Modeling Approach

Monzur Hossain, Mahbubur Rahman, and Md. Atiqur Rahman

4.1 Introduction

The domestic price of energy products including electricity, oil and natural gas has long been administered in Bangladesh. The government provides subsidies to all these energy products at various rates. Natural gas is the

M. Hossain (✉)
Bangladesh Institute of Development Studies (BIDS), Dhaka, Bangladesh

M. Rahman
Bangladesh Institute of Development Studies (BIDS), Dhaka, Bangladesh

University of Portsmouth, Portsmouth, UK

Md. A. Rahman
Bangladesh Institute of Development Studies (BIDS), Dhaka, Bangladesh

University of New Mexico, Albuquerque, NM, USA

M. Hossain (ed.), *Bangladesh's Macroeconomic Policy*,
https://doi.org/10.1007/978-981-15-1244-5_4

primary source of energy (85–90 percent),[1] and the government supplies it to the people at a subsidized price (after buying it at a higher price from gas companies). On the other hand, although the selling price of natural gas to the power (electricity) generation companies is not that much subsidized, the government provides massive subsidies for the power sector as it supplies electricity to the people and others at a rate lower than the market price. Power generation is also dependent on imported diesel or furnace oils, the price of which is also administered to be lower than the actual price. Therefore, the government of Bangladesh incurs a large amount of expenditure in the form of subsidies every year for the energy sector. Against the backdrop of an overwhelming burden of subsidies, the Bangladesh government has intensified reforms of energy prices in recent times to bring fiscal discipline.[2]

Though there is a fear about the depletion of natural gas reserves, a significant increase in gas production was observed between 2001 and 2008, with total output reaching 596 billion cubic feet in 2008. This increase of gas production obviously increases tax revenues from international oil companies. The tax revenue received from international oil companies (IOCs) was over Bangladeshi taka (BDT) 29.5 billion ($433 million) in 2007 compared to BDT 4.25 billion ($290 million) in 2000. The retail gas price had increased by 15–20 percent between 2000 and 2005, though tariff adjustment for the gas sector has not taken place since 2005. However, after July 2009, gas price had increased by about 10 percent and price of feed gas (the gas supplied to CNG filling stations) had increased by 400 percent.

The subsidies to fossil fuels and electricity, which have been escalating rapidly in recent years, have been creating pressure on the government's budgetary allocations. In FY2012, the government spent BDT

[1] Bangladesh's energy sector is highly dependent on natural gas. About 57 percent (i.e. inclusive of captive power generation) of the country's natural gas production is used in power generation. The number of consumers of electricity and the quantity of electricity consumption have increased during 1994–2008. The total number of connections has increased from 2.2 million in 1994 (i.e. electrification rate of 10 percent) to over 4.7 million by 2001 (electrification rate of over 17 percent), and the majority of new consumer connections were provided by Bangladesh Rural Electrification Board (REB). By 2008, the total number of electricity consumers had reached 10.6 million (i.e. electrification rate of over 37 percent) and the total electricity consumption grew by 181 percent over the period at a rate of 7.1 percent per annum.

[2] The term "energy" is used to cover all commercial sources (e.g. electricity), petroleum products (e.g. octane, diesel, kerosene, furnace oil and other products) and natural gas, that the government subsidizes.

81.4 billion (US$ 944 million) as energy subsidies. However, Global Subsidies Initiative (GSI) estimated the cost of subsidies at BDT 148.9 billion (US$1.7 billion) in FY2012, which is much higher than the reported one (Mujeri, Chowdhury and Sahana 2014). The reason is that GSI took into account off-budget subsidies such as low-interest rate loans that the government provides to the Bangladesh Power Development Board and the Bangladesh Petroleum Corporation.

In the context of burden of subsidies and fiscal imbalances, the government has made several rounds of revisions of energy prices in recent years. This has led to sharp reactions among various quarters on its possible consequences on the economy. While upward energy price revision is expected to be inflationary from the consumers' and producers' perspective, allocative efficiency and diminishing fiscal burden could have an offsetting effect on the price level. Therefore, a partial analysis may not be appropriate to gauge the proper impact of energy prices on various economic indicators. From these concerns, this study aims to assess the impact of energy price adjustments under a macro-econometric modeling framework.

This study analyzes the impact of energy price changes on major macroeconomic variables, such as growth, inflation, fiscal balances and external balances in Bangladesh, with the help of a macro-econometric policy simulation model. This study also attempts to examine the pattern of growth or inflation if a particular set of policies are adopted under certain exogenous conditions. Five major channels of transmission are considered in the model: the macroeconomic channel, price channel, fiscal channel, trade channel and production channel. The effect of energy price changes on macroeconomic outcomes could be predicted with alternative scenarios of deregulations of domestic energy prices, particularly to the outcomes for growth, inflation, fiscal balances and external balances. The prediction has been done for the period FY2015 to FY2021 in line with the Seventh Five Year Plan period (2015–2019) and Perspective Plan, 2021.

The chapter is organized as follows. After the introductory remarks of the present chapter, Sect. 4.2 provides a brief review of the relevant literature on energy price shock, transmission channels and macro-econometric models. Section 4.3 then analyzes the trends of energy prices and subsidies in Bangladesh. Section 4.4 discusses the macroeconomic models in Bangladesh. The model framework is discussed in Sect. 4.5. Section 4.6 discusses the variables of interest while Sect. 4.7 tests the simulation results and checks for validity of the model. Finally, Sect. 4.8 concludes the chapter with some significant policy recommendations.

4.2 Energy Price Shock and Transmission Channels: A Conceptual Framework

Energy price shock has both expenditure and investment side responses. Consumption expenditures may be directly affected by energy price changes through different channels. For example, higher energy prices might reduce discretionary income, and it also might cause consumers to postpone irreversible purchases of consumer durables etc. (see Bernanke 1983; Pindyck 1990). There has been no consensus on how energy price changes affect one's livelihood in the long run. One stream of argument is that the redistribution (partially mostly) of income from the refiners to consumers happens through higher wages or higher stock returns on domestic energy companies. Apart from that, higher energy prices simply transfer income from one consumer to another. Another argument is that energy price shocks may lead to fall in energy consumption due to precautionary savings motive of the consumers from the concerns of a greater likelihood of future unemployment and income losses. This effect will have general equilibrium consequences on employment and real income. Though there is an additional operating cost effect at the advent of energy price hike as households tend to delay or forego purchases of energy-related durables. However, as Hamilton (1988) argued, the scope of uncertainty effect is broader than that of operating cost, because it is limited only to specific consumer durables. These effects might affect aggregate demand of an economy (Bresnahan and Ramey 1993). Several studies found evidences of cutbacks and shifts in demand in response to energy prices (Herrera 2007; Edelstein and Kilian 2007).

In addition to cutbacks or shifts in consumer expenditures, energy price hike has effect on investment expenditures of firms too (Hamilton 2008). For example, an increase in the price of energy raises the marginal cost of production depending on the cost share of energy. This will cause a reduction of demand for the firm's output. Therefore, by responding to reduced demand and higher energy costs, firms might cut down on their investment expenditures. Thus, uncertainty effect of energy price shocks has both supply-side and demand-side implications.

In the face of uncertainty and the reallocation effect due to energy price changes, there is a high likelihood that macroeconomic aggregates will respond asymmetrically because the net response of these effects would vary. While energy price increases correspond to an amplified response of macroeconomic aggregates, the corresponding response to falling energy prices will be lesser. Therefore, a macro-econometric modeling exercise involving all the important sectors of the economy could potentially capture the net effect of energy price changes to the economy.

4.3 Energy Price and Subsidy Scenario in Bangladesh

The Government of Bangladesh, like many other countries, has been providing subsidies for decades in a number of areas including agriculture, petroleum products, electricity, natural gas, health, education and food. Despite the fact that subsidies create extra pressure on exchequers, they have wide-ranging impacts on the distribution of wealth within a country, economic growth and the environment. However, the government makes readjustments sporadically to energy prices (Fig. 4.1) to bring it close to the market price level.

In Bangladesh, while food subsidies dominated until the early 2000s, non-food subsidies including energy subsidies started dominating the subsidy basket thereafter (Fig. 4.2). Subsidies in non-food items have been increasing over time and reached about BDT 15 billion in 2011–2012. A study estimated that almost 90 percent of total subsidies accounted for energy subsidies in recent times, mostly due to the escalation of subsidies in quick rental power plants (Fig. 4.2).

4.4 Macro-Econometric Models in Bangladesh

Several attempts have been made so far to construct Macroeconomic models for Bangladesh. Islam (1965) conducted one of the first studies of the macroeconomic model for the Pakistan economy, in which East Pakistan (present Bangladesh) was treated as a region. The objectives of Islam's study were to formulate economic models of Pakistan, undertaking statistical estimation, collecting, organizing and processing both published and unpublished data systematically.

The empirical works on constructing macro-econometric models of Bangladesh economy have been intensified in the 1980s mainly to aid the policymakers in rebuilding the economy after the shattered first decade of independence during the 1970s. Rashid (1981) developed a short-run macro-econometric model for Bangladesh economy with the primary

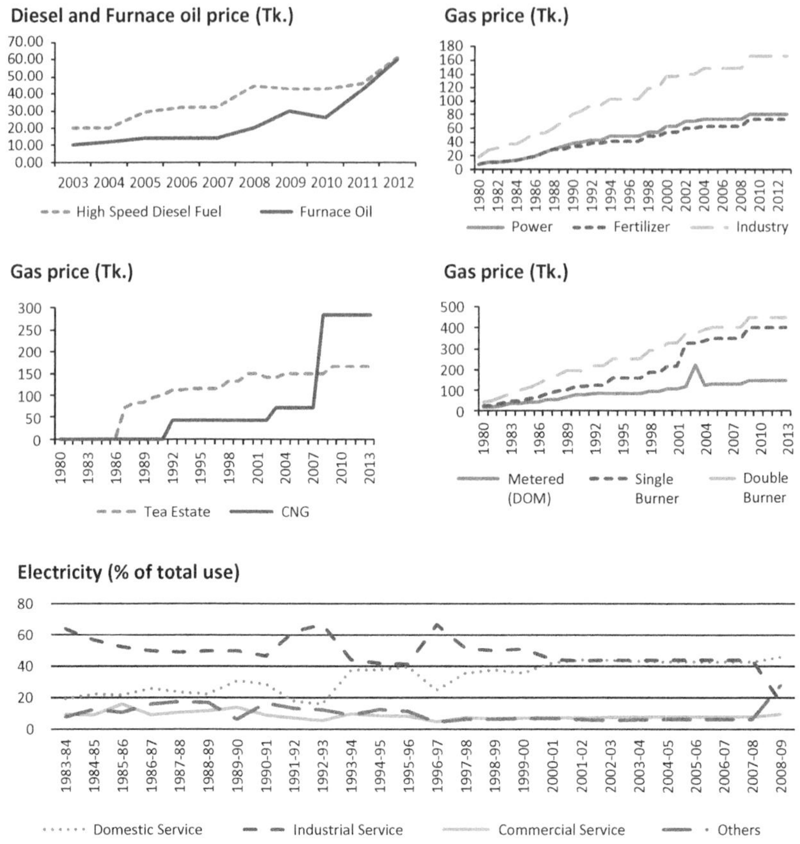

Fig. 4.1 Energy price and electricity usage patterns in Bangladesh. (Sources: Bangladesh Energy Regulatory Commission (BERC); Petrobangla; Titas Gas and various issues of Newspapers)

objective of understanding the workings of the economy. Though the model lacks rigorousness, it was the beginning of an attempt to quantify macro-economic impact on the Bangladesh economy.

Parikh (1983) constructed a macroeconomic model of the Bangladesh economy using the Keynesian approach of price rigidity with quantity rationing. The model also explicitly delineated the structure of the economy and its interdependence between various sectors of the economy.

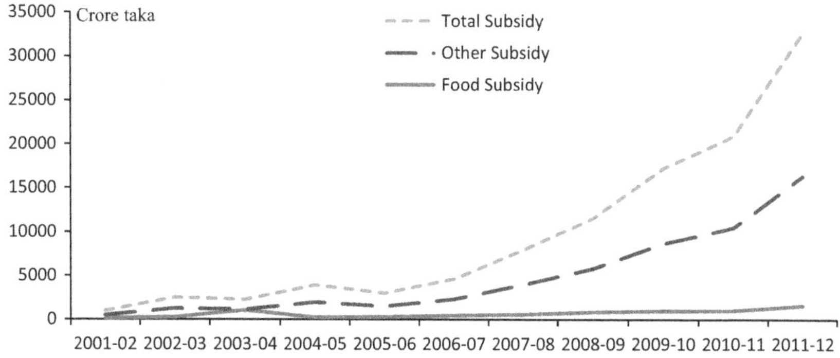

Fig. 4.2 Pattern of subsidies in Bangladesh. (Source: Bangladesh Bureau of Statistics (BBS); Bangladesh Institute of Development Studies (BIDS))

One of the important features of the model was that it included the weather factor. However, Parikh's Model is confined to strict functional forms. One criticism of Parikh's model is that it did not test the equations and, therefore, no definite policy suggestions were offered. Chowdhury (1986) used the vector autoregression (VAR) technique as an alternative approach to forecasting the macroeconomic model in the context of Bangladesh's economy. However, the model was once again restricted into functional form and no estimation of the parameters was carried out.

Rahman and Shilpi (1996) developed a dynamic macroeconomic model for the Bangladesh economy concerning five economic blocks, such as expenditure, fiscal, money and finance, trade and aggregate supply block. Chowdhury, Dao and Wahid (1995) analyzed the relationship between money, output, prices and exchange rate for Bangladesh using a VAR model with quarterly data over 1974–1992 period. They found, among other things, monetary policy to be significant in explaining output, and monetary policy and inflation jointly determine the exchange rate.

More recently, Basher and Haque (2000) have developed a simulated macro-econometric model for Bangladesh economy. Their model consisted of five important sectors of Bangladesh Economy: demand, fiscal, money and finance, trade and supply side. It has also included remittance income as an endogenous factor in the model. The model was estimated using annual data from 1974 to 1997. Quin, Razzaque and Rahman (2006) constructed a small macro-econometric model with seven macro-economic blocks, but they used quarterly data. As most of the macro variables in Bangladesh are only available on an annual level, they have manipulated them on an ad hoc basis to generate a quarterly scale. Thus, their policy shocks' results based on such quarterly data have less credential. Rahman and Khatun (2011) also used almost the same seven blocks to construct another macro-econometric model, but they used annual data to give shocks of monetary policy changes on some macroeconomic outcomes.

However, in Bangladesh, so far, no such attempt has been made to develop a macro-econometric model to capture energy price shocks on the economy. Thus, we attempt to develop a dynamic macro-econometric model for Bangladesh with a special focus on energy price adjustments. The model has been developed in order to assess an economy-wide impact of energy price adjustments by linking possible effects on production, consumption as well as government expenditure, which might have a balancing effect on economic output.

4.5 The Model Framework

Macro-econometric model is a simultaneous equations system model developed for policy simulation following basically Tinbergen (1967) and Klein and Goldberger (1955). In this exercise, attempts will be made to capture the impact of energy price shocks on various macroeconomic indicators of Bangladesh. The model is a reduced form with some equations and identities.

There are several blocks in the model viz. the macroeconomic, government, trade, price, monetary and production (Fig. 4.3). The macroeconomic block comprised equations involving the nominal gross domestic product (GDP), private consumption and private investment to GDP ratio. The government block is comprised of equations determining the combined current expenditure, the combined revenue receipts of the government along with the public investment and the fiscal deficit. The external block is comprised of equations determining the export, import, net capital inflow, exchange rate, trade balance and change in foreign exchange reserve. The monetary block involves equations regarding the public borrowing and the rate of interest and the change in high-powered and narrow money.

The model has been applied to study the macro-behavior of the energy price changes and macro-relationships of the energy sector with rest of the economy. The model is, therefore, constrained to address some of the

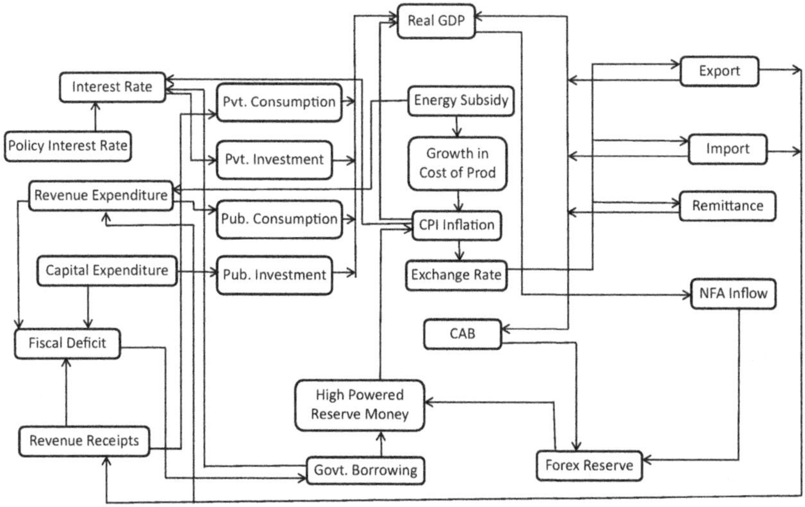

Fig. 4.3 Flow chart of the model (Note: CAB = Current Account Balance)

issues like relative price impacts, energy efficiency, technological changes, alternative fuels and the linkages with financial markets.

The model has been developed to link up the macroeconomic consequences of the changes in the government energy expenditures. As most of the variables have a two-way causality with others, the model involves simultaneous equation framework. This model will give us a scope of policy appraisal of the Bangladesh economy. In accordance with a set of putative assumptions which place a greater consideration to real phenomena, the prime focus of the model is to shed light on the inflationary consequences in connection with the growth aspects on the basis of some conditional factors. The shortcoming of the model is that it exerts no effort to underline the perceptions of the economic agents regarding the expectations of policy interventions which is dominant for the efficiency of this kind of interventions.

There are 72 behavioral and technical equations and 66 variables. PcGive and PcGets software have been used to estimate the behavioral and technical equations (Hendry and Doornik 2001; Hendry and Krolzig 2001). A brief description of some key behavioral and estimated technical equations is shown in Appendix 4C.

4.6 Variables of Interest

The key policy variables included in the model are: revenue and capital expenditure to GDP ratio, the rate of change in administered prices (apart from oil), the weighted average tariff rate for energy, public debt to GDP ratio, the ratio of government borrowing from market over the central bank and the change in foreign exchange reserve. The data comes from various government sources including the Bangladesh Bureau of Statistics (BBS), Bangladesh Bank and Ministry of Finance.

We have used several exogenous variables in the model, such as the growth of output in OECD (Organisation for Economic Co-operation and Development) countries as a group as well as in the USA, China and the Middle East, the rainfall index, the capital-output ratio and the costs of production in terms of wage, rent and interest costs. The outcome variables include the GDP growth rate, the inflation rate, the current account deficit to GDP ratio and the fiscal deficit to GDP ratio as well as some other key macroeconomic ratios, such as the trade deficit relative to GDP, the combined tax and non-tax revenue to GDP ratio and the budget deficit to GDP ratio. The variables used in the model are listed in Appendix Table 4.4.

4.7 Model Simulation Results

We run two types of simulations here. In the first case, we evaluate the predictive accuracy of the macro-econometric model, both within and out of the sample. The second type of simulation is used to evaluate policy shocks in response to energy price changes, particularly on some key economic indicators. All simulation exercises are done using the software *Winsolve.*

4.7.1 Validity Check of the Model

4.7.1.1 Within-Sample Validity

Within-sample (1985–2011) predictive accuracy (or validity) of the model is checked by the mean percentage error (MPE) and the root mean square percentage error (RMSPE). They are computed as follows:

$$MPE = \frac{1}{T}\sum_{t=1}^{T}\left(\frac{Y_t^s - Y_t^a}{Y_t^a}\right), \quad RMSPE = \sqrt{\frac{1}{T}\sum_{t=1}^{T}\left(\frac{Y_t^s - Y_t^a}{Y_t^a}\right)^2}.$$

Table 4.1 Statistics of within-sample (1980–2011) validity

Variable	*MPE*	*RMSPE*
Private Consumption at Constant Price	−0.017	0.025
GDP at Constant Price	−0.048	0.059
Net Foreign Asset	−0.474	2.171
Gross National Product (GNP) at Constant Price	−0.038	0.049
Consumer Price Index (CPI)	0.021	0.069
Government Revenue	−0.032	0.092
Producer Price Index (PPI)	−0.007	0.073
Govt. Consumption at Constant Price	0.018	0.119
Private Investment at Constant Price	−0.066	0.145
Value Addition in Agriculture Sector at Constant Price	−0.033	0.044
Value Addition in Industrial Sector at Constant Price	0.040	0.085
Value Addition in Service Sector at Constant Price	−0.037	0.044
Current Account Balance	−0.465	2.433
Export at Constant Price	0.042	0.113
Import at Constant Price	−0.008	0.100
Narrow Money	0.031	0.113

Source: Authors' estimation

Where Y^s and Y^a are the simulated and actual values of an endogenous variable respectively and T is the number of simulated periods. We first run a dynamic simulation that predicts endogenous variables using predicted values of other related endogenous variables from the lagged period and exogenous variables. Then predicted and actual values of endogenous variables are used to compute MPEs and RMSPEs. Table 4.1 presents the estimated MPEs and RMSPEs for some key endogenous variables. We see that they are reasonably low in almost all cases, which indicates that within-sample validity of the model is high. Two variables, namely net foreign asset and current account balance, have high estimates of MPE and RMSPE, indicating a low level of predictive power. One possible explanation could be that the values of these two variables are often negative, which might have driven to have high estimates of MPE and RMSPE. The predicted and actual series of variables are shown in Figs. 4.4 and 4.5. We view that most of the variables are predicted well, as they are close to actual series.

4.7.1.2 Out-of-Sample Validity

We run stochastic simulations to know the out-of-sample (2012–2021) performance of the model. Under these simulations, the bootstrap method is used to give random shocks into individual endogenous variables, but for the out-of-sample period, random shocks are generated from individual residuals of variables for within-sample period (to note, residuals are differences between actual series and predicted series generated from the dynamic simulation for within sample). One thousand stochastic simulations/replications are run through bootstrapping. One hundred quintiles are computed to compare the magnitudes of out-of-sample forecasts because within-sample uncertainty captured by residuals makes variations at out-of-sample forecasts.

Figures 4.6 and 4.7 demonstrate out-of-sample forecasts of some of the key variables at 3rd, 50th and 97th quintiles. The 50th quintiles represent mean simulated values, while 3rd and 97th quintiles represent the 95 percent confidence intervals. In Figs. 4.6 and 4.7, we see that variables with low confidence intervals or low magnitudes of variations are predicted well within the sample. Two extreme examples are private consumption at a constant price and current account balance. The former has the highest within-sample prediction (as RMSPE, which is better than MPE, is the lowest in Table 4.1), which makes a low magnitude at out-of-sample predictions. The latter has the lowest within-sample prediction (as RMSPE is the highest in Table 4.1) but has a high level of magnitude at out-of-sample predictions. However, the out-of-sample performance of the model seems quite good as we see in Figs. 4.6 and 4.7.

4.7.2 *Results from Policy Shocks/Simulations*

It has been estimated roughly that an increase of gas, fuel and electricity prices by around 40, 15 and 25 percent respectively, will help the government withdraw subsidy almost entirely from the energy sector. We use these estimated/predicted energy prices' changes to give policy shocks into the model. We have simulated the model with two alternative scenarios as shown in Table 4.2. When we assume that changes in energy prices will sustain forever or prices will not come back to normal levels after changes caused by subsidy withdrawal, then the shocks are called

Table 4.2 Energy price adjustments and alternative scenarios

	Shocks Applied to 2015–2021	
	Scenario-1 (percent)	*Scenario-2 (percent)*
Gas price	40	80
Fuel price	15	30
Electricity price	25	50

Note: The assumptions are based on current trends of price adjustments

impulse shocks. Scenario-1 and Scenario-2 in Table 4.2 imply impulse shocks for an extended period (2015–2021).

To know the effects of shocks on the economy, we first obtain base solutions or base predicted values of the variables for out-of-sample period, after running a dynamic simulation for out-of-sample period without any changes of energy prices. Then, we run two dynamic simulations for out-of-sample period applying two types of shocks and compare them with the baseline scenario. Figure 4.8 shows percentage changes of predicted values of some key variables under four types of shocks from base values. Four scenarios in the figure include both step shocks and impulse shocks. As opposed to impulse shocks, step shocks imply that shocks under two scenarios in Table 4.2 happen only in one period, 2015. As a result, while impulse shocks imply that simulated values do not come back to the baseline values, step shocks (as happened for one period) allow simulated values to come back to the baseline values after some periods. In Fig. 4.8, scenarios-1 and 2 imply step shocks, and scenarios-3 and 4 imply impulse shocks.

In addition to Fig. 4.8, Table 4.3 also reports the simulated values of some selected indicators as a result of some energy shocks as shown in Table 4.2, but Table 4.3 shows the averages of simulated values over the three out-of-sample periods (2015, 2015–2019 (seventh five year plan period), 2015–2021 (perspective plan period of the government)) estimated under impulse shocks. Results under scenarios-1 and 2 in Table 4.3 are comparable with percentage changes under scenarios-3 and 4 in Fig. 4.8. Scenarios-3 and 4 in Fig. 4.8 show that due to the energy price increase, inflation will increase and subsequently real GDP growth will fall slightly, but nominal GDP rises as consumer price index rises. Government budget/fiscal deficit will decrease slightly as a result of the energy price increase as expected. However, note that all changes due to shocks are applicable if other variables remain normal. If other policy variables also change simultaneously, effects on the economy might be different.

In Table 4.3, the results suggest that a combination of energy price increase (Scenario-1: 40 percent of the gas price, 15 percent of fuel price and 25 percent of electricity price) will decrease GDP growth rate by about 0.4 percent (e.g. (5.78–5.56)/5.78) and increase of inflation rate by 0.5 percent over the period 2015–2019. Similarly, an increase of energy price at a higher rate (Scenario-2: 80 percent of the gas price, 30 percent of fuel price and 50 percent of electricity price) will decrease GDP growth rate by about 0.44 percent and increase inflation rate by 0.8 percent over the same period. Thus, any upward revision of energy prices will be slightly inflationary and as a result, the real GDP growth rate will fall slightly during the predicted period.

Table 4.3 Effects of energy price increases on some key variables

		Baseline	*Scenario-1*	*Scenario-2*
GDP growth (Constant price)	2015	6.07	5.95	5.85
	2015–2019	5.78	5.56	5.41
	2015–2021	5.69	5.42	5.24
Inflation rate	2015	4.55	5.89	6.96
	2015–2019	4.40	5.38	6.14
	2015–2021	4.40	5.19	5.81
Government revenue to GDP	2015	0.119	0.118	0.117
	2015–2019	0.118	0.117	0.116
	2015–2021	0.118	0.117	0.116
GDP growth (Current price)	2015	10.02	10.68	11.22
	2015–2019	9.59	10.34	10.95
	2015–2021	9.44	10.07	10.57

Source: Authors' estimation

4.8 Concluding Remarks

This study attempts to analyze the economy-wide impact of energy price adjustments applying a macro-econometric model. The model initially analyzes macroeconomic data for the period 1980–2011. Within-sample validation and out-of-sample predictions imply that the model fits well and it can be used for policy simulations through assumed shocks. Considering the current gap between subsidized and government's buying price of energy, reasonable alternative scenarios of price shocks were derived and subsequently applied. The simulated results are drawn for the period 2015–2021, making it consistent with the Seventh Five Year Plan and the Perspective Plan. The results suggest that an upward revision of energy prices will be slightly inflationary and as a result, the real GDP growth rate will fall slightly during the predicted period.

The simulations suggest that a combination of energy price increase (Scenario-1: 40 percent of gas price, 15 percent of fuel price and 25 percent of electricity price) will decrease GDP growth rate by about 0.4 percent and increase inflation rate by 0.5 percent over the period 2015–2019. Similarly, an increase of energy price at a higher rate (Scenario-2: 80 percent of the gas price, 30 percent of fuel price and 50 percent of electricity price) will decrease GDP growth rate by about 0.44 percent and increase inflation rate by 0.8 percent over the same period. Thus, any upward revision of energy prices will be inflationary to some extent and as a result, the real GDP growth rate will fall slightly during the predicted period, and vice-versa. A note of caution is required in explaining the result because it is based on the ceteris paribus assumption. The GDP growth and inflationary situation might improve if changes in other macroeconomic indicators take place along with energy price adjustments.

Appendix 1

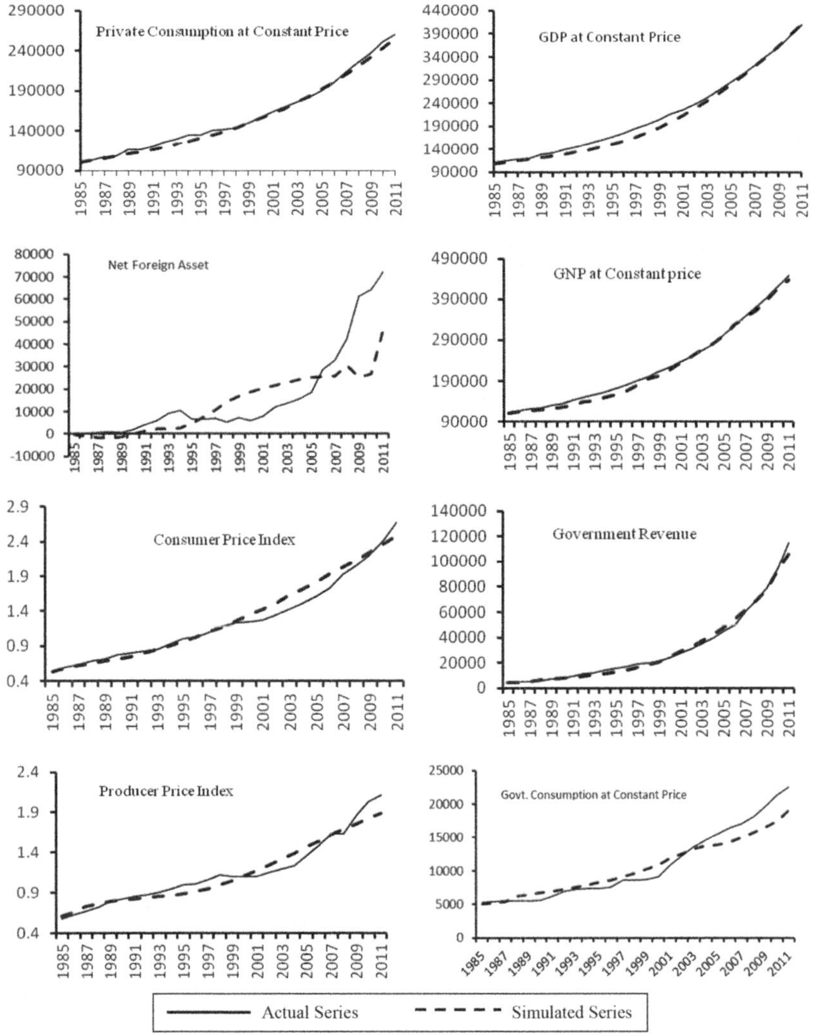

Fig. 4.4 Actual series and simulated series derived from dynamic simulation (1985–2011). (Source: Authors' estimation)

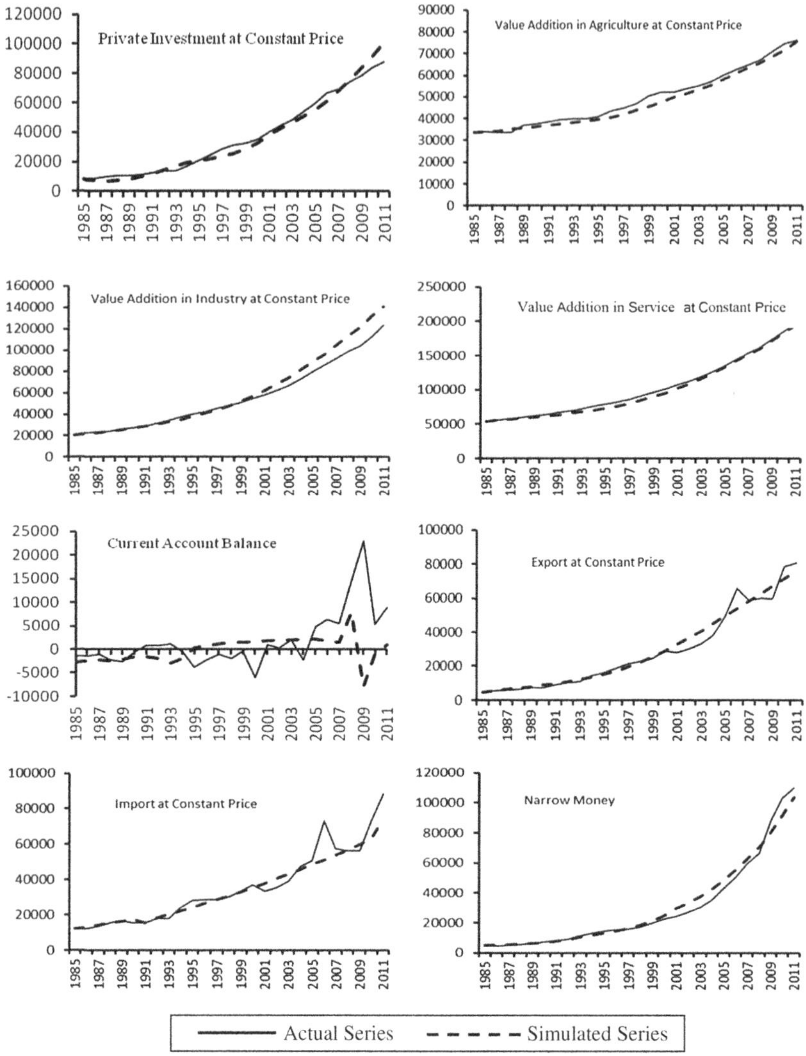

Fig. 4.5 Actual series and simulated series derived from dynamic simulation (1985–2011) (Cont.) (Source: Authors' estimation)

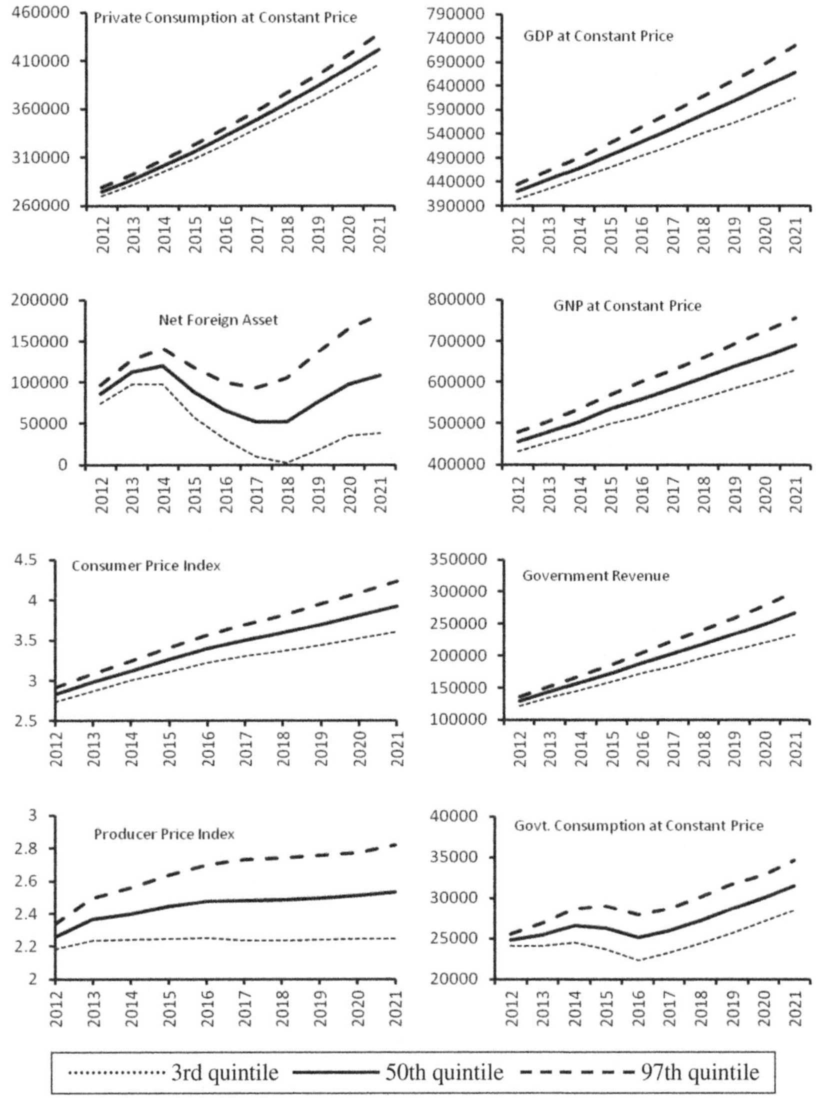

Fig. 4.6 Out-of-sample predicted values from stochastic simulations (2012–2021). (Source: Authors' estimation)

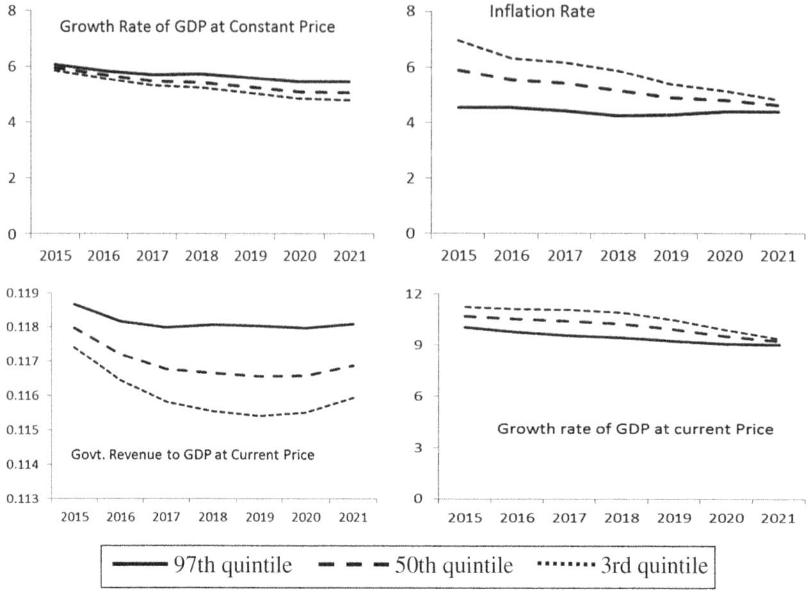

Fig. 4.7 Out-of-sample predicted values of selected indicators from stochastic simulations (2012–2021). (Source: Authors' estimation)

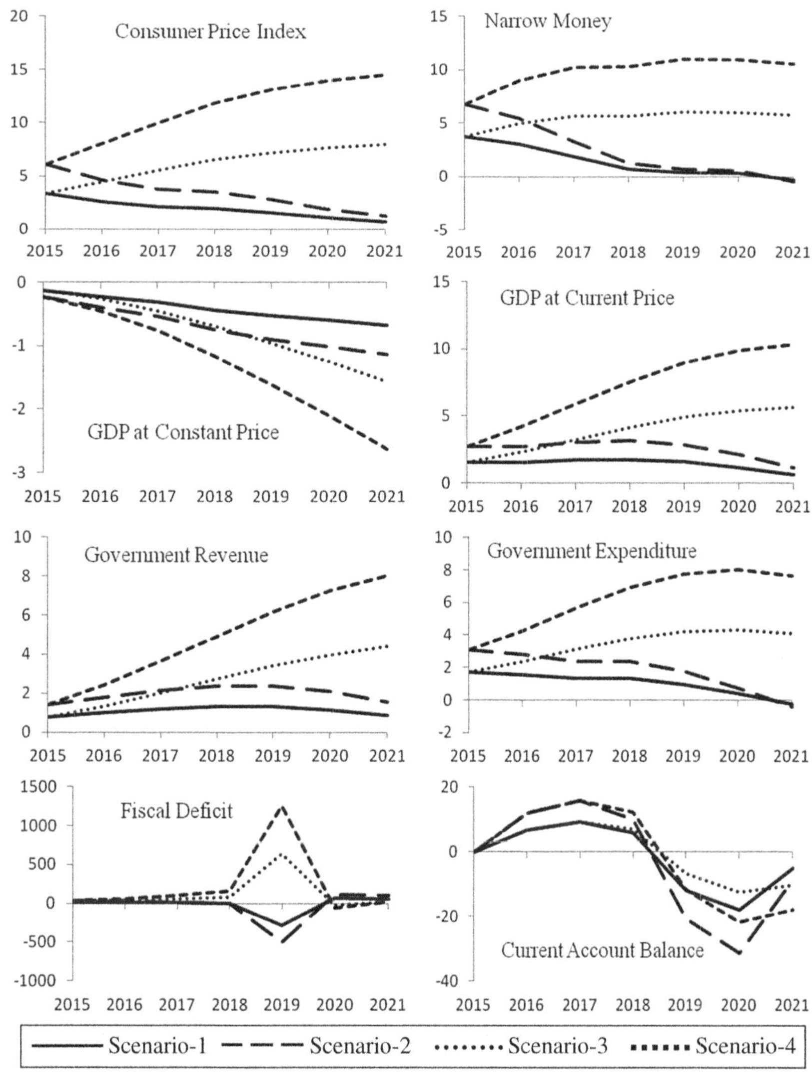

Fig. 4.8 Effects of energy price changes on some key variables (percent changes from base). (Source: Authors' estimation)

Appendix 2

Table 4.4 Variables definition of the model and units of data

Variables	*Name*	*Unit*
PCONc	Private Consumption at Constant Price	Mil/BDT
PCON	Private Consumption at Current Price	Mil/BDT
NFIAc	Net Factor Income from Abroad at Constant Price	Mil/BDT
NFIA	Net Factor Income from Abroad at Current Price	Mil/BDT
GDPc	GDPs at Constant Price	Mil/BDT
GDP	GDPs at Current Price	Mil/BDT
GTAX	Govt. Tax Revenue	Mil/BDT
NFA	Net Foreign Asset	Mil/BDT
IRD	Interest Rate on Deposit	Mil/BDT
IRL	Interest Rate on Lending	Mil/BDT
GNPc	GNPs at Constant Price	Mil/BDT
GNP	GNPs at Current Price	Mil/BDT
DDEBT	Govt. Domestic Debt	Mil/BDT
FDEBT	Govt. Foreign Debt	Mil/BDT
DEBT	Total Govt. Debt	Mil/BDT
DCCB	Domestic Credit of Central Bank	Mil/BDT
DCDMB	Domestic Credit of Deposit Money Bank	Mil/BDT
ER	Exchange Rate	Mil/BDT
GREV	Total Govt. Revenue	Mil/BDT
GREXP	Govt. Revenue Expenditure	Mil/BDT
GEXP	Total Govt. Expenditure	Mil/BDT
GDEF	Govt. Budget Deficit	Mil/BDT
cGDEF	Cumulative Govt. Budget Deficit	Mil/BDT
P_C	CPI	
P_GDP	GDP Deflator	
P_INV	Investment Deflator	
P_M	Import Deflator	
P_X	Export Deflator	
P_P	Producer price Index	
GCONc	Govt. Consumption at Constant Price	Mil/BDT
GCON	Govt. Consumption at Current Price	Mil/BDT
GINVc	Govt. Investment at Constant Price	Mil/BDT
GINV	Govt. Investment at Current Price	Mil/BDT
PINVc	Private Investment at Constant Price	Mil/BDT
PINV	Private Investment at Current Price	Mil/BDT
INVc	Investment at Constant Price	Mil/BDT
INV	Investment at Current Price	Mil/BDT
CP	Credit to Private Sector	Mil/BDT
VA1	Value Added in Agriculture at Current Price	Mil/BDT
VA1c	Value Added in Agriculture at Constant Price	Mil/BDT
VA2	Value Added in Manufacturing at Current Price	Mil/BDT

(*continued*)

Table 4.4 (continued)

Variables	*Name*	*Unit*
VA2c	Value Added in Manufacturing at Constant Price	Mil/BDT
VA3	Value Added in Service at Current Price	Mil/BDT
VA3c	Value Added in Service at Constant Price	Mil/BDT
BR	Bank Rate	
IRRIG	Irrigated area	
REM	Remittance at Current Price	Mil/BDT
CAB	Current Account Balance	Mil/BDT
X	Export at Current Price	Mil/BDT
Xc	Export at Constant Price	Mil/BDT
M	Import at Current Price	Mil/BDT
Mc	Import at Constant Price	Mil/BDT
RAIN	Rainfall	
FCPI	Foreign Consumer Price Index	
FGDPc	Foreign GDP at Constant Price	
M0	Currency in Circulation	
M1	Narrow Money	
M2	Broad money	
ADc	Aggregate Demand at Constant Price	Mil/BDT
P_ad#OIL#lit	Administered oil Price per liter	
K	Capital Formation at Current Price	Mil/BDT
Kc	Capital Formation at Constant Price	Mil/BDT
GPW	Weighted Price of Gas	
FPW	Weighted Price of Fuel	
EPW	Weighted Price of Electricity	
ifeq	Winsolve code to capture structural break	

Appendix 3

Regression Results Under Different Blocks

Macroeconomic Block

Private Consumption at Constant Price

$$\Delta \log(\text{PCONc}) = 0.03892 - 0.3356 * \Delta \log(\text{PCONc}(-1)) - 0.07153 * \text{ECM\_PCONc}$$

$$\begin{aligned}\text{ECM\_PCONc} = {} & \log(\text{PCONc}(-1)) \\ & - 0.95 * \log(\text{GNPc}(-1) - \text{GTAX}(-1) / (\text{GNP}(-1) / \text{GNPc}(-1))) \\ & - 0.05 * \log((\text{DDEBT}(-1) + \text{M0}(-1) + \text{NFA}(-1)) / \text{P\_C}(-1)) \\ & + 0.001 * (\text{IRD}(-2) - 100 * \text{dlog}(\text{P\_C}(-2)))\end{aligned}$$

Diagnostic Tests:

Sigma	0.0155215
R^2	0.353919
AR 1-2 test	F(2,23) = 0.34059 [0.7149]
ARCH 1-1 test	F(1,23) =0.0066794 [0.9356]
Normality test	Chi^2(2) = 6.6762 [0.0355]*
hetero test	F(4,20) = 0.43762 [0.7799]
hetero-X test	F(5,19) = 0.40672 [0.8381]
RESET test	F(1,24) = 0.67548 [0.4192]

Note: *, ** indicate significance at 1% or higher and below 1% level, respectively

Private Investment at Constant Price

$$\begin{aligned}\Delta \log(\text{PINVc}) = {} & -1.678 + 0.4878 * \Delta \log(\text{PINVc}(-1)) \\ & + 0.363 * (\log((\text{DCCB}(-2) + \text{DCDMB}(-2)) / \text{P\_INV}(-2)) \\ & - \log((\text{DCCB}(-3) + \text{DCDMB}(-3)) / \text{P\_INV}(-3))) \\ & - 0.3807 * \text{ECM\_PINVc}\end{aligned}$$

$$
\begin{aligned}
ECM\_PINVc = {} & \log\left(PINVc\left(-1\right)\right) - \log\left(GNPc\left(-1\right)\right) \\
& + 0.001 * \left(IRL\left(-2\right) - 100 * d\log\left(P\_INV\left(-2\right)\right)\right) \\
& - 0.85 * \log\left(time\left(1981\right)\right)
\end{aligned}
$$

Diagnostic Tests:

Sigma	0.0447481
R^2	0.463892
AR 1-2 test	F(2,17) = 0.12531 [0.8830]
ARCH 1-1 test	F(1,17) = 0.19853 [0.6615]
Normality test	Chi^2(2) = 1.4364 [0.4876]
Hetero test	F(6,12) = 1.3098 [0.3244]
Hetero-X test	Not enough observations
RESET test	F(1,18) = 0.66885 [0.4241]

Private Investment at Current Price

$$
\begin{aligned}
\Delta\log\left(PINV\right) = {} & \log\left(PINVc\right) + \log\left(PINV\left(-1\right) / PINVc\left(-1\right)\right) \\
& - 0.2808 * \left(\log\left(PINV\left(-1\right) / PINVc\left(-1\right)\right) - \log\left(PINV\left(-2\right) / PINVc\left(-2\right)\right)\right) \\
& + 0.2077 * d\log\left(P\_M\right) + 0.6601 * \log\left(VA2\left(-3\right) / VA2c\left(-3\right)\right) \\
& - \log\left(VA2\left(-4\right) / VA2c\left(-4\right)\right)\Big) - 0.1749 * ifeq\left(1999\right) \\
& - 0.1899 * ECM\_PINVc
\end{aligned}
$$

$$
\begin{aligned}
ECM\_PINV = {} & \log\left(PINV\left(-1\right) / PINVc\left(-1\right)\right) \\
& - 0.5 * \log\left(P\_M\left(-1\right)\right) - 0.5 * \log\left(VA2\left(-3\right) / VA2c\left(-3\right)\right)
\end{aligned}
$$

Diagnostic Tests:

Sigma	0.0334281
log-likelihood	58.1777
AR 1-2 test	F(2,21) = 2.2873 [0.1263]
ARCH 1-1 test	F(1,21) = 0.38265 [0.5428]
Normality test	Chi^2(2) = 1.3126 [0.5188]
Hetero test	F(9,13) = 1.0978 [0.4259]
Hetero-X test	Not enough observations
RESET test	F(1,22) = 2.0178 [0.1695]

Production Block

Value Added in Agriculture Sector in Constant Prices

$$\Delta\log(VA1c) = 0.6802 * \Delta\log(VA3c) - 0.3325 * \Delta\log(IRRIG) + 0.2721 * \Delta\log(IRRIG(-1)) - 0.574 * ECM\_VA1c$$

$$ECM\_VA1c = \log(VA1c(-1)) - 2.21093 + 0.142550 * \log(VA2c(-1)) - 0.842551 * \log(VA3c(-1)) - 0.0572921 * \log(RAIN(-1))$$

Diagnostic Tests:

Sigma	0.0166401
log-likelihood	77.1142
AR 1-2 test	F(2,22) = 0.77360 [0.4735]
ARCH 1-1 test	F(1,22) = 0.14526 [0.7068]
Normality test	Chi^2(2) = 3.4625 [0.1771]
Hetero test	F(8,15) = 0.13374 [0.9963]
Hetero-X test	F(14,9) = 0.16939 [0.9983]
RESET test	F(1,23) = 0.47500 [0.4976]

Value Added in Agriculture Sector in Current Prices

$$\log(VA1) = \log(VA1c) + \log(VA1(-1)/VA1c(-1)) + 0.01868 + 0.7142 * d\log(P\_P) - 0.121 * ifeq(1992) - 0.4091 * ECM\_VA1$$

$$ECM\_VA1 = \log(VA1(-1)/VA1c(-1)) - 0.90 * \log(P\_P(-1))$$

Diagnostic Tests:

Sigma	0.0265619
R^2	0.816459
AR 1-2 test	F(2,24) = 3.7882 [0.0372]*
ARCH 1-1 test	F(1,24) = 0.34507 [0.5624]
Normality test	Chi^2(2) = 1.2792 [0.5275]
Hetero test	F(5,20) = 2.4039 [0.0732]
Hetero-X test	F(6,19) = 2.0532 [0.1080]
RESET test	F(1,25) = 0.12616 [0.7254]

Note: *, ** indicate significance at 1% or higher and below 1% level, respectively

Value Added in Manufacturing Sector in Constant Prices

$$\begin{aligned}\Delta \log(VA2c) = {} & 0.1754 + 1.176 * \Delta \log(VA3c) \\ & + 0.1336 * \big(\log(Kc(-1) * (VA2(-1) / GDP(-1))) \\ & - \log(Kc(-2) * (VA2(-2) / GDP(-2)))\big) \\ & + 0.05199 * \Delta \log(Xc) + 0.04261 * \Delta \log(Xc(-3)) \\ & - 0.07246 * ECM\_VA2c\end{aligned}$$

$$\begin{aligned}ECM\_VA2c = {} & \log(VA2c(-1)) - 0.40 * \log(Kc(-1) * (VA2(-1) / GDP(-1))) \\ & - 0.30 * \log(VA3c(-1)) - 0.05 * \log(time(1981))\end{aligned}$$

Diagnostic Tests:

Sigma	0.0113262
R^2	0.797123
AR 1-2 test	F(2,20) = 0.062210 [0.9399]
ARCH 1-1 test	F(1,20) = 0.37028 [0.5497]
Normality test	Chi^2(2) = 1.3067 [0.5203]
Hetero test	F(10,11) = 0.44105 [0.8960]
Hetero-X test	Not enough observations
RESET test	F(1,21) = 2.7510 [0.1121]

Value Added in Manufacturing Sector in Current Prices

$$\begin{aligned}\Delta \log(VA2) = {} & \Delta \log(VA2c) + 0.4812 * \Delta \log(P\_P) \\ & + 0.2821 * \Delta \log(P\_M) - 0.6683 * ECM\_VA2\end{aligned}$$

$$\begin{aligned}ECM\_VA2 = {} & \log(VA2(-1) / VA2c(-1)) - 0.60 * \log(P\_P(-1)) \\ & - 0.20 * \log(P\_M(-1)) - 0.26 * \log((VA3(-1) / VA3c(-1)) / \\ & (VA1(-1) / VA1c(-1)))\end{aligned}$$

Diagnostic Tests:

Sigma	0.0222731
log-likelihood	75.5262
ARCH 1-1 test	F(1,26) = 0.59667 [0.4468]
Normality test	Chi^2(2) = 2.2523 [0.3243]
Hetero test	F(6,21) = 0.29711 [0.9314]
Hetero-X test	F(9,18) = 0.60531 [0.7768]
RESET test	F(1,27) = 1.4544 [0.2383]

Value Added in Service Sector in Constant Prices

$$\Delta \log(VA3c) = -0.2502 + 0.3651 * \Delta \log(ADc) + 0.2943 * \Delta \log(ADc(-2)) - 0.3582 * ECM\_VA3c$$

$$ECM\_VA3c = \log(VA3c(-1)) - \log(ADc(-1))$$

Diagnostic Tests:

Sigma	0.0176603
R^2	0.262108
AR 1-2 test	F(2,23) = 0.65276 [0.5300]
ARCH 1-1 test	F(1,23) = 2.5233 [0.1258]
Normality test	Chi^2(2)= 8.7262 [0.0127]*
Hetero test	F(6,18) = 0.97352 [0.4708]
Hetero-X test	F(9,15) = 1.5891 [0.2055]
RESET test	F(1,24) = 14.622 [0.0008]**

Note: *, ** indicate significance at 1% or higher and below 1% level, respectively

Value Added in Service Sector in Current Prices

$$\log(VA3) = \log(VA3c) + \log(VA3(-1)/VA3c(-1)) + 0.02006 + 0.0587 * (\log(VA3(-3)/VA3c(-3)) - \log(VA3(-4)/VA3c(-4))) - 0.06095 * (\log(GCON(-1)/GCONc(-1)) - \log(GCON(-2)/GCONc(-2))) + 0.5333 * \mathrm{dlog}(P\_C) - 0.3753 * ECM\_VA2$$

$$ECM\_VA2 = \log(VA3(-1)/VA3c(-1)) - \log(P\_C(-1)) + 0.107812 * \log(P\_M(-1)) - 0.000175127 * \log(time(1981))$$

Diagnostic Tests:

Sigma	0.025641
R^2	0.47869
AR 1-2 test	F(2,21) = 0.53202 [0.5951]
ARCH 1-1 test	F(1,21) = 1.0179 [0.3245]
Normality test	Chi^2(2) = 8.5870 [0.0137]*
Hetero test	F(8,14) = 0.53672 [0.8104]
Hetero-X test	Not enough observations
RESET test	F(1,22) = 0.022487 [0.8822]

Note: *, ** indicate significance at 1% or higher and below 1% level, respectively

GNP in Constant Prices

$$\begin{aligned}\log(GNPc) = {} & \log(GNP) - \log(GNP(-1)/GNPc(-1)) - 0.01598 \\ & - 0.3451 * (\log(VA1/VA1c) - \log(VA1(-1)/VA1c(-1))) \\ & - 0.266 * (\log(VA2/VA2c) - \log(VA2(-1)/VA2c(-1))) \\ & - 0.1756 * (\log(VA3/VA3c) - \log(VA3(-1)/VA3c(-1))) \\ & + 0.8726 * ECM\_GNPc\end{aligned}$$

$$\begin{aligned}ECM\_GNPc = {} & \log(GNP(-1)/GNPc(-1)) - 0.277787 \\ & * \log(VA1(-1)/VA1c(-1)) - 0.397247 \\ & * \log(VA2(-1)/VA2c(-1)) - 0.374275 \\ & * \log(VA3(-1)/VA3c(-1))\end{aligned}$$

Diagnostic Tests:

Sigma	0.01162
R^2	0.85793
AR 1-2 test	F(2,24) = 3.3388 [0.0526]
ARCH 1-1 test	F(1,24) = 0.15256 [0.6995]
Normality test	Chi^2(2) = 21.323 [0.0000]**
Hetero test	F(8,17) = 3.8100 [0.0098]**
Hetero-X test	F(14,11) = 7.0421 [0.0013]**
RESET test	F(1,25) = 1.6042 [0.2170]

Note: *, ** indicate significance at 1% or higher and below 1% level, respectively

Net Factor Income from Abroad

$$\Delta \log(NFIA) = 0.25469 - 0.47142 * \Delta \log(NFIA(-2)) \\ -0.03110 * ECM\_NFIA$$

$$ECM\_NFIA = \log(NFIA(-1)) + 1.45 * \log(ER(-1) * (FCPI(-1) / P\_P(-1))) \\ -4.95 * \log(time(1981))$$

Diagnostic Tests:

Sigma	0.098694
R^2	0.491495
AR 1-2 test	F(2,23) = 0.27155 [0.7646]
ARCH 1-1 test	F(1,23) = 0.35577 [0.5567]
Normality test	Chi^2(2)= 1.9064 [0.3855]
Hetero test	F(4,20) = 0.26558 [0.8966]
Hetero-X test	F(5,19) = 0.71541 [0.6196]
RESET test	F(1,24) = 1.5517 [0.2249]

Government Block

Government Revenue at Current Prices

$$\Delta \log(GREV) = 0.1493 + 0.5011 * \Delta \log(GTAX) - 0.3717 * ECM\_GREV$$

$$ECM\_GREV = \log(GREV(-1)) - \log(GTAX(-1))$$

Diagnostic Tests:

Sigma	0.0210324
R^2	0.709137
AR 1-2 test	F(2,26) = 0.80690 [0.4571]
ARCH 1-1 test	F(1,26) = 1.0230 [0.3211]
Normality test	Chi^2(2) = 1.2843 [0.5262]
Hetero test	F(4,23) = 0.13251 [0.9688]
Hetero-X test	F(5,22) = 0.18297 [0.9661]
RESET test	F(1,27) = 0.15531 [0.6966]

Government Tax Revenue in Current Prices

$$\Delta\log(GTAX) = -0.6725 + 0.9238 * \Delta\log(GNP) + 0.11 * ifeq(2000) + 0.1289 * ifeq(2010) - 0.2135 * ECM\_GTAX$$

$$ECM\_GTAX = \log(GTAX(-1)) - \log(GNP(-1)) - 0.20 * \log(time(1981))$$

Diagnostic Tests:

sigma	0.044885
R^2	0.477251
AR 1-2 test	F(2,23) = 0.67129 [0.5208]
ARCH 1-1 test	F(1,23) = 0.47496 [0.4976]
Normality test	Chi^2(2) = 0.41815 [0.8113]
hetero test	F(6,18) = 3.2838 [0.0232]*
Hetero-X test	Not enough observations
RESET test	F(1,24) = 0.12942 [0.7222]

Note: *, ** indicate significance at 1% or higher and below 1% level, respectively

Government Consumption in Constant Prices via Deflator Equation

$$\log(GCONc) = \log(GCON) - \log(GCON(-1)/GCONc(-1)) - 0.5141 * (\log(GCON(-1)/GCONc(-1)) - \log(GCON(-2)/GCONc(-2))) - 0.3882 * (\log(VA3/VA3c) - \log(VA3(-1)/VA3c(-1))) + 0.3163 * ECM\_GCONc$$

$$ECM\_GCONc = \log(GCON(-1)/GCONc(-1)) - \log(VA3(-1)/VA3c(-1))$$

Diagnostic Tests:

Sigma	0.0201784
log-likelihood	73.6253
AR 1-2 test	F(2,24) = 4.8118 [0.0175]*
ARCH 1-1 test	F(1,24) = 8.3306 [0.0081]**
Normality test	Chi^2(2) = 6.4245 [0.0403]*
Hetero test	F(6,19) = 1.2507 [0.3255]
Hetero-X test	F(9,16) = 1.8906 [0.1277]
RESET test	F(1,25) = 3.7072 [0.0656]

Note: *, ** indicate significance at 1% or higher and below 1% level, respectively

Government Consumption in Current Prices

$$\Delta \log(GCON) = 0.607 * \Delta \log(GREV(-1)) + 0.4478 * (\log(GEXP2(-3)/GREV(-3)) - \log(GEXP2(-4)/GREV(-4))) - 0.06818 * ECM\_GCON$$

$$ECM\_GCON = \log(GCON(-1)) - \log(GREV(-1)) + 0.007 * \log(time(1981))$$

Diagnostic Tests:

Sigma	0.0321337
log-likelihood	58.1162
AR 1-2 test	F(2,23) = 0.16220 [0.8512]
ARCH 1-1 test	F(1,23) = 3.7558 [0.0650]
Normality test	Chi^2(2) = 6.1587 [0.0460]*
Hetero test	F(6,18) = 2.2078 [0.0901]
Hetero-X test	F(9,15) = 1.8334 [0.1438]
RESET test	F(1,24) =0.00063080 [0.9802]

Note: *, ** indicate significance at 1% or higher and below 1% level, respectively

Government Revenue Expenditure in Current Prices

$$\Delta \log(GREXP) = -0.3806 + 3.488 * \Delta \log(GREV) + 2.391 * \Delta \log(GREV(-1)) - 1.05 * ECM\_GREXP$$

$$ECM\_GREXP = \log(GREXP(-1)) - 0.90 * \log(GREV(-1)) - 0.20 * \log(time(1981))$$

Diagnostic Tests:

sigma	0.119731
R^2	0.712494
AR 1-2 test	F(2,10) = 1.8132 [0.2129]
ARCH 1-1 test	F(1,10) = 0.090820 [0.7693]
Normality test	Chi^2(2) = 1.5656 [0.4571]
hetero test	F(6,5) = 4.9169 [0.0507]
Hetero-X test	Not enough observations
RESET test	F(1,11) = 0.18669 [0.6740]

Government Development Expenditure/Public Investment in Current Prices

$$\Delta\log\left(\text{GINV}\right) = -0.09583 + 0.4212 * \Delta\log\left(\text{GINV}\left(-1\right)\right) + 0.7257 * \Delta\log\left(\text{DEBT}\right) - 0.8892 * \text{ECM\_GINV}$$

$$\text{ECM\_GINV} = \log\left(\text{GINV}\left(-1\right)\right) - 0.85 * \log\left(\text{DEBT}\left(-1\right)\right)$$

Diagnostic Tests:

Sigma	0.104452
R^2	0.379036
AR 1-2 test	F(2,24) = 0.10207 [0.9034]
ARCH 1-1 test	F(1,24) = 1.0435 [0.3172]
Normality test	Chi^2(2) = 5.2643 [0.0719]
Hetero test	F(6,19) = 0.81166 [0.5738]
Hetero-X test	F(9,16) = 1.0888 [0.4217]
RESET test	F(1,25) = 0.83655 [0.3691]

Domestic Debt in Current Prices

$$\Delta\log\left(\text{DDEBT}\right) = -0.30577 * \Delta\log\left(\text{DDEBT}\left(-2\right)\right) - 0.02328 * \text{ECM\_DDEBT}$$

$$\text{ECM\_DDEBT} = \log\left(\text{DDEBT}\left(-1\right)\right) - 0.86 * \log\left(\text{FDEBT}\left(-1\right)\right) - 3.50 * \log\left(\text{IRL}\left(-1\right)\right)$$

Diagnostic Tests:

Sigma	0.461213
log-likelihood	17.0237
AR 1-2 test	F(2,24) = 0.27567 [0.7614]
ARCH 1-1 test	F(1,24) = 0.40827 [0.5289]
Normality test	Chi^2(2) = 7.8212 [0.0200]*
Hetero test	F(4,21) = 1.5550 [0.2230]
Hetero-X test	F(5,20) = 1.1913 [0.3486]
RESET test	F(1,25) = 0.072401 [0.7901]

Note: *, ** indicate significance at 1% or higher and below 1% level, respectively

Foreign Debt in Current Prices

$$\begin{aligned}\Delta\log(\mathrm{FDEBT}) = 0.2611*(\log(-\mathrm{cGDEF}(-1)) - \log(-\mathrm{cGDEF}(-2)))\\ +1.094*(\mathrm{NFA}/(\mathrm{DCCB}+\mathrm{DCDMB}) - \mathrm{NFA}(-1)\\ /(\mathrm{DCCB}(-1)+\mathrm{DCDMB}(-1))) + 0.6283\\ *(\mathrm{NFA}(-2)/(\mathrm{DCCB}(-2)+\mathrm{DCDMB}(-2))\\ -\mathrm{NFA}(-3)/(\mathrm{DCCB}(-3)+\mathrm{DCDMB}(-3)))\\ +0.9381*\Delta\log(\mathrm{ER}) - 0.4557*\mathrm{ECM\_FDEBT}\end{aligned}$$

$$\begin{aligned}\mathrm{ECM\_FDEBT} = \log(\mathrm{FDEBT}(-1)) - 4.13062 - 0.358651*\log(-\mathrm{cGDEF}(-1))\\ -0.748811*\log(\mathrm{ER}(-1)) - 0.998,947\\ *(\mathrm{NFA}(-2)/(\mathrm{DCCB}(-2)+\mathrm{DCDMB}(-2)))\end{aligned}$$

Diagnostic Tests:

Sigma	0.04332
log-likelihood	50.9196
AR 1-2 test	F(2,21) = 1.1516 [0.3353]
ARCH 1-1 test	F(1,21) = 0.014222 [0.9062]
Normality test	Chi^2(2)= 0.82357 [0.6625]
hetero test	F(10,12) = 0.31343 [0.9623]
Hetero-X test	Not enough observations
RESET test	F(1,22) =0.0032061 [0.9554]

Trade Block

Exports in Constant Prices

$$\begin{aligned}\Delta\log(\mathrm{Xc}) = 0.218 - 0.738*(\log(\mathrm{ER}(-3)*(\mathrm{FCPI}(-3)/\mathrm{P\_P}(-3)))\\ -\log(\mathrm{ER}(-4)*(\mathrm{FCPI}(-4)/\mathrm{P\_P}(-4))))1.53*\\ \Delta\log(\mathrm{FGDPc}(-2)) - 0.21*\mathrm{ECM\_Xc}\end{aligned}$$

$$\begin{aligned}\mathrm{ECM\_Xc} = \log(\mathrm{Xc}(-1)) - 1.18773*\log(\mathrm{ER}(-1)*(\mathrm{FCPI}(-1)/\mathrm{P\_P}(-1)))\\ -0.314626*\log(\mathrm{FGDPc}(-1)) - 0.427229*\log(\mathrm{time}(1981))\end{aligned}$$

Diagnostic Tests:

Sigma	0.0875171
R^2	0.444844
AR 1-2 test	F(2,21) = 0.42347 [0.6602]
ARCH 1-1 test	F(1,21) = 0.088985 [0.7684]
Normality test	Chi^2(2) = 5.4857 [0.0644]
Hetero test	F(6,16) = 0.61355 [0.7165]
Hetero-X test	F(9,13) = 0.60779 [0.7705]
RESET test	F(1,22) = 0.016296 [0.8996]

Imports in Constant Prices

$$\begin{aligned}\Delta\log(Mc) = {} & 0.07807 + 0.3333 * \Delta\log(Mc(-2)) + 0.8252 * \mathrm{dlog}(Xc) + 0.3675 \\ & * \Delta\log(Xc(-1)) - 0.3387 * \mathrm{dlog}(Xc(-2)) - 0.339 \\ & * (\log(ER * (FCPI / P\_P)) - \log(ER(-1) * (FCPI(-1) / P\_P(-1)))) \\ & + 0.6117 * (\log(ER(-3) * (FCPI(-3) / P\_P(-3))) \\ & - \log(ER(-4) * (FCPI(-4) / P\_P(-4)))) - 0.7889 * ECM\_Mc\end{aligned}$$

$$\begin{aligned}ECM\_Mc = {} & \log(Mc(-1)) - 0.50 * \log(PCONc(-1) + GCONc(-1) + PINVc(-1)) \\ & - 0.50 * \log(Xc(-1)) + 0.24 * \log(ER(-1) * (FCPI(-1) / P\_P(-1)))\end{aligned}$$

Diagnostic Tests:

Sigma	0.0590461
R^2	0.837801
AR 1-2 test	F(2,18) = 0.56582 [0.5777]
ARCH 1-1 test	F(1,18) = 0.61494 [0.4431]
Normality test	Chi^2(2) = 1.9212 [0.3827]
Hetero test	F(14,5) = 0.58687 [0.8016]
Hetero-X test	Not enough observations
RESET test	F(1,19) = 0.29780 [0.5916]

Current Account Balances in Current Prices

$$\begin{aligned}\Delta(CAB) = {} & -1432 - 0.3742 * \Delta(CAB(-1)) - 0.8206 * (X(-2) - M(-2) \\ & -X(-3) + M(-3)) - 0.9523 * (X(-3) - M(-3) - X(-4) + M(-4)) \\ & - 0.3758 * ECM\_CAB\end{aligned}$$

$$ECM\_CAB = CAB(-1) + 1656 + 0.17 * (X(-1) - M(-1))$$

Diagnostic Tests:

Sigma	2256.73
R^2	0.821872
AR 1-2 test	F(2,21) = 0.034961 [0.9657]
ARCH 1-1 test	F(1,21) =0.00063578 [0.9801]
Normality test	Chi^2(2) = 2.3322 [0.3116]
Hetero test	F(8,14) = 0.43740 [0.8792]
Hetero-X test	Not enough observations
RESET test	F(1,22) = 0.11957 [0.7328]

Money Block

Money in Circulation

$$\Delta \log(M0) = -0.4268 * \Delta \log(M0(-2)) + 0.7671 * \Delta \log(M1) + 0.2727 * \Delta \log(M1(-2)) - 0.1009 * ECM\_M0$$

$$ECM\_M0 = (\log(M0(-1)) - \log(M1(-1))$$

Diagnostic Tests:

Sigma	0.0361518
log-likelihood	55.3886
AR 1-2 test	F(2,22) = 0.40415 [0.6724]
ARCH 1-1 test	F(1,22) = 0.17126 [0.6830]
Normality test	Chi^2(2)= 4.9178 [0.0855]
Hetero test	F(8,15) = 1.1826 [0.3705]
Hetero-X test	F(14,9) = 1.3256 [0.3421]
RESET test	F(1,23) = 5.6891 [0.0257]*

Note: *, ** indicate significance at 1% or higher and below 1% level, respectively

Narrow Money

$$\Delta \log(M1) = \Delta \log(P\_C) - 0.7956 - 0.2771 * (\Delta \log(M1(-3)) - \Delta \log(P\_C(-3))) + 1.365 * \Delta \log(ADc(-2)) - 0.2475 * ECM\_M1$$

$$ECM\_M1 = \log(M1(-1) / P\_C(-1)) - \log(ADc(-1)) + 0.008 * (IRL(-1) - 100 * \Delta\log(P\_C(-1))) - 0.30 * \log(time(1981))$$

Diagnostic Tests:

Sigma	0.0662882
R^2	0.404229
AR 1-2 test	F(2,22) = 1.0763 [0.3581]
ARCH 1-1 test	F(1,22) = 0.53500 [0.4722]
Normality test	Chi^2(2) = 2.9824 [0.2251]
Hetero test	F(6,17) = 0.68394 [0.6651]
Hetero-X test	F(9,14) = 2.9895 [0.0326]*
RESET test	F(1,23) = 11.561 [0.0025]**

Note: *, ** indicate significance at 1% or higher and below 1% level, respectively

Broad Money

$$\Delta\log(M2) = +0.2416 * \Delta\log(M2(-1)) + 0.574 * (\log(DCCB + DCDMB + NFA) - \log(DCCB(-1) + DCDMB(-1) + NFA(-1))) - 0.1783 * ECM\_M2$$

$$ECM\_M2 = \log(M2(-1)) - \log(DCCB(-1) + DCDMB(-1) + NFA(-1))$$

Diagnostic Tests:

Sigma	0.0361319
log-likelihood	58.6296
AR 1-2 test	F(2,25) = 9.9780 [0.0007]**
ARCH 1-1 test	F(1,25) = 24.204 [0.0000]**
Normality test	Chi^2(2) = 8.5917 [0.0136]*
Hetero test	F(6,20) = 3.7812 [0.0111]*
Hetero-X test	F(9,17) = 2.5962 [0.0432]*
RESET test	F(1,26) = 0.62176 [0.4375]

Note: *, ** indicate significance at 1% or higher and below 1% level, respectively

Net Foreign Asset

$$\Delta(\text{NFA}) = \Delta(\text{NFA}(-1)) + 1061 + 0.7546 * \Delta(\text{CAB}) - 0.4242 * \Delta(\text{CAB}(-2)) - 0.6238 * \text{ECM\_NFA}$$

$$\text{ECM\_NFA} = \Delta(\text{NFA}(-1)) - \text{CAB}(-1)$$

Diagnostic Tests:

Sigma	1548.26
R^2	0.897147
AR 1-2 test	F(2,22) = 0.43728 [0.6513]
ARCH 1-1 test	F(1,22) = 3.3356 [0.0814]
Normality test	Chi^2(2) = 0.38018 [0.8269]
Hetero test	F(6,17) = 3.9846 [0.0113]*
Hetero-X test	F(9,14) = 4.2894 [0.0076]**
RESET test	F(1,23) = 25.473 [0.0000]**

Note: *, ** indicate significance at 1% or higher and below 1% level, respectively

Domestic Credit of Central Bank

$$\Delta\log(\text{DCCB}) = 0.1453 + 0.9768 * (\log(\Delta(\text{DDEBT}) + 50{,}000) - \log(\Delta(\text{DDEBT}(-1)) + 50{,}000)) - 0.1238 * \text{ECM\_DCCB}$$

$$\text{ECM\_DCCB} = \log(\text{DCCB}(-1)) + 22 - 2.52 * \log(\Delta(\text{DEBT}(-1)) + 50{,}000) - 1.22 * \log(\text{time}(1981))$$

Diagnostic Tests:

Sigma	0.204798
R^2	0.236123
AR 1-2 test	F(2,25) = 0.065650 [0.9366]
ARCH 1-1 test	F(1,25) = 0.11489 [0.7375]
Normality test	Chi^2(2) = 2.8479 [0.2408]
Hetero test	F(4,22) = 2.3240 [0.0884]
Hetero-X test	F(5,21) = 1.7748 [0.1618]
RESET test	F(1,26) = 3.0232 [0.0939]

Domestic Credit of Deposit Money Banks

$$\Delta \log(DCDMB) = 1.209 * \Delta \log(INV) - 0.2178 * ECM\_DCDMB$$

$$ECM\_DCDMB = \log(DCDMB(-1)) + 2.10 - 1.23 * \log(INV(-1)) + 0.001 * (IRL(-1) - 100 * \Delta \log(P\_C(-1)))$$

Diagnostic Tests:

Sigma	0.0353202
log-likelihood	52.9967
AR 1-2 test	F(2,23) = 0.23524 [0.7923]
ARCH 1-1 test	F(1,23) = 0.047610 [0.8292]
Normality test	Chi^2(2) = 6.2479 [0.0440]*
Hetero test	F(4,20) = 1.9279 [0.1450]
Hetero-X test	F(5,19) = 1.7251 [0.1773]
RESET test	F(1,24) = 2.2865 [0.1436]

Note: *, ** indicate significance at 1% or higher and below 1% level, respectively

Deposit Rate

$$\Delta(IRD) = +0.5785 * \Delta(BR) + 0.09656 * \Delta(ER) - 0.09438 * \Delta(ER(-3)) - 0.5344 * ECM\_IRD$$

$$ECM\_IRD = IRD(-1) + 2.52 - 0.82 * BR(-1) - 0.08 * ER(-1)$$

Diagnostic Tests:

Sigma	0.380562
AR 1-2 test	F(2,20) = 0.037920 [0.9629]
ARCH 1-1 test	F(1,20) = 1.0457 [0.3187]
Normality test	Chi^2(2) = 1.9972 [0.3684]
Hetero test	F(8,13) = 0.43143 [0.8818]
Hetero-X test	F(14,7) = 0.18466 [0.9964]
RESET test	F(1,21) = 0.13951 [0.7125]

Lending Rate

$$\Delta(\text{IRL}) = 0.7863 * \Delta(\text{IRD}) - 0.2139 * \text{ECM\_IRL}$$

$$\text{ECM\_IRL} = \text{IRL}(-1) - 11 - 0.70 * \text{IRD}(-1) + 0.28 * \log(\text{DDEBT}(-1))$$

Diagnostic Tests:

Sigma	0.427457
AR 1-2 test	F(2,23) = 0.92255 [0.4117]
ARCH 1-1 test	F(1,23) = 0.019697 [0.8896]
Normality test	Chi^2(2) = 7.9926 [0.0184]*
Hetero test	F(4,20) = 2.0860 [0.1207]
Hetero-X test	F(5,19) = 1.7556 [0.1704]
RESET test	F(1,24) = 1.2794 [0.2692]

Note: *, ** indicate significance at 1% or higher and below 1% level, respectively

Price Block

GDP Deflator

$$\begin{aligned}\Delta\log(\text{P\_GDP}) = {} & 0.4667 * \Delta\log(\text{P\_GDP}(-1)) + 0.1885 * \Delta\log(\text{P\_GDP}(-3)) \\ & + 0.6552 * (\log((\text{PCON} + \text{GCON} + \text{INV}) / (\text{PCONc} + \text{GCONc} + \text{INVc})) \\ & - \log(\text{PCON}(-1) + \text{GCON}(-1) + \text{INV}(-1))) / \\ & (\text{PCONc}(-1) + \text{GCONc}(-1) + \text{INVc}(-1)) \\ & - 0.3345 * (\log((\text{PCON}(-1) + \text{GCON}(-1) + \text{INV}(-1)) / \\ & (\text{PCONc}(-1) + \text{GCONc}(-1) + \text{INVc}(-1))) \\ & - \log((\text{PCON}(-2) + \text{GCON}(-2) + \text{INV}(-2)) / \\ & (\text{PCONc}(-2) + \text{GCONc}(-2) + \text{INVc}(-2))) - 0.3353 * \text{ECM\_P\_GDP}\end{aligned}$$

$$\begin{aligned}\text{ECM\_P\_GDP} = {} & \log(\text{P\_GDP}(-1)) - 0.91 \\ & * \log((\text{PCON}(-1) + \text{GCON}(-1) + \text{INV}(-1)) \\ & / (\text{PCONc}(-1) + \text{GCONc}(-1) + \text{INVc}(-1)))\end{aligned}$$

Diagnostic Tests:

Sigma	0.00875871
log-likelihood	92.3715
AR 1-2 test	F(2,20) = 0.045236 [0.9559]
ARCH 1-1 test	F(1,20) = 1.0296 [0.3224]
Normality test	Chi^2(2) = 0.83493 [0.6587]
Hetero test	F(10,11) = 1.0692 [0.4539]
Hetero-X test	Not enough observations
RESET test	F(1,21) = 1.1421 [0.2973]

Consumer Price Index

$$\Delta \log(P\_C) = 0.03688 + 0.3802 * \Delta \log(P\_P) + 0.1699 * \Delta \log(P\_M) + 0.1917 * \Delta \log(P\_M(-1)) - 0.3982 * ECM\_P\_C$$

$ECM\_P\_C = \log(P\_C(-1)) - 0.33 * \log(P\_P(-1)) - 0.18 * \log(P\_M(-1)) - 0.26 * \log(M2(-1)/GDPc(-1)) - 0.03 * \log(GPW2(-1)) - 0.04 * \log(FPW2(-1)) - 0.06 * \log(EPW2(-1))$

Diagnostic Tests:

Sigma	0.0177119
R^2	0.658657
AR 1-2 test	F(2,20) = 0.22329 [0.8019]
ARCH 1-1 test	F(1,20) = 0.37002 [0.5498]
Normality test	Chi^2(2) = 2.0840 [0.3528]
Hetero test	F(8,13) = 0.75906 [0.6432]
Hetero-X test	Not enough observations
RESET test	F(1,21) = 2.6695 [0.1172]

Producer Price Index

$$\Delta \log(P\_P) = 0.364239 * \Delta \log(P\_P(-1)) + 0.321486 * \Delta \log(P\_P(-3)) + 0.229704 * \Delta \log(P\_M(-2)) - 0.214906 * ECM\_P\_P$$

$$ECM\_P\_P = \log(P\_P(-1)) + 1.20 - 0.46 * \log(P\_M(-1)) - 0.25 * \log(GPW2(-1))$$

Diagnostic Tests:

Sigma	0.0354513
log-likelihood	55.9365
AR 1-2 test	F(2,22) = 1.3451 [0.2811]
ARCH 1-1 test	F(1,22) = 0.37581 [0.5461]
Normality test	Chi^2(2) = 5.2604 [0.0721]
Hetero test	F(8,15) = 0.65827 [0.7194]
Hetero-X test	F(14,9) = 0.77607 [0.6765]
RESET test	F(1,23) = 0.18601 [0.6703]

Investment Deflator

$$\Delta \log(P\_INV) = 0.4952 * \left(\log\left(VA3(-2) / VA3c(-2)\right) - \log\left(VA3(-3) / VA3c(-3)\right)\right) - 0.1624 * ifeq(1999) - 0.4997 * ECM\_P\_INV$$

$$ECM\_P\_INV = \log\left(P\_INV(-1)\right) - 0.60 * \log\left(VA2(-1) / VA2c(-1)\right) - 0.35 * \log\left(VA3(-1) / VA3c(-1)\right) - 0.001 * IRL(-2)$$

Diagnostic Tests:

Sigma	0.0282803
log-likelihood	63.8363
AR 1-2 test	F(2,24) = 0.32778 [0.7237]
ARCH 1-1 test	F(1,24) = 0.068873 [0.7952]
Normality test	Chi^2(2) = 0.45551 [0.7963]
Hetero test	F(5,20) = 0.68335 [0.6414]
Hetero-X test	F(6,19) = 0.54284 [0.7693]
RESET test	F(1,25) = 2.3988 [0.1340]

Export Deflator

$$\Delta \log(P\_X) = -0.219 * \Delta \log\left(P\_X(-1)\right) + 0.4864 * \left(\log\left(VA2(-3) / VA2c(-3)\right) - \log\left(VA2(-4) / VA2c(-4)\right)\right) + 0.4109 * \Delta \log(P\_M) - 0.2565 * ECM\_P\_X$$

$$ECM\_P\_X = \log(P\_X(-1)) - 0.5 * \log(P\_M(-1)) \\ - 0.5 * \log(VA2(-1) / VA2c(-1))$$

Diagnostic Tests:

Sigma	0.0246245
log-likelihood	66.1403
AR 1-2 test	F(2,22) = 0.40800 [0.6699]
ARCH 1-1 test	F(1,22) = 0.025071 [0.8756]
Normality test	Chi^2(2) = 7.7422 [0.0208]*
Hetero test	F(8,15) = 1.0970 [0.4166]
Hetero-X test	F(14,9) = 3.7995 [0.0250]*
RESET test	F(1,23) = 1.9806 [0.1727]

Note: *, ** indicate significance at 1% or higher and below 1% level, respectively

Import Deflator

$$\Delta\log(P\_M) = 0.0191048 + 0.767812 * \Delta\log(P\_X) - 0.136711 * ECM\_P\_M$$

$$ECM\_P\_M = \log(P\_M(-1)) + 4.34921 + 0.261571 * \log(time(1981)) \\ - 0.673132 * \log(FCPI(-1)) - 1.37486 * \log(ER(-1))$$

Diagnostic Tests:

Sigma	0.0311255
R^2	0.598272
AR 1-2 test	F(2,26) = 0.051444 [0.9500]
ARCH 1-1 test	F(1,26) = 0.30609 [0.5848]
Normality test	Chi^2(2) = 6.3204 [0.0424]*
Hetero test	F(4,23) = 2.9677 [0.0410]*
Hetero-X test	F(5,22) = 5.8836 [0.0013]**
RESET test	F(1,27) = 0.86269 [0.3612]

Note: *, ** indicate significance at 1% or higher and below 1% level, respectively

References

Bangladesh Economic Review. (2005, 2006, 2007, 2008). *Finance Division, Ministry of Finance, Dhaka, Government of the People's Republic of Bangladesh.*

Bank, B. (2006, 2007, 2008). *Economic trends (various issues)*. Dhaka: Statistics Department, BB.

Basher, S. A., & Haque, A. E. (2000). *BANSIM – A Computer based Simulation Model for Bangladesh Economy, Environment and Development Services.* Institute of Development, Environment and Strategic Studies, North South University.

Bernanke, B. S. (1983). Non-monetary effects of the financial crisis in the propagation of the Great Depression.

Bresnahan, T. F., & Ramey, V. A. (1993). Segment shifts and capacity utilization in the US automobile industry. *The American Economic Review, 83*(2), 213–218.

Chowdhury, A. R. (1986). Vector autoregression as an alternative macro-modelling technique. *The Bangladesh Development Studies*, 21–32.

Chowdhury, A. R., Dao, M. Q., & Wahid, A. N. (1995). Monetary policy, output and inflation in Bangladesh: A dynamic analysis. *Applied Economics Letters, 2*(3), 51–55.

Davis, S. J., & Haltiwanger, J. (2001). Sectoral job creation and destruction responses to oil price changes. *Journal of Monetary Economics, 48*(3), 465–512.

Edelstein, P., & Kilian, L. (2007). The response of business fixed investment to changes in energy prices: A test of some hypotheses about the transmission of energy price shocks. *The BE Journal of Macroeconomics, 7*(1).

Hamilton, J. D. (1988). A neoclassical model of unemployment and the business cycle. *Journal of Political Economy, 96*(3), 593–617.

Hamilton. (2008). Oil and the macroeconomy. In L. E. Blume & S. N. Durlauf (Eds.), *The new Palgrave dictionary of economics* (2nd ed.). London: Palgrave Macmillan.

Hendry, D. F., & Doornik, J. A. (2001). *Empirical econometric modelling using PcGive 10.* London: Timberlake Consultants.

Hendry, D. F., & Krolzig, H. M. (2001). *Automatic econometric model selection using PcGets.* London: Timberlake Consultants Ltd.

Herrera, A. M. (2007). *Inventories, oil shocks and macroeconomic behavior.* Department of Economics, Michigan State University.

Islam, N. (1965). *A short-term model for Pakistan economy.* Karachi: Oxford University Press.

Klein, L. R., & Goldberger, A. S. (1955). *Econometric model of the United States, 1929–1952.* Amsterdam: North-Holland Publishing Company.

Lee, K., & Ni, S. (2002). On the dynamic effects of oil price shocks: A study using industry level data. *Journal of Monetary Economics, 49*(4), 823–852.

Mujeri, M.K., Chowdhury, T.T. and Sahana, S. (2014). *Energy Sector in Bangladesh: An Agenda for Reform*, The International Institute for Sustainable

Development. available at: https://www.iisd.org/gsi/sites/default/files/ffs_bangladesh_agenda.pdf

Parikh, A. (1983). Construction of a macroeconomic model of the Bangladesh economy. *The Bangladesh Development Studies, 11*, 1–16.

Pindyck, R. S. (1990). *Irreversibility, uncertainty, and investment* (No. w3307). National Bureau of Economic Research.

Quin, D., Razzaque, A., & Rahman, M. M. (2006). *A small quarterly macroeconometric model of Bangladesh*. Manila: Asian Development Bank (ADB).

Rahman, M. M., & Khatun, R. (2011). *A small macroeconometric model of the Bangladesh economy*. Manchester: The University of Manchester.

Rahman, S. H., & Shilpi, F. J. (1996). *A macroeconometric model of the Bangladesh economy: Model, estimation, validation and policy simulation. Research monograph no. 17*. Dhaka: Bangladesh Institute of Development Studies.

Rashid, M. A. (1981). A macro-econometric model of Bangladesh. *The Bangladesh Development Studies, 9*, 21–44.

Statistics, B. B. O. Various years. *Statistics Division, Ministry of Planning, Dhaka, Government of the People's Republic of Bangladesh.*

Tinbergen, J. (1967). *Economic policy, principles and design*. Amsterdam: North Holland Publishing Company.

PART II

Monetary and Fiscal Policy

CHAPTER 5

Assessing the Effectiveness of Monetary Policy in Bangladesh

Monzur Hossain and Md. Wahid Ferdous Ibon

5.1 Introduction

An analysis of the effectiveness of monetary policy of a country is important to understand its goals, instruments and channels. The common intended goal of monetary policy is to maintain a stable inflation and provide support to higher growth. For the appropriate choice of monetary policy instruments, it is important for the monetary authorities to know when and how their policy-induced changes in monetary variables affect aggregate output and inflation through one or more channels, such as the interest rate channel, the exchange rate channel, the asset price channel and the credit channel (see Mishkin 1996).[1]

[1] The credit channel again can be decomposed into the bank lending channel and the balance sheet channel.

We thank Marjan Hossain for her excellent research assistance.

M. Hossain (✉)
Bangladesh Institute of Development Studies (BIDS), Dhaka, Bangladesh

Md. W. F. Ibon
Department of Economics, University of Dhaka, Dhaka, Bangladesh

M. Hossain (ed.), *Bangladesh's Macroeconomic Policy*,
https://doi.org/10.1007/978-981-15-1244-5_5

Though the monetary policy in developed economies is being formulated with a main objective of maintaining a stable output gap and inflation gap, the challenges in the developing world is different. Monetary policy in developing countries usually works on how to augment the capacity to maintain stable inflation and support higher growth in a weak monetary transmission mechanism. With certain limitations, the monetary policy strategy of Bangladesh over time mainly concentrates toward achieving the goal of price stability and higher growth combining both conventional and non-conventional approaches. However, it is a challenge for developing countries like Bangladesh to find a stark balance between monetary stimulus and macroeconomic stability in the pursuit of higher economic growth. Recognizing the importance of fiscal policy in achieving macroeconomic stability and higher growth, policy coordination between monetary and fiscal authorities is thus very important.

Bangladesh Bank, the central bank of Bangladesh, formulates monetary policy with key objectives of maintaining price stability and supporting high growth. In the conduct of its monetary policy, Bangladesh Bank started releasing monetary policy statements twice a year since 2006. For a targeted rate of inflation, Bangladesh Bank considers reserve money (RM) and broad money (M2) as operating and intermediate targets, respectively. Accordingly, they use different rates such as repo, reverse repo rates, bank rate, cash reserve requirement (CRR) and statutory liquidity requirement (SLR) as policy instruments. The targets often go beyond the limit set forth in the monetary policy statements. Therefore, it is important to assess the effectiveness of monetary policy in Bangladesh in terms of its intended outcomes.

In this chapter, we thus make an attempt to assess the effectiveness of monetary policy in Bangladesh using various relevant econometric techniques, such as structural vector autoregression (SVAR) model, impulse response functions (IRFs) and variance decomposition techniques. In the analysis, we use monthly time series data of the relevant variables for the period 1989 (January)–2018 (December), allowing three foreign blocks (world rice price, world crude oil price and federal fund rate) along with seven domestic blocks in order to identify monetary transmission channels in Bangladesh.

This chapter is organized as follows. After introduction, Sect. 5.2 reviews literature and Sect. 5.3 discusses the conduct of monetary policy in Bangladesh. Section 5.4 discusses data and methodology. Section 5.5

discusses the results and Sect. 5.6 develops a policy matrix in order to support effective monetary policy. Section 5.7 concludes the chapter.

5.2 Literature Review

Extensive research on the effectiveness of monetary policy is rather limited in Bangladesh. Available studies, mainly conducted by Bangladesh Bank officials, have primarily focused on identifying various transmission channels (i.e. credit channel, interest and exchange rate channel, and so on) of monetary policy. All existing studies in the context of Bangladesh have looked into the monetary policy effectiveness through domestic variables/ blocks (Ahmed and Islam 2004; Younus 2004, 2005, 2017; Alam 2015) with only exception (Afrin 2017) which has included both domestic and foreign variables into the model.

Both Ahmed and Islam (2004) and Younus (2004) have used vector autoregression (VAR) technique on quarterly time series data and found weak and no evidence of credit channel in Bangladesh, respectively. Ahmed and Islam (2004) have also found similar weak evidence of the existence of exchange rate channel of monetary transmission in Bangladesh. They have checked the robustness of such weak existences of credit and exchange rate channel by using a sub-sample and found similar results. Younus (2005) has found contrasting results compared to Younus (2004). Using a simple correlation matrix method, it showed that both deposit and credit channels exist in Bangladesh, indicating that macroeconomic variables like price level and output can be influenced by the central bank through the use of the level of bank deposit and credit.

Alam (2015) looked into the effect of policy rate (i.e. treasury bill rate) on gross domestic product (GDP), price level and exchange rate in Bangladesh. This paper identifies that an increase in policy rate is followed by expected consequences. For instance, an unexpected rise in three-month T-bill rate decreases output and increases the value of Bangladeshi currency. Not only policy rate, but also money supply has significant effect on output and price level growth in Bangladesh (Younus 2017).

Another recent study, Afrin (2017), has applied the SVAR technique with monthly data from 2003 to 2014 and found significant effect of domestic variables (i.e. bank credit and exchange rate) and foreign variables (i.e. world rice price) on macroeconomic aggregates like GDP and price level. This chapter has identified a "stabilizing role" of central bank in response to a domestic credit boom.

On the other hand, in regard to monetary policy effectiveness in other countries, analyzing monetary data using vector error correction model (VECM) and IRFs for India, Bhattacharya et al. (2011) have argued that interest rate hike has no direct impact on GDP. However, exchange rate appreciates following an increase in interest rate in India. They have found that the exchange rate appreciation lowers the general price level. Two other studies (Ghosh and Rajan 2007; Khundrakpam 2007) have also found similar evidence of exchange rate pass-through in India. Not only exchange rate but also interest rate (policy rate) has been found to be effective in forming output growth and consumer prices (Kapur and Behera 2012).

Although exchange rate channel has been evident in developing countries like India, it is ineffective in Gulf Cooperation Council (GCC) countries (Cevik and Teksoz 2012). Using a SVAR model, they showed that the exchange rate channel is not present in GCC countries (i.e. change in exchange rate does not affect non-hydrocarbon output and consumer prices). However, interest rate and bank lending do affect non-hydrocarbon output and consumer prices.

Thao (2017) have used a non-recursive SVAR model to figure out the monetary transmission channels in Vietnam. In order to assess the effect of World Trade Organization (WTO) accession in 2007, this chapter has divided the sample period into pre- and post-2007 and adopted the same technique to check for transmission channels and their relative effectiveness in Vietnam. In both sample periods, credit channel has been identified as relatively more effective rather than interest rate channel in Vietnam. According to this chapter, exchange rate, world rice price and world crude oil price are also important determinants in shaping GDP and price levels in Vietnam. Other studies (Hung and Pfau 2009; Nguyen 2014; Raghavan and Silvapulle 2008) have also used VAR/SVAR techniques and found more or less similar results in case of Vietnam and Malaysia.

Kilinc and Tunc (2014) have adopted SVAR model to analyze the effect of both domestic (interest rates and risk premium) and foreign (commodity prices and global demand) shocks on output and inflation in Turkish economy. They have found both domestic and foreign shocks to have significant impact on Turkish GDP and inflation formation.

Overall, the above studies have mostly used various specifications of VAR and SVAR models to identify monetary transmission channels. In terms of data, studies belong to two groups: (i) with only domestic variables, and (ii) with both domestic and foreign variables. Few studies have used quarterly data whereas a few have attempted with monthly data. Allowing foreign shocks into the model is uncommon in the context of Bangladesh, perhaps due to her less exposure to international markets. However, as the country has achieved lower middle income status and is likely to be graduated from the least developed country (LDC) status by 2024, it is important to take foreign shocks into consideration while analyzing the effectiveness of monetary policy variables in the context of her growing integration with global financial market.

5.3 Conduct of Monetary Policy in Bangladesh

The conduct of monetary policy in Bangladesh Bank can be judged by inflationary developments, private sector credit growth and liquidity situation in the banking sector. How much the policy rates are effective in achieving these targets is the crux of assessing the effectiveness of monetary policy.

Under the Financial Sector Reform Program (FSRP) of the 1990s, the monetary policy framework that is taken up by the Bangladesh Bank is mostly market-based and focuses on influencing the target variables through a supply and demand framework. Bangladesh Bank doesn't have direct control over money supply and thus influences money supply by using direct monetary instruments (bank rate, credit ceiling, SLR and CRR) and indirect monetary instruments (TB auctions, repo and reverse repo agreements) to impact the broad money M2 via money multiplier. The basic mechanism used for this is the control of liquidity via the repurchase agreements, reverse repo and treasury bill auctions. These, then, have an impact on the inter-bank call money rate for overnight money market transactions. Repo introduces money into the system and reverse repo reduces the money supply, and through this, the liquidity situation is controlled by the Bangladesh Bank. Direct instruments, such as CRR and SLR and bank rates are also used to influence money supply albeit infrequently. Before the 1990s, direct control of various instruments like credit and interest rates were more prevalent but after the 1990s, more indirect instruments like repo and reverse repo were used. Apart from influencing inflation, the monetary policy also influences the asset prices and returns of the financial markets.

In the conduct of monetary policy, Bangladesh Bank sets a safe limit of the M2 growth target in line with the projected GDP growth and expected inflation. Once the safe limit has been determined, Bangladesh Bank attempts to clear the money market by changing the nominal stock of money M2. The relationship between broad money and reserve money allows the RM to be used as an operating target to reach the M2 via the money multiplier, for which Bangladesh Bank has to monitor constantly the factors like currency-deposit ratio, reserve-deposit ratio and the excess reserve-deposit ratio.

A change in currency-deposit ratio usually means that the checkable deposits are being converted into currency, and since currency doesn't undergo multiple expansions unlike checkable deposits, the money multiplier declines, and so does the broad money. Currency holding usually depends on the income and the deposit interest rate. Financial innovations, increased number of bank branches and lower costs of financial transactions also have impact on the currency-deposit ratio.

The reserve-deposit ratio can be changed by the Bangladesh Bank through the use of CRR. Before the 1990s financial reform, CRR was used frequently as a tool, but its role was shrinked after the introduction of government T-bill auctions in 1995. The average excess reserve-deposit ratio measures the behavior of the banks and their efficiency at managing funds. Because excess reserves are used as a means of damage control, in case of unexpected outflow of deposits or any abnormal behavior in the money market. However, as excess reserves do not earn any interest income, and therefore banks choose to reduce the excess reserve ratio through efficient fund management.

5.3.1 Inflation

In Bangladesh the behavior of food and non-food inflation is quite opposite and goes beyond the traditional pattern of same trend, as is observed in many other countries. While non-food inflation has been declining, food inflation has been increasing. Headline inflation continuously remains within a range of 7–8 percent during the decade. Monetary policy has been apparently effective in curbing non-food inflation, but the main component of inflation is food inflation on which monetary policy remains largely ineffective. Food inflation contributes to more than 65 percent in overall inflation (Mortaza and Hasnayen 2008). Overall inflation is found to be biased toward food inflation as it follows the trend of food inflation. Therefore, as food inflation is largely affected by supply side constraints, the role of monetary policy in curbing inflation in Bangladesh is somewhat limited. As a fact, during the period 2012–2014, broad money growth declines from 20 percent to about 15 percent, but inflation remains the same, which points to the fact that the main policy objective remains unfulfilled (Figs. 5.1 and 5.2).

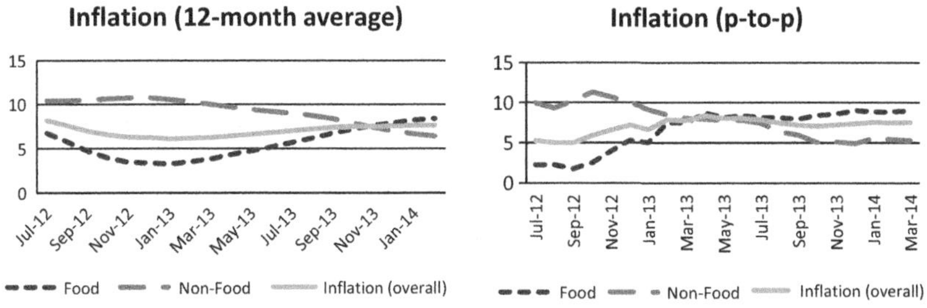

Fig. 5.1 Inflationary episodes

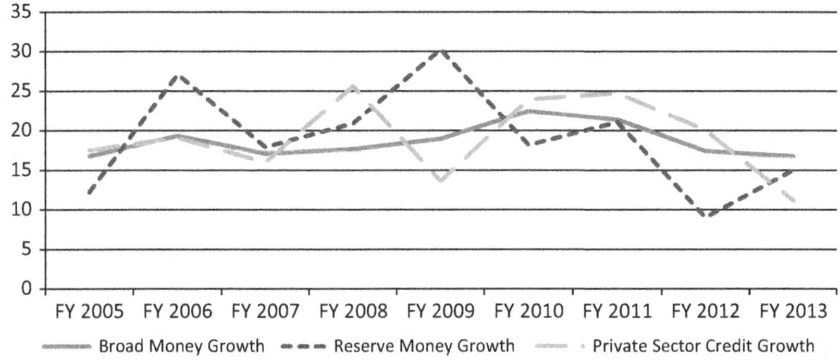

Fig. 5.2 Money supply and private credit growth

5.3.2 *Private Sector Credit Growth and Private Investments*

It is still heavily contested as to how much impact, if any, monetary policy has on private sector investments through either the "money" channel or the alternative "credit" channel. Khan (2010) argues that in developing countries, the underdeveloped financial systems and weak interest rate responsiveness of aggregate spending provide a very limited scope for traditional money transmission processes through the interest rate channel. However, the working of monetary policy via asset side of balance sheets of banks is raising the validity of credit channel.

The distinction between money view and credit view is resolved to some extent by Khan (2010). The transmission process in monetary policy was traditionally analyzed by focusing on monetary aggregates. On the other hand, credit view assesses the role of credit markets in the said transmission of monetary policy. In financially underdeveloped economies, the credit view offers better insights into long-term growth to policymakers. Tightening of monetary policy causes banks to reduce loans and securities. This reduction is extensive to the point that banks reduce and reallocate total loan portfolios, and in turn the amount spent by the recipients of said loan would start to reduce as they are unable to find alternative sources of finance due to decline of bank credit, which is in line with the money view.

In line with above views, monetary policy has a role to stimulate growth for which private sector credit growth is an important determinant. Note that private investment has been stagnant at around 21–22 percent of GDP for the last one decade or so, which is well below the required target at 25 percent or more set in the sixth and seventh Five-Year Plans. The effectiveness of monetary policy in influencing money supply and interest rates will likely have effect on private sector credit growth, which is also closely associated with private investments. Higher economic growth hinges on higher private investment. Private investment and private credit have positive relationship, and thereby lower private credit growth hurts economic growth. However, despite a higher target set in Monetary Policy Statements (MPSs), a lower growth of private credit has been achieved in most of the years. As one can see from Fig. 5.2, private credit growth is not consistent with M2 growth.

5.3.3 *Liquidity Management*

Over the last decade, banks often experience excessive liquidity buildup or liquidity crisis—both the situations indicate problem with monetary policy management. A fall in private credit and govt credit from the banking sector, increase of net foreign asset (NFA) due to increased remittances, and buying dollar from domestic market are the key reasons for excessive liquidity, while the vice versa represent liquidity crisis in the banking sector. Fall in private credit is attributed to lack of investment demand, restrictive credit regime and banks' reluctance to reduce interest rate.

Bangladeshi commercial banks have been relying mainly on deposit for the supply of loanable funds in the absence of bond market. Credit-deposit ratio often hovers around 0.8–0.85 though the actual values often differ from the policy targets, which indirectly points to problem with monetary policy formulation. A high non-performing loan ratio (NPL) in the Bangladeshi banking sector (10.33 percent of total outstanding loan in March 2019) is another problem that also creates problems for interest rate structure that makes the monetary policy instruments less effective. This, in other words, is indicating that the transmission channels via interest rate changes are weak (Table 5.1).

Table 5.1 Sector-wise interest rate structure and different policy rates

Rates	*June 2013 (percent)*	*June 2014 (percent)*	*June 2018 (percent)*
A. Interest rate structure			
Savings fixed deposits (diff maturity)	11–12.5	8.5–10	8–9.5
Industry loan	15–17	15.5–17	13–15.5
Housing loan	15–19	15–19	12–14.5
Consumer credit	15.5–19.5	16–18	12.5–15.5
Trade financing	16–18	16–18	12–15
B. Policy rates			
Repo	7.25	7.25	6
Reverse repo	5.25	5.25	4.75
Govt. treasury bills	8.13–11.54	6.82–10.60	2.85–5.89
Govt. treasury bonds	10.94–12.48	8.52–12.48	3.42–8.82

5.4 Data and Methodology

The normal transmission channel of monetary policy is that an increase in money supply would cause a reduction in interest rate; this would lead to increase in investment and thereby higher aggregate demand and higher GDP. Along the way there may be some increase in inflation, depending on constraints on the supply side. Conversely, a reduction in money supply would cause an increase in interest rate, fall in investment and aggregate demand leading to lower inflation and possibly lower GDP. However, in the context of investment climate and weaker monetary policy transmission channels, the acceleration of GDP growth is affected by the country's overriding development objective, rather than the monetary policy framework alone.

Therefore, to assess the effectiveness of monetary policy in Bangladesh, we have used a monthly dataset collected from International Financial Statistics (IFS) and Bangladesh Bank database for the period 1989 (January)–2018 (December). Our dataset includes ten time series variables and two blocks. The foreign block includes (1) world crude oil price (OIL), (2) world rice price (RICE) and (3) US federal fund rate (FED), and the domestic block variables (4) gross domestic product (GDP), (5) consumer price index (CPI), (6) broad money supply (M2), (7) central bank policy rate (CBPR), (8) lending interest rate (LR), (9) bank credit (CRE) and (10) nominal exchange rate of taka (NER). Figures 5.8, 5.9 and 5.10 present the dataset in raw, logarithmic and logarithmic first difference form, respectively.

In order to perform a SVAR model, we first perform various diagnostic tests, such as Augmented Dickey–Fuller (ADF) test, Johansen co-integration test and VAR stability test. As our dataset is a time series of 360 periods (1989 M1–2018 M12), there is a possibility that the variables are non-stationary in level form (Dickey and Fuller 1979). In order to check for this, we have performed ADF test (see Table 5.6) for all the variables and found that most of them are non-stationary (integrated of order one) in level form and are stationary (integrated of order zero) in first difference form. Interest rate variables like FED, CBPR and LR are found to be stationary in the level form. We have taken first difference of the variables that are non-stationary of order one before estimating SVAR model so that all the variables of SVAR satisfy stationarity condition (i.e. zero-unit root).

Before estimating parameters of SVAR, we have performed a stability test (see Table 5.7 and Fig. 5.11) and found that our proposed SVAR model satisfies stability condition when the lag length is two (02). Moreover, trace statistic and maximum eigenvalue statistic for various specifications (see Table 5.8) confirm that the SVAR model is cointegrated. Finally, we perform a non-recursive[2]-type reduced form SVAR using the standard specification following Kim and Roubini (2000), Pham (2016) and Thao (2017). The SVAR model looks like:

$$A\begin{bmatrix} u_{oil} \\ u_{rice} \\ u_{fed} \\ u_{gdp} \\ u_{cpi} \\ u_{m2} \\ u_{cbpr} \\ u_{lr} \\ u_{cre} \\ u_{neer} \end{bmatrix} = B\begin{bmatrix} e_{oil} \\ e_{rice} \\ e_{fed} \\ e_{gdp} \\ e_{cpi} \\ e_{m2} \\ e_{cbpr} \\ e_{lr} \\ e_{cre} \\ e_{neer} \end{bmatrix},$$

[2] In a non-recursive specification, any element of the matrix A can take non-zero value (i.e. not only the past information, but also the possibility of unexpected shocks can affect policy-makers' decisions), whereas in a recursive specification, matrix A is assumed to be a lower triangular one (i.e. policymakers use only the available information while designing policies.).

where matrix A is the contemporaneous coefficient matrix, B is the variance-covariance matrix of residuals, *u* indicates stochastic errors and *e* indicates structural innovations (Table 5.2).

Moreover, we use IRF and variance decomposition techniques to analyze the data.

Table 5.2 Contemporaneous coefficient matrix and variance-covariance matrix

	A. Matrix A									
	Independent variable									
	OIL	*RICE*	*FED*	*GDP*	*CPI*	*M2*	*PR*	*LR*	*CRE*	*NER*
OIL	1.00	0.00	0.00	0.00	0.00	0.00	0.00	0.00	0.00	0.00
RICE	0.00	1.00	0.00	0.00	0.00	0.00	0.00	0.00	0.00	0.00
FED	NA	0.00	1.00	0.00	0.00	0.00	0.00	0.00	0.00	0.00
GDP	NA	NA	0.0	1.00	0.00	0.00	0.00	0.00	0.00	0.00
CPI	NA	0.00	0.0	NA	1.0	0.00	0.00	0.00	0.00	0.00
M2	0.00	0.00	0.00	NA	NA	1.00	0.00	0.00	0.00	0.00
PR	0.00	0.00	NA	NA	NA	0.00	1.00	NA	0.00	0.00
LR	0.00	0.00	0.00	0.00	0.00	0.00	NA	1.00	NA	0.00
CRE	0.00	0.00	0.00	0.00	NA	NA	NA	NA	1.00	NA
NER	NA	NA	NA	NA	NA	NA	NA	0.00	0.00	1.00
	B. Matrix B									
	OIL	*RICE*	*FED*	*GDP*	*CPI*	*M2*	*PR*	*LR*	*CRE*	*NER*
OIL	NA	0.00	0.00	0.00	0.00	0.00	0.00	0.00	0.00	0.00
RICE	0.00	NA	0.00	0.00	0.00	0.00	0.00	0.00	0.00	0.00
FED	0.00	0.00	NA	0.00	0.00	0.00	0.00	0.00	0.00	0.00
GDP	0.00	0.00	0.00	NA	0.00	0.00	0.00	0.00	0.00	0.00
CPI	0.00	0.00	0.00	0.00	NA	0.00	0.00	0.00	0.00	0.00
M2	0.00	0.00	0.00	0.00	0.00	NA	0.00	0.00	0.00	0.00
PR	0.00	0.00	0.00	0.00	0.00	0.00	NA	0.00	0.00	0.00
LR	0.00	0.00	0.00	0.00	0.00	0.00	0.00	NA	0.00	0.00
CRE	0.00	0.00	0.00	0.00	0.00	0.00	0.00	0.00	NA	0.00
NER	0.00	0.00	0.00	0.00	0.00	0.00	0.00	0.00	0.00	NA

5.5 Empirical Results

5.5.1 *Money Supply and GDP Growth*

The contemporaneous coefficient matrix of the SVAR model in Table 5.3 highlights some interesting caveats to the role of monetary policy in Bangladesh. The effect of positive world oil price shock on Bangladesh's GDP and CPI is negative. However, the magnitude is not statistically significant at 5 percent level. This indicated that Bangladesh's output and price levels are not in general affected by world crude oil price, which is obvious because Bangladesh administers oil prices through subsidies. Also Bangladesh's GDP is not significantly affected by world rice price hike. This finding is not surprising because Bangladesh is now self-sufficient in rice production. The impact of M2 on GDP is found to be negative and significant in Bangladesh highlighting a dubious role of broad money and private investments, which casts doubt about the role of monetary policy in stimulating GDP growth. For the sample period, NER has been found to be negatively affected by a rise in GDP, which is also expected because Bangladesh strongly intervenes in the foreign exchange market to keep the NER almost fixed.

Increase in money supply has significant negative effect on bank credit in Bangladesh. However, an increase in money supply contributes to an

Table 5.3 Contemporaneous coefficient matrix of SVAR model

	Independent Variable									
	OIL	RICE	FED	GDP	CPI	M2	PR	LR	CRE	NER
OIL	1.00	0.00	0.00	0.00	0.00	0.00	0.00	0.00	0.00	0.00
RICE	0.00	1.00	0.00	0.00	0.00	0.00	0.00	0.00	0.00	0.00
FED	-0.650 (0.201)	0.00	1.00	0.00	0.00	0.00	0.00	0.00	0.00	0.00
GDP	-0.036	-0.009	0.0	1.00	0.00	0.00	0.00	0.00	0.00	0.00
CPI	-0.001	0.00	0.0	0.004	1.0	0.00	0.00	0.00	0.00	0.00
M2	0.00	0.00	0.00	-0.033 (0.008)	-0.124 (0.072)	1.00	0.00	0.00	0.00	0.00
PR	0.00	0.00	-0.016	0.024	6.011 (2.111)	0.00	1.00	0.136	0.00	0.00
LR	0.00	0.00	0.00	0.00	0.00	0.00	-0.677	1.00	0.769 (5.179)	0.00
CRE	0.00	0.00	0.00	0.00	0.024	-0.132 (0.023)	0.001	-0.0003	1.00	0.901 (0.038)
NER	-0.001	0.008	0.0003	-0.022 (0.004)	0.003	0.386 (0.025)	-0.0003	0.00	0.00	1.00

Note: Highlighted cells indicate statistically significant (at 05 percent level) coefficients. Numbers in the parentheses are standard errors. Variables in the column (row) are independent (dependent)

increase in the NER of taka. Policy rate follows the retail rate (lending rate) (i.e. increase in the lending rate leads to an increase in the policy rate), but the association is not statistically significant.

Therefore, contemporaneous coefficients of SVAR model in this section suggest that money supply negatively affects private credit, and so does GDP growth. This, in other words, indicates somewhat ineffectiveness of monetary policy instruments. However, since the variables are subject to be influenced by their lagged effect, further assessments are made in the following sections using variance decomposition and IRFs.

5.5.2 *Responses of Domestic Variables to Various Shocks*

The estimated impulse response functions of Bangladesh's GDP and CPI on three external shocks, namely, oil price, rice price and federal fund rate are shown in Fig. 5.3. Positive innovations to oil price in international market causes Bangladesh's GDP to increase in the first month, and then it decreases in the second month to increase again in the following month. Responses of GDP to world rice price are mostly negative except a positive impulse during the third month of world rice price hike. Such effects dwindle after 9–10 months. The effect of a rise in federal fund rate on Bangladesh's GDP is rather very limited. It wipes out in first two months and the response is not significant. All three foreign shocks affect Bangladesh's CPI inflation mostly in a positive direction. For instance, a rise in world rice price results in an increase in Bangladesh's CPI between second and seventh months. However, in the long run, such foreign shocks do not persist and are statistically insignificant.

5.5.3 *Responses of GDP and CPI on Domestic Shocks*

The estimated impulse responses of GDP to four domestic shocks (i.e. shock in central bank policy rate, broad money supply, bank credit and NER of taka) are shown in Fig. 5.4. Among the four shocks, broad money supply or M2 has relatively larger impact on GDP, as visible from above IRFs. GDP falls in the first month of positive innovations to money supply and then it increases in the following month. However, such short-term responses die out in about six months. Other domestic shocks like exchange rate, bank credit and policy rate affect GDP mostly in positive direction although the responses are very poor. The results are consistent with contemporaneous SVAR coefficients.

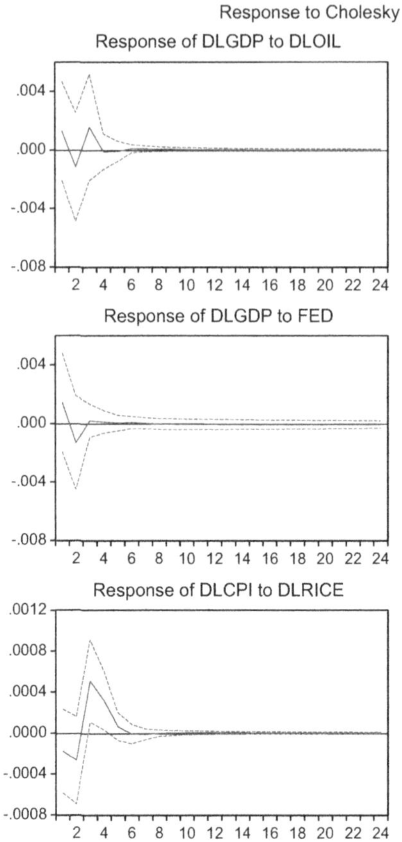

Fig. 5.3 Responses of GDP and CPI to foreign shocks

Figure 5.5 describes CPI's responses to the domestic shocks. As expected, an expansionary monetary policy causes the general price level to rise in the short run. Positive and significant effect of expansionary monetary policy on CPI persists for about a quarter and then decays to zero. Positive innovations to NER of taka affects CPI mostly positively except a negative spike during third month. Innovations in policy rate and bank credit have positive impact on CPI in initial months. However, responses are statistically insignificant. Therefore, the effects are short-lived and warrants dynamic adjustments of monetary policy instruments.

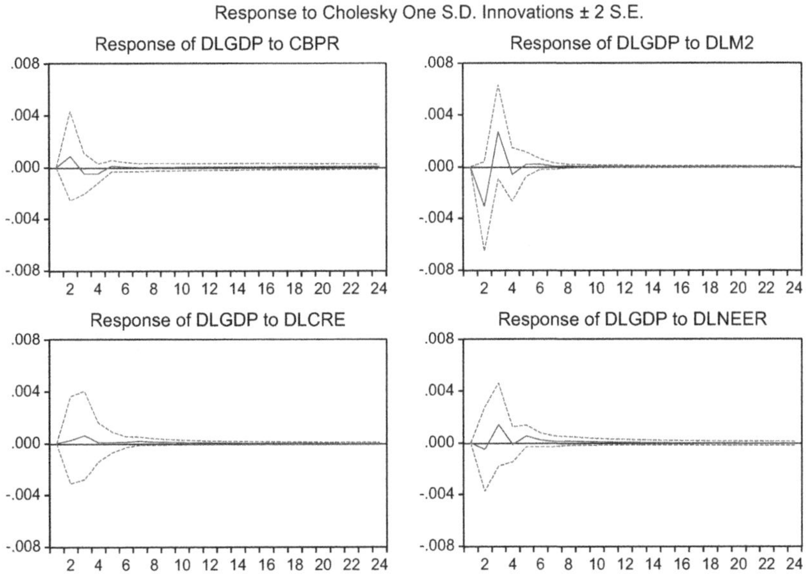

Fig. 5.4 Responses of GDP to domestic shocks

At this point we look into the responses of monetary variables (i.e. money supply and central bank policy rate) to three foreign shocks. Innovation in federal fund rate seems to have long-run effect on both money supply and policy rate. Following a positive shock in the FED rate, Bangladesh's policy rate increases tremendously and persists even after 24 months. This response becomes statistically significant after 10 months of the shock. Hence, FED rate does not have significant impact on Bangladesh's policy rate in the short run. However, it has a strong positive effect on policy rate in the long run. This finding can also be verified by the variance decomposition of policy rate of Bangladesh (see Appendix). Positive innovation in FED rate has negative effect on Bangladesh's broad money supply in the long run, and effects persist even after 24 months of innovation in FED rate. International oil price has insignificant positive effects on Bangladesh's policy rate. It responds to oil price more in the long run. Hike in international crude oil and rice price produces, respectively, bell shape and inverse bell shape IRF for broad money supply of Bangladesh. However, these responses are not significant (Fig. 5.6).

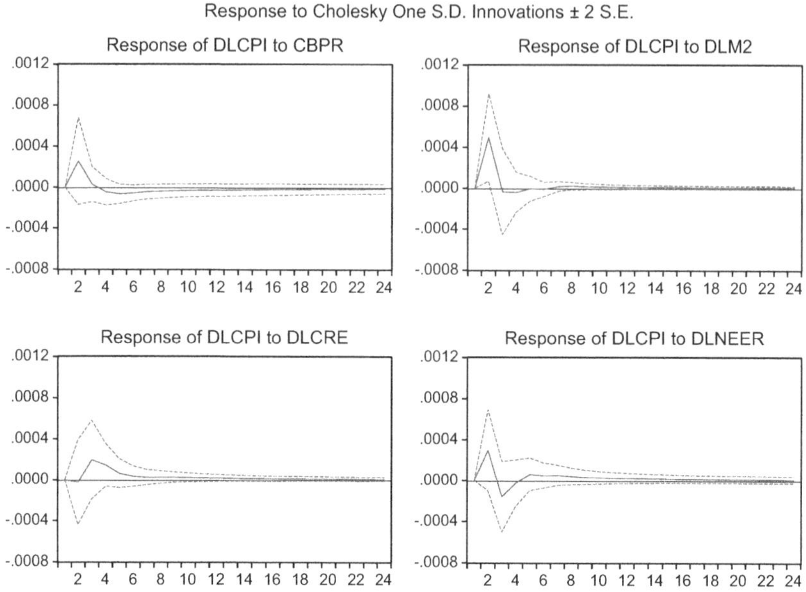

Fig. 5.5 Responses of CPI to domestic shocks

Figure 5.7 explores some interesting points. Positive innovation in money supply significantly and positively affects bank credit. However, the large increase in bank credit due to an expansionary monetary policy gets reduced substantially in about ten months. This points to the fact that money supply affects bank credit, which can also be confirmed by decomposing the variance of bank credit (see Appendix). Expansionary monetary policy affects NER of taka negatively and significantly. Such effects persist for about four months. Variance decomposition of NER also confirms the similar findings (see Appendix). Innovation in money supply negatively affects policy rate in Bangladesh, with a persistent effect even after 24 months of the shock in money supply. Exchange rate has a profound impact on bank credit in Bangladesh. IRF shows that a positive innovation in NER of taka positively and significantly affects bank credit. Bank credit increases sharply during the first four months and then slowly decays. Such effects persist even after 24 months of exchange rate shock. Variance decomposition of exchange rate also confirms this finding that exchange rate has a long-run effect on policy rate in Bangladesh (see Appendix).

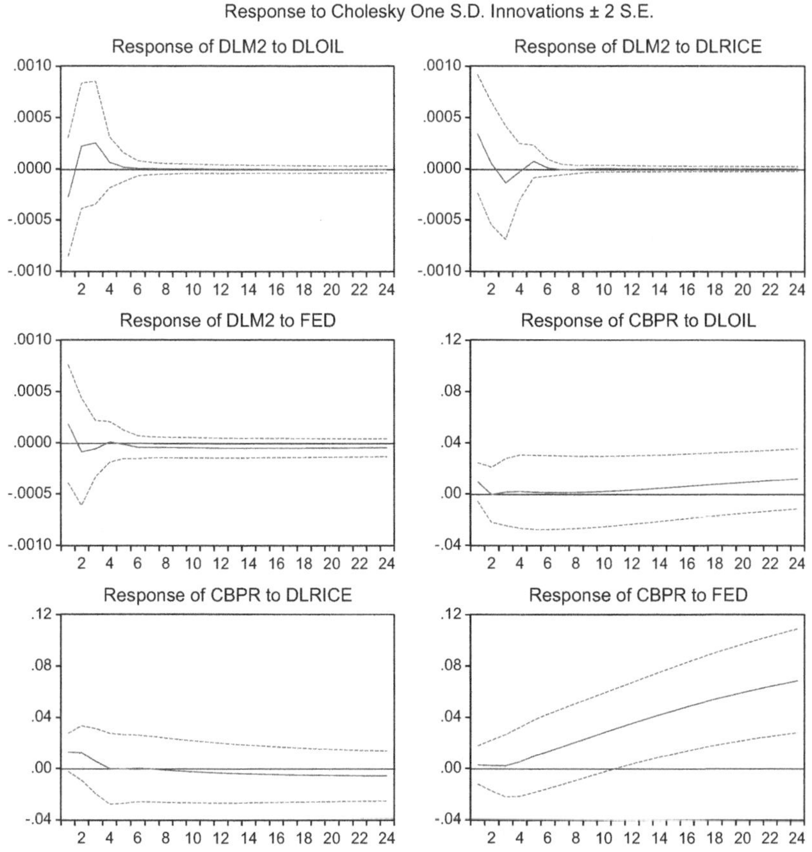

Fig. 5.6 Responses of money supply and policy rate to foreign shocks

5.5.4 *Impact of Money Supply (M2) on Inflation and Private Credit*

Using ten years' data (2005–2014), we perform variance decomposition analysis to assess the impact of money supply on food and non-food inflation (Table 5.4). The analysis shows that M2 explains only 5 percent variation in food inflation and 18 percent variation in non-food inflation in a year. This clearly implies that the role of monetary policy in containing inflation in Bangladesh is rather limited. On the other hand, the analysis shows that money supply growth has quick impact on

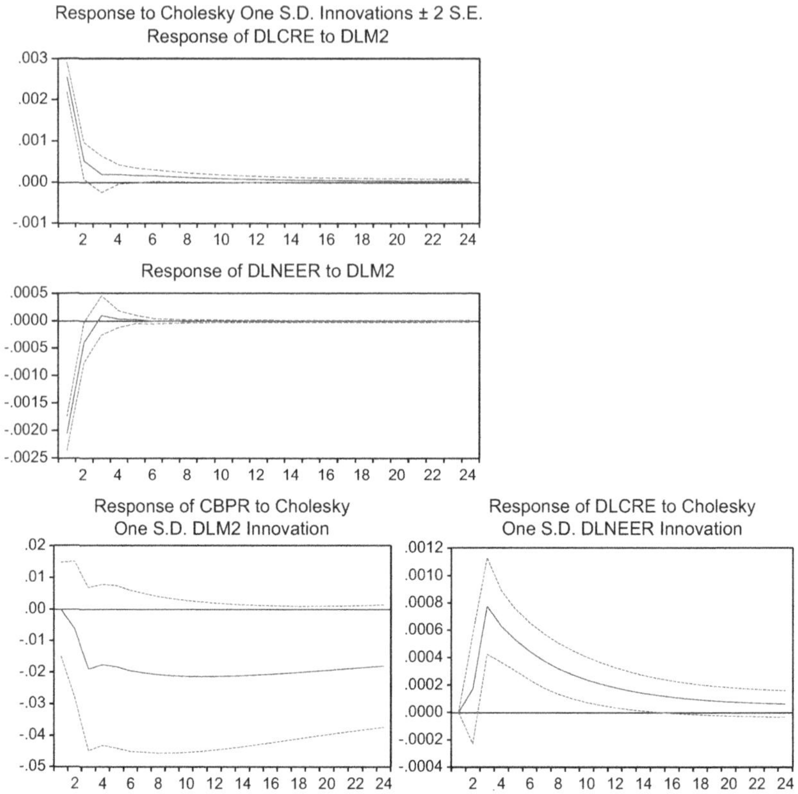

Fig. 5.7 Responses of monetary policy to monetary shocks

private credit growth, about 7 percent variations of credit in 3 months and 10 percent in 6 months, which is also consistent with IRFs in the previous sections.

5.6 Monetary Policy Tools and Implications

In the formulation of monetary policy, some structural policy issues are needed to be addressed to achieve intended outcome of monetary policy. Financial sector reforms, exchange rate management, complementarity between fiscal and monetary policy, credit allocation, and so on might help to implement monetary policy in a more effective way. In order to apply the available policy tools judiciously, a matrix of expected outcomes with limitations of the measures has been developed below (Table 5.5).

Table 5.4 Contribution of money supply to inflation and private credit growth

A. Food inflation

Period	S.E.	M2_GROWTH	FOOD_PP
1	1.78	100.00	0.00
3	2.12	99.97	0.02
6	2.34	99.95	0.04
9	2.42	99.95	0.05
12	2.45	99.94	0.05

B. Non-food inflation

Period	S.E.	M2_GROWTH	NON_FOOD_PP
1	1.73	100.00	0.00
3	1.98	99.41	0.58
6	2.15	93.97	6.028
9	2.27	86.84	13.15
12	2.35	81.63	18.36

C. Private credit

Period	S.E.	M2_GROWTH	PRIVATE SECTOR CREDIT
1	1.717519	100.0000	0.000000
3	2.054673	93.32430	6.675700
6	2.293391	90.52616	9.473835
9	2.393174	89.77648	10.22352
12	2.434445	89.51234	10.48766

5.7 Conclusions

This chapter evaluates the effectiveness of monetary policy in Bangladesh in light of the intended dual objectives of maintaining price stability and supporting faster economic growth with poverty reduction. Overall, our analysis suggests that monetary transmission channels are weak, and therefore, monetary policy is less effective in achieving its intended dual objectives, such as growth and price stability. In the conduct of monetary policy in Bangladesh, the choice of target variables is the major constraint. Administered interest rates and directed credit allocation make it difficult to use them as target variables. This situation implies that, practically, the only target variable Bangladesh Bank can seek to influence is the broad money supply. The weak link between money supply and interest rate reveals the fact that the financial system of Bangladesh is not largely competitive and efficient. The banks, particularly the private

Table 5.5 Policy matrix

Policy tools	*Intended outcome*	*Possible limitations*	*Evidence on effectiveness*	*Recommended policy responses*
Interest rate policy	Higher investment, low inflation, smooth monetary policy transmission	Stickiness due to oligopolistic bank structure; excess liquidity if capped; market distortion due to higher NSD rates	Effective in the short run	Greater efficiency in the financial sector; lower bad loans; lower operating costs of banks and so on; use monetary policy instrument, such as CRR, SLR to reduce interest rate
Sterilized intervention	Prevent nominal and real appreciation while neutralizing the growth of base money	Rising quasi-fiscal cost; higher interest rates that attract additional inflows; Unable to prevent real appreciation over the medium term due to eventual inflation	Some evidence of effectiveness in the short term, but not in the medium to long term	Use sterilized intervention as a short-run measure
Greater exchange rate flexibility	Effective monetary policy for macroeconomic management; discourage speculative attacks; higher economic growth	Loss of international price competitiveness	Limited intervention to smooth the pace of appreciation or depreciation may be effective	Greater flexibility with frequent but small interventions
Complementarity between fiscal and monetary policy	Contain inflationary pressure; encourage public investments; prevent real appreciation	Lack of flexibility and timeliness; reduction of the provision of some basic services and infrastructure investment; possibility of a positive signaling effect to attract additional investments	Some evidence of effectiveness in keeping better growth performance	Exploit the automatic stabilizer function of the budget; the government may implement planned infrastructure investment and basic services delivery without increasing spending out of higher tax revenues or reducing tax rates
Financial sector reforms	Greater transparency; financial depth; responsiveness of interest rate; proper functioning credit market	Not intended for short run	Short-run	Better supervision; prudent regulations; Basel conditions
Agricultural and SME credit	Foster economic growth	Banks unwillingness; conducive environment; Lower financial inclusion	Effective	Medium- to long-run outcome; greater allocation of refinancing schemes; revise interest rate structure; policy guidelines for effective use of refinancing schemes

Source: Authors' compilation

ones, collusively determine the lending rate with little regard for money supply conditions. Therefore, the role of monetary policy has been less effective for accelerating growth.

Further, money supply has no discernible impact on inflation mainly due to the fact that inflation in Bangladesh is dominated by food inflation, which is less likely to be affected by money supply. Moreover, in an open, import-dependent economy like Bangladesh, domestic prices are largely influenced by international prices. Hence, monetary policy instruments, such as cash reserve and statutory liquidity requirements and operations in treasury bonds, cannot exert significant influence on the target variable, namely, money supply. Therefore, the role of monetary policy in containing inflation is somewhat less effective. From this point of view, to contain inflation, a complementarity between fiscal and monetary policy is important.

Commercial banks in Bangladesh typically maintain large excess liquidity in absence of alternative investment options, particularly due to underdeveloped bond market. In this situation, it would be less useful to expand money supply through reduction in cash reserve requirement/statutory liquidity requirement or treasury bond operations, if extra demand for investment is not created. Note, however, that the relationship between interest rate and investment is not straightforward in Bangladesh. Similarly, reasonable increases in cash reserve/statutory liquidity requirements or treasury bond operations would not be of much help in inducing banks to restrain credit since they will indulge in excess liquidity. The above analysis clearly points to the fact that monetary policy has been less effective in accelerating growth or containing inflation in the context of structural weaknesses of the financial system in Bangladesh. Though monetary policy appears to be effective in most cases for the short-term period, it is important for the monetary policy authority to work on making transmission channels more effective with dynamic adjustments to policy instruments. Accommodative monetary policy needs to be pursued with greater coordinated support from fiscal authority.

Appendix

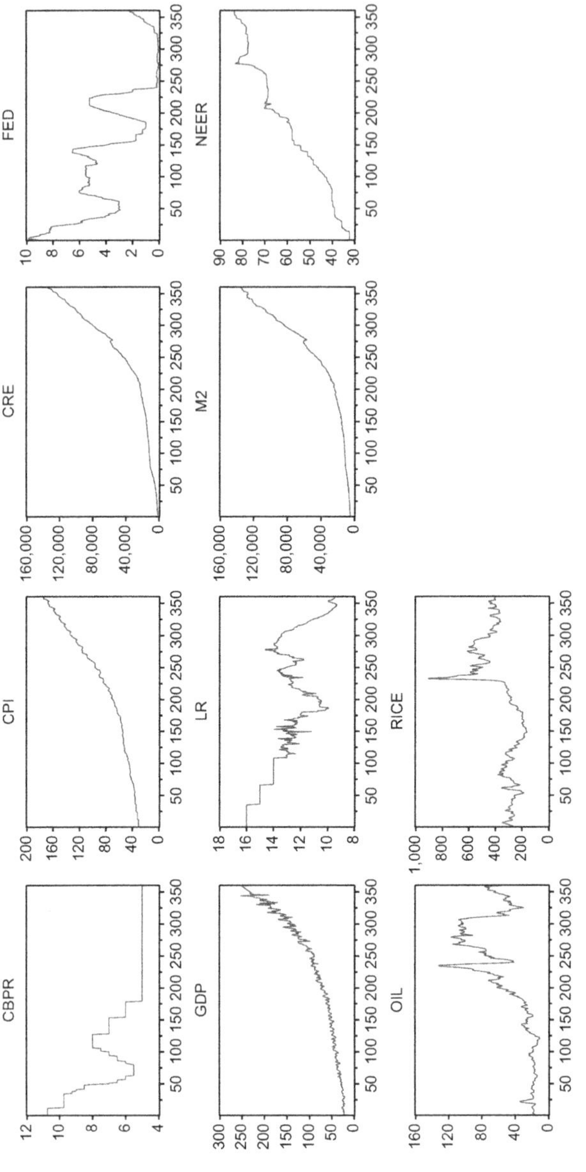

Fig. 5.8 SVAR model variables in raw form

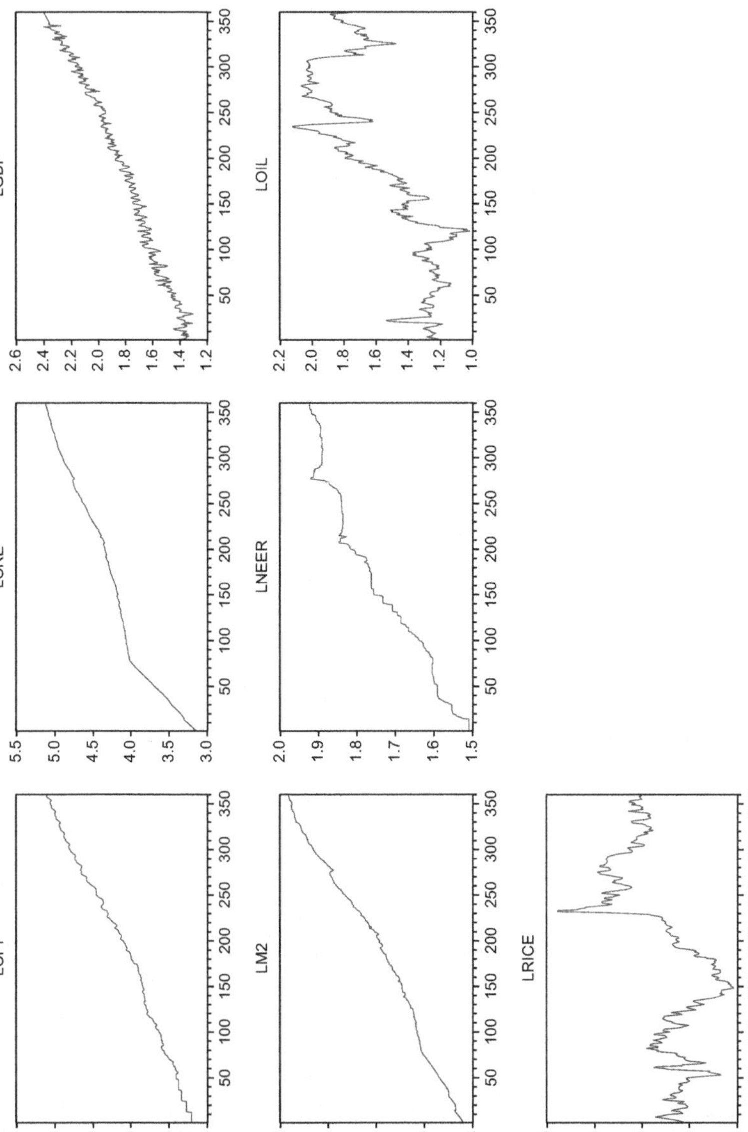

Fig. 5.9 SVAR model variables in logarithmic form (not including CBPR and LR)

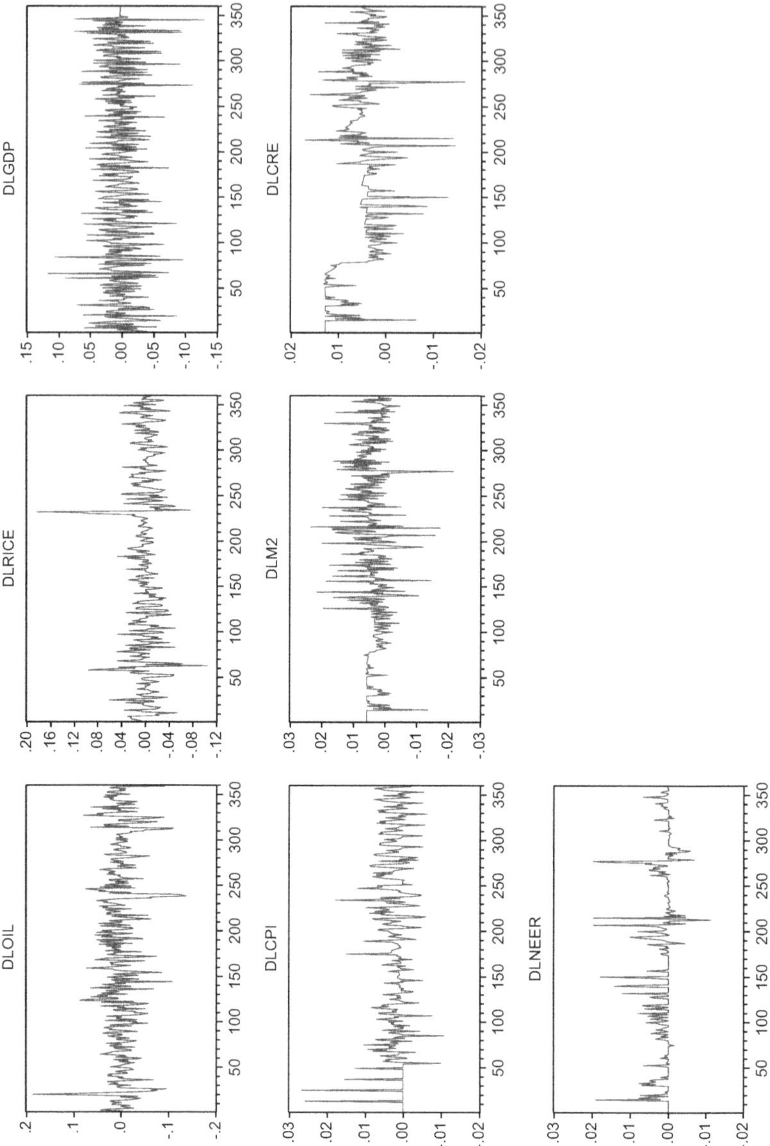

Fig. 5.10 SVAR model variables in logarithmic first difference form (not including CBPR and LR)

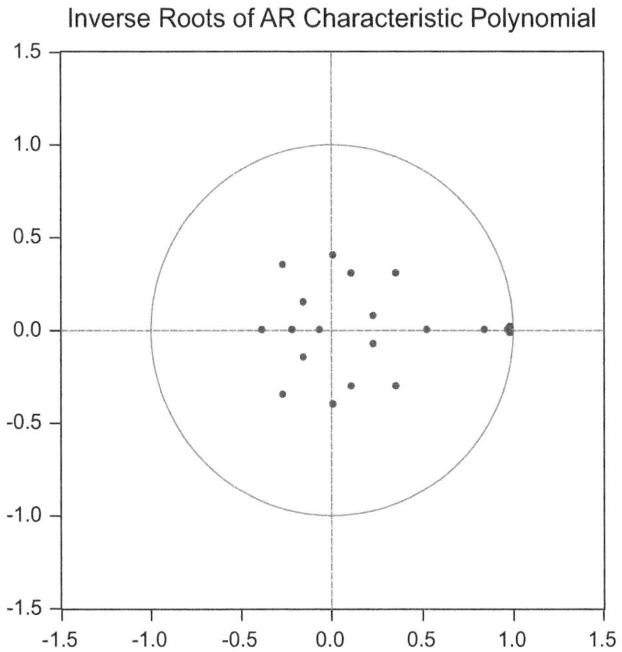

Fig. 5.11 SVAR model stability analysis

Table 5.6 ADF test results

Variable	*Level form*	*First difference form*
LOIL	I(1)	I(0)
LRICE	I(1)	I(0)
FED	I(0)	I(0)
LGDP	I(1)	I(0)
LCPI	I(1)	I(0)
LM2	I(1)	I(0)
CBPR	I(0)	I(0)
LR	I(0)	I(0)
LCRE	I(1)	I(0)
NER	I(1)	I(0)

Note: I(1) and I(0) indicate that the variable is integrated (at 5 percent level) of order one and zero, respectively

Table 5.7 SVAR model stability analysis

Roots of characteristic polynomial
Endogenous variables: DLOIL DLRICE FED DLGDP DLCPI DLM2 CBPR LR DLCRE DLNER
Exogenous variables: C
Lag specification: 1 2
Date: 03/17/19 Time: 11:05

Root	Modulus
0.985038 + 0.016534i	0.985177
0.985038 − 0.016534i	0.985177
0.972232	0.972232
0.843991	0.843991
0.526439	0.526439
0.356975 + 0.304276i	0.469057
0.356975 − 0.304276i	0.469057
−0.263900 + 0.349601i	0.438023
−0.263900 − 0.349601i	0.438023
0.012954 − 0.401032i	0.401241
0.012954 + 0.401032i	0.401241
−0.381024	0.381024
0.111520 − 0.304123i	0.323925
0.111520 + 0.304123i	0.323925
0.232681 + 0.074652i	0.244363
0.232681 − 0.074652i	0.244363
−0.149902 + 0.149937i	0.212018
−0.149902 − 0.149937i	0.212018
−0.210977	0.210977
−0.060373	0.060373

No root lies outside the unit circle
VAR satisfies the stability condition

Table 5.8 Johansen co-integration test results

Sample: 1360
Included observations: 356
Series: DLOIL DLRICE FED DLGDP DLCPI DLM2 CBPR LR DLCRE DLNER
Lags interval: 1–2
Selected (0.05 level[a]) number of cointegrating relations by model

Data trend:	None	None	Linear	Linear	Quadratic
Test type	No intercept No trend	Intercept No trend	Intercept No trend	Intercept Trend	Intercept Trend
Trace	7	7	7	7	7
Max-Eig	7	7	6	6	6

[a]Critical values based on MacKinnon-Haug-Michelis (1999)

References

Afrin, S. (2017). Monetary policy transmission in Bangladesh: Exploring the lending channel. *Journal of Asian Economics, 49*, 60–80.

Ahmed, S., & Islam, M. E. (2004). The monetary transmission mechanism in Bangladesh: Bank lending and exchange rate channels. *The Bangladesh Development Studies, 30*, 31–87.

Alam, M. R. (2015). Effectiveness of monetary policy in Bangladesh. *The Journal of Developing Areas, 49*(2), 363–372.

Bhattacharya, R., Patnaik, I., & Shah, A. (2011). Monetary policy transmission in an emerging market setting (IMF Working Papers, 1–25). Available at: https://www.imf.org/~/media/Websites/IMF/imported-full-text-pdf/external/pubs/ft/wp/2011/_wp1105.ashx

Cevik, S., & Teksoz, K. (2012). *Lost in transmission? The effectiveness of monetary policy transmission channels in the GCC countries. Middle East Development Journal, 5*(3), 1350018–1.

Dickey, D. A., & Fuller, W. A. (1979). Distribution of the estimators for autoregressive time series with a unit root. *Journal of the American Statistical Association, 74*(366), 427–431.

Ghosh, A., & Rajan, R. S. (2007). How high is exchange rate pass-through in India? Has it changed over time? *The Journal of International Trade & Economic Development, 16*(3), 373–382.

Hung, L. V., & Pfau, W. D. (2009). VAR analysis of the monetary transmission mechanism in Vietnam. *Applied Econometrics and International Development, 9*(1), 165–179.

Kapur, M., & Behera, H. K. (2012). *Monetary transmission mechanism in India: A quarterly model.* Germany: University Library of Munich.

Khan, S. (2010). *The design and effects of monetary policy in sub-Saharan African countries.* Washington, DC: Peterson Institute for International.

Khundrakpam, J. K. (2007). *Economic reforms and exchange rate pass-through to domestic prices in India* (No. 225). Bank for International Settlements.

Kilinc, M., & Tunc, C. (2014). *Identification of monetary policy shocks in Turkey: A structural VAR approach* (No. 1423).

Kim, S., & Roubini, N. (2000). Exchange rate anomalies in the industrial countries: A solution with a structural VAR approach. *Journal of Monetary Economics, 45*(3), 561–586.

MacKinnon, J. G., Haug, A. A., & Michelis, L. (1999). Numerical distribution functions of likelihood ratio tests for cointegration. *Journal of Applied Econometrics, 14*, 563–577.

Mishkin, F. S. (1996). *The channels of monetary transmission: Lessons for monetary policy* (No. w5464). National Bureau of Economic Research.

Mortaza, M. G., & Hasnayen, S. (2008). Inflation accounting across income groups: Does inflation hurt the poor more in Bangladesh? *Bangladesh Bank Quarterly, 5*(3), 30–41.

Nguyen, H. T. (2014). *Monetary transmission mechanism analysis in a small, open economy: The case of Vietnam*. Australia: University of Wollongong.

Raghavan, M., & Silvapulle, P. (2008, July). Structural VAR approach to Malaysian monetary policy framework: Evidence from the pre-and post-Asian crisis periods. In *New Zealand Association of Economics, NZAE Conference* (pp. 1–32).

Thao, Bach Thi Nhat. (2017). *An evolution of monetary policy in Vietnamin, 1998–2016: An SVAR approach*. Bachelor's thesis, unpublished, Aalto University School of Business, Mikkeli Campus.

Vu, G., Nguyen, T., Duong, T., & Pham-Hi, D. (2016). Impacts of government spending shock on Vietnamese macroeconomic aggregate variables: DSGE and SVAR models. *Communications in Mathematics and Applications, 7*(4), 343–359.

Younus, S. (2004). The impact of monetary policy on the bank portfolio in Bangladesh. *Bank Parikrama, 27*, 29.

Younus, S. (2005). *Monetary transmission through bank portfolio in Bangladesh*. Policy Note Series PN, 603.

Younus, S. (2017). Monetary transmission channels in Bangladesh: Evidence from a floating exchange rate regime. *The Journal of Developing Areas, 51*(2), 255–272.

CHAPTER 6

A Review of Public Expenditures in Bangladesh: Evidence on Sustainability and Cyclicality

Zahid Hussain and Monzur Hossain

6.1 Introduction

The importance of fiscal policy as a tool in macroeconomic management can hardly be over-emphasized. Ever since the Keynesian Revolution in economics, leading to the birth of macroeconomics as a separate branch of study, the role, conduct and effectiveness of fiscal policy have been major preoccupations of economic research. With the post-World War II emergence of many independent nations, fiscal policy has assumed a new role in building physical and social infrastructure in developing economies. Its

We would like to acknowledge the research support provided by Afroza Alam, Research Analyst, World Bank Dhaka office.

Z. Hussain (✉)
The World Bank, Dhaka, Bangladesh
e-mail: zhussain@worldbank.org

M. Hossain
Bangladesh Institute of Development Studies (BIDS), Dhaka, Bangladesh

M. Hossain (ed.), *Bangladesh's Macroeconomic Policy*,
https://doi.org/10.1007/978-981-15-1244-5_6

traditional role in correcting market failures, that appear to be ubiquitous in these countries, has also attracted renewed focus.

The developmental role of fiscal policy raises the question of sustainability to the forefront. The debt crisis in the Latin American economies made it clear that public spending backed by excessive debt creation can create hurdles that economies can overcome at very high costs. There is no alternative to aligning public spending with the economy's ability to mobilize domestic resources and debt finance in ways that preserve fiscal space and do not unduly pass on the financial burden to the future generation.

The traditional stabilization role of fiscal policy goes back to the very fundamental question of whether its design and associated political economy are consistent with such role. Ideally, stabilization requires fiscal expansion when economy is slowing down, and a fiscal contraction when economy is overheating. This can happen automatically if there are mechanisms in place that allow taxes and public spending to respond in stabilizing direction, when the state of the economy warrants so. However, research shows, unlike the advanced economies, that this is often not the case in developing economies.

Bangladesh does well on fiscal sustainability. The joint World Bank-International Monetary Fund (IMF) Debt Sustainability Analysis (DSA) in 2019 suggests that Bangladesh be at low risk of external or domestic debt distress assuming no major slippage in macroeconomic management. Bangladesh also maintains procyclicality of fiscal policy. The correlation between the cyclical components of tax revenues and expenditure with the cyclical component of gross domestic product (GDP) is positive, although it is statistically significant only in case of tax revenues. Both the correlation and cointegration coefficients suggest that the current and annual development program (ADP) expenditures be procyclical (Beyer and Milivojevic 2019).

In this chapter, we attempt to review the conduct of fiscal policy in Bangladesh, and in that context, we discuss the pattern of fiscal policy indicators as well as identify the possible risks associated with it. We also provide some policy recommendations based on the assessment that are important to address in order to maintain a sustained growth.

The chapter is organized as follows. After Introduction, Sect. 6.2 reviews the public expenditures in Bangladesh. Section 6.3 discusses the revenue structure and tax system of the country. In Sect. 6.4, we have discussed public debt situation and fiscal sustainability aspects, and in Sect. 6.5, cyclicality of fiscal policy. Section 6.6 discusses revenue mobilization and expenditure effort in currently advanced economies when they were less prosperous, and Sect. 6.7 highlights deficit financing in Bangladesh. Finally, Sect. 6.8 provides conclusion and some policy recommendations.

6.2 A Review of Public Expenditures[1]

The most striking feature of public expenditure in Bangladesh is its low level relative to GDP, when compared with countries at a similar level of development. It has struggled to maintain pace with growth in the size of the economy. Public expenditure grew by an annual average of around 8 percent during 2010–2018. There were significant increases in both recurrent and development expenditure in real terms. The priority shifted toward investment, as the government took on large projects in the transport and energy sectors. Public investment grew at an annual average of 14 percent, while recurrent expenditure grew by 6 percent per year. This led to increase in the share of development spending from 33 to 40 percent of total expenditures. Revealed expenditure priorities in both the recurrent and development budgets are broadly in line with the government's development strategy. Investment expenditures including those of state-owned enterprises, as reported in the national accounts, increased as a share of GDP from 5.8 percent in FY12 to 8 percent in FY18.

Despite increases in public investments, recurrent expenditures continue to dominate the central government budget. With the increase in pay and allowances, pensions and gratuities, and grants-in-aid outpacing revenue growth in recent years, fiscal space has eroded because of the stickiness or irreversibility of the expanded subsidies and grants. The economic justification for some of the existing subsidies is not immediately obvious, since there is no pressing case for a sustained fiscal stimulus or mitigation of negative externalities. Some subsidies (such as agricultural subsidies targeted to small and marginal farmers), certainly not all, may be justified on grounds of inclusion. Changing composition of debt toward expensive sources of domestic financing has led to rapid increases in interest expenses in recent years.

While Bangladesh has been able to provide public services with comparatively low public expenditures, concerns about expenditure effectiveness remain. These concerns are particularly salient in the social sectors. Enrollment and completion rates at primary and secondary education levels are comparable to those of upper middle-income and high-income countries, but learning and health outcomes are well below par. Education

[1] This section draws from the comprehensive assessment of fiscal trends provided in the World Bank, The Public Expenditure Review Update 2015, while updating the data available since this review was published.

and health services remain underfunded and would benefit from higher budget allocations. Bangladesh's current level of spending on health and education is below that of aspirational peers, but efficient in terms of generating output. However, there is evidence that a shortage of funds has generated inefficiencies that constrain the sectors' ability to address future expenditure needs. For one, there is a shortage of qualified medical personnel, as Bangladesh has fewer doctors and nurses per capita than peer countries. With utilization rising, pressure on the limited number of doctors has increased, resulting in long wait times, comparatively short consultations and an increasing reliance on the private sector, which risks equity in the system. The health system lacks the capital necessary to address a growing incidence of non-communicable diseases.

Public investment is channeled through the ADP mainly while sizable expenditures are also made outside the ADP stream (Fig. 6.1a, b). The share of public investment through non-ADP segment has increased steadily during the recent years. In practice, both ADP and non-ADP segments contain elements of recurrent and capital spending.[2] This practice nurses fragmentation and poses questions for the planning and execution efficiency. The sectors that benefit from the largest shares of the ADP budget are transport and communications, energy, and social development, with transport becoming particularly important in recent years, absorbing around a quarter of ADP.

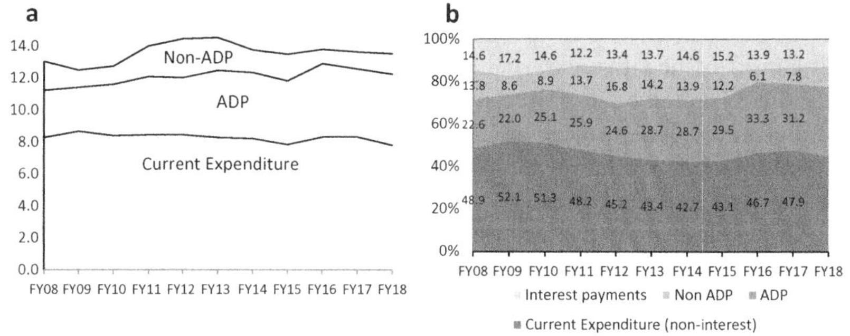

Fig. 6.1 Public expenditure. (**a**) Public expenditures as percent of GDP. (Source: Ministry of Finance). (**b**) Share of various types public expenditures. (Source: Ministry of Finance)

[2] See World Bank (2010).

An ineffective public investment management system constrains capital expenditure by limiting capital budget execution rates. Capital budgets and capital spending exhibit similar patterns in most sectors. Budgeted capital expenditure increases significantly every year, accompanied by a concurrent decrease in budget execution rates—from over 83.8 percent in FY10 to 78 percent in FY18. Significant spike in development expenditure in the fourth quarter, and especially in June, each fiscal year, has become a recurring phenomenon. The expenditure spikes are related to a lack of effectiveness in implementing and managing the development budget. Ministries, divisions and agencies face pressures to compensate for the low budget execution rates in the period leading up to the year end, and the collective impact of several financial accounting issues causes the backloading of expenditure within each fiscal year.

This pattern can largely be explained by an ineffective public investment management system that delays project execution. The delays reflect constraints at the project selection and implementation stage. At the project selection stage, an absence of robust and standardized independent review processes and ad hoc budget allocations to capital projects, driven in many cases by political rather than technical considerations, contribute to delays. Similarly, the absence of a clear system of scrutiny often results in approval of projects without feasibility studies. The implementation stage is constrained by the lack of a carefully designed implementation work plan, which undermines project management. Furthermore, weak cash management does not allow for the anticipation of cash shortfalls, which can lead to frequent cash rationing for capital projects. Improving capital spending thus requires comprehensive reforms to Bangladesh's public investment management system.

Bangladesh achieved average fiscal deficits of 3.1 percent of GDP over the past decade, varying within a narrow band. The deficit was well below the South Asia average of 4 percent. The low deficit was partly by design and partly by default. Low deficit together with strong economic growth resulted in low and declining public debt as a share of GDP. Public debt declined steadily from 37 percent of GDP in FY08 to 31 percent of GDP at the end of FY18, among the lowest in South Asia. The 2019 joint DSA of the IMF and the World Bank found that public debt was sustainable, even in the event of large shocks, including significant borrowing to finance new power plants and partially recapitalize state-owned banks (Fig. 6.2).

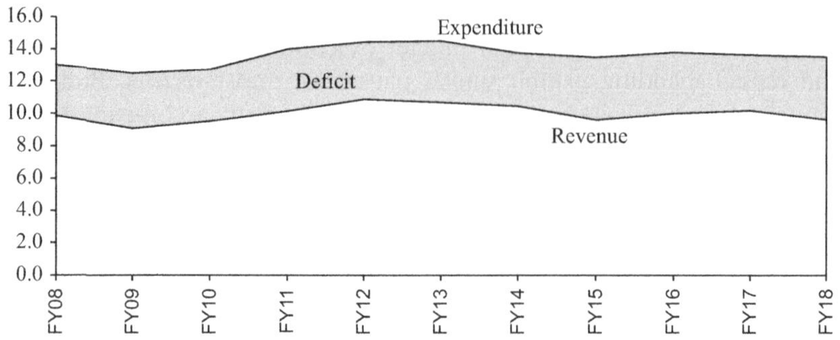

Fig. 6.2 Fiscal balance as percent of GDP. (Source: Ministry of Finance)

In assessing Bangladesh's low fiscal deficit relative to the South Asian average (Table 6.1), several important caveats should be kept in mind. The major reason behind low deficit is low public expenditures, despite increasing more than 2 percentage points of GDP in the last five years. Low revenues limit resources available for investment in expanding and maintaining strategic infrastructure as well as social expenditures. The energy mix is becoming increasingly expensive, at a time when demand for electricity is surging. Passing on the high costs to consumers is politically difficult, which results in an increasing subsidy burden. Also, the sound record in fiscal discipline stems partly from a lack of capacity to spend allocated resources in the development budget.

Considering the cross-country regularity that government spending tends to rise more than proportionately with income levels, Bangladesh public expenditure to GDP ratio falls short of what is typically observed in other countries at Bangladesh's income levels (Fig. 6.3a). This represents a leaner government that avoids the efficiency and welfare costs of bloated state bureaucracies and overextended government programs, which so often characterize both developing and industrial economies. Low levels of public spending have helped maintain low employment levels in the civil service by international comparisons. Bangladesh civil service is also small when compared to other South Asian countries, and its size has remained unchanged for several years.

Bangladesh's apparently low level of public spending need also be seen in the context of its extremely high population density. There is strong empirical evidence at the international level that larger countries have smaller government consumption as a share of GDP. Sharing non-rivalrous

Table 6.1 Fiscal trends compare well with other countries in the region

Indicator (percent GDP)	*FY08*	*FY09*	*FY10*	*FY11*	*FY12*	*FY13*	*FY14*	*FY15*	*FY16*	*FY17*	*FY18*	*South Asia 2017*
General government revenue	9.9	9.1	9.5	10.2	10.9	10.7	10.4	9.6	10.0	10.2	9.6	20.7
General government expenditure	13.0	12.5	12.7	14.0	14.4	14.5	13.8	13.5	13.8	13.6	13.5	24.7
Overall budget deficit	−3.2	−3.4	−3.2	−3.9	−3.6	−3.8	−3.3	−3.9	−3.8	−3.5	−3.9	−4.0
Primary deficit	1.3	1.2	1.4	2.1	1.6	1.8	1.8	1.8	1.9	1.7	2.2	−1.8
General government debt	37.2	36.2	34.9	34.0	32.7	32.1	31.7	31.8	31.5	30.6	31.1	56.7

Sources: Ministry of Finance, IMF and the World Bank

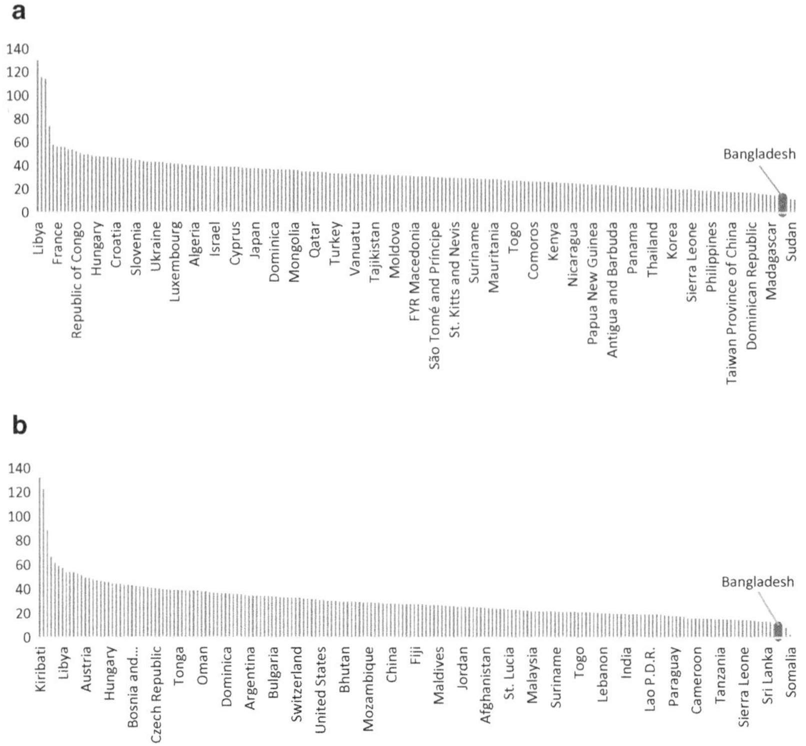

Fig. 6.3 (**a**) Bangladesh's position in the world at public expenditure (average expenditure, 2013–2017, percent GDP). (Source: IMF, World Economic Outlook). (**b**) Bangladesh's position in the world at public-sector revenue (average revenue, 2013–2017, percent GDP). (Source: IMF, World Economic Outlook)

public goods over larger population results in lower per capita costs of provision.[3] In particular, there appear to be strong scale effects of population on public expenditure on education, public order and safety, general public services, and transportation by central government. There is also evidence that the returns to scale are in the public employment needed to achieve

[3] Shelton, Cameron A., "The Size and Composition of Public Expenditure", Graduate School of Business, Stanford University, October 21, 2004.

the distribution of public goods rather than the goods themselves.[4] This can explain why Bangladesh has succeeded in maintaining the delivery of a reasonable amount of public services with a civil service that is small compared to countries at a similar level of development. While Bangladesh's high population density helped exploit scale economies, there remain several concerns pertaining to the effectiveness of public functions, limited coverage of public goods and services, inadequate manpower utilization, the sizable share of wage bill broadly defined[5] vis-à-vis budgetary funding and competing demands for non-wage inputs on government's limited budgetary resources from priority sources. More importantly, while rigorous and updated functional reviews of the government are not available, there are indications of problems in the manpower structure and skill-mix.

6.3 Revenue Structure and Development Financing

While total government expenditure has increased from 12.5 percent in 1990 to about 13.5 percent in 2018, the tax-GDP ratio has increased from 6 percent to about 10 percent during the same period. With an increased level of government expenditure coupled with increased tax revenue, the direct contribution of aid in financing fiscal deficit has declined from 80 percent in 1990 to about 40 percent in 2015 (Fig. 6.4). This suggests that the overwhelming importance of aid in maintaining fiscal stability has been declining over time in the context of increased capacity of domestic resource mobilization (Fig. 6.4).

It is important to note here that the tax-GDP ratio in Bangladesh is the lowest even among the South Asian Association for Regional Cooperation (SAARC) countries. The lower growth of tax revenue over time indicates that there was a possibility of fiscal unsustainability in the absence of foreign assistance. It is true that the dependence on foreign aid in financing fiscal deficit has decreased over time, but it is still significant in managing inter-temporal fiscal policy of the government.

Bangladesh's revenue effort is among the lowest in the world. Averaging less than 11 percent of GDP over the period 2010–2018, only Sudan has

[4] For example, costs per student in primary and secondary schools in Bangladesh are one of the lowest in the world, reflecting very high student-teacher and student to classroom ratios.

[5] Including pension, subvention, and separation liabilities.

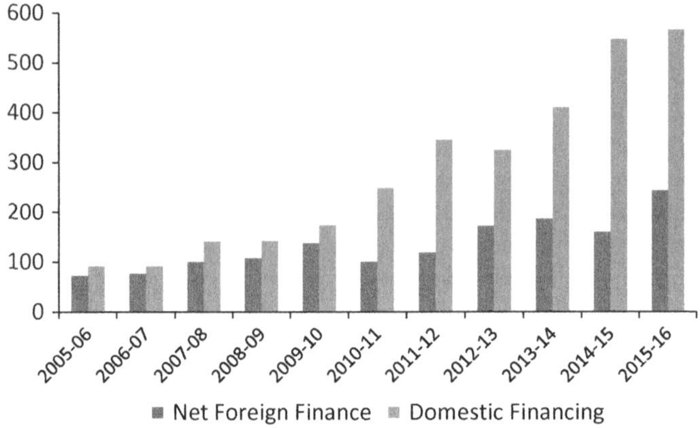

Fig. 6.4 Trends of domestic and foreign financing (in billion Tk.). (Source: National Board of Revenue (NBR) and Economic Relations Division (ERD)

lower public-sector revenues as a share of GDP than Bangladesh (see Fig. 6.3b). Not surprisingly, with low fiscal deficits, this results in correspondingly low public expenditure. Though a temporary rise of revenue performance over FY10–FY12 was observed, it has since tapered off.

6.3.1 *Tax Revenues*

Revenues did grow almost in proportion to nominal GDP growth in the past decade. In most cases, the achievements for individual tax categories have fallen short of expectations of the seventh five year plan (7FYP) so far. Non-tax revenues have been constant at less than 2 percent of GDP over the decades. Trade liberalization and the introduction of the value added tax (VAT) reduced dependence on customs duty while increasing the relative importance of domestic taxes like VAT and direct taxes. The expected target for 2021 is to raise revenue to 15 percent of GDP (Fig. 6.5).

The key strategies that the National Board of Revenue (NBR) adopts include improvement of revenue collection efforts through capacity building of NBR, income tax and VAT automation, organizing tax and VAT fairs, digitalizing tax payment system, and so on. Analysis of tax efforts and tax buoyancy for Bangladesh suggests that it ranks lowest among a sample of 50 developing countries. The estimated overall tax effort is about 0.5 (less than unity) indicating that the country is yet to utilize its full capacity of tax revenue collection. The estimated tax buoyancy ratio is 1.235 indicating that

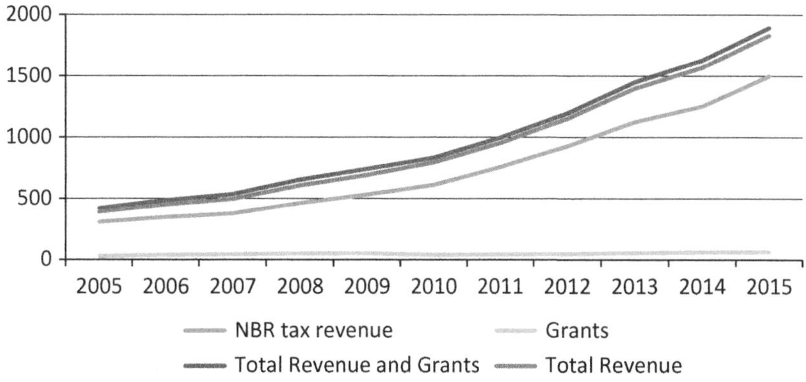

Fig. 6.5 Breakdown of sources of revenue 2005–2015 in billions of taka

tax revenue is highly responsive to GDP growth, and thus, strong efforts can be made to increase revenue collection (Begum 2007; Hossain 2017). Overall, there are scopes of higher revenue collection, if proper strategies are put in place.

Implementation of the Tax Modernization Plan has stumbled because of delays in the computerization of the tax system. Difficulties in implementation of the new VAT law (enacted in 2012) apprehend the VAT modernization efforts, which was a commitment of the government while receiving Extended Credit Facility (ECF) from the IMF. The key challenges of revenue collection include the country's narrow tax base, with wider exemptions and tax holidays (Fig. 6.6).

The main sources of tax should be income tax and VAT. Expansion of the tax base would enable the taxation of more individuals and companies within the tax net. As about 8 million Micro, Small and Medium Enterprises (MSMEs) are now operating, most of which are not registered.[6] One strategy thus could be to bring them under tax net through encouraging them to register. A tax incentive mechanism can be developed for the MSMEs that are registered and have trade licenses. The FY20 Budget has ambitious targets for bringing more individuals and companies under the tax net. This would certainly help to move the stagnating revenue-GDP ratio toward the 15 percent target. But the initiatives and incentives that are in place will need major overhauling to enhance the tax potential on the domestic side (Tables 6.2 and 6.3).

[6] Economic Census, 2013 (BBS 2013).

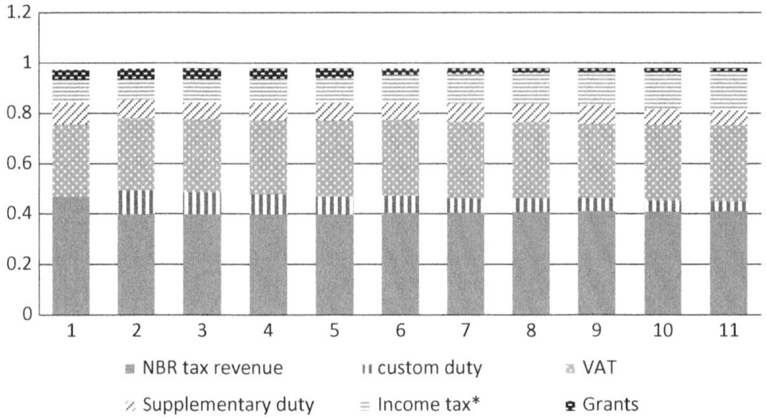

Fig. 6.6 Share of tax and non-tax revenue in total taxes 2005–2015. (Source: NBR)

Table 6.2 Revenue structure (tax-GDP ratio) in the Seventh Five-Year Plan Period (FY16–FY20)

As percent of GDP	*FY14*	*FY15*	*FY16*	*FY17*	*FY18*	*FY19*	*FY20*
	Actual		*Revised budget*			*7FYP period projection*	
Total revenue	10.4	10.8	12.1	13.5	14.3	15.1	16.1
Total tax revenue	8.6	9.3	10.6	11.5	12.3	13.1	14.1
NBR tax revenue	8.3	8.9	10.3	11.1	11.9	12.7	13.7

Note: 7FYP=Seventh Five-Year Plan Period 2016–2020

Table 6.3 Major components of revenue under the 7FYP Period (FY16-FY20)

As percent of GDP	*FY14*	*FY15*	*FY16*	*FY17*	*FY18*	*FY19*	*FY20*
	Actual	*Revised budget*			*7FYP period*		
Customs duty	1.0	1.0	1.1	1.2	1.2	1.2	1.3
Vat+SD	4.5	4.6	5.4	5.7	6.4	6.6	7.0
Income tax	2.6	3.2	3.7	4.1	4.3	4.9	5.4
Others	0.1	0.1	0.1	0.1	0.1	0.1	0.1
Non-NBR tax	0.3	0.4	0.3	0.4	0.4	0.4	0.4
Non-tax revenue	1.8	1.5	1.5	2.0	2.0	2.0	2.0

Source: National Board of Revenue and Seventh Plan Projections

Note: SD=Supplementary Duty

6.3.2 Tax System in Bangladesh

The tax system in Bangladesh shares characteristics commonly found in most other developing countries. The rate of growth of tax revenues tends to fall short of the rate of expansion in the size of the economy, unless discretionary measures are taken for enhancing revenue realization by adjusting the rate structure or expanding the tax base. The tax policy framework is inadequate, and the pace of administrative modernization is slow with a high degree of fragmentation and weak enforcement mechanisms. Incremental reforms introduced in bits and pieces have brought only marginal changes to the system. The overall policy framework is replete with exemptions, incentives and special regimes, allowing significant scope for tax officials and political elites to exercise discretion whenever convenient.

Overcoming resistance to policy and administrative modernization is the biggest challenge brought home most vividly by the recent attempts to implement the VAT law passed in 2012. The original law intended to increase reliance on voluntary compliance, moving away from a largely "control"-based system that relies heavily on physical monitoring of taxpayers to enforce compliance. The multifarious amendments to the new VAT law in 2019 will allow tax officials to retain substantial discretion, thus nurturing opportunities for abuse of the system, rent seeking and revenue losses.

Tax administration is fragmented. It remains divided into three autonomous divisions based on the type of tax rather than tax functions: direct tax, VAT and customs. The inadequacies and inefficiencies of such a system sustains room for collusion and abuse. It allows the large taxpayers to use political influence to minimize their tax burden. In the judicial system, lower levels of the appeals process are characterized by widespread abuse. Cases that escalate to the higher courts are subject to high costs and inordinate processing delays. This fosters informal means for tax evasion as no taxes can be collected while cases are pending.

6.4 Public Debt and Fiscal Sustainability

The public sector deficit and the burden of public debt have important macroeconomic implications. In addition to crowding out private investment and hence affecting adversely the growth prospects, it can contribute to the persistence of inflation through monetization of deficit and/or vicious spirals of debt and deficit. The sustainability of fiscal position is an important dimension of fiscal policy, which attempts to answer the question of whether the current fiscal position can be sustained without exploding or imploding debt. However, assessing the sustainability of the fiscal policy is never straightforward and depends critically on assumptions concerning the future path of several macroeconomic variables. Fiscal sustainability assessments attempt to estimate the magnitude of medium- or long-run inconsistencies in fiscal policy, and the size of the fiscal adjustment needed to achieve stabilization of the public sector debt-GDP ratio.

Strong growth performance (Fig. 6.7a) has resulted in Bangladesh's external debt falling steadily by about 1 percentage point of GDP per year, reaching less than 31.1 percent of GDP at the end of FY18 (Fig. 6.7b). This, however, was largely offset by a rise in the domestic financed component of the deficit both as a share of government debt stock and relative to GDP. Net foreign financing of the deficit declined significantly from around 4.8 percent of GDP in the 1990s to well under 1.2 percent of GDP in FY18 while net domestic financing increased from around 1.6 percent of GDP in 2000 to 3.5 percent in FY18. Thus, the stability in the government debt stock relative to GDP in recent years is attributable entirely to a decline in external debt, even though the debt pipeline has been growing rather rapidly. The decline in external debt to GDP ratio reflects predominantly the inability to get the funds released due to weak implementation capacity.

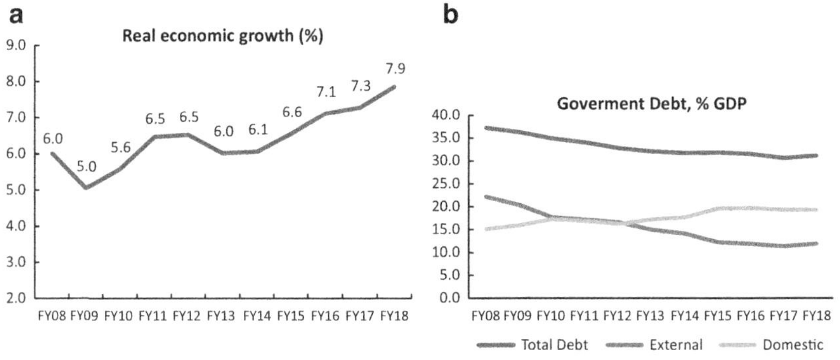

Fig. 6.7 (**a**) Bangladesh's growth performance. (Source: Bangladesh Bureau of Statistics (BBS)). (**b**) Trends of public debt. (Source: IMF, ERD and World Bank staff calculation)

Fiscal sustainability in the long run is defined as that path of primary deficit that would keep the debt-GDP ratio constant at some specified level, which may be the initial debt level or some measure of "optimal" debt. Annex discusses the analytics of the long-run sustainability condition. Calculations based on Eq. 6.7 in Annex are used below to assess Bangladesh's long-run fiscal sustainability. This requires establishing benchmarks for nominal interest rate, inflation, growth and seigniorage.

Interest Rate Bangladesh's cost of public debt servicing is relatively modest. The interest bill was well below 5 percent of the total debt stock until recently but has risen to 5.9 percent in FY18. In FY19, total interest payment is projected to be about 1.9 percent of GDP, which represents about 5.9 percent of the FY19 beginning of period debt stock. Most of Bangladesh's public debt is highly concessional external debt (67 percent of total external debt at end of FY17). As Bangladesh makes further transition on the middle-income path, less of its debt would be concessional and its older debt would be rolled into newer debt at higher interest rates. Thus, benchmarking an interest rate for Bangladesh that would apply to long-run steady state at the current effective rate could be quite misleading. Interest rate on National Savings Certificate (3 years maturity) is 11.5 percent (Fig. 6.8).

Inflation Rate The consumer price index (CPI) inflation rate in Bangladesh was 5.8 percent in FY18. It declined to 5.5 percent in FY19. Given Bangladesh's low single digit inflation record in the last decade, a working assumption is that inflation rate would be in the 6–6.5 percent range in perpetuity.

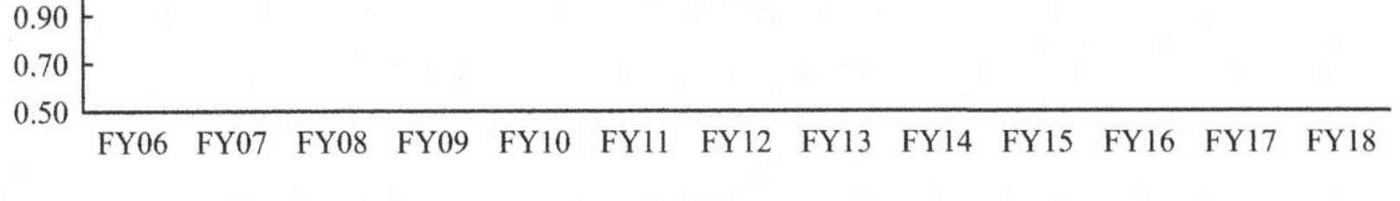

Fig. 6.8 Primary balance as percent of GDP. (Source: Ministry of Finance)

Growth Bangladesh averaged real GDP growth of 6.5 plus percent during last five years despite slowdown in reforms, industrial disasters hurting Bangladesh's image abroad and external shocks. It is therefore reasonable to assume an average GDP growth of at least 6.5 percent.

Seigniorage Seigniorage is the change in reserve money, which, in Bangladesh, ranged between 0.4 and 2.6 percent of GDP during FY10–18 (Fig. 6.9). In FY18, base money constituted 10.4 percent of GDP. Combining this with inflation and growth assumptions implies that seigniorage would be about 1.3 percent of GDP.

Combining the assumptions about nominal interest rate, growth, inflation and the monetary base along with the fact that Bangladesh's initial debt was 31.2 percent of GDP lead to the result that Bangladesh can achieve fiscal sustainability along with a constant 31 percent debt to GDP ratio by running a primary deficit of 1.3 percent of GDP. This is obviously very dependent on the assumptions of the analysis. Table 6.6 in Annex presents a range of primary balances corresponding to varying nominal interest rates and real GDP growth rates.[7] The estimated primary balance is most sensitive to the assumptions about growth and interest rates. At any given nominal interest rate, for each additional percentage point of growth, the government has room to run a 0.2–0.3 percentage point of GDP larger primary deficit. For each additional percentage point on the interest rate, the required reduction in primary deficit is about 0.3–0.4 percentage point of GDP. This indicates that if Bangladesh were to suffer a sustained rise in interest rates or a sustained decline in GDP growth, it would need to run a substantially smaller primary deficit, or even a primary surplus, to keep the debt ratio stable at the current level.

Bangladesh's primary deficit increased from 1.8 percent of GDP in FY13 to 2.2 percent in FY18, well beyond the level consistent with maintaining the current debt ratio for any plausible path of growth and nominal interest rate. The primary deficit declined to 1.7 percent of GDP in FY17, but it increased to over 2.2 percent in FY18. This level is sustainable when GDP growth is 7 percent or above, while effective nominal interest rate is 8 percent or lower. Bangladesh can afford to bear some increases in financing cost without risking fiscal sustainability if growth is sustained at 7 plus percent.

[7] This table was produced by using the fiscal sustainability model presented in the World Bank, Public Expenditure and Institutional Review 2010. The analytical derivation of the model is reproduced in Annex for ease of reference.

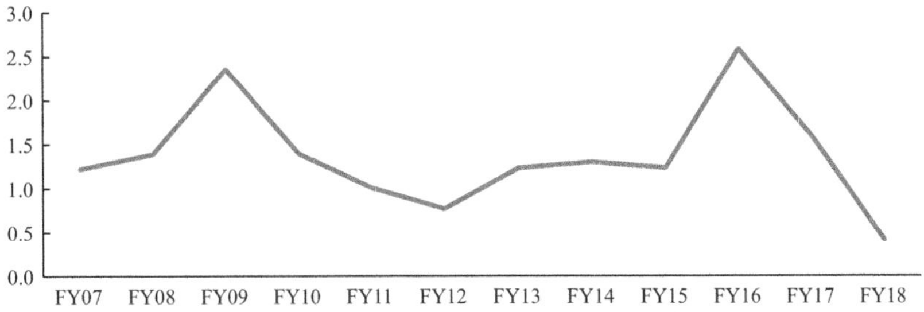

Fig. 6.9 Change in reserve money, percent of GDP. (Source: Bangladesh Bank)

6.4.1 Low Risk of Debt Distress

The joint World Bank-IMF DSA in 2018 reaffirmed that Bangladesh is at low risk of external or domestic debt distress assuming no major slippage in macroeconomic management.[8] Bangladesh's public debt remains within acceptable limits in terms of GDP, revenues and exports over the medium to long term.[9] However, this assumes a baseline that could be considered optimistic, including real economic growth of 7 percent each year for the next 20 years, and well-contained fiscal deficits (as well as inflation of 5–6 percent each year).

There is no room for complacence. Caution is needed, particularly considering the low revenue and the risk that interest payments may rise, as external financing conditions tighten, and thus crowd out other essential expenditure. An alternative scenario considering the consequences of failing to introduce the new VAT law, as originally designed, without losing its revenue increasing features with no consolidation in expenditure shows that the fiscal deficit would widen, leading to higher domestic borrowing

[8] The discussion in this section is based on the results of the joint World-IMF Debt Sustainability Analysis reported in the IMF, Article IV Report (2018).

[9] As described in ibid., standard shocks include "(i) a two-year reduction in economic growth by one standard deviation based on historical performance; (ii) a two year reduction in export value growth by one standard deviation based on historical performance; (iii) a two year reduction in inflation by one standard deviation based on historical performance; and (iv) a permanent 30 percent nominal exchange rate depreciation, as well as combinations of these scenarios."

costs. There would consequently be a significant deterioration in all standard debt sustainability indicators, and the debt trajectory would lose some resilience. This implies that in the absence of a boost to tax revenues through the implementation of tax reforms or other means, to keep the primary deficit on a sustainable path, a significant cut in public expenditure would be needed, with potential consequences for economic growth and poverty reduction.

As highlighted in the DSA, external risks include contracting large amounts of short-term debt, a protracted slowdown in key export markets, a rapid build-up of non-concessional debt, or a combination thereof. The fiscal stance is vulnerable to several exogenous shocks.[10] Other assessments find that fiscal sustainability may be threatened by increasing international fuel prices and exchange rate depreciation, along with increased domestic interest rates. Direct energy subsidies estimated at 0.6 percent of GDP in FY14 and 0.5 percent in FY16, and fertilizer subsidies close to 1 percent of GDP, in the context of rising international price of urea,[11] whose price tends to track that of oil, would have a significant impact on fiscal balances. An increase in the price of oil and urea at around 30 percent is estimated to increase the deficit by around 0.6 percent of GDP on average over a five-year period, and lead to a cumulative increase in the debt stock by around 3 percent of GDP over the period.[12] Similarly, a permanent 10 percent depreciation in the taka/US$ exchange rate would increase the fiscal deficit by around 0.8 percent of GDP and increase the stock of debt by over 6 percent of GDP over five years. An increase in domestic interest rates by around 130 basis points is estimated to increase the fiscal deficit by around 0.3 percent of GDP and increase public debt by 1.3 percent of GDP over five years. A combination of these, or other risks discussed below, occurring around the same time could be particularly problematic, especially if the government is unable to issue enough debt to finance costs.

[10] This section is based on findings in Medina, 2015. *Assessing Fiscal Risks in Bangladesh.* IMF Working Paper WP/15/110.

[11] An organic compound commonly used in fertilizer.

[12] Compared to the baseline projections used.

6.4.2 *Loan Guarantees and Pensions Pose Additional Risks*

Until FY12, guarantees tended to be small and related to agricultural credit. However, after FY12, there was a steep increase in guarantees, provided primarily to state-owned commercial banks (SOCBs) for lending to non-financial state-owned enterprises (SOEs). The stock of government guaranteed debt rose from 3.5 percent of GDP in FY14 to over 5 percent by end-FY15, of which guarantees to SOCBs represented 30 percent of the total. Guarantees have since declined to 2 percent of GDP in FY18, due largely to a decline in guarantees to the energy sector, thanks to reduced global oil prices.

The dominant banking sector is characterized by poor asset quality. Stress testing by Bangladesh Bank indicates that loan defaults are the most significant risk on capital adequacy. Sensitivity is particularly high to the top large borrowers. Default by the top three large borrowers results in 23 banks falling below the minimum regulatory capital to risk (weighted) asset ratio (CRAR). The SOCBs and specialized development banks (SDBs) pose a financial and fiscal stability risk. SOCBs and SDBs underperform on capital adequacy, non-performing loans (NPLs) and profitability.[13] State-owned banks suffer from weak internal controls and risk management practices, as well as significant inefficiencies.

Pension payments to civil servants has recently been one of the fastest growing items in the national budget. There has been almost a ninefold increase since FY07. It increased by 284 percent during FY15–19. Pension expenditure accounted for almost half of total pay and allowances in the FY19 budget. The unfunded nature of the government pension system, the early retirement age and the method by which pension benefits are calculated pose serious contingent liability problems that could undermine fiscal sustainability. There are around 1.2 million public servants, of whom up to 40,000 retire each year. Demographic trends are likely to drive up the number of retirees each year. The General Provident Fund (GPF) is a mandatory defined contribution scheme for civil servants. Pension accounts accrue interest at around 12 percent per year and retiring civil servants can withdraw their full account balance as gratuity. In addition, civil servants can borrow up to 80 percent of their contributions at any time. As the number of retirees increases, meeting the withdrawals may prove to be a fiscal burden.[14]

[13] See Bangladesh Bank, Financial Stability Report 2018 for more details.

[14] WB, Public Expenditure Review Update 2015.

6.5 Cyclicality of Fiscal Policy

Developing countries tend to increase spending or reduce taxes in good times and cut spending or increase taxes during periods of recession (Martorano 2018). The procyclical bias in fiscal policy could be a reflection of the inability to access external finance in time, and weak institutions that cannot contain overspending when growth is high. Typically, the spending movements relative to the output gap is used to define the cyclicality of spending. If government spending decreases with a positive output gap, that is, when actual output is above its potential, it is countercyclical. If the spending increases instead, it is procyclical. If public spending increases more than proportional with GDP, there is a so-called voracity effect (Tornell and Lane 1999).[15] For taxes, it is important to differentiate between tax rates and tax revenue. The tax rate is an instrument rather than an outcome, which makes it the right variable to study instrument cyclicality. The response of the tax revenue to changes in GDP, on the other hand, is an outcome and depends on the tax revenue buoyancy. It depends on the structure of the tax system and can be influenced only indirectly by changing the tax structure. The revenue buoyancy together with the cyclicality of government spending is fundamental to assess whether fiscal policy stimulates or dampens demand with the business cycle. A proportional change of tax revenue and government spending leaves the tax-to-GDP ratio unchanged. A more than proportional response of the tax revenue leads to a reduction in the deficit ratio. A large short-run revenue buoyancy means that taxes act as automatic stabilizers. The long-run revenue buoyancy is important for the impact of economic growth on long-term fiscal sustainability.

Beyer and Milivojevic (2019) report correlation coefficients between the fiscal variables and GDP in the South Asian countries. The correlations are reported in terms of cyclical components and in terms of growth rates.[16] They find that most governments in South Asia, including

[15] "Powerful groups interact dynamically via a fiscal process that effectively allows open access to the aggregate capital stock. This leads to a "voracity effect," by which a shock, such as a terms of trade windfall, perversely generates a more-than-proportionate increase in fiscal redistribution and reduces growth." See Aaron Tornell and Philip R. Lane, "The Voracity Effect", *American Economic Review*, Vol. 89, No. 1, March 1999.

[16] For the former, they detrend variables with the Hodrick-Prescott filter using the standard smoothing parameter for annual data. In the robustness section, they also present results for a different filter that avoids many of the shortcomings of the typical procedure.

Bangladesh, tend to spend more when GDP growth accelerates. The analysis of the co-movements between growth rates, rather than cyclical components, yields similar results. The procyclicality of public spending increased after the Global Financial Crisis in all countries except Sri Lanka. The inflation tax seems non-cyclical in most South Asian countries, as no statistically significant relationship in either direction emerged. Like for public expenditure, the cyclical components of tax revenue and GDP move closely together in most countries in the region. In Bangladesh, there is no correlation between the two series (−0.07).[17]

Their regression results, based on a data panel for all South Asian countries and a model with country fixed effects, show that, for every additional percentage point of growth, public spending increases by 1.16 percentage points and the relationship is statistically significant at the 5 percent level. A 1 percent increase in GDP growth translates into a 0.85 percent increase in tax revenue, that is, the tax buoyancy is below one. The voracity effect is now even larger. For every additional percentage point of economic growth, government spending in South Asia increases by 1.28 percent. The result for the short-term inflation tax cyclicality does not differ significantly from the estimate above, whereas the tax revenue buoyancy, at 0.95, is getting closer to one. In addition, it is statistically significant at the 5 percent level. Estimates of the long-run relationship suggest roughly proportional movements in the long run for spending and tax revenue, although the latter is not statistically significant.

Annual data reconfirm similar procyclicality of fiscal policy in Bangladesh. As Table 6.4 shows, the correlation between the cyclical components of tax revenues and expenditure with the cyclical component of GDP is positive, although it is statistically significant only in case of tax revenues. Positive correlation of tax revenues, meaning when GDP is above its trend, tax revenues are also above their trend, suggests tax revenues act as automatic stabilizers. But this result is not confirmed by the cointegration coefficients where the sign is negative. This means, in the long run, when GDP is above trend, tax revenues are below trend. Both the correlation and cointegration coefficients suggest that the current and ADP expenditures are procyclical.

[17]The results are similar when analyzing the coefficient between growth rates of the tax revenue and GDP (0.65, 0.43, and 0.06, respectively). The correlation between these two variables is statistically significant in India and Nepal. It is also positive in Bhutan, Sri Lanka, and Pakistan, but not statistically significant.

Table 6.4 Correlation and cointegration between fiscal variables and GDP growth (cyclical)

Fiscal variables (cyclical)	*Correlation coefficient*	*Cointegrating coefficients*
Tax revenue	0.39*	−6.24*
Current expenditure	0.10	5.01*
Annual development program	0.10	8.93*

Source: MoF and BBS

Data: Based on annual growth data from 1991 to 2018. Cyclical components are calculated as the deviation of the actual data from a trend computed using the Hodrick-Prescott filter with the standard smoothing parameter for annual data (6.25)

*The result is significant at $p < 0.05$

The above findings suggest that fiscal policy in Bangladesh amplifies boom-and-bust cycles. When growth accelerates, both tax revenue and government spending increase, but spending increases stronger than revenue. Larger tax revenue does not significantly impact subsequent economic activity, but larger public spending does. The latter further accelerates economic growth. When the economy slows, the deceleration is amplified by contractionary fiscal policy. Such amplification of boom-and-bust cycles appears to be especially severe in Bangladesh. In addition, in Bangladesh, tax revenue and economic growth are not significantly correlated, meaning that government misses out on much needed revenue and taxes fail to act as automatic stabilizers. Political distortions or borrowing constraints can explain a procyclical fiscal policy. Arguably, the spending needs of South Asian countries are immense and postponing spending in times of high growth to preserve fiscal space for times of low growth comes with costs.[18] Reallocating away from current spending toward capital spending could benefit growth. Growth-oriented fiscal expenditure reforms also tend to result in a more stable macroeconomic environment (Carrère and De Melo 2012). It is also argued that fiscal policy would benefit from stronger institutions framing budget implementation, more realistic fiscal plans and stronger public financial management.

[18] Developing this argument in a macroeconomic model would allow assessing the welfare implication of South Asia's procyclical fiscal policy.

6.6 Lessons from Advanced Economies

Are the low tax to GDP and expenditure to GDP ratios in Bangladesh an aberration, or are they corollaries of the low state of development of the economy? Even with substantial concessional financing, government spending is lower than by peer and advanced economies' standards. A recent contribution by Izvorski and Karakulah (2019) shows comparisons between today's developing countries, and today's advanced economies can provide aspiration but not pertinent recommendations about policies and institutions. They show that comparisons with advanced economies when they were less prosperous and would have been considered low-income or lower middle-income provides fresh insights. Using government spending a century ago by fourteen of today's advanced economies, they highlight four lessons for developing countries. These lessons, as articulated by the authors, are summarized below.

Governments can advance development even with low levels of government spending. Today's low-income countries spend more than twice on average than today's advanced economies spent more than a century ago (Fig. 6.10). This difference reflects the lack of the tax instruments and

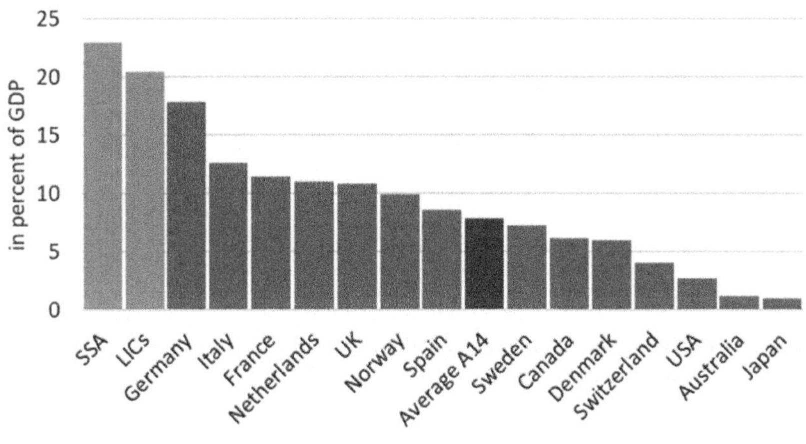

Fig. 6.10 Governments of today's low-income countries spent more on average in 2018 than today's advanced economies did in 1900 (percent of GDP). (Source: Ivailo Izvorski and Kenan Karakulah (2019))

systems countries have today.[19] Moreover, society's expectations from the government were much different then.[20] However, even with low level of government spending, economic development was brisk in most of the Advanced 14 at the turn of the twentieth century, with infrastructure improvements financed by private capital and the strong expansion of primary and secondary education. Thus, while working on strengthening domestic taxation and raising more revenues to finance public goods, the priority needs to be on improving the business environment to attract private capital—mobilizing private finance for development.

Developing economies need to focus on building fiscal and market institutions. Government spending in the Advanced 14 increased substantially since 1960, as they reevaluated the role of government amid rapid industrialization and globalization (Fig. 6.11). New taxes became com-

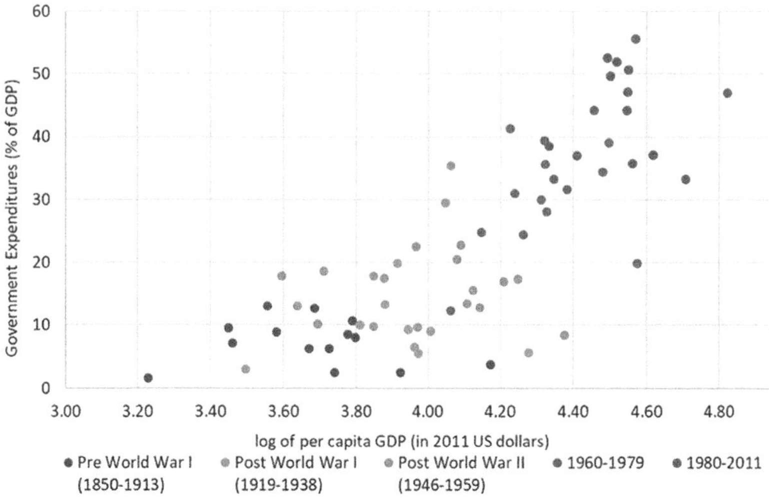

Fig. 6.11 Government spending of the Advanced 14 rose significantly in the twentieth century (percent of GDP). (Source: Ivailo Izvorski and Kenan Karakulah (2019))

[19] According to Izvorski and Karakulah (2019), from 1850 until the early 1900s, customs duties and excises provided the bulk of government revenues, while the personal income tax and VAT were not introduced in countries until later.

[20] Izvorski and Karakulah (2019) show that in 1900, for example, spending on unemployment, health, pensions, and housing amounted to only 1.1 percent of GDP in the Scandinavian countries on average and to 0.7 percent of GDP in the US.

monplace. The shift from agrarian to industrial to post-industrial economies required different worker skills. Economic disruptions reshaped governments in the past, as appears to be happening now with the changing world of work, leading to a large expansion of social insurance and spending on social protection.

While increasing government spending, developing economies must make a choice between the extent of redistribution and government services. Both the level and variability of government spending among the advanced economies have increased. Before 1913, spending among the advanced economies ranged from less than 2 percent of GDP in Japan to 13 percent in Italy, or a span of 11 percentage points. Currently, the span of spending among the advanced economies is 39 percentage points: from 17.3 percent in Hong Kong to 56.4 percent in France. Robust growth can happen with a smaller or a larger government, in general. Too large of a redistribution, however, can create substantial disincentives to work and invest, or lead to tensions between formal and informal workers, employees of large companies or SOEs and small private firms. This danger now is clearer than ever: the changing world of work is conflicting with persistent informality in developing countries like Bangladesh where social protection systems cover only tiny part of the population.

Government spending has been countercyclical since World War II in almost all advanced economies. Countercyclical fiscal policy is considered a must for today's developing countries, especially for those with abundant natural resources. However, as demonstrated earlier, there is overwhelming evidence that fiscal policy has been consistently procyclical in developing countries, resulting in macroeconomic imbalances, unproductive debt build-ups and ongoing instability (Fig. 6.12).

6.7 Deficit Financing in Bangladesh

Bangladesh maintains a steady budget deficit within 5 percent of GDP. Both domestic bank borrowing and non-bank borrowing are the primary sources of financing budget deficit in Bangladesh. Treasury bills and bonds comprised 17.6 percent and 52.9 percent of the total government's domestic debt stock, respectively, in 2015. The National Savings Directorate (NSD) instruments play an important role in deficit financing accounting about 34.5 percent of the total debt stock (Table 6.5).

In the context of Bangladesh's graduation from LDC status in 2024 and achievement of lower middle-income status in 2015, in addition to

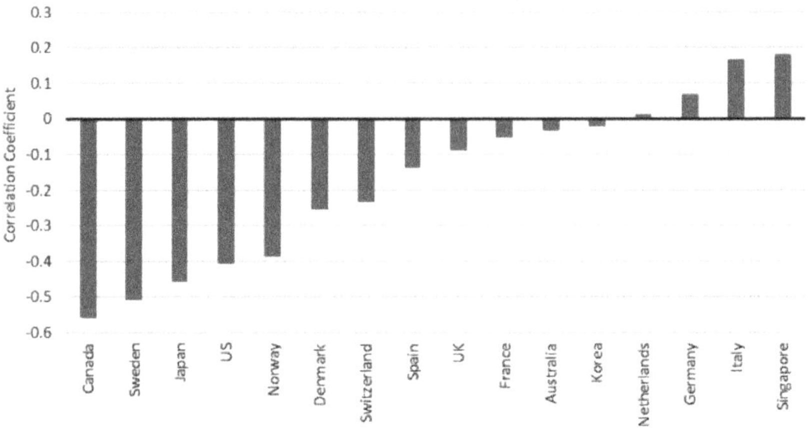

Fig. 6.12 Government spending has been countercyclical in today's advanced economies, 1950–2011 (percent of GDP). (Source: Ivailo Izvorski and Kenan Karakulah (2019))

Table 6.5 Bangladesh: public domestic debt, 2015

	In billions of taka	*In percent of total domestic debt*
Central government	2928	96.3
Overdraft at Bangladesh Bank	0	0.0
Ways and means advances from Bangladesh Bank	24	0.8
Treasury bills	331	10.9
Treasury bonds	1148	37.8
Checks issued but not cashed	113	3.7
Directorate of National Savings instruments	1048	34.5
General provident fund	264	8.7
SOEs		
Net liabilities to the banking system	111	3.7
Total	3039	100.0
(Percent of GDP)	20.1	

Source: Bangladesh Bank and IMF staff estimates

NBR revenues, alternative sources of resource mobilization needs to be explored. The bond market is almost non-existent and, therefore, development of bond market is an important strategy for mobilizing domestic resources. Sovereign wealth bonds and diaspora bond, linking CSR activities to development finance, climate change finance, and so on could be the alternative sources of development finance. A detailed analysis on alternative sources will be provided in a separate chapter.

6.8 Conclusions

The assessment in this chapter highlights that Bangladesh's efforts of maintaining fiscal discipline has been commendable. The fiscal stance has remained robust despite numerous pressures placed on scarce public resources due to recurring natural disasters; unpredictably changing global prices of food, fuel and fertilizer; and, more recently, the influx of Rohingyas. The central government's fiscal stance is sustainable at the current and projected levels of the fiscal deficit.

However, procyclicality of fiscal policy is not conducive for development in the long run. Countercyclical fiscal policy in the short run can help support aggregate demand and growth during cyclical downturns. Conversely, fiscal contraction can cool down an economy facing the risk of overheating. Advanced economies have used taxes and government spending to smooth the business cycle, particularly in the post-World War II era. Apart from economic stabilization, fiscal policy plays a critical role in facilitating and stimulating economic growth in the medium and long term. Public spending on roads, ports, and digital connectivity affects the productivity of the entire economy. Last but not the least, experience shows that fiscal policy is particularly important as a redistributive tool without which growth can hardly be made inclusive. Public investments in education and health can foster growth by building human capital, thus ensuring fiscal sustainability while augmenting the productive capacity of the poor.

Limited fiscal space, which is linked to rigidities in the budget, continues to constrain allocations for important economic sectors including health, education and social protection over time. Moving forward, it would be important to factor into fiscal policy long-term considerations such as the impact of an aging society. Moreover, demands of a country moving up the income ladder to improve the social and physical infrastructure will exert pressures in the medium to long term. The development of a comprehensive multi-year strategy and action plan is important for domestic revenue mobilization. It will help articulate Bangladesh's vision for the evolution of its tax system. Shifting to a function-based tax administration from a type of tax system can enhance efficiency while providing better services to taxpayers.

Non-financial and financial SOEs' debt is a key fiscal risk. The government effectively services the debt of state-run entities that receive current and capital transfers for public-guaranteed debt. Key factors weighing on the country's vulnerability are its growing exposure to foreign currency-denominated non-concessional debt for mega projects and large refinancing risks vis-à-vis low fiscal and external buffers. Containing non-discretionary spending and improving the efficiency of allocation mechanisms to enhance value for money are other important priorities. This includes increasing the efficiency and effectiveness of public spending in energy, transport, education, health, and social protection and improving prioritization and efficiency of public investment by strengthening public investment management. Staying in the same path will leave very limited room to deal with the consequences of domestic and external shocks or natural disasters.

Annex

Framework for Long-Run Sustainability Assessment

The following is a reproduction from the World Bank, Public Expenditure and Institutional Review 2010.

The government's flow budget constraint can be written as

$$b_t = (1+r)b_{t-1} - x_t - \sigma_t, \tag{6.1}$$

where b_t is the end-of-period stock of real debt, x_t is the real primary balance, and σ_t is the real value of seigniorage revenue.

Forward iteration on this equation combined with the condition

$$\lim_{j\to\infty}(1+r)^{-(j+1)} b_{t+j} = 0 \tag{6.2}$$

implies

$$b_{t-1} = \sum_{i=0}^{\infty}(1+r)^{-(i+1)}(x_{t+i} + \sigma_{t+i}) \tag{6.3}$$

This is the government's lifetime budget constraint. It states that the government finances its debt at the end of period $t-1$ by, from date t forward, raising seigniorage revenue and running primary surpluses with an equal present value.

The most basic tool for fiscal sustainability analysis uses a steady-state version of this lifetime budget constraint. To begin, consistent with the presentation in most World Bank and IMF documents, it is useful to rewrite (6.3) in terms of stocks and flows expressed as fractions of GDP. Let y_t represent real GDP, define $\bar{b}_t = b_t / y_t, \bar{x}_t = x_t / y_t$ and $\bar{\sigma}_t = \sigma_t / y_t$. Given this notation, Eq. 6.3 can be rewritten as

$$\bar{b}_{t-1} y_{t-1} = \sum_{i=0}^{\infty} (1+r)^{-(i+1)} \left(\bar{x}_{t+i} + \bar{\sigma}_{t+i} \right) y_{t+i} \text{ or}$$
$$\bar{b}_{t-1} = \sum_{i=0}^{\infty} (1+r)^{-(i+1)} \left(\bar{x}_{t+i} + \bar{\sigma}_{t+i} \right) \frac{y_{t+i}}{y_{t-1}} \tag{6.4}$$

Imagine a steady state in which (i) real GDP grows at a constant rate g, so that $y_t / y_{t-1} = 1+g$, (ii) the primary surplus as a fraction of GDP is a constant $\bar{x}$, and (iii) seigniorage as a fraction of GDP is a constant $\bar{\sigma}$. In this case, Eq. 6.4 reduces to

$$\bar{b}_{t-1} = \sum_{t=0}^{\infty} \left(\frac{1+g}{1+r} \right)^{i+1} \left(\bar{x} + \bar{\sigma} \right) \tag{6.5}$$

Assuming $r > g$, (6.5) reduces to

$$\bar{b}_{t-1} = \bar{b} \equiv \left(\bar{x} + \bar{\sigma} \right) / \bar{r} \tag{6.6}$$

where $\bar{r} = (r-g) / (1+g)$.

Equation (6.6) can be used in two ways. First, one could make reasonable assumptions about the values of $\bar{x}, \bar{\sigma}, r$ and g based on historical trends in the country's fiscal accounts as well as typical historical values of seigniorage revenue, the real interest rate and the real growth rate. Together these assumptions can be mapped into an estimate of $\bar{b}$ using Eq. 6.6. If the government's actual stock of debt exceeded this estimate, then the government's finances could be argued to be unsustainable. Alternatively, Eq. 6.6 can be rewritten as

$$\bar{x} = r\bar{b}_{t-1} - \bar{\sigma}. \tag{6.7}$$

Given estimates of $\bar{r}$ and $\bar{\sigma}$ and data on the size of the government's actual debt stock, b_{t-1}, Eq. 6.7 can be used to determine the necessary size of the primary balance to ensure fiscal sustainability. That is, rather than setting $\bar{x}$ equal to some historical average, one can determine the value that $\bar{x}$ would need to take in the future to maintain sustainable finances.

A final interpretation of Eq. 6.7 is that if $\bar{x}$ were set consistent with it, then the debt-GDP ratio would remain constant in the steady state. In other words, when $\bar{x}$, $\bar{\sigma}$, r and g are constant and $\bar{x}$ is given by (6.7), not only will the government's finances be sustainable, but it will also be true that $\bar{b}_t$ will be constant and equal to $\bar{b}$.

How to calculate $\bar{\sigma}$? Assume base money is a constant fraction of GDP: ${M_t}/{P_t}\, y_t = \bar{m}$; inflation is constant at some rate π, and real growth is constant at the rate g, so that

$$\begin{aligned} \bar{\sigma} &= \frac{M_t - M_{t-1}}{P_t y_t} = \frac{M_t}{P_t y_t} - \frac{P_{t-1} y_{t-1}}{P_t y_t} \frac{M_{t-1}}{P_{t-1} y_{t-1}} \\ &= \bar{m} - \frac{1}{(1+\pi)(1+g)} \bar{m} = \frac{\pi + g + \pi g}{(1+\pi)(1+g)} \bar{m} \equiv \bar{\sigma}. \end{aligned} \tag{6.8}$$

With assumptions and projections regarding inflation, growth and the size of base money, one gets a benchmark value for $\bar{\sigma}$.

Table 6.6 Calculations of sustainable primary balances for a range of real GDP growth and interest rates

	Growth									
	−0.036	*0.040*	*0.045*	*0.050*	*0.055*	*0.060*	*0.065*	*0.070*	*0.075*	*0.080*
Nominal interest rate	0.030	−0.029	−0.031	−0.032	−0.034	−0.036	−0.038	−0.039	−0.041	−0.043
	0.040	−0.026	−0.028	−0.030	−0.031	−0.033	−0.035	−0.037	−0.039	−0.040
	0.050	−0.023	−0.025	−0.027	−0.029	−0.030	−0.032	−0.034	−0.036	−0.038
	0.060	−0.020	−0.022	−0.024	−0.026	−0.028	−0.029	−0.031	−0.033	−0.035
	0.070	−0.017	−0.019	−0.021	−0.023	−0.025	−0.027	−0.028	−0.030	−0.032
	0.080	−0.014	−0.016	−0.018	−0.020	−0.022	−0.024	−0.026	−0.028	−0.029
	0.090	−0.012	−0.014	−0.015	−0.017	−0.019	−0.021	−0.023	−0.025	−0.027
	0.100	−0.009	−0.011	−0.013	−0.015	−0.016	−0.018	−0.020	−0.022	−0.024
	0.110	−0.006	−0.008	−0.010	−0.012	−0.014	−0.016	−0.017	−0.019	−0.021
	0.120	−0.003	−0.005	−0.007	−0.009	−0.011	−0.013	−0.015	−0.017	−0.018
	0.130	0.000	−0.002	−0.004	−0.006	−0.008	−0.010	−0.012	−0.014	−0.016

References

Bank, B. *Treasury bill/bond auctions*. Retrieved May 30, 2015 from: http://www.bangladesh-bank.org/monetaryactivity/treasury.php

Bayraktar, N., Le, T. M., & Moreno-Dodson, B. (2014). Analysis of tax revenue and incidence in Sri Lanka. *World Bank. 2015c*. The World Bank.

BBS. (2013). *Economic Census-2013*. Dhaka: Bangladesh Bureau of Statistics.

Begum, L. (2007). *A panel study on tax effort and tax buoyancy with special reference to Bangladesh* (Working paper no. 715). Dhaka: Policy Analysis Unit (PAU) Research Department, Bangladesh Bank.

Beyer, R., & Milivojevic, L. (2019). *Fiscal policy and economic activity in South Asia*. World Bank Policy Research Working Paper (8792).

Calderón, C., & Servén, L. (2014). *Infrastructure, growth, and inequality: An overview*. Washington, DC: The World Bank.

Carrère, C., & De Melo, J. (2012). Fiscal spending and economic growth: Some stylized facts. *World Development, 40*(9), 1750–1761.

Department of National Savings. (2015, May 30). *5 Years Bangladesh Sanchayapatra*. Retrieved from: http://www.nationalsavings.gov.bd/5_year_s.htm

Devarajan, S., Swaroop, V., & Zou, H. F. (1996). The composition of public expenditure and economic growth. *Journal of Monetary Economics*, 37(2), 313–344. Available from: http://www1.worldbank.org/publicsector/pe/pfma07/ShantaVinayHengfu.pdf

Hossain, M. (2017). *Resource mobilization strategies and action plan for Bangladesh*. Dhaka: United Nations Development Program (Unpublished).

IMF. (2014). *Fourth review under the three-year arrangement under the extended credit facility—Staff report and debt sustainability analysis update*. Washington, DC: International Monetary Fund. Available from: http://www.imf.org/external/pubs/ft/scr/2014/cr14149.pdf

IMF. (2015, April). *World economic outlook database*. Washington, DC: International Monetary Fund. Available from: https://www.imf.org/external/pubs/ft/weo/2015/01/weodata/index.aspx

Izvorski, I., & Karakulah, K. (2019, February 2019). *4 lessons for developing countries from advanced economies' past, BROOKINGS*. Retrieved from https://www.brookings.edu/blog/future-development/2019/02/20/4-lessons-for-developing-countries-from-advanced-economies-past/

Khwaja, M. S., & Iyer, I. (2014). *Revenue potential, tax space, and tax gap: A comparative analysis*. The World Bank. Available from: http://hdl.handle.net/10986/18806

KPMG. (2015, May 28). *Tax tools and resources*. Retrieved from: https://home.kpmg/vg/en/home/services/tax1/tax-tools-and-resources.html

Le, T. M., Moreno-Dodson, B., & Bayraktar, N. (2012). *Tax capacity and tax effort: Extended cross-country analysis from 1994 to 2009*. The World Bank. Available from: http://hdl.handle.net/10986/12094

Martorano, B. (2018). Cyclicality of fiscal policy in Latin America over the period 1990–2015. *Review of Development Economics, 22*(1), 67–90.

Medina, L. (2015). *Assessing fiscal risks in Bangladesh* (No. 15–110). International Monetary Fund. Available from: http://www.imf.org/external/pubs/ft/wp/2015/wp15110.pdf

Ministry of Finance. (2012). *Year End Report on Fiscal Position: Fiscal Year 2011–12*. Government of Bangladesh. Available from: http://www.mof.gov.bd/en/budget/year_end_fiscal/year_end_report_2011_12.pdf

Ministry of Finance. (2013). *Year End Report on Fiscal Position: Fiscal Year 2012–13*. Government of Bangladesh. Available from: http://www.mof.gov.bd/en/budget/year_end_fiscal/year_end_report_2012_13.pdf

National Board of Revenue (NBR). (2010). *Outline of Tax Modernization Plan (2011–2016)*. Government of Bangladesh. Available from: http://www.nbr-bd.org/tender/NBR_Modernisation_Plan_Final_draft.pdf

Planning Commission. (2010a). *Outline Perspective Plan of Bangladesh 2010 to 2021: Making vision 2021 a reality*. Government of Bangladesh. Available from: http://www.un-bd.org/docs/Final_Draft_OPP_June_2010.pdf

Planning Commission. (2010b). *Sixth Five Year Plan*. Government of Bangladesh. Part 1 available from: http://www.unicef.org/bangladesh/Six-Five-Year-Plan-2012-Final.pdf. Part 2 available from: http://www.plancomm.gov.bd/wp-content/uploads/2013/09/SFYP_Part-2.pdf

Planning Commission. (2012). *Perspective Plan of Bangladesh 2010 to 2021: Making vision 2021 a reality*. Government of Bangladesh. Available from: http://www.plancomm.gov.bd/wp-content/uploads/2013/09/Perspective-Plan-of-Bangladesh.pdf

Tornell, A., & Lane, P. R. (1999). The voracity effect. *American Economic Review, 89*(1), 22–46.

World Bank. (2010). *Bangladesh—Public expenditure and institutional review: Towards a better quality of public expenditure—Main report*. Washington, DC: The World Bank. Available from: http://hdl.handle.net/10986/2875

World Bank. (2012). *World development indicators*. Washington, DC: The World Bank. Available from: http://data.worldbank.org/data-catalog/world-development-indicators

World Bank. (2014). *A public investment management review and reform road map for Bangladesh*. Washington, DC: The World Bank.

World Bank. (2015a, June). *Public expenditure review update*.

World Bank. (2015b). *Towards new sources of competitiveness in Bangladesh: A Bangladesh diagnostic trade integration study*. Washington, DC: The World Bank.

World Bank. (2015c). *Bangladesh development update*. Dhaka: The World Bank. Available from: https://openknowledge.worldbank.org/handle/10986/21777

World Bank. (Forthcoming-a). *Systematic country diagnostic*. Washington, DC: The World Bank.

World Bank. (Forthcoming-b). *Fiscal space for health in Bangladesh*. Washington, DC: The World Bank.

World Bank/IFC. (2014). *Doing business report 2015: Going beyond efficiency*. Washington, DC: The World Bank. Report and data available from: http://www.doingbusiness.org/

World Economic Forum. (2014). *The global competitiveness report 2014–15*. Davos: WEF. Available from: http://www3.weforum.org/docs/WEF_GlobalCompetitivenessReport_2014-15.pdf

CHAPTER 7

Effectiveness of Fiscal Policy in Stimulating Economic Growth: An Empirical Study on Bangladesh

Selim Raihan and Iffat Anjum

7.1 Introduction

Economic growth in a country is contingent upon both public and private sectors. During the Great Depression of 1930s and its aftermath, Keynes (1936) brought attention to the vital role of public sector in stimulating the economy. Keynesian economists emphasized on the importance of government policies in closing the gap between potential and actual level of outputs in the economy. Over the last decade, significant changes have emanated in global development thinking not as mere growth but sustainability, and inclusiveness of growth became the focus. Public sector plays a central role in supporting economic development, while ensuring that growth is sustainable and equally beneficial to people from all walks. The

S. Raihan (✉)
Department of Economics, University of Dhaka, Dhaka, Bangladesh

South Asian Network on Economic Modeling (SANEM), Dhaka, Bangladesh

I. Anjum
South Asian Network on Economic Modeling (SANEM), Dhaka, Bangladesh

M. Hossain (ed.), *Bangladesh's Macroeconomic Policy*,
https://doi.org/10.1007/978-981-15-1244-5_7

role of government is crucial in pursuing the development goals in national as well as global contexts. The global development agenda of Sustainable Development Goals (SDGs) highlight the role of public sector in financing and implementing the 17 Goals within 2030. Especially in less developed countries, the government has to take the lead in setting the structure for boosting economic activities of the economy and to enable private sector to perform well. Government policy translated into macroeconomic stability is essential for sustaining higher economic growth.

One of the most important tools the government has at its disposal to influence the economy is the fiscal policy. Effective use and implementation of fiscal policy is crucial for maintaining macroeconomic stability of a country. Macroeconomic issues related to fiscal policy such as budget deficit, government spending on social and physical infrastructure, public debt, tax rates and so on are at the core of economic debate in developing as well as developed economies. The key instruments of fiscal policy include government expenditure and taxation through which government exerts influence over various indicators of macroeconomic performance of the economy such as aggregate demand, inflation, money supply, unemployment, economic growth, and so on. There are two types of fiscal policy: expansionary fiscal policy, which refers to increasing government expenditure, lowering taxes, increasing transfer payments and so on, aiming at boosting economic activities; and contractionary fiscal policy, which refers to reducing government expenditure, higher taxes, decreased transfer payments and so on, stabilizing the economy.

Bangladesh has been experiencing an average growth rate of around 6 percent for almost past two decades, paving the way toward achieving lower middle income country status in 2015. Being the 43rd largest economy in the world in terms of nominal gross domestic product (GDP) and with a per capita GDP of $1610 in 2017, the country is now aspiring to become upper middle income country within 2030. The impressive economic growth in Bangladesh has been driven mostly by exports, remittance inflow, as well as domestic consumption demand. A major component of aggregate demand of a country is the government expenditure. Bangladesh's fiscal policy has mostly been expansionary in nature, with government expenditure exceeding government revenue and resulting in budget deficit. Government expenditure can effectively be divided into two components—government's consumption expenditure and investment expenditure. This chapter focuses on government consumption component. Bangladesh has one of the lowest tax-GDP ratios in the world and second lowest in South Asia. Moreover, the tax effort in Bangladesh is staggeringly low, showing that there is scope for generating much higher tax revenues.

This chapter aims to explore the impact of government consumption and government tax revenues on economic growth of Bangladesh using empirical analysis. The objective and importance of the study is twofold. First, although there exists a number of literatures examining the effectiveness of fiscal policy in Bangladesh, none took a production function approach to look into it. Secondly, with tax-GDP ratio of Bangladesh being one of the lowest in the world, the study reveals important policy implications about the impact of increased tax efforts on the long-run growth of the country.

The chapter is organized as follows. Section 7.2 reviews the relevant literature. Section 7.3 discusses the methodology, and Sect. 7.4 discusses the results. Section 7.5 provides conclusion and recommendations.

7.2 Literature Review

The effectiveness of fiscal policy in stimulating the economic activities and maintaining macroeconomic stability of a country has received considerable policy and research interests. Fiscal policy is an important tool at the disposal of the government to mitigate short-run fluctuations in aggregate output and employment, as well as recovering from any shock to move toward the long-run economic growth. There are two contrasting economic schools of thought regarding the role of fiscal policy in economic development: one asserts that different forms of government spending on social as well as physical infrastructures have positive effect on economic development, while the other school of thought highlights that government regulations and taxation create distortions in the market. The debate between these two views has been fueled by mixed empirical evidence offered by different studies on the relationship between public expenditure and economic growth.

That expansionary fiscal policy is a useful tool to stimulate economic activities, which was first argued by Keynes in his 1936 book *The General Theory of Employment, Interest and Money.* Keynes argued that national output increases as a consequence of an increase in the government spending, while Wagner's Law (Wagner 1883) states that the size of the government expenditure increases with economic growth. A number of literatures shed light on these two schools of thoughts. With the upsurge of endogenous growth theories, there has been a number of empirical studies looking into the long-run growth effects of fiscal variables. Endogenous growth theories offer the framework for exploring effectiveness of fiscal policy in stimulating growth and expect that public spending and taxation have both short-run and long-run impacts on growth. Barro and Sala-I-Martin (1992) discussed the effects of fiscal policy in a variety of endogenous growth models. Barro (1990) found a negative relationship between the share of government spending in GDP and economic growth. Using the data of 98 countries for the period 1960–1985, Barro (1991) found an inverse relationship between growth and share of government consumption in GDP.

Kormendi and Meguire (1985) used post-WWII data of 47 countries for their analysis and showed that there is no significant relationship between the average growth rate of real GDP and average growth rate of government consumption expenditure. Easterly and Rebelo (1993) studied empirical relationship among fiscal variables and the rate of growth and found no distinct relationship between public spending and growth. Connolly and Li (2016) conducted a panel data analysis on data of 34 OECD (Organisation for Economic Co-operation and Development) countries for the period 1995–2011. Their findings indicate a lack of significant relationship between government consumption spending and economic growth. Landau (1983) found a statistically significant negative relationship between the share of government consumption expenditure in GDP and the rate of growth of real per capita GDP. A positive association between GDP growth rate and size of government expenditure was found in a study conducted by Ram (1986) using the data of 115 countries over the period 1960–1980. Kyissima et al. (2017) conducted a time series analysis to examine the long-run and short-run relationship between government expenditure and economic growth in Tanzania using data of 1996–2014. Employing error correction model (ECM) and Granger causality test, the study found positive and significant relationship between government spending and growth in the long run, with granger causality test revealing uni-directional causality between the two variables.

A number of empirical studies concluded that taxes have detrimental impact on economic growth. Examining the effects of fiscal policy on economic growth of 22 OECD countries for the period 1970–95, Kneller et al. (1999) showed that distortionary taxation negatively affects growth. On the other hand, Barro and Sala-i-Martin (1992) showed that tax policy that encourages investment can have positive effect on growth. A number of country-specific studies were conducted to examine the relationship between government tax revenue and growth. Ojong et al. (2016) examined the impact of tax revenue on growth of Nigeria using data of 1986–2010 and found that there is evidence of significant positive relationship. Another study conducted by Babatunde et al. (2017) to explore the effects of taxation on the growth of Africa using data of 2004–2013 revealed that tax revenue has a positive and significant relationship with GDP. Engen and Skinner (1992) found strong and negative effects of both government spending and taxation on growth using a sample of 107 countries for the period 1970–85. While some studies concluded that government consumption and taxation have negative impact on growth, other studies found evidence of positive and significant effect. This study contributes to existing literature by providing empirical evidence from Bangladesh on the effects of government consumption and government tax revenue on economic growth using a time series analysis.

7.3 Methodology

The study looks into both short-run and long-run effects of fiscal policy instruments on economic growth of Bangladesh, using the vector error correction model (VECM) and Johansen cointegration technique. After conducting augmented Dickey-Fuller (ADF) and Phillips-Perron (PP) unit root tests to check for the stationarity properties of the time series variables, lag order selection test has been carried out to establish appropriate lag length to be used for the analysis. The cointegration rank of the models has been determined with the help of Johansen cointegration test, which also helped establish the existence of long-run causal relationships in the models. VECM has been employed to analyze disequilibrium adjustment in the short run, followed by Granger causality test and an investigation of the impulse response functions (IRFs).

7.3.1 Data

This study explores the effects of fiscal policy on economic growth in the context of Bangladesh economy using time series data of real GDP, government current consumption, stock of capital in the economy, laborer (number of persons engaged in economic activities) and tax revenues for the period 1980–2017. Data for abovementioned variables have been obtained from Penn World Table (PWT) version 9, World Bank's World

Development Indicators (WDI) database and Statistical Yearbooks of Bangladesh for different years. All variables have been converted into log form to conduct the analysis.

7.3.2 Model

The study employs the production function approach of the growth model as depicted in Eq. 7.1.

$$lnGDP = \propto_0 + \propto_1 lnK + \propto_2 lnL + \varepsilon. \tag{7.1}$$

Where,

lnGDP = log of real GDP
lnK = log of capital stock
lnL = log of labor
ε = error term representing other factors that might affect dependent variable that are not included in the model

In the augmented models 7.2 and 7.3, two fiscal policy variables have been added to Eq. 7.1.

$$lnGDP = \propto_0 + \propto_1 lnK + \propto_2 lnL + \propto_2 lngovcon + \varepsilon. \tag{7.2}$$

$$lnGDP = \propto_0 + \propto_1 lnK + \propto_2 lnL + \propto_2 lngovrev + \varepsilon. \tag{7.3}$$

Where,

lngovexp = log of real government consumption
lngovrev = log of real government revenue

The VECM model of Eq. 7.2 is used to capture the association between real GDP and government consumption, and VECM model of Eq. 7.3 is used to capture the relationship between real GDP and government tax revenue.

7.4 Results and Analysis

7.4.1 Unit Root Tests

There is a possibility of time series variables exhibiting spurious relationships due to the non-stationary characteristics of the variables. To check that possibility, we conducted ADF and PP unit root tests to check the stationarity properties of all variables.

A graphical presentation of the trends in the variables in their level forms is shown in Fig. 7.1. All the time series variables (log of real GDP, log of capital stock, log of labor, log of government current consumption and log of government revenue) exhibit upward trend with respect to time, which indicates non-stationary properties of the time series variables.

After examining the trends in these variables in their level forms, first difference of these variables has been generated. As depicted in Fig. 7.2, the first difference forms of these variables do not exhibit any trend with respect to time, indicating stationarity.

In both ADF (Dickey and Fuller 1979) and PP (Phillips and Perron 1988) unit root tests, the null hypothesis states that the time series has a unit root, implying non-stationarity of the variable. The alternative hypothesis is that there is no unit root in the time series, therefore the time series is stationary. The test statistic is compared to the critical values. The null hypothesis is rejected if the test statistic value exceeds the critical value in absolute value. The corresponding p-value is consulted to determine the level of significance at which the null hypothesis is rejected.

Table 7.1 presents the results obtained from the ADF unit root tests conducted on all the time series variables included in Eqs. 7.2 and 7.3. After conducting unit root tests on the level form of the variables, same tests have been conducted on their first difference form. The results of the ADF tests indicate that although all variables are non-stationary in their level form, they are stationary in first difference form.

The results of the PP tests shown in Table 7.2 reconfirm the findings of the ADF tests. All variables are found to be non-stationary in level form and stationary in first difference form. The results indicate that the variables are integrated of order one, that is, I(1), as they are stationary in first difference form.

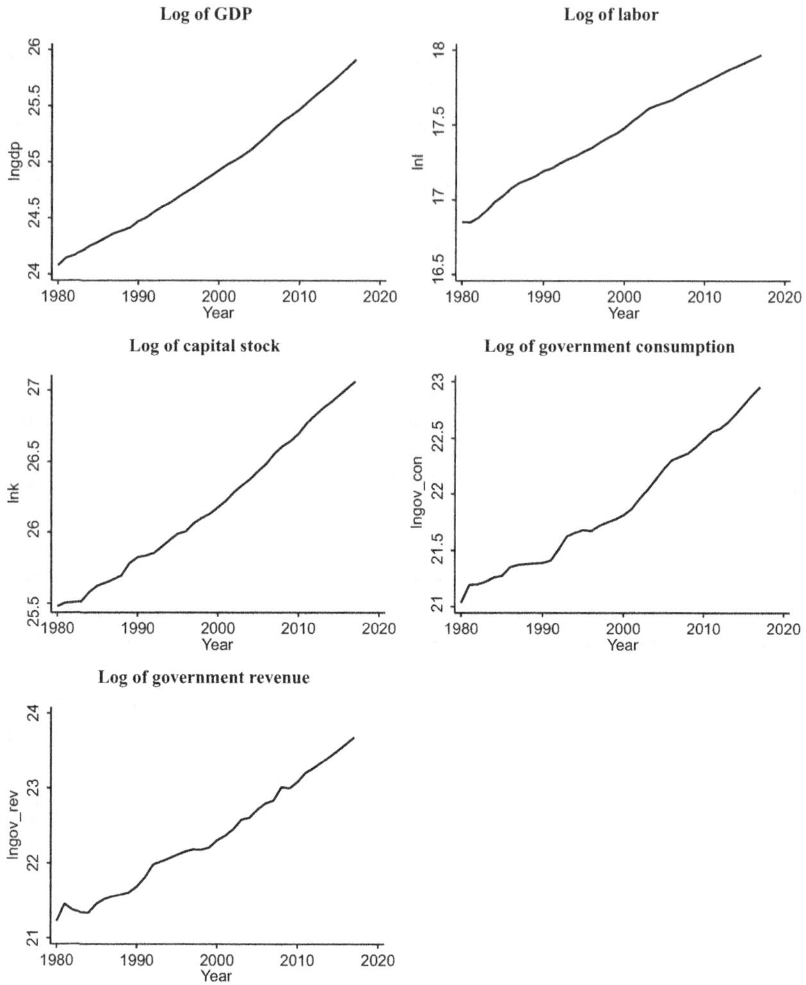

Fig. 7.1 Trend in the variables in their levels

7.4.2 Lag Length Selection Test

Before proceeding with the cointegration test and VECM, appropriate lag length needs to be determined for each model. For this purpose, lag order selection test has been conducted. The statistics commonly used to determine the appropriate lag length are log ratio (LR), final prediction error

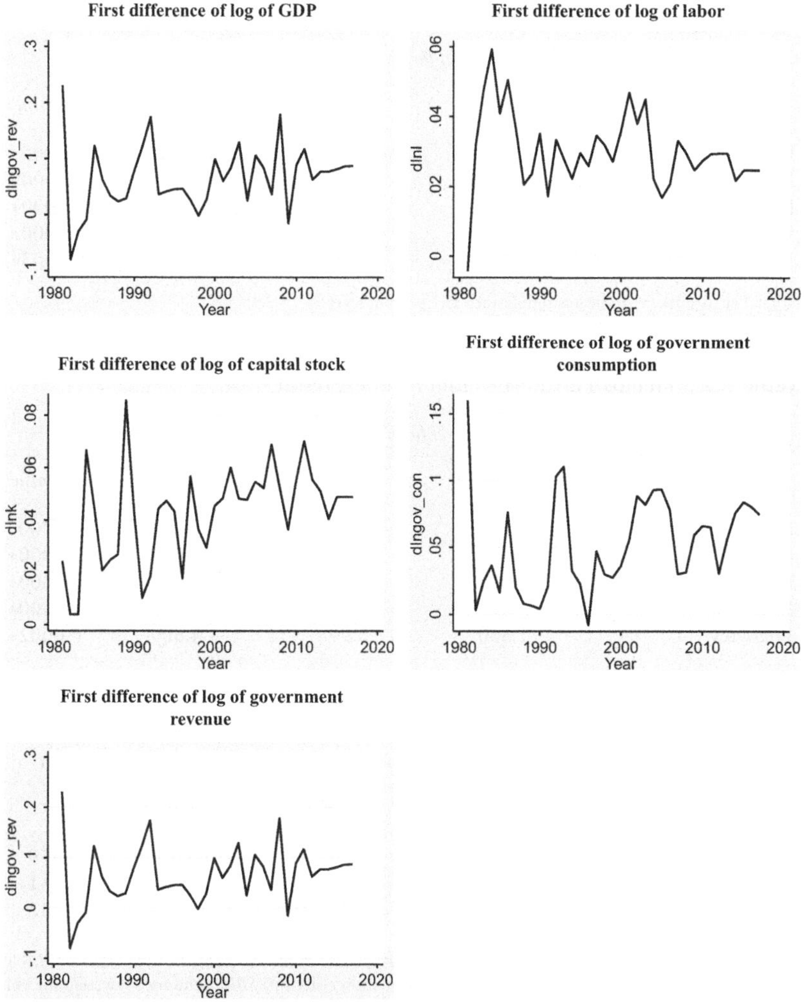

Fig. 7.2 Trend in the variables in their first difference

(FPE) (Akaike 1969), Akaike's information criterion (AIC) (Akaike, A New Look at the Statistical Model Identification, 1974), Schwarz's Bayesian information criterion (SBIC) (Schwarz 1978) and Hannan-Quinn information criterion (HQIC) (Hannan and Quinn 1979) statistics. While AIC and FPE are suitable for sample size of less than 60, HQIC is more suitable for sample size of more than 120 (Liew 2004).

Table 7.1 ADF unit root test result

Variable	*Level form*		*First difference form*	
	Test statistic	*P-value*	*Test statistic*	*P-value*
lnGDP	3.308	1.000	−8.001	0.0000*
lnK	2.008	0.999	−9.638	0.0000*
lnL	−0.025	0.956	−7.063	0.0000*
Lngovcon	−2.177	0.215	−6.942	0.0000*
Lngovrev	1.608	0.998	−4.439	0.0003*

Note: The asterisk (*) indicates significance at 1 percent level

Table 7.2 Phillips-Perron (PP) unit root test result

Variable	*Level form*		*First difference form*	
	Test statistic	*P-value*	*Test statistic*	*P-value*
lnGDP	5.935	1.000	−7.867	0.0000*
lnK	2.249	0.999	−9.717	0.0000*
lnL	−0.026	0.956	−6.940	0.0000*
Lngovcon	−2.251	0.188	−6.950	0.0000*
Lngovrev	1.530	0.998	−4.509	0.0002*

Note: The asterisk (*) indicates significance at 1 percent level

Table 7.3 Lag length selection test for model of government consumption

Lag order	*LL*	*LR*	*FPE*	*AIC*	*HQIC*	*SBIC*
0	195.423		0.00	−10.635	−10.573	−10.459
1	443.552	496.260	0.00	−23.531	−23.224	−22.651*
2	464.869	42.633*	0.00*	−23.826*	−23.273*	−22.243

Note: The asterisk (*) indicates lag order selected by respective criterion. Here, *LL* log likelihood, *LR* log ratio, *FPE* final prediction error, *AIC* Akaike's information criterion, *SBIC* Schwarz's Bayesian information criterion, *HQIC* Hannan-Quinn information criterion

Tables 7.3 and 7.4 show the lag order selection statistics for models of government consumption and government revenue, respectively. For the purpose of this study, the appropriate lag length to be used for the model of government consumption is two, and for the model of government revenue, lag length of one is used.

Table 7.4 Lag length selection test for model of government revenue

Lag order	*LL*	*LR*	*FPE*	*AIC*	*HQIC*	*SBIC*
0	187.504		0.00	−10.195	−10.133	−10.019
1	427.459	479.91*	0.00*	−22.636*	−22.329*	−21.757*
2	436.524	18.13	0.00	−22.251	−21.699	−20.668

Note: The asterisk (*) indicates lag order selected by respective criterion. Here, *LL* log likelihood, *LR* log ratio, *FPE* final prediction error, *AIC* Akaike's information criterion, *SBIC* Schwarz's Bayesian information criterion, *HQIC* Hannan-Quinn information criterion

7.4.3 *Cointegration Test*

The chapter employs Johansen cointegration test to determine the existence and number of cointegrating rank for the model. Before conducting the Johansen cointegration test, lag order selection test has been conducted to determine appropriate lag length to be used for the cointegration test. After considering the LR, FPE, AIC, SBIC and HQIC statistics, appropriate lag length has been determined for the Johansen cointegration test.

Following Johansen cointegration technique, two tests are used to determine the presence as well as number of cointegrating relationship among the variables. These two tests are trace test (Johansen, Statistical Analysis of Cointegration Vectors, 1988) and maximum eigenvalue test (Johansen and Juselius 1990). In both tests, the null hypothesis states that there exists at least n number of cointegrating relationships among the variables in the long run, and the alternative hypothesis is that there are more than n numbers of cointegrating relationship. If the test statistic value is greater than the critical value, we can reject the null hypothesis in favor of the alternative hypothesis.

The results of the Johansen cointegration tests conducted for models of government consumption and government revenue are presented in Tables 7.5 and 7.6, respectively. The results reveal that there is existence of at least two cointegrating relationships among the variables in these two models. This implies that VECM can be applied, and meaningful conclusion can be drawn from the analysis.

To examine the long-run association among the variables, Johansen cointegration technique has been used. The existence of cointegrating relationship among the variables tells us that there is long-run causal, not

Table 7.5 Johansen cointegration test for model of government consumption

Maximum rank	*Trace statistic*	*5 percent critical value*	*Max-eigen statistic*	*5 percent critical value*
0	88.093	39.890	49.036	23.800
1	39.058	24.310	28.215	17.890
2	10.843*	12.53	10.132	11.440
3	0.711	3.840	0.711	3.840

Note: The asterisk (*) indicates rejection of null hypothesis at 5 percent level of significance

Table 7.6 Johansen cointegration test for model of government revenue

Maximum rank	*Trace statistic*	*5 percent critical value*	*Max-eigen statistic*	*5 percent critical value*
0	188.029	39.890	144.779	23.800
1	43.251	24.310	30.940	17.890
2	12.310*	12.530	11.835	11.440
3	0.475	3.840	0.475	3.840

Note: The asterisk (*) indicates rejection of null hypothesis at 5 percent level of significance

spurious, relationship among the variables in both models. The result of the Johansen test reveals that there is positive and significant long-run causal relationship between real GDP growth and government consumption and between real GDP growth and government tax revenue.

7.4.4 Vector Error Correction Model

The VECM is used in various literatures to investigate the short-run dynamics and long-run causal relationship among variables. If there exists at least one cointegrating relationship among the variables, a vector error correction model can be applied. The error correction term in VECM shows the speed of adjustment from the short-run state of variables to their long-run equilibriums. A negative and significant coefficient of error correction term indicates that the model is converging to its long-run equilibrium, while a positive and significant coefficient of error correction term may imply structural change in the variable. An insignificant coefficient of error correction term, on the other hand, indicates to the insignificance of the short-run disequilibrium. The individual coefficients serve to capture the short-run effects.

Table 7.7 VECM result of model of government consumption

Dependent variable: D_lnGDP				
Variable	*Coefficient*	*Standard error*	*t-statistics*	*P-value*
Error correction term (ECM)	−0.128**	0.054	−2.380	0.017
D_lnK	−0.029	0.104	−0.280	0.779
D_lnL	−0.083	0.146	−0.570	0.567
D_lngovcon	−0.032	0.049	−0.660	0.512

Note: ***, ** and * indicate statistical significance at the 1, 5 and 10 percent levels, respectively

Table 7.8 VECM result for model of government revenue

Dependent Variable: D_lnGDP				
Variable	*Coefficient*	*Standard error*	*t-statistics*	*P-value*
Error correction term (ECM)	−0.140***	0.029	−4.830	0.000
D_lnK	−0.043	0.096	−0.450	0.656
D_lnL	−0.109	0.135	−0.810	0.417
D_lngovrev	−0.045*	0.027	−1.660	0.096

Note: ***, ** and * indicate statistical significance at the 1, 5 and 10 percent levels, respectively

Tables 7.7 and 7.8 present the VECM results for the models of government consumption and government revenue, respectively. The VECM results reveal a negative and significant error correction term for both models. The individual coefficients show that, in the short run, the effect of government consumption on economic growth is found to be negative and insignificant. However, in the short run, government tax revenue is found to have a negative and significant effect on real GDP growth.

7.4.5 *Causality Test*

To investigate the direction of the causal relationship among the variables, we carried out Granger causality test. Granger causality test examines whether there exists any uni-directional or bi-directional causality between variables, under the null hypothesis of no Granger causality, against the alternative hypothesis of existence of Granger causality (Granger 1969). The findings of pairwise Granger causality tests (Tables 7.9 and 7.10) suggest that government consumption and government tax revenue have bi-directional causal relationships with economic growth.

Table 7.9 Granger causality test for model of government consumption

Equation	*Excluded*	*chi2*	*df*	*Prob > chi2*
Dlngdp	dlnl	17.553	2	0.000
Dlngdp	dlnk	3.118	2	0.210
Dlngdp	dlngov_con	5.997	2	0.096
Dlngdp	ALL	22.854	6	0.001
Dlnl	dlngdp	6.218	2	0.045
Dlnl	dlnk	1.189	2	0.552
Dlnl	dlngov_con	2.576	2	0.276
Dlnl	ALL	15.993	6	0.014
Dlnk	dlngdp	2.693	2	0.260
Dlnk	dlnl	4.405	2	0.111
Dlnk	dlngov_con	0.1753	2	0.916
Dlnk	ALL	9.511	6	0.147
dlngov_con	dlngdp	5.345	2	0.069
dlngov_con	dlnl	0.365	2	0.833
dlngov_con	dlnk	5.713	2	0.057
dlngov_con	ALL	15.520	6	0.017

Table 7.10 Granger causality test for model of government revenue

Equation	*Excluded*	*chi2*	*df*	*Prob > chi2*
Dlngdp	dlnl	15.540	2	0.000
Dlngdp	dlnk	2.427	2	0.297
Dlngdp	dlngov_rev	5.814	2	0.098
Dlngdp	ALL	18.131	6	0.006
Dlnl	dlngdp	15.894	2	0.000
Dlnl	dlnk	0.961	2	0.618
Dlnl	dlngov_rev	10.785	2	0.005
Dlnl	ALL	27.133	6	0.000
Dlnk	dlngdp	5.330	2	0.070
Dlnk	dlnl	4.943	2	0.084
Dlnk	dlngov_rev	0.607	2	0.738
Dlnk	ALL	10.057	6	0.122
dlngov_rev	dlngdp	6.371	2	0.094
dlngov_rev	dlnl	2.743	2	0.254
dlngov_rev	dlnk	2.647	2	0.266
dlngov_rev	ALL	9.814	6	0.133

7.4.6 Impulse Response Function

The study also attempted to explore the dynamic nature of model by employing IRFs resulting from the vector autoregression (VAR) analysis. The purpose of IRF is to find the response of one variable to a shock or impulse in one of the other variables in the model. These functions are particularly useful to the policy makers to understand the effects of a shock in policy variables. In generating impulse response functions, a shock is given to the impulse variable in period one, in order to generate an impact or response in the dependent variable of interest.

For the analysis in this chapter, a time period of eight has been chosen to generate the IRFs. While looking at the IRF s generated from applying basic VAR on the model of government consumption (shown in Fig. 7.3), it was found that, in the short run, real GDP decreases responding to a change in government consumption However, once it recovers from the said shock, real GDP remains stable in the long run. Similarly, Fig. 7.4 reveals that after an immediate increase in response to a change in government tax revenue, real GDP converges back to its long-run equilibrium path.

7.5 Conclusion and Policy Recommendations

The study employs VECM and Johansen cointegration technique to study the effectiveness of fiscal policy instruments on economic growth of Bangladesh in the long run and short run using time series data of 1980–2017. The study also uses granger causality test to investigate the direction of long-run causality among the variables of interest and finds that there is bi-directional causality between economic growth and government consumption as well as between economic growth and government tax revenue in the long run. The existence of cointegrating relationship revealed by the Johansen conintegration test indicates that the long-run relationship among the variables is not spurious, but meaningful. Also by looking into the impulse response functions, the study gains valuable insight on short-run dynamics of the model. The IRFs reveal that although, in the short run, real GDP decreases responding to an impulse in government consumption and increases responding to a change in government tax revenue, once it recovers from the said shock, the real GDP remains stable in the long run. Finally, as portrayed by the VECM results, there is

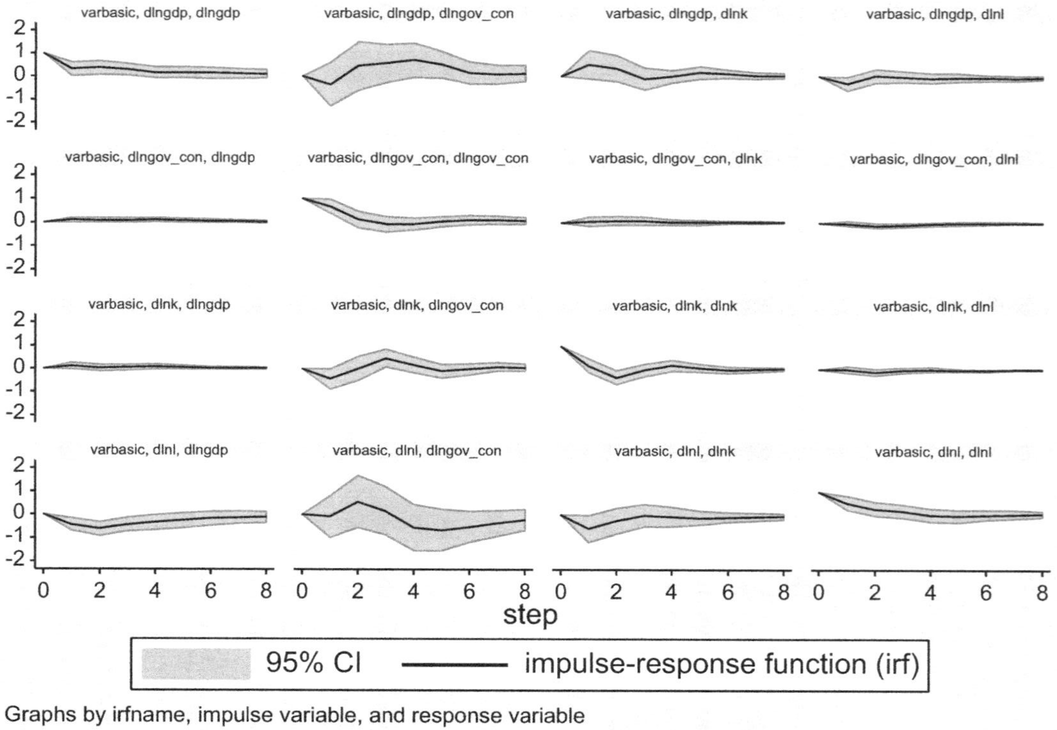

Fig. 7.3 Impulse response function (IRF) showing the impact of a shock on government consumption on real GDP growth rate

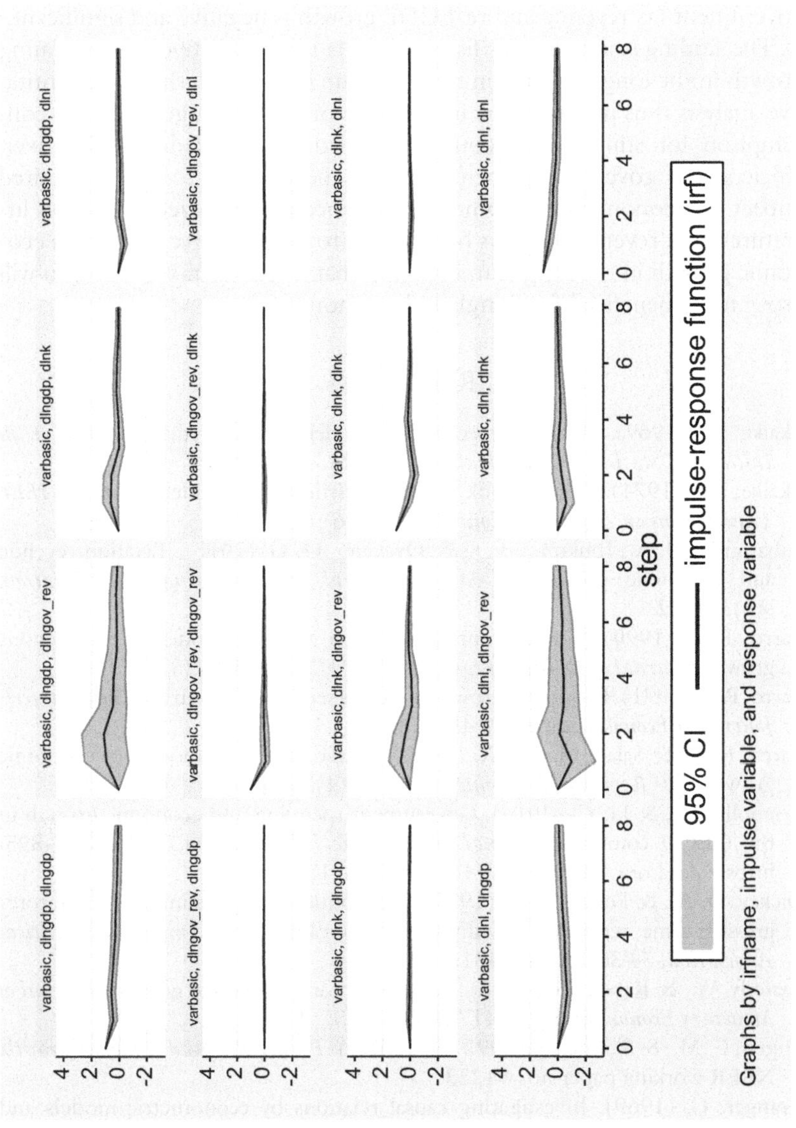

Fig. 7.4 Impulse response function (IRF) showing the impact of a shock on government tax revenue on real GDP growth rate

negative and insignificant relationship between government consumption and real GDP growth in the short run, while that relationship between government tax revenue and real GDP growth is negative and significant.

The findings suggest that fiscal policy is more effective in stimulating growth in the long run than in the short run in Bangladesh. The quantitative analysis thus points to the importance of increasing government consumption for stimulating economic growth in Bangladesh. Moreover, efficiency of government spending must be ensured to obtain desired impact on economic development, as has been emphasized in various literatures. Tax revenue also has been found to have positive impact on economic growth in the long run, implying that increased tax-GDP ratio will prove to be beneficial for Bangladesh economy.

References

Akaike, H. (1969). Fitting autoregressive models for prediction. *Annals of the Institute of Statistical Mathematics, 21*(1), 243–247.

Akaike, H. (1974). A new look at the statistical model identification. *IEEE Transactions on Autometic Control, AC-19*(6), 716–723.

Babatunde, O. A., Ibukun, A. O., & Oyeyemi, O. G. (2017). Taxation revenue and economic growth in Africa. *Journal of Accounting and Taxation, 9*(2), 11–22.

Barro, R. J. (1990). Governemnt spending in a simple model of endogenous growth. *Journal of Political Economy, 98*(5PT 2), S103–S125.

Barro, R. J. (1991). Economic growth in a cross section of countries. *The Quarterly Journal of Economics., 106*(2), 407–443.

Barro, R. J., & Sala-I-Martin, X. (1992). Public finance in models of economic growth. *The Review of Economic Studies, 59*(4), 645–661.

Connolly, M., & Li, C. (2016). Government spending and economic growth in the OECD countries. *Journal of Economic Policy Reform, 19*(4), 386–395. https://doi.org/10.1080/17487870.2016.1213168.

Dickey, D. A., & Fuller, W. A. (1979). Distribution of the estimators for autoregressive time series with a unit root. *Journal of the American Statistical Association, 74*(366a), 427–431.

Easterly, W., & Rebelo, S. (1993). Fiscal policy and economic growth. *Journal of Monetary Economics, 32*(3), 417–458.

Engen, E. M., & Skinner, J. (1992, December). *Fiscal policy and economic growth.* NBER working paper no. w4223.

Granger, C. (1969). Investigating causal relations by econometric models and cross-spectral methods. *Econometrica, 37*(3), 424–438.

Hannan, E. J., & Quinn, B. G. (1979). The determiantion of the order of an autoregression. *Journal of the Royal Statistical Society, Series B, 41*(2), 190–195.

Johansen, S. (1988). Statistical analysis of cointegration vectors. *Journal of Economic Dynamics and Control, 12*(2–3), 231–254.

Johansen, S., & Juselius, K. (1990). Maximum likelihood estimation and inference on cointegration with applications to demand for money. *Oxford Bulletin of Economics and Statistics, 52*(2), 169–210.

Keynes, J. M. (1936). *The general theory of employment, interest and money*. London: Macmillan.

Kneller, R., Bleaney, M. F., & Gemmell, N. (1999). Fiscal policy and growth: Evidence from OECD countries. *Journal of Public Economics, 74*(2), 171–190.

Kormendi, R. C., & Meguire, P. G. (1985). Macroeconomic determinants of growth. *Journal of Monetary Economics, 16*(2), 141–163.

Kyissima, K. H., Pacific, Y. K., & Ramadhan, A. A. (2017). Government expenditure and economic growth in Tanzania: A time series analysis. *International Journal of Development and Economic Sustainability, 5*(1), 11–22.

Landau, D. (1983). Governemnt expenditure and economic growth: A cross country study. *Southern Economic Journal, 49*(3), 783–792.

Liew, V. K.-S. (2004). Which lag length selection criteria should we employ? *Economics Bulletin, 3*(33), 1–9.

Ojong, C. M., Anthony, O., & Arikpo, O. F. (2016). The impact of tax revenue on economic growth: Evidence from Nigeria. *IOSR Journal of Economics and Finance, 7*(1), 32–38.

Phillips, P. C., & Perron, P. (1988). Testing for a unit root in time series regression. *Biometrika, 75*(2), 335–346.

Ram, R. (1986). Government size and economic growth: A new framework and some evidence from cross-section and time-series data. *American Economic Review, 76*(1), 191–203.

Schwarz, G. (1978). Estimating the demension of a model. *Annals of Statistics, 6*(2), 461–464.

Wagner, A. (1883). Three extracts on public finance. In R. A. Musgrave & A. T. Peacock (Eds.), *Classics in the theory of public fiannce* (pp. 1–15). London: Macmillan.

CHAPTER 8

Financing Infrastructure Investment Through Spillover Tax Revenue Sharing: Evidence from Some Asian Countries

Naoyuki Yoshino, Monzur Hossain, N. Hendriyetty, and Solani Lakhia

8.1 Introduction

Infrastructure investment is the key to achieve higher economic growth. Asia remains the engine of the global economy, but maintaining the region's economic vibrancy will require, among others, more investments in infrastructures (the International Monetary Fund's (IMF) latest "Regional Economic Outlook: Asia and the Pacific", 2019). The Asian region

N. Yoshino (✉)
Asian Development Bank Institute (ADBI), Tokyo, Japan

Keio University, Tokyo, Japan
e-mail: nyoshino@adbi.org; yoshino@econ.keio.ac.jp

M. Hossain
Bangladesh Institute of Development Studies (BIDS), Dhaka, Bangladesh

N. Hendriyetty • S. Lakhia
Asian Development Bank Institute (ADBI), Tokyo, Japan
e-mail: nhendriyetty@adbi.org

M. Hossain (ed.), *Bangladesh's Macroeconomic Policy*,
https://doi.org/10.1007/978-981-15-1244-5_8

witnessed growth at 5.6 percent in 2018 and 5.4 percent in 2019. Bangladesh is not an exception.

Bangladesh is one of the fastest growing economies in Asia. The Bangladesh economy has been growing at an impressive rate of over 6 percent since the last decade and her progress in attaining several Millennium Development Goals (MDGs) and Sustainable Development Goals (SDGs) especially in social sectors was markedly better than the neighboring countries, including India. Given the accelerated pace of growth against the backdrop of various economic reforms undertaken in the 1990s onward, the importance of aid in Bangladesh's development process has decreased to a great extent. The declining trend of aid in Bangladesh is consistent with the global scenario. For example, as a percentage of gross national income (GNI), official development assistance (ODA) has been dwindling in developing South Asia, especially in India, Pakistan, Bangladesh and Sri Lanka. The declining trend of aid is thus attributable to the improved economic performance of Bangladesh, which is evident from her achievement of the lower middle income status in 2015, and subsequent graduation target from the least developed country (LDC) status by 2024. In the context of declining aid, the country is in dire need of financial resources to meet the infrastructure investment demand (see Table 8.8 in appendix).

For achieving the middle income status and subsequent success in SDG implementation, there has been a growing demand for development investment, and therefore mobilization of resources and broadening the resource base are important agenda for the Government of Bangladesh. For this purpose, the country needs a set of clear, systematic, predictable and well-coordinated broad-based strategies to ensure a sustainable resource base for implementing development programs in Bangladesh (Hossain 2017).

The Seventh Five Year Plan (SFYP) of Bangladesh presents the overall financial estimates, particularly investment requirements, to achieve the objectives of the plan. The plan (GoB 2016) envisions a large expansion in public investment, especially from domestic sources, and a similarly ambitious expansion in private investment. While 78 percent of the total financing is estimated to be mobilized from the private sector, the remaining 22 percent will be financed from public sources. Overall, gross investments are set to increase by 32 percent of gross domestic product (GDP) on average per annum during the SFYP period, of which 24.7 percent is expected to come from private sector and 7.3 percent from public sector. While the current public sector investment is about 7 percent of GDP (which is very close to the target), the main challenge is to increase private sector investment, which has been stalled at about 22 percent of GDP for quite a long time.

Among the projected resource requirements for implementing the Plan, 90 percent of the total financing requirements is expected to be met from domestic sources and the remaining 10 percent from external sources. Table 8.8 in appendix depicts several quantitative investment targets that require strong resource mobilization policies for the financing of further development. With regard to domestic resources, an ambitious growth of total government revenues has been projected from the existing 10.7 percent to 16.1 percent of GDP (i.e. from Tk. 1.690 to Tk. 4.728 trillion in 2020). Tax revenue is predicted to achieve 14.1 percent of GDP in the plan from the previous 9.3 percent, which will require to increase the tax revenue three-fold from Tk. 1.406 trillion to Tk. 4.052 trillion. With regard to private resource acquisition from external sources, foreign direct investment (FDI) growth has also been projected to a significant rise, from 0.9 percent to 3 percent of GDP, leading to a six-fold increase from US$1.7 billion to US$ 9.6 billion. A significant surge in private sector infrastructure investment is expected from 0.2 percent to 1 percent of GDP in Public-Private Partnerships (PPPs). It is thus important for the government to articulate proper policies and strategies in order to achieve these challenging targets.

This chapter makes an attempt to identify the ways to encourage more domestic private investments in infrastructure with particular focus on the use of spillover tax revenue. Sharing spillover revenue with private investors is expected to increase the rate of return of the investors and considering various positive externalities, this approach is expected to create a win-win environment for both the government and private investors (Yoshino, Nakahigashi and Pontines, 2017). Considering cost reduction in infrastructure investment as another key for success, this chapter also proposes to use land trust for acquisition of land from landowners to minimize the cost and delay in implementation of infrastructure projects.

The chapter is organized as follows. Section 8.2 reviews the need for infrastructure in Bangladesh and other Asian countries, while Sect. 8.3 reviews private savings aspects in Asian countries. Section 8.4 discusses spillover benefits of infrastructure investments, and Sect. 8.5 explains how to estimate spillover benefits. Section 8.6 shows the ways of measuring and sharing spillover revenues. Section 8.7 discusses some innovative financing approaches available in Asia, and Sect. 8.8 concludes the chapter.

8.2 Infrastructure Needs in Bangladesh and Asia

8.2.1 Infrastructure Needs in Bangladesh

Bangladesh is ranked 109th with regard to infrastructure quality (WEF 2018). For maintaining the impressive growth of over 7% for a long time, the country needs to allocate more resources for infrastructure investments. Based on the simple Harrod-Dommer model exercise, the country needs to achieve investment at a rate of about 35 percent of GDP to achieve more than 8 percent GDP growth in the coming years. The government undertook various infrastructure mega projects in the areas of Energy, Telecommunication, Transport Airport, Transport Ports, Transport Rail, Transport Road and Water. The investment plan and financing need are shown in Table 8.1.

Table 8.1 Sector-wise investment need in Bangladesh

Sector	*Investment plan*	*Financing need*
Power sector	Targeted electricity production within *2024*: 30,000 MW Length of main grid: 120,000 km Expected new distribution line: 8000 km	US$6–7 billion investment is required in renewable energy ~US$60 billion investment is required in technology
Roads infrastructure	Average speed: 21–27 km/h Annual losses due to inefficiency in road transport: >US$3 billion	Investment required in this sector: ~US$136 billion
Economic zones	Proposed number of economic zones under *BEZA* (*Bangladesh Economic Zones Authority*): 100 Expected jobs to be supported under this capacity: 10 million Expected amount of export earnings through economic zones: US$40 billion	Investment required in economic zones: ~US$25 billion
Water	400 billion liters of water is wasted every year <15 percent of people have access to clean drinking water	~US$62 billion investment is required in this sector

Source: Werner (2018)

Table 8.2 Estimated infrastructure needs in Asia

	Baseline total (US$ in billion)	*Percent of GDP*	*Climate adjusted (US$ in billion)*	*Percent of GDP*
Central Asia	33	6.8	38	7.8
East Asia	919	4.5	1071	5.2
South Asia	365	7.6	423	8.8
Southeast Asia	184	5.0	210	5.7
The Pacific	2.8	8.2	3.1	9.1
Asia and Pacific	1503	5.1	1744	5.9

Source: Asian Development Bank (2017)

8.2.2 Infrastructure Needs in Growing Asia

There are huge infrastructure needs in many Asian countries. If they were financed by public money alone, huge budget deficits would arise and fiscal sustainability would be lost. An estimate of climate-adjusted infrastructure investment needs suggests that South Asia needs investment equivalent to about 9 percent of its GDP, whereas Southeast Asia needs the same about 6 percent of its GDP (Table 8.2). Private sector financing will, thus, be the key to satisfy the huge demand in infrastructure investment in developing countries, such as in Bangladesh.

If foreign private investors supplied finance for infrastructure investment, several risks, such as exchange rate risks and political uncertainties would be associated with it in the future. Therefore, instead of foreign companies, the government has to rely on domestic infrastructure companies for investments and eventually government would have to take over their losses for compensation. This type of financing in the form of PPP has not been found to be very successful in Bangladesh, considering a meagre investment of 0.2 percent of GDP under the approach. Therefore, alternative approaches for financing infrastructure investments need to be explored.

8.3 Private Savings for Private Investments: Way Forward

In 1997, the Asian financial crisis hit Korea, Thailand, Indonesia and several other Asian countries. In those days, domestic savings were not so large in many Asian countries. Foreign investors came to the Asian region for a higher rate of return and created an economic bubble in Asia. The bubble was burst because of sudden capital outflows from Asia, which created a big financial shock in the Asian region. However, in recent years, domestic savings in Asia have increased thanks to steady economic growth in the Asian region (Table 8.3). However, investment-savings gap for most of the countries except Singapore is not enough to cater to the needs of additional investment financing.

Various kinds of savings instruments are available in the Asian region. The financial sector of most of the Asian countries are dominated by banks. Bank deposits are the main means of domestic savings in Asia. Considering very low exposure to insurance, pension funds, mutual funds, and so on, Asia must strive for developing these long-term financial instruments in order to provide long-term security to the people. Further, these funds will pave the way for mobilizing long-term finance for infrastructure investments.

A few examples of Japanese innovative approaches in mobilizing insurance might be worth noting here. Right after World War II, there were many widows who lost their husband during the war in Japan. The government employed them as sales ladies for life insurance. They visited companies and houses to ask people to prepare for their retirement and educate them about the importance of life insurance. In that way, Japan achieved one of the biggest shares of insurance in households' savings.

Post offices started to collect deposits and postal life insurance. Private insurance companies focused more on large cities and big companies. Since agricultural farmers and employees in small businesses were left behind, post office insurance provided life insurance products for those who were not covered by private insurance companies.

Table 8.3 Average domestic savings and investment rate in Asia

	Savings rate/GDP (%)			*Investment rate/GDP (%)*		
Country	*2012*	*2015*	*2017*	*2012*	*2015*	*2017*
China	49.7	47.5	46.0	47.2	44.7	44.6
Malaysia	30.9	28.2	28.5	25.7	25.1	25.6
Singapore	46.8	43.5	44.5	29.9	26.5	28.5
Thailand	27.6	30.4	33.9	28.0	22.4	22.8
Bangladesh	29.9	29.0	29.6	28.3	28.9	30.5

Source: IMF, World Economic Outlook Database, World Development Indicators

Note: Savings rate = gross national saving/GDP; investment rate = gross capital formation/GDP

However, bank deposits are dominant in many Asian countries including Bangladesh in the absence of strong pension and insurance funds (Fig. 8.1). Long-term savings, such as insurance and pension funds, must be promoted as these long-term savings would be the most suitable financing sources for infrastructure investment (Fig. 8.2).

However, private investors are usually discouraged due to the low rate of return from infrastructure investments. Further, various risks are associated with infrastructure investments. Most of the discussion surrounding infrastructure investments was focused on (i) how to share the risks between the government and the private sector, and (ii) how to reduce

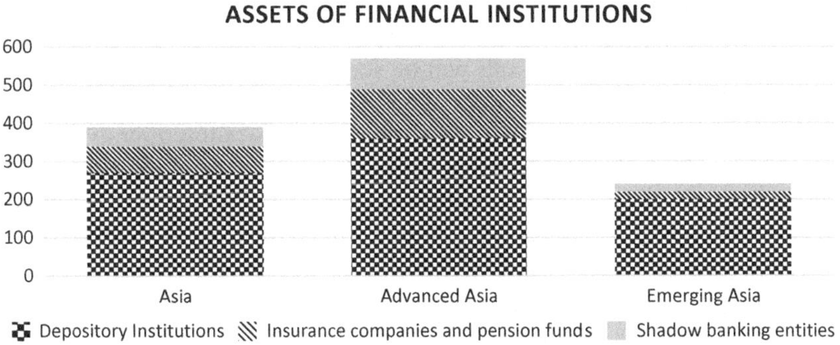

Fig. 8.1 Dominance of bank deposits in Asian regions and a small share of insurance in Asia. (Source: IMF)

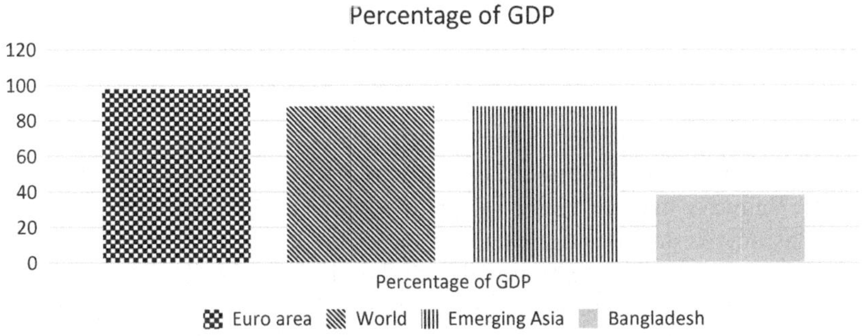

Fig. 8.2 Bank's provision of domestic credit to the private sector (2016). (Source: World Bank)

various risks associated with infrastructure investment. Therefore, various stimuli are needed to encourage private investors to participate in public infrastructure projects.

8.4 Spillover Benefits of Infrastructure Investments

This section discusses ways to increase the rate of return on infrastructure investment to attract long-term investors. Good infrastructure creates huge spillover effects in any region. For example, new roads will make it possible for farmers to ship their products at much cheaper costs and much faster. New railways will bring business into the region and result in faster commutes to large cities. New apartments will be constructed. New restaurants and shopping malls will be started. New employment will be generated along new railway lines. Therefore, property tax, corporate tax, individual income tax and sales tax revenues will rise subsequently.

In the past, in Japan and other selected countries, in addition to user charges, land capture was an important source of revenues in the railway sector. When a new railway was planned to be constructed, railway companies used to purchase the land from farmers along the planned railway. The railway companies used to make money by selling those land to individuals for housing or commercial businesses once the railway was constructed. Similar methods were used in the US when their railways were in the process of expansion to the west in the seventeenth century.

However, the land capture brings only one-time gain to the railway companies. The railway company purchases the land before the railway is constructed and sells it for housing, commercial buildings, and so on, after the railway is constructed. Thus, railway companies do not receive continuous income flows from the land.

It is important to have continuous inflow of revenues for infrastructure developers and investors in infrastructure. In addition to user charges, spillover tax revenues from infrastructure could be a good source of revenues. Railways make it easier for people to have access to cities. Various establishments and businesses are expected to be created along the railways, which will ultimately contribute to spillover revenues.

In the past, all these tax revenues were collected by the government (either by the local government or by the central government) and they were not returned to infrastructure investors. However, these spillover tax

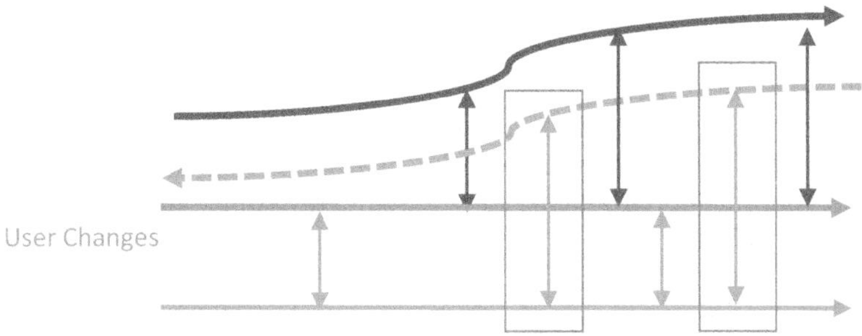

Fig. 8.3 Return in infrastructure

revenues are obtained due to the development of new infrastructure such as railways, roads, water supply, and so on.

If infrastructure companies rely only on user charges, as is shown in Fig. 8.3, their return would be much lower as shown in green line. However, it is possible to increase their rate of return if a portion of spillover revenues is shared among the investors.

Private participation in infrastructure has been advocated from the time when "PFIs (private financial initiatives)" came into existence in the UK. However, most of the discussions were on how to mitigate risks and how to share the risks associated with infrastructure investment. There was not much discussion on how to increase the rate of return for a long period of time. Spillover tax revenues can be a continuous source of a rising rate of return from infrastructure investments.

Water supply will create huge spillover effects in the region. New apartments can be constructed. New commercial buildings can be set up. This will provide huge development along the water supply. If water supply were to be financed by private investors, they will expect a reasonable rate of return to secure their investment. If all the revenues from infrastructure investments were received as user charges, water prices would go up. However, water is a basic amenity for everybody. A water company cannot raise its price. However, private investors in water supply require a high rate of return. There are internal conflicts between users and investors in infrastructure.

Roads contribute to the development of new residential areas, and farmers can sell their products much more quickly and at lower costs to cities. However, there were no revenues from regular roads. In the past, government was the only body that could finance road construction since there were no revenues. If government spends so much money on road construction, other government spending must be cut, or budget deficits will rise. Fiscal sustainability of the government would be jeopardized. Ordinary roads do not generate any such income; however, if a highway is developed across regions, it would contribute to huge spillover economic development, and consequently contribute to large spillover tax revenues.

8.5 Estimates of Spillover Effects

This section discusses the methods of estimates of spillover effects. Yoshino and Abidhadjaev (2017) developed a method to compute spillover effects from infrastructure investments. The three cases include a railway in Uzbekistan, a high-speed railway in Kyushu island of Japan and a highway in Manila city (Yoshino et al. 2018a, b). All of these estimates were obtained by using the difference-in-difference method.

In the case of Uzbekistan's railway, the economic growth in the non-affected region rose from 8.3 percent to 8.5 percent, indicating only 0.2 percent growth. On the other hand, the region along the railway (affected region) witnessed a 2.2 percent GDP growth from 7.2 percent to 9.4 percent. The two regions exhibit a 2.0 percent difference in their economic growth. In other words, as shown in Table 8.4, the railway contributed to a 2.0 percent increase in GDP growth because of its spillover effects compared to other regions, which resulted in huge tax revenues to the government. A detailed analysis can be found in Yoshino and Abidhadjaev (2017).

In the case of the highway in Manila city, the three cities along the highway received three times higher tax revenues after four years of operation (Yoshino and Pontines 2015). Tax revenues in Batangas city went up to 1209.61 million Peso compared to the period before the construction of highway, as shown in Table 8.5.

For the case of high-speed railway in Japan, corporate tax, income tax and other tax revenues (including property tax revenues) were compared in three periods, namely, (i) the construction period, (ii) the operation period without good connectivity, and (iii) the operation period with good connectivity to Osaka and Tokyo. Total tax revenues, personal income tax revenues, corporate tax revenues and other tax revenues (including property tax revenues) were compared for three different periods. When the construction started, many speculators who antici-

Table 8.4 Numerical estimation of the difference in difference coefficient using regional data for Uzbekistan, 2005–2008 and 2009–2012

Region group	*Outcome*	*Pre-railway period*	*Post-railway period*	*Difference*
Non-affected group	Average GDP growth rate (percent)	8.3	8.5	0.2
Affected group	Average GDP growth rate (percent)	7.2	9.4	2.2
Difference				2.0

Source: Yoshino and Abidhadjaev (2017)

Notes: The affected group includes the regions of Samarkand, Surkhandarya, Tashkent and the Republic of Karakalpakstan. The rest of the observations are included in the non-affected group
GDP-gross domestic product

Table 8.5 Calculated increase in business tax revenues for the beneficiary group relative to non-beneficiary group (Peso in million)

Years	T−*2*	T−*1*	T	T+*1*	T+*2*	T+*3*	T+*4*
Lipa City	134.36	173.50	249.70	184.47	191.81	257.35	371.93
Ibaan	5.84	7.04	7.97	6.80	5.46	10.05	12.94
Batangas City	490.90	622.65	652.83	637.83	599.49	742.28	1209.61

Source: Yoshino and Pontines (2015)

pated rising property values started to purchase the land along the high-speed railways. Property tax revenues went up significantly. Construction companies engage many workers in constructions, which contributed to rise of income of the workers. As a result, personal income tax revenues and corporate tax revenues also have increased. However, during the operation period of no connectivity with large cities of Osaka and Tokyo, personal income tax revenues and corporate tax revenues went down compared to the period of construction. However, the good connectivity with Osaka and Tokyo brought businesses and passengers into the region, which has significantly increased corporate income and individual income taxes in the region. Property tax revenues kept on rising due to expected increase in property values resulting from speculation, as is shown in Fig. 8.4.

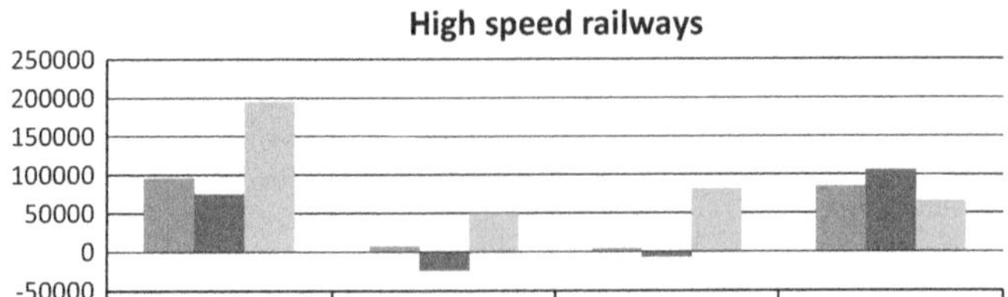

	ΔTotal Tax	ΔPersonal Income Tax	ΔCorporate Tax	ΔOther Taxes
Construction (1991-2003)	94896	7447	3435	84012
Operation 1 (2004-2010)	75131	-23843	-6883	105858
Operation 2 (2011-2013)	194790	49860	80998	65102

Fig. 8.4 Connectivity increased tax revenue. (Source: Yoshino and Abidhadjaev 2017)

8.6 Measuring Spillover Effects and Sharing the Revenues

8.6.1 Measuring Spillover Benefits

A dummy variable was introduced before the infrastructure was constructed and after the operation had been started by taking the difference of the tax revenues between two regions. One region was along the infrastructure and another region was the one where there was no impact of infrastructure investment. The example is given in Table 8.4. Difference in GDP or difference in tax revenues was statistically estimated in Yoshino and Abidhadjaev (2016a, b, 2017), and Yoshino, Helble and Abidhadjaev (2018a). However, these econometric estimations are time-consuming and the choice of the region, selection of explanatory variables, and so on, is not easy in practice.

The spillover effects therefore can be simply estimated using the difference-in-difference method defined as follows (Source: Yoshino and Abidhadjaev 2017) (Fig. 8.5).

1. Compute the national average growth rate of tax revenues for each tax item, such as corporate tax, personal income tax, property tax, sales tax, and so on.
2. Compute the growth rate of each tax revenue along the newly constructed infrastructures such as road, highways, railways, water supply, and so on.

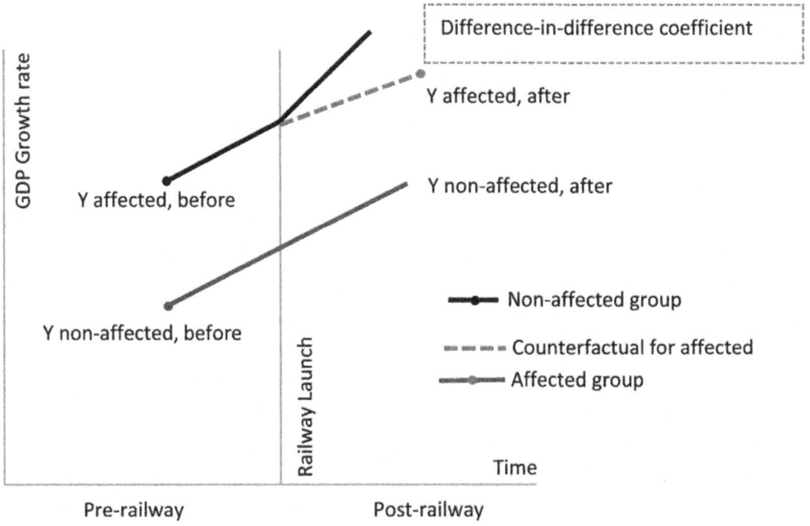

Fig. 8.5 Spillover effects

3. Take the difference between (2) and (1) by defining the difference as spillover effects. But these exercise has to be done for baseline and endline periods.

Infrastructure investment is the key to generate higher tax revenues for the government. The proposed method here argues that the local and central governments do not need to deduct their existing tax revenues earnings; they can only share a part of the incremental tax revenues with private investors who invested in the infrastructure. The proposed methods of returning the spillover tax revenues will encourage development of rural regions and create an ownership among the investors. In Bangladesh, many infrastructure investments are financed by the central government, which generates huge spillover tax revenues. However, if tax zones are segregated in a way to collect tax revenues across various mega infrastructures, it is possible to estimate spillover tax revenues generated from those projects, which can later be shared with the investors as part of their return.

8.6.2 *Sharing Spillover Revenues*

How much percent of spillover tax revenues should be returned to private investors? An accurate share between the government and the private sector can be determined from theory. The translog production function will give us the distinction between direct effects and indirect effects (= spillover effects).

Table 8.6 shows the estimates of spillover effects of infrastructure investment in the case of Japan (Nakahigashi and Yoshino 2016). The share of spillover effects through inducing private capital and employments in Japan was between 66.1 and 68.9 percent. Therefore, in the case of Japan, the government should retain 31.1–33.9 percent of spillover tax revenues and the private investors should be allocated the rest 66.1–68.9 percent of spillover tax revenues. Accurately speaking, the share between public sector and private sector has to be computed in each case of investments. However, in practice, it is not easy to run translog production function for every projects, as shown in Table 8.6. Therefore, a simple way would be to share the spillover tax revenues, say 50 percent of spillover tax revenue, among the private investors. In case of multiple projects implementing at a similar time, the spillover revenue can be shared according to their proportion of investments.

It is expected that sharing spillover revenue among the private investors for a stipulated period will increase the rate of return for the investors, which would be much higher than the one that they receive under the current system, such as PPP or Build-Operate-Transfer (BOT). The share

Table 8.6 Japanese macroeconomic estimates of spillover effects

Time period	*1956–60*	*1966–70*	*1976–80*	*1986–90*	*1996–2000*	*2006–10*
Direct effect of infrastructure investment	0.696	0.638	0.359	0.215	0.135	0.108
Spillover effect through private capital (Kp)	0.452	0.493	0.270	0.174	0.110	0.085
Spillover effect through employment (L)	1.071	0.814	0.448	0.247	0.154	0.125
Spillover effects of infrastructure investment (%)	68.644	67.210	66.691	66.222	66.094	66.139

Source: Nakahigashi and Yoshino (2016)

of spillover tax revenues will push both private investors and government to work hard to develop the region along each infrastructure.

8.6.3 Ways to Accelerate Spillover Effects by Infrastructure

The impact of education infrastructure project could generate even bigger spillover effects for the stakeholders, such as investors, government, landowners, farmers, businessmen both from the small and medium enterprises (SMEs) and from start-ups. Yoshino and Abidhadjaev (2016a, b) show that secondary school education and university education together with infrastructure investments contribute toward higher GDP in the region as estimated by use of data from 40 countries (Table 8.7).

Technological progress and innovations are very important in the education system, especially in engineering education. Traditionally, in order to get the best education, youngsters have to attend good schools (it is very competitive to enter such schools in Asian countries). With the expansion and advancement of technology, it is rather convenient for youngsters and even for others to listen to the best lectures and learn from best teachers through the internet and smartphones from anywhere they live. It is important for governments to provide technology facilities and encourage students and school leavers to make use of these facilities for personal growth.

Table 8.7 Positive spillover effects by good education together with infrastructure investments (secondary school and university education)

Dependent variable: log difference GDP per capita in 1991–2010			
Regression number	REG. 1	REG. 2	REG. 3
Variables	Coef.	Coef.	Coef.
lnY_1991	−0.06 (−0.54)	−0.14 (−1.35)	−0.14 (−1.38)
ln(*n*+g+*d*)	−3.09 (−0.59)	−5.75 (−1.23)	−4.36 (−0.77)
ln(*Kg*)	0.23 (1.17)	0.31 (2.00)	0.53 (3.30)
ln(Sec)			0.00 (0.46)
ln(*Kg*)*ln(Sec)	0.20 (1.59)		
ln(UNI)			0.21 (2.07)
ln(*Kg*)*ln(Uni)		0.24 (2.76)	
Constant	−0.28 (−0.33)	0.56 (0.69)	0.48 (0.57)
Number of observations	*44*	*44*	*44*
R-squared	*0.21*	*0.3*	*0.3*
F-statistic	*2.62*	*4.14*	*3.29*

Source: Yoshino and Abidhadjaev (2016a, b)

The relation of education and technology to the region's economic growth could be expressed in the production function as *Y* = *A* F(*Kp*, *L*, *Kg*), where *Y* = regional *GDP*, *A* = technological progress, *Kp* = private capital, *L* = labor, *Kg* = infrastructure. If technological progress (*A*) goes on, the regional output which is created by infrastructure investment will further rise. Human capital development (*L*) will enhance regional output resulting from spillover effects.

Theoretically, over time, the function would be as follows:

$$Y_t = AF\left(K_{pt}, L_t, K_{gt}\right) \tag{8.1}$$

$$Y_{t+1} = AF\left(K_{p.t+1}, L_{t+1}, K_{gt}\right) \tag{8.2}$$

$$Y_{t+n} = AF\left(K_{p.t+n}, L_{t+n}, K_{gt}\right) \tag{8.3}$$

* * *

Now changes in *Y* with respect to changes in public infrastructure (*Kg*) over time *t* are as follows:

$$\frac{dY_{t+n}}{dKg_t} = A.\frac{\partial F}{\partial K_{pt}}.\frac{\partial K_{p.t+n}}{\partial K_{gt}} + A.\frac{\partial F}{\partial L_{t+n}}.\frac{\partial L_{t+n}}{\partial k_{gt}} + A\frac{\partial F}{\partial K_{gt}} \tag{8.4}$$

where $A.\frac{\partial F}{\partial K_{pt}}.\frac{\partial K_{p.t+n}}{\partial K_{gt}} + A.\frac{\partial F}{\partial L_{t+n}}.\frac{\partial L_{t+n}}{\partial k_{gt}}$ represents the spillover effects of investment in a particular area.

Therefore, this chapter would suggest that Asian countries start internet education for all levels from secondary to university, including engineering education. Professors and lecturers can deliver lectures through internet, which can be broadcast all over the country afterward. This technique will benefit students and people in regions and villages. People can learn basic technical skills, languages and gain knowledge on many aspects of industries and vocations. There are many other innovative ways by which a government can generate significant spillover benefits in a cost-effective manner.

8.7 Some Innovative Approaches to Finance Infrastructure Investments

8.7.1 Hometown Trust Funds to Promote SMEs and Start-Up Businesses

At this juncture, the authorities should think beyond building infrastructure. Even if the infrastructure is available, most SMEs find it difficult to receive financial support for their start-ups. Banks and financial institutions are often reluctant to lend money to start-ups, because it is very risky. To address SMEs financing woes, Bangladesh can take a lesson from Japan's "hometown investment trust funds." Some 20 years ago, Japan was able to create such funds, which helped Japan to create a generation of new entrepreneurs afterwards.

These funds had two primary objectives: one, to provide money for start-ups, especially for women who wanted to start their own businesses such as restaurants and shops; two, to start internet-based selling portals where the villagers could sell their products to markets outside their villages. Through internet marketing, they have been able to capture a large clientele around the country, thanks to well-built infrastructure that allowed them to deliver goods and products without much delay.

8.7.2 Land Trust for Smoothening Land Acquisition

Acquisition of lands for development projects has been a major barrier in many Asian countries including Bangladesh. Hossain and Yoshino (2018) showed that there is ample scope for implementing land trust in Bangladesh particularly in the areas of real estate management in cities, rebuilding old-town areas, delta plan management, which will reduce the prices of land, ensure sustainable land management as well as attract private investments. Landowners are usually reluctant to give their lands for development projects. We suggest setting up a land trust which can bring a solution for this. The land trust was created in Japan many years ago and, accordingly, the owners can retain their ownership of land but can lease the land (for 99 years, for example) for constructing building or other infrastructures. By doing this, the owner can ensure a reasonable flow of income over the years (Fig. 8.6).

Under the land trust method, landowners entrust their land to trust banks and the trust banks manage the land. For instance, in the case of agricultural land, the trust bank aids young farmers who wish to farm the

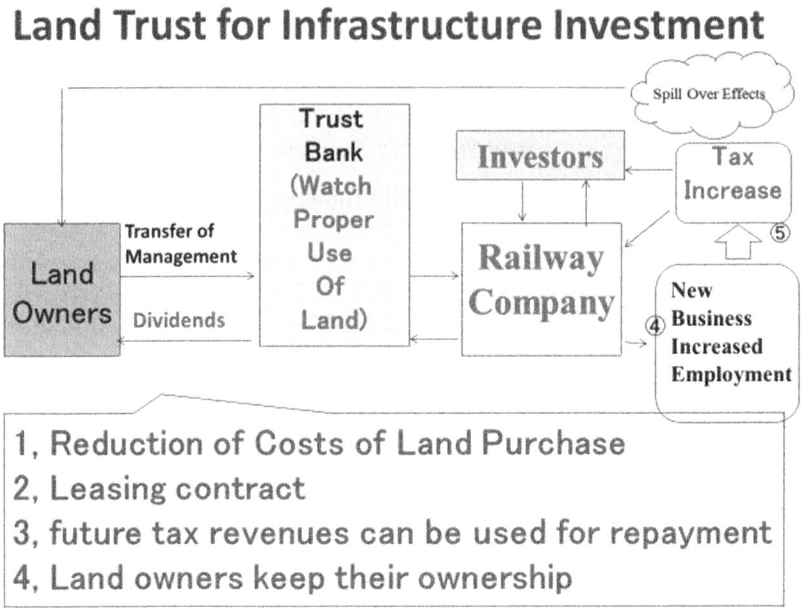

Fig. 8.6 Spillover benefits from land trust

large consolidated land to use it and increase the utility. The landowners receive part of the profit as dividends. The consolidation of land leads to higher profits for landowners. The proposed framework allows for usage rights allowing owners to maintain their ownership right whilst increasing their profit by leasing land for infrastructure and development projects (Yoshino et al. 2018b).

The practice is to consolidate assets owned by individuals, entrust them to the trust bank and make better use of the assets. It has a similar function to trust of money. Consolidating money to operate more effectively is the same as consolidating assets owned by individuals who are not able to maximize the utility of their assets by themselves or do not have the know-how, therefore entrusting them to the trust bank in order to increase the utility of the assets.

This is one of the best ways for providing usage rights to infrastructure companies and for city planning. Further, the acquisition costs of land will significantly reduce, which will thereby reduce one-time costs of infrastructure developers. They need only to pay for resettlement costs of landowners and can pay an annual rent for 99 years to landowners.

Spillover tax revenues from infrastructure projects can be used to finance these rental payments to landowners.

8.7.3 City Infrastructure

When developing infrastructure, many countries, policymakers, builders and contractors overlook about the city planning aspects. City planning is imperative for construction of sustainable infrastructure. This can ensure positive spillover effects of the infrastructure investment. Traditionally, infrastructure is considered only from a construction perspective. However, it goes much beyond simple construction. It is pertinent to address the capability of the proposed infrastructure to develop the region, cascading the benefits to multiple communities. Such projects should allocate areas or zones for markets, shops, residencies and manufacturing industries. That kind of zoning will help create a good city.

8.7.4 Carbon Tax for Environmental Protection Associated with Infrastructure

Yoshino and Taghizadeh-Hesary (2017) propose to charge tax on CO_2 and other exhaustion gases to promote green finance. Charging tax on CO_2, NOx and other exhaustion gases will reduce pollution in the region. Satellite photos can estimate the amount of gases produced by each infrastructure and its users.

Yoshino and Taghizadeh-Hesary propose how these pollution taxes can be introduced into green infrastructure, which, in turn, will promote investment in green infrastructure. Additional methods should be introduced to reduce bad environmental consequences associated with infrastructure investments.

8.8 Conclusions

There is a huge need of infrastructure investment to facilitate faster growth in Asia, particularly in Bangladesh. This chapter highlighted various options to attract private investors in infrastructure investment, which is in most cases done by the central or local governments. Considering the underdeveloped bond, pension and insurance funds in many Asian countries including Bangladesh, there is a strong need to develop these markets to finance infrastructure investments. Countries should reduce bank dependency, which is costly for financing investments. There is no denying that infrastructure creates huge spillover benefits, and also higher tax revenues. This chapter argues that if spillover tax revenues are shared equally between the government and private investors, private investors will be attracted more to invest in public infrastructures, because this will increase their rate of return on top of user charges. In support of this argument, we draw examples of some infrastructure projects of Japan, Uzbekistan and the Philippines. We also show how to calculate spillover tax revenues and what should be the appropriate percentages to share with private investors.

Apart from spillover revenue sharing argument, in this chapter, we have discussed some innovative financing approaches, such as Japan's hometown investment fund for financing SMEs, land trust approaches for sustainable land management, city infrastructure and carbon tax provision for environmental protection.

In the context of growing Asian economies with shrinking opportunities of financing, market-based financing solutions can solve infrastructure bottlenecks and accelerate growth momentum in Asian countries. Though implementation of the proposed method of sharing spillover revenues involves many operational challenges, it is expected that countries can overcome those challenges with their own initiatives, keeping in mind the positive benefits of infrastructure investments.

Appendix

Table 8.8 Financing of Seventh Five Year Plan investment (FY 2016 prices)

Item: amount in billions	*Total for five years (percent of total)*	*Yearly average*	*Percent of GDP*	*Public (percent of total)*	*Private (percent of total)*
GDP at current prices	–	US$252.0	–	–	–
Total investment	Tk. 31,902.8 (US$409)	US$80.6	32.0	Tk. 7252.3 (US$19.0) (22.7 percent)	Tk. 24,650.5 (US$61.6) (77.3 percent)
Domestic resources	Tk. 28,851.0 (US$370) (90.4 percent)	US$62.2	24.7	Tk. 1277 (US$13.8) (22.0 percent)	Tk. 4493.2 (US$48.) (88.0 percent)
External resources	Tk. 3051.8 (US$39) (9.6 percent)	US$18.4	7.3	Tk. 173.5 (US$5.2) (28.4 percent)	Tk. 436.8 (US$13.2) (71.6 percent)

Source: GoB: Planning Commission, Seventh Five Year Plan, 2015

References

ADB. (2017). *Meeting Asia's infrastructure needs.* Manila: Asian Development Bank. Sourced from: https://doi.org/10.22617/FLS168388-2

GoB. (2016). *7th five year plan.* Ministry of Planning, Government of the People's Republic of Bangladesh.

Hossain, M. (2017). *Identifying strategies and plan of action for resource mobilization.* A report prepared for Economic Relations Division, Ministry of Finance (unpublished).

Hossain, M., & Yoshino, N. (2018, December 10–11). *Sustainable land management in Bangladesh: Operationalizing land trust and delta management policies.* Presented in a conference titled Sustainable land management in Asia: Achieving SDGs, held in Asian Development Bank Institute, Tokyo.

International Monetary Fund. Research Department. *World economic outlook.* International Monetary Fund, various years.

Nakahigashi, M., & Yoshino, N. (2016). Changes in economic effect of infrastructure and financing methods. *Public Policy Review, Ministry of Finance, Policy Research Institute, 12*(1), 47–68.

Werner, W. J. (2018, October). *Infrastructure Bangladesh: Private sector engagement.* Presentation at DCCI on 'Destination Bangladesh: Gateway to growth and development' programme.

Yoshino, N., & Abidhadjaev, U. (2016a). *Impact of infrastructure investment on tax: Estimating spillover effects of the Kyushu high-speed rail Line in Japan on regional tax revenue.* (ADBI Working paper no. 574). Tokyo: Asian Development Bank Institute.

Yoshino, N., & Abidhadjaev, U. (2016b). Explicit and implicit analysis of infrastructure investment: Theoretical framework and empirical evidence. *American Journal of Economics, 6*(4), 189–199.

Yoshino, N., & Abidhadjaev, U. (2017). An impact evaluation of investment in infrastructure: The case of a railway connection in Uzbekistan. *Journal of Asian Economics, 49*, 1–11.

Yoshino, N., & Nakahigashi, M. (2004). The role of infrastructure in economic development. *ICFAI Journal of Managerial Economics, 2*, 7–24.

Yoshino, N., & Pontines, V. (2015). *The "highway effect" on public finance: Case of the STAR highway in the Philippines.* ADBI working paper 549. Tokyo: Asian Development Bank Institute. Available: http://www.adb.org/publications/highway-effect-public-financecase-star-highway-philippines/

Yoshino, N., & Taghizadeh-Hesary, F. (2017). *Alternatives to bank finance: Role of carbon tax and hometown investment trust funds in developing green energy projects in Asia.* ADBI working paper 761. Tokyo: Asian Development Bank Institute. Available: https://www.adb.org/publications/alternatives-bank-finance-role-carbon-tax-and-hometowninvestment-trust-funds

Yoshino, N., Nakahigashi, M., & Pontines, V. (2017). Attract private financing to infrastructure investment by injecting spillover tax revenues. *Nomura Journal of Asian Capital Market, 1*(2), 4–9.

Yoshino, N., Helble, M., & Abidhadjaev, U. (2018a). *Financing infrastructure in Asia and the Pacific: Capturing impacts and new sources.* Asian Development Bank Institute.

Yoshino, N., Paul, S., Sarma, V., & Lakhia, S. (2018b). *Land acquisition and infrastructure development through land trust laws: A policy framework for Asia* (No. 854). ADBI working paper series.

Yoshino, N., Hendriyetty, N. and Lakhia, S. (2019). Quality Infrastructure Investment: Ways to increase the rate of return for infrastructure investments. Policy Brief, T20 Japan Task Force 4: Economic Effects of Infrastructure Investments and Its Financing, Tokyo, 2019.

PART III

International Trade and Finance

CHAPTER 9

Trade Liberalization Policies and Trade Performances in Bangladesh: An Empirical Evaluation

Monzur Hossain

9.1 Introduction

The current impressive trade and economic performances are thought to be the result of various trade policy reforms undertaken over time. Bangladesh started various trade policy reforms in the 1980s, but major efforts were made in the early 1990s. The key objectives of the reforms were to scale down and rationalize tariffs, remove quantitative restrictions (QRs) and eliminate import licensing requirements. At the same time, Bangladesh made attempt to unify exchange rates and allow a more flexible exchange rate system. In 1994, Bangladesh agreed to make current account transactions convertible as part of International Monetary Fund's (IMF's) Article IV consultations. Trade liberalization in Bangladesh was done broadly in three major areas: (i) liberalization of imports through removal of QRs, (ii) reductions in nominal and effective tariffs, and (iii) adoption of a unified and moderately flexible exchange rate regime. The overarching objectives of these policies were to promote growth and employment through industrialization.

M. Hossain (✉)
Bangladesh Institute of Development Studies (BIDS), Dhaka, Bangladesh

M. Hossain (ed.), *Bangladesh's Macroeconomic Policy*,
https://doi.org/10.1007/978-981-15-1244-5_9

The liberalization of imports was done primarily via removal of QRs in phases. Significant progress was made in removing QRs in the 1990s compared with the 1980s. Whereas nearly 26 percent of all HS-4-digit items (here, HS stands for Harmonized Commodity Description and Coding Systems) were subject to QRs in 1990, now only 122 items (or 10 percent of items) covering about 2 percent of imports remain restricted, for trade and non-trade reasons. However, the progress toward increasing liberalization was evident in the Import Policy Order (IPO) of 1995–97 and the subsequent IPO 1997–2002. Overall, since 1990, trade-related QRs have been progressively removed, leaving some 2.2 percent of total HS-4-digit tariff lines (and 0.5 percent of import value) subject to trade-related prohibitions or bans as of 2002. These restrictions are currently limited to only three categories: agricultural products (chicks, eggs, salt), packaging materials and textile.

As a result of liberalization efforts, Bangladesh saw a significant improvement of trade performance, which has become double to a 30 percent of the gross domestic product (GDP) in the 1990s and increased further to about 50 percent in 2015. The growing openness to international trade has brought significant economic gains, notably an expansion of exports strong enough to cover imports and maintain the trade deficit at sustainable levels. Trade liberalization shifted the country from a highly restrictive system focusing on import substitution to a more dynamic, export-oriented system transforming the economy to embark on export-led growth trajectories.

The favorable trade policies helped Bangladesh make a successful transformation in trade composition from agricultural products to commodity products, particularly the ready-made garments (RMG). Import liberalization policies provide easier access to imported inputs that facilitated the growth of some other industries such as plastic, processed food, footwear, chemicals, printing, and so on (Bakht 2001). Still, the share of trade in GDP is not very satisfactory compared to some Southeast Asian countries. The lack of export diversification, problem with trade policy, inadequacy of trade infrastructure, technological innovation and national and international production networks are some of the key reasons behind such retreat.

The relevance of discussion on agricultural trade is of importance in the context of dominant agrarian base of the economy. Import liberalization policies allowed the country to import agricultural inputs more easily with cheaper prices, which has mainly contributed to impressive food grain production, particularly rice production. The striking part of liberalization is that average unweighted nominal protection level in agriculture has been reduced from more than 76 percent in 1992 to 31 percent in 2000 and further to 18.5 percent in 2008. However, the reduction of average weighted protection rate was also noteworthy—they fell from more than 33 percent in 1991 to 12 percent in 1999 and 5.5 percent in 2008. The discussion here suggests that there are still scopes of further liberalization.

In the context of above discussion, the pertinent research questions that emerge are: How have the trade patterns of Bangladesh been, both in terms of composition and volume, changing over time since 1990? Are trade patterns including agricultural trade consistent with trade and exchange rate liberalization policies? Can the impressive trade performances be explained as the outcome of trade liberalization? This chapter aims to address these questions by reviewing trade reform policies in Bangladesh and assessing the impact of such policies on trade performances.

The chapter is organized as follows. After the Introduction, Sect. 9.2 reviews the trade liberalization policies pursued by Bangladesh in different phases since her independence in 1971. Section 9.3 analyzes trade performances of Bangladesh in terms of export and import pattern over time. Section 9.4 assesses the impact of exchange rate liberalization and cash incentive policies on exports. Finally, Sect. 9.5 provides conclusions and policy recommendations.

9.2 Review of Trade Liberalization Policies

In the early decade of independence, Bangladesh followed a restrictive trade regime and an import substitution industrialization strategy. During the decade, trade regime was characterized by high tariffs and QRs on imports. Trade liberalization started at a substantial scale from the middle of the 1980s, but on a partial basis particularly as part of conditionality under the structural adjustment reform programs of the World Bank and the IMF. At that time, reform measures were taken to simplify import procedures, reduce and harmonize tariff rates, remove restrictions on repatriation of profit and income from foreign investment, and so on. The highest customs duty rate was reduced from 350 percent in 1990 to 32.5 percent in 2003 and 25 percent in 2011. At present, QRs are applicable only to non-trade aspects, such as health, environment, culture, national security, and so on. The number of operative tariff slabs was reduced from 24 in the 1980s to 5 in 2010, and the (unweighted) average customs duty rate was reduced from 100 percent in 1985 to 57 percent in 2000 and 15 percent in 2010. Thus, the trade liberalization policies undertaken by the Bangladesh government over the course of time 1972 to 2000 can be described in three phases. The three phases of trade reforms are briefly discussed below.

9.2.1 *Phase-I (1972–1975): Restrictive Trade Regime*

After the independence in 1971, the first Bangladesh government pursued highly restrictive trade and exchange rate policies partly because of uncertainty in various economic and socio-political structure of a new state and lack of capacity in handling liberalized environment. The nature of protection included quantitative restrictions, high tariff rates, and a fixed but overvalued exchange rates. The protectionist trade regime continued till 1976 with a view to controlling import levels and providing protection to domestic industry.

In this protectionist regime, there were provisions for import and export licensing. The government would allocate foreign exchanges on a discretion to importers through a tedious process of import licensing. For exporters, the Export Performance License was issued to use a certain proportion of their export earnings for import purposes through an Import Entitlement Certificate. As the Export Performance License premium was reflected in their exchange earning, there was a *de facto* dual exchange rate in practice.

During this period, most agricultural commodities were on the restricted or banned lists of imports. Some restrictions were imposed on the export of agricultural products and also export duties were applied to some agricultural exports. The liberalization of trade and exchange rate policy, however, was started from the mid-1970s with slightly strengthened institutional capabilities of the country.

9.2.2 *Phase-II (1976–1990): Partially Liberalized Trade Regime*

The progress in trade liberalization slowed down in the 1980s, particularly with respect to reductions in import tariffs. Major reforms in exchange rate policy took place in the 1980s. In mid-1979, Bangladesh adopted a limited flexible exchange rate policy by fixing the taka to a basket of currencies of major trading partners. Earlier, it was fixed to British Pound-Sterling. Import payment procedure was also made flexible at that time. Import payment at the official exchange rate was rapidly reduced, and an increasing proportion of import payments was made at the rate of the secondary exchange market. About 40 percent of all imports were financed out of this source, while the share of secondary exchange market in non-aid imports reached nearly 70 percent at the end of 1989 (Ahmed et al. 2007).

The export licensing system was simplified substantially in 1986 by the introduction of Export Performance Benefit. This allows the beneficiary exporters to directly cash their benefit entitlement at their banks. These policies contributed to the rapid growth of non-traditional exports during the 1980s, as well as a rapid expansion of the secondary wage earners scheme market. A wide range of agricultural commodities benefited from the Export Performance Benefit incentives. However, exports of raw jute were not included in the Benefit scheme and thus suffered directly from the overvalued exchange rate. The secondary exchange market helped narrow down the gap between the official and the wage earners scheme rate. Eventually, the two rates were unified in 1992, which marked the end of the Export Performance Benefit arrangement (Rahman 1992). During this phase of reform, some progress had been made, and thus a window opened up for further liberalization.

9.2.3 *Phase-III (1990s): Liberalized Trade Regime*

9.2.3.1 Import Liberalization Policies

Trade liberalization in the early 1990s caused a substantial decline in tariff rates. Import tariffs and total tax incidence on the import of major agricultural commodities declined sharply during the 1990s and 2000s (Table 9.1). While tariffs (unweighted) for agricultural commodities were declined from 25.5 percent in 2000 to 18.5 percent in 2008, tariffs for industrial commodities declined from 22 percent in 2000 to 13.5 percent in 2008. Duties on capital goods, consumer goods and intermediate goods declined substantially during 2000–2008, while duties on raw materials remained almost the same during the same period. Further, duties on capital goods, consumer goods, intermediate goods and raw materials declined markedly during 2010–2015, while duties on industrial goods remained largely the same during this period. However, during 2010–2015, tariffs (unweighted) for agricultural commodities increased from 19.4 percent to 20.1 percent.

As part of import liberalization, ban or restriction has been withdrawn on a substantial number of commodities at the HS-4-digit level. As a result, the number of import-restricted item reduced from 752 during 1985–1986 to only 63 during 2003–2006. Since the list includes both trade and

Table 9.1 Tariff rates for different goods

Item/category	*Tariff year*	*2000*	*2005*	*2008*	*2010*	*2015*
	Trade year	*2002*	*2004*	*2008*	*2010*	*2015*
Capital goods	Simple average	13.04	9.35	7.71	7.30	5.40
	Weighted average	8.91	13.87	8.43	7.54	6.63
Consumer goods	Simple average	30.03	20.13	20.05	19.73	17.99
	Weighted average	29.19	17.12	18.52	16.28	18.47
Intermediate goods	Simple average	22.14	15.96	14.31	13.97	11.88
	Weighted average	18.59	29.68	14.78	10.60	12.91
Raw materials	Simple average	14.71	12.25	13.88	11.66	9.30
	Weighted average	9.32	3.44	4.03	2.53	4.88
WTO HS agricultural commodities	Simple average	25.46	17.73	18.52	19.4	20.1
	Weighted average	11.28	7.35	5.56	5.4	5.2
WTO HS industrial	Simple average	21.91	15.29	13.58	14.3	13.7
	Weighted average	19.64	23.7	14.01	13.4	12.2

Source: World Integrated Trade Solution (WITS)

Note: WTO = World Trade Organization

non-trade-related items, in particular, the number of trade-related banned items has declined substantially from 275 in 1985–1986 to 5 in 2003–2006.

All QRs on agricultural products have been removed in the 1990s. Tariff lines of all products that faced QRs were brought down to only 2 percent in 1994 and zero in subsequent years. Private sector was allowed to import rice and wheat in the early 1990s, which ended the long-standing government's monopoly on food grain imports. Also, the ban on the export of fine quality rice was lifted, though the ban continued for the export of coarse rice. These liberalization policies have impacted positively the growth of import of rice and other food items (Fig. 9.1).

Import liberalization usually lowers costs in downstream industries, expands their output and thereby exports and triggers a push for industrialization. It is, therefore, imperative to focus on the impact of growth of imported raw materials on the production and export structure and the employment creation in the manufacturing sector during the liberalization period. An improvement in technical efficiency is considered as an important source of growth of output (Leibenstein 1966) through proper allocation of resources. The degree of efficiency determines whether a firm might survive or stagnate or fail over time (Jovanovic 1982). Though this chapter does not focus on these aspects of trade liberalization, various studies already reflected on it (Raihan 2008; Ahmed and Sattar 2004).

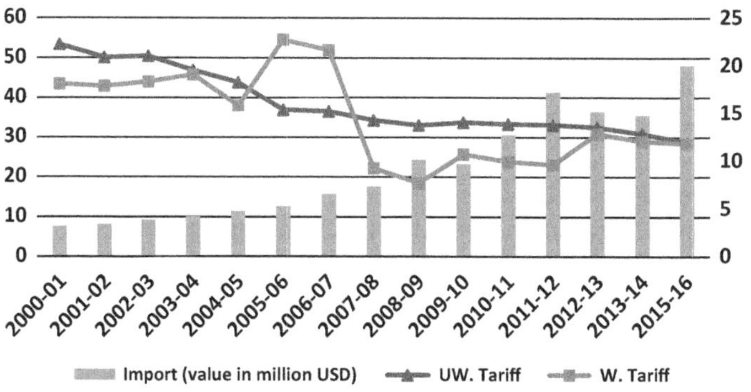

Fig. 9.1 Tariffs and import growth. Notes: Import values are expressed in million US dollar; Tariff rates are presented in percentage (secondary vertical axis). (Source: World Integrated Trade Solution (WITS))

Box 9.1 Some Key Export Promotion Policies

Restructuring of the export credit guarantee scheme (ECGS)
Utilization of foreign exchange by exporters
Export promotion fund (EPF)
Flexible time limit for adjustment of export credit
Rebate on insurance premium
Income tax rebate on export earnings
Payment of duty drawback through commercial banks
Bonding facilities for export-oriented industries
Duty-free import of capital machinery by export-oriented industries
Bonded warehouse facilities
Duty drawback scheme
Tax holiday

Sources: Export policy order (various issues); Bangladesh Bank (FE Circulars, various issues)

9.2.3.2 Export Promotion Policies

Various measures have been taken over time to promote and diversify exports. Measures include cash incentives to some traditional and non-traditional items, restructuring export credit guarantee schemes, creating of export promotion fund, introduction of duty drawback and bonded warehouse facility, income tax rebate to certain extent, and so on (see Box 9.1). Moreover, subsidized interest rate (7 percent) and undervalued exchange rate are some of the important policy supports given to exporters.

Cash Incentives (Subsidies) for Exporting Products

Bangladesh government has been providing various incentives including cash incentives to exporters in order to increase the volume as well as value of exports since 1994. Initially, it was for export of jute goods produced by government and non-government jute mills, and export-oriented local textiles. Later, the scope and extent of the cash incentive program were expanded in order to encourage exporters for product and market diversification, particularly for non-traditional items. Cash incentive for leather goods (100 percent export-oriented industries) was introduced in April 2000. Cash incentive facility started for export of agricultural goods, particularly for frozen shrimps and other fish, agro product (vegetables/fruits) and processed agro products from December 2000. Other products that enjoy cash incentive benefits so far are bone meal, bicycle, commodities made of hogla, straw, coir of sugarcane, potato, eggs and day-old chicks of poultry industries, liquid glucose produced at Ishwardi Export Processing Zone (EPZ) (from December 2005), light engineering products (from February 2006), and halal meat (from December 2006).

However, the rate of cash incentive varies across commodities (Table 9.9 in Appendix). The government makes changes to rates and sectors time to time, however, on an ad hoc basis, sometimes with pressure from business communities without properly evaluating the impact of cash incentives on export performances.

Cash incentives are provided on net freight on board (FOB) value of the selected commodities exported (shipped) during a year. Export value is calculated using a fixed price set by the Bangladesh Bank. Annual disbursement of money provided as cash incentive for agricultural and non-agricultural commodities has increased over time. The total amount of cash subsidy paid was US$132 million in 2002, which was increased to US$417.7 million in 2015–2016. However, the process of disbursement of cash subsidies involves corruption and inefficient allocation for which full benefits of cash incentives could not be realized.

In Bangladesh, although total export has increased five times between 2002 and 2016, total ratio of cash subsidy to total exports remained almost the same throughout the period (Table 9.2). The benefit as a ratio of promoted exports is nearly 1 percent over the years, which appears to be a negligible amount that could hardly influence export performance.

Table 9.2 Benefits generated from export subsidies

Product	*FY 2002–2003*	*FY 2005–2006*	*FY 2009–2010*	*FY 2010–2011*	*FY 2015–2016*
Total exports (in million US$)	6548	10,526	16,204	22,924	34,240
Total manufactured exports (in million US$)	6086	9753	15,517	20,838	32,974
Total cash subsidy (in million US$)	132.37	89.74	171.4	191.4	417.700
Benefits as a ratio of promoted exports	0.02	0.01	0.01	0.01	0.012
Real effective exchange rate (REER) index (decrease indicates depreciation): 10 currency basket	92.27	83.86	97.74	89.4	137.950

Sources: Authors' calculation; Bangladesh Bank; Ministry of Finance (MoF); FY = fiscal year

9.2.4 Trade Liberalization: Regional Scenarios

It can be observed from Table 9.8 that Bangladesh's nominal import protection level is comparable to other South Asian countries. Tariff reduction in Bangladesh during the early 2000s was slower than other South Asian neighbors. However, recently Bangladesh has made a good progress in bringing down its tariff structure to the regional level. In particular, Bangladesh's most-favored nation (MFN) applied tariff (ad valorem) for agricultural goods (17.52 percent as against 20.62 percent in South Asia) is the lowest in South Asia, but slightly higher than the low-income country level. Trade restrictive indices (TRIs), calculated by the World Bank, suggest that Bangladesh is the least restricted in South Asia (11.33 vs. 11.75) and even among low-income countries (Table 9.8 in Appendix).

Although Bangladesh has been rated as a moderate restrictive country until recently, the average nominal protection rate level is now comparable to other South Asian countries. However, there is scope for further trade liberalization as high regulatory duties are often placed on an ad hoc basis.

9.3 Trade Performances of Bangladesh

Trade performance of a country can be best judged by its trade intensity (trade to GDP ratio) indicators. These reflect the extent of integration of a country with the global economy. As Fig. 9.2 shows, trade intensity has

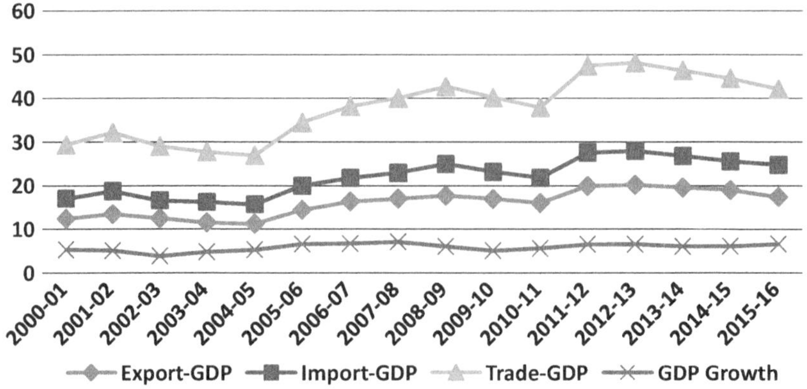

Fig. 9.2 Trade pattern in Bangladesh. (Source: The World Bank)

reached 45 percent of the country's GDP and its average figure is around 44 percent (excluding trade in service) in the 2006–2010 period. Trade intensity (trade openness) of Bangladesh made a phenomenal growth in 2006–2010 despite global economic crisis during that period. It is worth noting that during 2006–2015, export intensity has made a slight progress, increased from 17 percent in 2006–2010 to about 18.5 percent in 2011–2015 (Table 9.3). At the same time, the gap between export and import intensities has also increased. Widening of the gap between export and import intensities can be explained by the increase of import dependence as well as increased global price of imports relative to its exports.

Another explanation is the increased import-dependent exports by shifting from indigenous raw material-based export products to imported raw material-based garment exports. Import intensity has increased magnanimously from about 13 percent in 1981–1985 to 27.6 percent in 2011–2015. The capacity to import has elevated due to improved export capacity as well as increased inflow of remittance income of migrant workers. One of the important indicators of global integration is the import penetration ratio. This has increased to 24 percent in 2006–2010 from 11.8 percent in 1981–1985. Although it takes 20 years for it to be doubled, the driving forces behind it were import liberalization policies and increased domestic demand for better quality imported items.

Table 9.3 Indicators of trade pattern (average percentage)

Economic phases	*Trade intensity*	*Export intensity*	*Import intensity*	*Import penetration ratio*	*Terms of trade (ToT)*
1981–1985	16.848	3.958	12.890	11.820	–
1986–1990	16.780	4.907	11.873	11.090	92.780
1991–1995	22.551	7.988	14.563	13.640	98.600
1996–2000	30.042	11.951	18.091	17.050	98.060
2001–2005	34.600	13.584	21.017	19.540	81.820
2006–2010	43.937	17.691	26.246	24.150	91.080
2011–2015	46.106	18.470	27.636		85.980

Source: Bangladesh Bureau of Statistics (BBS); Bangladesh Economic Review, Ministry of Finance, various issues

Notes: Intensity is measured as percentage of GDP; different base years were used in calculating terms of trade; import penetration is calculated as the ratio of import/(GDP-exports+imports)

9.3.1 *Trade Balance and Coverage of Imports by Exports*

Trade balance is an indicator of trade performance of a country. Trade balance as a percentage of GDP reflects whether and how much a country is dependent on foreign aid or external income other than exports of goods for her development. One can observe that the government on average has been facing trade deficit of around US$7500 million per annum. Trade deficit has escalated from US$1733 million in 1981–1985 to US$7486 million in 2006–2010, that is, 27.5 percent per period. It is worth noting that proportion of trade balance to GDP hovers around 6–8 percent in all the periods. Compared to this, normalized trade balance has decreased substantially. Import coverage ratio has also increased significantly from about 31 percent in 1981–1985 to about 76 percent in 2011–2015, indicating an enhanced productive capacity of Bangladesh (Table 9.4).

The current account balance (CAB) has largely been negative until 2004 and afterwards until 2016 it was positive in Bangladesh (Fig. 9.3, right scale). For the last two years (2017–2018), current account deficit has widened substantially with the increase of import payments mainly due to import of rice in the face of shortfall of rice production, import of capital machineries and goods mainly to support implementation of some mega infrastructure projects, coupled with the decrease of exports and remittances in recent years. Though large and persistent current account deficit is a cause of concern, the current situation in Bangladesh is not that much worrying as this appears to be consistent with macroeconomic fundamentals.

Table 9.4 Trade balance (average) and coverage of imports by exports

Economic phases	*Trade balance as percent of GDP*	*Normalized trade balance*	*Growth of trade balance*	*Coverage of imports by exports in percent*
1981–1985	−8.93	−0.53	−0.74	30.91
1986–1990	−6.97	−0.41	1.07	41.6
1991–1995	−6.58	−0.29	15.43	54.75
1996–2000	−6.14	−0.21	−2.62	66.14
2001–2005	−7.43	−0.21	17.73	64.47
2006–2010	−8.56	−0.19	13.15	65.96
2011–2015	−7.31	−0.57	6.24	75.61

Source: Author's calculation

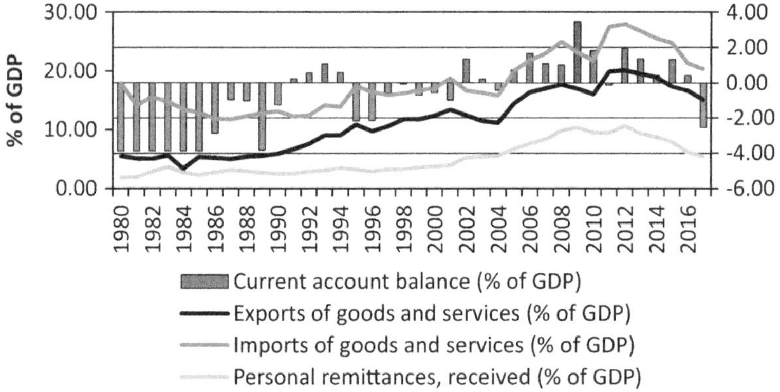

Fig. 9.3 Current account balance and trade pattern. (Sources: Bangladesh Bank; Ministry of Finance, 2018)

9.3.2 Dynamics of Exports and Imports

The dynamism in international trade in Bangladesh started during 1980–1981, when the exports of primary products started declining with the increase of export of manufacturing items, particularly the RMG products. The country registered a sizeable proportion of manufactures export and import as percentage of total merchandise export and import, respectively (96 percent vs. 63 percent) in 2015 implying its progress toward industrialization (Table 9.5). RMG has been the major export item (Fig. 9.4). Food import varies between 15 and 19 percent of total imports, while food export remains miniscule.

Table 9.5 Exports and imports as percentage of merchandise exports and imports

Year	*Manufactures exports (percent of merchandise export)*	*Food export (percent of merchandise export)*	*Manufactures import (percent of merchandise import)*	*Food import (percent of merchandise import)*	*Trade in service (percent of GDP)*	*Share of trade in global trade (percent)*
1990	77.49	14.31	55.85	18.95	3.62	0.05
1995	85.15	10.45	69.14	17.30	5.88	0.07
2000	90.51	7.61	67.65	16.48	5.17	0.10
2005	91.77	6.18	64.94	15.6	5.75	0.09
2010	91.69	4.03	64.09	17.42	5.93	0.12
2015	95.81	2.71	63.17	16.56	5.62	0.19

Source: The World Bank

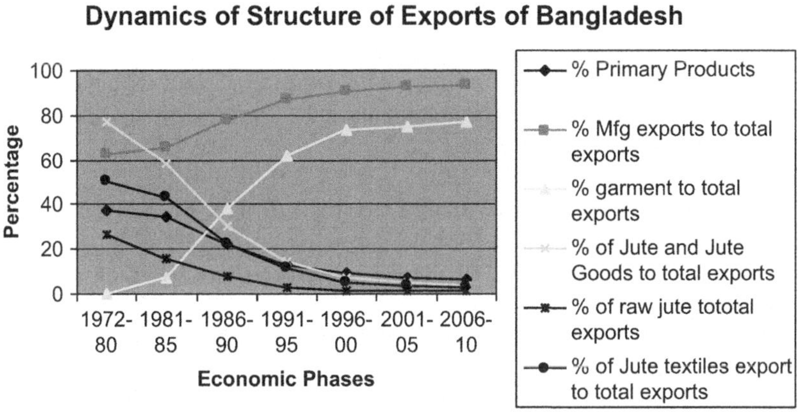

Fig. 9.4 Export dynamics. (Source: Export Promotion Bureau (EPB), Bangladesh)

As Table 9.5 shows, manufactures, particularly merchandise export (about 95 percent), dominate the export basket, while the share of manufactures is about 64 percent in merchandise imports. Food export has been on a declining trend, while food import has been stable at about 17 percent of merchandise import. Trade in services as percentage of GDP has been increasing, but slowly.

Since 2000, Bangladesh had made a remarkable progress in increasing its share in global exports and imports, which together accounts for about 0.19 percent. Bangladesh's trade share in global trade has doubled since

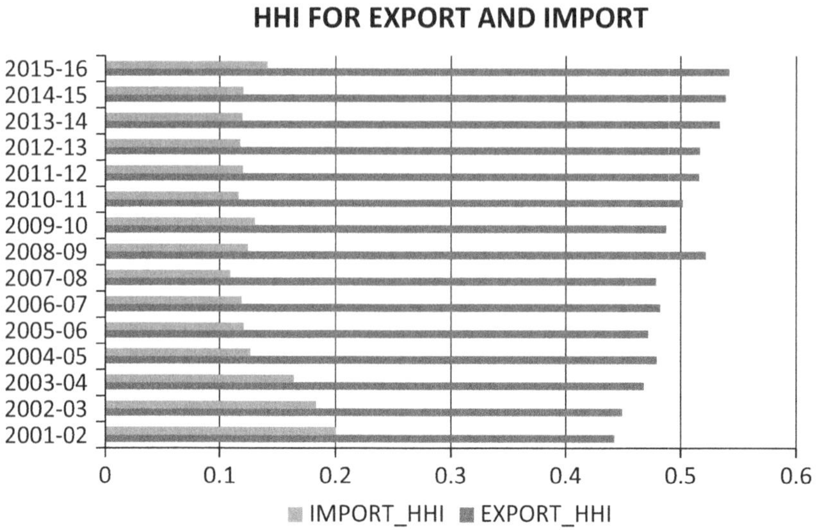

Fig. 9.5 Import and export concentration ratio for Bangladesh, 2005–2015. (Source: Author's calculation)

2000, which is impressive, thanks to the growth of RMG exports. Compared with some other least developed countries (LDCs), the progress is remarkable in terms of increased global share of trade (exports and imports).

However, within the manufacturing sector, lack of export diversity remains a measure of least development, as evident in Fig. 9.5. Estimated export and import concentration ratios, measured in terms of Herfindahl-Hirschman index (HHI), show that export concentrations are much higher than import concentration. The estimated concentration for export is about 0.50, while it is slightly over 0.1 for import in FY 2015–2016. Higher export concentration is due to the dominance of RMG in the export basket, which accounts for around 80 percent exports of Bangladesh. High concentration in exports implies that the country is more vulnerable to external shocks, and therefore Bangladesh needs to diversify its export basket.

9.3.3 Evolving Markets and Export Diversification

It appears that in most cases both volume and value of exports of products that enjoy cash incentives have been on a rising trend, but not significantly. Even, market destinations for these products are not the same for all the years, indicating that these products could not maintain access to a particular market for long time (Fig. 9.7 in Appendix). In the cases of vegetables, bicycle, leather products and frozen shrimp, a single market dominates for quite a long time; however, in the cases of potato, fruits, tobacco and jute products, destinations have been changing each year. These might have happened for several reasons including tariff structure of those markets, inability to maintain sanitary and phytosanitary standards of those markets, and so on. However, this issue needs to be analyzed further in greater detail.

Considering current slow pace and lower extent of diversification, it is hard for the existing sectors, such as leather, pharmaceuticals, light engineering, chemicals, and so on to take over the place of the RMG sector. What could be the sector that has the potential to take over RMG? East Asian experience can guide us.

The trade specialization of some East Asian countries like Japan, the ASEAN 4 and now Southeast Asian economies may be explained by the "Flying Geese pattern" (Akamatsu 1962). Their specialization follows a trend—initially they have specialized in manufacturing nondurable consumer goods like apparel, and then to durable consumer goods, and then to capital goods of higher value. The industrial transformation that has happened in East Asia could provide a lesson to Bangladesh about its future direction of industrialization as well as export diversification (Fig. 9.6). Bangladesh's specialization in RMG with having no other such potential sector could pave the way for specialization in a different sectors like the hardware and electronics sector. The reason is that the information and communication technology (ICT) sector requires human capital, along with low level of technology, which could allow a country to specialize in hardware and electronics. The hardware segment of the information technology (IT) industry has the largest number of firms, approximately 10,000, but it also appears that this sector is intensely amalgamated with assembling and repairing services (Hossain 2017). Most of these firms sell computer and computer-related accessories, and roughly 60,000 PCs and laptops are sold per month in Bangladesh. There are lots of electronics assembling firms that are now selling their products in domestic market, where only a few are involved in manufacturing of electronics items. Walton is a good example. If the firms are provided with proper incentives and policy support, they might make a strong case for next exporting giant after the RMG.

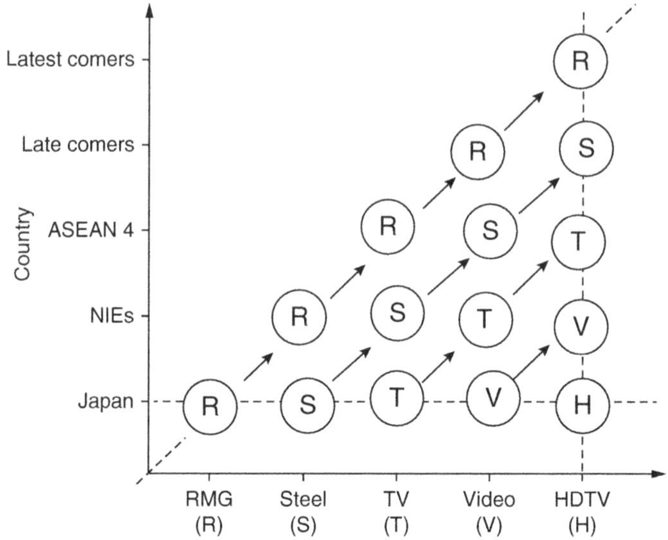

Fig. 9.6 Flying geese industrial pattern of East Asia. Note: The graph is drawn following Lopez-Acevedo and Robertson (2016)

9.4 Evaluation of Policies

In this section we evaluate the impact of exchange rate and cash incentives of Bangladesh's export as part of assessing the impact of trade policies.

9.4.1 Exchange Rate and Trade Performance

In this section, we attempt to examine the effect of exchange rate on exports. There are two primary determinants of export demand (Dornbusch 1988; Hooper and Marquez 1993). First is the foreign income variable which measures the economic activity and the purchasing power of the trading partner country ("income effect"). Second is the relative price or the terms to trade variable ("price effect"). Since real exchange rate volatility might have affected exports, exchange rate volatility is an additional factor that needs to be explicitly taken into account ("volatility effect"). Incorporating these determinants, we can derive a simple export demand function as follows:

$$x_t = \alpha_0 + \alpha_1 \cdot y_t^{world} + \alpha_2 \cdot p_t^{world} + \alpha_3 \cdot V_t + \varepsilon_t, \qquad (9.1)$$

where x_t is the natural logarithm of real export (total export is deflated by the export price index) of Bangladesh, y_t^{world} is the natural logarithm of the trade-weighted sum of the real GDP of eight key trading partners, p_t^{world} is the trade-weighted sum of terms of trade of key trade partners, V_t is the real exchange rate volatility measured as the two-quarter moving average standard deviation[1] and ε_t is an error term.

Applying the augmented Dickey-Fuller (ADF) test, we find that all series, such as x_t, y_t and p_t exhibit I(1) process except V_t which is I(0). Thus, we go for estimating cointegration equations considering V_t as exogenous variable. The results are shown in Table 9.6. We estimate the short-term adjustment factors including real effective exchange rate (REER) volatility under the vector error correction model. As apparel (knitwear and woven garments) constitutes major share of Bangladesh's export, we estimate separate cointegrating equations for knitwear and woven for their main destinations, such as the US and the EU. Signs of the coefficients are consistent with the theoretical predictions. The volume of exports (imports) to a foreign country ought to increase as the real income of the trade partner (destination country) rises, and vice versa. So we expect $\alpha_1>0$. A rise (fall) in the terms of trade of a trade partner will cause the domestic goods to become less (more) competitive than foreign goods; therefore, exports will fall (increase) and imports will rise (fall). So we expect $\alpha_2 < 0$.

The results show that overall exports from Bangladesh are inversely related to international prices and statistically significant, implying that price support is crucial for the export sector. Export of knitwear and woven garments constituted around 70 percent of total exports in 2007, of which 70 percent were exported to the US (23 percent) and the EU market (47 percent). The estimation of demand functions for knitwear and woven garments in the US and the EU market shows a significant impact of price and income on woven and knitwear exports, respectively. As a result, woven exports have experienced sharper decline than knitwear in these markets in the latter half of 2008 in the face of global economic recession. Although income is also found to be significant for export demand of the USA and the EU for knitwear and woven, exports of these items are expected to be less affected by the current global recession due to their low income elasticity.

[1] V_t is calculated as follows: $V_t = \left[\frac{1}{m}\sum_{i=1}^{m}\left(\ln REER_{t+i-1} - \ln REER_{t+i-2}\right)^2\right]^{1/2}$.

Table 9.6 Estimated cointegrating equations for exports from Bangladesh (quarterly data: 2000Q1–2008Q4)

	Total export (world)	*USA*			*EU*		
		USA market (USA)	*Knitwear to USA*	*Woven to USA*	*EU market (EU)*	*Knitwear to EU*	*Woven to EU*
Long-term equations:							
Income	1.69	0.02	0.03	0.01	0.014	0.009	0.002
(destination)	(0.375)	(0.004)	(0.006)	(0.003)	(0.0008)	(0.006)	(0.0008)
	[1.69]	[12.96]***	[12.23]***	[9.67]***	[9.88]***	[16.89]***	[2.93]*
Terms of trade	−13.32	−0.016	−0.012	−0.02	−0.057	0.012	−0.06
(destination)	(2.30)	(0.0008)	(0.01)	(0.006)	(0.019)	(0.016)	(0.02)
	[9.60]***	[1.20]	[1.20]	[8.91]***	[5.64]**	[0.53]	[6.15]***
Constant	49.91	−0.07	−0.32	0.05	0.225	−0.067	−0.22
Short-term equations:							
REER Volatility	0.11 (0.04)**	0.0003 (0.0002)**	0.00007 (0.0001)	−0.0001 (0.0001)	0.0003 (0.0002)	0.000006 (0.0005)	0.0002 (0.0002)
Error Correction Term	−0.19 (0.22)	−0.7 (0.30)**	−0.80 (0.33)**	−0.91 (0.24)***	−1.54 (0.27)***	−2.17 (0.43)***	−1.71 (0.26)***
Constant	−0.08 (0.06)	−0.0003 (0.0004)	0.0002 (0.0005)	0.0002 (0.0004)	0.001 (0.005)	0.001 (0.001)	0.001 (0.0002)***

Notes:

1. At most 1 cointegrating equation is significant at both 1 percent and 5 percent level
2. *, **, *** indicates 10 percent, 5 percent and 1 percent level of significance. Standard errors are in parentheses. Chi-square values are reported in third brackets
3. Chi-square values are obtained by imposing cointegrating restrictions on coefficients (Chi-square critical values: at 1 percent = 6.63; at 5 percent= 3.84; at 10 percent = 2.70)
4. REER volatility is used, respectively, for world, US and EU

Although REER volatility has significantly positive effect on overall exports, the impact is very low (Table 9.6). The low magnitude of the coefficient of volatility indicates that the less the REER volatility, the more the positive impact on overall exports. This finding calls for the stabilization of the REER, particularly the foreign exchange market. Thus, price competitiveness and exchange rate management play a critical role in export promotion in Bangladesh.

9.4.2 *Impact of Cash Incentives on Export Performance*

The impact of subsidy on export has been a contentious issue. On the one hand, it is argued that export subsidy creates "trade distortions" by affecting trading patterns among trading partners. Moreover, it escalates fiscal burden of the government, as well as leads to both inefficiency and inequity in resource allocation as it leads to regressive transfers from the exchequer to a section of industry. On the other hand, export subsidies can be justified from the viewpoint of welfare maximization. Various arguments in favor of export subsidies include neutralization of import duties, supporting the infant-industry and capital market imperfections and use of these by one's counterpart. In many countries where only one or two exporting products dominate the total exports, subsidies are used as a means for expansion and diversification of exports. However, the impact of export subsidy is mixed in the literature. Evidence from India does not justify the application of subsidies on exports (Panagariya 2000). Further, from the experiences of Mexico and Brazil, export subsidies are proved to be a costly instrument of export diversification. However, it is widely argued that export subsidies worked well in East Asia for export expansion and diversification.

For the analysis, quarterly data are used for the period 2000–2009.[2] Equation 1 is used again adding log (cash incentives). REER volatility has a significant and positive impact on exports to the USA, while it is not significant in terms of exports to the EU. The low magnitude of the coefficient of volatility indicates that Bangladesh maintains a stable REER that makes a positive impact on exports.

Cash incentives provided to exporters have no significant effect on total exports to both the EU and the US markets, although the sign is positive

[2] Only quarterly data are available from Bangladesh Bank. A longer and monthly time series of cash incentives, if available, would produce better results.

Table 9.7 Impact of cash incentives on exports, 2000Q1–2008Q2

	Total export (VEC-1)		*Total export (VEC-2)*
Long-term equation:			
US income	4.85 (0.45)***	EU income	1.30 (0.17)***
US price	−1.24 (0.69)*	EU price	−20.63 (3.44)***
Constant	−31.93	Constant	92.58
Short-term equation:			
Vol_REER	0.05 (0.02)**	Vol_REER	0.028 (0.03)
Cash incentives	0.01 (0.05)	Cash incentives	0.04 (0.06)
Error correction term	−1.76 (0.28)***	Error correction term	−0.29 (0.22)

Notes: At most 1 cointegrating equation is significant at both 1 percent and 5 percent level. *, ** and *** indicates 1 percent, 5 percent and 10 percent level of significance, respectively

(Table 9.7). This was expected as cash subsidy given to exports is negligible in amount, which could hardly influence exports. However, the impact could be assessed more rigorously by analyzing product-specific longer time series data.

9.5 Conclusions and Policy Recommendations

This chapter makes an in-depth review and analysis of trade policies pursued by Bangladesh over time and how the policies contribute to trade performances of the country. Trade liberalization was done in phases since her independence in 1971, while major reform measures were undertaken in the 1990s. Bangladesh has made a substantive liberalization in the tariff structures and eliminating QRs. Trade liberalization policies contributed positively toward impressive trade performances of Bangladesh. Trade intensity of Bangladesh witnessed a phenomenal growth, 12 percent in 1990 to 50 percent in 2016, and the trade showed resilience during global economic crisis in 2008–2010. This evidence indicates an increased trade capacity of the economy despite declining aid flow of the economy. The country has been able to improve its capacity to import, which is not only due to increased exporting capacity but also because of increased domestic demand, thanks to higher inflow of remittance income of migrant workers and spending on public infrastructures. The export basket still remains highly concentrated in RMG products, implying less diversification of exports over time. Though various cash incentives are provided to promote exports of non-traditional products, such incentives are not found effective partly due to its insignificant amount and partly due to its allocative inefficiencies.

Recognizing the limitations of the private sector in delivering trade capacity-building services and trade-related infrastructure, international assistance could play an important role to eliminate trade barriers by strengthening public sector capacities. "Aid for Trade" could be one such international assistance mechanism for trade-capacity building. Considering East Asian transformation of industrial sector, after the RMG, Bangladesh could see its huge potential in the ICT sector that could pave the way for specialization in electronics sector. At present, though many electronic assembling plants are now operating in Bangladesh, proper incentives and support could help elevate them into manufacturing plants, which will boost export earnings from the sector. Anti-export biases still remain in some sectors. The tariff structures are still non-predictable, and therefore a proper tariff incidence needs to be analyzed. Therefore, there are scopes of further liberalization of trade sector by eliminating anti-export biases and rationalizing supplementary duties and tariffs. Further liberalization, improving trade infrastructure and technical capacities, and efficient trade policy are some of the future policy agenda that can take trade performances one step ahead.

Appendix

Table 9.8 Trends in average MFN applied tariff rates in developing and industrial countries, 2000–2010 (unweighted in percent)

Country/group	*2000*	*2001*	*2002*	*2003*	*2004*	*2005*	*2006*	*2007*	*2008*	*2009*	*2010*
Afghanistan					4.2		6.2	6.2	6.2		
Bangladesh	22.2	21.0	21.0	19.5	18.2	15.5	15.5	14.5	14.8		
Bhutan	15.4	15.4	17.7		22.2	22.2		17.7	16.0		
India	32.7	30.9	28.4		28.4	16.0	14.5	14.0	9.7	10.1	
Maldives	21.3	21.1	21.3	21.2	21.1	21.3	21.4		21.5	21.5	
Nepal	14.2	14.7	14.6	14.8	14.8	14.7	12.5	12.4	12.7	12.4	12.4
Pakistan	23.6	20.2	17.2	16.8	16.2	14.6	14.8	14.9	14.0	14.7	
Sri Lanka	9.3	8.9	8.9	8.7	9.9	11.3	11.0	10.7		10.1	9.3
Lao, PDR	9.3	9.5			8.7	7.0	6.5	5.8	9.3		
Cambodia	17.0	16.7	16.3	16.3	15.6	14.1		12.5	12.4		
Vietnam	15.1	15.2	14.2	13.7	13.9	13.0	11.9	11.7	8.0		7.1

(*continued*)

Table 9.8 (continued)

Country/group	*2000*	*2001*	*2002*	*2003*	*2004*	*2005*	*2006*	*2007*	*2008*	*2009*	*2010*
Memo: simple average											
Developing countries (134)	14.9	13.6	13.3	12.5	11.1	11.3	10.4	10.4	10.4	10.0	8.9
Low income (34)	15.4	14.9	14.6	14.1	12.4	14.2	12.7	12.1	12.4	12.1	11.2
Middle income (100)	14.8	13.2	12.8	11.8	10.7	10.5	9.6	9.8	9.7	9.2	8.0
High income non-OECDs (19)	6.9	7.3	7.5	5.1	4.0	5.5	6.0	7.3	5.8	4.1	7.8
High income OECDs (11)	3.8	4.4	3.9	3.7	3.3	3.3	3.2	2.9	2.8	3.1	2.8
World, all above co. (164)	12.9	11.9	11.6	10.6	9.5	9.9	9.3	9.4	9.2	8.7	8.1

Sources: UNCTAD TRAINS database (through WITS); WTO IDB database (through WITS); WTO IDB CD ROMs, various years and Trade Policy Review—Country Reports in various issues, 1990–2005; UNCTAD Handbook of Trade Control Measures of Developing Countries—Supplement 1987 and Directory of Import Regimes 1994; World Bank Trade Policy Reform in Developing Countries since 1985, WB Discussion Paper #267, 1994 and World Development Indicators, 1998–2006; The Uruguay Round: Statistics on Tariffs Concessions Given and Received, 1996; OECD Indicators of Tariff and Non-Tariff Trade Barriers, 1996 and 2000; and IMF Global Monitoring Tariff data file 2004

Notes: All tariff rates are based on unweighted averages for all goods in ad valorem rates, or applied rates, or MFN rates whichever data is available in a longer period

Table 9.9 Rate of cash incentives (export subsidy) provided for export of different products (in percent)

Product	*FY 2001–2002*	*FY 2002–2003*	*FY 2003–2004*	*FY 2004–2005*	*FY 2005–2006*	*FY 2006–2007*	*FY 2007–2008*	*FY 2008–2009*	*FY 2009–2010*	*FY 2010–2011*	*FY 2011–2012*
Potato		15	15	15	20	10	10	10	10	10	20
Tobacco		10	10	10	10	10	10	–	–	–	
Leather product	15	15	15	15	15	15	15	15	17.5	15	12.5
Jute product	7.50	7.50	7.50	7.50	7.50	7.50	7.50	7.50	10	10	10
Handloom		15	10	5							
Agro product (veg)		15	25	25	30	20	20	20	20	20	20
Agro product (fruit)		20	25	25	30	20	20	20	20	20	20
Crushed bone	15	15	15	15	15	15	15	15	15	15	15
Bicycle	15	15	15	15	15	15	15	15	15	15	15
Frozen shrimp and other fish	10	10	10	10	10	10	10	10 (Jul–Mar), 12.5 (Apr–June)	12.50	10	10
Halal meat						20	20	20	20	20	20
Home textile						5	5	5	5	5	5
Poultry hatching egg and day old chick						15	15	15	15	15	15
Commodities made of hogla, straw, coir or sugarcane						15–20	15–20	15–20	15–20	15–20	15–20
Light engineering products						10	10	10	10	10	10
Ship										5	5
Crust leather										3	3
Finished leather										4	4
Pet bottle										10	10

Source: Bangladesh Bank, FE Circulars

Fig. 9.7 Evolving markets for exporting (subsidized) products. Notes: Value of exports in thousand taka. (Source: Bangladesh Bank; Export Promotion Bureau (EPB))

References

Ahmed, S., & Sattar, Z. (2004). Impact of trade liberalisation: Looking at the evidence. *Economic and Political Weekly, 36*, 4059–4067.

Ahmed, N., Bakht, Z., Dorosh, P. A., & Shahabuddin, Q. (2007). *Distortions to agricultural incentives in Bangladesh* (No. 1856-2016-152627).

Akamatsu, K. (1962). A historical pattern of economic growth in developing countries. *The Developing Economies, 1*(1), 3–25.

Bakht, Z. (2001). Trade liberalization, exports and growth of manufacturing industries in Bangladesh. In M. M. Huq & J. Love (Eds.), *Strategies for industrialization: The case of Bangladesh*. Dhaka: University Press Ltd.

Dornbusch, R. (1988). *Exchange rates and inflation*. Cambridge, MA: MIT Press.

Hooper, P., & Marquez, J. R. (1993). *Exchange rates, prices and external adjustment in the United States and Japan* (No. 456). Washington, DC: Board of Governors of the Federal Reserve system.

Hossain, M. (2017). Labor market and skills gap analysis for the ICT sector in Bangladesh. *BIDS study report*, skills for employment investment program, Ministry of Finance, Government of Bangladesh.

Jovanovic, B. (1982). Selection and the evolution of industry. *Econometrica: Journal of the Econometric Society*: 649–670.

Leibenstein, H. (1966). Allocative efficiency vs. X-efficiency. *The American Economic Review, 56*, 392–415.

Lopez-Acevedo, G., & Robertson, R. (Eds.). (2016). *Stitches to riches?: Apparel employment, trade, and economic development in South Asia*. Washington, DC: The World Bank.

Panagariya, A. (2000). *Evaluating the case for export subsidies* (Policy research working paper series 2276). Washington, DC: The World Bank.

Rahman, S. H. (1992). *Trade policies and industrialization in Bangladesh: An assessment*. Dhaka: Mimeo, Bangladesh Institute of Development Studies.

Raihan, S. (2008). *Trade liberalization and poverty in Bangladesh*. Working paper no. 15. Macao Regional Knowledge Hub, December.

CHAPTER 10

Analysis of Trade Pattern, Market Access and Trade Potential in Bangladesh

Monzur Hossain and Narayan Chandra Nath

10.1 Introduction

Bangladesh's trade performance, after 2000, has been very impressive which is thought to be the result of trade liberalization and increased trade capacity of the country. The share of trade in gross domestic product (GDP) has increased significantly from about 12 percent in 1991 to about 50 percent in 2015, showing the growing importance of trade in the economy. The success in stimulating trade in recent years can be described by the fact that Bangladesh has managed to carve out an export niche in the global division of labor by exploiting its comparative advantage derived from particular resources, such as ready-made garments (RMG). The country has been able to diversify its exports—shifting from agricultural products in the 1970s and 1980s to RMG in the 1990s onward, thanks to preferential market access to the US and the EU markets. However, exports remain highly concentrated in garment products for more than a decade, and therefore diversification of export basket is a concern, particularly from the point of safeguarding the country's export from any external shock. Apart from this fact, rapid growth of apparel export has triggered the growth of accessories and packaging

M. Hossain (✉) • N. C. Nath
Bangladesh Institute of Development Studies (BIDS), Dhaka, Bangladesh

M. Hossain (ed.), *Bangladesh's Macroeconomic Policy*,
https://doi.org/10.1007/978-981-15-1244-5_10

industries, most of which benefited from import liberalization policies (Bakht 2001). Easier access to imported inputs facilitated the growth of some other industries such as plastic, processed food, footwear, chemicals, printing, and so on, and the growth of exports of these items is gradually increasing. Still the share of trade in GDP is far from satisfactory compared to some Southeast Asian countries. The reasons of such retreat could be the lack of export diversification, market access, lack of trade infrastructure, anti-export bias, technological innovation and inability of creating production networks, nationally and internationally.

On average, during 2006–2010, exports of goods and services grew by an annual average rate of 15.1 percent, whereas imports grew by an average of 25 percent. However, during 2010–2015, export growth has slowed down, mainly due to shrinkage of global demand for apparels emanating from global economic recession and to some extent, local political uncertainities. The most spectacular thing is that global financial crisis, in 2007–2008, could not hurt export performance immediately as was expected, which is thought to be the result of product specialization (particularly low-end products-base) and timely taken stimulus measures by the government.

Bangladesh made a successful transformation in trade composition by shifting its specialization from agricultural product to manufacturing commodities over time. Though agricultural trade dominated trade basket in the 1970s and 1980s, the share of agriculture in the overall trade volume started declining with the emergence of the RMG industry in the early 1980s, particularly when liberalization process started. The major exporting agricultural commodity was jute and jute goods, which has lost attractiveness because of fierce competition from synthetics as well as lack of proper research and development for jute and jute goods. While agriculture constituted around 21 percent of total trade in the 1980s, the share dropped to 11.1 percent in 2011. Food grain production, particularly rice production, has increased threefold since Bangladesh's independence, mainly due to increased availability and affordability of agricultural inputs because of import liberalization policies. This has decreased import dependency on food substantially nowadays. The average unweighted nominal protection level in agriculture fell from more than 76 percent in 1991–1992 to 31 percent in 1999–2000 and 18.5 percent in 2008; on the contrary, the average weighted protection rate fell from more than 33 percent in 1990–1991 to 12 percent in 1998–1999 and 5.5 percent in 2008 (Ahmed et al. 2007).

Regional trade integration has come to the forefront in the face of global financial crisis in 2007–2008. South Asian Free Trade Arrangement

(SAFTA) has not been proved effective and, therefore, some South Asian countries have signed bilateral free trade agreements, though Bangladesh has not signed any bilateral free trade agreements yet. The South Asian Association for Regional Cooperation (SAARC) countries' share of trade in the world is very small and insignificant (around 3.6 percent) compared to other regions, such as East Asia (around 20 percent) and the EU area (around 25 percent). Despite being a highly liberalized region, intra-regional trade in South Asia is also negligible. One of the reasons for this unsatisfactory situation is that these countries have similar trade structure and they compete each other in the global market with similar products. Further, existence of some non-tariff and para-tariff barriers also restrict the growth of intra-regional trade to some extent. Greater cooperation in different areas of trade is expected to contribute to greater intra-regional share of trade among the SAARC countries in the future, which will help encounter any global economic or financial crisis.

This chapter thus addresses the following pertinent research questions regarding trade pattern and performance in Bangladesh: How the trade patterns of Bangladesh, both in terms of composition and volume, have been changing over time? Are trade patterns including agricultural trade consistent with trade and exchange rate policies? Is there any change in spatial pattern of trade over the period? And what is the status of intra-regional trade? To this end, this chapter examines the trade pattern including export and import pattern of Bangladesh over time, analyzes evolving markets and explores the possibilities of trade opportunities for Bangladesh, discusses various aspects of international trade and food security of Bangladesh and provides policy recommendations on trade policies and pattern. For the analysis, revealed comparative indices (RCIs) for products as well as geographies and a trade potential index (TPI) for selected countries have been estimated.

The chapter is organized as follows. After the introduction, Sect. 10.2 discusses the trade pattern and provides an analysis of exports and imports. Section 10.3 provides an analysis of evolving markets and opportunities for Bangladeshi exports. It also estimates a trade potential index. Section 10.4 provides conclusions and policy recommendations.

10.2 Trade Pattern in Bangladesh

Trade openness (intensities) is the prime indicator of trade pattern and trade performance of a country reflecting the extent of integration of a country with the global economy. Trade intensity (trade to GDP ratio) has reached about 50 percent of the country's GDP, and its average figure is around 44 percent (excluding trade in service) in recent times. It is interesting to note that in the two phases of structural adjustment program and privatization program under New Industrial Policy of 1982 and 1986, trade intensity remains stagnated at only 16.7 percent. Gradually, it increased to 23 percent in 1991–1995 due to substantial liberalization move. In fact, trade intensity of Bangladesh made a phenomenal growth in 2006–2010 despite global economic crisis during that period. It is worth noting that during 1981–2010, export intensity has made a steady progress, increased from about 4 percent in 1981–85 to about 17 percent in 2006–10. At the same time, the difference between export and import intensities had also increased. Widening of the gap between export and import intensities can be explained by the increase of import dependence as well as increased global price of imports relative to its exports.

10.2.1 Analysis of Exports

10.2.1.1 Structure and Growth of Exports of Commodities

In general, consumer goods dominated the export basket overwhelmingly. Consumer goods along with materials for consumer goods constitute about 98.5 percent of exports during 2011–2015. The picture has not changed since the beginning of the 1980s. In terms of different categories of exports, such as high-tech products, primary products, intermediate products and capital equipment, picture has not changed much over time indicating a low level of export diversification (Table 10.1). Though proportion of primary products in the export basket decreased, proportion of intermediate products or capital equipment or high-tech products did not increase. The share of high-tech products and capital equipment remained stagnated at less than 1 percent indicating a low level of technological diffusion of the economy.

Bangladesh demonstrated a tremendous success in knitted and woven garments export since the 1990s. While in the 1970s, jute and jute goods constituted about 77 percent, in the period of 2006–2010, and afterwards, garments constituted about 80 percent of total exports (Fig. 10.1). From the very insignificant proportion of 7 percent in 1981–1996, garments and textiles export rose steadily to over 80 percent in recent times. In knitted garments, it occupies third place in the world, followed by Hong Kong and China. Though it made a remarkable success in both

Table 10.1 Structure of exports by types of commodities

	Percent share in exports			
Period	*Percent share of consumers goods in exports (average)*	*Percent share of material for consumer goods in exports (average)*	*Percent share of capital goods in exports (average)*	*Percent share of materials for capital goods (average)*
1981–1985	68.5	29.4	1.0	1.1
1986–1990	74.4	23.4	1.5	0.7
1991–1995	81.2	16.4	1.7	0.6
1996–2000	90.2	8.5	0.7	0.6
2001–2005	89.3	10.0	0.4	0.3
2006–2010	84.3	13.6	0.6	0.5
2011–2015	87.0	11.5	0.8	0.7

Source: Estimated from the data of Bangladesh Economic Review

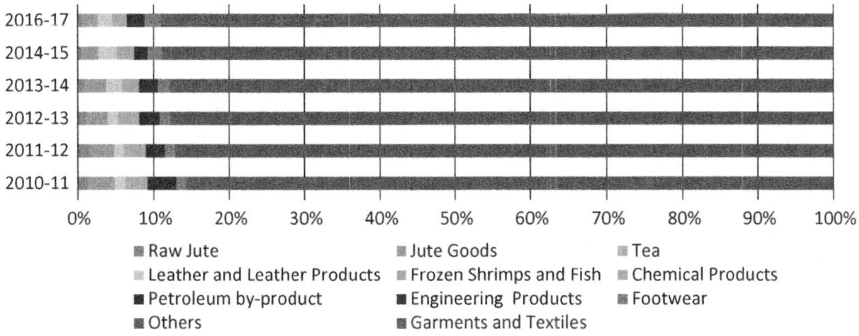

Fig. 10.1 Export concentrations. (Source: Bangladesh Bank)

knitted and woven garments, its main categories are not more than five. In knitted garments, T-shirts and pullovers (80 percent) and, in woven garments, shirts, jackets and trousers are the major products (86 percent). However, export potentials of RMG have not yet got exhausted, rather the sector can move forward comfortably with background experiences for a number of years with accumulated skill of about 5000 entrepreneurs and 4 million garment workers and thousands of accounting and managerial professionals.

There are many products yet to be developed. Again, in the same category of products, it can go for higher quality products. Aggressive marketing drive with brand name of Bangladeshi companies is a feasible option. In this context, economic diplomacy and investment for international marketing need to be facilitated by the government. One note of caution is that it is very risky to rely on a single product, for which exports might become vulnerable in the face of any global market change.

Detailed structure of exporting commodities shows that the share of traditional exports has fallen, while the share of woven and knitted garments has substantially increased (Table 10.9 in Appendix). Knitted garments superseded woven garments in recent years and the share of woven garments has virtually declined from 50 percent in 1991–1995 to 38 percent in 2006–2010. It is worth noting that RMG has played a crucial role in uplifting the country's export earnings in the last two decades with greater diversification within the sector. However, as Ahmed and Sattar (2004) argued, existence of anti-export bias in trade policy also deters the expected export growth of other sectors.

It is interesting to see that the proportion of traditional exports has been growing rapidly in recent years. For example, jute goods and raw jute exports grew at the rate of 20.4 percent and 26.5 percent, respectively, in the period of 2006–2010. Though proportion of non-garments declined from 62 percent in 1981–1985 to 32 percent in 2006–2010, they depicted a positive growth of 13.4 percent during the same period. Thus, not only the performance of garments was noteworthy, performance of other sectors is also appreciable in the face of global economic crisis. Other products except paper board and tea seem to be still prospective despite decline in their growth of exports (Table 10.9 in Appendix).

10.2.1.2 Structure and Growth of Exports by Market Destinations

Only nine countries constitute about 75 percent share of total exports of Bangladesh during 1991–2010, which was 38 percent in 1981–1985 (Fig. 10.2). The share of other countries than these nine countries has declined from 62 percent in 1981–1985 to 25 percent in 2006–2010. In the period of 1996–2005, the share of other countries was abysmally lower at 19 percent only. A country like the USA alone accounts for 25 percent of total exports. Three European countries, the UK, Germany and France together buy 25 percent of total export products. Thus 50 percent of exports destined to just four markets show that exports in these four markets have been increasing over time. Bangladesh's export is thus concentrated not only in a very few commodities but also in a very few markets.

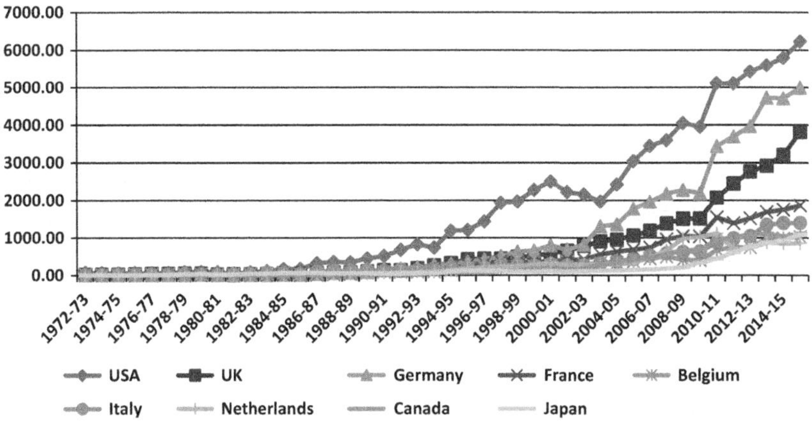

Fig. 10.2 Exports to important market destination (million US dollar). (Sources: Bangladesh Bank; Export Promotion Bureau)

This calls for diversification of markets too, to avoid instability and vulnerability of export earnings.

In order to minimize the risk of export concentration, diversification of export commodities in the currently accessible developed markets is definitely a possible option to pursue. For this, the import demand of these developed countries needs to be studied closely at detailed product categories in order to get access to these markets. Further, Bangladesh needs to explore new markets including emerging economies like China, India, Brazil, Russia and Korea and African countries. As currently exports are concentrated in only nine markets, there is an immense potential for market expansion for Bangladeshi exports (Fig. 10.2).

10.2.2 Analysis of Imports

10.2.2.1 Composition and Growth of Imports by Commodities and Countries

The composition of imports has changed substantially over time with significant shifts from primary goods to consumer goods. The share of consumption goods increased from 31 percent in 1981–1985 to 57 percent

Table 10.2 Structure of imports by commodity (in percent)

Category (average)	*1981–85*	*1986–90*	*1991–95*	*1996–00*	*2001–05*	*2006–10*	*2011–15*
Primary goods Import	27.9	19	12.1	12.3	12.3	13.8	11.5
Rice import	3.1	2.1	2.0	3.0	1.5	1.8	0.7
Wheat import	11.5	9.3	3.5	2.5	2.3	2.9	2.2
Oil seeds import	0.1	0.6	1.2	1.0	0.6	0.6	0.9
Raw cotton import	9.9	4.5	3.1	2.4	3.0	2.7	2.0
Crude petroleum	3.4	2.6	2.3	3.3	4.9	5.8	5.7
Major intermediate goods	23.3	16.2	16.4	14.5	19.0	21.9	22.7
Edible oil	9.5	5.3	3.1	3.0	3.6	4.3	3.7
Petroleum products import	6.6	4.7	4.1	4.8	8.5	9.0	8.4
Fertilizer import	4.0	1.9	2.5	1.4	1.9	3.4	3.2
Clinker import	1.3	2.5	2.6	1.2	1.4	1.5	1.5
Staple fiber import	0.2	0.2	0.6	0.5	0.5	0.5	1.8
Yarn import	1.4	1.6	3.6	3.6	3.1	3.2	4.1
Capital machinery import	29.6	34.2	29.7	9.3	8.4	6.9	6.6
Other imports	19.0	31.0	42.0	64.0	60.0	57.0	59.2

Source: Bangladesh Economic Review (various issues), Ministry of Finance

in 2006–2010. Next important item of import is intermediate goods constituting about 22 percent in the recent period. Its share was 23.3 percent in 1981–1985. The share of primary goods has substantially declined from 28 percent in 1981–1985 to 12 percent in 2011–2015. The share of capital goods in import basket has also substantially declined to about 7 percent in 2011–2015 from 30 percent in 1981–1985 (Tables 10.2 and 10.10). Bangladesh has comparative advantage in exporting non-rice products and, therefore, the commercialization of non-rice food products could be an important policy agenda for agricultural diversification and food security (Dorosh and Shahabuddin 2005).

10.2.3 Composition and Growth of Imports by Sources of Their Supply

A major portion of imports of Bangladesh comes from only nine countries (Table 10.3). Two suppliers, India and China, together constitute one-third of imports of Bangladesh. Though India and China constituted only 6.2 percent in 1986–1990, they have come up strongly to outbid other suppliers in the subsequent periods, mainly because it is relatively cheaper to import consumer goods from these markets. The share of imports from

Table 10.3 Growth of imports (average) by sources of their supply

Country	*Fiscal year*					
	1986–90	*1991–95*	*1996–00*	*2001–05*	*2006–10*	*2011–15*
India	3.0	8.8	13.2	13.9	13.8	18.6
China	3.2	5.6	7.9	10.4	15.9	17.7
Singapore	6.7	6.1	5.8	8.7	5.9	6.9
Japan	13.3	9.8	7.9	6.2	4.1	1.7
Hong Kong	3.3	6.9	5.7	4.6	3.6	4.3
Taiwan	0	2.8	4.3	3.6	2.3	4.2
S. Korea	2.9	5.8	4.5	3.8	3.3	3.7
USA	7.2	5.2	4.1	2.5	2.1	1.7
Malaysia	1.2	1.1	1.8	1.9	3.5	3.5
Others	59.1	50.2	44.8	44.4	37.5	32.5
Total	100	100	100	100	100	100
Top nine sources of imports	40.9	49.8	55.2	55.6	62.5	67.5

Source: Estimated from the data of Bangladesh Economic Review, Ministry of Finance

top nine countries has increased from 40.9 percent in 1986–1990 to 67.5 percent in the 2011–2015 period. The share of imports from other countries compared to these nine countries has sharply declined from 59 percent to 32 percent during the period. A compound annual growth of imports is also reported in Table 10.8.

While the share of nine countries in import basket has increased, the growth of imports from other countries has also increased considerably in the recent period (Table 10.3). Imports from countries like Malaysia, South Korea and Japan have increased along with predominant supply from India and China. A high growth of imports can be observed from India, China and Malaysia. Growth of imports from the USA is also stably high. Major contribution to import growth of Bangladesh has come from top nine suppliers (67.5 percent). However, India and China alone accounted for 37 percent growth of imports.

10.3 Evolving Markets and Opportunities: An Analysis

This section analyzes evolving markets and opportunities for Bangladesh through estimating different sets of standard indices, like revealed comparative advantage (RCA), geographic RCA and TPI. The findings based on these indices will help identify potential products and markets.

10.3.1 *Indicator of Revealed Comparative Advantage and Specialization Pattern*

The RCA index reflects a country's comparative advantage or disadvantage in terms of different products and regions. The RCA indices are popularly used in the trade literature for evaluating the trade performance and specialization of a country. A quantitative comparison can be made between different products of a country and the rest of the world. A change in the indicator of comparative advantage may reflect both a shift in specialization and a variation in trade performance. Therefore, in the context of highly concentrated export basket and escalating trade deficits, Bangladesh needs to invest along the lines of its dynamic comparative advantage to expand and diversify exports.

The modified Balassa revealed comparative advantage (BRCA) index and standardized revealed comparative advantage have been estimated as analytical tools to uncover changes in comparative advantage patterns over time and of the products. We further estimated trade specialization index to see whether the products are specialized in the lines of their comparative advantage. The analysis uses time series data of a wider range of commodity groups and market destinations to make a dynamic assessment of comparative advantage of Bangladesh in the global market.

BRCA can be expressed as:

$$\mathrm{BRCA}_{\mathrm{i}} = \frac{bX_i / bX_T}{wX_i / wX_T}$$

where bX_i = Bangladesh's export of product i, bX_T = total export of Bangladesh, wX_i = world export of product i and wX_T = world total exports.

Using the RCA, a symmetric RCA, namely the symmetric Balassa index (SBI) can be estimated as follows:

$$\mathrm{SBI} = (\mathrm{BRCA} - 1) / (\mathrm{BRCA} + 1).$$

A country would be considered to have a comparative advantage or disadvantage in products depending on whether the ratio of BRCA is greater or less than 1. It ranges from 1 to infinity when it enjoys comparative advantage, but zero to one when it has comparative disadvantage for the products. To address asymmetric values of the index, symmetric RCA indexes for different products are calculated. The SBI ranges from −1 to 1. The estimated index and changes in pattern of index are shown in Table 10.11.

The estimated RCA and SBI indexes show that Bangladesh has been enjoying high RCA in knitted garments, woven garments, jute and jute goods, other textile articles, frozen fish, leather, footwear and headgear and parts (Table 10.4). Our estimates show that about one-fourth (24.7 percent) of 1571 products at four-digit level enjoy comparative advantage in the world market as their average RCA is around 20 and average symmetric RCA is around 0.90. Trade specialization index of these products is on average around 0.75 (Table 10.5). But these product categories reflect are subject to high concentration in terms of products (88 percent share for three products) and market destination (55 percent for three markets). The analysis indicates that attention needs to be given not only on RCA of products for specialization, but also on diversification of export items and market destinations. This is important for ensuring sustainability of export earnings on a long-term basis.

During the same period, traditional export commodities including tea and leather lost their previous comparative advantage. The sectors which came into dynamism were footwear, ceramic products, household articles including tableware and kitchenware, light engineering, pharmaceuticals, bicycle, tent, home textiles, and vegetables.

Table 10.4 Pattern of changes of revealed comparative advantage of 98 products at 2-digit level during 2005–2009

Type of changes in comparative advantage	*No of products*	*Percent*
Stably high and increased	5	5.10
Advantage lowered	4	4.08
Shift from disadvantage to advantage	3	3.06
Disadvantage reduced	7	7.14
Shift from advantage to disadvantage	8	8.16
Increased disadvantage	24	24.49
Shift from advantage to disadvantage	47	47.96
Total	98	100.00

Source: Authors' calculation

Note: Though the data are somewhat outdated, the situation has not changed much over time as discussed in previous sections. Data are taken from United Nations Conference on Trade and Development (UNCTAD)

Table 10.5 Revealed comparative advantage (RCA), trade specialization index, and concentration ratios for Bangladeshi exports (out of 1571 Products), 2009

Products having comparative advantage	*RCA*	*Symmetric RCA*	*No of products*	*percent total products*	*Exports in thousand US$*	*Percent of total*	*Trade specialization index*	*Product concentration*	*Concent. ratio of markets*
Knitted garments	36.00	0.95	102	6.49	7,754,376	45.42	1.03	69	44
Non-knit garments	30.00	0.94	114	7.26	6,381,134	37.37	1.01	67	64
Other textile articles	12.20	0.85	49	3.12	688,265	4.03	0.99	51	41
Headgear and parts	14.50	0.87	10	0.64	98,200	0.58	0.96	100	83
Vegetable fibers and fabrics	113.50	0.98	15	0.95	387,707	2.20	0.87	91	49
Leather	6.10	0.72	19	1.21	167,457	0.98	0.71	94	61
Fish	5.10	0.67	45	2.86	482,667	2.87	0.96	91	49
Footwear	2.00	0.33	22	1.40	226,449	1.33	0.74	85	51
Tobacco and manufactured thereof	1.10	0.05	5	0.32	49,238	0.29	0.69	98	43
Fertilizer	1.10	0.05	2	0.13	59,378	0.35	−0.74	100	81
Mating materials	1.00	0.00	5	0.32	2727	0.02	1.00	98	43
All	20.24	0.91	388	24.70	16,297,598	95.00	0.75	86	55
Potential products									
Ceramic products	0.80	−0.11	16	1.02	34,579	0.35	−0.03	95	50
Pharmaceuticals	0.10	−0.82	15	0.95	36,253	0.21	−0.56	92	37
Plastic products	0.10	−0.82	39	2.48	38,742	0.23	−0.86	68	58
Non-woven,, felt, twine	0.70	−0.18	20	1.27	15,787	0.09	−0.30	71	76
Leather goods	0.40	−0.43	19	1.21	20,158	0.12	0.24	59	69
Meat, fish and food prep.	0.40	−0.43	7	0.45	20,344	0.12	0.88	99	50
Carpets and other floor cover	0.60	−0.25	11	0.70	7769	0.05	0.61	90	49
Artificial flowers	0.30	−0.54	7	0.45	1071	0.01	0.41	96	88

Source: Authors' calculation. Calculated from United Nations International Trade Statistics Database (UN Comtrade) data

The challenges for Bangladesh are to increase price and non-price competitiveness and find new potential industries and markets for promoting exports of the country in the face of global competition. Since comparative advantage is a major determinant of trade expansion, the country's trade policy should be consistent with the dynamics of comparative advantage. As the analysis of aggregate trade data cannot uncover exactly which products are resembling better competitiveness, a TPI has thus been estimated in the next section to identify trade potentials of the locally produced commodities.

10.3.1.1 Geographic RCA or Specialization Index

Geographic specialization index (GSI) is estimated to identify the RCA in a particular market and geographic specialization. The most commonly used index for this is Balassa geographic specialization index, which is expressed as follows:

$$GSI = \frac{bX_a / bX_w}{wX_a / wX_w}$$

where wXw = export of the world, wXa = export of the world to the market 'a', bXa = Bangladesh export to market 'a' and bXw = Bangladesh export to the world.

A country is said to have specialized with comparative advantage in the exports in region 'a', if GB is greater than 1. A symmetric Balassa (SGB) index is estimated as:

$$SGB = \frac{GB - 1}{GB + 1}$$

The estimated symmetric Balassa geographic specialization index for Bangladesh reveals that Bangladesh has comparative advantage in export to the North America and the Western Europe (Table 10.6). The standardized trade specialization index (STSI) has been estimated for both the commodity and the geographic specialization of a country (Table 10.5). Bangladesh had comparative advantage in 19 percent of products at two-digit level and 10 percent at four- and six-digit levels in 1998, which increased in 2009 indicating that some products having disadvantages in

Table 10.6 Geographic revealed comparative advantage of Bangladesh's exports, 1988–2009

Geographical area	*Balassa RCA*				*Symmetric Balassa index*			
	1988	*1993*	*1998*	*2009*	*1988*	*1993*	*1998*	*2009*
North America	1.620	1.900	1.770	2.300	0.230	0.310	0.270	0.390
Western Europe	0.710	0.990	1.090	2.400	−0.170	−0.001	0.046	0.410
Other industrialized countries	0.790	0.400	0.380	0.400	−0.110	−0.420	−0.440	−0.420
Africa	1.870	0.570	0.192	0.320	0.300	−0.270	−0.670	−0.510
Developing Asia	1.090	0.540	0.430	0.650	0.050	−0.290	−0.400	−0.210
Other developing America	0.120	0.080	0.810	0.135	−0.770	−0.850	−0.850	−0.070

Source: Authors' calculation

1998 transformed into advantageous position in 2009. As far as geographical trade specialization is concerned, Bangladesh has been geographically specialized in two regions: the EU and North America, especially the US. They are the two most specialized regions for Bangladesh's international trade reflecting the RMG export destinations (Table 10.6).

Bangladesh does not enjoy geographic comparative advantage in Asian countries except Thailand; however, it enjoys slight geographical advantage with Vietnam, Laos and Cambodia among other South Asian countries. The gravity of Bangladesh's disadvantage with the Philippines and the Middle East is small but high for Asian giants like Japan, China, India and Korea Republic. This raises question regarding effectiveness of export promotion efforts in these countries.

10.3.2 Trade Potential Index

As was discussed in the previous section, the analysis of comparative advantage cannot fully uncover the potentiality of products or markets. Therefore, it is necessary to analyze trade potentials in a different setup. There are different approaches to estimate trade potential for a country. For example, gravity analysis is used to assess trade potential at aggregate level, whereas TPI helps calculate potential at disaggregated product level.

TPI is a scoring system which allows the analysis to focus on trade potential while taking cognizance of import demand, import trends, growth rates and unit values rather than focusing solely on trade potential values (Rensburg and Letswalo, 2010). Following the methodology used by Rensburg and Letswalo (2010), we have estimated TPI for Bangladesh. However, we have modified the criteria of calculating "indicative trade potential" for our estimation. First, we assign a score of either 1 or 0 according to the trade indicators contained in the database. This score is, then, summed up to obtain a total score. A score of 0 would indicate the least trade potential, while a score of 5 would indicate the greatest trade potential (see Box 10.1).

Box 10.1 Calculation of the Trade Potential Index

- **Import growth**: If imports by Bangladesh to any of the selected country happened in 2015, a score of 1 is allocated. The absence of import is allocated a score of 0. The existence of any trade relationship (import or export) is considered a significant factor in furthering trade.
- **Export growth**: A positive growth rate in the value of exports over a five-year period will be awarded a score of 1, while no or negative growth will be awarded a score of 0.
- **Growth in export demand**: A positive growth of exports to the rest of the world measured over a five-year period will be allocated 1. No growth or negative growth rates are awarded a score of 0.
- **Growth in import demand**: A positive growth of imports from the rest of the world measured over a five-year period will be allocated 1. No growth or negative growth rates are given a score of 0.
- **Indicative trade potential**: A rule of thumb is set for this purpose: if the country's total import on that particular product line is 10 times higher than Bangladesh's export of that product to that specific country, a score of 1 is allocated. Trade potential with a lower value or with no or negative trade potential values are allocated a score of 0.

Source: Rensburg and Letswalo (2010).

The methods of calculating TPI is discussed in Box 10.1. For the purpose of calculating TPI for Bangladesh, first we have selected some countries based on top 30 export destinations of Bangladesh (at 2-digit HS level) for the period 2002–2007[1]. We have then selected the countries for which Bangladesh's export growth has registered a growth of more than 50 percent. We have ended up of a country group of 12 through this process (Table 10.7). Then, finally, we have calculated TPI with these countries at HS-6-digit level using the UN Comtrade database through World Integrated Trade Solution (WITS). However, due to lack of sufficient information, TPI for Indonesia could not be calculated.

The summary of the estimated TPI for Bangladesh has been reported in Table 10.7. Highly potential commodities include garments and its

Table 10.7 Trade potential index for Bangladesh (number of items at 6 digit HS level)

SL no.	*Country name*	*TPI score*						*Share of 5 in total (percent)*
		5	*4*	*3*	*2*	*1*	*Total items*	
1	Australia	151	34	4			189	79.89
2	Austria	46	42	3			91	50.55
3	Canada	43	71	107	62	16	299	14.38
4	China	101	197	72	11		381	26.51
5	Denmark	63	50	23	6	1	143	44.06
6	Germany	177	151	74	16	3	421	42.04
7	India	221	130	79	15	2	447	49.44
8	Italy	187	109	44	14	2	356	52.53
9	Mexico	34	37	30	7		108	31.48
10	Pakistan	35	69	24	16	5	149	23.49
11	Spain	117	72	28	5	3	225	52.00
12	Turkey	57	51	18	2		128	44.53

Source: Authors' estimation based on 2007 data

Note: The TPI is measured against a potential score of 5. A score of 0 would represent the lowest end of the scale and the least trade potential whilst a score of 5 would indicate the greatest trade potential

[1] Since our objective here is to introduce a method in order to identify trade potential of a country, the method can be replicated to recent data. As Bangladesh's export basket has not changed that much since 2007, the results are assumed to be valid till now.

accessories, plastic, light engineering, pharmaceuticals, chemicals, tableware/kitchenware, frozen food, and so on.[2] Therefore, to harness the potentiality of these products, it is important to improve domestic production capacity, liberalized environment, international production network and efficient incentive structure.

Table 10.7 also reveals that a large number of products have immense potential for trade in a number of countries. In terms of number of items with very high trade potential, India ranks in the first place; countries like Italy, Germany, Australia, Spain and China are also very potential market for a number of products. Among these countries, Australia can be considered as the most potential market for Bangladesh as 80 percent of 189 items exported in the year 2007 have very high potential for Australia. The other promising markets where Bangladeshi exporters can explore are Austria, India and Turkey. However, the underlying condition is that despite potentials, Bangladeshi products must maintain importing countries quality standards, sanitary and phytosanitary restrictions in order to get access to these potential markets.

To summarize, the estimated RCA and SBI indexes show that Bangladesh has been enjoying high RCA in knitted garments, woven garments, jute and jute goods, other textile articles, frozen fish, leather, footwear, headgear and parts. But these product categories are facing high concentration in terms of not only of products (88 percent share for three products) but also of market destinations (55 percent for three markets). Therefore, more attention requires not only on RCA of products for specialization, but also on diversification of export items and market destinations. This is important for ensuring sustainability of export earnings on a sustainable basis.

On the other hand, TPI indicates that for Bangladesh a large number of products have vast potential for trade in a number of countries like India, Italy, Germany, Australia, Spain and China. However, to get access to these promising markets, a high quality of these potential products needs to be maintained in line with sanitary and phytosanitary restrictions in these countries. A review of tariff and para-tariff structures of these countries is also important to achieve competitiveness.

[2] The list of potential items is not given in this paper, but can be provided upon request.

10.4 Conclusions and Policy Recommendations

Bangladesh has made a good progress in gaining share of trade in GDP in recent years, but her share in global and regional trade is still insignificant. Her exports are less diversified concentrating to mainly ready-made garments, thereby exposed to external shocks. To enhance Bangladesh's share in global trade, more integration with sub-regional economies, diversification of exports, trade liberalization and greater market access would be the right policy options. Other than the RMG products, agro-processed food, pharmaceuticals, leather and footwear, plastic, ceramics, light engineering, electrical and electronics, and so on need proper attention and policy support in order to diversify exports of Bangladesh.

The estimated revealed comparative advantage (RCA) indices indicate that attention needs to be paid not only on RCA of products for specialization, but also on diversification of export items and market destinations. For diversification of export basket, the government has been providing cash incentives to exporters of certain traditional and non-traditional products since 1996. Both volume and value of exports of subsidized products (those enjoy cash incentives) have been on a rising trend over the period of time, albeit marginally. It is, thus, necessary to analyze the incentive and support structures in order to achieve maximum benefits out of it. Thus, streamlining of cash incentives is required both in terms of its amount and operational modalities.

Despite having potentials of many Bangladeshi products in various markets, they could not enter due to poor quality standard or poor institutional quality of the country. Therefore, for greater market access, the underlying condition is that Bangladeshi products have to maintain importing countries' quality standards by reviewing their sanitary and phytosanitary measures in detail. In this regard, development and capacity strengthening of relevant institutions, such as Bangladesh Standard and Testing Institution (BSTI) is in the center point of discussion.

The effective rate of protection suggests that though rice is strongly import substitutable, it is not strongly exportable. Among the non-rice crops, pulses, potato and vegetables are strongly exportable as well as highly import substitutable. Thus commercialization of non-rice food products may be an important policy issue in agricultural diversification and food security. There are two important factors determining the future prospects of such exports: one relates to the tariff barriers in the importing countries, and the other relates to sanitary and phytosanitary restrictions. Sanitary and phytosanitary measures seem to be more important for Bangladeshi exporters of these products. It is important to ensure that Bangladesh undertakes necessary measures to meet sanitary and technical standards of the importing countries. Appropriate institutions and technical expertise need to be built up for ensuring the safety and quality of exports. Further study may be undertaken to examine what efforts have been made so far in Bangladesh to meet such requirements in the importing countries.

The challenges for Bangladesh are to increase price and non-price competitiveness and find new potential industries and markets for vitalizing the exports of the country in the face of acute global competition. Drawing conclusions based on only analyzing comparative advantage index or trade potential index may be misleading if they are not matched with the country's overall trade policy and productive capacity. The trade policy of Bangladesh has long been criticized for various reasons, such as the lack of time-bound initiatives, unpredictable tariff structure, market distortionary policies and existence of anti-export bias. Therefore, a robust and well-analyzed trade policy needs to be devised to bring dynamism in the trade structure of a middle-income country context.

Increasing productive capacities, establishing production networks and linkages could be important policy stimuli for enhancing export diversification. In order to increase productive capacity, the following measures can be undertaken:

(i) Strengthening national capacity to undertake analysis of competitive potential at the product and subsector level
(ii) Establishing the quality and conformity assessment infrastructure required to increase exports
(iii) Providing special attention to productive sectors with high export potential to upgrade product and production quality and comply with standards and regulations
(iv) Allocating sufficient fund for research and development (R&D) of agro-processed products
(v) Developing troubleshooting mechanism in cases where export products encounter technical barriers and advising on technical solutions to problems
(vi) Building capacities of existing research institutions, such as Bangladesh Agriculture Research Institute (BARI), BSTI, Bangladesh Council for Scientific and Industrial Research (BCSIR), and so on.

Appendix

Table 10.8 Compound growth of imports by sources of supply (in percent)

Country	*Fiscal year*				
	1986–1990	*1991–1995*	*1996–2000*	*2001–2005*	*2006–2010*
India	24.7	39.7	−6.7	14.4	19.4
China	15.6	33.3	−5.3	23.4	22.9
Singapore	11.5	−4.7	19.6	1.9	8.3
Japan	16.8	15	−0.4	−9.8	12.4
Hong Kong	35.9	21.3	3.9	4.3	6.4
Taiwan			15.6	1.6	3.4
S. Korea	18.5	19.8	−3.4	0.9	14.9
USA	6.1	10.9	−0.4	7.3	10.2
Malaysia	11	6.4	11.9	16.9	35.2
Others	10.1	8.2	10.1	10.1	12.7
Total	12.3	13.5	4.8	8.9	16.4
Top nine sources	15.6	11.1	7.6	8.3	8.3

Source: Estimated from data of BBS

Table 10.9 Average percentage share of individual export items

Export items	1981–85	1986–90	1991–1995	1996–00	2001–05	2006–10	Observation
Raw jute	15.91	9.7	3.6	1.93	1.09	1.27	Substantial decline
Tea	6.72	3.34	1.66	0.73	0.25	0.07	Substantial decline
Frozen food	8.67	12.33	7.77	6.44	5.03	3.48	Stable and prospective
Agriproduct	1.03	1.68	0.51	0.54	0.51	0.97	Slight increase
Other primary commodities	1.1	0.8	0.69	0.35	0.29	0.58	Slight decrease
Total primary goods	33.43	27.84	14.23	10	7.16	6.38	Substantial decline
Jute goods	46.09	27.98	12.94	6.29	3.67	2.82	Substantial decline
Total jute and jute goods	62	37.68	16.54	8.22	4.76	4.08	Substantial decline
Leather	8.91	11.87	6.75	4.02	3.13	1.75	Substantial decline
Leather goods	0	0	0.49	0.67	0	0	Prospective
Footwear	0	0	0.41	0.59	0.29	0.58	Increased and prospective
Nathalie and furnace oil	4.69	1.36	0.97	1.66	7.16	6.38	Increased
Woven garments	3.9	34.26	50.41	53.14	48.42	37.6	Substantial increase
Knitwear	0	0.19	8.78	18.49	26.72	39.16	Substantial increase
Total garments	3.9	34.46	59.2	71.62	75.13	76.76	Substantial increase
Chemical products	1.06	2.11	2.22	1.86	1.6	1.35	Stable
Fertilizer	0.91	1.79	7.4	1.61	0	0	Declined
Pharma	0.02	0.01	0.07	0.1	0.05	0	Stably low
Paper prod	1.02	0.78	0.14	0	0	0	Decline
Handicraft	0.36	0.34	0.29	0.14	0.08	0.04	Stably low
Engineering products	0.29	0.46	0.4	0.27	0.36	1.52	Slight increase
Specific textiles	0.07	0.14	1.14	0.96	0	0	Stably low
Other mfg.	0.1	0.21	1.15	3.43	8	7.09	Increased
Total mfg exports	66.57	79.75	85.77	90	92.83	92.5	Substantial increase
Total exports	100	107.59	100	100	100	100	
Total export exec garments	96.1	73.13	40.8	28.38	24.87	23.24	Substantial decline
Total manufactured exports except garments	62.67	45.29	26.57	18.38	17.7	16.87	Substantial decline

Source: Calculated from the data of Export Promotion Bureau (EPB)

Table 10.10 Growth of imports by commodities (%)

Category	*1981–1985*	*1986–1990*	*1991–1995*	*1996–2000*	*2001–2005*	*2006–2010*
Growth rate of primary goods import	–9	4	19	14	27	–7
Growth rate of rice import	139	83	402	271	87	–71
Growth rate of wheat import	–4	3	–1	25	23	19
Growth rate of oil seeds import	8	664	28	–6	17	–1
Growth rate of raw cotton import	–21	9	–2	20	25	–12
Growth rate of crude oil	–5	20	23	15	26	9
Growth rate of major intermediate goods	–13	13	13	7	26	1
Growth rate of edible oil	–12	5	17	13	25	4
Growth rate of petroleum products import	–13	11	14	19	28	–1
Growth rate of fertilizer import	–12	61	1	1	49	13
Growth rate of clinker import	26	16	5	19	20	–2
Growth rate of staple fiber import	114	40	24	–3	23	4
Growth rate of yarn import	13	15	36	–3	21	3
Growth rate of capital machinery import	4	10	10	–2	27	–1
Growth rate of consumption imports	33	21	17	14	13	11

Source: Estimated from the data of Bangladesh Bureau of Statistics (BBS)

Table 10.11 Pattern of changes in revealed comparative advantage of major items of 98 product categories of exports of Bangladesh

Commodities industry (Bangladesh)	*2005 RCA*	*2006 RCA*	*2007 RCA*	*2008 RCA*	*2009 RCA*	*Pattern of change*
00 All industries						
62 Articles of apparel, accessories, not knit or crochet	27.2	28.1	29.8	40	36	Stable; high
61 Articles of apparel, accessories, knit or crochet	30.9	30	29.1	32	30.1	Stable; high
03 Fish, crustaceans, mollusks, aquatic invertebrates nes	8.1	15	11	13.8	12.2	Increased
53 Vegetable textile fibers nes, paper yarn, woven fabric	115	9	121	7.7	5.1	Positive though declined
63 Other made textile articles, sets, worn clothing and so on	9.6	108	10.6	129.5	114	Increased substantially
41 Raw hides and skins (other than furskins) and leather	9.8	9.8	9.6	8.4	2	Declined though positive
87 Vehicles other than railway, tramway	0.1	8.8	4.5	2.1	6.1	Shift to high advantage
31 Fertilizers	4.4	1.5	0.1	0.1	0.1	Shift to disadvantage
64 Footwear, gaiters and the like, parts	1.6	0.1	1.8	18.3	14.5	Increased substantially
58 Special woven or tufted fabric, lace, tapestry and so on	6.6	8	0.1	1.2	0.1	Shift to disadvantage
07 Edible vegetables and certain roots and tubers	2.2	0.1	0.1	0.5	1.1	Lowered advantage
65 Headgear and parts thereof	16.5	13.3	7.5	0	1.1	Lowered advantage
52 Cotton	1.3	2.6	2	0.1	0	Shift to disadvantage
27 Mineral fuels, oils, distillation products and so on	0	0	0.1	0.1	0.1	Reduced disadvantage
56 Wadding, felt, nonwovens, yarns, twine, cordage and so on	4.2	3.4	12.8	1.1	0.1	Shift to disadvantage
39 Plastics and articles thereof	0.2	0.9	0.2	0	0.8	Reduced disadvantage
28 Inorganic chemicals, precious metal compound, isotopes	0.9	1.2	1.3	0.1	0	Disadvantage increased
72 Iron and steel	0.2	0.1	1.4	0	0.2	Stable; disadvantage

(*continued*)

Table 10.11 (continued)

Commodities industry (Bangladesh)	*2005 RCA*	*2006 RCA*	*2007 RCA*	*2008 RCA*	*2009 RCA*	*Pattern of change*
84 Boilers, machinery	0	0.6	0.1	0.9	0	Stable; disadvantage
08 Edible fruit, nuts, peel of citrus fruit, melons	0.9	0.1	3	0.7	0.4	Disadvantage increased
55 Manmade staple fibers	1.3	2.6	2.8	0.6	0.4	Shift to disadvantage
69 Ceramic products	1.1	0.2	0.5	0.2	0.2	Shift to disadvantage
06 Live trees, plants, bulbs, roots, cut flowers and so on	2.2	0.9	1.4	0	0.4	Shift to disadvantage
24 Tobacco and manufactured tobacco substitutes	1.1	0.1	0.1	0.1	0.1	Shift to disadvantage
09 Coffee, tea, mate and spices	1.4	0	0.3	0.4	0.3	Shift to disadvantage
90 Optical, photo, technical, medical and so on apparatus	0.1	0.1	1	0.2	0.7	Reduced disadvantage
49 Printed books, newspapers, pictures and so on	0.6	0.8	0.1	0.5	0.2	Disadvantage increased
30 Pharmaceutical products	0.1	0.5	0.9	0.6	0	Disadvantage increased

Source: Authors' calculation. Adapted from the data of UNCTAD of 2005–09

References

Ahmed, S., & Sattar, Z. (2004). Impact of trade liberalization: Looking at the evidence. *Economic and Political Weekly, XXXIX*(36), 4059–4067.

Ahmed, N., Bakht, Z., Dorosh, P. A. & Shahabuddin, Q. (2007). *Distortions to agricultural incentives in Bangladesh* (Working Paper 32). The World Bank, Washington D.C. Available at: http://documents.worldbank.org/curated/en/724601468177569404/National-spreadsheet-for-agricultural-distortions-in-Bangladesh

Bakht, Z. (2001). Trade liberalization, exports and growth of manufacturing industries in Bangladesh. In M. M. Huq & J. Love (Eds.), *Strategies for industrialization: The case of Bangladesh.* Dhaka: University Press Ltd.

Bangladesh Economic Review. (Various issues). Ministry of Finance, Government of the People's Republic of Bangladesh.

BBS. (Various years). Bangladesh Bureau of Statistics, Dhaka. Web: http://www.bbs.gov.bd/

Dorosh, P. A., & Shahabuddin, Q. (2005). Trade liberalization and food security in Bangladesh. In S. C. Babu & A. Gulati (Eds.), *Economic reforms and food security: The impact of trade and technology in South Asia*. New York: Haworth Press.

EPB. (Various years). Export Promotion Bureau, Government of the People's Republic of Bangladesh. Web: www.epb.gov.bd

Rensburg, G., & Letswalo, J. (2010). Country market study: Saudi Arabia. Retrieved from: http://s3.amazonaws.com/zanran_storage/www.nda.agric.za/ContentPages/110659005.pdf

UNCTAD. (Various years). United Nations Conference on Trade and Development, Geneva. Web: https://unctadstat.unctad.org/EN/

CHAPTER 11

Exchange Rate Management Under Floating Regime in Bangladesh: An Assessment

Monzur Hossain and Mansur Ahmed

11.1 Introduction

While the advantages of freely floating regime are well known, it is still debated whether this regime is suitable for less developed countries. The problem of destabilizing speculation and consequent excessive exchange rate volatility appears to be exacerbated in developing countries, making a floating regime unsuitable, particularly in the absence of a resilient and developed financial system (Grenville and Gruen 1999). After the Asian and Latin American crises in the 1990s, there has been a growing tendency among countries to adopt a corner regime—either a fixed or a floating regime. However, many studies document that the way developing countries float is not consistent with the characteristics of clean floats (Hossain 2009; Hausmann et al. 2001; Hernandez and Montiel 2003).

M. Hossain (✉)
Bangladesh Institute of Development Studies (BIDS), Dhaka, Bangladesh

M. Ahmed
The World Bank, Washington, DC, USA
e-mail: Mahmed10@worldbank.org

M. Hossain (ed.), *Bangladesh's Macroeconomic Policy*,
https://doi.org/10.1007/978-981-15-1244-5_11

Bangladesh adopted a freely floating regime on May 30, 2003 by abandoning the adjustable pegged system.[1] The transition to the floating regime was smooth, experiencing a depreciation of less than 1 percent from June 2003 to April 2004. Exchange rate kept on depreciating gradually from mid-2004, and it had reached at Tk. 70/USD in 2006 from Tk. 58/USD in 2003, accounting for a 20 percent depreciation. After that, the exchange rate remained fairly stable between taka 68 and 69 per USD for quite a long period before it had jumped to about Tk. 75/USD in 2010 and continued so until it made another shorter leap to around Tk. 80/USD in 2012 (Fig. 11.1). It, thus, appears that sporadic adjustments are made in the exchange rate market. Now the questions are: Is this behavior consistent with the characteristics of a floating regime? Or, can the behavior of the nominal exchange rate (NER) be explained in a way that the authority allows the nominal bilateral rate to move to its equilibrium level and then intervene only to prevent excessive volatility around that level?

In Bangladesh, exporters often demand depreciation to offset domestic price and wage inflation and regain competitiveness. However, depreciation has both positive and negative effects on the economy, such as on output and inflation. First, depreciation directly affects the rate of inflation.

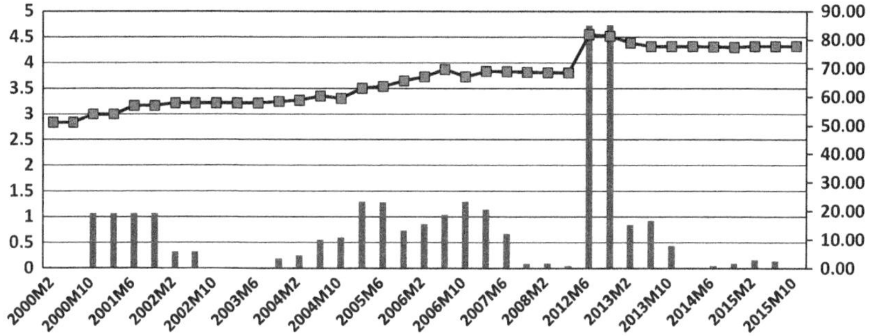

Fig. 11.1 Nominal exchange rate movement and its volatility. (Source: Bangladesh Bank)

[1] Historically, Bangladesh had been maintaining various pegged exchange rate regimes, such as pegged to pound sterling (£):1972–1979; pegged to a basket of major trading partners' currencies (£ as the intervening currency) 1980–1982; pegged to a basket of major trading partners' currencies (US$ as the intervening currency): 1983–1999; crawling band: 2000–2003; floating exchange rate: May 30, 2003–present.

The impact of depreciation on inflation will depend on the level of the pass-through. Second, depreciation affects output through a *balance sheet* effect: the depreciation increases the cost of repayment of foreign currency-denominated debt, reducing profits in this period, and thus the capital stock and output in the second period. Third, a larger depreciation will result in a decrease in interest rates. Thus, a larger depreciation increases output in the second period, since the reduction in interest rate eases the credit constraint (we call this *the credit channel* effect). The overall effect on income will depend on which of the two channels, balance sheet or credit channel, dominate. If the credit channel dominates over the balance sheet channel, depreciation is expansionary. Otherwise, it is contractionary.

Against this backdrop, the monetary authorities usually choose to keep the exchange rate nominally fixed or almost fixed, by intervening in the foreign exchange market. Occasional intervention in the foreign exchange market is not bad at all, particularly for developing countries like Bangladesh if the intervention is targeted to achieve some economic objectives such as stable inflation or trade competitiveness. However, it is dangerous if NER moves along a continuum for a long time—it may create distortions in the market, for example, *irrational exuberance*, which include strong growth, accelerating inflation, rising international reserves and gradual overvaluation. This situation would be troublesome for the economy if it proceeds too far. Therefore, it is important to assess the exchange rate management practices in the context of pursuing floating regime. The main concern here is whether Bangladeshi taka is overvalued and to what extent through assessing the behavior of the *real effective exchange rates* (REERs).

The main objectives of this study are: (i) to characterize the exchange rate policies Bangladesh is currently pursuing, (ii) to evaluate the appropriateness of such policies in the light of both contemporary international and domestic economic conditions, and (iii) to provide some alternative policy options that might be of assistance in managing exchange rates under the floating regime. The study takes into account behavior of both the nominal and real exchange rates (RERs), behavior of economic fundamentals, intervention activities, exchange rate market pressure, exchange rate pass-through, exchange rate misalignment, and so on. This chapter uses data from various secondary sources including Bangladesh Bank, International Financial Statistics (IFS) of International Monetary Fund (IMF) and Direction of Trade Statistics (DOT) of the IMF.

This chapter is organized as follows: Sect. 11.2 reviews the literature on exchange rate issues of Bangladesh. Section 11.3 analyzes the behavior of the NER by focusing on the behavior of interest rates and international reserves during floating and pre-floating regimes. In Sect. 11.4, we assess the *de facto* exchange rate regime of Bangladesh by characterizing the extent of intervention in the foreign exchange market. In Sect. 11.5, we estimate an exchange market pressure index (EMP index) to understand how frequently exchange rate shocks are observed and explore the determinants of that shock and estimate the exchange rate pass-through coefficients to understand the impact of exchange rate changes on domestic price changes. In Sect. 11.6, the behavior of the REER and nominal effective exchange rate (NEER) and its implication for international price competitiveness are analyzed, and concurrantly, we estimate the equilibrium RER and its misalignment. Section 11.7 provides conclusions and some policy recommendations based on our findings that could act as guiding principles for exchange rate management in Bangladesh.

11.2 Literature Review

This section surveys empirical contributions on various aspects of exchange rate policies in Bangladesh. Hossain (2002) investigates the exchange rate responses to inflation in Bangladesh for the period 1973–1999. He finds that the effect of devaluation on inflation during the fixed exchange rate regime was not significant, and he claims the results to be robust for the whole sample period. By analyzing the movement of the RER and trade balance in Bangladesh for the period 1973–1996, Hossain (1997) finds that the continued inflows of foreign capital—foreign aid and overseas worker's remittances—have caused an appreciation of the RER by increasing the relative demand for non-tradable.

Rahman and Basher (2001) have estimated the equilibrium RER as well as exchange rate misalignment for the period 1977–1998. They find that trade liberalization and increase in debt service burden results in a real depreciation of the currency; while increase in capital inflow, improvement in terms of trade (TOT) and increase in government consumption of non-tradables result in a real appreciation of the currency. From the estimated long-run equilibrium RER, they find that Bangladesh currency was considerably overvalued until the late 1980s. However, the RER broadly was in equilibrium during the 1990s. An

Asian Development Bank (ADB) study concludes that the misalignment between the actual and equilibrium exchange rate for the period 1997–2001 has been small and has progressively narrowed since 1998 (ADB 2002). During 2001, the misalignment was only 2.2 percent.

Prior to adopting floating exchange rate regime, Islam (2003) concludes that the economic and institutional prerequisites of a floating exchange rate regime are not met in Bangladesh. Some recent studies have tried to explain the behavior of NERs of Bangladesh after its transition to the floating rate regime. By doing a correlation analysis, Rahman and Barua (2006) explore the possible explanation of the exchange rate movement. They finds that there is a strong correlation (−0.40) between depreciation and export-import gap as a share of reserves, and letter of credit (L/C) openings for imports also have a positive correlation (0.45) with volatility of the exchange rate, implying that the higher the L/C openings, the more volatile the exchange rate. They conclude that high seasonal demand for foreign currency because of increased import bills, systematic withdrawal of excess liquidity by Bangladesh Bank and relatively faster expansion of credit and higher interest rates on various national savings instruments are the reasons behind the interest rate hike in the money market and depreciation of the NER.

Younus and Chowdhury (2006) make an attempt to analyze Bangladesh's transition to floating regime and its impact on macroeconomic variables. They find that output growth in Bangladesh performed well in the intermediate and floating exchange rate regimes. Inflation is lower in the intermediate regime despite higher money supply and exchange rate depreciation. They also find that currency depreciation boosted export growth in the floating regime.

Chowdhury and Siddique (2006) have analyzed the exchange rate pass-through to domestic inflation in Bangladesh. Analyzing the data for the period 1997:07 to 2005:03, they have not found any significant pass-through effect of exchange rate in Bangladesh. They have applied vector autoregression (VAR) technique in their analysis. If their findings are correct, its policy implication would be to allow the currency to depreciate further in order to give a boost to the economy. The findings, however, appear to have been affected by measurement errors.

The above survey, however, indicates that there is a dearth of studies that cast a systematic and comprehensive assessment of contemporary exchange rate policies of Bangladesh, particularly after adopting the floating exchange rate regime.

11.3 Exchange Rate Management in Bangladesh

This section describes the behavior of the NERs by focusing on three aspects of exchange rate management: (i) the stock of reserves, (ii) the extent to which Bangladesh uses these reserves to stabilize the exchange rate, and (iii) the extent to which interest rates are used to stabilize the exchange rate. Figure 11.1 plots NER movements (level) as well as volatility of NER, measured by the six-month moving average standard deviation. The figure shows that during intermediate regime (adjustable pegged regime before 2003), NER moves occasionally because of official devaluation, and for the first six months of the floating regime, NER remained almost fixed. It is observed that from April 2004, NER was somewhat volatile, but remained fairly stable after March 2006. In June 2012, there was an upward jump of NER which continued till 2013, and after that the NER again remained very stable.

Is the stability of NER attributable to market driving forces consistent with economic fundamentals or is it due to artificial market intervention? To assess the situation, the conventional way is to look at relative volatilities of the exchange rate, reserves and interest rates. It is better to look into relative volatilities, because comparisons based solely on the volatility of exchange rates alone, or of reserves alone, could be misleading. The exchange rate could be more volatile simply because it is subject to larger external shocks. Comparing exchange rate volatilities does not provide a complete idea of the willingness of the authority to defend its parity. It may be the case that the central bank is intervening in the foreign exchange market to keep the exchange rate within certain limits, while during the period of less volatility, the authority is letting the exchange rate float independently. Similarly, comparing volatility of reserves may be problematic too. It is possible for reserves during a particular period to be relatively stable due to the absence of shocks that would have warranted a movement in the exchange rate, or in case the authority intervenes heavily, if a shock warrants it. However, a possible drawback of using relative volatilities is that, one does not know if the ratio is high because of the numerator being unusually high or the denominator unusually low. But intervention in the foreign exchange market is not the only channel that monetary authorities apply to influence movements in the exchange rate. They can also influence exchange rate market by tightening or loosening monetary policy. We, therefore, analyze relative volatility of exchange rates and also interest rates to assess the degree to which monetary authorities are willing to let the exchange rate float freely.

For measuring volatility, we use the standard deviation of the level of each of the three indicators, the exchange rate, international reserves and interest rates. For example, for reserve volatility, we use the standard deviation of the stock of reserves, normalized by the dollar value of the stock of base money (M0) and for measuring volatility of interest rates, we consider the standard deviation of call money interest rate. Table 11.1 presents the volatility of reserves, exchange rates as well as volatility of market (call money) interest rate and respective relative volatilities—relative volatility of exchange rate over international reserves and the relative volatility of exchange rate over interest rate.

The estimates in Table 11.1 suggest that, except for the period 2006–2008, the NER remained more volatile in other periods, and relative volatility of international reserves and call money rates in those periods were also higher, indicating a strong effort of intervention from Bangladesh Bank to keep the market stable.

The comparison of volatility of NERs against some major trading partner currencies using the coefficient of variation shows that Bangladeshi taka remained stable against all other trading partner's currencies except the US dollar (Table 11.2). This also highlights the importance of the US dollar as an invoice currency in Bangladesh.

Table 11.1 Relative volatilities of the nominal exchange rate, international reserve and call money rate (monthly data)

	Volatility of NER (Tk./ per US$)			*Volatility of reserve*	*Volatility of interest rate*			*Rel. vol (ER/ res)*	*Rel. vol (ER/ IR)*
	Std. dev.	*Max.*	*Min.*	*Std. dev.*	*Std. dev.*	*Max.*	*Min.*		
Pre-floating regime (Jan 2000–May 2003)	2.65	57.9	51.0	0.052	2.97	16.75	4.25	50.96	0.89
Floating regime (Jun 2003–Feb 2006)	3.03	67.13	57.9	0.046	3.30	15.97	4.95	65.57	0.92
Floating regime (Mar 2006–June 2008)	0.71	70.27	67.11	0.061	3.62	21.54	6.9	11.64	0.20
Floating regime (2010–2015)	2.92	81.9	71.2	0.062	3.21	13.88	9.29	47.1	0.91

Source: Authors' calculation

Note: ER indicates Exchange rate and IR indicates interest rate

Table 11.2 Comparison of volatility of exchange rates (coefficient of variation)

	Taka/US dollar	*Taka/ Rupee*	*Taka/ RMB*	*Taka/ Pound*	*Taka/ Yen*	*Taka/ Euro*	*Taka/ Sing $*
Pre-floating regime (Jan 2000–May 2003)	0.047	0.019	0.050	0.066	0.039	0.101	0.039
Floating regime (Jun 2003–Feb 2006)	0.500	0.065	0.057	0.075	0.055	0.069	0.065
Floating regime (Mar 2006–Nov 2008)	0.110	0.063	0.055	0.058	0.064	0.076	0.050
Floating regime 2010–2015	0.040	0.125	0.062	0.045	0.165	0.077	0.062

Source: Bangladesh Bank

Table 11.3 Sale and purchase of foreign exchange by Bangladesh Bank (in million USD)

	2003–04	*2004–05*	*2005–06*	*2006–07*	*2007–08*	*2008–09*	*2010–15*
Sale	0.00	459.00	413.10	0.00	735.50	70.00	962.00
Purchase	313.95	147.10	0.00	649.50	202.50	815.20	17,580.00
Net injection	−313.95	311.90	413.10	−649.5	533.00	−745.20	−16,618.00

Source: Bangladesh Bank

Note: -ve indicates buying US$

The findings in Tables 11.1 and 11.2 indicate that the way Bangladesh manages exchange rate is, by and large, not consistent with the characteristics of freely floating exchange rate regime. The extent of intervention in the foreign exchange market in order to keep the NER almost fixed or to allow it to move within a very narrow range is evident from Table 11.3. Though the intervention in the foreign exchange market is a common practice all over the world, it breaks the norm of a *de jure* regime if it continues in one direction for a long time, which is not clear from the analysis provided in this section. Therefore, it is necessary to follow a technical *de facto* regime classification criterion.

11.4 *De Facto* Regime Classification for Bangladesh

It is recognized in the literature that countries, particularly non-OECD (Organisation for Economic Co-operation and Development) countries, often deviate from their official exchange rate commitments. To capture

Table 11.4 *De facto* regime classification criteria

	σ_e	$\Delta\sigma_e$	σ_r
Inconclusive	Low	Low	Low
Flexible	High	High	Low
Dirty float	High	High	High
Crawling peg	High	Low	High
Fixed	Low	Low	High

Source: Levy-Yeyati and Sturzenegger (2005)

the deviation, some authors, thus, made attempts to characterize the *de facto* regimes of the countries. At least three *de facto* regime classifications are available so far (see Levy-Yeyati and Sturzenegger 2005; Bubula and Otker 2002; and Reinhart and Rogoff 2004). All these *de facto* classifications take the following three variables into account, *exchange rate volatility* (σ_e), *volatility of exchange rate changes* ($\Delta\sigma_e$) and *volatility of reserves* (σ_r). In this study, we follow the Levy-Yeyati and Sturzenegger (2005) method in Table 11.4.

Table 11.4 sets the criteria according to textbook description. Flexible exchange rates are characterized by little intervention in the exchange rate markets together with unlimited volatility of NER. Conversely, a fixed exchange rate regime occurs when the NER does not move while reserves are allowed to fluctuate. A crawling peg corresponds to the case where changes in the NERs occur with stable increments (i.e. low volatility in the rate of the exchange rate) while active intervention keeps the exchange rate along that path. A dirty float should be associated with the case in which volatility is relatively high across all variables, with intervention only partially smoothing exchange rate fluctuations.

Following the methodology adopted by Levy-Yeyati and Sturzeneger (2005), we estimate *exchange rate volatility* by monthly absolute percentage change of NER (σ_e), *volatility of exchange rate changes* ($\Delta\sigma_e$) by the standard deviation of monthly percentage change of NER, and *volatility of reserves* (σ_r) by the absolute change of reserves in classifying a *de facto* regime. A word of caution is in order for reserves. Reserves are notoriously difficult to measure, and there is usually a large difference between changes in reserves and interventions. Therefore, we take particular care in reserves for intervention. First, we define net reserves in dollar by subtracting foreign liabilities from foreign assets and deflating it by the NER (e_t) as follows.

$$R_t = \frac{Foreign\ Assets_t - Foreign\ Liabilities_t}{e_t}.$$

Next, we measure the monthly intervention in the foreign exchange market, r_t, as follows:

$$r_t = \frac{R_t - R_{t-1}}{Monetary\ Base_{t-1}(M_0)/e_{t-1}}.$$

Our measure of volatility here is the average of the absolute monthly change in r, that is, the average of the absolute monthly change in net international reserves relative to the monetary base in the previous month, in dollars.

The estimates of volatility are shown in Table 11.5 for the period 2000–2015. Following the classification criteria, we identify the *de facto* exchange rate regime of Bangladesh for the period 2000–2003:5 as an adjustable pegged regime. The behavior of the nominal NERs and reserves for the first ten months of the *de jure* floating regime was puzzling (inconclusive) as volatilities of all the three variables were fairly low, which cannot be explained from the textbook context. One of the reasons perhaps is that Bangladesh Bank intervened in the market not by buying or selling dollars, but by imposing some quantitative restrictions on LC margins. On the other hand, the period 2004:5 to 2006:12 was characterized by high NER volatility with high reserve volatility, which indicates that the *de facto* exchange rate regime was a *dirty float*. The *de facto* analysis of

Table 11.5 *De facto* classification of exchange rate regime in Bangladesh, 2000–2015

Period	σ_e	$\Delta\sigma_e$	σ_r	*Comments*
Jan 2000–May 2003	0.33 (L)	1.28 (H)	4.56 (H)	Adjustable peg
June 2003–April 2004	0.22 (L)	0.31 (L)	1.15 (L)	Inconclusive
May 2004–Dec 2006	1.05 (H)	1.23 (H)	3.65 (H)	Dirty float
Jan 2007–June 2008	0.15 (L)	0.18 (L)	5.97 (H)	Fixed
2010–2015	1.8 (H)	0.05 (L)	5.79 (H)	Crawling peg

Source: Authors' calculation

Notes: We term an indicator high (H) if it exceeds its long-term estimates, otherwise it is termed as low (L). Long-term estimates are $\sigma_e = 0.98$, $\Delta\sigma_e = 1.16$ and $\sigma_r = 4.15$

exchange rate regime for the period (2007:1–2008:6) reveals that the behavior of exchange rates is closer to a fixed (pegged) exchange rate system. Finally, *de facto* analysis of exchange rate regime for the recent period 2010–2015 reveals a crawling pegged system. Despite some limitations of *de facto* regime classifications, it may be concluded that Bangladesh's exchange rate policy is not consistent with a freely floating regime. Rather, it can be broadly defined as a managed floating regime.

The deviation from the floating regime commitment may happen due to a country's vulnerability to high exchange rate pass-through as well as having high frequency of exchange rate shocks. Both the issues can be explored by assessing the exchange rate market pressure and pass-through effect.

11.5 Behavior of Nominal Exchange Rate

11.5.1 Exchange Market Pressure

The exchange market disequilibrium can be captured by the changes in international reserves or changes in exchange rates or combination of both. Under the fixed and floating regime, the extent of imbalance in the Forex market can be estimated more directly by looking at the changes in reserves and changes in exchange rates, respectively. However, in a managed floating or an intermediate regime, monetary authorities usually allow either changes in reserves or exchange rate or combination of both in order to restore equilibrium in the foreign exchange market. The monetary approach to the balance of payments (BOP) suggests that exchange market disequilibrium arises when there is an excess demand for domestic money. Based on this proposition, Girton and Roper (1977) proposes an EMP index as the weighted sum of monthly changes in NER and monthly changes in the stock of international reserves scaled by monetary base in order to capture disequilibrium in the foreign exchange market. The Girton-Roper model has been extensively applied to many countries (see, Modeste 1981; Bahmani-Oskooee et al. 1998; Taslim 2003).

Given that Bangladesh has been maintaining a managed floating regime instead of a pure float as evident from our analyses in the previous sections, in this section we use the composite variable EMP as proposed by Girton and Roper (1977) to study the interaction between monetary variables and external sector, and the severity of exchange rate shocks in Bangladesh during the period 2000:1 to 2015:7.

We computed the EMP index by calculating the weighted sum of monthly changes in nominal exchange rate and monthly changes in the stock of international reserves scaled by monetary base. The weights are inversely proportional to the relative variances of NER changes and international reserve changes. As proposed by Eichengreen, Rose and Wyplosz (1996), a standardized indicator of crisis (IC) can be calculated based on EMP as: $IC = \frac{EMP - \mu_{EMP}}{\sigma_{EMP}}$. According to them, a crisis is signaled if IC > 1.5, while Kaminsky and Reinhart (1999) set a critical value of 3 for the IC. Both EMP and IC indices are plotted in Fig. 11.2.

Figure 11.2 shows that EMP is positive in Bangladesh during the 2000–2010; however, in 2010–2013 the EMP was negative. During 2005–2006 and 2010–2012, the extent of imbalance in the foreign exchange market was severe. It appears from the index IC that shocks were more frequent and several times it crossed the crisis threshold during the period 2005–2006, and 2010–2012 periods, which can be characterized as the turbulent periods. However, after 2012, the market has been able to neutralize EMP.

The main theoretical proposition of Girton and Roper (1977) is that the domestic money market equilibrium, if disturbed, is restored through some combination of the currency depreciation/appreciation and reserves

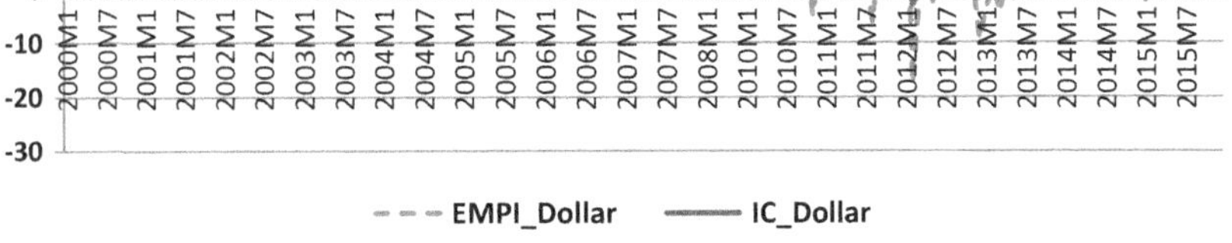

Fig. 11.2 Exchange market pressure index (2000–2015). (Source: Authors' calculation)

outflow/inflow. The excess domestic money supply will cause a combination of currency depreciation and reserves outflow while excess domestic money demand will cause some combination of currency appreciation and reserves inflow to restore the money market equilibrium. Therefore, it may be hypothesized a positive and contemporaneous impact of shock to domestic credit growth upon EMP—an increase in domestic credit causes the exchange rate to depreciate or the foreign exchange reserves to deplete or some combination of the two. To this end, we plot the percentage change in net foreign asset (NFA) and net domestic asset (NDA) in Fig. 11.3 to see the relationship.

From Fig. 11.3, it may be concluded that intervention was almost sterilized for the period 2005:8 to 2007:9 and after 2012. Comparing Figs. 11.2 and 11.3, a positive relationship between domestic credit growth (or growth of money supply) and exchange market shock is observed. That is, when Bangladesh Bank chooses to increase domestic money supply, some combination of reserve depletion or currency depreciation occurs. The situation deteriorates in the absence/ineffectiveness of interest rate channel of monetary policy transmission, which leads to sterilized interventions that ultimately contributes to exchange rate shocks.

From Figs. 11.2 and 11.3, we may conclude that sterilized intervention in Bangladesh causes extra pressure on the foreign exchange market. However, an incomplete sterilized intervention is seen from 2007:9

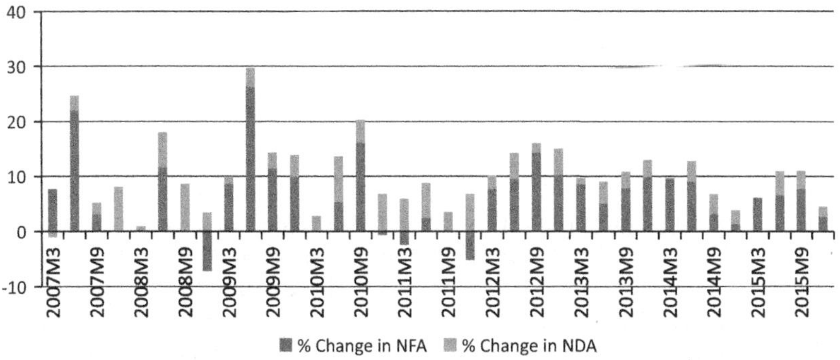

Fig. 11.3 Percentage change in net foreign assets (NFA) and percentage change in net domestic assets (NDA). (Source: Monthly Economic Trends)

onward, which might have contributed to an increase in inflation.[2] Therefore, if there is a likelihood of EMP, it would be a good option for Bangladesh Bank to tighten the money supply through interest rates channel. In what follows, Bangladesh Bank should work hard on making the financial sector more competitive in order to ensure smooth transmission of monetary policy stimuli through the interest rate channel, and only then can they enjoy the "low inflation benefit" of non-sterilized interventions. At the same time, tight monetary policy must be accompanied by fiscal adjustments; otherwise, it might increase the burden on the intertemporal budget and may, thus, be counterproductive.

11.5.2 *Exchange Rate Pass-Through*

Exchange rate pass-through is usually estimated to explain exchange rate movements. We estimate the pass-through effect for Bangladesh using a simple methodology applied for Australia by de Brouwer and Ericsson (1995), for Mexico by Garces-Diaz (2001) and for a cross-country analysis by Hausmann et al. (2001). Although for drawing the complete picture of exchange rate pass-through requires a complete paper, we take a simplistic approach here to estimate the pass-through coefficients using data for the period 2000–2008 just to see whether the intervention in the foreign exchange market is done in order to contain inflationary effects on Bangladesh economy. Our sample period includes intermediate exchange rate regime (2000:1 to 2003:5) also, because during this period exchange rates were allowed to move within a narrow band.

We consider the model of domestic prices using a mark-up equation as follows:

$$P = \alpha W^{\theta} F^{\gamma}, \tag{11.1}$$

where P is domestic price, W wages, F international prices in domestic currency (obtained by multiplying the exchange rate with an index of international prices) and α, θ, and γ are three parameters representing mark-up and the long-run elasticity of wages and external prices. By taking the natural logarithm of the above equation, it is possible to estimate the

[2] In a recent monetary policy statement (July 19, 2009), Bangladesh Bank admitted that they purchased 1.48 billion dollar in 2008–2009 from the currency market, most of which remains unsterilized.

long-run relationship among wages, international prices and local prices. Since we do not have monthly data for wages, we estimate the following long-run equation:

$$p = ln(\alpha) + \gamma f, \tag{11.2}$$

where lower case letters represent the log of the corresponding upper case variables defined above.

All the series we use are monthly and can be described as having a unit root process. Hence, we need to study the long-run relationship between internal and external prices using cointegration analysis. To understand the speed of adjustment, we also estimate the error correction model.

We measure p using the log of the consumer price index (CPI) of Bangladesh and use three different definitions of f. In the first definition, we add the log of the US dollar exchange rate to the log of an index of international non-fuel commodity prices (from IFS). In the second definition, we substitute the index of commodity prices by the US CPI, and in the third definition, we substitute commodity price index by the Indian CPI. Table 11.6 reports the results.

Table 11.6 shows that the long-run pass-through coefficient is very high and significant for Bangladesh. It is 0.87 for international price, 1.26 for the US price, and 0.95 for the Indian prices, which indicates that a change in international or the US or Indian prices will almost completely translate into a change in domestic prices. The estimated ECT is negative and significant—the speed of adjustment to equilibrium is 2 percent for international prices and 3 percent for the US prices, while it is 4 percent for Indian prices. Although our result is based on a simple univariate analysis, we find

Table 11.6 Estimates of inflation pass-through

	Changes in international prices	*Changes in the US prices*	*Changes in the Indian prices*
γ	0.87 (0.14)***	1.26 (0.15)***	0.95 (0.09)***
Constant	2.96	6.37	3.61
Error correction term (ECT)	−0.02 (0.005)**	−0.03 (0.01)**	−0.04 (0.02)**

Source: Authors' estimation based on data covering the period 2000–2008

***, ** indicate significance at 10 percent and 5 percent level, respectively

that exchange rate pass-through has some role in explaining the low volatility (stability) of exchange rate in Bangladesh, particularly after March 2006, when the world was facing high inflationary episodes.

11.6 Behavior of the REER and NEER

The REER is the inflation-adjusted and trade-weighted exchange rate, which is used as a popular index to determine international trade competitiveness of a country. On the other hand, NEER is a trade-weighted index, which is also used to represent trade competitiveness. This section is devoted to a discussion of the movements of both the REER and the NEER. Following Bangladesh Bank's procedure, we calculated the REER and the NEER considering the year 2000 as base and using trade weights of eight major trading partners (see Table 11.9 of the Appendix), namely, the US, the UK, Japan, the EU, China, India, Hong Kong and Singapore.[3] We have also estimated bilateral RERs against major trading partners.

Figure 11.4 plots the REER and bilateral RER. It shows that the REER depreciated around 20 percent over the years in an unstable fashion. During the fixed regime, 2000–2003, the REER moved in tandem with

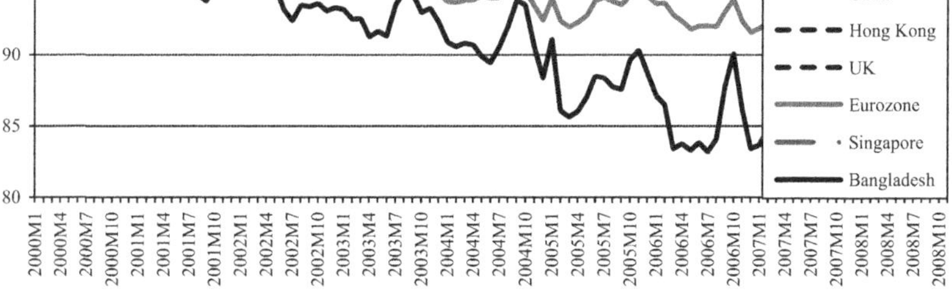

Fig. 11.4 Bangladesh's aggregate and bilateral REERs based on CPI (2000 = 100) (a rise indicates real appreciation)

[3]The analyses and results in this section are adapted from the authors' previous work (Hossain and Ahmed 2009).

the price differential and the movement of the US dollar vis-à-vis major currencies. The taka gained competitiveness during 2000–2003 because of the continued lower inflation differential as well as occasional devaluations. However, during the turbulent period of the floating regime (2004–2006), the taka remained competitive because of high depreciation as well as US dollar depreciation vis-à-vis major currencies despite high inflation differentials (with high domestic inflation). From 2006, the REER shows an appreciating trend, but for a brief period. With almost a stable NER of the dollar in the period 2006–2008, the REER shows slightly upward trend because of high inflation differentials and US dollar depreciation vis-à-vis major currencies. It is also observed from the trend of the REER that some periodic adjustments of taka/dollar exchange rate might have contributed to the overall trend of depreciation. Since there is a long-term trend in the REER movement, it suggests that the REER might have been overvalued to some extent.

Figure 11.4 also shows that the bilateral RER against the euro exhibits higher volatility with an overall depreciating trend. However, all other trading partners' RERs remained stable. It appears that Bangladesh competitiveness vis-à-vis the EU is particularly unstable.

It may be noted that the calculation of the REER using CPI may contain measurement error because CPI may not be the right index for this purpose. Since wholesale price index (WPI) contains largely tradable goods while CPI is more heavily weighted toward non-tradable goods, this phenomenon translates into a long-term rise of CPI relative to WPI. Therefore, the REER based on CPI is likely to underestimate the economy's competitiveness to the extent that this internal price movement is significant (relative to its trading partners). If an increase in the price of non-tradable relative to tradable is due to greater productivity growth in the second sector than the first, such increases lead to real appreciation in the RERs. This is well known as the Balassa-Samuelson effect. Does this effect exist in Bangladesh?

To address the issue, first we calculate the ratio of CPI to WPI, which is shown in Fig. 11.5, and then we calculate the REER based on WPI[4] in Fig. 11.6 using the same weights as in the case of the CPI-based REER. Figure 11.5 shows that internal price movements are persistently higher in Bangladesh and a sharp rising trend is observed since 2003:5; however, the WPI-based REER showed slightly appreciating trend from

[4]WPI is available only up to May 2006 with the base 1973. Here we calculate WPI considering the base period 2000 in order to make it consistent with the REER.

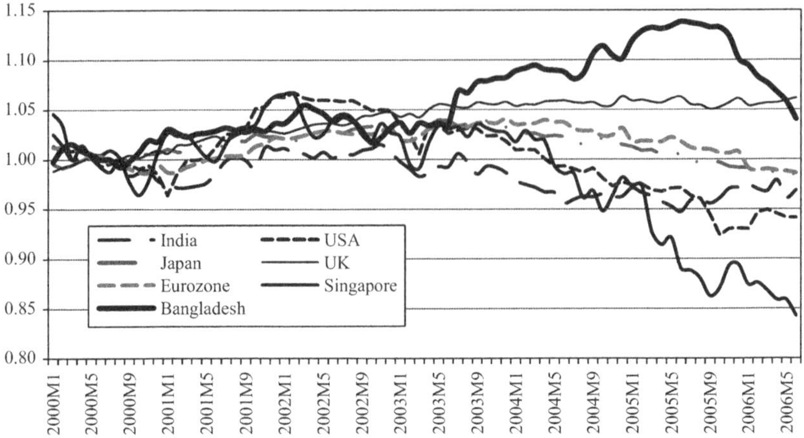

Fig. 11.5 CPI/WPI for selected countries (WPI: 2000=100)

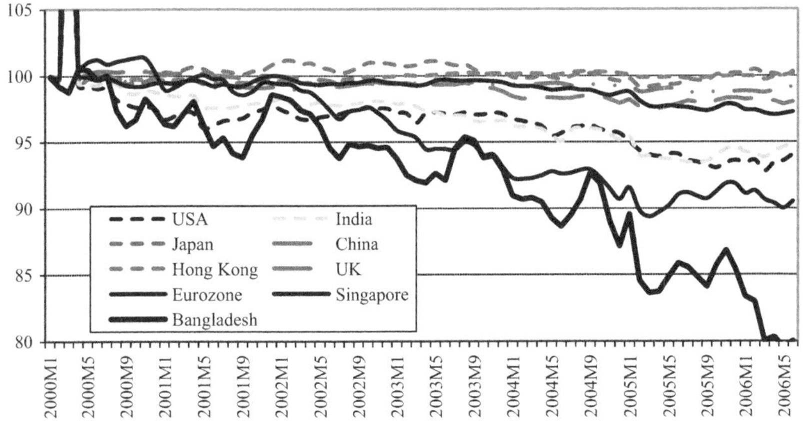

Fig. 11.6 Bangladesh's aggregate and bilateral REERs based on WPI (a rise indicates real appreciation)

that period that provides an indication of the Balassa-Samuelson effect on Bangladesh economy.

It is interesting to see that the REER (based on WPI) depreciated in line with the rising pattern of relative prices, implying that Bangladesh maintains competitiveness by offsetting price inflation (Fig. 11.6).

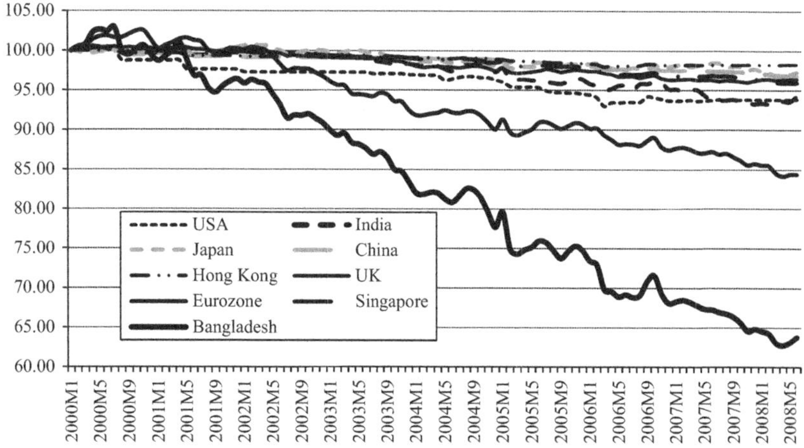

Fig. 11.7 Bangladesh's aggregate and bilateral NEERs (a rise indicates appreciation)

Comparing the patterns of the CPI-based REER and WPI-based REER, it may be concluded that WPI-based REER better predicts the competitiveness of Bangladesh. However, lack of WPI data would be a big problem for further simulation.

The behavior of the NEER also shows the same depreciating but unstable trend (Fig. 11.7). The NEER is a trade-weighted index without being adjusted for inflation. This index has particular importance in stabilizing the pace of competitiveness, especially when the currencies of the trading partners are more volatile.

11.6.1 Equilibrium REER and Misalignment

The next question is whether the actual RER is overvalued or undervalued compared to the long-run equilibrium exchange rate.[5] We employ the

[5] Two approaches have been widely used to estimate equilibrium the REER: the fundamental equilibrium exchange rate (FEER) and the BEER. Generally two different sets of variables are used in estimating FEER and BEER (Clark and MacDonald 1999). FEER models consider variables that affect the equilibrium current and capital account balances, such as real incomes of the domestic country and the partner countries. FEER also takes into account factors affecting national savings and investment. BEER, on the other hand, puts

behavioral equilibrium exchange rate (BEER) approach to estimate the long-run equilibrium REER with a view to estimating the actual over- or undervaluation of exchange rate in terms of the macroeconomic fundamentals and to assess the appropriateness of current managed floating exchange rate regime in Bangladesh.

Following Clark and MacDonald (1999) and Baffes, Elbadawi and O'Connel (1999), a simple reduced form equation is examined:

$$lreer_t = f\left(ltot_t,\ lnfa_t,\ rird_t,\ bd_t\right), \tag{11.3}$$

where *lreer* is log of the REER of Bangladesh, *ltot* represents log of TOT of the country, *lnfa* represents NFAs to capture the effects of external resources balances on equilibrium, *rird* is the real interest rate differential (RIRD) with the trading partner countries, and *bd* is the budget deficit that represents the fiscal balance of Bangladesh government. For the analysis, vector error correction model (VECM) has been used.

Quarterly data are used covering the period from 2000Q1 to 2008Q2, mainly to see the effect of country's transition to floating rate regime. The TOT, defined as the relative price of exports to imports, has been calculated from the mirror data of trading partners using trade as weight. The NFAs have been taken as a proxy to capture the effect of capital account balance on the REER. RIRD has been calculated by deducting the US RER from Bangladeshi RER, where both RERs have been derived through subtracting respective inflation rate from nominal lending rate on advances. The fiscal balance of the government has been proxied by Bangladesh's fiscal deficit, expressed as a ratio of gross domestic product (GDP). The data have been compiled from various issues of Economic Trends, Bangladesh Bank Quarterly and IMF's International IFS.

11.6.2 Estimation Results

Before applying VECM, we need to confirm that all variables under consideration have to be integrated at order of one so that first difference of the variables should be stationary. To check the order of integration of the series, two well-known unit root tests, namely, the augmented Dickey-Fuller (ADF)

emphasis on the variables of the macroeconomic fundamental such as TOT shocks, fiscal stance, RIRD, and so on.

Table 11.7 ADF and PP tests for unit root[a]

Variables	*ADF*	*PP*	*Variables*	*ADF*	*PP*
Lreer	−3.25**	−1.39	Δ*lreer*	−6.53*	−6.93*
Ltot	−2.25	−1.89	Δ*ltot*	−5.08*	−7.60*
Lnfa	−3.35*	−2.20	Δ*lnfa*	−3.52*	−3.69*
Rird	−2.05	−1.97	Δ*rird*	−3.07*	−2.88*
Bd	−0.86	−1.52	Δ*dbd*	−2.95*	−5.48*

Notes: 1. Δ implies first difference of the respective variables. 2. * and ** imply significant at 5 and 10 percent level, respectively, using MacKinnon critical value

[a]ADF and PP tests for *lreer*, *ltot*, *lnfa* and *rird* are based on the inclusion of an intercept as well as a linear time trend. However, since no clear trend was found for the Δ*rird*, Δ*bd*, Δ*lreer*, Δ*ltot*, and Δ*lnfa* and ADF, and PP tests are performed without the trend term

and Phillips-Perron (PP) tests, have been employed. There seems to be a consensus in the cointegration literature that the PP test is preferable to ADF.

In Table 11.7 we report the ADF and PP test results to see the order of integration of the related variables.[6]

In Table 11.7, the absolute values of ADF statistics on the level of variables, except *lreer* and *lnfa*, are smaller than that of the critical values implying that these variables are considered non-stationary. When first differences of these variables are considered, the test statistics on Δ*ltot*, Δ*rird* and Δ*dbd* exceed the critical values. Thus, *ltot*, *rird* and *bd* are integrated of order one. In the case of *lreer* and *lnfa*, ADF statistics exceed the critical values implying that variables are stationary in their level. On the other hand, in case of Δ*lreer* and Δ*lnfa*, ADF statistics exceeded critical values. However, according to the PP test, all variables are found to be non-stationary at their levels and stationary at their first difference, which indicates that all variables are integrated at order one.

For the presence of cointegration between REER and the macroeconomic fundamentals, Johansen (1988) and Juselius (1992) multivariate cointegration tests are performed. Four lags were selected for VAR following the likelihood ratio statistic adjusted for degrees of freedom and Akaike *information* criterion (AIC). The result from the Johansen (1995) procedure to test for the existence and number of cointegrating equations is presented in Table 11.8. The Johansen's trace test for the cointegrating

[6]A time series is integrated of order d [usually denoted as ~I(d)]. d is the number of times the series needs to be differenced in order to become stationary.

Table 11.8 Johansen test for cointegrating rank

Maximum rank	*Trace statistics*	*01 percent critical value*
0	112.62	66.52
1	55.33	45.58
2	19.53	29.75
3	7.17	16.31
4	0.34	6.51

Source: Authors' calculation

rank from Table 11.8 evidenced that at least two significant cointegrating vectors exist in the system.[7] The presence of two cointegrating vectors confirms the long-run relationship between the REER and macroeconomic fundamentals over the sample period 2000Q1–2008Q2.

Based on the estimated cointegrating vector, the long-run equilibrium equation can be written as:

$$\begin{array}{llllll} lreer = 13.19 - 1.938\ ltot & +\,0.040\ lnfa & -\,0.012\ rird & -\,0.023\ bd & -\,0.006t \\ \text{s.e.} \qquad\qquad\quad (0.18) & (0.010) & (0.001) & (0.002) & (0.001) \end{array}$$

where standard errors are given in parentheses. Most coefficients of the cointegrating vector are plausible in magnitude, statistically significant and correctly signed based on economic theory. From the results, the following conclusions can be drawn.

- Any improvements in TOT will have depreciating effect on the real effective exchange rate. A 1 percentage point increase in TOT is associated with 1.94 percentage point depreciation of the REER in the long run.
- Increased NFAs will put pressure on the currency to appreciate, and 1 percentage point increase in NFAs will cause 0.04 percentage point appreciation in the REER in the long run.

[7]The presence of multiple cointegrating vectors makes it difficult to give an economic interpretation of the estimated relationships. Moreover, due to small sample size, we could not carry out the analysis with multiple cointegrating vectors.

- RIRD will worsen the exchange rate, and 0.012 percentage point depreciation of REER will be associated with 1 percentage point improvement in RIRD.
- As expected, Bangladesh's fiscal deficit as a ratio of GDP leads to depreciation of the REER, and the magnitude of the depreciation in REER is 0.023 percentage point due to 1 percentage enhancement of budget deficit.
- As Montiel (1997) suggested, a time trend is used to capture the impact of productivity growth, that is, the Balassa-Samuelson effect.[8] The effect suggests that productivity improvements will, generally, be concentrated in the tradable sector and thus lead to an appreciation. The sign of *t* is negative and significant, that is, the productivity differential is negative, which implies a higher productivity for tradable sectors that may contribute to the real appreciation. This confirms the presence of Balassa-Samuelson effect.
- The estimated ECT is found to be negative (−0.70) and significant. This implies that the speed of adjustment to the equilibrium is very high for each quarter, which is 70 percent.

11.6.3 Exchange Rate Misalignment

The estimated long-run relationship of the REER and macroeconomic fundamentals allow us to estimate the equilibrium REER from the VECM specifications. The long-run elasticities have been applied to the actual values of the macroeconomic fundamentals in a given period and a series of equilibrium exchange rates is obtained. The overvaluation or undervaluation of the exchange rate can be assessed by deriving the equilibrium 'sustainable' real effective exchange rate and subtracting it from the actual real effective exchange rate. As sharp fluctuation in macroeconomic fundamentals is usual, equilibrium REER based on the actual values of macroeconomic fundamentals will also show sharp fluctuation. This leads us to estimate a 'sustainable' equilibrium REER, which gives an estimate of departure from actual REER in the medium-term framework. Sustainable values of the fundamentals have been derived through three quarterly moving averages.

[8]The Balassa-Samuelson effect can come from two sources: (1) productivity differential between the domestic tradable and non-tradable sectors and (ii) productivity growth differentials relative to trading partners.

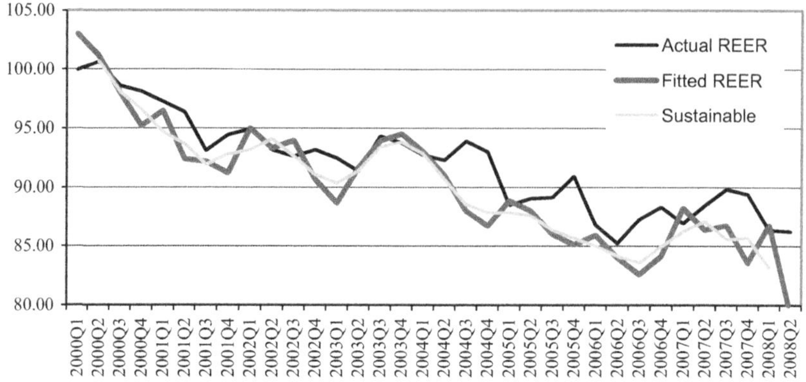

Fig. 11.8 Actual and equilibrium REER

Figure 11.8 depict these RER and overvaluation of the taka. The observed RER seems to have been overvalued since 2004:Q2. For 2007–2008; it appears that the REER remains overvalued on an average 3 percent. This indicates that the exchange rate remains very close to the equilibrium as warranted by the economic fundamentals for the period of analysis. A further analysis can be done by applying our methods discussed here.

11.7 Conclusions and Policy Recommendations

This chapter analyzes exchange rate management approaches under a floating rate regime in a comprehensive manner. It analyzes both the behavior of the NER and the RER. Although Bangladesh was committed to maintaining a freely floating regime, our findings suggest that its exchange rate policies were not consistent with the characteristics of freely floating regime. Generally speaking, Bangladesh pursues a managed floating rate regime. Given the *thin* foreign exchange market, high exchange rate pass-through and exchange rate shocks EMP. It appears to be difficult for Bangladesh to maintain a freely floating regime.

Given the vulnerable financial system, this study suggests that it is better for Bangladesh to continue a managed floating regime with frequent and small interventions. Simultaneously, Bangladesh Bank needs to work on developing mechanisms for inflation targeting policies, ensuring efficiency in the financial system, and building necessary institutions in order to manage exchange rates efficiently.

It seems that currently exchange rates are managed on an ad hoc basis without having clear targets or objectives. However, this management can be rated as good as the exchange rate remains very close to its equilibrium as warranted by economic fundamentals. Certainly there is scope to improve exchange rate management under a managed floating regime.

There are at least three channels identified in this study by which exchange rate instability can be transmitted to the domestic economy.

(i) *Pass-through (inflation) effect*: A high pass-through coefficient is estimated for Bangladeshi taka. A 1 percent change in international prices translates almost 100 percent of that change into domestic prices. Since Bangladesh's trade is dominated by imports, a depreciation of taka easily translates inflation into the domestic economy. This high exchange rate pass-through is also likely to increase the external debt burden.

(ii) *Competitiveness effect*: Although Bangladesh has achieved average competitiveness, it is not stable. The behavior of Euro seems to be an important source of instability. Regarding the long-term determinants of the REER, an increase in NFAs leads to REER appreciation, that is, the loss of international price competitiveness. An improvement of TOT works in favor of REER depreciation because of the substitution effect due to increase in import prices.

(iii) *Domestic credit effect*: This is an indirect channel through which the exchange rate is affected in Bangladesh. An increase in domestic credit causes the exchange rate to depreciate or the foreign reserves to deplete or some combination of the two, leading to EMP. It is observed that sterilized intervention causes extra pressure in the foreign exchange market.

Therefore, Bangladesh Bank should keep the above three indicators into consideration while managing exchange rates. Note that there is no simple formula for exchange rate management to achieve two important goals of exchange rate management, *competitiveness* and *price stability*, simultaneously (Ohno 1999). In the absence of a solid consensus on the proper target of exchange rate management, we propose to adopt the following pragmatic policies:

Stabilization of REER: In normal times, the exchange rate should be managed so as to stabilize overall competitiveness. For this purpose, the REER index, properly constructed to measure the average competitiveness of the tradable sectors, should be constantly monitored. To stabilize the REER, adjustments must be made against movements of other currencies as well as of inflation differentials. *This can be accomplished either by a prescribed formula or more informally through timely corrections.*

REER basket: Currently there are eight currencies in the REER basket. Since Bangladesh's commodity trade is dollar-denominated, *we propose to create a REER basket of four major currencies including the US dollar, the euro, the UK pound sterling and the Japanese yen with proper weights.* This kind of basket would be easier to manage and monitor. Although trade with Japan is not significant, Japanese yen should be included because it matters for debt burden, official development assistance (ODA), and grants.

Crisis management: Bangladesh has not yet faced any currency crisis, and therefore the capacity of exchange rate management has not been tested. With gradual economic development, shocks such as sudden shifts in foreign direct investment (FDI), export demand or the TOT, large business swings, significant resource discovery (or loss), major natural disasters, and so on may occur. In that case *a trigger mechanism needs to be adopted for additional adjustments.* On the other hand, in the face of a currency attack or other severe financial turmoil in the region or in the global economy, REER stabilization policy may be suspended temporarily to minimize contagion, credit crunch, reversal of capital flows, and so on. However, *during a crisis or global economic meltdown, it is better to stabilize the NEER instead of the REER when other trading partner currencies are fluctuating against each other.*

Accumulation of reserves: To maintain managed floats, Bangladesh needs to accumulate a sufficiently large stock of reserves. Has reserve accumulation already proceeded beyond the optimal point? Since the standard practice is to maintain international reserve for three months import payments, the reserve position in recent times (2015–2018) has met the necessary condition, but it is not sufficient. For maintaining stability in the foreign exchange market, it is necessary to accumulate additional reserves. In this context, the management of capital flows is very important for avoiding any crisis. Since maintenance of large stocks of reserves is a costly activity, *exchange rate stabilization policies should be based on frequent and small adjustments rather than large and rare ones.*

Institutional development: The foreign exchange market of Bangladesh is in an embryonic stage and thin in terms of daily transactions. Currency forward market and other derivatives are absent. Bangladesh Bank still controls the market by following net open dollar position of commercial banks. However, as the economy embarks on a middle-income growth path, the market will need to be expanded, and forward transactions will need to be entertained. Therefore, to reap the maximum benefits of the managed floating regime, there is no alternative to building institutions and bringing efficiency and depth to the foreign exchange market. Particularly, it is necessary to develop inter-bank bond markets as well as capital markets with further financial liberalization.

Appendix

Table 11.9 Trade weights used in the REER calculation

Country	*Weights*
China	0.0699
Singapore	0.0850
India	0.1734
USA	0.2155
UK	0.0739
EU	0.2318
Hong Kong	0.0598
Japan	0.0906

Source: Bangladesh Bank, Younus (2009)

References

ADB. (2002). *Quarterly economic update (March)*. Dhaka: Asian Development Bank, Bangladesh Resident Office.

Baffes, J., O'Connell, S. A., & Elbadawi, I. A. (1999). *Single-equation estimation of the equilibrium real exchange rate*. Washington, DC: The World Bank.

Bahmani-Oskooee, M., Martin, M. A. G., & Niroomand, F. (1998). Exchange rate sensitivity of the demand for money in Spain. *Applied Economics, 30*(5), 607–612.

Bubula, M. A., & Ötker, M. I. (2002). *The evolution of exchange rate regimes since 1990: Evidence from de facto policies* (No. 2-155). International Monetary Fund.

Chowdhury, M. I., & Siddique, S. F. (2006). *Exchange rate pass-through in Bangladesh* (Policy Analysis Unit Working Paper Series No: WP, 607).

Clark, P. B., & MacDonald, R. (1999). Exchange rates and economic fundamentals: A methodological comparison of BEERs and FEERs. In *Equilibrium exchange rates* (pp. 285–322). Dordrecht: Springer.
de Brouwer, G., & Ericsson, N. R. (1995). Abstract for RDP9510: Modelling Inflation in Australia. Reserve Bank of Australia.
Eichengreen, B., Rose, A. K., & Wyplosz, C. (1996). *Contagious currency crises* (No. w5681). National Bureau of Economic Research. Available at https://www.nber.org/papers/w5681
Garces-Diaz, D. G. (2001). *Was NAFTA behind the Mexican export Boom (1994–2000)?*. Available at SSRN 261586.
Girton, L., & Roper, D. (1977). A monetary model of exchange market pressure applied to the postwar Canadian experience. *The American Economic Review, 67*(4), 537–548.
Grenville, S., & Gruen, D. (1999). Capital flows and exchange rates. In *Capital flows and the international financial system* (p. 109). Available at https://rba.gov.au/publications/confs/1999/pdf/grenville-gruen.pdf
Hausmann, R., Panizza, U., & Stein, E. (2001). Why do countries float the way they float? *Journal of Development Economics, 66*(2), 387–414.
Hernandez, L., & Montiel, P. J. (2003). Post-crisis exchange rate policy in five Asian countries: Filling in the "hollow middle"? *Journal of the Japanese and International Economies, 17*(3), 336–369.
Hossain, A. (1997). The real exchange rate, production structure, and trade balance: The case of Bangladesh. *Indian Economic Review, 32*, 155–177.
Hossain, M. M. A. (2002). *Exchange rate responses to inflation in Bangladesh* (No. 2-166). International Monetary Fund.
Hossain, M. (2009). Institutional development and the choice of exchange rate regime: A cross-country analysis. *Journal of the Japanese and International Economies, 23*(1), 56–70.
Hossain, M., & Ahmed, M. (2009). An assessment of exchange rate policy under floating regime in Bangladesh. *The Bangladesh Development Studies, 32*, 35–67.
Islam, M. A. (2003). *Exchange rate policy of Bangladesh: Not floating does not mean sinking*. CPD Occasional Paper series.
Johansen, S. (1988). Statistical analysis of cointegration vectors. *Journal of Economic Dynamics and Control, 12*(2–3), 231–254.
Johansen, S. (1995). *Likelihood-based inference in cointegrated vector autoregressive models*. Oxford: Oxford University Press on Demand.
Juselius, K. (1992). Testing structural hypotheses in a multivariate cointegration analysis of the PPP and the UIP for UK. *Journal of Econometrics, 53*(1–3), 211–244.
Kaminsky, G. L., & Reinhart, C. M. (1999). The twin crises: The causes of banking and balance-of-payments problems. *American Economic Review, 89*(3), 473–500. Available at https://www.aeaweb.org/articles?id=10.1257/aer.89.3.473

Levy-Yeyati, E., & Sturzenegger, F. (2005). Classifying exchange rate regimes: Deeds vs. words. *European Economic Review, 49*(6), 1603–1635.

Modeste, N. C. (1981). Exchange market pressure during the 1970s in Argentina: An application of the Girton-Roper monetary model: a note. *Journal of Money, Credit and Banking, 13*(2), 234–240.

Montiel, P. J. (1997). Exchange rate policy and macroeconomic management in ASEAN countries. In J. Hicklin et al. (Eds.), *Macroeconomic issues facing ASEAN countries*. Washington, DC: IMF.

Ohno, K. (1999). *Exchange rate management in developing Asia: Reassessment of the pre-crisis soft dollar zone* (No. 1). ADBI Research Paper series.

Rahman, M. H., & Barua. S. (2006). Recent experiences in the foreign exchange and money markets. Policy Note 0703, published in the *Bangladesh Bank Quarterly*, III (4).

Rahman, A. A., & Basher, S. A. (2001). Real exchange rate behaviour and exchange rate misalignments in Bangladesh. *The Bangladesh Development Studies, 27*, 69–93.

Reinhart, C. M., & Rogoff, K. S. (2004). The modern history of exchange rate arrangements: A reinterpretation. *The Quarterly Journal of Economics, 119*(1), 1–48.

Taslim, M. A. (2003). A monetary approach to exchange market disequilibrium in Australia: 1975–97. *Australian Economic Papers, 42*(2), 183–196.

Younus, S., & Chowdhury, M. I. (2006). *An analysis of Bangladesh's transition to flexible exchange rate regime*. Policy Analysis Unit, Research Department, Bangladesh Bank.

CHAPTER 12

Determinants of Capital Flows to Least Developed Countries: Lessons for Bangladesh

Monzur Hossain

12.1 Introduction

Considering the global aid scenario and declining aid trend in Bangladesh and other least developed countries (LDCs), official aid alone is not adequate to accelerate economic growth, alleviate poverty and achieve other Sustainable Development Goals (SDGs) in these countries. It is important to stress that financing SDGs would require increasing the investment rate above the domestic saving rate, and bridging the respective financing gap with additional financing from abroad. Mobilizing resources from both public and private sources for financing development involves challenges and, therefore, it is important for these countries to understand the dynamics of capital flows.

Various initiatives including Brussels Program of Action (BPoA) and Istanbul Program of Action (IPoA) have been undertaken under the auspices of the United Nations (UN) to facilitate official aid to developing countries. In a discussion of capital flows dynamics, it is necessary to highlight the possible processes and challenges that impede the successful implementation of BPoA and IPoA. The BPoA was adopted in 2001 with

M. Hossain (✉)
Bangladesh Institute of Development Studies (BIDS), Dhaka, Bangladesh

M. Hossain (ed.), *Bangladesh's Macroeconomic Policy*,
https://doi.org/10.1007/978-981-15-1244-5_12

an aim to improve LDCs'[1] share in global trade, foreign direct investment (FDI) and financial flows during 2001–2010. The program set specific goals and targets with time bound policy actions to be adopted by the LDCs and their development partners in support of the goals. A review of the program, however, highlighted that commitments made by both the LDCs and their development partners largely remained unfulfilled (UNESCAP 2010). The donor countries did not fulfill their commitments (in the BPoA) on the disbursement of official development assistance (ODA) equivalent to 0.2 percent of their GNP during the decade. To some extent, donors' stringent conditions dampened LDCs' opportunities to receive additional fund. Moreover, in the advent of global financial crisis in 2007–2008 and subsequent recession in developed countries, LDCs found them in a more vulnerable situation because of their higher reliance on exports, aid and external debt. In the context of difficulties faced by LDCs in implementing BPoA, the IPoA was adopted for the subsequent decade 2011–2020, which charts out strategies for the sustainable development of LDCs with a focus on enhancing their productive capacities. Under IPoA, one of the important strategies for LDCs would be to attract more capitals (both private and official), which critically depends on understanding of the underlying factors influencing capital flows in these countries. The objective of this paper is, therefore, to identify the factors that influence capital flows to this group of developing countries.

A widespread view holds that FDI, portfolio equity, foreign aid and external debt in a country's external finance are important determinants of economic performance, and to some extent, propensity to crises. Then, what are the determinants of capital flows? Recipient countries receive funds for investment which are not normally available from domestic sources, while investing countries receive a higher return than that of the developed world. In this context, interest rate differentials could explain capital flows. On the other hand, official funds from donor agencies or

[1] Least developed countries (LDCs) are defined based on the following three criteria: (i) *Low-income criterion* based on a three-year average estimate of the gross national income (GNI) per capita (under \$750 for inclusion, above \$900 for graduation); (ii) *human resource weakness criterion* involving a composite Human Assets Index (HAI) based on indicators of (a) nutrition, (b) health, (c) education and (d) adult literacy; and (iii) *economic vulnerability criterion* based on indicators of the instability of agricultural production, the instability of exports of goods and services, the economic importance of non-traditional activities (share of manufacturing and modern services in GDP), merchandise export concentration and the handicap of economic smallness. There are now 49 countries in the LDC group.

countries are made available only when receiving countries could fulfill certain conditions related to governance, institutional reform and macroeconomic stability. LDCs often find these conditions difficult to fulfill, and, therefore, they fail to receive required fund from donors.

Review of literature suggests that while a set of studies focuses on the determinants of capital flows, other sets of studies focus on the persistence of capital flows. From analytical perspective, these two issues imply dynamic characteristics of capital flows. Moreover, proper care is necessary to encounter endogeneity bias in explaining capital flows. If the dynamic capital flows are analyzed in a static model, it will not provide an unbiased assessment of the factors associated with capital flows. This study, thus, takes into account these problems in estimation by applying the Arellano-Bond generalized method of moments (GMM) dynamic panel regression model to capital flows to a panel of 48 LDCs (the list are given in the Appendix II) for the period 1991–2012. The GMM estimator considers the explanatory variables and the difference of the lagged dependent variables as instrument in the level equation. The lagged dependent variable is the instrument in the first-difference equation. Hence, the Arellano-Bond GMM estimator provides unbiased estimates of coefficients by encountering both persistency and endogeneity issues in the model.

There are two important qualifications of this chapter. *One*, it estimates the determinants and persistency effect of capital flows—whether capitals are temporary or irreversible. *Two*, it assesses the determinants of capital flows to these countries particularly in the context of BPoA and IPoA. As this group of countries is diverse in nature (e.g., natural-resource endowment, landlocked, island, etc.) and level of economic development, some of them receive higher capitals, but others do not. Why? This study attempts to provide answer to this question.

The findings of this study suggest that macroeconomic stability, trade openness, financial sector development, natural resource abundance and political stability are the key determinants of capital flows (FDI and debt) to LDCs. While FDI flows are of natural resource-seeking in African LDCs, it is mostly efficiency-seeking (related to financial sector development) in Asia. The study also finds a positive link between capital inflows and political institutions, which are consistent with some recent studies for emerging and developed countries (e.g. see Faria and Mauro 2009). For official aid flows, secondary school enrollment has emerged as an important determinant. The GMM estimators suggest that capital flows in LDCs are less persistent, implying a limited scope of capital flows for financing development activities in LDCs.

The rest of the chapters are organized as follows. Section 12.2 reviews the literature on capital flows. Section 12.3 describes the data, presents the empirical strategy and reports the main results. Section 12.4 concludes the chapter.

12.2 A Brief Review of Literature on Capital Flows

Four types of capital usually flow to developing countries: (i) portfolio equity flows, such as bond and equity (i.e. developing country company share purchase); (ii) commercial bank lending from developed to developing countries; (iii) FDI, physical investment by non-residents to developing countries and (iv) official flows consisting aid, grants, concessional and non-concessional credits given to developing countries by donor agencies and countries. Among these four types of capital flows, first two types require developed financial system and, therefore, are less relevant to the LDCs. In the cases of most LDCs, there are restrictions in place on foreign commercial bank borrowing as well as portfolio investment, particularly from the fear of crisis due to sudden reversals. However, FDIs and official flows are two major sources of capital flows to developing countries.

Many previous studies have sought to identify the determinants of capital flows including FDI flows. Studies based on interest rate differentials provide evidence that such differentials could explain capital mobility only among developed countries (Montiel 1993). In contrast, both net and gross capital flows to developing countries respond to economic fundamentals, official policies and financial market imperfections. In a cross-section of 40 advanced and developing countries, Alfaro et al. (2008) find that institutional quality is a key determinant of total capital flows. In a panel of advanced and developing countries, Albuquerque (2003) finds the share of FDI in total flows to be negatively and significantly associated with good credit risk ratings, but unrelated to indicators of institutional quality. In contrast, in a cross-section of advanced and developing countries, Hausmann and Fernandez-Arias (2000) find no relationship with institutional quality. Applying a gravity model of bilateral FDI stocks—drawn from OECD (Organisation for Economic Co-operation and Development) data—and bank loan stocks to a sample of about 10 source countries and 20 recipient countries, Wei (2001) finds that weaker institutions are associated with less FDI and more bank loans.

In a recent cross-section study, Faria and Mauro (2009) find that equity-like liabilities as a share of countries' total external liabilities are positively and significantly associated with indicators of educational attainment, openness, natural resource abundance and institutional quality. Regarding the nature of capital flows, Sarno and Taylor (1999) show that equity, bond and official flows are relatively less persistent than bank credit and FDI flows. This finding is important from the perspective of sudden stops and reversals of capital flows.

Other studies have identified a number of additional factors that may influence FDI. Such factors include human capital, natural resources, economic size and openness. Human capital may act as a stronger "pull" factor for FDI (Borensztein et al. 1998) than other forms of capital such as portfolio equity or debt. Natural resources may also attract FDI to a greater extent (Hausmann and Fernandez-Arias 2000; Lane and Milesi-Ferretti 2001). Larger economic size (proxied by measures such as total gross domestic product (GDP)) also attracts FDI, which provides an opportunity to better serve the local market (possibly circumventing trade barriers). Finally, openness may reduce the need for "tariff hopping" FDI, though countries having quota-free market access of products may be an attractive destination for FDI, which may be called "efficiency-seeking" FDI. Wei and Shleifer (2000), Wei (2001) and Wei and Wu (2002) find that weak institutions tilt capital inflows toward bank loans and away from FDI, consistent with their hypothesis that foreign direct investors are less likely to be bailed out than the foreign banks in the event of a crisis.

12.3 Empirical Analysis

This section briefly describes the data, presents the empirical strategy and reports the results. Appendix I describes the data sources and variables in greater detail.

12.3.1 Description of Variables and Data Sources

The objective of this study is to examine the determinants of capital flows to LDCs. Hence, the following three dependent variables are considered: (i) net FDI inflows, (ii) net external debt and (iii) official aid flows. *FDI* is the sum of equity capital, reinvestment of earnings, other long-term capital and short-term capital as shown in the balance of payments (BOPs). *Total external debt* is debt owed to non-residents repayable in foreign currency, goods or services. *Total external debt* is the sum of public, publicly guaranteed and private nonguaranteed long-term debt, IMF credit and short-term debt. Short-term debt includes all debt having an original maturity of one year or less and interest in arrears on long-term debt. Therefore, external debt includes bank borrowing also. *Net* ODA consists of disbursements of loans made on concessional terms (net of repayments of principal) and grants by official agencies of the members of the Development Assistance Committee (DAC), by multilateral institutions and by non-DAC countries to promote economic development and welfare in countries and territories in the DAC list of ODA recipients. It includes loans with a grant element of at least 25 percent (calculated at a rate of discount of 10 percent). The data cover the period 1991–2012. Figure 12.1 displays the trend of external debt, net FDI flows, net financial flows and aid as percentage of gross national income (GNI) across regions, which provides a preliminary understanding of capital flows to LDCs.

This study considers the similar set of explanatory variables that are used in empirical studies including Faria and Mauro (2009). The explanatory variables considered include the level of economic development (GDP per capita in the US dollars at constant 2000 prices), openness (sum of imports and exports over GDP), natural resources (exports of fuels and/or metal and ore exports), human capital (percentage of population over 25 that has attended some secondary schooling), financial development (private credit to GDP or M2 to GDP), inflation, real exchange rate, political system and electoral competitiveness (Executive Index of Electoral Competitiveness (EIEC)).

The source of data, in most cases, is the World Development Indicators (WDIs) of the World Bank. Data on political variables is collected from data on political indices (DPI) of the World Bank (Beck et al. 2001, updated in 2013). The sources and definitions are discussed in Appendix I in greater detail. Table 12.1 reports correlation between variables used in this study.

The focus of our analysis is the LDCs. Therefore, the whole sample consists of 48 countries defined as LDCs by the UN as of 2012. In addition, two groups of countries, namely, African and Asian LDCs, are analyzed separately. The reason for looking at both samples separately is twofold. First, LDCs in these two regions are characterized by diverse geopolitical and economic conditions. Some Asia-Pacific LDCs are landlocked and island countries, which are highly vulnerable to external shocks because of their dependence on highly concentrated exports and tourism. On the other hand, some African LDCs have been suffering from civil war, which are vulnerable to domestic real shocks. Second, the

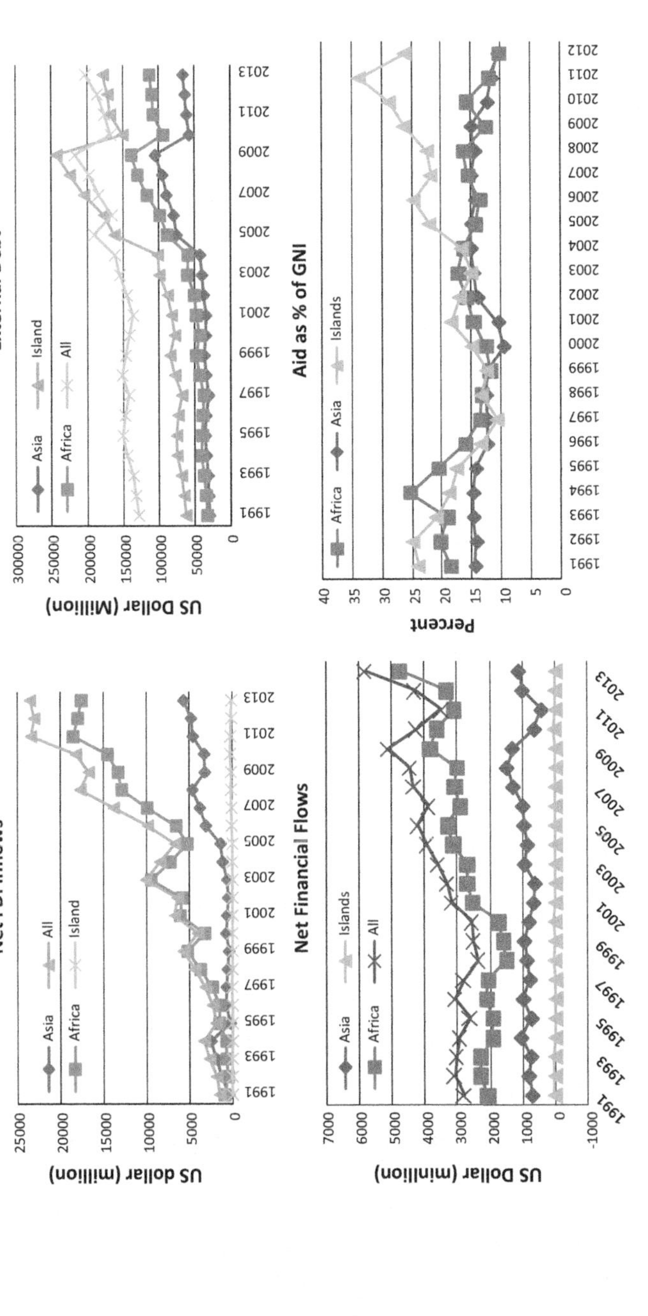

Fig. 12.1 Trend of capital inflows, 1991–2013. (Source: The World Bank)

Table 12.1 Pair-wise correlations of variables (averages)

	Net capital inflows	*External debt*	*FDI*	*GDP*	*GDP per capita*	*Institutional quality*	*Openness*	*Natural resource*	*Political system*	*LIEC*	*Financial development (M2/GDP) (1)*	*Financial development (Credit/ GDP)(2)*
External debt	0.49***	1.00										
FDI	0.07**	0.36***	1.00									
GDP	0.67***	0.74***	0.25***	1.00								
GDP per capita	−0.19***	−0.17***	0.30***	−0.06	1.00							
Institutional quality	0.02	−0.27***	−0.21***	−0.12***	0.05	1.00						
Openness	−0.29***	−0.28***	0.18***	−0.22***	0.50***	0.08**	1.00					
Natural resource	−0.04	0.15***	0.22***	−0.02	0.16***	−0.45***	0.10	1.00				
Political system	0.07**	−0.02	0.04	−0.04	0.03	0.03	0.01	−0.42***	1.00			
Financial Development (1)	−0.09***	−0.09***	−0.08**	−0.04	0.00	−0.07*	0.20***	−0.14***	0.01	−0.02	1.00	
Financial Development (2)	−0.07*	−0.03	−0.06	−0.04	−0.08**	−0.21***	0.01	0.02	0.02	0.01	0.90***	1.00

Source: Author's estimation

Note: ***, ** and * indicate significance at 1 percent, 5 percent and 10 percent level respectively; LIEC = Legislative Index of Electoral Competitiveness

bulk of FDIs in Africa is of the resource-seeking type, as it was mainly diverted to oil and other natural resource extraction, while FDI directed toward Asian LDCs is mostly efficiency and quota-seeking, as it was mainly diverted to manufacturing sector. Hence, such grouping of countries will help control heterogeneity among developing countries of the same region in the analysis.

12.3.2 Methods of Analysis

For estimating capital flows to LDCs, a dynamic panel GMM estimator has been applied. The reason is that a GMM, or difference GMM estimator can encounter endogeneity problem as well as short-panel bias. Arellano and Bond (1991) make a first difference to the panel data and then use the endogenous (or predetermined) lagged variables' levels to instrument for the transformed lagged dependent variable. The lagged levels provide little information about the first differences when the underlying series are relatively stationary and, therefore, are weak instruments (Arellano and Bover 1995; Blundell and Bond 1998). To overcome the problem, Arellano-Bover and Blundell-Bond GMM employ additional moment conditions based on the lagged variables' first differences (in addition to their levels) to increase the efficiency of the estimation. Therefore, to increase the efficiency of the estimates as well as to capture dynamics of capital flows, the Arellano-Bover/Blundell-Bond GMM model has been applied in the analysis. The regression model is thus specified as:

$$CI_{it} = \alpha + \beta x_{it} + \gamma PI_{it} + \lambda FI_{it} + \varepsilon_{it}, \tag{12.1}$$

where α is the constant factor, x_{it} represents a vector of macroeconomic factors, PI represents political institutional factors and FI represents financial institutions-related factors.

The Arellano-Bover/Blundell-Bond GMM model provided tests for AR(1) and AR(2) in first differences. The model introduces first order serial correlation; however, the test for "no second order serial correlation" for the disturbances of the first-differenced equations is important for testing the consistency of the GMM estimates. It has been observed that there exists first order serial correlation, but not the second order serial correlation in the estimated results. Further, the Sargan (1958) test has been applied to test the joint validity of moment conditions (the presence of over-identification) and to identify optimal lag. The tests confirm that the instruments used are orthogonal to the error term, that is, over-identification is rejected.

12.3.3 The Results

The determinants of capital flows—net FDI flows, external debt (gross capital flows) and official aid (as percent of GNI)—are reported in Tables 12.2, 12.3 and 12.4, respectively. The Arellano-Bond GMM estimates show a clear sign of persistence in capital flows to LDCs.

We begin by focusing on the determinants of the net FDI flows to the LDCs in the whole sample for the whole period, and sub-periods: 1991–2000 and 2001–2012 (Table 12.2). For the whole sample, per capita GDP, financial development, proxied by domestic credit to GDP ratio, and trade openness (total export and import to GDP ratio), fuel export and political system (−ve sign indicates presidential system) are significantly associated with FDI inflows to the LDCs. Inflation rate and per capita GDP are negatively and significantly associated with FDI inflows. While the same variables are significant for FDI inflows in 1991–2000, only openness, human capital development and financial sector development are significant for the period 2000 onward. The results show that net FDI flows are moderately persistent—the effect is 0.38, indicating that last year's net FDI inflows will amplify current FDI inflows by 38 percent. However, for the period 2000–2012, FDI flows were less persistent. Thus, the behavior of FDI inflows in the LDCs has changed in the 2000s, as FDI inflows are not directed toward countries having natural resources, rather it were diverted to the LDCs having higher trade openness, human capital and financial depth. The results are consistent with Faria and Mauro (2009) and Hausmann and Fernandez-Arias (2000).

Regional variations are significantly evident in case of FDI inflows. While per capita GDP, trade openness, fuel export, secondary school enrolment ratio (human capital) and political system are the determinants of FDI inflows in Africa, only per capita GDP and human capital are found to be significant for Asian LDCs. FDIs are slightly more persistent in Asian LDCs than African LDCs. It appears that FDIs in Africa are associated with more stringent conditions than those in Asia.

As expected, external debt is found to be highly persistent in all model specifications—the persistent effect is about 0.60 (Table 12.3), implying that 60 percent of total debts are not repaid. Financial development is sig-

Table 12.2 Determinants of net FDI inflows

	All (1991–2012)	*All (2001–2012)*	*All (1991–2000)*	*Africa (1991–2012)*	*Asia (1991–2012)*
Lagged FDI flows	0.38 (0.037)***	0.13(0.11)	0.36(0.04)***	0.36(0.04)***	0.41(0.07)***
Per capita GDP	0.22(0.047)***	0.0011(0.062)	0.33(0.06)***	0.20(0.05)***	0.20(0.07)***
Inflation	−0.00025(0.00022)	−0.00017(0.00017)	−0.025(0.02)	−0.0003(0.0002)	−0.007(0.02)
Openness	0.14 (0.02)***	0.17(0.03)***	0.18(0.02)***	0.20(0.02)***	0.006(0.14)
RER	0.00015(0.0003)	0.00046(0.0009)	0.00002(0.0003)	−0.0004(0.0006)	0.00005(0.0002)
Fuel export	0.086(0.03)***	−0.006(0.06)	0.13(0.04)***	0.14(0.04)***	−0.045(0.04)
Ore and metal export	0.018(0.02)	0.017(0.03)	0.05(0.03)	0.008(0.02)	0.095(0.12)
Financial development	0.013(0.03)	−0.11(0.04)***	0.03(0.03)	−0.004(0.03)	0.02(0.03)
Enrol-Sec	−0.014(0.04)	0.22(0.06)***	0.10(0.05)**	0.12(0.06)**	−0.07(0.03)**
Political system	−2.14(0.90)**	−0.50(0.90)	−2.15(2.03)	−2.83(1.13)	−1.7(1.3)
EIEC	−0.096(0.20)	−0.24(0.25)	0.05(0.29)	−0.02(0.24)	0.14(0.34)
Constant	−6.48(1.74)***	0.35(1.78)	−15.32(2.91)***	−11.07(2.02)***	4.97(2.3)***
N	499	206	293	369	130

Source: Author's estimation

Note: *** and ** indicate significance at 1 percent and 5 percent level respectively

Table 12.3 Determinants of external debt, 1991–2012

	All (1991–2012)	*All (2001–2012)*	*All (1991–2000)*	*Africa (1991–2012)*	*Asia (1991–2012)*
Lagged ext. debt	0.56(0.036)***	0.64(0.06)***	0.56(0.05)***	0.54(0.04)***	0.83(0.06)***
Per capita GDP	−0.56(0.34)*	−0.22(0.30)	−0.15(0.64)	−0.65(0.4)	−0.7(0.4)
Inflation	0.0042(0.0014)***	0.04(0.08)	0.004(0.002)**	0.004(0.002)***	−0.05(0.09)
Openness	0.44(0.13)***	−0.09(0.11)	1.36(0.30)***	0.62(0.2)***	−0.05(0.08)
RER	−0.002(0.002)	−0.0009(0.001)	−0.008(0.006)	−0.002(0.004)	−0.002(0.0007)
Fuel export	−0.60(0.3)***	−0.17(0.34)	−0.24(0.60)	−0.6(0.33)***	0.44(0.34)
Ore and metal export	−0.12(0.2)***	−0.43(0.20)**	−0.08(0.30)	−0.13(0.2)	−2.81(2.6)
Financial development	0.71(0.2)***	0.52(0.20)**	0.10(0.40)	0.90(0.2)***	0.5(0.2)**
Enrol-Sec	−1.25(0.43)***	−1.01(0.34)***	−2.34(0.95)***	−2.73(0.62)	0.7(0.2)**
Political system	−1.81(6.7)	6.04(7.3)	−13.55(9.8)	−1.3(9.17)	47.13(22.7)**
EIEC	−0.25(1.43)	1.4(1.6)	−1.6(2.32)	0.75(1.65)	−20.83(8.07)***
Constant	38.59(14.34)***	45.94(16.22)***	18.03(26.6)	49.97(13.95)***	25.11(15.01)*
N	377	164	213	283	94

Source: Author's estimation

Note: ***, ** and * indicate significance at 1 percent, 5 percent and 10 percent level respectively

Table 12.4 Determinants of official aid flows, 1991–2012

	All (1991–2012)	*All (2001–2012)*	*All (1991–2000)*	*Africa (1991–2012)*	*Asia (1991–2012)*
Lagged aid: GNI	0.50(0.03)***	0.5(0.03)***	0.43(0.08)***	0.53(0.04)***	0.71(0.04)***
Per capita GDP	−0.005(0.08)	0.14(0.08)	−0.13(0.15)	−0.004(0.9)	0.5(0.11)
Inflation	0.0002(0.0004)	−0.01(0.03)	0.0002(0.0004)	0.0002(0.0004)	−0.04(0.04)
Openness	−0.04(0.03)	−0.09(0.03)***	0.2(0.08)***	0.04(0.04)	0.0002(0.03)
RER	−0.001(0.0004)	−0.0009(0.0004)	−0.002(0.002)	0.002(0.0007)	−0.0007(0.0003)
Fuel export	0.02(0.05)	0.008(0.06)	−0.04(0.13)	0.03(0.07)	0.03(0.07)
Ore and metal export	0.003(0.03)	0.009(0.04)	−0.02(0.06)	0.01(0.04)	0.04(0.20)
Financial development	0.005(0.04)	0.008(0.05)	−0.2(0.09)**	0.07(0.05)	0.2(0.05)***
Enrol-Sec	−0.13(0.06)**	−0.09(0.07)	−0.4(0.2)**	0.2(0.1)**	−0.2(0.07)***
Political system	0.6(1.5)	−1.97(2.0)	0.99(2.5)	0.5(2.3)	0.6(1.4)
EIEC	−0.05(0.3)	1.06(0.4)***	−0.97(0.5)*	0.07(0.35)	0.2(0.54)
Constant	14.9(2.6)***	12.93(3.7)***	15.44(5.43)***	14.6(3.24)**	3.6(3.91)
N	502	289	213	368	134

Source: Author's estimation

Note: ***, ** and * indicate significance at 1 percent, 5 percent and 10 percent level respectively; RER = Real Exchange Rate

nificantly associated with the total foreign debt in all model specifications. Openness and inflation rate are positively significant, indicating that macroeconomic stability and trade liberalization policies may be crucial for receiving more external debts by the LDCs. Natural resource abundance is negative and significant to total external debt, indicating that countries having natural resources are relatively less reliant on external loans or grants. Almost the same results are obtained while they were analyzed for African LDCs; however, only financial sector, human capital and political system matter for external debt flows to Asian LDCs. Thus, there have been significant differences between African and Asian LDCs in the determinants of external debts.

Finally, persistence and determinants of aid flows are examined (Table 12.4). Aid inflows are significantly and moderately persistent for the whole sample period (0.50), as well as for both the regions with higher persistence in Asian LDCs (0.71). That is, aid disbursements have lagged behind commitments as evidenced from the persistency rate causing less than potential development impact and eventual lower rates of return to investments than appraised (Rahman and Hossain 2014). While for African LDCs, only human capital development is significant for receiving higher aid, both financial sector and human capital are significant for Asian LDCs. The reason is that development in social sectors including secondary school enrolment has been deemed as positive outcome of aid in many developing countries. However, it is difficult to tag aid effectiveness with macroeconomic outcome due to data problems and endogeneity biases. Nevertheless, pipeline has been built up with undisbursed aid in many LDCs due to poor project implementation capacity that led to delays and cost escalation. In many cases, both donors and the government are at loggerheads on real reason for implementation delay. Is it the stringency of loan conditions that the donor has imposed or the failure of responsible government agencies to fulfill loan conditions agreed upon by both sides? These are the reasons that might have led to the findings that only a few variables can significantly explain aid flows to the LDCs.

To summarize the findings, the determinants of various types of capital inflows vary significantly across regions. The result indicates that the behavior of capital flows to the LDCs, particularly FDI and external debt, is contingent upon various factors including macroeconomic stability, financial sector development, trade openness, natural resource abundance and political system or democratic environment. For official aid, secondary school enrollment has been the key determinants of official aid flows.

Since the LDCs are constrained by external financing for development and donors provide differential treatments to different LDCs as part of receipt of external capital, a consistent set of criteria needs to be adopted under the IPoA. As all the LDCs do not have the same level of natural resources, continuous efforts for maintaining macroeconomic stability, developing the financial sector and liberalizing trade regime could be important policy options for the LDCs in order to receive more capitals in a sustainable manner.

12.4 Concluding Remarks

This chapter provides some explanations to the question of why some LDCs receive more capitals than the others. The findings suggest that the determinants of both FDI and external debt are almost the same—macroeconomic stability, financial sector development, trade openness, natural resource abundance and political stability. The study, however, could not find any significant relationship between official aid flows and macroeconomic outcome; rather it establishes a link between aid flows and social sector development. The reason could be that the effectiveness of aid could be better judged in terms of social sector outcome. As all the LDCs do not have the same level of natural resources, continuous efforts for maintaining macroeconomic stability, developing the financial sector and liberalizing trade regime could be important policy options for the LDCs in order to receive more capitals in a sustainable manner. Thus, the results suggest for appropriate policies aimed at improving macroeconomic and financial environment along with political stability in order to ensure more capital flows to LDCs.

The findings of this study reveal that the determinants of capital flows vary significantly across regions. Furthermore, as donors provide differential treatments to different LDCs as part of disbursing external capital, a consistent set of criteria based on the findings of this study needs to be adopted under the IPoA for equitable distribution of capital among the LDCs. Otherwise, like BPoA, most of the commitments regarding external capital will be likely to remain unfulfilled. Though it is evident that natural resource-endowed countries have certain comparative advantages to attract more capitals/FDIs, others could capitalize their advantage through proper utilization of export potentials and market size. It is, thus, important for all the LDCs to enhance their productive capacity to attract more foreign capitals as outlined in the BPoA and subsequent IPoA. The results of this paper thus underscore the need of a set of consistent indicators for successful implementation of IPoA for enhancing development in the LDCs including Bangladesh.

A framework of linkages between national, sector and project level programming and monitoring indicators has to be devised on the basis of the various national plans and the SDGs that will serve as the basis of the cooperation with the International Development Partners. Keeping these issues in mind, an action plan should be developed which might take into account the following aspects of development cooperation: (i) planning, budgeting, monitoring, reporting and evaluation; (ii) broadening the resource base; (iii) framework of dialogue; (iv) integrated financing strategy; (v) reliable database on development cooperation and (vi) capacity building for resource mobilization. For meeting up financing gap for implementing the SDGs, Bangladesh and other LDCs should strive for mobilizing financing from alternative sources, such as by strengthening the South-South Triangular Cooperation, issuing diaspora bond, sovereign bond and GDP-indexed bond, in addition to existing available sources.

Appendix I

Dependent Variables

Net FDI inflows, external debt and aid inflows as percent of GNI are used as dependent variables. Data are taken from World Development Indicators (WDI), the World Bank.

Independent Variables

GDP Per Capita
Constant US dollars in 2000 for all available years between 1991 and 2007. Source: World Development Indicators, World Bank.

Financial Development
Private credit divided by total GDP for all available years between 1991 and 2007. Source: World Development Indicators, World Bank.

Natural Resources
Fuel export and percentage of ore, metals and fuels in total exports for all available years between 1991 and 2007. Source: World Development Indicators, World Bank.

Openness
Sum of imports and exports divided by total GDP for all available years between 1991 and 2007. Source: World Development Indicators, World Bank.

Human Capital
Percentage of total population over 25 who attended at least some secondary schooling. Sources: World Development Indicators (WDI), the World Bank.

Political Institutional Variables

The following political institutional variables are taken from the data on political indices (DPI) of the World Bank (see Beck et al. 2001; revised in 2013).

Political System
Codes

Presidential	0
Assembly-elected president	1
Parliamentary	2

Systems with unelected executives get a 0. Systems with presidents either elected directly or by an electoral college (whose *only* function is to elect the president), and there is no prime minister, also receive a 0. In systems with both a prime minister (PM) and a president, the following factors are considered in order to categorize the system:

(a) *Veto power*: president can veto legislation and the parliament needs a supermajority to override the veto.
(b) *Appoint prime minister*: president can appoint *and* dismiss prime minister and/or other ministers.
(c) *Dissolve parliament*: president can dissolve parliament and call for new elections.
(d) *Mentioning in sources*: If the sources mention the president more often than the PM, this serves as an additional indicator to call the system presidential (Romania, Kyrgyzstan, Estonia and Yugoslavia).

The system is presidential if (a) is true, or if (b) and (c) are true. If no information or ambiguous information on (a), (b), (c), then consider (d). Countries in which the legislature elects the chief executive are parliamentary (2), with the following exception: if that assembly or group cannot easily recall him (if they need a two-third vote to impeach, or must dissolve themselves while forcing him out) then the system gets a 1.

Executive Indices on Electoral Competitiveness (EIEC)
Executives who are (1) elected directly by population, or (2) elected by an electoral college that is elected by the people and has the sole purpose of electing the executive, are scored on the above scale. • Executives elected by bodies other than these are given the same score that the electing body would get. Even if the electing body is not the actual "legislature" that is tracked in the LIEC (such as an appointed electoral college), the competitiveness of that body is used to score the executive. • This means that competitively elected prime ministers get 6 or 7. The chief executives of Communist nations (the chairman of the Communist Party) are given a 3, because they are elected by the Party Congress, electing bodies which they do not appoint. Executives elected by small, appointed juntas or by appointed electoral colleges get 2.

Appendix II: List of Sampled 48 LDCs Across Regions

Africa (33)		*Asia (14)*	*Latin American and Caribbean (1)*
1. Angola	17. Liberia	1. Afghanistan	1. Haiti
2. Benin	18. Madagascar	2. Bangladesh	
3. Burkina Faso	19. Malawi	3. Bhutan	
4. Burundi	20. Mali	4. Cambodia	
5. Central African Republic	21. Mauritania	5. Kiribati	
6. Chad	22. Mozambique	6. Lao PDR	
7. Comoros	23. Niger	7. Myanmar	
8. Congo, Dem. Rep.	24. Rwanda	8. Nepal	
9. Djibouti	25. Senegal	9. Sao Tome and Principe	
10. Equatorial Guinea	26. Sierra Leone		
11. Eritrea	27. Somalia	10. Solomon Islands	
12. Ethiopia	28. South Sudan	11. Timor-Leste	
13. Gambia, The	29. Sudan	12. Tuvalu	
14. Guinea	30. Tanzania	13. Vanuatu	
15. Guinea-Bissau	31. Togo	14. Yemen, Rep.	
16. Lesotho	32. Uganda		
	33. Zambia		

Note: Maldives and Samoa were in the panel until 2011 and 2014 before their graduation, and South Sudan has been included in the list recently. Vanuatu and Equatorial Guinea are set to be graduated within next few years

References

Albuquerque, R. (2003). The composition of international capital flows: Risk sharing through foreign direct investment. *Journal of International Economics, 1*(2), 353–383.

Alfaro, L., Kalemli-Ozcan, S., & Lolosovych, V. (2008). Why doesn't capital flow from rich to poor countries? An empirical investigation. *Review of Economics and Statistics, 90*(2), 347–368.

Arellano, M., & Bond, S. (1991). Some tests of specification for panel data: Monte Carlo evidence and an application to employment equations. *Review of Economic Studies, 58*(2), 277–297.

Arellano, M., & Bover, O. (1995). Another look at the instrumental variable estimation of error-components models. *Journal of Econometrics, 68*(1), 29–51.

Beck, T., Clarke, G., Groff, A., Keefer, P., & Walsh, P. (2001). New tools in comparative political economy: The Database of Political Institutions. *World Bank Economic Review, 15*(1), 165–176.

Blundell, R., & Bond, S. (1998). Initial conditions and moment restrictions in dynamic panel data models. *Journal of Econometrics, 87*(1), 115–143.

Borensztein, E., De Gregorio, J., & Lee, J. (1998). How does foreign direct investment affect economic growth? *Journal of International Economics, 45*(1), 115–135.

Faria, A., & Mauro, P. (2009). Institutions and the external capital structure of countries. *Journal of International Money and Finance, 28*, 367–391.

Hausmann, R., & Fernandez-Arias, E. (2000, March). *Foreign direct investment: Good cholesterol?* New Orleans: Inter-American Development Bank. Mimeo.

Lane, P., & Milesi-Ferretti, G. M. (2001). External capital structure: Theory and evidence. In H. Siebert (Ed.), *The world's new financial landscape: Challenges for economic policy*. Berlin/Heidelberg: Springer.

Montiel, P. (1993). *Capital mobility in developing countries* (PRE Paper 1103). Policy Research Department, World Bank.

Rahman, S. H., & Hossain, M. (2014). Whither aid in Bangladesh. In S. Ahmed, M. Alamgir, M. K. Mujeri, & A. Rahman (Eds.), *Bangladesh: Vision 2030*. Dhaka: Bangladesh Institute of Bank Management. 2015.

Sargan, J. D. (1958). The estimation of economic relationships using instrumental variables. *Econometrica, 26*(3), 393–415.

Sarno, L., & Taylor, M. P. (1999). Hot money, accounting labels and the permanence of capital flows to developing countries: An empirical investigation. *Journal of Development Economics, 59*, 337–364.

UNESCAP. (2010). Asia-Pacific regional review of the Brussels program of action for the least developed countries for the decade 2001–2010: Dhaka outcome document.

Wei, S. J. (2001). Domestic crony capitalism and international fickle capital: Is there a connection? *International Finance, 4*(1), 15–45.
Wei, S. J., & Shleifer, A. (2000). Local corruption and global capital flows. *Brookings Papers on Economic Activity, 31*(2), 303–346.
Wei, S. J., & Wu, Y. (2002). Negative alchemy? Composition of capital flows, and currency crises. In S. Edwards & A. Frankel (Eds.), *Preventing currency crises in emerging markets* (pp. 461–506). Chicago: The University of Chicago Press.

CHAPTER 13

Aid, Macroeconomic Stability and Economic Development in Bangladesh

Sultan Hafeez Rahman and Monzur Hossain

13.1 Introduction

The role of external assistance in macroeconomic stability and economic development in developing countries has received great attention in the aid effectiveness literature. Evaluating the impact of aid on growth or development is not straightforward. Modeling the relationship involves unpacking the specific effects of macroeconomic variables. The related technical problems such as endogeneity and omitted variables pose challenges even setting aside the problems of data. Political economy issues add to these complexities. However, various rigorous micro-level impact evaluations of aid effectiveness with large data sets have been conducted to assess intervention-oriented outcomes. These evaluations have mainly examined specific outputs, impacts and outcomes in aid-funded projects, and the bulk of the empirical evidences at the micro level shows that aid is effective.

S. H. Rahman (✉)
BRAC Institute of Governance and Development, BRAC University, Dhaka, Bangladesh

M. Hossain
Bangladesh Institute of Development Studies (BIDS), Dhaka, Bangladesh

M. Hossain (ed.), *Bangladesh's Macroeconomic Policy*,
https://doi.org/10.1007/978-981-15-1244-5_13

The failure of the empirical literature in assessing the impact of aid on macroeconomic performance has given rise to what Mosley et al. (1987) termed as the "micro-macro paradox". Burnside and Dollar (2000) find that the positive impact of aid on economic growth depends on sound macroeconomic policies (fiscal, monetary, trade and exchange rate policies). That sound macroeconomic performance forms the "bedrock" of a strong and inclusive economic growth strategy is by now well accepted. Equally important are sound institutions which design and implement them. There is significant empirical research showing the importance of institutions and social capital on aid effectiveness. Many studies report a positive and statistically significant effect of institutional quality on economic growth. High corruption and lack of transparency, both tend to be common in developing countries, erode the quality of institutions and hence tend to undermine social capital accumulation, economic growth and, to some extent, aid effectiveness. Weak institutions even affect donor-driven reform agenda (Addison and Baliamoune-Lutz 2006).

Usually developing countries depend on aid to maintain macroeconomic stability, particularly external and domestic deficits. Such aid often comes with policy conditionalities which typically involve adjustments in tax and expenditure policies, tariff and exchange rate policies, sectoral policies, and so forth. Thus, macroeconomic stability is a target of aid conditionalities. In theory, if they are implemented effectively, they would contribute significantly to growth and welfare.

Bangladesh is not an exception. It has been receiving aid since its independence in 1971. Once termed as a "basket case", it is now a development paradox. On average, Bangladesh has received official aid of between US$1 billion and US$1.5 billion annually during the period 1972–2016. The changing structure of aid in Bangladesh over time might shed light on its importance in the economy. Food and commodity aid dominated the aid basket in the 1970s and 1980s, when it was much needed, which has now declined sharply with improvement in food production. Since the 1990s, donor support focused mainly on development project and program aid linked to agreed policy reforms. As growth accelerated with the advent of economic reforms, the importance of aid has declined.

Bangladesh undertook major trade and financial liberalization programs as part of the structural adjustment reforms supported by the World Bank and the International Monetary Fund (IMF). Adoption of current account convertibility in March 1994 and floating exchange rate, a *de facto* "managed float" system in June 2003 as part of exchange rate and trade policy liberalization along with financial sector liberalization agreed with the IMF for its support under Enhanced Structural Adjustment Facility (ESAF) and Poverty Reduction Growth Facility (PRGF), respectively, improved the domestic investment climate growth and balance of payments (BOPs). The impressive growth that Bangladesh has achieved is credited mainly to its solid macroeconomic management. Besides, in the context of bilateral donor assistance, it complemented the multilateral donor reform programs. A good example was the adoption of reform policies in project management, procurement and implementation, which led to positive development outcomes.

This chapter attempts to assess the role of aid in macroeconomic stability and economic development; specifically, it investigates the role of foreign aid in maintaining external balance and fiscal sustainability, and economic development. Considering the difficulties in establishing causal relationship, this chapter relies on addressing the questions through descriptive analysis and draws insights consistent with economic theory.

The chapter is organized as follows. Section 13.2 reviews some relevant literature in the context of aid effectiveness. Section 13.3 discusses trends and composition of aid in Bangladesh, and Sect. 13.4 assesses the role of aid in macroeconomic performance. Section 13.5 discusses aid performance in selected sectors, and Sect. 13.6 discusses the donors' assessment of aid performance in Bangladesh. Section 13.7 reflects on the political economy of aid, and Sect. 13.8 presents concluding remarks.

13.2 Literature Review

The empirical literature on effectiveness of aid is inconclusive. Yet the interest around aid effectiveness issues has revived in the context of further progress with the Millennium Development Goals (MDGs) and subsequent Sustainable Development Goals (SDGs). An important aspect of assessing aid effectiveness is to what extent aid has contributed to the intended purpose. At the micro level, it is less complicated to test aid effectiveness by looking at specific outcomes in aid-funded projects. The issue, however, is more complex at the macro level. Due to this *micro-macro paradox*, no empirical regularity has so far emerged on this topic (Mosley et al. 1987).

Burnside and Dollar (2000) argue that the presence of good policies (good fiscal, monetary and trade policies) is important to achieve a positive impact of aid on economic growth. The link between growth and aid is, in most cases, empirically unstable—it changes if the sample, the control variables or the model specifications change (e.g. Lensink and White 2001; Hansen and Tarp 2000, 2001; Antipin and Mavrotas 2006). Another strand in the literature emphasizes the role of institutions and social capital on aid effectiveness. Most of the studies find a positive and statistically significant effect of institutions (institutional quality) on growth. They argue that if institutions matter for investment decisions this is the link through which institutions contribute to growth. (e.g. Easterly and Levine 1997; Alesina et al. 2003; Easterly et al. 2006; Baliamoune-Lutz 2005).

Aid effectiveness in Bangladesh has not been studied rigorously yet. Quibria and Ahmed (2007) highlight several aspects of aid effectiveness in Bangladesh on the basis of qualitative arguments. The challenges of analyzing aid effectiveness, as discussed earlier, are twofold: (i) in case of micro-level analysis, it is difficult to link project outcomes with national-level development indicators, which is also dependent on a good impact analysis of the project (technicality aspect), and (ii) with a certain share of development projects, it is very difficult to gauge their impact at the macro level as aid is linked to various policies and objectives (policy aspect).

However, at the micro level, the scenario is not very clear either. Questioning the diminishing marginal return aspect of aid, Radelet (2006) argues that aid should generate intended sectoral outcome if it is properly allocated to the relevant sectors. However, this is not the case in many instances. Thus, the changing sectoral allocation of aid in a country with stronger institutions should provide an indication of its role in fostering development of the country. However, proper assessment of aid effectiveness by donors in the light of the Paris Declaration could be a better source of our understanding to the development impact of aid, if it is done in an unbiased manner.

13.3 Trends and Composition of Foreign Aid

After independence in 1971, Bangladesh faced daunting challenges, such as large and rapidly growing population, lack of resources, anemic domestic saving and investment rates, large food deficit, high illiteracy, infant and maternal mortality as well as inadequate access to safe water and sanitation. Initially a large amount of aid was required to finance essential imports (trade gap) including food and the much needed reconstruction investments (saving-investment gap). Aid levels started declining since the

1990s, but they were primarily devoted to investments in growing sectors underpinning accelerated growth of the economy from 3–4 percent gross domestic product (GDP) growth annually, to 6–7 percent GDP growth annually. It was also a prudent financial portfolio management decision by the government to finance investments from concessional aid rather than from high-cost borrowing (domestic and foreign). This kept debt sustainability at a manageable level (Table 13.1).

The declining trend of aid in Bangladesh is in line with the global experience (Fig. 13.1). As a percentage of gross national income (GNI) and ODA has been declining in South Asia, such as in India, Pakistan, Bangladesh and Sri Lanka, the flow of aid is still high in conflict-ridden countries, such as in Afghanistan and in resource-poor smaller countries like Nepal, Bhutan and the Maldives. Bangladesh received much lower amount of aid compared to its least developed country (LDC) counterparts (Fig. 13.2). This is attributable to improving economic performance of Bangladesh as the country is very close to graduating from LDC status to middle-income country. This is consistent with the experiences of countries that have sound macroeconomic fundamentals.

13.3.1 Composition of Aid Over Time

Bangladesh receives four types of aid: project aid, budget support aid, commodity aid and food aid. The transformation of the Bangladesh econ-

Table 13.1 Average official development assistance (ODA), (1972–2015)

Time period	*1972–1980*	*1981–1990*	*1991–2000*	*2001–2010*	*2011–2015*
Average ODA (current) (million US$)	774.98	1451.94	1390.20	1352.54	2255.02
Average ODA (Constant 2015) (million US$)	2353.74	2711.02	1774.58	1419.81	2072.70

Source: World development indicators (WDI), World Bank data

Note: Net official development assistance (ODA) consists of disbursements of loans made on concessional terms (net of repayments of principal) and grants by official agencies of the members of the Development Assistance Committee (DAC) by multilateral institutions and by non-DAC countries to promote economic development and welfare in countries and territories in the DAC list of ODA recipients. It includes loans with a grant element of at least 25 percent (calculated at a rate of discount of 10 percent)

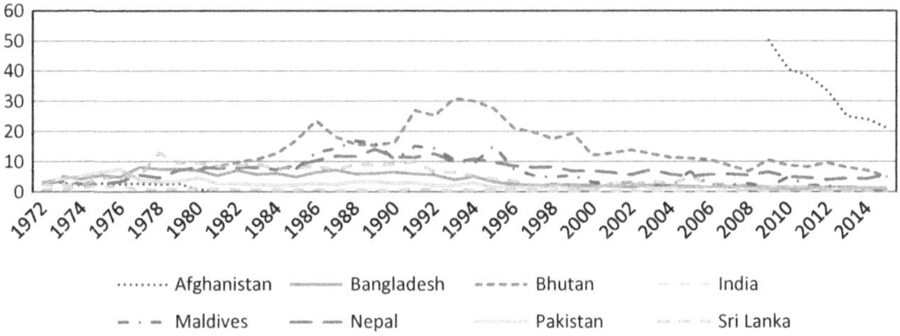

Fig. 13.1 Aid as percent of GNI in South Asian Association for Regional Cooperation (SAARC) countries (1972–2015). (Source: World development indicators, World Bank)

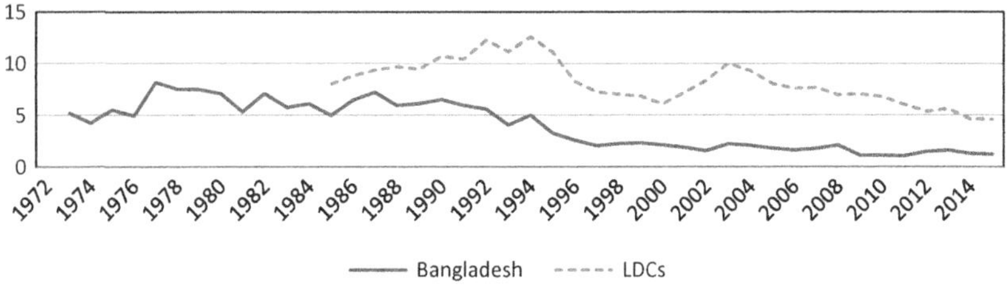

Fig. 13.2 Comparison of aid flows between Bangladesh and the LDCs (percent of GNI) (1972–2015). (Source: World development indicators, World Bank)

omy happened in a series of steps, which has been reflected in the changing composition of aid over time (Fig. 13.3). Food aid has declined due to reaching a status in self-sufficiency with increased food production. Similarly, commodity aid has also significantly reduced after 2004–2005, due to increased export earnings, tax revenue growth and consistent rise in foreign remittances. There was no inflow of commodity aid since the period of 2005–2006; hence, thereafter, project aid constitutes about 99 percent of the total aid, and the rest only about 1 percent is food aid.[1]

Historically, the share of project aid has remained within 25 percent of total project value across sectors. A shift in aid allocation to different sectors has also been observed, over time, with a shift of development priority

[1] During the 1980s, while food and commodity aid was seen to dominate the aid basket at 51.1 percent, project aid comprised 48.9 percent. As Bangladesh matured over the years, the composition of aid showed a shift, with project aid taking over the main portion of aid.

of the government. The key sectors that received higher aid allocations in the 1990s were power, transport, water resources, industry, oil, gas and mineral resources. From 2000 onward, some sectors like industry, oil, gas extraction and water resource got less project aid allocation in the context of the changing scenario (Fig. 13.4). Along with infrastructure projects, aid also went to various projects that are related to MDG/SDG targets such as health, education and rural development (poverty reduction). The composition of aid appears to be changing with the development priorities of the country.

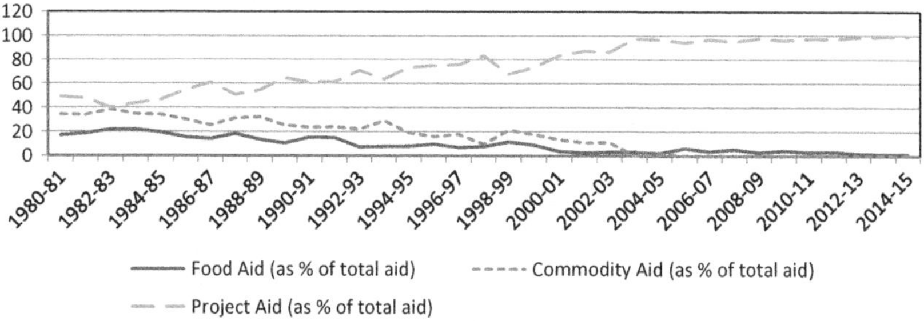

Fig. 13.3 Trends of food, commodity and project aid. (Source: Flow of external resources 2014–2015, Economic Relations Division (ERD), Ministry of Finance (MoF))

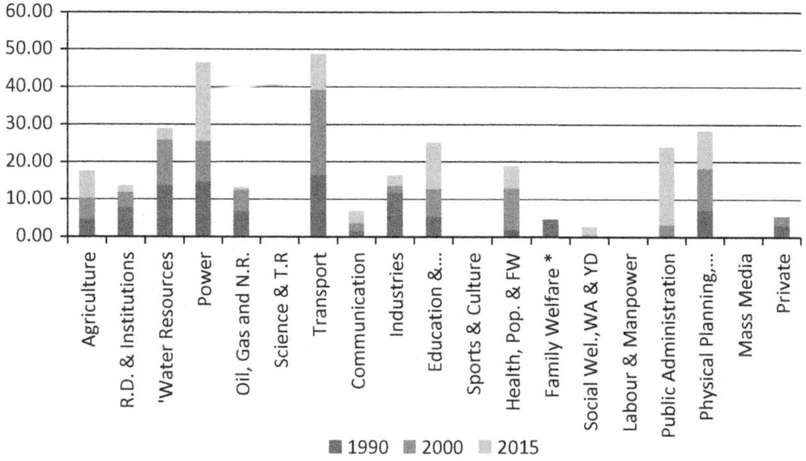

Fig. 13.4 Percentage share of project aid to different sectors. (Source: Flow of external resources 2014–2015, Economic Relations Division, Ministry of Finance)

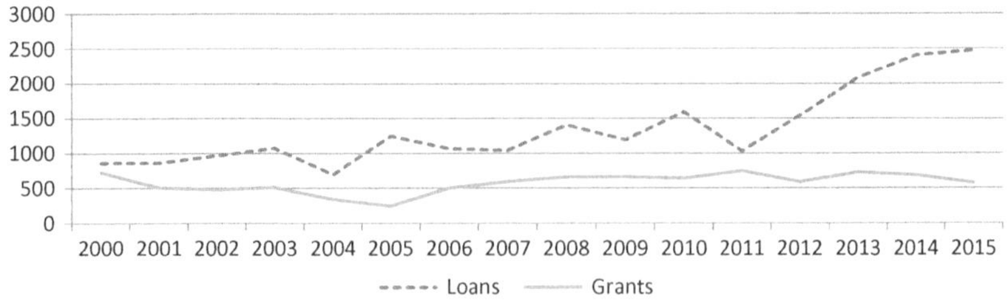

Fig. 13.5 Loans versus grants (US$ million). (Source: Economic Relations Division (ERD), Ministry of Finance)

13.3.2 Changing Scenario in Aid Composition: Grant Versus Loan

The composition of foreign aid disbursements shows a decline in the portion of grants, with subsequent increase in the share of loans (Fig. 13.5). During the year 2000, the portion of loans occupied 54.3 percent of total aid ($861.9 million), which increased to 81.2 percent ($2472.2 million) during 2015. During the same period, grants occupied 45.7 percent of total aid, which declined to 18.8 percent of the total aid disbursed.

13.3.3 Gap Between Disbursements and Commitments

The pipeline, commitment and disbursement figures are currently being reported in a misleading way in the official report of ERD, "Flow of External Resources into Bangladesh" (ERD 2012). Though the opening pipeline consists of commitments for several years, the existing reporting structure does not reflect that perspective. Moreover, the figures on annual commitments and disbursements are also misleading because they do not match the year-on-year figures. As the Fig. 13.6 shows, disbursements exceed commitments in some points, indicating that previous year's committed aid can be disbursed in the preceding year. Therefore, for making aid data reporting more effective, aid data on actual commitment and disbursements for a particular year may be reported, and an analysis of the pipeline should be made in a way that can reflect clearly the implementation period of the projects that are in the pipeline.

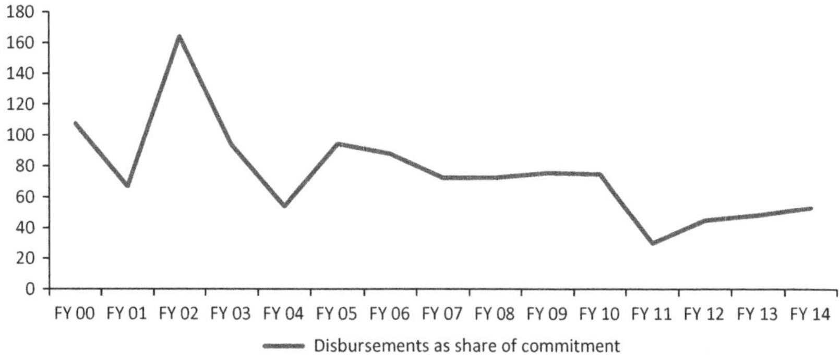

Fig. 13.6 Disbursements as a share of ODA commitments (2000–2014: percent). (Source: Economic Relations Division (ERD), Ministry of Finance)

Despite the reporting problem, there exists a gap between the disbursements and commitments which might have led to a substantial amount of the committed aid to remain in the pipeline. Low level of disbursements often hinders the progress in project implementation, which leads to cost escalation and delayed project outcome. Figure 13.6 shows that, recently, the rate of disbursements of committed aid declined to below 40 percent.

A perennial problem of sluggish project implementation results in slow aid disbursement. This usually ends up in a time and cost overrun that might have negative impact on aid utilization. Efficient utilization of financial assistance or effective project implementation can be hindered by certain factors. Faulty project design leads to a revision of Development Project Proposal (DPP) or Technical Project Proposal (TPP) before project commencement, which delays project implementation start date. Challenges in the land acquisition process as well as procurement-related bottlenecks tend to hinder the rate of project implementation. Lack of coordination in projects within sectors or government agencies also is a factor. Delay in the approval of awarding contracts, appointing consultants, fund release and lack of coordination among co-financers (multi-donors funded projects) are often cited as some of the common causes of slow disbursement in various newspapers and government budget documents. Worse still, slow reforms in enhancing the aid delivery mechanisms over a long period have resulted in these factors becoming a set of structural constraints.

13.3.4 Changing Pattern of Donors

13.3.4.1 Traditional Donors

Multilateral donor agencies such as Asian Development Bank (ADB), World Bank (International Development Association (IDA)) and UN System are the main sources of foreign assistance to Bangladesh, while contribution from bilateral sources, such as the governments of Japan, the UK and Canada, is also significant. The World Bank (IDA) and ADB have continued to be the large multilateral donors for Bangladesh, providing assistance largely from their concessional windows. However, the terms and conditions of the multilateral donors have become hardened in recent times, with Bangladesh's prospect of graduation from LDC status. As a result, ADB is now classifying Bangladesh as a blend country, which allows Bangladesh to borrow from both concessionary and non-concessionary windows, considering its strength in repayment of loans.

The volume of multilateral aid has surpassed that of bilateral aid over time (Fig. 13.7). From 1999 to 2014, the percentage share of multilateral aid has increased with decline of bilateral aid. As of 2015, multilateral aid comprised 68.9 percent of total aid, while the share of bilateral aid was 31.1 percent.

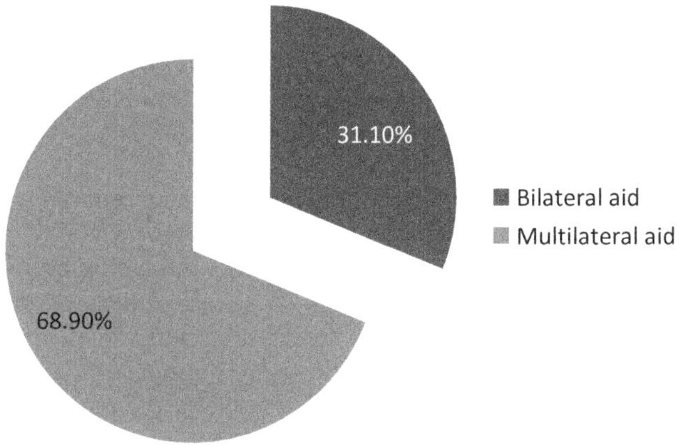

Fig. 13.7 Composition of aid provided by donors (as of 2015). (Source: Economic Relations Division (ERD), Ministry of Finance)

13.3.4.2 Non-Traditional Donors

Over time, a good number of new but non-traditional donors have emerged, such as China, India, the Islamic Republic of Iran, Kuwait, Malaysia, Saudi Arabia, Turkey and United Arab Emirates. These emerging countries introduce line of credit for countries like Bangladesh which have geopolitical importance. Nonetheless, Bangladesh also maintains strong relations with DAC member countries, such as Japan and Republic of Korea.

13.3.4.3 Private Sector Donors

In order to accelerate economic growth, alleviate poverty and fulfill other SDGs, official aid alone cannot be considered an adequate funding source. The private sector needs to be focused as a driver toward growth and employment generation. If aid efforts were dedicated toward catalyzing innovative financing solutions for the private sector, it could lead to private sector development. Funding the SDGs would require increasing the investment rate above the domestic saving rate, as well as utilizing additional foreign financing to bridge the financing gap. Among private sector flows, workers' remittances, foreign direct investment (FDI), portfolio debt, equity flows, lending from foreign banks and philanthropic funding from various private sector donors like Melinda-Gates foundation, corporate social responsibility (CSR) activities and other foundation activities could be noteworthy.

13.3.5 Sectoral Allocation of Aid

Historical share of project aid in the annual development programs (ADP) across sectors shows that the allocation remained almost within the 15 percent of total project value. The key sectors that receive higher aid allocations in Bangladesh are power, transport, education and health. Since the 1990s, project aid has declined substantially for sectors like agriculture, water resources, oil and gas and family welfare. Beyond infrastructure, an increasing share of aid has been allocated to sectors contributing to the achievement of MDG targets such as health, education and rural development (poverty reduction) (Fig. 13.8).

Although the allocation of foreign aid in different sectors appears to be smaller in terms of total sectoral expenditure, foreign aid matters in many big infrastructure projects. For example, foreign aid has been deemed necessary to implement various big infrastructure projects for a number of

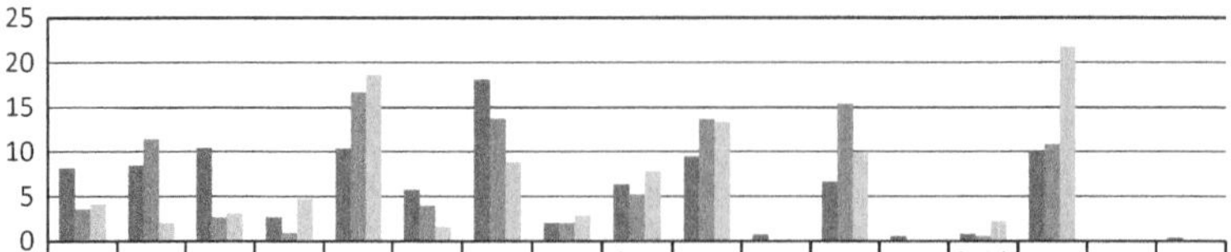

	Agriculture	Rural Development & Institution	Water Resources	Industries	Power	Oil, Gas & Mineral Resources	Transport	Communication	Physical Planning, Water Supply & Housing	Education & Religion	Sports & Culture	Health, Population & Family Welfare	Mass Media	Social Welfare, Women Affairs & Youth Dev.	Public Administration	Science & Technology	Labour & Manpower
1990s	8.13	8.4	10.36	2.61	10.27	5.66	18.09	1.95	6.29	9.39	0.68	6.56	0.5	0.73	10	0.04	0.34
2000s	3.49	11.37	2.59	0.83	16.68	3.93	13.69	1.95	5.2	13.63	0	15.36	0.03	0.48	10.77	0	0
2011-2015	4.0067	1.9716	3.0485	4.6522	18.566	1.4802	8.7481	2.7929	7.768	13.386	0	9.6689	0	2.159	21.742	0	0

Fig. 13.8 Percentage share of aid to different sectors. (Source: Bangladesh Economic Review (BER), various issues)

reasons: (i) providing foreign exchange requirement for financing foreign procurement of goods and services required for the project, (ii) providing investment financing on concessionary terms, (iii) releasing local resources for other social priorities, (iv) transferring technology through project design and implementation, (v) employing foreign experts with knowledge and experience not available in the country, (vi) ensuring synergy with other important foreign aid-financed projects, (vii) insulating growth-inducing investments from the hazards of political maneuvering that characterize annual budget allocation process and (viii) proper monitoring and evaluation of the project. While there are problems with implementation across the board, past experience suggests that donor-funded projects are better managed and implemented than those that are funded by local sources. Over time, some big infrastructure projects have been implemented well in Bangladesh, with significant contribution from foreign assistance, such as first and second Meghna Bridges in Demra and Daudkandi, Buriganga Bridge in Keraniganj, Bangabandhu Jamuna Bridge and the Dhaka-Chittagong highway. These projects have created positive development outcomes in terms of improved transportation and communication as well as increased economic activities in the surrounding regions. These projects have laid the foundation for the development of economic corridors and economic zones in Bangladesh. Thanks to the bridges over several rivers, the Dhaka-Chittagong belt has emerged as the first true economic corridor of Bangladesh, notwithstanding the teething problem of the new access-controlled Super Expressway. So, from the perspective of Bangladesh, dealing with multilateral donors for important projects sometimes appears to be cumbersome due to multifaceted conditions attached to aid financing. Moreover, Bangladesh's graduation from LDC, which is expected in 2024, will make ODA costlier than now.

13.4 Aid and Macroeconomic Performance

The impact of aid on macroeconomic performance will be examined in terms of whether or not foreign assistance (i) augments domestic savings to finance increased investments, (ii) helps to maintain fiscal sustainability and (iii) provides additional foreign exchange to finance import payments and contribute to viable BOPs.

13.4.1 Savings and Investment

Domestic savings and investments were low in the 1970s before these picked up in the 1980s. Notwithstanding the level and rate of savings (domestic and national), aid always had a role in total investments (physical asset accumulation) even in the paradoxical case when national savings exceeded total investments (Fig. 13.9). Without aid investments, public investment, especially, would have been lower, and so would growth performance. There was a policy shift toward privatization and promotion of the public sector in the late 1970s. As a result, investment in both public and private sectors grew at nearly 15 percent annually in real terms in the late 1970s and early 1980s, though this growth did not sustain for a longer period.

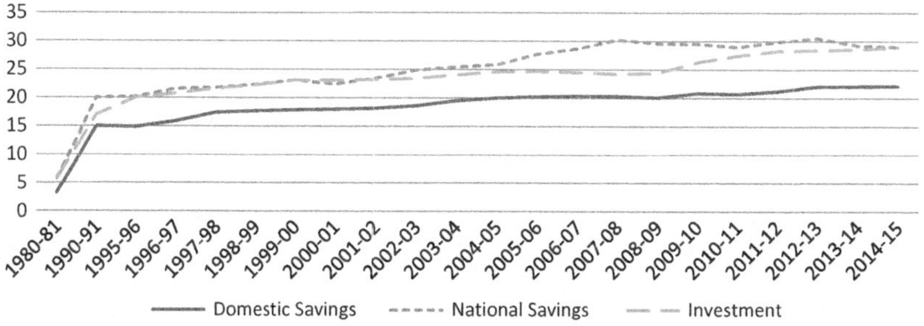

Fig. 13.9 National savings, domestic savings and investment rate (as percent of GDP). (Source: Bangladesh Economic Review, various issues)

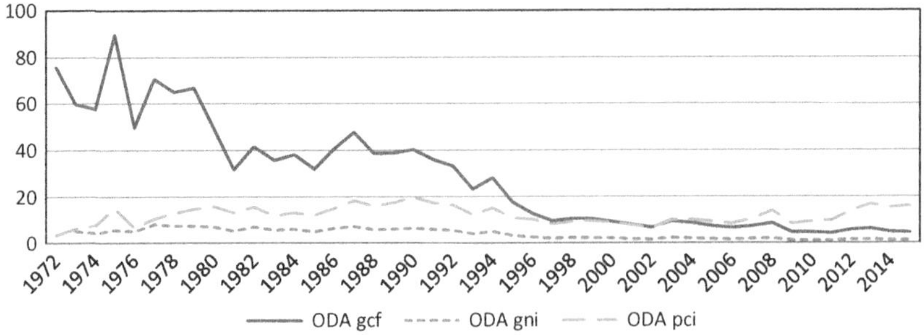

Fig. 13.10 ODA as percent of GNI, gross capital formation (GCF) and per capita income (PCI). (Source: World Development Indicators, World Bank)

However, a more comprehensive macroeconomic reform started in the early 1990s in the face of a transition to parliamentary democracy. The reforms of the 1980s and 1990s[2] helped reduce fiscal and external deficits to a sustainable level, consistent with the level of aid availability. There has been a significant improvement in saving and investment performance in the 1990s compared with 1980s. In the latter period, saving and investment were associated with increase in aid relative to investment (gross fixed capital formation (GFCF)), whereas in the 1990s, saving and investment increased despite decline in aid (Figs. 13.9 and 13.10).

The decline of aid, both in relative terms (Fig. 13.10) and in absolute terms (Table 13.1), reflects some positive aspects of the economy including improving BOPs, exploding overseas employment and remittances along with growing reserves. Bangladesh economy continued to perform well over time bypassing negative impacts of several global financial crises, oil price shocks, food price spike and natural calamities. It would be fair to say that aid has had a positive impact on growth in Bangladesh,

[2]While the policy reforms in the 1980s aimed at withdrawal of food and agricultural subsidies, privatization of state-owned enterprises, financial liberalization and withdrawal of quantitative import restrictions, the reforms of the early 1990s were particularly aimed at moving toward an open economy, such as making the current account convertible, reducing import duties generally to much lower levels and removing virtually all controls on the movements of foreign private capital. In addition, on the fiscal front, value added tax (VAT) was introduced in the 1990s. As indicated earlier, reforms of the early 1990s led to an improvement in macroeconomic indicators.

though more analytical work is needed to establish correlation and/or causality in a more credible way.

In the early 1980s, domestic savings and the investment saw a downward trend when the external aid climate deteriorated (Figs. 13.9 and 13.10). A major policy shift of the early 1980s was the adoption of market-oriented liberalization against the backdrop of serious macroeconomic imbalances. Decline in foreign aid and severe deterioration of terms of trade (TOT) were the key reasons of such imbalances.

While the net inflow of foreign assistance further declined to around 2 percent of GNI, both investment and saving rates and consequently the growth performance of the country have improved. The investment scenario has improved significantly in the 1990s. The ratio of investment to GDP, which was less than 17 percent in the 1980s, increased to about 23 percent at the end of the 1990s. Since the public sector investment hovers around 6–7 percent of GDP over time, the increase was mainly due to private sector investment. Private investment ratio in recent years (2015–2018) increased to around 21–22 percent with the same level of public investment (6–7 percent of GDP), indicating that no crowding out happened due to public investments. As foreign aid goes mainly to public investments, particularly in infrastructure investments, aid indirectly facilitates private investments, and so does private sector-led growth.

There are criticisms of reform programs initiated in the 1980s in consultation with multilateral donors. In the early 1990s, for example, the marked increase in the domestic savings rate might be the result of aggregate demand deficiency, which was reflected in stalled private investment, near-zero inflation along with a buildup of international reserves. The uncertainty created by policy reforms as part of aid package, which had no preannounced targets or timetable, could have been a contributing factor (Mahmud 2006).

Though there were criticisms about the effectiveness of the Structural Adjustment Program of the 1980s, subsequent trend of key economic variables, however, suggests that the apprehension about policy reforms was somewhat misplaced because the economy started embarking on higher growth trajectories in subsequent periods with benefits of policy reforms started in the 1980s and afterwards. While the average GDP growth was 3.7 percent annually during the 1980s, it increased to 4.4 percent in the first half of the 1990s, and further to 5.2 percent in the second half of the 1990s. During the 2000s, the country achieved impressive economic growth, about 6 percent on average, which was thought to be the positive outcome of reforms undertaken in the 1980s and 1990s.

13.4.2 Fiscal Stability

Aid finances fiscal deficits and contributes to tax revenue earnings by financing imports and spurring growth. During the 1980s, the fiscal deficit came down from 6.6 percent of GDP to 5.4 percent in the 1990s, and later, in most of the years, the fiscal deficit remained within 5 percent of GDP. While total government expenditure has increased from 12.5 percent of GDP in 1990 to about 16 percent of GDP in 2015, the tax-GDP ratio has increased from 6 percent of GDP to over 9 percent of GDP during the same period (Fig. 13.11). With an increased level of government expenditure coupled with increased tax revenue, the direct contribution of aid in financing fiscal deficit has declined from 80 percent in 1990 to 28 percent in 2015. Net foreign financing in deficit finance was more than 75 percent before 1990, indicating an overwhelming importance of aid in maintaining fiscal stability during that period in Bangladesh (Fig. 13.12).

It is important to note here that the tax-GDP ratio in Bangladesh has been the lowest even among the SAARC countries. Given the lower

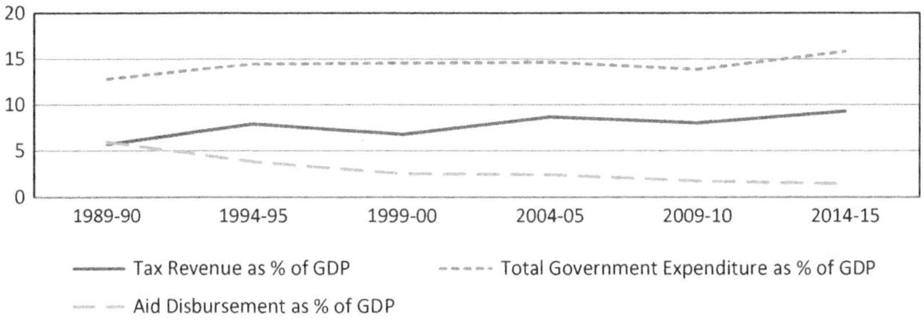

Fig. 13.11 Fiscal indicators. (Source: Bangladesh Economic Review, various issues)

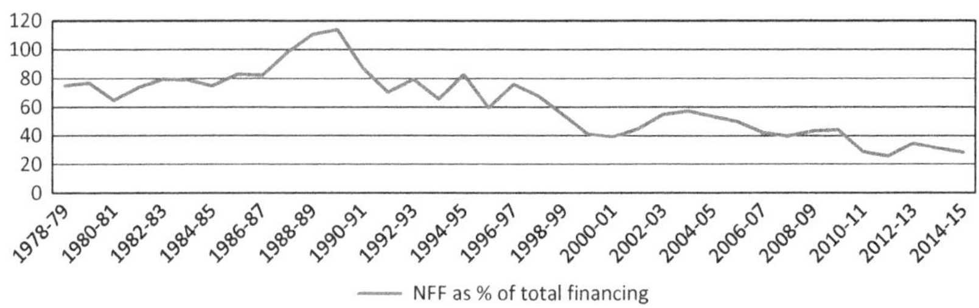

Fig. 13.12 Net foreign financing in deficit finance (percent). (Source: Bangladesh Economic Review, various issues)

growth of tax revenue over time, there was a possibility of fiscal unsustainability, particularly in the absence of foreign assistance. Though the dependence of foreign aid in financing fiscal deficit has decreased over time, its role is still significant in managing intertemporal fiscal policy of the government.

13.4.3 External Stability

Aid-financed infrastructure and aid-supported policy reforms spearheading external openness and integration with the global economy played an important role in growth of trade. The export-GDP ratio increased from less than 6 percent in the latter half of the 1980s to the current level of above 15 percent. With increase in imports, the trade openness of the economy (i.e. the combined ratio of imports and exports to GDP) has increased to about 48 percent in recent years, sustaining a higher growth performance of the economy.

Until 1992, net ODA was contributing significantly to Bangladesh's foreign exchange reserve buildup, as it was higher than the reserve (without grant) of the country. Since 1993, foreign exchange reserve has been surpassing the ODA, with a significant contribution from overseas remittances and export earnings (Fig. 13.13). Thus, ODA contributed positively to the BOP in the 1970s, 1980s and 1990s; however, its significance in maintaining a viable BOP has been declining since 2000, mainly because of higher remittance receipts and export earnings from the ready-made garments (RMG).

Trade balance gives an idea about dependence on foreign aid or external income rather than on exports of goods. A better view of export/import relation is indicated by normalized trade balance, as shown in Table 13.2. Trade deficit has escalated from US$1733 million in 1981–1985 to US$9783 million in 2011–2015, accounting 13.7 percent growth per five-year period. The average annual growth of trade deficit has increased substantially in the periods 2001–2005, 2006–2010 and 2011–2015. It is worth noting that the proportion of trade balance to GDP hovers around 7 percent in all the periods. However, import coverage ratio (coverage of import payments by export earnings) has increased significantly from about 31 percent in 1981–1985 to about 76 percent in 2011–2015, indicating that foreign aid was an important source of foreign exchange requirement to cover import payments until 1990. Thus, foreign aid has contributed to maintaining viable BOP that resulted in sustained level of economic growth (Table 13.2).

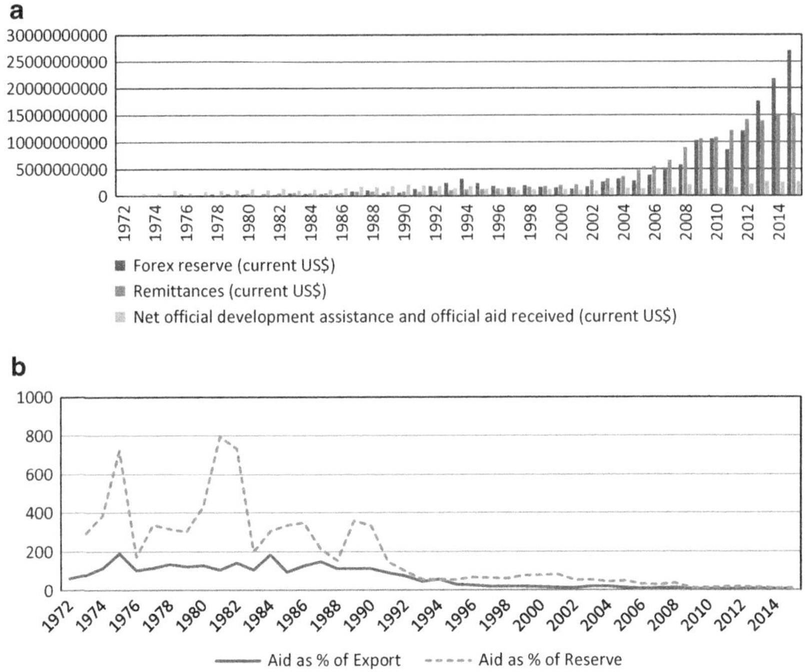

Fig. 13.13 (**a**) Remittances, foreign reserve and ODA. (Source: World Development Indicators, World Bank) (**b**) Aid as percentage of foreign reserves and exports. (Source: World Development Indicators, World Bank)

Table 13.2 Trade balance (average) and coverage of imports by exports

Economic phases	*Trade balance as percent of GDP*	*Normalized trade balance (X-M/ X+M)*	*Growth of trade balance*	*Trade balance in million US$*	*Coverage of imports by exports in percent*
1981–1985	−8.93	−0.53	−0.74	−1733.0	30.91
1986–1990	−6.97	−0.41	1.07	−1919.8	41.6
1991–1995	−6.58	−0.29	15.43	−2357.7	54.75
1996–2000	−6.14	−0.21	−2.62	−2775.6	66.14
2001–2005	−7.43	−0.21	17.73	−4333.4	64.47
2006–2010	−8.56	−0.19	13.15	−7464.5	65.96
2011–2015	−7.31	−0.14	6.24	−9783.1	75.61

Source: Author's calculation using data from BBS: X=Exports; M=Imports

Trade liberalization policies coupled with floating exchange rate policies has contributed positively to the external sector performance. Sound macroeconomic management with stable inflation has helped Bangladesh to reduce its dependency on aid as well as build a strong foreign exchange reserve position, which gives a cushion against any external shock. In achieving such good progress in macroeconomic management, not only the amount of aid but also the policy prescriptions supported by multilateral agencies as part of aid package contributed positively to overall macroeconomic stability of the country.

Aid has, thus, been playing an important and direct role in maintaining external sector stability until 1990. While aid was more than 200 percent of reserve until 1993, it started declining and reached 9.5 percent of reserve in 2015. Similarly, while aid was more than 100 percent of export earnings until 1993, thereafter it started declining, and it was only about 7.6 percent of export earnings in 2015. The importance of aid, perhaps, has reduced with good external sector performance (Fig. 13.13b).

The analysis in this section suggests that foreign aid has played an important direct role on macroeconomic management until 1990. Afterward, although the amount of aid has declined, its relevance has not declined as aid now comes with policy packages that helped Bangladesh maintain macroeconomic stability and build sound institutions.

13.5 Impact of Aid on Economic Development

The progress in social sector can be attributed to public investments in social sectors and in appropriate policies. The role of aid in social sectors can, thus, be examined in the light of contribution of aid in different sectors. Bangladesh has shown significant improvements in key social indicators such as fertility, life expectancy, school enrollment (primary) and child immunization, and has successfully eradicated polio and measles which still infect some neighboring countries (Table 13.3). Bangladesh has made remarkable progress across several MDG goals with some help from donor-driven projects. It has made remarkable achievements in meeting several MDG targets such as reducing poverty gap ratio, attaining gender parity at primary and secondary education, under-five mortality rate reduction, containing HIV infection with access to antiretroviral drugs, children under five sleeping under insecticide-treated bed nets, detection and cure rate of TB under directly observed therapy (DOTs), and so on.

Table 13.3 Progress of social indicators in Bangladesh, 1972–2015

Item	*1972*	*1980*	*1990*	*2000*	*2010*	*2012*	*2015*
Secondary school enrollment (percent gross)	20.46	18.63	20.24	47.8	49.89	53.45	63.42
Secondary school enrollment (percent net)	–	15.58	–	44.61	46.04	48.08	57.14
Primary school enrollment (percent gross)	63.28	69.79	80.56	–	102.30	–	111.09
Primary school enrollment (percent net)	70.37	67.54	72.03	–	91.55	90.51	90.50
Fertility rate	6.93	6.36	4.55	3.12	2.28	2.21	2.13
Immunization, DPT (percent of children aged 12–23 months)	–	–	69	82	94	94	97
Immunization, measles (percent of children aged 12–23 months)	–	–	65	74	88	88	94
Improved sanitation facilities (percent of population within access)	–	–	–	25.35	39.93	42.76	46.92
Life expectancy at birth	47.03	53.48	58.40	65.32	70.20	71.04	72.16
Malnutrition prevalence, weight for age (percent of children under 5)	–	–	61.5	42.3	36.8	31.9	32.6
Malnutrition rate (children under 5 per thousand)	–	–	63.4	50.8	41.4	42	36.1
Mortality rate (per one thousand live births)	147	133	99.7	64	38.9	35	29.8

Source: World Development Indicators, World Bank Data, United Nations Children's Fund (UNICEF) Data

In the 1970s and 1980s, the best use of aid was in sectors like agriculture, water resource and family welfare including family planning. As a result, Bangladesh was able to make a significant progress in these areas, particularly in raising agricultural production, reducing population growth and improving water supply and sanitation, as well as oil and gas extraction and supply.

With good progress in these sectors, the donors shifted the concentration to sectors that were linked to MDGs after 2000. Consequently, health, education and rural development (poverty reduction) got priority (Fig. 13.14).

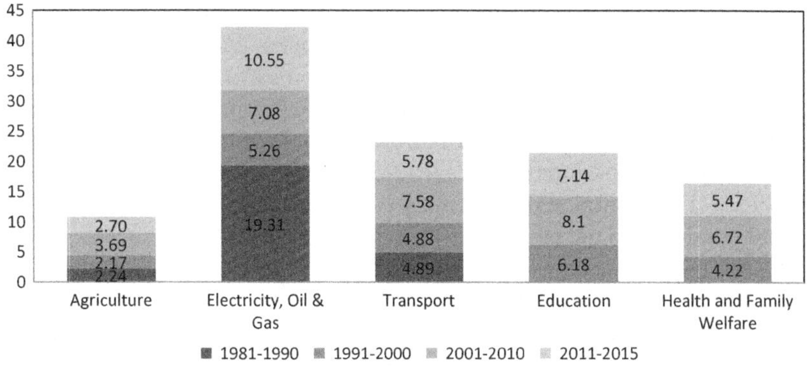

Fig. 13.14 Sectoral growth rate of GDP (percent). (Source: Bangladesh Economic Review, various issues)

13.6 Donor Evaluation of Aid Effectiveness in Bangladesh

To support more results-based aid, the Paris Declaration in 2005 underscored the need for global commitments for both donor and partner countries in terms of scale-up, untying and monitorable set of indicators. The Declaration sets five core principles: ownership, alignment, harmonization, management for results and mutual accountability. In addition, it identifies 12 monitorable indicators to deal with some of the major aid effectiveness issues.

The multilateral donors have been evaluating their aid by surveying recipient countries in the light of principles of aid effectiveness set in the Paris Declaration. As a multilateral regional lender, ADB finds its aid highly effective in Bangladesh in the context of medium-term targets set in the Declaration. Bangladesh has achieved all the targets since 2005, which were supposed to be achieved in 2010. Thus, ADB's aid is almost aligned to the Declaration (ADB 2010).

On the other hand, being the largest lender (around $13.0 billion in 2012), the evaluation made by the World Bank (IDA) suggests that the results of aid are not quite satisfactory, and it blamed the government for its failure to implement reforms. It also suggests that "a core constraint in the development process in Bangladesh was the government itself and its unwillingness to enforce the needed public sector reforms (World Bank 1998b, p. 56)." Despite the unhappiness of the World Bank in terms of reform programs pursued by Bangladesh, it has been widely acknowledged that

World Bank's reform programs as part of aid conditionality have influenced in shaping up the country's institutions and policies. As part of World Bank's structural reform programs, Bangladesh pursued various trade and financial reforms from late 1980s, particularly to promote private sector development. These reforms were addressed at removing the distortions in trade, pricing, credit allocation and interest rates. In terms of aid effectiveness indicators of the Paris Declaration, World Bank's evaluation suggests that Bangladesh could not maintain the targeted level in some areas until 2007, such as ownership, reliable public financial management (PFM), result-oriented frameworks and joint country analytic work (World Bank 2011).

Since 1973, UNDP has been supporting projects in three major areas: crisis prevention and recovery, democratic governance and poverty reduction and MDG achievement. The United Nations Development Programme (UNDP) aid amounted to US$289.5 million during 2004–2009. UNDP's independent evaluation in 2010, which is done once after every five years, suggests that most interventions during 2005–2010 reflected national priorities in Bangladesh. The UNDP report also suggests that UNDP-funded projects have been able to generate positive outcomes in different areas (UNDP 2010). During 2005–2010, it has been observed that UNDP financed various programs on rural and urban poverty reduction (e.g. Rural Employment Opportunities for Public Assets (REOPA), and Urban Partnerships for Poverty Reduction (UPPR), and so on), confidence building in Chittagong Hill Tracts, local government decentralization, disaster management and the like. During this period, Bangladesh has been able to reduce poverty significantly, from over 40 percent to about 31 percent and the credit certainly goes to some extent to UNDP-financed programs (UNDP 2010). However, analyzing UNDP's Union Parishad Governance Project (UPGP) interventions, Hossain and Roy (2019) show that although the UPGP has improved the administrative governance of Union Parishads, functional governance involving citizens remains weak, and therefore, due to partial improvement of governance framework, UPGP does not appear to have a significant impact on the overall local economic development and service delivery of UPs. Therefore, it is difficult to conclude that all the donor-sponsored projects have derived their intended outcomes properly.

Among donor assessments, the outcome of ADB and UNDP interventions appears to be in line with partner expectations, while the World Bank has an issue with the gap it sees between reform programs pursued by the Bangladesh government and what was suggested by the Bank as part of the aid package. There is no denying that the Bangladesh government has pursued substantial trade and financial liberalizations in the 1990s—may be not fully in line with the suggestions made by the lender. The reason for an apparent gap is partly due to political and economic sensitivity of those activities, and partly due to lack of ownership of the suggested reforms. Nonetheless, the current level of economic growth—more than 6 percent in the 2000s—is mainly attributed to the reforms undertaken in the 1990s, a clear indication of lagged effects in terms of qualitative changes made through institution building and improvement of governance in addition to quantitative impacts on the economy.

13.7 Reflections on the Political Economy of Aid

The UN First Development Decade launched the era of development assistance to developing countries. Half a century later, another high point was reached when the world's leaders met at the Millennium Summit in 2000 and declared the MDGs as the set of goals which the developing countries must achieve by 2015, with economic assistance that would be provided to them. The MDGs represented a new aid paradigm, based on a broader and coherent narrative of what constitutes successful development compared with the "Washington Consensus", which was more narrowly focused on economic factors to accomplish macroeconomic adjustment, trade liberalization and the expansion of market for goods, services and factors. Consequently, the focus of attention of the international financial institutions (IFIs) and bilateral aid agencies in "measuring" the success of aid turned to the MDGs. The focus of governments, too, rapidly turned to the MDGs. The convergence on development goals has since shaped the aid process. The much "maligned" aid conditionality—especially "hard" conditionality—contained in the structural adjustment programs of donors in the 1980s gradually shifted to a "lighter touch" approach and was generally welcomed by the developing countries. Judging by the enthusiasm with which it was received by the developing countries, and the achievement by many of them of the eight core MDGs ahead of 2015, and others who are likely to achieve them as well, aid effectiveness is likely to have improved.

In-country, it is not possible to separate aid allocation from the fiscal decision-making process, and hence aid decisions are influenced by political factors and not just by plan priorities. Thus, the choice of project investments in roads is often influenced by politics, as also the choice of constructing roads across the country at the expense of railways and inland water ways, both of which might be strong contenders if economic welfare was given due weightage by policy planners. While there is evidence of positive local economic effects of road building, there is little analysis of which of the alternative transport investments might have resulted in greater welfare gains. The negative externalities (environmental costs) of road building (e.g. obstruction of natural water flows causing excessive flooding) must also be factored into this calculation. Excessive investment in roads may well have distorted resource allocation. A specific example of the high economic costs of diverting resources to roads at the expense of rail and waterways is the current state of connectivity between Dhaka and Chittagong—the fastest growing eastern corridor of the country. Twenty years ago, goods could be transported by road to Chittagong Port from Dhaka (a distance of about 250 km) in 6–7 hours; today, it takes 8–12 hours. Slow connectivity in a vital growth corridor is a major constraint to the country's growth.

The failure to raise the tax/GDP ratio to 18–20 percent and the gross national saving rate to over 30 percent at present reflects poorly not only on public policy choices but also on aid effectiveness. Macroeconomic stability alone is not good enough. Donors must rethink tax and revenue reforms to make aid more effective. This requires innovative ideas and convergence of incentives of governments and taxpayers to make compliance easier. Bangladesh should be able to graduate from external assistance well under two decades. This requires not only strong government commitment but also donor focus on these crucial targets. Donors need to be more responsive to country needs. Long response times in delivering aid to the recipient and large cost overruns due to delays in aid projects and programs remain a "chronic" problem and make the "effective costs" of aid higher than the projected financial costs at the time investment decisions are made. There is a keen awareness of these issues associated with aid. This, thus, remains an area of improvement for donors. A better combination of the quantum, quality and delivery speed of aid can significantly enhance aid effectiveness. On the side of recipients like Bangladesh, improvements in ADP implementation in terms of country ownership, sustainability of results and technical analysis of cost-benefit must be ensured.

13.8 Conclusions

The paper assesses the role of aid in Bangladesh in terms of achieving macroeconomic stability and economic development. The overall effectiveness of aid has been evaluated here in terms of the resultant improved economic performance and subsequent decline in the importance of aid.

The gross national savings rate has increased from below 10 percent in 1980, to about 30 percent in recent years, with increased level of tax-GDP ratio, which paves the way for superior growth performance of the economy. The ratio of investment to GDP, which was less than 17 percent in the 1980s, increased to about 23 percent at the end of the 1990s, and further to 31 percent in 2016. The increase was mainly due to private investment, which has risen from less than 10 percent of GDP in 1980 to about 22–23 percent in recent times, indicating that public investments with support from foreign aid did not crowd out private investments. Rather, aid has played a catalytic role in public investment in infrastructure development that has led to private-sector-oriented growth.

It has been shown that aid has played an important role in attaining fiscal stability over time. While total government expenditure has increased from 12.5 percent in 1990, to about 16 percent in 2011, fiscal deficit remained within the limit of 5 percent of GDP in all the periods. The tax-GDP ratio has increased from 6 percent to just over 10 percent during the same period. With an increased level of government expenditure coupled with increased tax revenue, the contribution of aid in financing the fiscal deficit has decreased from 80 percent in 1990 to 40 percent in 2011, indicating an overwhelming importance of aid in maintaining fiscal stability in Bangladesh before 1990.

Aid was contributing significantly to Bangladesh's foreign exchange reserve build-up until 1990, as it was higher than the reserve (without grant) of the country. Since 1993, foreign exchange reserve has started surpassing the ODA, with a significant contribution from overseas remittances and export earnings. Thus, ODA contributed positively to the BOP in the 1970s, 1980s and 1990s—the periods which laid the foundation for the sustained higher GDP growth in the latter two decades. However, significance of aid in maintaining a viable BOP has been declining since 2000, mainly because of higher remittance receipts and export earnings from the RMGs. In attaining sound macroeconomic management, not only the volume of aid but the attached policy reforms also played an important role.

Apart from sound macroeconomic performance, Bangladesh has shown significant improvements in key social indicators with donor supports, such as fertility, life expectancy, school enrollment (primary) and child immunization, and has successfully eradicated polio and measles. Bangladesh has already met several targets of MDGs like reducing poverty gap ratio, attaining gender parity at primary and secondary education, under-five mortality rate reduction and containing HIV infection, and is in good track of achieving SDG targets. Progress in the social indicators can be attributed to sectoral investments made by the government over time with significant contribution from foreign aid. While foreign aid made up a significant part of investments in sectors like energy, transport, water and sanitation in the 1980s and 1990s, it now contributes significantly to sectors like education and health.

Bangladesh's strong economic progress over the past four decades has virtually made aid much less important. From being a heavily aid-dependent country at birth, the share of foreign aid is down to about 2 percent of GNI. Bangladesh—a country arrogantly dubbed as a "basket case" by Kissinger in 1972 because of its heavy reliance on food imports and high poverty incidence—has graduated from food aid. Being a borderline food self-sufficient country today, it imports food grain for food security purposes only. Commodity aid, once significant in financing imports, has also become insignificant. However, there is no reason to believe that aid/ODA in all aspects played its intended role duly. In some cases, aid-driven projects suffer from a lack of ownership and well-defined sustainability of results. Independent impact evaluation of donor-driven projects in many instances was not done properly, which therefore led to misleading conclusion of the results of the projects, and based on the faulty results, same or similar projects were continued or undertaken. Though, on the whole, aid contributed positively to development, it would have contributed more if the constraints were controlled more efficiently. Therefore, more efforts are needed from the part of the government on the choice of aid-dependent projects and its long-term goals. Greater attention by donors to the local context, government ownership, more implementable institutional reforms in the rapidly evolving economic context, effective monitoring and evaluation to improve aid disbursement and achieve stronger results is needed, while Bangladesh remains on track to graduating from aid-dependency over the next decade.

Bangladesh is, however, well advised to continue relying on aid to finance infrastructure development, since it requires low-cost financing for a long period to support its sustainable growth. This is necessary because investment in infrastructure requires lower cost—longer-term capital, which is crucial for Bangladesh at this stage. It can graduate fully out of external assistance once the country is able to access international financial markets to borrow at reasonable costs for longer maturities. This is the main reason for China and India to borrow from multilateral development Banks such as the ADB, and the World Bank and IMF. Bangladesh must also borrow to protect against vulnerabilities in its external sector, and to strengthen its investments in counteracting climate change impacts.

References

ADB. (2010). *Aid effectiveness report and the way forward.* Manila: Asian Development Bank.

Addison, T., & Baliamoune-Lutz, M. (2006). Economic reform when institutional quality is weak: The case of the Maghreb. *Journal of Policy Modeling, 28*(9), 1029–1043.

Alesina, A., Devleeschauwer, A., Easterly, W., Kurlat, S., & Wacziarg, R. (2003). Fractionalization. *Journal of Economic Growth, 8*(2), 155–194.

Antipin, J. E., & Mavrotas, G. (2006). *On the empirics of aid and growth: A fresh look* (no. 2006/05). Research paper, UNU-WIDER, United Nations University (UNU).

Baliamoune-Lutz, M. (2005). *Institutions, social capital, and economic development in Africa: An empirical study.* International Centre for economic research working paper series, 18, 2007-05.

Burnside, C., & Dollar, D. (2000). Aid, policies, and growth. *American Economic Review, 90*(4), 847–868.

Easterly, W., & Levine, R. (1997). Africa's growth tragedy: Policies and ethnic divisions. *The Quarterly Journal of Economics, 112*(4), 1203–1250.

Easterly, W., Ritzen, J., & Woolcock, M. (2006). Social cohesion, institutions, and growth. *Economics and Politics, 18*(2), 103–120.

ERD. (2012). *Flow of external resources into Bangladesh.* Dhaka: Economic Relations Division, Ministry of Finance.

Hansen, H., & Tarp, F. (2000). Aid effectiveness disputed. *Journal of International Development, 12*(3), 375–398.

Hansen, H., & Tarp, F. (2001). Aid and growth regressions. *Journal of Development Economics, 64*(2), 547–570.

Hossain, M., and Roy, P.K. (2019). Does democratic local governance facilitate local economic development? Evidence from Bangladesh. *Local Government Studies.* Online available March 5. https://doi.org/10.1080/03003930.2019.1583561

Lensink, R., & White, H. (2001). Are there negative returns to aid? *Journal of Development Studies, 37*(6), 42–65.
Mahmud, W. (2006). *Monitoring donor support to poverty reduction strategy in Bangladesh: Rethinking the rules of engagement*. Dhaka: Economic Research Group and Commonwealth Secretariat.
Mosley, P., Hudson, J., & Horrell, S. (1987). Aid, the public sector and the market in less developed countries. *The Economic Journal, 97*(387), 616–641.
Quibria, M. G., & Ahmad, S. (2007). *Aid Effectiveness in Bangladesh* (No. 10299). University Library of Munich, Germany.
Radelet, S. (2006). *A primer on foreign aid*. Available at SSRN 983122.
UNDP. (2010). *Assessment of development results, Bangladesh*. New York: United Nations Development Program.
World Bank. (2011). *The World Bank and aid effectiveness—Performance to date and agenda ahead*. Washington, DC: The World Bank.

CHAPTER 14

Macroeconomic Determinants of Remittances and Implications for Economic Growth: Evidence from Bangladesh

Shubhasish Barua and Farhana Rafiq

14.1 Introduction

International remittance has become the most reliable source of foreign exchange in many developing countries. In Bangladesh, flows of remittances have been the most influential component for balance of payment (BOP) management and building up foreign exchange reserves. Even during the recent global financial crisis, remittances remained the most robust source of foreign finance. Moreover, remittance is directly linked with the well-being of households in recipient countries. Empirical evidence shows that remittance is an effective tool for reducing poverty and increasing consumption level of the recipient households.

S. Barua (✉)
Department of Development Studies, University of Dhaka, Dhaka, Bangladesh

F. Rafiq
Department of Economics, American International University-Bangladesh, Dhaka, Bangladesh
e-mail: Farhana_r@aiub.edu

M. Hossain (ed.), *Bangladesh's Macroeconomic Policy*,
https://doi.org/10.1007/978-981-15-1244-5_14

During the 2000s, inflows of remittances were growing at a spectacular speed with a growth rate of 19.4 percent on average annually.[1] However, things have changed in recent times. Over the last five years, the growth of remittances has slowed down to just 7 percent on average. In order to understand the recent downturn of foreign remittances, we have to look at the factors that influence the flows of remittances. Remittance transfers from host to home country take place through both formal and informal channels. The formal channels include banks, post office and money transfer operators, withdrawal from automated teller machines (ATMs) in the home country. In the official channels, a range of instruments are used for transferring money through formal channels such as electronic transfer, demand draft, travelers' check, telegraphic transfer, postal order and other payment methods. In addition to formal channels, historically informal methods have played an important role in the transfer of remittances. Informal channels include hundi or hawala-based transfers, personally carried cash without declaration during travelling back home or money transferred through friends and relatives.

The chapter has three specific objectives. Firstly, to examine the role of conventional macroeconomic factors in determining the inflows of remittances. Secondly, to evaluate the impact of financial sector development on the inflows of workers' remittances. Finally, to investigate the existence and sign of long-run relationship between remittances and gross domestic product (GDP).

A strand of studies identified a set of macroeconomic factors that influence the flows of workers' remittances from host to home countries. The fundamental factors among them include the level of migration stock of the home country in a particular host country and income differential between host and home country (or the level of income in the host and home country). In addition to these basic determinants, interest rate differential or deposit interest rates, and inflation rate differential between home and host country also play an important role in determining remittance flows.

Inflows of remittances through official channels in contrast to unofficial channels bear important macroeconomic implications. Remittances transferred through formal channels increase the foreign exchange reserves of the home country, whereas money sent through *hundis* does not contribute in building up the reserves. Another important implication of using informal channel is that such money can be used for cross-border smuggling, money laundering or other underground economic activities. The

[1] Year implies fiscal year, which starts at the month of July and ends at the month of June in the following year. For instance, the year 2001, implies fiscal year 2000–2001.

other concern is that such informal systems can be used to facilitate terrorist financing activities. As these informal transfers are not officially recorded, they will tend to distort the policy-making process as well. Several factors influence the choice of remittance-sending channel—transaction cost and time for remittance transfer, ease of transferring money, exchange rate differential between official and curb market, capacity of regulatory bodies and related rules and regulations. With this backdrop, interventions such as reducing the transaction cost of remittance transfer and increasing the accessibility of financial services can play a significant role in increasing the flows of workers' remittances.

In this context, expansion of bank branches can enhance the flows of workers' remittances through official channels in multiple ways. First, account-to-account transfer through banks generally requires the sender to have a bank account in the host country and receiver in the home country. Second, money transferred through registered money transfer operators (MTOs) can be collected in bank branches with proper identification documents. Third, bank branches with ATM facilities can also be used for withdrawal of cash from a personal bank account in home country. Moreover, availability of bank branches increases the access to financial services such as savings instruments to the recipient families, which can encourage the migrant workers to send more money for saving purposes. The expansion of bank branches coupled with the rising level of income in the home country will increase the number of depositors in the commercial banks of the home country. Because of these facilities, expansion of bank branches can significantly encourage the use of official channels for remittance transfer and, thereby, increasing the inflows of workers' remittances in the home country.

This chapter uses inflows of remittances through official channels only and examines the role of financial sector development in home country that can influence the flows of remittances through formal channels while controlling for macroeconomic determinants of remittances. To explore the role of macroeconomic factors and financial sector development in the host country, this chapter uses a panel dataset of bilateral remittance flows from 12 major host countries to Bangladesh over the period 2005–2017. The bilateral data on annual remittances are matched with the corresponding host country-specific macroeconomic factors and home country characteristics to construct the dataset for empirical analysis. Using a panel data fixed effects regression framework, we found that income differential between the host countries and the home country has no significant impact on workers' remittances. This result implies that altruism did not play a strong role in increasing the transfer of remittances during 2005–2017 period. In contrast, we found that financial sector development in the home country measured by number of bank branches has positive impact on remittances over this period. The conclusion remains the same even after controlling for financial development indicator for the host countries. We also tested the sensitivity of this finding with alternative indicators, including number of depositors with commercial banks, number of ATMs and financial institutions access index. The results confirm the importance of financial sector development in enhancing the remittance flows.

We also examined whether there is a long-run relationship between workers' remittances and GDP of Bangladesh. As Bangladesh has been experiencing a stable growth rate of GDP and sharp increase in the flows of workers' remittances over the sample period, exploring the relationship between the variables over the long run can provide us useful policy implications. For the purpose of this analysis, we used time series data on aggregate remittance flows and GDP of Bangladesh from 1981 to 2017. Using Johansen cointegration approach, we found that there is a positive long-run relationship between aggregate flows of workers' remittances and GDP of Bangladesh.

The rest of the chapter is organized as follows. Section 14.2 discusses the literature on determinants of workers' remittances and impact of remittances on economic development of the home country. Section 14.3 explains the determinants of workers' remittances which are used in this study, and Sect. 14.4 formulates the empirical framework for regression analysis. Section 14.5 shows the empirical results, and Sect. 14.6 concludes the chapter.

14.2 Literature Review

Motivations for remittance transfer are generally analyzed from two different perspectives—"altruism" and "portfolio motive". The first one treats remittances as altruistic transfer that are motivated by remitters' concern for their families in the home country and increases during times of economic hardship at home. The latter considers transfer of remittances as a type of capital flow and motivated by remitters' willingness to diversify their asset between the host and the home country. The altruistic perspective suggests that remittance flows are countercyclical that increases during economic downturn. In contrast, the portfolio approach is used to explain the procyclical behavior of remittances.

A strand of studies found evidence in favor of altruistic motive to remit the countercyclicality of remittance flows. A few studies used income differential between the host and home country to examine the significance of altruistic motive to remit. Schiopu and Siegfried (2006) and Barua, Majumder, and Akhtaruzzaman (2007) found significant evidence in favor altruistic motive to remit using this approach. The former did not observe any role of portfolio motive, while the latter found some evidences in favor of this view. Using a panel dataset of remittances from 21 western European countries to 7 European neighboring countries, Schiopu and Siegfried (2006) showed that income differential between the host and home country has a positive effect on remittance flows. Using a similar framework in a panel data of remittance flows from ten major host countries of Bangladeshi migrant workers, Barua, Majumder, and Akhtaruzzaman (2007) also found altruism as the main motivation of remittance transfer. Using a balanced panel dataset of bilateral remittance flows, the authors showed that income differential has a strong positive impact on flows of workers' remittances in Bangladesh during 1993–2004. This study is closely related to these two studies but focuses not only on the role of macroeconomic determinants but also on the role of financial sector development in the home country.

Chami et al. (2005) emphasized that remittance should be treated as compensatory transfer rather than capital flows. Based on a panel data of 49 countries, the authors find that the income gap between the home country and the USA is negatively correlated with the flows of workers' remittance, which implies that remittance transfer increases with lower income in the home country relative to the USA.

Many studies tested altruistic motive to remit using income in the home country. Using agricultural GDP as a measure of economic hardship in the home country and Johansen cointegration test, Bouhga-Hagbe (2006) showed that flows of remittances are negatively correlated with agricultural GDP in the long run. Chamon, Semblat and Morant (2005) showed that remittances in Samoa are positively correlated with income growth in host countries and negatively with income growth in home country. As discussed above, the negative correlation between home country growth and remittances supports the view that remittance flows are countercyclical. Quartey and Blankson (2004) also found that remittances behave countercyclically in Ghana, meaning remittances increase during economic downturn and vice versa. Vargas-Silva and Huang (2005), using data for several countries, observed that remittances are more responsive to economic conditions of host countries than home countries.

The main finding of the above discussion is that altruistic motive to remit is a dominant reason behind remittance transfer resulting in countercyclical pattern of remittances. Our study contributes to this literature from at least two grounds. Firstly, we reexamined the role of macroeconomic determinants of workers' remittances during flexible exchange rate regime in Bangladesh. Secondly, we explored the role of financial development in increasing the flows of workers' remittances in Bangladesh.

Worker remittances tend to accelerate the pace of economic development with increased domestic saving and investment in the recipient countries. In our study, we have also tried to set the relationship between remittances and economic growth. Various studies on the effect of remittances to economic growth have shown diverse results. However, growth prospects and the investment climate matter for achieving greater benefits of remittances in migrant home countries. Remittances positively affect savings and investment, which in turn leads to an increase in income and reduction in poverty (Adams 1998; Adams and Page 2003).

Studies showed that workers' remittances have positive impact on growth and poverty. Some studies showed that worker remittances contribute in poverty reduction by smoothing consumption of recipient households (Adams 1991; Jongwanich 2007). Giuliano and Marta (2009) found that workers' remittances can have a positive impact on economic growth of the countries where financial sector is not well developed by facilitating credit access among the poor and encouraging investment. Based on a sample of 36 African countries, Fayissa and Nsiah (2010) also found a positive association between workers' remittances and economic growth. However, the impact of workers' remittances on economic growth is mixed in South and South East Asian economies (Habib and Nourin 2006). The authors observed that there is a negative relationship between remittances and per capita GDP growth in four of their sampled countries: Thailand, Sri Lanka, India and Indonesia, whereas the converse is true in the other three countries: Bangladesh, Pakistan and the Philippines.

Impact of remittances on economic growth can be observed through investment channel. Remittances can encourage investment in physical and human capital and contribute to the development of the financial system of the home country that ultimately stimulate economic growth (Chami et al. 2008; World Bank 2006). For example, remittances can ease financing constraint and thereby increase domestic investment rate. Moreover, a significant portion of remittances are spent on acquiring education and nutrition leading to higher rate of human capital accumulation, which improves total factor productivity and subsequent growth. However, Sobiech (2019) highlighted that the impact of remittances on growth depends on the level of financial development of the receiving countries. In particular, the paper found that only economies with less developed financial sector can benefit from the inflows of remittances.

In contrast, some studies highlighted that the effect of remittances on economic growth could be negative. For instance, outflows of skilled work force from the home country, appreciation of the real exchange rate (RER) and moral hazard problem arising from remittances could have negative impact on economic growth (World Bank 2006; Jahjah et al. 2003; Chami et al. 2008).

A few studies examined the macroeconomic impact of remittances in Bangladesh. Stahl and Habib (1989) calculated the multiplier effect of remittances for Bangladesh for the period of 1976–1988 and argued that remittances can contribute to growth by encouraging production of consumption and intermediate goods domestically. Using Johasnsen cointegration test Paul and Das (2011) document a long-run positive relationship between remittances and GDP. They, however, find no short-run effect of remittance on output growth. Against this backdrop, Rahman et al. (2006) reported that remittances have short-run positive impact on Bangladesh's GDP growth and employment. Siddique, Selvanathan and Selvanathan (2012) also found that remittances positively affect economic growth in Bangladesh.

However, a phenomenal growth of remittances and a significant change in the composition of the use of remittances in Bangladesh over the years warrant a rigorous evaluation of its impact on various economic indicators. From that perspective, it is important to reexamine the relationship between remittances and growth in Bangladesh.

14.3 Data and Variables

14.3.1 Framework for Identifying Macroeconomic Determinants of Remittance

14.3.1.1 Workers' Remittances

We obtained annual data on bilateral flows of remittances in BDT from major host countries to Bangladesh from the Bangladesh Bank website in fiscal year basis. For analysis purposes, we converted remittances data from BDT to US dollar by dividing with average BDT/USD exchange rate. We used remittance data for 12 major host countries of Bangladeshi migrants—Australia, Bahrain, Republic of Korea, Kuwait, Malaysia, Oman, Qatar, Saudi Arabia, Singapore and the United Arab Emirates (UAE), the United Kingdom (UK) and the USA.

14.3.1.2 Migration Stock

The literature on determinants of remittance shows that the stock of migrants in the sending country is a fundamental determinant of the size of the remittance flows. However, bilateral migration stock data for Bangladesh are not available in yearly basis for most of the major host countries of Bangladeshi migrants. We constructed bilateral migration stock data of Bangladesh for each of the host countries using multiple sources. For 9 out of the 12 major host countries, we used Bureau of Manpower, Employment and Training (BMET) database for collecting yearly overseas employment as a measure of bilateral outflows of migrant workers from Bangladesh.[2] However, the amount of return migrants from the host countries to Bangladesh is not available in this database. In order to estimate the net bilateral migration from Bangladesh, we calculated the ratio of bilateral migration flows to Bangladesh and migration from Bangladesh from the online database of *Proceedings of the National Academy of Sciences of the United States of America* (PNAS), who estimated migration flow data at five-year interval from 1990 to 2015. In the next stage, yearly bilateral net migration flows from Bangladesh are estimated by multiplying the yearly BMET overseas employment data with the corresponding ratio of return migration at five-year interval. Finally, the yearly estimates of bilateral migration stocks are calculated by taking the cumulative sum of net migration for each host country from 1987 onward.[3] We obtained yearly migration stock data for rest of the three host countries from OECD International Migration Database and used the *stock of foreign-born population by country of birth* from this database as migration stock.

However, not only the migration stock but also its compositional feature bears important implications for the bilateral flows of remittances. The first issue in compositional feature is the skill mix of migrant workers. According to BMET data, less skilled laborers constitutes around half of the unskilled overseas employment. The impact of the higher share of the less skilled workers on the flows of remittances is not unambiguous. On the one hand, the less skilled workers may transfer a higher share of their relatively low income in the host country; on the other hand, if income and human capital are positively correlated, the higher share of less skilled

[2] These nine countries are Bahrain, Republic of Korea, Kuwait, Malaysia, Oman, Qatar, Saudi Arabia, Singapore and United Arab Emirates and rest of the three countries are Australia, United Kingdom and United States).

[3] The dataset can be downloaded from https://www.oecd.org/els/mig/keystat.htm.

workers will reduce the amount of remittances (Schiopu and Siegfried 2006). The latter study showed that the size of the average remittances reduces with the share of unskilled laborers. However, due to non-availability of bilateral migration data by skill category or duration of stay in the host country of the migrants, we cannot test these hypotheses directly.

14.3.1.3 Income Differential

In order to capture the altruistic motive, we include income differential as a proxy variable, which is measured by the ratio of GDP per capita based on purchasing power parity (PPP) between the host country (j) and the home country. The yearly data on per capita GDP at PPP in international dollars are taken from the World Development Indicators (WDI) database. This measure, by accounting for non-tradables, has two particular advantages over other measures. Firstly, it provides a better understanding of the income gap between the home and host countries. Secondly, it reflects the goods and services that can be purchased in home country with the amount of remittances transferred to the recipients. The expected sign of the coefficient of income differential is positive, implying that the flows of remittances increase with the income gap between the sending and receiving country.

14.3.1.4 Inflation Differential

The effect of inflation differential between the migrant home country and/or host country can be either positive or negative. The positive effect may arise if higher inflation in home country relative to host country induces the remitters to send more money to help the family for purchasing goods and services in home country. On the other hand, relatively higher inflation in the home country may indicate relatively higher risk and uncertainty in the home country, which might discourage them to send remittances. Inflation differential is thus important which is measured by taking difference between annual percentage change in the consumer price index (CPI) of home and the host country (j). The percentage changes of CPI data are collected from WDI database of the World Bank.

14.3.1.5 Return on Financial Assets

In order to capture the investment motive to remit, we include only deposit interest rate in the home country from WDI database. Due to non-availability of deposit interest rate data for several host countries, we could not construct the interest rate differential between host countries and home country. Therefore, we assume that an increase in the interest rate on deposit in home country is expected to encourage the remitters to send money in the home country for saving purposes.

14.3.1.6 Exchange Rate

Movement in the bilateral exchange rate between host and home country can influence the remittance-sending behavior. The ultimate effect of exchange rate changes on remittances depends on two opposing forces, wealth effect and substitution effect (Bouhga-Hagbe 2004). A depreciation of home currency leads to a decline in the prices of goods and services in the home country, in terms of host country currency. As a result, remitters can transfer less to buy the same amount of goods and services in the home country and can substitute the more expensive good in the host country with less expensive ones at the home country. On the other hand, depreciation of home currency leads to an increase in income of remitters in home country's currency, thereby encouraging them to buy more goods and services in home country. Bilateral exchange rate data are collected from online publication of Economic Trend.

Empirical evidence suggests that exchange rate depreciation stimulates inward flows of workers' remittances, holding other factors constant. In order to ensure the steady inflows of workers' remittances and competitiveness in the export market, Bangladesh Bank actively intervenes in the foreign exchange market by buying foreign currency to neutralize the appreciation pressure on domestic currency. The annual BDT/USD exchange rate soared by 11 percent in FY2012 (BDT 79.1) over the same period of FY2011 (BDT 71.2). This is the largest depreciation of domestic currency since the switching of exchange rate regime from fixed to floating mechanism in 2003. By intervening in the interbank market, Bangladesh Bank has managed to maintain the BDT/USD exchange rate at 78.60 taka per US dollar over the FY2012–2015 even in the face of appreciating pressure emanating from rapid growth of foreign capital. While an undervalued currency provides an incentive for the remitters and exporters, it can reduce the profitability of domestic industries that relies on imported intermediate inputs and capital machineries.

14.3.1.7 Access to Financial Services

One of the key objectives of this chapter is to examine the impact of an increase in access to financial services in the home country on the inflows of workers' remittances. To explore this issue, we used mainly number of commercial bank branches (per 100,000 adults) as a measure of financial sector development. We also used number of depositors with commercial banks (per 1000 adults), number of ATMs (per 100,000 adults) and financial institution access index to test the sensitivity of the results. All of these indicators are obtained from the WDI database except the last one.

14.3.2 Conceptual Framework: Channels of Remittances that Influence the Growth

14.3.2.1 Impact on Income Distribution

To understand the impact of remittance on poverty, it is important to understand the distribution of income and wealth in the home country. There exists a dynamic relationship between migration, remittances and inequality (Mckenzie and Rapoport 2007). The authors show that migration reduces inequality in communities with higher level of migration in the past. The cost of migration reduces over time because of networks affects. As a result, inequality increases in the initial stage, as only wealthier individuals are able to migrate at relatively higher cost and reduces with the expansion of migration networks.

14.3.2.2 Impact on Savings and Investment in Human Capital

Number of studies showed that remittances move countercyclically. However, others also argued that remittances can increase households' savings, reduce economic vulnerability and increase investment capacities. Moreover, remittances coming through formal channels can raise national savings rate, if the propensity to save of remittance receiving households is greater than that of non-immigrant households (Kapur 2005). Remittances can have long-term impact on poverty if remittances are used for investments in human capital. Utilization of remittances for health and education purposes can not only affect today's well-being but also promote human capital development.

14.3.2.3 Impact on Balance of Payment

From macroeconomic perspective, remittances improve the balance of payments as well as international reserve position of a country. Therefore, remittances can work as a shock absorber if there is any crisis of foreign exchange supply. Moreover, central bank can intervene in the foreign exchange market to stabilize the market in such a situation.

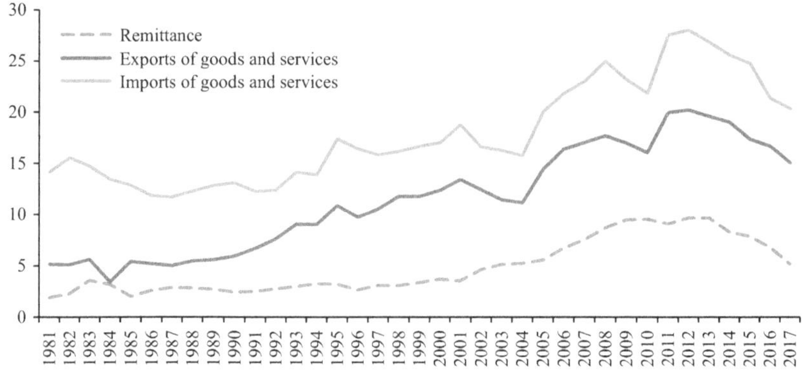

Fig. 14.1 Remittance, exports and imports as percent of GDP. (Source: Bangladesh Bank and WDI)

However, a note of caution is that a rapid growth of reserves through remittances might appreciate exchange rate and invite Dutch Disease–type situation. Therefore, a careful policy toward remittance use is necessary for better macroeconomic stability. Figure 14.1 shows that remittances played an important role in reducing the trade deficit in Bangladesh, in particular, since 2000s.

14.4 Econometric Strategy

(a) **For Assessing Determinants**

We investigate the role of financial development on the inflows of workers' remittances in a macroeconomic remittance determination model that controls for both altruistic and investment motive for remitting. The altruistic motive for remittance transfer is captured by income differential between the home and host countries, while the investment motive is controlled by the deposit interest rate in the home country. In addition to these key variables, we also controlled for bilateral exchange rate and inflation differential between the home country and each of the host countries.

The baseline specification for regression analysis takes the following form:

$$lnR_{jt} = \alpha + \alpha_j + \tau_t + \beta_1 lnMst_{jt-1} + \beta_2 rpgdp_{t-1} + \beta_3 infdf_{t-1} + \beta_4 ex_{jt-1} + \beta_5 ir_{t-1} + \varepsilon_{jt}, \quad (14.1)$$

where lnR_{jt} represents the log of remittances (in US dollar) from country j to the receiving country, Bangladesh, in year t, $lnMst_{jt-1}$ is the lagged log of migration stock of Bangladesh in the sending country j, $rpgdp_{t-1}$ is the lagged ratio of per capita GDP of the sending country (j) to the home country (in purchasing power parity), $infdf_{t-1}$ is the lagged difference of inflation rate between the host country j and the home country, ex_{jt-1} is the lagged bilateral nominal exchange rate between the host country j and Bangladesh, ir_{t-1} represents the lagged deposit interest rate in the home country. The model also includes a set of sending country fixed effects α_j and year fixed effects τ_t.

In order to explore the impact of financial sector development, particularly access to banking services on the inflows of workers' remittances, we include a measure of financial sector development in the home country in the preliminary specification:

$$lnR_{jt} = \alpha + \alpha_j + \tau_t + \beta_1 lnMst_{jt-1} + \beta_2 rpgdp_{t-1} + \beta_3 infdf_{t-1} + \beta_4 ex_{jt-1} + \beta_5 ir_{t-1} + FA_{t-1} + \varepsilon_{jt}, \quad (14.2)$$

where FA_{t-1} is an indicator for the access to financial services, measured either by commercial bank branches per 100,000 adults or depositors with commercial banks (per 1000 adults).

14.5 Empirical Results

14.5.1 Determinants of Workers' Remittances

Based on an unbalanced panel dataset of 12 major remittance-sending countries of Bangladesh, we estimated a macroeconomic model for remittance determination covering 2004–2017 period. We include source country fixed effects to control for unobserved time invariant heterogeneity across source countries and time dummies to account for macroeconomic shocks that are common to all source countries. Regression results, based on Eqs. (14.1) and (14.2), are presented in Table 14.1. Column (1) shows the estimation results of Eq. (14.1) without the deposit interest rate

Table 14.1 Panel fixed effect regression results of determinants of workers' remittances

	(1)	(2)	(3)	(4)	(5)	(6)
Log of migration stock	0.823**	0.823**	0.823**	0.823**	0.823**	0.823**
	(0.283)	(0.283)	(0.283)	(0.283)	(0.283)	(0.283)
Log of nominal exchange rate	0.958	0.958	0.958	0.958	0.958	0.958
	(0.648)	(0.648)	(0.648)	(0.648)	(0.648)	(0.648)
PCGDP differential (PPP)	0.053	0.053	0.053	0.053	0.053	0.053
	(0.033)	(0.033)	(0.033)	(0.033)	(0.033)	(0.033)
Inflation differential Hm-Ho	−0.035***	−0.035***	−0.035***	−0.035***	−0.035***	−0.035***
	(0.010)	(0.010)	(0.010)	(0.010)	(0.010)	(0.010)
Deposit interest rate (percent)		0.141**	0.032	0.050*		
		(0.046)	(0.025)	(0.026)		
Com. bank branches (per 100,000 adults)			0.589**		0.590**	
			(0.208)		(0.208)	
Depositor with com. banks (per 1000 adults)				0.002**		0.002**
				(0.001)		(0.001)
R-squared	0.72	0.72	0.72	0.72	0.72	0.72
N	151	151	151	151	151	151

Notes: ***, ** and * indicate statistically significant at the 1% level, 5% level; and 10% level, respectively

of home country. Column (2) shows the results based on Eq. (14.1). Columns (3) and (4) report the results for Eq. (14.2) with number of commercial bank branches and number of depositors in commercial banks, respectively, as indicators for access to financial services.

The first four variables are common in all the regressions and appear with expected signs of the coefficients. The signs and levels of significance of these coefficients remain unchanged across all columns. The estimated coefficients of the log of migration stock appears with a positive sign and statistically significant at 5 percent level in all regressions. The coefficients corresponding to log of nominal exchange rate and per capita GDP differential are positive but statistically insignificant in all the columns.

Inflation differential between the home and host country has a negative impact on the amount of remittances transferred to the home country, which is consistent with the idea that relatively higher inflation in the home country reflects the higher level of risks associated with investment in the home country and thereby discourages the remitters to transfer money in the home country. The results show evidence in favor of investment motive to remit, as the deposit interest rate coefficient always appears with a positive sign and statistically significant at 5 percent level in column (2) and 10 percent level in columns (4).

The coefficient related to our main variable of interest, number of bank branches per 100,000 adults, appears with a positive sign and statistically significant at 5 percent level in columns (3) and (5). Interestingly, the coefficient of deposit interest rate reduced considerably and became statistically insignificant after including the number of bank branches in home country as a financial development indicator in column (3). Therefore, in column (2), without the number of bank branches variable, the coefficient of deposit interest rate is biased upward because of a positive relationship between number of a bank branches and deposit interest rate. In column (5), we exclude the deposit interest rate from the regression to verify the sensitivity of the coefficient corresponding to financial access indicator. The sign of the coefficient *FA* slightly increases in column (5) compared to that in column (3). In columns (4) and (6), we use number of depositors in commercial banks as an indicator for access to financial services. The results are similar to that in the previous case.

One concern with the coefficients of financial development indicators in the home country in Table 14.1 is that we did not control for financial development in the host country. In Table 14.2, we include indicators for financial development in the host countries. In column (1), we control for number of commercial bank branches in the host countries and in column (2) number of depositors with commercial banks in the host countries. The financial development indicator for the home country in column (1) remains positive and statistically significant at 5 percent level even with the inclusion of commercial bank branches in the host countries. Though the coefficient of the latter itself appears with a positive sign, it is statistically insignificant in column (1). In column (2), we include number of depositors with commercial banks in the host countries as an indicator of financial development in the host countries. The coefficient itself turns out to be negative and statistically significant at 10 percent level. On the other hand, coefficient of number of depositors in the home country remains positive but turns statistically insignificant.

Table 14.2 Fixed effect regression results with host country financial development

	(1)	(2)	(3)	(4)	(5)	(6)
Log of migration stock	0.883**	0.497***	0.823**	0.999**	0.812**	0.977***
	(0.374)	(0.103)	(0.283)	(0.362)	(0.285)	(0.282)
Log of nominal exchange rate	0.907	1.555	0.958	0.676	1.386*	0.445
	(0.679)	(1.019)	(0.648)	(0.782)	(0.730)	(1.095)
PCGDP differential (PPP)	0.051	0.021	0.053	0.053	0.058	0.069***
	(0.032)	(0.011)	(0.033)	(0.034)	(0.036)	(0.021)
Inflation differential Hm-Ho	−0.035**	−0.035**	−0.035***	−0.041***	−0.032***	−0.004
	(0.011)	(0.012)	(0.010)	(0.011)	(0.009)	(0.015)
Com. bank branches (home)	0.577**					
	(0.233)					
Com. bank branches (host)	0.029					
	(0.047)					
Deps. with com. banks (home)		0.002				
		(0.001)				
Deps. with com. banks (host)		−0.001*				
		(0.000)				
Number of ATMs (home)			0.129**	0.128**		
			(0.045)	(0.047)		
Number of ATMs (host)				−0.0004		
				(0.004)		
Financial institution access index (home)*100					0.159**	0.196***
					(0.068)	(0.047)
Financial institution access index (host)*100						0.100*
						(0.048)
R-squared	0.69	0.79	0.72	0.69	0.72	0.81
N	134	59	151	124	139	118

Notes: ***, ** and * indicate statistically significant at the 1% level, 5% level; and 10% level, respectively

We also perform a series of robustness check on our baseline findings. Our main results remain consistent in robustness analysis and confirm the role of access to financial services as one of the main determinants of the flows of workers' remittances in Bangladesh. In column (3) of Table 14.2, we included number of ATMs (per 100,000 adults) in the home country, and in column (4), we add number of ATMs in the host country along with the former. In column (5), we use financial inclusion access index for the home country as an indicator for financial development, and in column (6), we add the same variable for the host countries. In all these four cases, the financial development indicators in the home country appear with a positive sign and statistically significant at 5 percent level.

14.5.2 Long-Run Relationship Between Remittances and GDP

In this section, we explore the relationship between GDP and remittances in the long-run. Figure 14.2 presents natural log of real GDP and the natural log of remittances over the period 1981–2017.

From the above figure, we can hypothesize that there is a long-run positive relationship between remittances and GDP. The question is whether this relationship is positive and statistically significant or not. We examined this question using Johansen cointegration test in the next section.

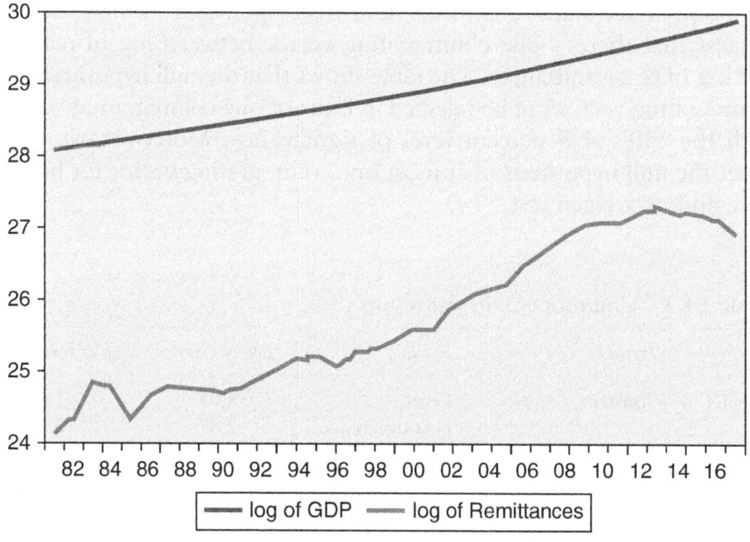

Fig. 14.2 Log of GDP (real) and log of remittances 1981–2017 (FY)

Unit Root Test

The variables must be tested for presence of unit root before performing the cointegration test. We used augmented Dickey-Fuller test (ADF) to examine stationary property of the variables. Table 14.3 reports unit root test results using ADF test. In panel-1, we report the results with constant only option and in panel-2 with constant and trend for both level and first difference form of the variables. The ADF test results show that all the series are integrated of order one or I(1). The null hypothesis of unit root could not be rejected for both log of real GDP and log of real remittances in level form.

As the variables of interest are integrated of order 1, we can use cointegration test to examine the long-run relationship between them. As the Johansen test is sensitive to lag length, the optimal lag length for the VAR system needs to be determined before performing the test. We obtained the appropriate lag length based on an unrestricted VAR model in level form using Akaike information criterion (AIC). We found that the VAR system requires five lags in level form to obtain uncorrelated residuals. The cointegration test is carried out assuming linear trend in data, and an intercept in the cointegrating equation and test VAR.

Table 14.4 shows cointegration test results for log of real GDP and log of real remittances from 1981 to 2017 period. Panel-1 and Panel-2 show the cointegration results based on trace test and maximum max-eigenvalue test. Both trace statistic (λ trace) and max-eigenvalue (λ max) statistics suggest that there is one cointegrating vector between log of real GDP and log of real remittances. The table shows that the null hypothesis of no cointegrating vector can be rejected in favor of one cointegrating vector in both the cases at 5 percent level of significance. Moreover, we cannot reject the null hypothesis of at most one cointegrating vector for both the trace and max-eigen test.

Table 14.3 Unit root (ADF) test results

	Trend	*Form*	*Log of GDP*	*Log of remittances*
Panel-1	Constant	Level	8.07	−1.07
		First difference	−2.87	−5.00
Panel-2	Constant and trend	Level	−0.26	−1.43
		First difference	−4.92	−4.96

Table 14.4 Johansen cointegration test results

Hypothesized no. of CE(s)	*Eigen value*	*Trace statistic*	*5 percent critical value*	*Prob.***	*Eigen value*	*Max-Eigen statistic*	*5 percent critical value*	*Prob.***
	Panel-1				Panel-2			
None *	0.49	22.45	15.49	0.00	0.49	21.85	14.26	0.00
At most 1	0.02	0.61	3.84	0.44	0.02	0.61	3.84	0.44

Notes: 1. Both trace and max-eigenvalue tests indicate 1 cointegrating eqn(s) at the 0.05 level
2. * denotes rejection of the hypothesis at the 0.05 level
3. ** MacKinnon-Haug-Michelis (1999) p-values

Table 14.5 Normalized cointegrating coefficients

Log of GDP	*Log of remittances*
1	−0.136 (0.076)

Note: Standard error in parentheses

Therefore, there is a long-run equilibrium relationship between log of real GDP and log of remittances. Existence of a single cointegrating vector indicates that real GDP and real remittances display long-run co-movement, that is, there is a long-run equilibrium relationship between the variables. Table 14.5 shows normalized cointegration coefficients. By normalizing the cointegration equation on real GDP, we observe that remittances and GDP are positively correlated in the long run.

14.6 Conclusions

Using an unbalanced panel data of bilateral remittance flows from 12 major host countries to Bangladesh over the period 2005–2017, we explored the role of macroeconomic factors and financial development in the home country on the flows of workers' remittances in Bangladesh. The set of macroeconomic determinants capture both altruistic motive and investment motive to remit, in addition to other macroeconomic factors. Based on the results from fixed effects regression model, we observed that conventional macroeconomic determinants such as income differential between host and home country and bilateral exchange rates were not influential in determining the flows of workers' remittances in Bangladesh. On the other hand, deposit interest rate in the home country that represents investment motive to remit also turned insignificant after including our main indicator for financial development in the home country.

One of the key findings of the chapter is that the number of commercial bank branches (per 100,000 adults), the main indicator of financial development in the home country, has a considerable positive impact on flows of remittances in Bangladesh. The role of financial development in the home country remains positive and statistically significant even with the measure of financial development in the host countries as well as with alternative indicators.

Among the macroeconomic variables, inflation differential between home and host country appears with a negative sign and remains statistically significant in all regression. The implication of this finding may be that an increase in risk and uncertainty in the home country relative to host country discourages the remitters to transfer money to the home country. On the other hand, we did not find any significant influence of bilateral exchange rate on the flows of workers' remittances over the sample period.

To explore long-run relationship between remittances and GDP, we used time series data on workers' remittances from 1981 to 2017. Using Johansen cointegration test, we found that there is a positive long-run relationship between remittances and GDP, which highlights the importance of remittances for macroeconomic development in Bangladesh.

References

Adams, R. H. (1991). *The effects of international remittances on poverty, inequality, and development in rural Egypt* (Vol. 86). Washington, DC: International Food Policy Research Institute.

Adams, R. H., Jr. (1998). Remittances, investment, and rural asset accumulation in Pakistan. *Economic Development and Cultural Change, 47*(1), 155–173.

Adams, R. H., & Page, J. (2003). *International migration, remittances, and poverty in developing countries* (Vol. 3179). Washington, DC: World Bank Publications.

Barua, S., Majumder, M. A., & Akhtaruzzaman, M. (2007). *Determinants of workers' remittances in Bangladesh: An empirical study*. Policy Analysis Unit (PAU), Bangladesh Bank Working Paper No. WP, 713.

Bouhga-Hagbe, M. J. (2004). *A theory of workers' remittances with an application to Morocco*. International Monetary Fund.

Bouhga-Hagbe, M. J. (2006). *Altruism and workers' remittances: Evidence from selected countries in the Middle East and Central Asia*. IMF working paper, WP/06/130, International Monetary Fund.

Chami, R., Fullenkamp, C., & Jahjah, S. (2005). Are immigrant remittance flows a source of capital for development? *IMF Staff Papers, 52*(1), 55–81.

Chami, R., Barajas, A., Cosimano, T., Fullenkamp, C., Gapen, M., & Montiel, P. (2008). *Macroeconomic consequences of remittances* (Occassional Paper 259). Washington, DC: International Monetary Fund.

Chamon, M., Semblat, R., & Morant, A. (2005). *Samoa: Selected issues and statistical appendix*. International Monetary Fund.

Fayissa, B., & Nsiah, C. (2010). The impact of remittances on economic growth and development in Africa. *The American Economist, 55*(2), 92–103.

Giuliano, P., & Marta, R. (2009). *Journal of Development Economics, 90*(1), 144–152.

Habib, N., & Nourin, S. (2006). *Remittances and real investment: An appraisal on south and south east Asian economies*. Bangkok: Faculty of Economics, Chulalongkorn University, Asian Institute of Technology.

Jahjah, M. S., Chami, M. R., & Fullenkamp, C. (2003). *Are immigrant remittance flows a source of capital for development* (No. 3-189). International Monetary Fund.

Jongwanich, J. (2007). *Workers' remittances, economic growth and poverty in developing Asia and the Pacific countries*. Bangkok: United Nations Publications.

Kapur, D. (2005). Remittances: The new development mantra? In *Remittances: Development impact and future prospects* (pp. 331–360). Washington, DC: World Bank.

Mckenzie, D., & Rapoport, H. (2007). Network effects and the dynamics of migration and inequality: Theory and evidence from Mexico. *Journal of Development Economics, 84*(1), 1–24.

Paul, B. P., & Das, A. (2011, September). The remittance-GDP relationship in the liberalized regime of Bangladesh: Cointegration and innovation accounting. *Theoretical and Applied Economics, 18*(9), 41–60.

Quartey, P., & Blankson, T. (2004, December). Do migrant remittances minimize the impact of macro-volatility on the poor in Ghana?. In *Final report submitted to the global development network*. Available at http://www.imf.org/external/np/res/seminars/2005/macro/pdf/quarte.pdf

Rahman, M., Mustafa, M., Islam, A., & Guru-Gharana, K. K. (2006). Growth and employment empirics of Bangladesh. *The Journal of Developing Areas*, 99–114.

Schiopu, I. C., & Siegfried, N. (2006). *Determinants of workers' remittances: Evidence from the European neighbouring region*. Working paper series (No. 688) European Central Bank (ECB).

Siddique, A., Selvanathan, E. A., & Selvanathan, S. (2012). Remittances and economic growth: Empirical evidence from Bangladesh, India and Sri Lanka. *Journal of Development Studies, 48*(8), 1045–1062.

Sobiech, I. (2019). Remittances, finance and growth: Does financial development foster the impact of remittances on economic growth? *World Development, 113*, 44–59.

Stahl, C. W., & Habib, A. (1989). The impact of overseas workers' remittances on indigenous industries: Evidence from Bangladesh. *The Developing Economies, 27*(3), 269–285.

Vargas-Silva, C., & Huang, P. (2005). *Macroeconomic determinants of workers' remittances: Host vs. home country's economic conditions,* Western Michigan University.

World Bank. (2006). *Global economic prospects: Economic Implications of Remittances and Migration.* Washington DC: World Bank

PART IV

Finance and Growth

CHAPTER 15

Financial Liberalization, Financial Development and Economic Growth: An Analysis of the Financial Sector of Bangladesh

Monzur Hossain

15.1 Introduction

Bangladesh started its journey after the independence in 1971 with a small financial sector having dominance of the informal sector. The dominance continued even in the late 1980s when 63 percent of total credit was supplied by the informal sector (Rahman 1992). Afterwards, the dominance of informal financial sector started declining with the development of formal financial sector through various reform measures. Moreover, NGO-MFIs sector emerged in the 1980s and captured a certain portion of the informal market. More private banks came into operation in the 1980s in consequence of necessary financial deregulations, which also contributed to the declining role of informal financial sector gradually. The key financial deregulations included interest rate deregulations, withdrawal of restrictions on trade financing, allowance of private

M. Hossain (✉)
Bangladesh Institute of Development Studies (BIDS), Dhaka, Bangladesh

M. Hossain (ed.), *Bangladesh's Macroeconomic Policy*,
https://doi.org/10.1007/978-981-15-1244-5_15

and foreign banks, and so on, which have been contributed to making the sector vibrant and more competitive. Consequently, substantial financial development has taken place with a significant growth of credit, deposit and broad money to GDP ratios.

Historically, the financial sector in Bangladesh is dominated by banks. Starting with only nine private commercial banks in the 1980s, the sector has expanded with a handful of 59 commercial banks along with 33 non-banking financial institutions in 2018. The capital market is still in a rudimentary stage consisting of two stock exchanges, namely, Dhaka and Chittagong and, therefore, does not have enough maturity and depth to play a significant role in the financial sector. Despite having an expanded financial sector, still a large section of the rural population depends on the semi- and in-formal financial institutions for financial services, though the trend has been changing. Over one-third of the adult population now has access to banks, and financing of small businesses is still heavily relied on semi- or informal financial sector. The formal financial sector has been expanding rapidly with various innovations and technological improvement over time, and therefore the gap between the formal and informal sectors has been considerably narrowing down in recent years.

Though financial liberalization in the 1990s brought significant and qualitative changes in the financial sector of Bangladesh, its intended effect on bringing efficiency and competitiveness in the financial sector is still dubious. Hossain (2012) argued that financial liberalization initiated in the 1990s seems to have led to a widening interest rate, spread as opposed to the conventional wisdom. Distortions in the loan market, institutional weaknesses and the poor policy environment are mainly responsible for this. The existing literature assesses the impact of financial liberalization on growth via financial deepening. It is to be noted that while financial deepening affects access to finance, liberalization affects the incentives related to credit deployment (Abiad et al. 2008). Financial liberalization reduces the role of the government allowing greater role of the market in allocation of resources that lead to a greater efficiency in the market. On the other hand, financial deepening refers to an increase in the volume of credit and is typically measured by indicators such as M2, credit to the private sector or stock market capitalization relative to GDP.

To assess the impact of financial liberalization, one needs to look into three indicators: (i) the movement of real interest rates, (ii) the volume of intermediation and (iii) the efficiency of intermediation. Different types of methodologies can be adopted to examine these indicators. Against this backdrop, this chapter discusses the following three aspects of financial development: (i) the status of formal, semi-formal and informal financial sector and their linkages; (ii) the impact of financial liberalization on financial development and financial deepening and subsequent impact on economic growth and (iii) the impact of financial liberalization on the efficiency of the financial sector.

This chapter is organized as follows. Section 15.2 provides an overview of the financial sector, and Sect. 15.3 discusses various aspects of financial reforms. Section 15.4 discusses the impact of financial development on economic growth. Section 15.5 concludes the chapter.

15.2 An Overview of the Financial Sector

The financial sector of Bangladesh can be categorized into three sectors in terms of types of institutions, such as the informal sector, semi-formal sector and formal sector. A brief overview of these sectors is given below.

15.2.1 The Informal Financial Sector

By the informal financial sector, we usually refer to the institutions and transactions that are not operating under the jurisdiction of the financial system officially endorsed. The financial services in the informal sector mainly offer financial services of savings collection and lending. Non-commercial financial transactions between friends and relatives is also included in the informal sector. The most prominent institutions in this sector are deposit collectors, moneylenders and credit associations. Apart from deposit collection or on loan extension, there are some informal institutions of both services, which are generally open only to their members.

Though it is difficult to estimate the extent of informal credit, several studies were conducted earlier in the 1980s and 1990s to estimate the size and volume of the informal credit market. With the development of the formal financial system, importance of informality has been shrinking. However, there are evidences that informal credit market still has a role in rural Bangladesh. One study conducted in 1986 estimated that about 64 percent of total credit (Tk 14.1 billion) was transacted in the informal financial sector (The Rural Credit Survey, BIDS, 1986). Afterward, to the best of our knowledge, no such bigger study was conducted on the informal credit market. However, with the development of the financial sector, obviously the proportion of informal credit has come down significantly. A BIDS survey on SME financing (BIDS 2018) shows that the loan from

Table 15.1 Sources of financing for SMEs in the last five years (2013–2018)

	Amount of loan taken (BDT)	*Percent*	*Interest rate (average)*
Loan from banks	4776433.5	38.15	10.91
Loan from personal sources	1346593.7	10.75	6.85
NGOs/microfinance institutions	6128918.8	48.96	15.30
Others	266,250	2.12	12.13

Source: BIDS Survey 2018 on the Evaluation of the Activities of SME Foundation

personal sources and other informal sources constitute about 12.87 percent of total loan portfolio of a small firm (Table 15.1), indicating a shrinking role of informal financial source. While about 49 percent of SME loan comes from NGO-MFIs, about 38 percent loan comes from banking sector. So currently about 87 percent of total credit of the SME sector comes from formal financial system. The interest rate for personal sources is quite low compared to other sources, and interest rate for NGO-MFIs remains the highest. Except for interest rate for personal loan, the other sectors remain almost integrated in terms of interests charged on loan. The depth of informal financial market can, thus, be judged by the extent of SME financing. Therefore, according to BIDS SME survey, informal sources currently supply about 13 percent of total credit, particularly for the small businesses (Table 15.1).

There are several discernible characteristics of informal financial sector. Usually the financial transactions of the informal financial sector are small in size and frequent in nature. Informal financial institutions rely on personal relations with customers and repeated transactions as part of risk-reducing strategies. The emergence of the NGO-based microcredit sector in Bangladesh has been reducing the importance of the informal financial sector in the economy. With the development of various types of formal financial services and institutions, such as NGO-MFIs, credit cooperatives, agent banking, mobile financial services, and so on, linkage between formal and informal financial institutions has also been growing and contributing to syphoning off informality to a greater extent. As a result, the maturity and depth of the financial sector has increased at a significant level.

A greater linkage between formal and informal sectors can be viable for both the firms and households as well as for well-functioning of the financial system. There are various models that allow a viable linkage between formal and informal sector. SME Foundation's credit wholesale program is an example where SME Foundation provides fund to commercial banks at a rate (say 5 percent) lower than bank lending rate to disburse to SMEs at a single digit rate (say 9 percent). Here SME Foundation helps banks to identify borrower firms, which act as an implicit credit guarantee. Another example could be the solar home system (SHS) program of Infrastructure Development Company Ltd. (IDCOL). IDCOL provides refinancing to NGOs who sell SHS to customer on credit at 12 percent, though they receive fund from IDCOL at 6–8 percent (Hossain 2019). There are many other such examples. Women's World Banking is such a mechanism that has been operating in some 50 countries to extend loans to women through commercial banks with the use of a guarantee mechanism. In many cases, such linkages work even in a better way than the existing formal system. Since these linkages are being developed on innovations, a careful and well-thought mechanism is necessary to derive maximum benefits out of it.

15.2.2 Semi-Formal Financial Sector

Microfinance institutions (MFIs) largely fall in the category of semi-formal financial institutions. By definition, the semi-formal institutions are those that are registered and often regulated to some degree, but not strictly under the prudential regulations. These institutions do not have mandate to operate as formal bank, though their role is pivotal in bridging gap between informal and formal financial sectors. However, over time the linkage between MFIs and banks has been on a rising trend in the context of financial collaboration through increased sophistication in the financial sector.

In Bangladesh, microcredit program has been implemented mainly by NGOs and Grameen Bank. Moreover, some commercial banks and special programs of Bangladesh government have the features of microcredit programs. About 692 licensed NGO-MFIs and Grameen Bank operate with a network of 17,241 branches and 33.17 million members (Table 15.2). The top 20 NGOs and Grameen Bank together have a 75 percent share of the microcredit market as of 2013, though the share of other NGO-MFIs has been on a rise (Khalily and Islam 2014). However, only Grameen Bank represents about 25 percent of total savings and loan of the sector. The microcredit program provides opportunities to about 33 million poor people to be engaged in income generating activities. It is to be noted that the microcredit institutions in Bangladesh are now being regulated by the

Table 15.2 Microcredit activities of NGO-MFIs

	Grameen Bank			*Licensed NGO–MFIs*			*Aggregate*		
Year	*2011*	*2012*	*2013*	*2011*	*2012*	*2013*	*2011*	*2012*	*2013*
Number of branches	2565	2567	2567	18,066	17,977	14,674	20,631	20,544	17,241
Number of members (million)	8.36	8.36	8.54	26.08	24.64	24.60	34.44	33.00	33.14
Number of borrowers (million)	6.58	6.71	6.74	20.65	19.31	19.27	27.23	26.02	26.01
Loans disbursement (billion taka)	108.54	118.61	126.02	303.18	456.02	432.28	411.72	574.63	558.30
Loans outstanding (billion taka)	75.29	80.32	84.38	173.79	211.32	257.01	249.08	291.64	341.40
Loans outstanding as percentage of loan disbursement (percent)	69.4	67.7	66.96	57.3	46.3	59.5	60.5	50.8	61.1
Borrowers per branch	2565	2613	2625	1143	1074	1313	1319	1267	1509
Clients per branch	3259	3257	3327	1444	1371	1676	1670	1606	1922

Sources: Grameen Bank; Microcredit Regulatory Authority 2010–2013; Khalily (2016)

Microcredit Regulatory Authority (MRA), which was established under an Act in 2006.

Numerous studies have so far been conducted on the impact of microcredit on poverty reduction in Bangladesh. It is well recognized that MFIs in Bangladesh have played a significant role in delivering financial services to the poor and women, at very low loan default rates. Collateral-free group-based lending and mobilization of savings are the key features of microfinance programs that helped them achieve greater outreach. Khandker (2005) finds that microfinance helps reduce poverty of female participants and contributes to overall poverty reduction at the village level that invigorates the rural economy. Therefore, this sector contributes not only to poverty reduction but also to deepening and diversifying the financial system. With proper policies and strategies, the semi-formal sector could play much better role in providing greater access to finance for small businesses and creating opportunities for productive investment.

15.2.3 The Formal Financial Sector

15.2.3.1 Banking Financial Institutions

The formal financial sector of Bangladesh is dominated by the banks. The banking sector comprises 59 banks (as of 2018) including 6 state-owned commercial banks (SCBs), 42 private commercial banks (PCBs), 2 specialized banks (SBs) and 9 foreign commercial banks (FCBs). The growth of banks over time does not follow any systematic pattern, and new licenses for banks get momentum when new political government comes into power. Therefore, some periods saw a surge in number of banks, which is why it is difficult to justify the growth of banks fully from economic grounds (Fig. 15.1).

After the financial liberalization, the intermediation has increased quite significantly in Bangladesh. Banks' asset as a percentage of GDP has increased from 33 percent in 1997 to about 60 percent in 2015, which clearly indicates a greater depth of financial intermediation in the country. Though overall Non-performing loan (NPL) ratio has decreased over time, banks return on asset (RoA) and return on equity (RoE) have not changed that much. The role of SCBs has declined with emergence of PCBs. The SCBs' share in total assets has declined from 54 percent in 1998 to 31 percent in March 2009 and further to 27.5 percent in 2016 (Table 15.8 in Appendix). Private banks' share in total credit (asset) has risen from 33 percent in 1998 to 63 percent in 2009 and further to 64.5

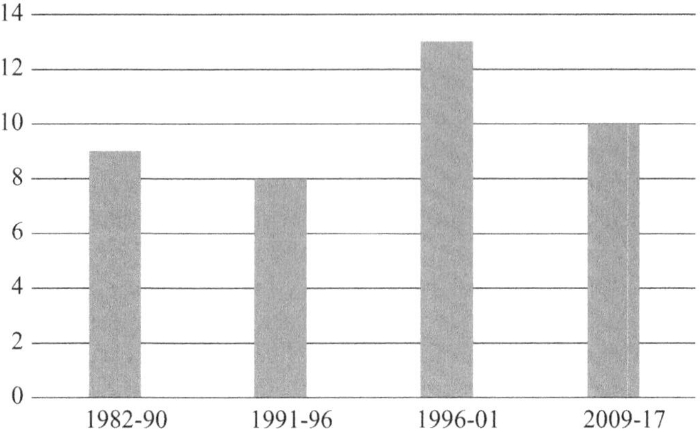

Fig. 15.1 Approval of new commercial banks over time. (Source: Bangladesh Bank, Annual Report, various issues)

percent in 2015. But PCB's share in total deposit has substantially increased from 29.71 percent in 2009 to 64.5 percent in 2015, which is mainly for allowing government organizations to deposit money in PCBs. However, still a large section of the people (about 65 percent) does not have access to formal banking services due to concentration of private banks in urban or semi-urban areas. Private banks tend to be concentrated in the urban areas and cities, though their branches in rural areas have been increasing over time (from 30 percent in 2009 to 40 percent in 2015). Furthermore, various rules and regulations of deposits, lengthy loan approval procedure, voluminous loan application procedure, requirement of guarantor and collateral, and so on discourage a large section of rural population to avail banking services. Rural people are mainly served by SCBs having 63 percent branches in rural areas, which run on government subsidies. As Table 15.3 shows, RoE has been declining for all types of banks during 2009–2015, which is partly due to stagnant investment demand as well as partly due to entry of new banks in the market that has created unhealthy competition among the banks for deposit mobilization.

NPL ratio has been the most worrying part of Bangladeshi banking sector. Though the ratio has been declining at aggregate level (Table 15.3), bank-specific data show that NPL ratio is still at a very alarming level (above 20 percent) for SCBs and DFIs (Fig. 15.2). While the classified loan as percentage of total loan has decreased over time, the proportion of bad loan as percentage of total classified loan has remained almost the

Table 15.3 Performance indicator of all banks

	Total asset (taka in billion)	*Total asset to GDP ratio*	*Gross NPL ratio*	*Expenditure to income (EI) ratio*	*Return on asset (ROA)*	*Return on equity (ROE)*
1997	472	33.7	37.49	95.31	0.63	12.95
2001	1100.1	43.4	29.7	87.9	0.75	17
2005	2042.8	55.1	13.6	92.1	0.6	12.4
2010	4855.1	53	11.5	75.2	1.8	21.0
2011	5867.6	55.6	10.4	67.5	1.5	17.0
2012	7030.7	58.6	14.7	72.5	0.6	8.2
2013	8000.2	59.5	14.1	76.8	0.9	11.0
2014	9143.1	60.3	16.8	76.5	0.8	8.1
2015	10314.6	59.5	14.3	80.2	0.8	10.5

Source: Annual Report, Bangladesh Bank, various issues

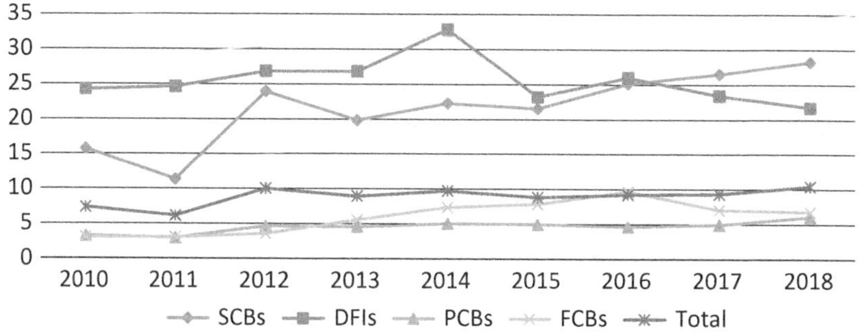

Fig. 15.2 Gross NPL ratio for banks. (Source: Annual Report, Bangladesh Bank, various issues)

same, which is over 80 percent (Table 15.9, Appendix). So SCBs are plagued by bad loan culture and, therefore, the government has to recapitalize these banks every year from exchequers.

Two specialized banks, namely Bangladesh Krishi Bank (BKB) and Rajshahi Krishi Unnayan Bank (RAKUB), were created especially to provide financial services to the farmers for their agricultural development. They disbursed about 33 percent of total agricultural credit in 2016, which was about 52 percent in 2008 (Bangladesh Bank Annual Report, various issues). PCBs are now being engaged more in recent times in providing agricultural credit, as their share now stands at about 50 percent. However, despite good objectives, these banks (BKB and RAKUB) could not provide services at the expected level due to weak governance structure. Therefore, inefficiencies and corruption sometimes divert funds away from agricultural purposes.

15.2.3.2 Corporate Governance and Management Efficiency of the Banks

Corporate governance in the banking sector is now a big concern. Though some measures relating to corporate governance were taken limiting the number of family members and their tenure in the board of directors and introducing a provision for independent directors representing depositors' interests, time-to-time change of these provisions in favor of owners' interest holding back the growth and efficiencing of the banking sector. The nomination of board of directors in the SCBs from political concerns without judging their expertise and experiences is one of the reasons of deteriorating health of these banks. Political pressure and a heinous corruption nexus between bankers and customers often lead to loan approvals that turn into NPL. Poor bank corporate governance is, thus, largely responsible for higher NPL.

Management efficiency (ME) or operating efficiency (OE), could be two other aspects that might be of concern while assessing the performances of the banking sector. Banks usually strive for lower efficiency ratios, as they indicate higher earnings for lower spending. As Table 15.4 shows, for the period 2003–2008, OE and ME are higher for private commercial banks compared to SCBs and SBs, which is misleading in the sense that efficiency level for the SCBs and SBs has been historically worse than others'. One reason behind this result could be the window dressing practices of SCBs and SBs.

Table 15.4 Management and operating efficiency of the banking sector

	PCBs		*SCBs*		*FCBs*		*SBs*	
Year	*ME*	*OE*	*ME*	*OE*	*ME*	*OE*	*ME*	*OE*
2003	0.12	0.12	0.07	0.07	0.10	0.10	0.01	0.01
2004	0.08	0.08	0.05	0.05	0.06	0.06	0.00	0.00
2005	0.08	0.08	0.06	0.06	0.06	0.06	0.00	0.00
2006	0.10	0.10	0.06	0.06	0.07	0.07	0.01	0.01
2007	0.10	0.10	0.04	0.04	0.07	0.07	0.03	0.03
2008	0.09	0.09	0.06	0.06	–	–	0.04	0.04

Note: Author's estimate; management efficiency (ME) = interest expense/total loans; operating efficiency (OE) = total operating expense/net Income after tax

Table 15.5 Structure, assets, liabilities and deposits of NBFIs

	2009	*2010*	*2011*	*2012*	*2013*	*2014*	*2015*
No. of NBFIs	29	29	31	31	31	31	32
Government-owned	1	1	2	3	3	3	3
Joint-venture	8	8	8	10	10	10	10
Private	20	20	20	18	18	18	19
New branches	20	20	53	8	7	7	15
Total branches	88	108	161	169	176	183	198
Total assets	193.8	251.5	288.4	333.9	436.3	517.6	563.8
Total liabilities	164.4	206.8	235.7	274.3	350.4	423.1	465.5
Liabilities-assets ratio	84.8	82.2	81.7	82.2	80.3	81.7	82.6
Total deposit	80.8	94.4	112.6	145.4	198.3	245.7	271.8
Deposit as percent of total liabilities	49.2	45.7	47.8	53.0	56.6	58.1	58.4

Source: Bangladesh Bank

15.2.3.3 Non-bank Financial Institutions

The non-bank financial institutions (NBFIs) have been growing over time in Bangladesh and contributing importantly in strengthening financial system of Bangladesh. The main objective of these institutions is to provide term loans and meeting the long-term credit gap of the firms. The basic difference between NBFIs and BFIs is that NBFIs can collect only long-term deposits and also invest in long-term projects (Hossain and Shahiduzzaman 2002). Starting from 1981, currently in 2018, 33 NBFIs are operating in Bangladesh (Table 15.5). Though their growth in numbers is slow, their activities expanded significantly as their total asset and liabilities have increased to almost double during 2009–2015. In terms of assets and liabilities, NBFIs have been able to diversify their products significantly over time. The growth of the NBFIs and their activities appears to be impressive in a bank-dominated financial system.

Figure 15.3 compares RoEs of NBFIs and PCBs. Both the curves follow a similar pattern from 2008 onward though RoEs of NBFIs are a bit lower than their competitors. Higher cost of funds incurred by NBFIs may be a reason behind lower RoE. Weighted average RoEs of NBFIs and PCBs decreased to 5 percent and 10 percent in 2016, respectively. In terms of profitability, the performances of NBFIs have gone down in recent years, though their performance was better before 2008.

The share of classified lease/loan of NBFIs came down from 7.12 percent in 2007 to 5 percent in 2011 but again increased to 9 percent in

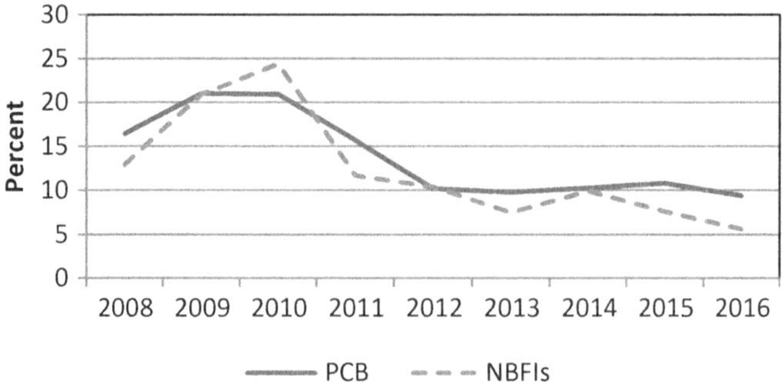

Fig. 15.3 ROEs of NBFIs and PCBs. (Source: BB Annual Report, various issues)

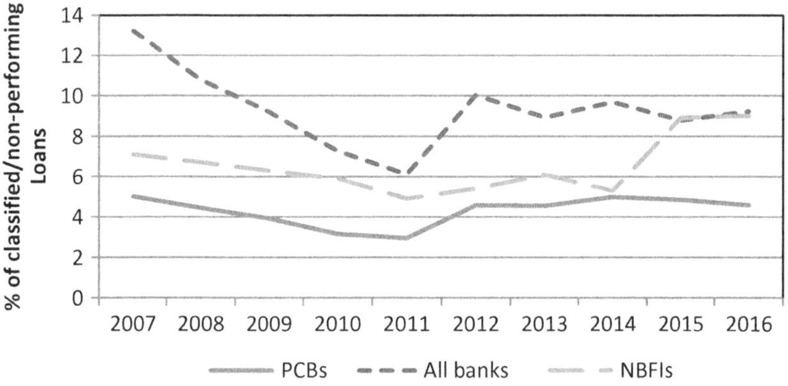

Fig. 15.4 Gross NPL to total financing of banks and NBFIs. Note: The figure for NBFIs is up to June 2016. (Source: Annual Report and Financial Institution Department, BB)

2014 onward. Figure 15.4 shows that classified loans of PCBs also showed the similar trend. Classified loans of PCBs had declined from 4.5 percent in 2007 to 2.9 percent in 2011 and again increased to about 5 percent in 2014. It may be noted that though NBFIs form a much newer market segment than PCBs, their share of classified loans is way above than that of PCBs and after 2014, it stays close to all banks' average level, which is alarming for future businesses of NBFIs.

15.2.4 Mobile Financial Service

With lack of availability of formal banks, people usually would depend on informal payment services, courier, post office, and so on to receive and send remittances. Mobile financial service (MFS) is a new addition to the financial services in Bangladesh, which became very popular in a short period of time in rural areas. MFSs, also known as mobile wallet, have been increasingly occupying an important place in day-to-day life and businesses in many developing countries including Bangladesh. According to World Bank's Global Findex data, although only 5.3 percent of individuals (age 15 or above) in the developing world have mobile money account in 2017, this figure is as high as 72.9 percent in Kenya and 50.6 percent in Uganda. In Bangladesh, 21.2 percent of the individuals have mobile money accounts and more than this proportion of people use MFS over the counter.

Within a short period since its inception in 2011, bKash has now over 28.5 million accounts (2017) and a quarter of a million agents, accounting for $16b worth of transactions per annum out of some $20b worth of mobile money services generated in an economy of $226bn. In other words, bKash accounts for 81 percent of the market while its nearest competitor, "Rocket" (floated by Dutch Bangla Bank) accounts for 17 percent. Most transactions are conducted "over the counter" (OTC) via bKash agents. Though as many as 16 bank companies got license for operating MFS in Bangladesh, only a few of them have been succeeded to capture a certain portion of the market while bKash remains the leader (Bangladesh Bank 2019). As MFS in Bangladesh is still (2019) limited to payments and transfer, people have to depend on formal and semi-formal financial institutions for basic financial services like deposits and credit. Further regulatory reforms allowing MFSs to involve in banking service and enabling a competitive environment would create a significant transformation in the financial sector of Bangladesh.

A BIDS survey (BIDS 2018) shows that although 98 percent of rural households have at least one mobile phone, only 38.4 percent have an account with an MFS. Among the households with mobile phones, 65.7 percent are found to use MFS, with 47.3 percent using bKash, and 25.5 percent using SureCash services. In contrast, among those who do not have a mobile phone, only 30 percent use MFS. The extent of account-holding among MFS users is 58 percent, and the remaining 42 percent of the MFS users are without an account. The latter group accesses MFS through agents. While banks do serve the rich more than the poor, MFIs and MFS tend to serve the rich and poor alike. From the poorest quintile,

44.8 percent households have access to MFIs and 36.0 percent to MFS. In contrast, in the richest quintile, 45.8 percent households have an account with MFIs compared to 41.2 percent with MFS. The poor seem to have an equal access to MFS as the rich.

15.3 Financial Sector Reforms

Before liberalization of the baking sector, the sector was characterized as a highly government-controlled, stifled and less diversified system. As a result, the system was vulnerable to shocks as it lacks capacity to manage the systemic and idiosyncratic risks in financial systems. Financial sector reforms, partly as donor-prescribed, started in the early 1990s to make the system more market-oriented and efficient, particularly the distressed government-owned banks. The reforms that have continued the decades of the 1990s have allowed private commercial banks, limited the scope of government intervention and strengthened prudential regulations.

As part of liberalization, from February 19, 1997, banks were given freedom to adjust interest rates. From July 12, 1999, further flexibility on interest rates was allowed as banks were permitted to differentiate interest rates among individual borrowers. The impact of financial liberalization can be best judged by the movement of real interest rate, volume of financial intermediation and efficiency of the financial sector. A significant upward fluctuations of real interest rates soon after liberalization indicate that liberalization induces a higher cost of intermediation (Fig. 15.5).

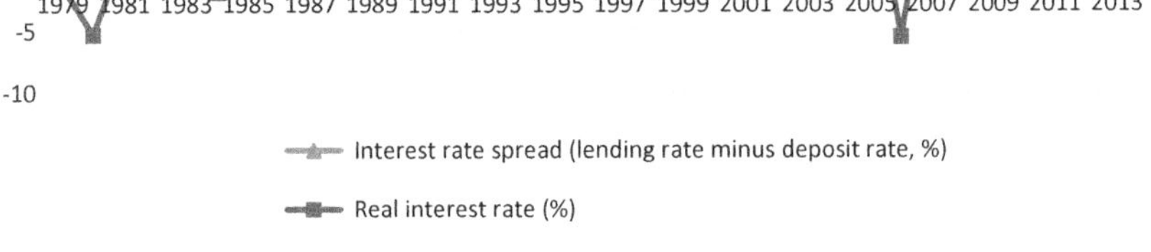

Fig. 15.5 Movements of real interest rate and interest spread

However, real interest rate alone cannot explain and hence we look into the movements of interest rate spread (IRS). Though IRS showed a declining trend in the latter half of the 1990s, it started increasing in the 2000s. It seems that liberalization has widened the IRS though it was supposed to decline and liberalization measures has not succeeded in significantly deepening or diversifying the financial sector. In fact, competition has not increased significantly in the banking sector in Bangladesh (Hossain 2012). Lack of competitiveness in determining interest rate is mainly attributed to the oligopolistic structure of the banking sector, and therefore Bangladesh Bank finds it difficult to implement monetary policies effectively.

To assess the loan market structure, we have estimated Herfindahl Index (HI) for loans and deposits for the period 1990–2012. As the major share of loan market was captured mainly by the SCBs from long time since the independence, as a result of financial liberalization, the market share started capturing by the PCBs gradually, and finally from 2005, PCBs outpaced SCBs (Fig. 15.6).

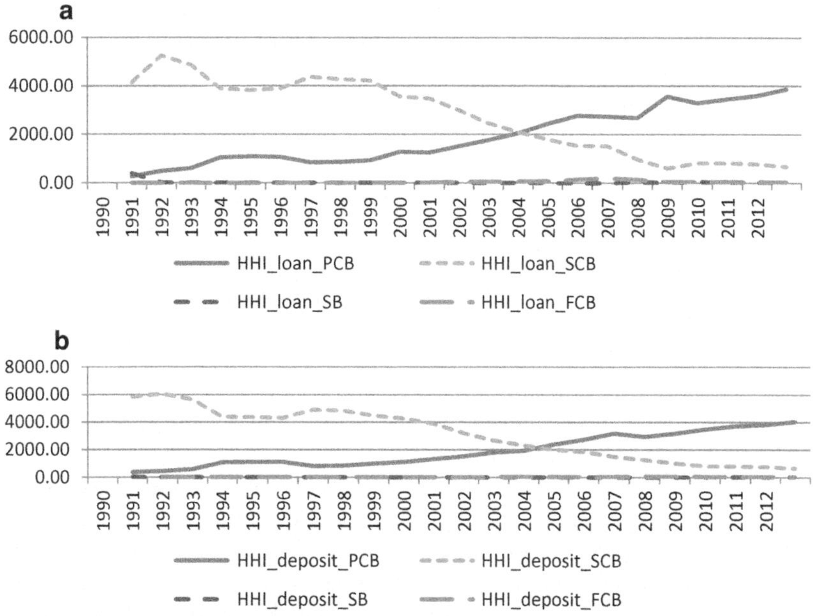

Fig. 15.6 Market concentration: Herfindahl Index. (**a**) HH Index for loans. (**b**) HH Index for deposits. Note: Author's estimate

Due to less effectiveness of monetary policy instruments in making market interest responsive, quite often Bangladesh Bank morally persuades the banks to reduce the interest rate spread at a rational level. To some extreme, Bangladesh Bank has also placed cap on both lending and deposit interest rates several times. And in 2018 at a new move, Bangladesh Bankers Association (an association of commercial banks) placed a cap on lending rate at 9 percent, and 6 percent on deposit rate. The important thing is that without making monetary transmission channels effective through bringing competition in the banking sector, these types of short-term measures would not be proved effective.

15.4 Financial Development and Economic Growth

There is a considerable amount of literature that highlighted the positive impact of a country's financial development on economic growth. Gurley and Shaw (1955) and later Goldsmith (1969) provided evidences of positive link between the real and financial sector. McKinnon (1973) and Shaw (1973) advocate for financial liberalization in order to obtain an efficient financial sector that could increase savings and real credit supply which in turn induces a higher volume of investment and faster economic growth. A large body of research on this topic convincingly established the fact that a well-developed and better functioning financial system supports faster economic growth. Development of the financial sector increases the overall efficiency of the financial institutions. A developed financial system reduces transaction costs, information asymmetries, market frictions and pool risk, which could stimulate economic growth by mobilizing savings and facilitating investment in an efficient manner. Hossain, Yoshino and Tagizadeh-Hesary (2018) show that local financial development through bank branch network expansion at the sub-district level improves the performances of SMEs and therefore contributes to economic growth.

As we have already observed, the financial liberalization measures of the 1990s have made a great stride in financial development of Bangladesh. Over time, financial rules and regulations have been liberalized and updated. As a result, the financial system has widened and deepened with improved financial development indicators. The key financial development indicators, such as deposit, credit and broad money to GDP ratios, displayed an increasing trend over time. These indicators have increased sub-

Table 15.6 Indicators of financial development

Period average	*Interest rate (lending)*	*Credit to private sector (percent of GDP)*	*Total deposits (percent of GDP)*	*Broad money (percent of GDP*	*Gross fixed capital formation (percent GDP)*	*GDP per capita at current US dollar*
1976–1980	11.09	6.59	14.86	19.03	10.44	160.0
1981–1985	13.68	13.67	20.23	24.54	10.51	192.0
1986–1990	14.71	19.08	24.75	28.67	13.87	242.0
1991–1995	13.90	16.58	23.07	26.68	17.93	283.0
1996–2000	13.83	23.17	26.7	31.01	21.51	353.0
2001–2005	12.33	28.83	35.08	40.02	22.63	395.0
2006–2008	13.40	34.5	45.0	45.0	24.4	565.5
2006–2010	12.68	32	33.32	41.45	26.20	460.86
2011–2015	12.73	38.05	41.84	50.8	28.53	780

Sources: Bangladesh Bank and Ministry of Finance

stantially from 6.6 percent, 14.9 percent and 19.0 percent, respectively, during 1976–1980 to 28.8 percent, 35.01 percent and 40.0 percent, respectively, immediate after the liberalization during 2001–2005. Such an improvement continued further to 38.05 percent, 41.84 percent and 50.8 percent during 2011–2015 (Table 15.6).

With a reasonable liberalized financial environment, the financial sector has been widened. In 2018, 59 commercial banks are operating with a combined network of over 9397 bank branches. The total asset of the banking sector stood at US$121 billion in 2015, which is almost half of Bangladesh's GDP. Private commercial banks dominate the banking sector, with 63.3 percent of the total banking sector assets in 2015. All these indicators indicate a reasonable development of the financial sector in Bangladesh (Table 15.7).

However, the level of financial inclusion is far from satisfactory. In Bangladesh, about one-third of the adults has a bank account (Bangladesh Bank 2016a). During 2010–2014, bank branch density has increased from 59 to 70 per 1000 sq. km. which is not satisfactory. While 53 percent of households have access to formal finance, considering financial services of quasi-formal and informal financial institutions, the proportion rises significantly to 89 percent (Khalily and Islam 2014). Bangladesh has been lagging behind other compara-

Table 15.7 Status of financial development in Bangladesh

Year	*ATM per 1000 sq.km.*	*ATM per 100,000 adults*	*Branches per 1000 sq.km.*	*Borrower per 100,000*	*Borrower per 100,000 adults*	*Deposit a/c per 1000 adults*	*Loan a/c per 1000 adults*	*Deposit to GDP ratio*	*Loan to GDP ratio*
2004	0.88	0.13	48.81	6.94	63.86	342.34	88.78	35.78	28.37
2006	2.54	0.35	50.8	6.92	66.61	362.95	91.92	39.18	32.02
2008	6.27	0.82	53.39	7.01	66.51	389.45	86.99	41.51	33.18
2010	16.29	2.06	59.06	7.47	66.73	474.07	88.81	46.89	39.10
2012	46.99	5.71	64.75	7.87	85.37	562.06	90.89	51.22	41.50
2014	79.31	9.27	70.47	8.23	81.62	628.87	86.72	51.46	37.30

Source: Financial Access Survey (FAS), IMF (2015)

tors in terms of financial deepening indicators. In 2015, the ratio of money supply (M2) to GDP, an indication of financial deepening, was 64.5 percent in Bangladesh compared to 189 percent in East Asia and the Pacific and 119 percent in high-income countries. The intermediary performance of the financial sector of Bangladesh was also not very satisfactory compared to its neighbors. For example, the ratio of private sector credit over GDP was 44 percent in 2015 in Bangladesh, compared to 47 percent in South Asia and 146.6 percent in high-income countries (The World Bank 2018). Though a certain level of development has occurred in the financial sector, further development in terms of financial deepening and inclusion will require development and reforms in required institutions.

The financial market of Bangladesh does not appear to be fully competitive. The behavior of interest rates indicates so. Interest rates, particularly lending interest rates, vary between 12 and 18 percent and interest spread varies between 5 and 8 percent. These figures are even higher than many developing country standards. It appears that financial liberalization have led to a widening interest rate spread (Hossain 2012). So, only financial liberalization doesn't seem enough to bring efficiency in the financial sector, and therefore measures are required to correct the existing distortions in the loan market and improve the weaknesses of required institutions to improve the situation.

Though the SBs have been gradually losing their higher share of the money market due to its high non-performing loans, managerial inefficiencies and a high-level of political and bureaucratic interventions, their contribution to provide banking services to rural areas, financing agriculture, is much higher compared to commercial banks. With government subsidies and directives, these SCBs still have 63 percent of their branches in rural areas, which is quite opposite in the cases of private commercial banks, in order to serve the rural people and businesses in spite of unviability of these branches (Bangladesh Bank 2016b).

It is noteworthy to mention that Bangladesh has achieved a remarkable progress in economic growth of 6 percent and more after 2005, which is widely thought to be the result of financial liberalization undertaken in the 1990s. All the financial development indicators, such as financial deepening (M2 as percent of GDP: m2_gdp), private sector credit by financial institutions to GDP (credit_fi/credit_bank) and bank branch per 10,000 adults, show an upward trend (Fig. 15.7). Such an improvement in financial development has been reflected in the growth of per capita GDP growth (i_y), industrial value added (ind_gva), and manufacturing value added (manf_gva) growth. With improved economic performances, recently in 2014, Bangladesh achieved lower middle-income status.

Going back to King and Levine (1993) study on finance-growth nexus, many cross-country studies have found a positive association between

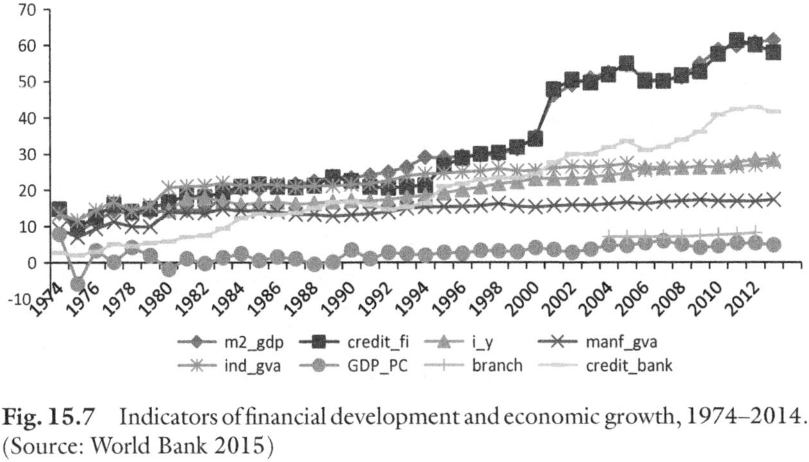

Fig. 15.7 Indicators of financial development and economic growth, 1974–2014. (Source: World Bank 2015)

finance and growth. A few studies in Bangladesh also showed similar positive results. Rahman (2004) finds a positive and statistically significant impact of financial development on both the investment-GDP ratio and per capita GDP in Bangladesh. The trends of credit to GDP and investment to GDP has positive association with financial development over time. However, further studies are needed to assess whether financial development generates an efficient allocation of financial resources across sectors.

15.5 Conclusions and Policy Recommendations

The financial sector in Bangladesh has experienced substantial reforms over time, particularly from the 1980s, which have contributed to deepening and widening of the financial sector. However, the benefits of financial liberalization have not yet been reaped fully due to institutional weaknesses. Despite having 59 commercial banks (including two new banks in the pipeline), only about one-third of the adult population has access to the banking service due to lack of branch network of these banks in rural areas, and therefore, a vast majority of people have to depend on semi-formal and informal financial sector. Only about 50 percent of credit demand for SMEs are now met by the banks. Banks' inability to diversify their products, lack of innovation, lack of operating and managerial efficiencies and poor bank branch network particularly in rural areas are some of the supply-side constraints to people's access to banking services. Among the demand-side constraints, lack of financial literacy, inability to save and higher transaction costs are important.

Interest rates, particularly lending interest rates, are thought to be very high and are not conducive to higher investments. Various initiatives of the governments including moral persuasion of the central bank, imposition of cap, and so on did not produce any good results. Less competitive structure of the financial sector, distortions in the financial market due to high interest structure of the national savings certificate, high ratio of non-performing loan, high operating costs of the banks, and so on are thought to be the key reasons behind the existing high interest rate structure in Bangladesh.

Non-performing loan ratio which is consistently over 10 percent of total outstanding loan is a big threat for the soundness of the financial system in Bangladesh. The NPL situation of the state-owned commercial banks (SCBs) is even worse—around 20–30 percent. Political patronization, weak corporate governance and corruption of the bankers are some of the key factors that are largely responsible for escalating NPL ratio. The corporate governance of the banks has become weaker by allowing family members in the board of directors of the commercial banks for a longer period and similarly appointing politically biased members in the board of state-owned banks. Such weak governance is one of the key reasons for piling up a big portion of NPL as they often intervene in loan approval process. Further, weak contract enforceability and lengthy and costly legal exercise are some of the structural weaknesses that contributes to high non-performing loans.

Therefore, it is important to enhance the quantity and quality of financial intermediation in the economy for enhancing economic development. Integration of various financial sectors, enhancing efficiency and continuous reform measures could better mobilize resources and finance development, essential maturity transformation between volatile savings and stable long-term investments. An efficient financial system with adoption of technologies is, thus, a compelling necessity to support the growing needs of investment as well as to improve better allocation of funds for productive investment.

SCBs have long been associated with negative images with rampant corruption, weak corporate governance and political interferences. Privatization of some of these banks could be the possible solution to these problems. The banking sector appears to lack some prudent regulations to establish depositors' rights in the face of new but troubled banks. It is, therefore, important for the government to strengthen deposit insurance scheme. Prudent regulations and legal framework for merger and acquisition policies also need to be streamlined in the context of growing demand for more new banks. By increasing operating and management efficiency, banks may make their products more competitive. The government should also make efforts to remove factors that are creating distortions in the financial market. Pervasive state intervention in the banking sector have to be stopped in order to improve risk management capacity as well as efficiency of the banks.

Appendix

Table 15.8 Comparative status of the banking sector in Bangladesh

Bank type	*Number*	*Number of branches*			*Percentage of total asset*	*Percentage of total deposit*	*Return on asset (percent)*	*Return on equity (percent)*
		Rural	*Urban*	*Total*				
A. In 2009								
State-owned banks (SCBs)	4	2146 (63.4 percent)	1240 (36.6 percent)	3386 (100 percent)	30.66	48.07	0.70	22.5
Private commercial banks (PCBs)	30	634 (30.3 percent)	1461 (69.7 percent)	2095 (100 percent)	53.71	29.71	1.37	16.37
Specialized banks (SBs)	5	1206 (88.5 percent)	157 (11.5 percent)	1363 (100 percent)	6.08	8.31	−0.17	−2.01
Foreign banks (FCBs)	9	0	56 (100 percent)	56 (100 percent)	9.55	13.91	2.94	17.75
Total	48	3986 (57.8 percent)	2914 (42.2 percent)	6900 (100 percent)	100.00	100.00		
B. In 2015								
State-owned banks (SCBs)	6	2324 (63.0 percent)	1366 (37.0 percent)	3690 (100 percent)	27.5	28.4	−0.04	−1.5
Private commercial banks (PCBs)	39	1714 (40.6 percent)	2512 (59.4 percent)	4226 (100 percent)	64.5	64.5	1	10.8
Specialized banks (SBs)	2	1296 (91.2 percent)	110 (7.8 percent)	1406 (100 percent)	2.8	2.9	−1.2	−5.8
Foreign banks (FCBs)	9	0	75 (100 percent)	75	5.2	4.3	2.9	14.6
Total	56	5334 (56.8 percent)	4063 (43.2 percent)	9397 (100 percent)	100.00	100.00	0.8	10.5

Source: Bangladesh Bank Annual Report; In 2009, two specialized banks Bangladesh Shilpa Bank and Bangladesh Shilpa Rin Sangstha were merged to form Bangladesh Development Bank Ltd. Since 2015 Bangladesh Development Bank Ltd. and BASIC Bank Ltd. are regarded as a state-owned commercial banks instead of specialized banks. Now Bangladesh Krishi Bank and Rajshahi Krishi Unnayan Bank are treated as specialized banks

Note: *SCB* state-owned commercial bank, *PCB* private commercial bank, *SB* specialized banks, *FCB* foreign commercial banks

Table 15.9 Classified, sub-standard, doubtful and bad/loss loans for all banks (2001–2016)

Year	*Total classified loans as percent of TL*	*Sub-standard loan as percent of TCL*	*Doubtful loans as percent of TCL*	*Bad/loss loans as percent of TCL*
2001	31.49	5.6	5.87	88.53
2005	13.55	8.66	6.96	84.37
2010	7.1	13.4	8.4	78.1
2015	8.8	8.9	6.5	84.6
2016	9.2	10.2	5.4	84.4

Source: Banking Regulation and Policy Department, FSR 2016, BB; *TL* total loan, *TCL* total classified loan

References

Abiad, A., Oomes, N., & Ueda, K. (2008). The quality effect: Does financial liberalization improve the allocation of capital? *Journal of Development Economics, 87*(2), 270–282.

Bangladesh Bank. (2016a). Bangladesh Bank annual report 2015–16.

Bangladesh Bank. (2016b). Schedule Banks Statistics, 2016.

Bangladesh Bank. (2019). Mobile financial service data. Available at https://www.bb.org.bd/fnansys/paymentsys/mfsdata.php

BIDS (2018). *Impact of mobile financial services in Bangladesh: The case of bKash.* Unpublished, Bangladesh Institute of Development Studies.

Goldsmith, R. W. (1969). *Financial structure and development* (No. HG174 G57).

Gurley, J., & Shaw, E. (1955). Financial aspects of economic development. *The American Economic Review, 45*(4), 515–538.

Hossain, M. (2012). Financial reforms and persistently high interest rate spread in Bangladesh: Pitfalls in institutional development? *Journal of Asian Economics, 23*(4), 395–408.

Hossain, M. (2019). Green finance in Bangladesh: Barriers and solutions. In J. Sachs et al. (Eds.), *A handbook on green finance: Energy security and sustainable development.* Singapore: Springer.

Hossain, M., & Shahiduzzaman, M. (2002, March). Development of non-bank financial institutions to strengthen the financial system of Bangladesh. *Bank Parikrama, XXVII*(1).

Hossain, M., Yoshino, N., & Taghizadeh-Hesary, F. (2018). *Local financial development, access to credit and SMEs' performance: Evidence from Bangladesh.* ADBI working paper 906. Tokyo: Asian Development Bank Institute. Available: https://www.adb.org/publications/local-financial-development-access-credit-smesperformance-bangladesh

IMF. (2015). *Financial access survey, 2015*. Washington, DC: International Monetary Fund.

Khalily, M. A. B. (2016). *Financial inclusion, financial regulation, and education in Bangladesh*, ADBI working paper, no. 621. Tokyo: Asian Development Bank Institute (ADBI).

Khalily, M. A. B., & Islam, M. S. (2014). *Access to finance in Bangladesh: An analysis of aggregate data*. Institute of Microfinance. Mimeo.

Khandker, S. R. (2005). Microfinance and poverty: Evidence using panel data from Bangladesh. *The World Bank Economic Review, 19*(2), 263–286.

King, R., & Levine, R. (1993). Finance and growth: Schumpeter might be right. *Quarterly Journal of Economics, 108*(3), 717–737.

McKinnon, R. I. (1973). *Money and capital in economic development*. Washington, DC: Brookings Institution.

Rahman, A. (1992). The informal financial sector in Bangladesh: An appraisal of its role in development. *Development and Change, 23*(1), 147–168.

Rahman, M. H. (2004). Financial development—economic growth nexus: A case study of Bangladesh. *The Bangladesh Development Studies, 30*(3/4), 113–128.

Shaw, E. (1973). *Financial deepening in economic development*. New York: Oxford University Press.

The World Bank. (2018). World Development Indicators database, 2018.

CHAPTER 16

Microfinance in Sustainable Development and Economic Growth in Bangladesh

M. A. Baqui Khalily

16.1 Introduction

In recent decades, two terminologies have occupied literature on economics and finance. They are sustainable growth and sustainable development. Sustainable growth refers to the maximum growth rate that can be maintained over time without distorting economic behavior, particularly of future generation. Attaining a sustainable economic growth rate may often have an adverse impact on environment and depletion of resources, leaving little for future generations. This brings the concept of sustainable development. Conceptually, it is a state of development where the present consumption needs (in a broad sense) are met without affecting the needs of future generations. The concept of sustainable development is not about environment only; it is much broader. It is also about creating and ensuring a society that is healthy, competitive and just for inclusive growth and resilience building.

M. A. Baqui Khalily (✉)
Department of Finance, University of Dhaka, Dhaka, Bangladesh

Institute of Inclusive Finance and Development (InM), Dhaka, Bangladesh

Department of Business Administration, University of Asia Pacific, Dhaka, Bangladesh

M. Hossain (ed.), *Bangladesh's Macroeconomic Policy*,
https://doi.org/10.1007/978-981-15-1244-5_16

Three elements are crucial in sustainable development—economic growth, inclusive society and environmental protection. An appropriate level of synchronization is required among these three elements. Therefore, an ideal or optimal state would be attaining sustainable growth through sustainable development. The core strategy is inclusive growth and development.

How do we attain sustainable development and growth? Factors that determine sustainable growth can be derived from both different economic theories and empirical evidences (e.g., Renelt 1991; Solow 1956; Bađun 2009; Mercieca 2010; Chirwa and Odhiambo 2016; Popov 2017). The critical factors that contribute to economic growth are higher savings and investment; investment in education, technology, health and infrastructure; development of the financial sector; induced policies for factor and product markets as well as institutional development. Access to finance is recognized as an important strategy for attaining sustainable development and growth.

Sustainable economic growth with higher level of investments and outputs via banking system does not necessarily imply sustainable development, as it does not guarantee access to all segments of society to financial and non-financial resources. High and sustainable growth can be ensured even under extremely skewed distribution of access to resources. This may still leave a large number of population on the margin outside the banking system. Two inhibiting factors—high transaction cost and high degree of risk due to the problem of asymmetric information—restrict the expansion of banking services in remote or rural areas as banks operate with maximum profit motive. As banks operate from their branch offices, clients are likely to access bank's financial services subject to transaction cost minimization. That means, clients are more likely to access branches nearer to their locations. On the other hand, because of profit maximization objective and loan production technology, banks are reluctant to provide small loans to millions. They may be better-off by providing collateral-based medium and large loans. Hence, banks and capital markets are likely to promote medium and large enterprises, and small loans to some extent. But their role is important for attaining sustainable economic growth through financing of the private sector. This is true in developing countries. However, people in the lower income strata are more likely to be excluded from the formal bank credit market.

Financial inclusion is increasingly becoming a policy priority for governments and a goal of the financial system. Access to financial services reflects the depth of financial outreach. A large body of research ranging from cross-country studies, industry-level studies, firm-level studies and time-series studies confirm that there is a positive link between financial development and economic growth.

The term "financial inclusion" refers to bringing the excluded low-income and poor households under the financial network through affordable financial products under new institutional arrangements. Financial inclusion is positively correlated with financial development and economic growth (e.g., Demetriades and Hussein 1996; Fry 1988; Gupta 1984; Levine 1997, 2005). Development of the financial sector and making financial services accessible to all can go a long way in reducing poverty (e.g., Beck et al. 2000; Honohan 2004; Rutherford 2000). Financial exclusion limits opportunities for employment and enterprise development and imposes a premium on the cost of basic services. Financial exclusion, thus, makes it difficult to reduce inequalities and alleviate poverty.

Therefore, considering the Sustainable Development Goals (SDGs)[1], sustainable development requires, on the one hand, financial inclusion of the excluded people in a country, and on the other hand, investment in social and economic institutions that will have positive impacts on growth and development.

In Bangladesh, the key new institutional arrangements are microfinance institutions. In a national survey, Khalily et al. (2015b) found that microfinance institutions (MFIs) are key players in promoting financial inclusion. They showed that around 78 percent of the households have access to financial services; of them 43 percent of the households have access to microfinance services. The effective role of microfinance institutions is better perceived when we look at the credit market: 38 percent of the households have access to micro credit market, while around 8 percent of the households have access to bank credit market. One of the critical findings that emerged from the study is the fact that banks are dominating players in urban areas, while MFIs are dominating players in rural areas. A little over 30 million members are under the network of MFIs. More flexibility has been introduced to the microfinance sector. It now offers individual loans of amounts as high as Tk.1.5 million. Micro and small enterprises can now access microfinance services, particularly in the rural

[1] The 2030 Agenda for Sustainable Development has a set of new Goals. The Goals suggest: (i) inclusive growth through inclusive finance; (ii) improved adaptation ability and resilience of the households in climate change related shocks; (iii) efficient use of maritime and land resources; (iv) community and integrated approach to sustainable development; (v) institutional development for a just, poverty-free and hunger-free sensitive society toward good governance and accountability of the participatory system; and (vi) redistribution of resources and development of micro and small enterprises.

areas. In 2017, the MFIs disbursed loans of over Tk. 12 billion. Micro savings now constitute 60 percent of loans outstanding. Therefore, financial inclusion through MFIs has contributed to financial development and increase in investment. This is likely to have an impact on attaining two core SDGs—poverty reduction and zero hunger—and the broad goal of economic growth.

The critical questions, therefore, are, what has been the impact of expanded financial inclusion through microfinance institutions on poverty alleviation? Does it contribute to economic growth? How does access to finance impact growth? These questions are addressed in this chapter both from the macro and micro perspectives. Based on the literature review and empirical evidences using Bangladesh data, we conclude that access to microfinance along with other services positively contributes to poverty reduction and economic growth. A longitudinal analysis of about 5000 households for a period of five years showed that 20 percent of the participating households have graduated from poverty on a sustainable basis over the project period, but it also showed that it takes about continuous participation of at least three years for possible impact of the project. However, households with access to microfinancial and non-financial services have higher probability of graduation from poverty than the households with access to microfinance services only. On the other hand, microfinance services impact economic growth through private investment and higher productivity of micro enterprises. Evidence shows that under certain assumptions, microfinance contributes to GDP growth at a rate between 12 and 17 percent.

The remaining part of the chapter is structured into five sections. Section 16.2 evaluates the role of MFIS in financial inclusion as an approach toward sustainable development in Bangladesh. In Sect. 16.3, impact of microfinance in sustainable development, particularly in poverty alleviation and food security, is evaluated. In Sect. 16.4, impact of microfinance on GDP in Bangladesh is evaluated. Finally, analysis and summary findings and policy implications are discussed in Sect. 16.5.

16.2 Financial Inclusion as an Approach to Sustainable Development in Bangladesh: The Role of MFIs

The basic objective of financial inclusion is to bring the excluded households, particularly the poor, under the financial system with alternate financial institutions, if required. The question is, why? People remain poor for lack of access to financial and non-financial resources. In other words, lack of entitlement makes people poor and less empowered (Sen 2018). As such, they are not able to access opportunities, and hence remain out of the socio-economic system for perpetual poverty. Given such reality, end of poverty has been identified as number 1 goal of sustainable development. The process of ending such poverty requires promotion of access to finance, particularly microfinance, and other non-financial interventions for poverty-stricken households.

With the experience of Grameen Model in Jobra, close to the University of Chittagong, Professor Muhammad Yunus clearly demonstrated that marginal benefit from access to microfinance would be positive and family wellbeing would accelerate (Khandker et al. 1995). It also showed that the poor are unable to access bank finance due to lack of collateral and entitlement to property. Successful experiment of Professor Yunus and subsequent emergence of microfinance institutions both in Bangladesh and in other countries including the USA demonstrated that inclusive finance is a requirement for poverty alleviation, and alternate institutional arrangements are required for providing financial services to the excluded poor households (Khandker 1998; Yunus 2007; Demirgüç-Kunt et al. 2017). Inclusive financial systems can benefit poor and disadvantaged people by providing them with broad access to credit eliminating price and/or non-price barriers. With investment in income generating activities, microcredit borrowers are likely to have higher income and higher amount of savings and increase in consumption (Dupas and Robinson 2013). It can also contribute to efficient allocation of financial and physical resources, economic growth, income and non-income inequalities, and the distribution of benefits in an economy (Fernando 2007).

Stuart Ratherford has worked in Bangladesh in the area of microfinance for a long time. In his most cited book *The Poor and Their Money*, he argues that the poor need financial services more than the non-poor, as they do not have savings. He showed that with appropriate financial instruments, poor households were able to save. On the other hand, because of the positive impact of access to finance by the poor households, income share of the poorer groups will increase and absolute poverty will decrease (Beck et al. 2000). In another study, Honohan showed that absolute poverty reduces at a higher rate for the poor with access to finance than the comparable counter-factual poor households.

In brief, inclusive finance reduces intensity of poverty, increases income, consumption and savings; and increases investment and assets. Such impacts ultimately contribute to inclusive growth. There are some evidences that show that microcredit does not have an impact on poverty alleviation, and when it does, it is because of entrepreneurial ability of the borrowers. But it certainly contributes to consumption smoothening and in turn to reducing food poverty (e.g., Banerjee et al. 2015). In most cases, the Randomized control trial (RCT) based studies were conducted over a limited period.

16.2.1 Outreach of Microfinance Institutions in Bangladesh

The whole argument has so far been to show that financial market has played a complimentary role in ensuring sustainable economic growth. Given the limited spill-over effects of private sector lending, it can be argued that financial inclusion is a necessary condition for sustainable development in Bangladesh. MFIs are more effective in ensuring a higher intensity of inclusive finance because of their wide branch network and operating model. Consequently, they contribute toward achieving the SDG goals, particularly goals 1 to 6.

Let me shed some light on the outreach of MFIs in Bangladesh. Some 692 MFIs are licensed and regulated by the Microcredit Regulatory Authority (MRA) under the Microcredit Regulatory Authority Act 2006. Since 2006, microfinance outreach has increased at a higher rate than the pre-2006 period. This is evident from the number of branches and the number of members enrolled (Table 16.1). Following the establishment of MRA, the number of branches and members has doubled during the past decade.

Consequently, annual loan disbursement has increased manifold, by over 12 times in the period 2006–17 (Table 16.2). Higher increase in disbursement of loans is due to increase in lateral entry of micro enterprises and micro enterprise loans. Loan outstanding has remained more or less at around 63 percent of the total annual disbursement. Annual average loan per borrower shows an increasing trend. Loan size that started with Tk. 2000 in 1980s is now around Tk. 28,000 by the end of 2016–17. Loan ceiling for individual borrower has also increased. Because of graduation and lateral entry of micro entrepreneurs, the loan ceiling has increased to Tk. one million. This is likely to have a larger impact on employment and economic growth, particularly in rural economic growth.

Considering high intensity of microfinance outreach, microfinance sector has higher penetration in financial market in Bangladesh. Khalily et al. (2015b) conducted a second round of national level survey on access to financial services over the same 9000 households surveyed in 2010. As such, it was a panel data set. The share of microfinance sector in providing financial services was higher (Table 16.3).

Table 16.1 Outreach of MFIs, 1999–2017

Year	*MFIs*	*Branches*	*Total members*
1999	533	3203	9,433,974
2000	585	3306	11,021,663
2001	629	4930	12,447,623
2002	656	5130	12,860,615
2003	720	5642	14,630,945
2004	721	7807	16,622,047
2005	690	7518	18,793,990
2006	611	9049	20,511,866
2007	535	12,096	23,955,424
2008	613	16,690	35,905,424
2009	745	17,407	35,707,896
2010	773	18,729	34,620,621
2011	695	17,851	33,062,340
2012	540	17,326	32,245,817
2013	550	17,702	32,008,923
2014	511	17,795	34,038,931
2015	506	18,635	36,232,279
2016	530	18,609	37,657,462
2017	510	19,166	39,216,816

Source: Bangladesh microfinance statistics, various issues, CDF

Table 16.2 Trends in loan disbursement and outstanding of MFIs, 1999–2017

Year	*Annual disbursement (in million Tk.)*	*Loan outstanding (in million Tk.)*	*Loan outstanding as percent of disbursement*	*Outstanding borrowers (in millions)*
1999	25,870	18,692	72.25	6.89
2000	33,171	21,903	66.03	7.98
2001	38,654	25,879	66.95	8.86
2002	44,357	29,988	67.6	9.46
2003	60,853	36,493	59.96	10.65
2004	69,163	44,346	64.11	11.96
2005	92,594	55,681	60.13	13.94
2006	124,446	73,176	58.8	16.09
2007	176,446	97,090	55.03	19.44
2008	311,060	126,635	40.71	29.79
2009	370,796	189,267	51.04	27.05
2010	371,816	221,667	59.62	27.20
2011	440,288	279,815	63.56	27.17
2012	498,101	311,044	62.45	25.95
2013	566,841	348,053	61.40	25.67
2014	647,216	409,966	63.34	27.24
2015	827,768	521,829	63.04	29.59
2016	955,772	611,618	63.99	30.61
2017	1207,538	770,465	63.82	32.45

Source: Bangladesh microfinance statistics, various issues, CDF

Table 16.3 Intensity of access to financial services by type of market, 2014 (percentage of households)

	Access to bank		*Access to MF*	
	2014 (three years)	*Aggregate (eight years)*	*2014 (three years)*	*Aggregate (eight years)*
National	42.57	55.43	46.91	61.32
Rural	40.49	54.73	47.34	63.90
Urban	49.76	57.85	45.43	52.41
Non-poor	49.79	61.83	45.72	59.93
Poor	24.19	39.11	50.57	65.58

Source: Khalily et al. (2015b)

Several interesting findings emerged from the survey. First, as expected, banks have higher market share in urban areas and MFIs have higher market share in rural areas in terms of percentage of households having access to financial services. Second, banks provide services more to non-poor households and MFIs offer services more to poor households. However, significant increase in the intensity of access to microfinance by the non-poor households was evident in the study. It is due to two factors—graduation of these households (HHs) from poverty, and lateral entry of non-poor HHs as micro enterprises. Third, day laborers and marginally self-employed (most cases outcome of micro credit) from poor households with no or at best primary education have more access to microfinance, while relatively more educated have access to bank financial services (Table 16.4). Fourth, it showed that higher percentage of households in the fourth and highest income quintile have more access to banks, while households in the lower quintile have access to microfinance. Fifth, it further showed that MFIs addressed both extremely poor and moderately poor households almost equally. Around 50 percent of these HHs do access microfinance services (Table 16.5).

Such clear demarcation of the clients between banks and microfinance suggests that the targeted groups for SDGs are addressed by the microfinance sector. It may be noted that financial services include deposit, credit and insurance. In case of microfinance, borrowers are required to be savers except in the case of lateral entrants. Micro credit and micro insurance will generally overlap, as micro insurance is linked to credit.

From the perspective of SDG number 1 (no poverty) and goal number 2 (no hunger), financial inclusion of poor households through MFIs

Table 16.4 Characteristics of households having any access to any financial services

Characteristics	*Aggregate access to any financial services*	*Access to formal finance*	*Access to microfinance*	*Access to informal finance*	*No access to financial services*
Occupation of household head					
Labor	75.46	23.39	56.91	25.52	24.54
Self-employment	83.71	46.87	53.07	24.37	16.29
Service/ professional	79.05	51.37	35.16	14.21	20.95
Education of HH head					
Illiterate	73.49	27.39	50.41	22.47	26.51
Up to 5	79.86	40.05	49.98	22.96	20.14
Up to 9	83.83	55.38	45.7	20.72	16.17
S.S.C	87.17	70	38.17	14.67	12.83
H.S.C	89.34	79.1	32.38	15.57	10.66
Above H.S.C	94.38	87.19	20.63	11.25	5.62
Income quintile					
Lowest	64.45	25.36	40.54	20.43	35.55
Second	78.06	29.18	54.59	25.35	21.94
Third	79.38	35.64	51.97	22.29	20.62
Fourth	83.9	49.07	47.88	19.63	16.1
Highest	90.28	73.7	39.24	17.83	9.72

Source: Khalily et al. (2015b)

Table 16.5 Access to credit by market type and poverty status

Poverty status	*Bank credit*		*Microcredit*	
	2014	*2010*	*2014*	*2010*
Extremely poor	4.24	5.26	42.18	44.52
Moderately poor	4.29	5.82	43.43	47.25
Non-poor	10.75	9.06	39.34	32.94
Total	8.95	7.99	40.10	36.64

Source: Khalily et al. (2015b)

appear to be more probable approach, as banks offer financial services largely to corporations and enterprises with little to targeted poor households. More than 60 percent of the rural households have access to microfinance services in Bangladesh, as is evident from Table 16.3 (Khalily et al. 2015b). In Bangladesh, in addition to providing financial services, MFIs also offer multi-dimensional non-financial social services.

16.2.2 *Types of Microfinance Services Offered in Bangladesh*

As noted earlier, microfinance sector in Bangladesh is different from those in other countries, even in many cases in other South Asian countries. MFIs in Bangladesh offer both financial and non-financial services. In most cases, non-financial services are linked with microfinance services. Over the last 30 years, MFIs in Bangladesh have evolved in addressing multi-dimensional needs of poor households. Starting with micro credits of very small amounts in the early 1980s, the loan size has increased. Loan products have diversified. Non-financial products have also diversified. All these diversifications have taken place in the context of sustainable poverty alleviation: it was family that was at the center of microfinance from the very beginning; it not only addressed short-term food poverty but also long-term sustainable poverty alleviation with a focus on empowerment and ownership of assets including education for children. Table 16.6 shows product diversification of MFIs over the last three decades.

Following information on 15 major social programs, the role of microfinance institutions in providing social services is presented in Box 16.1:

Different MFIs have undertaken different social programs based on the availability of funds and other ancillary services. Access to these programs will vary from one year to another. Therefore, considering cumulative figures, more than 60 percent of the members have access to different social programs.

Given the access of households to microfinance including credit, savings and insurance, and non-financial services including training, housing, education, empowerment, disaster management, health and other relevant services, the microfinance sector is likely to have impact on economic growth and multi-dimensional poverty at the household level.

Table 16.6 Product diversification of MFIs beyond traditional micro credit

	Product diversification	
Traditional micro credit	Savings	Credit for the ultra poor
	Micro enterprise	Credit for seasonal poverty
	Micro insurance	Housing credit
	Training	Education
	Technical assistance	Remittance
	Primary health care	Family planning
	Social awareness	Water and sanitation
	Climate change and disaster management	Forestation
	Credit for crop cultivation	Credit for livestock

Box 16.1 Role of Microfinance Institutions in Providing Social Services

- Over 68 percent of the MFIs offer *training* for the members in different areas;
- Over 54 percent of the MFIs offer *health care services*;
- Over 27 percent of the MFIs have specific program on building *houses* for the poor households in rural areas;
- Over 48 percent of the MFIs are engaged in *water and sanitation*;
- Although microfinance is oriented toward women, yet over 40 percent of the MFIs have a specific program for *women empowerment*;
- A little over 56 percent of the MFIs have *education* program for children;
- Over 35 percent of the MFIs are engaged in prevention of *child marriage*;
- About 30 percent of the MFIs are engaged in *forestation*, particularly in the southern region;
- A little over one-fourth of the MFIs provide *support to agriculture* through providing input and technical assistance services;
- Around 25 percent of the MFIs have *governance*-related programs;
- Over 25 percent of the MFIs are engaged in *disaster management and relief* efforts in the wake of disasters particularly in climate vulnerable areas;
- Around 22 percent of the MFIs have programs for *disabled children and women*;
- About 20 percent of the MFIs have programs for fighting *child and women trafficking*;
- About 20 percent of the MFIs have programs related to *family planning*; and
- Very recently, some major MFIs have undertaken programs for the growing elderly population in rural areas.

Source: Credit and Development Forum (2017)

16.3 Impact of Microfinance on Sustainable Development in Bangladesh

How does microfinance impact different outcomes at the household level? When poor households borrow, not the entire borrowed amount is fully utilized. A portion of the loan amount is used for consumption that takes the households out of short-run poverty, and a portion of the loan amount is utilized for productive purposes. It has been found that by and large, around 48 percent of the loan amount is utilized for productive purposes implying the creation of income generating assets. Compared to the counter-factual control groups, these households become better-off because of generated higher income and increase in investment. In many cases, we have found that non-borrowing households have more savings than those borrowing households, but their amount of investment is lower. That means, micro credit borrowers have higher investment. How is that possible? It is possible in two ways—investment of portion of borrowed amount in income generating assets and self-financing of investment from savings. Higher the amount of investment, higher the outcome of sustainable graduation from poverty. This is the story behind the successful graduation from poverty.

Khandker et al. (2016) showed with a panel data of three surveys covering a period of 20 years, between 1991/1992 and 2010/2011, that extreme poverty of the participating microfinance borrowers was 8 percentage point lower, and long-run graduation from poverty (sustainable poverty alleviation) was 10 percentage point higher than the non-microfinance households.

Ocasio (2012) showed that microfinance was more effective in capability enhancing services, as suggested by Sen, like health and education complement finance. This means, microfinance has a higher impact on socio-economic outcomes when households have access to both financial and non-financial services. As such, Ahmed and Khalily (2016) found that the multi-dimensional poverty index (MPI) was lower for microfinance households with access to multiple services. Similar evidence was also found by Khalily et al. (2015b).

Osmani et al. (2015) showed that the poverty rate in Bangladesh in 2010 would have been 46.3 percent higher compared to the actual rate of 33.1 percent, had there been no microfinance. Contribution toward self-employment and micro enterprises and increase in assets as well as higher factor productivity had contributed to this high contribution of microfinance in poverty alleviation. When referring to poverty reduction, the authors refer to long-run sustainable reduction in poverty.

In a recent paper, Ahmed et al. (2017) showed that the participating households in flexible microfinance programs had higher income, food consumption expenditure and savings than the counter-factual non-participants in north-western Bangladesh.

All these studies referred above were either cross-sectional or panel of few years. The analysis in this chapter is based on a longitudinal data set of some 5600 households. The data covers a period of five years from 2008 to 2013. Data was derived from the multi-dimensional Programmed Initiatives for Monga[2] Eradication (PRIME) program. Long-term panel data for six consecutive years (2008–2013) was available. As a result, the conventional problems of selection bias and unobservable characteristics could be eliminated in the impact assessment. Khalily et al. (2015a) assessed the impacts of PRIME on sustainable development goals including food security, economic outcomes and multi-dimensional poverty. The design of the PRIME contained both financial and non-financial interventions. The non-financial interventions included health care, technical assistance for income generating assets and training on different socio-economic issues.

16.3.1 Evidence from PRIME

Palli Karma-Sahayak Foundation (PKSF) designed a major program titled "Programmed Initiatives for Monga Eradication (PRIME)" in 2006 to address the issue of *monga* in the north-western region (greater Rangpur) of Bangladesh. It was designed following the census of monga-affected households. The benchmark data of some 350,000 households showed that around 90 percent of the households did not have three full meals during the period of monga (August–October). It means, the households coped with food insecurity through occasional starvation or

[2] The term '*monga*' refers to a state of extreme food insecurity. It is commonly associated with the greater Rangpur region where in the August–October period of every year, households experience *monga*. The word appears to be missing from the media in recent years because of the changing economic growth and development. Both macro and micro factors have contributed to such change. NGO-MFIs have played a key role in bringing the changes. Perhaps in 2006, the Rangpur region had the lowest microfinance penetration and now it has the highest rate of penetration. In Bangladesh, only 8 percent of households in the region could have three meals during monga time, and more than 40 percent struggle to have one meal a day. This has now changed. Therefore, Rangpur presents a case for understanding the role of microfinance in attaining SDGs.

food rationing.[3] During the monga time, many non-poor households also became food poor. Therefore, the immediate issue was of solving the problem of hunger (SDG number 2), and the long-run issue was of solving the problem of poverty on a sustainable basis (SDG number 1). In fact, when long-term poverty is solved, many of the SDGs are automatically attained. Long term impacts of PRIME were evaluated by InM from 2008. We present the findings of the study for the period 2008–2013 conducted over 5600 households. The households were classified into (i) program participants with access to both financial and non-financial services (PCP); (ii) program participants with access to financial services only (PCO), (iii) non-participant control households (NP); (iv) non-PRIME program participants with access to finance and non-finance interventions (NPCP) and (v) non-PRIME program participants with access to finance only (NPCO). We present here the evidence of the impact of PRIME on the PCP group in comparison to non-participants.

Food security was recognized as the primary goal of PRIME. Households were defined as food secured if the households had three full meals during the *monga* period. Following figures clearly demonstrate that participating households were much better-off than the control or non-participating households.

Figure 16.1 shows food security in normal time and Fig. 16.2 shows food security in monga time. All these households were homogenous in 2007 with only 10 percent of the HHs having three meals a day. In 2013, in other words, 70 percent of the PRIME HHs had three full meals in *monga* time compared with 55 percent of the non-participating HHs, although the households had a similar experience till 2010. Macroeconomic conditions may also have contributed to improving food security, among others. A program like PRIME has essentially contributed to solving the problem of hunger, thereby attaining goal number 2 of sustainable development. This would be possible only when we find that income (presented in Fig. 16.3) and total expenditure (both food and non-food expenditures) increased (presented in Fig. 16.4) more for the participating HHs.

Both the figures show that by the end of 2013, the total annual income was higher by Tk. 20,000 and total annual expenditures were higher by Tk. 13,000. This suggests that participating PRIME HHs, on an average,

[3] It may be noted that in 2006, the greater Rangpur region had the lowest intensity of microfinance penetration in Bangladesh. Only 38 percent of the households had access to microfinance.

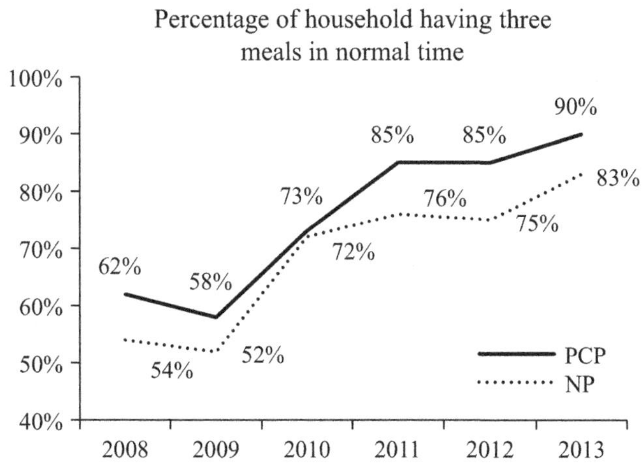

Fig. 16.1 State of food security in normal time

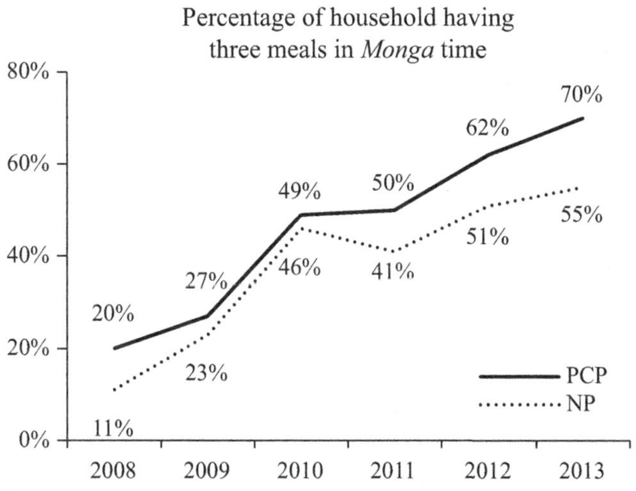

Fig. 16.2 State of food security in monga time

could finance expenditures by generated income. In such a situation, both investment (more from loans) and net savings will increase because of increase in net income. This is evident from Fig. 16.5 (trend in investment) and Fig. 16.6 (increase in net savings).

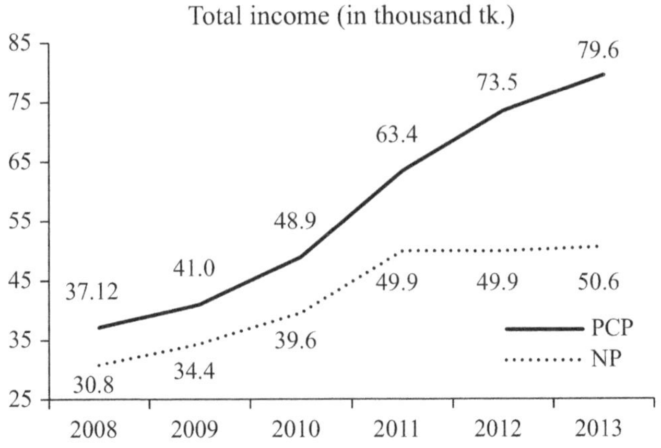

Fig. 16.3 Trends in total income

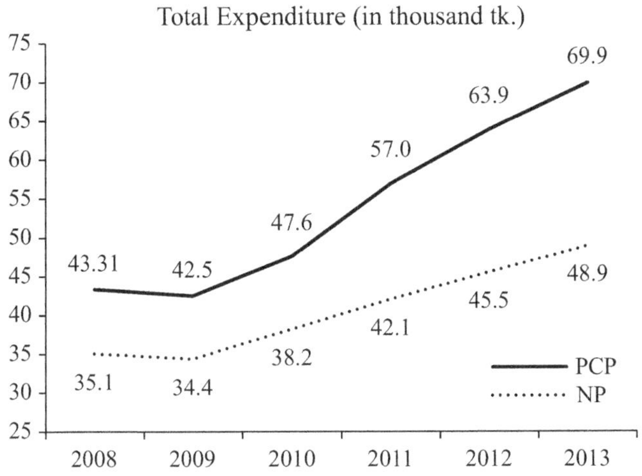

Fig. 16.4 Trends in total expenditure

The results are quite clear that ability to invest and save increased geometrically from 2011 for the participating PRIME HHs than for the non-participating control HHs. Considering the higher ability to invest and save, given the higher income and access to credit, one can perhaps intuitively conclude that a higher percentage of the participating HHs will

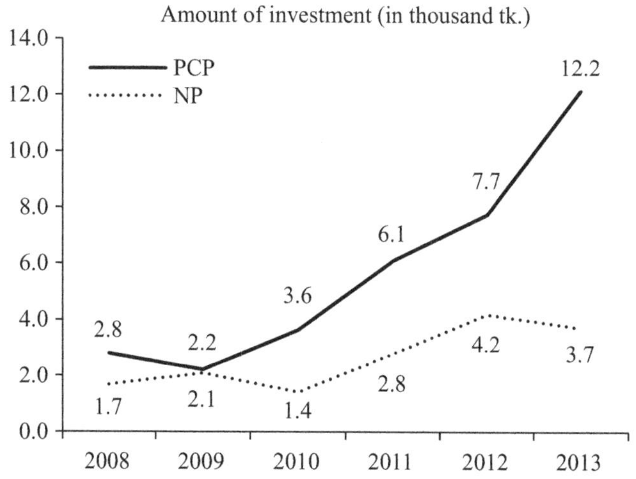

Fig. 16.5 Trends in investment

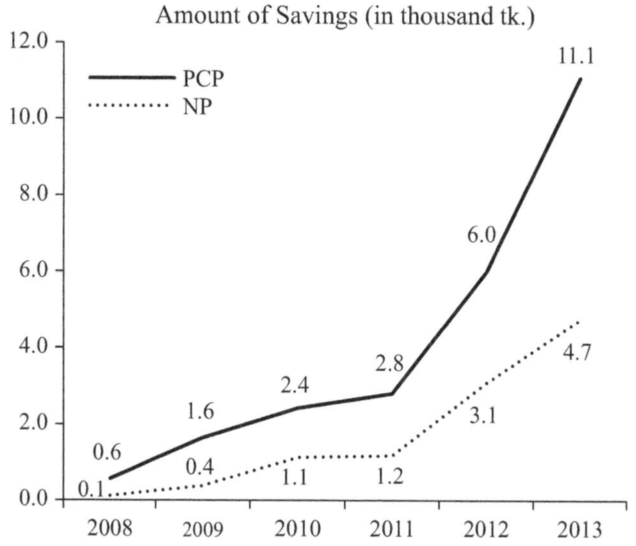

Fig. 16.6 Trends in savings amounts

be able to graduate sustainably from poverty. Figures 16.7, 16.8 and 16.9 demonstrate the impact of PRIME on intensity of poverty.

Several important findings can be derived from the figures. Even in 2008, two years after the program started, both participating and non-participating HHs were homogenous in the context of poverty status. Although poverty started to decline from 2009, the visible impact of PRIME was evident from 2011, three years after the program began. In the subsequent years, intensity of poverty—upper poverty (Fig. 16.7), lower poverty (Fig. 16.8) and food poverty (Fig. 16.9)—declined for the program participants with financial and non-financial interventions (PCP) at a higher rate than for the non-participants (NP). In 2013, the net impact of both lower and upper poverty reduction of PRIME (PCP) was 15 percentage points, and it was 11 percentage points in case of food poverty reduction. Certainly, the question arises, what would have happened if the HHs had received only finance? Khalily et al. (2015b) disaggregated the data and reassessed the impact of poverty. They showed that the intensity of poverty reduction reduced by 50 percent. Such decrease in poverty based on the cost of basic need method does not necessarily imply that these households have sustainably graduated from poverty. We define sustainable poverty reduction in the context of multi-dimensional poverty and term the households as sustainable graduated households from poverty, if they are below the deprivation benchmark.

Fig. 16.7 Trends in UPL. Note: *UPL* upper poverty line

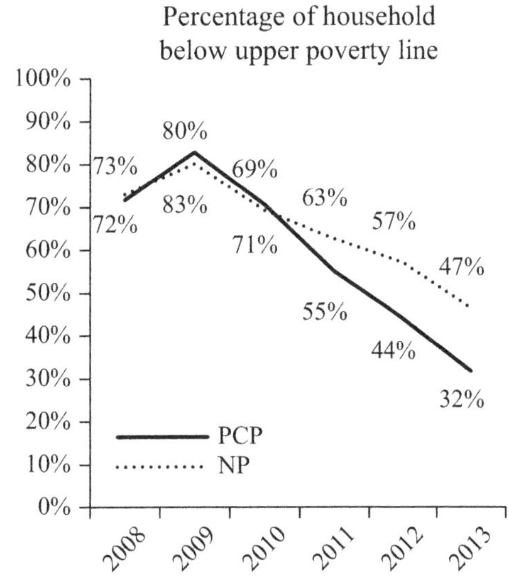

Fig. 16.8 Trends in LPL. Note: *LPL* lower poverty line

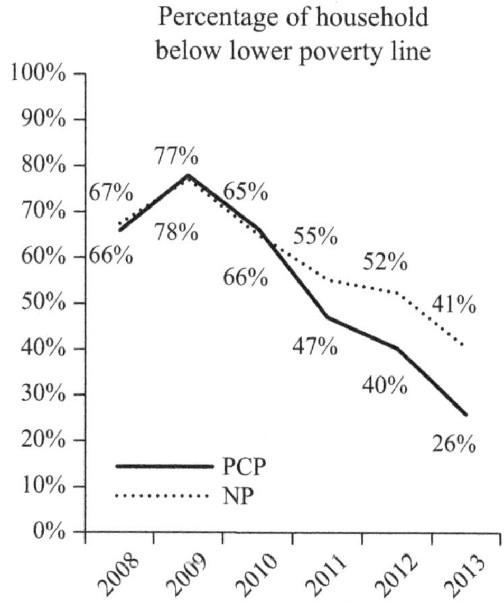

Fig. 16.9 Trends in FPL. Note: *FPL* food poverty line

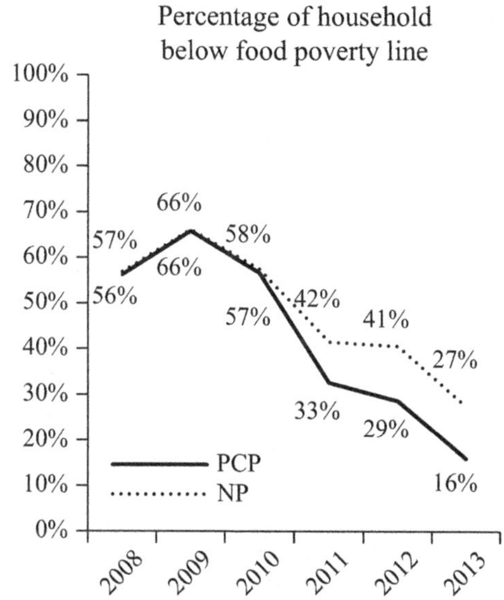

16.3.2 *Multi-Dimensional Poverty as a Proxy for Sustainable Graduation*

A simple cost of basic needs (CBN)-based poverty measure does not necessarily include all dimensions of poverty as noted in the sustainable development goals. Households with access to different resources—economic, financial, infrastructure and community resources—are more empowered and better capable of coping with vulnerability. Khalily et al. (2015b) estimated multidimensional poverty index (MPI) considering the dimensions as developed by Alkire-Foster (Alkire et al. 2015). They estimated MPI based on 20 items representing five dimensions—food poverty,[4] education, health, quality of life and social security. Their estimates showed that program participants (PCP) had lesser amount of deprivation than non-participants. As expected, the headcount ratio under consumption-based poverty was lower than deprivation-based poverty. Multi-average headcount under the former measure was 31.3 percent and it increased by 20 percentage point to 51.3 percent for program participants. But the rate increased by 29 percentage to 75 percent for non-participants. Consequently, the PRIME program had contributed to reducing multi-dimensional poverty by some 15 percentage points. Similar finding was also reported in Ahmed and Khalily (2016), but the question is who are the most benefitted—older participants or new participants?

We classified multi-dimensional poverty by the duration of participation. The results are reported in Table 16.7. It is quite evident that with increase in participation in PRIME, multi-dimensional poverty has systematically declined. It was only 15.02 percent for the PRIME participants with participation of over three years compared with 65.95 percent in the initial or base participation year. This was also corroborated by our Logit estimates. This means that the intensity of deprivation is lower for the participants with a longer duration in PRIME. Compared to the base or initial year, the odds ratio suggests that intensity of deprivation was seven times lower for the participants with a participation of over three years, after controlling for household characteristics and unobservable regional characteristics (Table 16.8).

[4]We have modified the dimensions of Alkire-Foster MPI. The Alkire-Foster MPI seems to consider that nobody is food poor, which is not true. A food poor can not graduate from multidimensional poverty. Therefore, we include 'Food Poverty' as another dimension. We considered that fewer items as used by Alkire-Foster will not capture any changes in deprivation in the intermediate term. As such, we have revised the items and our list includes 20 items.

Table 16.7 Intensity of multi-dimensional poverty by duration of participation in PRIME

Years of participation in PRIME as of year 2013	*Percentage*
Zero year	65.95
One to three years	19.03
More than three years	15.02

Table 16.8 Determinant of multi-dimensional poverty

Variables	*Intensity of deprivation*[a]
PRIME plus membership = zero year	Base
PRIME plus membership = One to three years	−0.0579***
	(0.0133)
PRIME plus membership = more than three years	−0.0705***
	(0.0145)

Figures in parentheses are standard errors

Level of significance: $***p < 0.01$, $**p < 0.05$, $*p < 0.1$

[a]Value of intensity of deprivation ranges from 0 to 1

The discussion reveals that microfinance contributes to different welfare outcomes. The question is, why? The mechanism at the household level is simple. It is through increase in savings and investment, multiple income opportunities, asset accumulation, skill development and technical assistance, and improvement in access to social institutions like education and health. These were evident from different studies in Bangladesh (see Khandker 1998; Khandker et al. 2016; Osmani et al. 2015; Khalily et al. 2015b; Ahmed et al. 2017). But not all households benefitted from participation in microfinance. Least benefitted groups were female-headed households, single income source depended day-labor households.

The evidence that microfinance along with non-financial services contributes to achieving sustainable development goals is likely to influence economic growth.

16.4 Impact of Microfinance on Economic Growth

Only in recent years, researchers have started addressing the issue of macroeconomic impact of microfinance. Such interest has arisen particularly because of the expanded scale and scope of microfinance services. Quite a number of studies (both theoretical and empirical) have been conducted on the macro impact of microfinance services.

Macroeconomic impacts have been assessed using both partial equilibrium and general equilibrium. Buera, Kaboskim and Shin (2012) used both the frameworks. They showed that impact outcomes differ. Using the partial equilibrium framework, they found that the aggregate output and capital increases but total factor productivity decreases. These impacts do not exist in general equilibrium framework. They reported that in general equilibrium, expanded microfinance services have only a marginal impact on per capita income because increase in total factor productivity was offset by lower capital accumulation. However, wages, interest rates and redistribution effects are more pronounced in general equilibrium analysis.

Expanded microfinance network and financial services along with non-financial interventions do contribute to improving the wellbeing of the participating households. Findings are diverse. Evidence suggests that expanded financial services complemented by non-financial services contribute to improved consumption smoothening and food security, increase in micro enterprise productivity and investment in agriculture and housing (e.g., Khandker et al. 2013; Khalily and Khaleque 2013; Imai and Azam 2012). These outcomes are quite expected if one examines the portfolio of microfinance institutions. As has been stated earlier, MFIs in Bangladesh offer diverse services: higher loan size for micro enterprises, training and technical assistance, and increase in the share of agricultural loans, loans for housing, health and education, among others. All these directly benefit the participating households and increase capital or wealth accumulation at the village or community level, bringing about a positive effect on products and factor markets. In other words, inter-sectoral flow of resources and capital accumulation as well as higher total factor productivity contributes to development. Donou-Adonsou and Sylwester (2015), through their theoretical framework, argued that expanded microfinance services can contribute to development through enterprise development and increase in output. They further argued that it will reduce income inequality and poverty. Using data from 71 developing countries, they showed that microcredit has positive impacts on economic growth and total factor productivity.

Khalily et al. (2015b) showed that over sixty percent of the households and Osmani et al. (2015) showed that more than 50 percent of the households had borrowed at least once in their lifetime from microfinance institutions. With such level of expansion of microfinance services, the annual disbursement has increased. More than Tk. 1200 billion was disbursed in 2016–2017 including almost 30 percent as micro enterprise loans with a ceiling of Tk. 1 million. With such an expansion, microfinance is certain to have both direct and indirect induced effects on the economy. What has been its contribution to the GDP? There are no empirical studies on the macro economic impact of microfinance in Bangladesh.

Sultan and Masih (2016) established causality between microfinance and GDP in Bangladesh. They showed that increase in micro credit has a significant positive impact on GDP growth of Bangladesh. However, they also demonstrated that growth also influences demand for micro credit. The authors, therefore, found a bi-directional relationship between microfinance and GDP growth.

The study by Raihan et al. (2017) is perhaps the pioneering study that examined the issue of impact of microfinance on GDP growth in Bangladesh using the statistic CGE framework. They estimated the impacts of microfinance on GDP growth under three scenarios. They are (i) flexible wage rates of both unskilled and skilled labor; (ii) assumption of fixed wage rate of unskilled labor and flexible wage rate for skilled labor; and (iii) assumption of fixed wage rate of both unskilled and skilled labor. The estimates of reduction in GDP growth rate are reported in Table 16.9 under the stated assumptions, had there been no microfinance services.

As reported in the Table 16.9, the real GDP growth in Bangladesh would fall between 8.9 and 11.9 percent, had there been no microfinance services. Such a fall will be even larger for the rural GDP. They estimated that the rural real GDP growth rate would reduce, under different scenarios, between 12.6 and 16.6 percent without the role of microfinance. Why would contribution of microfinance be so high in the growth of rural

Table 16.9 Estimates of reduction in GDP growth rate under different assumptions

GDP	*Assumption of flexible wage rate of both unskilled and skilled labor*	*Assumption of fixed wage rate of unskilled and flexible wage rate of skilled labor*	*Assumption of fixed wage rate of both unskilled and skilled labor*
Rural real GDP	−16.6	−14.0	−12.6
Real GDP	−11.9	−10.0	−8.9

Source: Raihan et al. (2017)

GDP? The authors built their estimates on the following information: (i) MFI capital operates through private investment; (ii) 47 percent of MFI credit goes to productive investment; (iii) MFI capital stock accounts for 9.89 percent of the total capital stock in the economy in 2012; (iv) 15 percent of micro credit is utilized in construction or maintenance of the house; and (v) total factor productivity of micro enterprises is 3.53 percent higher compared to counter-factual of no micro credit. However, the authors argued that macroeconomic impacts of microfinance on GDP growth was under-estimated for not able to consider under-employment and consumption smoothing out of microfinance, and human capital development as a result of higher income of the participating households.

Microfinance does have an impact on employment and wages. Rural wages increase due to increase in the flow of microfinance, as microfinance creates self-employment of the borrowers who were mostly otherwise employed in the labor market. As a result, supply of wage laborers reduce. Given the demand for laborers, such a fall in supply of laborer increase wages (Khandker et al. 1995). The result shows that there is a substitution of laborer from wage laborer to self-employment. Khalily et al. (2015b) showed that the average full-time employment created in micro enterprises was 1.63 persons. Based on this simple fact, it was estimated that microfinance might have created more than 10 million new jobs at the household and/or micro enterprise level.

The critical question is what is the transmission mechanism through which microfinance impacts GDP growth? Raihan et al. (2017) showed that absence of microfinance reduces capital stock with subsequent effects on the economy. First, fall in capital stock will cause fall in outputs in those microfinance–driven sectors, which will have an adverse impact on the decline in real GDP. Second, price of capital will increase, and wage and demand for labor will move upward to compensate for the fall in capital stock. Third, with higher prices of capital and labor, the primary factor cost will increase in the production process. Fourth, this increase in primary factor cost and intermediate input cost will lead to a fall in outputs in all sectors including non-MFI intensive sectors. Consequently, the real GDP will fall at a higher price. Higher price will be induced by increase in cost, which will have further impact on fall in real GDP. Finally, this higher cost and price of inputs will also adversely affect the real GDP through the foreign exchange market.

The underlying argument is the intensity of microfinance participation in financial and economic systems. Microfinance, because of its wide network of operations, contributes to financial development that leads to efficient allocation of resources, higher productivity, increase in capital investment and overall economic growth. Without the participation in microfinance, a vast number of low-income households remain outside the financial system. Therefore, an increase in the intensity of access to finance, both in-depth and outreach, contributes positively to sustainable economic growth (e.g., Alimukhamedova 2013). However, Alimukhamedova argued that this will start with the positive impact of microfinance in reducing income inequality and poverty.

From the evidence, it is quite clear that microfinance contributes to the GDP in Bangladesh. This is because of the intensity of services provided by MFIs. There has been product diversification over the last three decades. Loan size has increased, and so has the intensity of financial inclusion in Bangladesh. All the positive changes that have taken place in the microfinance sector have increased the intensity of financial development and productive investment.

16.5 Challenges and Policy Implications

Finance does play a role in sustainable growth and development. While banks and capital markets play a major role in developing the private sector and increasing the intensity of financial inclusion in urban areas for sustainable economic growth, these markets have a limited role in attaining sustainable development goals of no poverty reduction and no hunger. Microfinancial and non-financial services appear to be more effective in attaining several major goals of sustainable development through expanding the scale of operations, mostly in rural areas. Scaling up of microfinance services and increase in the microfinance network has contributed to increasing financial inclusion and promoting enterprises in rural areas. Because of the dominating presence of MFIs in financing different sectors like agriculture and rural enterprises and its inter-linkages with other sectors of the economy, microfinance has a diversified roles. Not only does it contribute to attaining sustainable development goals, it also contributes to economic growth and development. From the analysis, it appeared that microfinance has contributed to economic growth and development because of increase in financial development and capital assets as well as total factor productivity. In the years to come, the contribution of microfinance to the GDP will increase because of increase in loans for micro and small enterprises, and human capital development.

Finance is a powerful intervention for sustainable poverty alleviation. It is equally important for sustainable economic growth and redistribution of resources. Finance and non-financial interventions together with government policy support make finance more powerful in sustainable development. The ultimate outcome of sustainable development strategies is to make society more sensitive, just and rational for the welfare of today and tomorrow. The question is not about finance or non-financial services. The issue is, can non-financial services bring the desired changes without finance? Can finance alone bring about the desired level of sustainable development? The answer is, no. What is important in attaining sustainable development is augmenting the role of finance, including insurance, with the support of non-financial services and integration of both financial and non-financial services within a broad framework. Government needs to play a crucial role in integrating these financial and non-financial services within some alternate and competing institutional framework. But they are subject to some major challenges.

The most remarkable challenge will be *vulnerability due to climate change*. The best example would be vulnerability due to cyclones and tornados. When these shocks strike, they cause collateral damages for the HHs and environment. In 2009, Sidr struck the southern districts. In a recent study, Khalily et al. (2017) showed that only one-third of the households affected by Sidr could recover to the pre-Sidr situation. Some 20 percent could not recover at all. Others could recover partially of varying degree. Who could cope better? The study showed that households with access to microfinance had better coping ability. But the collateral damages caused by cyclones are much higher than the gains from participation in microfinance. With further loans in the post-disaster period, households were able to regain economic activities and generate income for maintaining livelihood. Access to microfinance can generate additional benefits, but it can be more effective when complimented by interventions for risk minimization.

Micro insurance becomes one of the major interventions that can be effective in attaining sustainable development goals. In Bangladesh, micro credit is linked to MFI managed informal micro insurance to cover the risk of credit liability in case of death of the borrower or spouse. Collateral damage is not covered. The critical issue is covering risk of property damage of the poor households due to climate change. Micro insurance can be effective in Bangladesh. In the Philippines, the regulatory authority has recognized micro insurance and promoted alternate institutional arrangements like mutual insurance of microfinance borrowers. They recognize damage to property and death in micro insurance. In Bangladesh, there is always a debate: who will do it? The insurance market has failed to provide services to these poor households or microfinance borrowers. Because of the conflict of interest, MFIs will perhaps not be institutions for providing microinsurance services. Alternate institutional arrangements, as in the Philippines, have to be examined and considered.

One of the major roles played by MFIs in Bangladesh is in general *financial literacy*. The borrowers know why and when to borrow, but in most cases, they are not aware of other financial instruments and institutions. Despite their participation in microfinance programs, their level of financial literacy is reasonably low. This is not about them but also about those with a low level of education. Khalily (2017) showed that financial literacy has a positive impact on financial inclusion and access to different institutions. He found that households in rural areas have limited financial literacy. From the perspective of solving the problem of asymmetric information and access to information, at least poor households need to be financially literate.

One of the interventions that has been identified in SDGs is the *role of the community*. It has come as a reference in some of the goals like community action. Community action will be required for adapting to climate change when individual household level action becomes ineffective. Linking finance with community level actions can make finance more effective. The reason that MFIs are successful in Bangladesh is their ability to integrate household level and community level interventions. As such, the government may need to deliver community level interventions, apart from building physical infrastructure, through MFIs when such integration is required for maximizing welfare of the poor households and development.

The role of microfinance in the GDP and in sustainable development is expected to increase at a faster rate in future because of the increasing investment in productive assets and human capital development. Increasing emphasis on micro and small enterprise financing, particularly in rural areas, will not only create employment opportunities and increase income, it will have sustainable impact on graduation from poverty and increase in GDP at a higher rate. What is needed is the complimentary role of the government to support the activities of microfinance institutions to finance more effectively. It should also be recognized that MFIs operate in a different segments of financial markets than the segments that banks operate in.

References

Ahmed, Q. K., & Khalily, B. (2016). Measuring multidimensional poverty based on evidence from programmed initiatives of monga eradication (PRIME) in North-Western Bangladesh. In Q. K. Ahmad & S. Ahmed (Eds.), *Bangladesh development: Some issues and perspectives, essays in honour of A M A Muhith*. Dhaka: Palok Publishers.

Ahmed, M., Khalily, B., Khaleque, M. A., & Nawal, S. N. (2017). Flexible micro finance program: Effectiveness and efficiency to reach the extreme poor. *Eurasian Journal of Business and Economics, 10*(20), 47–70.

Alimukhamedova, N. (2013). Contribution of microfinance to economic growth: Transmission channel and the ways to test it. *Business and Economic Horizons, 9*(4), 27–43.

Alkire, S., Roche, J. M., Ballon, P., Foster, J., Santos, M. E., & Seth, S. (2015). *Multidimensional poverty measurement and analysis*. Oxford: Oxford University Press.

Bađun, M. (2009). Intermediation by banks and economic growth: A review of empirical evidence. *Financial Theory and Practice, 33*(2), 121–152.

Banerjee, A., Karlan, D., & Zinman, J. (2015). Six randomized evaluations of microcredit: Introduction and further steps. *American Economic Journal: Applied Economics, 7*(1), 1–21.

Beck, T., Ross Levine, R., & Loayza, N. (2000). Finance and the sources of growth. *Journal of Financial Economics, 58*, 261–300.

Buera, F. J., Kaboski, J. P., & Shin, Y. (2012). *The macroeconomics of microfinance*. (Working Paper 17905). Cambridge: National Bureau of Economic Research.

Chirwa, T. G., & Odhiambo, N. M. (2016). Macroeconomic determinants of economic growth: A review of international literature. *South East European Journal of Economics and Business, 11*(2), 33–47.

Credit and Development Forum. (2017). *Bangladesh microfinance statistics*. Dhaka.

Demetriades, P. O., & Hussein, K. A. (1996). Does financial development cause economic growth? Time-series evidence from 16 countries. *Journal of Development Economics, 51*(2), 387–411.

Demirgüç-Kunt, A., Klapper, L., & Singer, D. (2017). *Financial inclusion and inclusive growth: Review of recent empirical evidence*. Policy research working paper: No. WPS 8040. Washington, DC: World Bank Group.

Donou-Adonsou, C. F., & Sylwester, K. (2015). Macroeconomic effects of microfinance: Evidence from developing countries. *Journal of Econometrics, 41*(1), 21–35.

Dupas, P., & Robinson, J. (2013). Why don't the poor save more? Evidence from health savings experiments. *American Economic Review, 103*(4), 1138–1171.

Fernando, N. A. (2007). *Low-income households' access to financial services: International experience, measures for improvement, and the future*. Manila: Asian Development Bank.

Fry, M. J. (1988). *Money, interest, and banking in economic development*. Baltimore: Johns Hopkins University Press.

Gupta, K. L. (1984). *Finance and economic growth in developing countries*. London: Croom Helm.

Honohan, P. (2004). Financial development, growth and poverty: How close are the links? In *Financial development and economic growth* (pp. 1–37). London: Palgrave Macmillan.

Imai, K. S., & Azam, M. S. (2012). Does microfinance reduce poverty in Bangladesh? New evidence from household panel data. *Journal of Development Studies, 48*(5), 633–653.

Khalily, M. A. B. (2002). *Impact of formal credit on agricultural production in Bangladesh*. Dhaka: Bureau of Business Research, University of Dhaka.

Khalily, M. A. B. (2013). *Impact of PRIME interventions at the household level—Fifth round*. Dhaka: Palli Karma-Sahayak Foundation (PKSF), Mimeo.

Khalily, M. A. B. (2017). Financial inclusion, regulation and education in Bangladesh. In N. Yoshino & P. J. Morgan (Eds.), *Financial inclusion, regulation and education: Asian perspectives*. Tokyo: Asian Development Bank Institute.

Khalily, M. A. B., & Khaleque, A. (2013). *Access to credit and productivity of enterprises in Bangladesh: Is there a causality*. Working paper no. 20. Dhaka: Institute of Microfinance.

Khalily, M. A. B., & Others. (2015a). *Impact of PRIME in Monga Mitigation in South West Bangladesh*, PKSF-InM., Mimeo.

Khalily, M. A. B., Mia, P., Akthar, N., & Hasan, M. (2015b). *Access to financial services in Bangladesh*. Dhaka: Institute of Microfinance.

Khalily, M. A. B., Schevens, H., & Hasan, M. (2017). Does ex-ante access to microfinance matter in coping and climate change adaptation in southern region in Bangladesh? Dhaka: Institute of Inclusive Finance and Development (InM).

Khandker, S. R. (1998). *Fighting poverty with microcredit: Experience in Bangladesh*. Oxford: Oxford University Press.

Khandker, S. R., Khalily, M. A. B., & Khan, Z. (1995). Credit programs for the poor: Household and intra-household impacts and program sustainability. In *Proceedings of the workshop*. Dhaka: Bangladesh Institute of Development Studies.

Khandker, S. R., Samad, H. A., & Ali, R. (2013). *Does access to finance matter in microenterprise growth? Evidence from Bangladesh*. Washington, DC: The World Bank.

Khandker, S. R., Khalily, M. B., & Samad, H. A. (2016). *Beyond ending poverty: The dynamics of microfinance in Bangladesh*. Washington, DC: The World Bank.

Levine, R. (1997). *Financial development and economic growth: Views and agenda.* Washington, DC: The World Bank.
Levine, R. (2005). Finance and growth: Theory and evidence. *Handbook of economic growth, 1*, 865–934.
Mercieca, P. (2010). Aid and economic growth in developing countries: A literature review. *Bank of Valletta Review, 41*, 1–22.
Ocasio, V. M. (2012). *Essays on the role of in financial deepening, economic growth and development.* Doctoral dissertation, Colorado State University. Libraries.
Osmani, S. R., Ahmed, A., Latif, M. A., & Sen, B. (2015). *Poverty and vulnerability in rural Bangladesh.* Dhaka: Institute of Microfinance and The University Press Limited.
Popov, A. (2017). *Evidence on finance and economic growth.* Working paper no. 2115. European Central Bank.
Raihan, S., Osmani, S. R., & Khalily, M. B. (2017). The macro impact of microfinance in Bangladesh: A CGE analysis. *Economic Modelling, 62*, 1–15.
Renelt, D. (1991). *Economic growth: A review of the theoretical and empirical literature* (Vol. 678). Washington, DC: World Bank Publications.
Rutherford, S. (2000). *The poor and their money* (pp. 6–7). New Delhi: Oxford University Press.
Sen, A. (2018). *Collective choice and social welfare.* Cambridge, MA: Harvard University Press.
Solow, R. M. (1956). A contribution to the theory of economic growth. *The Quarterly Journal of Economics, 70*(1), 65–94.
Sultan, Y., & Masih, M. (2016). *Does microfinance affect economic growth? Evidence from Bangladesh based on ARDL approach* (MPRA Paper No. 72123). Munich PErsonal RePEc Archive.
Yunus, M. (2007). *Banker to the poor: Micro-lending and the battle against world poverty.* New York: PublicAffairs.

CHAPTER 17

Development of Capital Market and Financing Future Growth in Bangladesh

Monzur Hossain

17.1 Introduction

A well-developed capital market is essential for financing future growth of an economy. It promotes private sector-led growth as well as it works as catalyst for deepening and diversifying the financial system. A well-functioning capital market is, thus, necessary for establishing an important link between financial development and economic growth. The capital market of Bangladesh is still in rudimentary stage in terms of its sophistication and depth. The country has two stock exchanges, namely, Dhaka Stock Exchange (DSE) and Chittagong Stock Exchanges (CSE). Though market capitalization has been on an increasing trend, the market already has experienced several crashes for which confidence of shareholders is still low on this market. Apart from this, secondary bond market has not yet been properly developed which deters long-term financing opportunities.

The regulatory framework of the capital market is maintained by the "Securities and Exchange Commission" (SEC) of Bangladesh, which was established on June 8, 1993, under the "Securities and Exchange Commission Act, 1993". The regulatory body often devises regulation on

M. Hossain (✉)
Bangladesh Institute of Development Studies (BIDS), Dhaka, Bangladesh

M. Hossain (ed.), *Bangladesh's Macroeconomic Policy*,
https://doi.org/10.1007/978-981-15-1244-5_17

a "learning by doing" basis. The activities of both the stock exchanges are autonomous non-profit in nature with Dhaka being the largest capital market of the country. The bourses operate in fully automated systems.

However, Bangladesh's capital market has seen a phenomenal growth in size, depth and maturity in recent years. Confidence of the investors was somewhat regained after the last crash in 2010 with various regulatory and institutional reforms undertaken by the SEC. Market capitalization increased from BDT 97.58 billion in FY2003 to BDT 3185.75 billion in FY2015, while DSE Broad Index (DSEX) posted around 3.2 percent compound annual growth rate (CAGR) during 2013–2015. Market capitalization in FY2015 is about 18.38 percent of GDP which was only 6 percent in 2003 (Tables 17.1 and 17.9). About 2.72 million beneficiary owners' (BO) accounts exist as of December 2017 (BSEC, Annual Report, various issues).

The role of capital market in industrial investment financing is still limited compared to bank finance. In FY2015, the amount of industrial term loans disbursed by banks and non-bank financial institutions (NBFIs) was at BDT 597.8 billion (of which the amount disbursed by NBFIs was BDT 77.3 billion) compared with only BDT 59.9 billion by new capital issued through private placements, public offerings and right offerings in the capital market. This is mainly due to underdeveloped secondary bond market.

The stock market in Bangladesh already experienced at least two crashes—one in 1996 and the other one in 2010. In both cases, some dishonest market players took benefits of thin capital market and policy inconsistencies of regulators. Though some of the perpetrators were identified, no actions were undertaken against them because of political patronization. However, after each of the crashes, SEC has taken some initiatives to strengthen the regulatory framework that has helped regain the confidence of the investors. During the global financial crisis in 2007–2008, while major global stock market indices declined by 30–60 percent, DSE general index (DGEN), the benchmark index of Dhaka Stock Exchange (DSE), decreased by only 7.1 percent in the year 2008, which is mainly due to its limited connectivity with global capital market.

Some of the key concerns for the development of the capital market include inadequate flow of securities with good fundamentals, corporate and government bonds; inadequate supply of professional investment analysts; slow growth of institutional investments, such as mutual funds, pension funds, insurance fund and professional portfolio manager fund; and weak monitoring and enforcement capacity of the regulator. Apart from these, the market also encounters some structural weaknesses that affect its overall development. For the development of the market, it is important to establish a sound secondary bond market and a well-developed government securities market. Moreover, improvement of efficiency in pricing mechanism and cost of listing and adequate information disclosure mechanism in order to ensure quality information are important for better functioning of the stock markets. Against the backdrop, this chapter focuses on the development trend of the capital market in Bangladesh, and challenges and opportunities with some policy recommendations.

The chapter is organized as follows. Section 17.2 reviews the relevant literature and Sect. 17.3 provides an overview of the capital market in Bangladesh. Section 17.4 discusses the market crash in 2010 and the role of the monetary policy in bursting stock bubble. Section 17.5 discusses the role of capital market on meeting long-term financing needs, and Sect. 17.6 provides some policy reform measures. Finally, Sect. 17.7 concludes the chapter.

17.2 Literature Review

The capital market is an integral part of financial system of any country, and it plays a significant role in the economic growth of the country. There exists a wide range of literature in support of the mutual relationship between capital market development and economic growth. Garretsen, Lensink and Sterken (2004) identified a potential positive relationship between economic growth and financial market's development. Their observations and findings suggest that a one percent improvement of economic growth rate leads to 0.4 percent rise in market capitalization/GDP ratio. Mohtadi and Agarwal (2001) conducted an analysis using panel data of 21 developing countries from 1977 to 1997 and showed that development of stock market is essential for long-run economic growth. They argued that while market liquidity (turnover ratio) contributes directly to growth, market size (capitalization ratio) works indirectly on growth by influencing investments. So, capital market and economic growth generally demonstrate an intricate two-way relationship.

In context of Bangladesh, Mia, Qamruzzaman and Ara (2014) investigated the dynamic relationship between stock market development and economic growth by using annual time series data from 2000 to 2013, and their studies reveal the existence of a long-run relationship between stock market development and economic growth in Bangladesh. And, the growth and development of stock market largely depends on the investment decisions of the investors. Sarbabidya and Saha (2018) conducted a field survey of DSE and CSE, and identified risk tolerance, true accounting information, past and present stock performance, earning per share, GDP and other macroeconomic issues of the country and political stability as important factors which have significant impact on the investment decisions in the stock market of Bangladesh. Masuduzzaman, Rahman and Ahammed (2013) pointed out that an integrated financial market can give rise to a sustainable growth in the capital stock market in the long run. Mujeri and Rahman (2009) highlighted that, for achieving a sustained rapid growth in the capital market, it is important to have a better liberalized, market based, effectively supervised and regulated financial sector. They also proposed to undertake policies in order to form a vibrant secondary debt market, develop institutional investors capable of providing comparatively long tenured funds and, at a more crucial note, improve efficient risk management.

Rahman, Islam, Hossain and Naser (2016) suggested that DSE is not efficient in the weak form (random walk). They also propose that DSE should emphasize on pursuing policies to facilitate the stockholders and investors in remaining updated about financial and non-financial information regarding the performance of listed companies in a timely manner, to improve the operation of DSE. Shah (2016) examined the impacts of the reform measures taken by the regulatory body of the stock exchanges, Bangladesh Security Exchange Commission (BSEC) under the second and third Capital Market Development Programs (CMDPs 2 and 3) on the capital market of Bangladesh. His findings suggest that under the CMDP 2, BSEC's state-of-the-art market surveillance system came into operation which increased the transparency of market transactions and had a significant impact on enhancing investors' confidence. The capital market reforms taken under CMDP 2 and the CMDP 3 are also expected to facilitate the development of bond and equity capital markets by mobilizing resources to more productive sectors, increasing the number of bond and equity issues, both primary and secondary, thereby, diversifying the financial instruments and broadening investor base. These measures will assist in the sustainable development of the capital market bringing balance to the bank-dominated financial system.

Macroeconomic environment also affects both financial and capital markets. Hossain and Rafiq (2012) analyzed the impact of inflation on the financial sector in Bangladesh. They showed that inflation has significant impact on the value of stocks and value traded. However, the rise in inflation decreases equity returns and market capitalization, as expected. Applying the threshold autoregressive conditional heteroscedasticity model, they showed that there is a threshold effect of inflation and a long-run negative inflation-finance relationship exists. Though inflation seems beneficial for financial indicators up to a certain level; after crossing the threshold level, it generates negative effect on various indicators such as bank assets, private credit and deposits as well as market capitalization, total issued capital and turnover.

17.3 An Overview of the Capital Market

The stock market in Bangladesh consists of two stock exchanges—DSE and CSE exchanges. Though DSE is bigger in terms of its capitalization and trading volume, over time CSE is also increasing its activities. While the number of listed securities in DSE was 559 in 2015, it was 298 in the CSE. Total market capitalization stood at BDT 3185.75 billion in the DSE and BDT 2496.85 billion in the CSE in 2015. Both the stock exchanges have shown steady progress in terms of all indicators of capital market over time. The analysis in this chapter are made using the data of DSE for the period 2000–2015, considering the fact that DSE is the key component of the capital market in Bangladesh.

Average daily turnover grew from BDT 66 million in 2003 to BDT 4156 million in 2015 (Table 17.1). As Fig. 17.1a shows, DSE general index started moving upward from 2006 and continued before the crash in 2010. The bullish behavior of the market at that period was attributed to overexposure of banks and financial institutions (FIs), speculative behavior of small investors and less participation of institutional investors. However, after the crash in 2010, the market seemed to have returned to its normal behavior (Fig. 17.1b).

Turnover velocity, measured as a ratio of turnover over market capitalization, also indicates the stock market bubble and burst situation. Yearly turnover velocity in recent years ranges around 40, which was 140 in 2011 indicating a drastic fall in market liquidity (Fig. 17.2).

The growth of companies listed in the securities market was not very much encouraging as around seven companies listed in each year on average. Market capitalization reached its highest level in 2010 at 31.16 percent of GDP (Table 17.1). And after 2011, it again fell below 20 percent and has remained so since then. In FY2015, market capitalization was 18.38 percent of GDP.

Table 17.1 Indicators of capital market development

Fiscal Year	*Listed companies*	*Issued capital (BDT million)*	*Market cap. (BDT million)*	*Market cap. as percent of GDP*	*Daily average turnover (BDT million)*	*General index/ broad index*
2003	251 (1.2 percent)	46,055 (27.64 percent)	97587.0 (33.68 percent)	2.93 percent	66 (−12.4 percent)	967.88 (16.55 percent)
2005	251 (−3.09 percent)	85722.6 (73.07 percent)	215421.9 (−4.22 percent)	5.18 percent	250 (26.26 percent)	1339.53 (−32.05 percent)
2010	273 (−9.00 percent)	806839.1 (32.86 percent)	2853892.2 (5.67 percent)	31.16 percent	9936 (186.84 percent)	6117.23 (−0.59 percent)
2015	292 (−10.43 percent)	1,127,410 (3.25 percent)	3,185,749 (−1.90 percent)	18.38 percent	4156.1 (−4.55 percent)	4507.58 (−1.65 percent)

Source: Bangladesh Securities and Exchange Commission, Annual Report (Various issues); Bangladesh Economic Review, various issues

[a]Percentage growth from previous year is in parenthesis

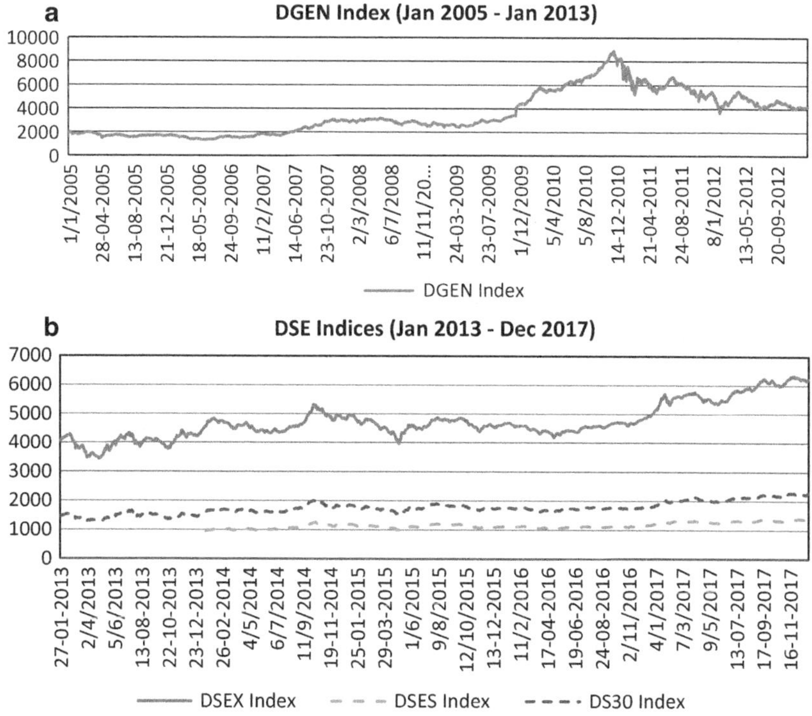

Fig. 17.1 DSE general index, 2005–2013. (Source: Data—DSE website. DSE replaced DSE general index (DGEN) with DSE broad index (DSEX) in January 2013. And DSE introduced DSE shariah index (DSES) in January 2015)

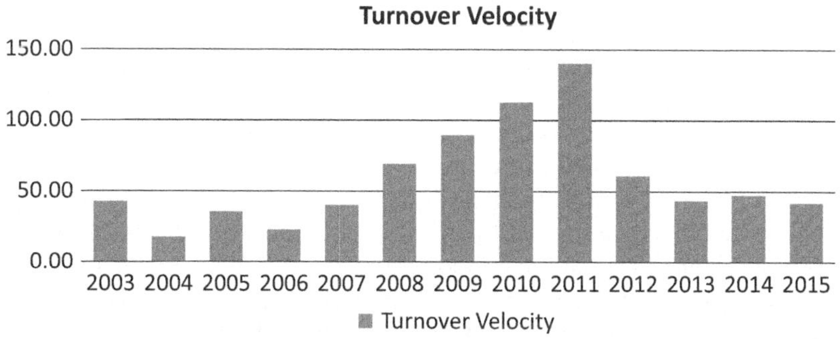

Fig. 17.2 Market liquidity in terms of turnover velocity. Note: Turnover velocity is calculated as a ratio of turnover over market capitalization. (Source: Economic Trends, Bangladesh Bank)

In regard to performance of different sectors, a shift can be observed before and after the crash in 2010. As the crash in 2010 is characterized partly by the dynamic inconsistency in Bangladesh Bank's policies regarding banks and FIs exposure to the market, the dominance of banks and financial institutions has reduced after 2010 (Table 17.2). In the new environment, some industries such as pharmaceuticals, fuel and power, cement and telecommunications sector overtook the position which is a good sign for industrialization of the country.

Mutual funds, pension funds and bonds play a vital role for strengthening capital market as well as the economy. There were 41 mutual funds with market capitalization of Tk. 30.4 billion in 2015. Market capital of the bond market was Tk. 555.2 billion compared to total market capitalization of Tk. 3185.7 billion (Table 17.3). Pension funds have not yet been floated in the market. Therefore, still the capital market in Bangladesh lacks enough maturity in terms of financing future growth prospects of the country.

17.3.1 Market Volatility: Risk and Return

The price-earning (P/E) ratio of most of the DSE shares depicts a substantial downfall throughout the years after December 2010 (Table 17.4). However, several sectors, such as service and real estate, jute, ceramic, food and engineering, have displayed a turnaround in fortune by December 2015. Though investors value P/E ratio most in making investment decisions, however, relying mainly on P/E is not appropriate because a higher P/E ratio is risky and may not reflect company fundamentals and, therefore, there is possibility of price fall in future.

The average volatility of DSEX (DSE broad index), as measured by standard deviation, was estimated to be 39.95 in December 2015 indicating a more stable state as depicted in Fig. 17.4. Figure 17.3 reports the daily fluctuation of broad price index and turnover at DSE. The marked lines in Fig. 17.4 represent the monthly standard deviation (volatility) of daily price indexes along with daily price indexes. From both the figures (Figs. 17.3 and 17.4), some episodes of market volatility is evident during 2013–2015 with a decreasing trend of price indexes. Volatility was substantially low during the second half of 2015, indicating a stable market condition in recent years. Therefore, P/E ratios and the volatility of DSE index can be used to assess the risks of the market.

Table 17.2 Sector-wise performance in the capital market (percent of total market capitalization) over 2003–2015

End of period	*Banks*	*Financial institutions*	*Mutual funds*	*Fuel and power*	*Pharmaceuticals*	*Services and real estate*	*Cement industries*	*Insurance*	*Telecommunications*	*Others*
2003	28.31	–	1.37	5.28	15.52	2.19	5.12	5.19	–	37.02
2005	46.27	–	1.06	1.91	15.25	0.81	14.71	3.93	–	16.6
2010	28.29	12.46	1.20	13.24	7.15	1.18	2.41	4.65	13.98	15.44
2015	13.55	5.60	1.07	14.29	14.30	0.78	7.19	2.79	17.21	23.22

Source: Monthly Economic Trends, Bangladesh Bank

Table 17.3 Indicators of mutual funds and bond market (DSE)

Fiscal year	*Listed mutual funds:*		*Bond market:*				
	Number of mutual funds	*Market capitalization (billion BDT)*	*Number of listed bonds*	*Government*	*Corporate*	*Debenture*	*Market capital (billion BDT)*
FY03	10	0.50	8	...	...	8	0.5
FY05	12	1.30	26	18	...	8	12.2
FY10	35	25.71	223	212	3	8	533.7
FY15	41	30.40	231	221	2	8	555.2

Source: Monthly review, various issues, Dhaka Stock Exchange Ltd; BSEC annual report, various issues

Table 17.4 Price earnings ratio of different sectors

Sector	*Sector-wise price earnings (P/E) ratio*							
	Dec-2004	*Dec-2005*	*Dec-2006*	*Dec-2007*	*Dec-2008*	*Dec-2010*	*Dec-2012*	*Dec-2015*
Bank	21.74	17.90	15.49	24.97	16.62	25.24	8.68	7.40
Financial institutions	–	33.83	7.88	15.13	25.26	47.27	15.19	15.13
Mutual fund	8.27	6.55	6.13	20.29	20.37	17.53	12.42	7.16
Engineering	18.62	14.14	17.34	28.57	30.24	50.10	19.08	29.53
Food and allied	10.11	9.13	18.69	23.28	16.93	27.30	20.99	30.30
Fuel and power	14.79	22.32	18.87	35.95	15.83	21.57	11.44	12.28
Jute	19.56	12.55	6.74	7.98	12.15	55.66	23.62	80.92
Textile	15.30	10.08	12.01	12.14	13.85	52.44	17.50	10.52
Pharmaceuticals	18.19	10.84	11.76	21.05	30.96	34.12	18.67	27.34
Paper and printing	1.82	4.69	6.62	6.23	9.36	126.93	29.85	16.70
Service and real estate	9.61	8.16	12.62	8.82	22.66	43.93	18.28	34.74
Cement	25.23	16.13	18.53	12.61	10.26	33.44	21.81	27.16
IT	25.11	10.46	11.12	15.25	46.52	64.91	22.92	17.44
Tannery	10.51	10.28	8.00	15.38	16.43	20.66	11.74	24.10
Ceramic	25.74	17.06	14.88	29.85	47.80	106.86	20.62	280.48
Insurance	26.92	20.87	10.24	15.59	21.81	64.64	22.25	10.55
Telecommunication	–	–	–	–	–	20.35	12.91	18.03
Travel and leisure	–	–	–	–	–	65.45	25.36	16.76
Miscellaneous	13.21	7.83	11.05	14.43	34.43	19.54	5.84	32.74
Market P/E	**18.40**	**13.85**	**14.51**	**23.58**	**18.42**	**29.16**	**12.10**	**15.24**

The sectors "Telecommunication" and "Travel and leisure" were incorporated in 2009 and 2010, respectively

Source: Monthly review, various issues, Dhaka Stock Exchange Ltd.

17.3.2 Mutual Funds and Their Performance

Mutual funds are the most widely known investment schemes around the world. In Bangladesh, 41 mutual funds were listed among the 555 listed securities in DSE as of December 2015. The market capitalization of all the mutual funds stood at BDT 30,420 million in December 2015, which was 19.5 percent higher compared to the same period in 2014. The share of mutual funds in total market capitalization (BDT 3185.7 billion) stood at merely 0.95 percent in 2015 indicating it as a less popular instrument in Bangladesh.

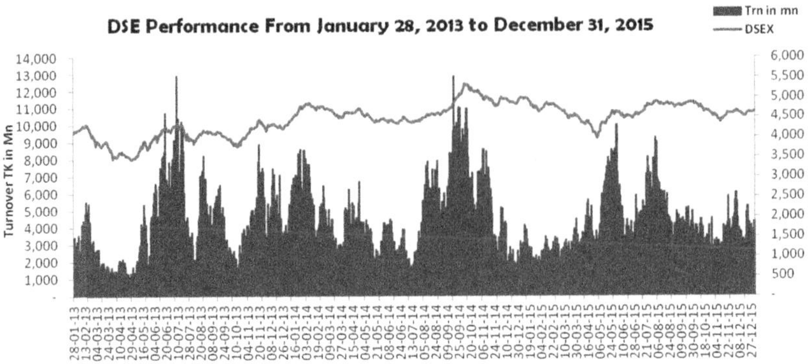

Fig. 17.3 Daily movement of price index and turnover at DSE. (Source: DSE monthly review and graphs—December 2015)

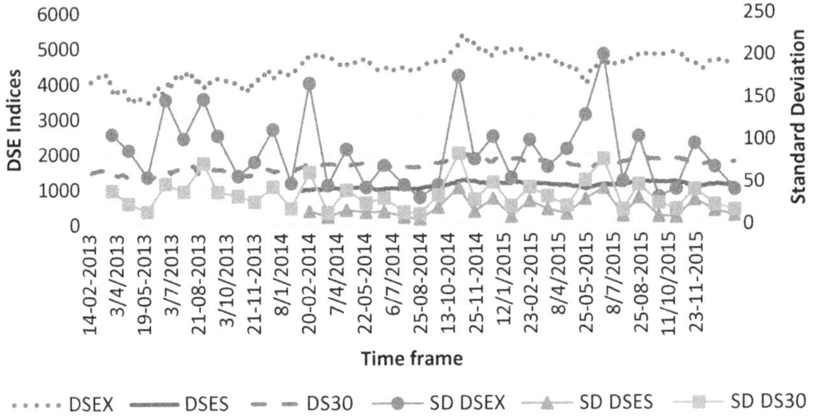

Fig. 17.4 Monthly standard deviation and daily price indexes. (Source: Data—DSE website)

Note that mutual fund performs a vital role in bringing transparency and stability in the market over the years. Total issued capital doubled in between 2010 and 2015, and compared to December 2003, it increased more than hundred folds by December 2015. In 2015, market capitalization stood at BDT 30,420 million, which was a nearly 50 times of what it was in 2003. Turnover fluctuated significantly because of the volatile nature of DSE. As evident in Table 17.5, P/E ratio of the mutual funds had been hovering around 8 before reaching its peak in 2010 at the advent of crisis. As in December 2010, the P/E ratio reached to double

Table 17.5 Key statistics of mutual funds

Time period	*No of mutual funds*	*Total issued capital (in million BDT)*	*Total market capitalization (in million BDT)*	*Turnover (in million BDT)*	*P/E ratio*
December 2003	11	395	664	27.86	8.48
December 2004	11	395	1046	55.98	8.27
December 2005	13	735	1521	61.48	6.55
December 2006	13	735	1537	378.24	6.13
December 2010	35	21,066	25,719	13588.72	17.53
December 2012	41	37,437	38,436	1845.48	12.42
December 2015	41	45,932	30,420	1074.55	7.16

Source: Monthly review, various issues, Dhaka Stock Exchange Ltd; CEIC data; BSEC annual report, various issues

digit figures by increasing nearly 200 percent from its December 2006 figure, mutual funds also showed some speculative characteristics.

17.3.3 *Regulatory Reforms and Frameworks*

In recent times, DSE has formulated certain rules and guidelines that ensure better functioning of the market. Some of the notable rules and guidelines are Membership Rules; Listing Rules; Corporate Governance Guidelines; Automated Trading Regulation, 1999; Settlement of Stock Exchange TR, 1999; Margin Rules, 1999; Member's Margin Regulation, 2000; and DSE (Board and Administration) Regulations, 2000 and 2013.

The SEC has made some progress in regulatory reform activities in a bid to develop and protect investors' interest by establishing transparency in the capital market though their effort still is not enough to strengthen the market.[1] A brief description of the major reforms undertaken in the capital market is briefly discussed below.

Establishment of Central Depository Systems (CDS) Up to December, 2017, a total of 2.72 million BO accounts were opened and 302 companies have been listed under CDS (DSE, monthly review). The introduction of CDS brought transparency in securities issuance and eased trading and settlement significantly. Moreover, it has reduced the settlement period of securities transactions substantially.

[1] The details of these rules and regulations are available in the website of DSE and can be reached through http://www.dsebd.org/

Imparting Training Programs The Commission, in association with the Dhaka and Chittagong Stock Exchanges, has so far arranged training for 173 authorized representatives of the members of DSE and 50 authorized representatives of the members of CSE. SEC also organizes the Investors' Education Program at its premise throughout the year for creating awareness among the investors of capital and securities markets. During July 2015–June 2016, a total of 720 investors participated in the program.

Enforcement Actions Enforceability of any rules and regulation is key to achieving higher success from those rules. The Commission claimed that they undertook 253 enforcement actions against the issuers and other market intermediaries during July 2015 to July 2016 against those who failed to comply with the securities-related rules.

Formation of FRC and BICM Government has formed an oversight body named "Financial Reporting Council (FRC)" under the "Financial Reporting Act (FRA), 2015" to ensure timely and quality financial disclosure statements. The Commission has established a training institute named "Bangladesh Institute of Capital Market (BICM)" in July 2008 in order to educate individual and institutional investors. However, the Institute lacks enough logistic and human resources to impart its intended duties. The capacity of the Institute needs to be enhanced to convert it into a center of excellence on capital market issues.

Establishment of Secondary Bond Market As already noted, still the capital market lacks a vibrant and active secondary bond market. Though some measures have been taken in regard to establishing secondary bond market by the Bangladesh Bank, it doesn't prove to be sufficient. The measures include the creation of a separate and exclusive platform for the PDs to enhance transaction of government bonds. However, despite guidelines regarding revaluation of treasury bills and bonds to encourage transaction of government securities, the situation has yet to improve. More efforts are needed to revamp secondary bond market in order to facilitate long-term infrastructure financing, which is critical for achieving higher economic growth.

17.3.4 Where Does Bangladesh Capital Market Stand: An International Comparison

Bangladesh's capital market is still small in size and relatively less liquid with compared to well-functioning international capital markets (Table 17.6,

Fig. 17.2). Comparing with capital markets of East Asian countries, Bangladesh's capital market is less liquid. However, it has a better place among the South Asian Association for Regional Cooperation (SAARC) countries (see also Table 17.10 in Appendix) (Table 17.7).

Table 17.6 Performance of the capital market in emerging and developed countries

Country	*Market capitalization as a percentage of GDP*	
	2006	*2015*
Philippines	56	81.57
Singapore	291	210.44
Malaysia	156	129.11
Thailand	68	86.89
Indonesia	38	41.04
Korea	94	89.04
China	34	74.00
Japan	108	111.38
The United Kingdom (UK)	160	107.5
Germany	57	50.83
The United States of America (USA)	146	138.34
Bangladesh	7.15	18.38

Source: McKinsey, International Monetary Fund (IMF), World Federation of Exchanges, World Bank

Table 17.7 International comparison of market liquidity

Country	*Market capitalization (USD billion)*		*Value of trade (USD billion)*		*Turnover velocity (percent)*	
	2006	*2015*	*2006*	*2015*	*2006*	*2015*
Philippines	68	239	11	38	16	16
Singapore	384	640	180	198	47	31
Malaysia	236	383	75	111	32	29
Thailand	140	349	101	271	72	78
Indonesia	139	353	49	75	35	21
Korea	834	1231	1342	1844	161	150
China	918	8188	736	39,326	80	480
Japan	4614	4895	5823	5572	126	114
Germany	1638	1716	2737	1445	167	84
USA	19,286	25,068	33,598	41,399	174	165
Bangladesh	30	40.08	7	1.16	23.3	3.5

Source: McKinsey, IMF, World Federation of Exchanges, Bangladesh Bank, World Bank

17.4 Stock Market Crash in 2010 and the Role of Central Bank: A Case Study

The way the stock market crash had happened in 2010 and the subsequent policy response showed by the regulators and Bangladesh Bank generated a widespread criticism. The instability in the stock market was observed from 2009, which continued till 2011. The market was bullish during 2009 and 2010 with 62 percent and 83 percent gain, respectively. At the advent of crisis, the market went down to 10 percent level in January and further 30 percent in February 2011. High stock market exposure of commercial banks in the stock market and subsequent efforts to reduce such exposure in association with monetary policy response contributed stock market crash in 2010 (Hossain 2011). Banks' exposure in the stock market at that time exceeded 20 percent or more.

A few issues warrant further analysis behind stock market crash. First, commercial banks' exposure to stock market exceeded at a level that was not expected. To dampen such exposure, Bangladesh Bank went for a limited time bound policy to restrain banks. Therefore, a sudden withdrawal (not in phases) created a panic in the market and ultimately created a shock in the market. Second, at the same time, a tightening of monetary policy was adopted, which had been a double debacle to the situation. Therefore, dynamic inconsistencies in policies arose that contributed to the crash.

To elaborate, Bangladesh Bank made it mandatory for all banks to maintain their investment in the stock market equivalent to 10 percent of their total deposit and to comply by December 2010, when in reality, the ratio was much higher than this level. Though the policy was announced in June/July, they were not asked to reduce it in phases. Bangladesh Bank also increased cash reserve ratio (CRR) in December 2010, which was a double debacle for the banks. Therefore, withdrawal of banks' large investments from the stock market appears to be the main reason for the 2010 crash in the capital market in Bangladesh.

Apart from inconsistencies in Bangladesh Bank's policies, weaknesses in regulatory framework and inadequacy of good investments played a key role in the crash. To reduce banks' exposure in the capital market, a soft landing (measures) approach was expected. The case of Japan in the early 1990s provides a lesson that the role of monetary policy in bursting stock market bubble is crucial (Hossain 2005). The actions of the Bank of Japan (BoJ) in bursting the bubble in the early 1990s caused a prolonged economic recession and led to the biggest banking crises in Japan. Though the action of the BoJ was intended to burst the real-estate asset price bubble, it had caused a crash in the Japanese stock and money markets too. The main efforts to stop the bubble in Japan included monetary tightening, new regulation on administering real asset prices and adoption of the Basel Accord of capital adequacy requirements. The Japanese crisis provide a lesson that any efforts of central bank to burst bubbles must depend on two aspects: (i) the degree of efficiency of the financial sector and (ii) the speed to burst the bubble must be aligned with the overall economic situation.

It is, therefore, important for Bangladesh Bank to formulate a long-term policy framework for the involvement of banks in the capital market by taking lessons from other similar cases.

17.5 Capital Market for Long-Term Financing

In the backdrop of the graduation from the LDC status, which is likely in 2024, Bangladesh is in pressure to look for alternative financing modes to finance its future development projects. Graduation from LDC will shrink Bangladesh's opportunity to avail lost-cost funding from multilateral donors, and in that context capital market could be an avenue for mobilizing financial resources for government's infrastructure projects. Capital market can be used to payback existing foreign debt by issuing bonds, finance green energy projects by issuing green bonds, and so on. However, only the government securities are sold over the counters in the secondary bond market in Bangladesh (Mujeri and Rahman 2009).

The size of the bond market is tiny in Bangladesh. Only 17 debentures were issued since 1987 through public offering, and no new debenture was issued after 1999. Among them eight are outstanding at present. However, due to inferior quality, trading of these debentures is negligible in the stock exchanges. Since December 2005, the trading of government treasury bonds has been started at DSE. As of January 2018, 8 debentures, 221 treasury bonds with different maturities and 1 corporate bond (floated in 2007 by the Islami Bank Bangladesh Limited, named IBBL Mudaraba Perpetual Bond) were being traded in the market.

To enhance the efficiency of the bond market, a few institutional measures are needed to be undertaken (Mujeri and Hossain 2011). It is important to develop a well-equipped *Primary Dealer System* to facilitate securities trading. Derivative markets are absent and therefore are needed to develop to hedge against exchange rate, interest and credit risks and promote institutional investors, such as pension and insurance funds, to increase demand for fixed income securities.

17.6 Some Recommended Policy Reforms

To improve the performances of the capital market, some structural measures are needed to be undertaken. The measures should include (i) increasing the number of merchant banks, (ii) establishing a commodity exchange, (iii) appointing efficient portfolio managers, (iv) improving internet/online trading facilities and (vi) providing access to high quality and credible corporate information. On top of this, a vibrant and strong regulator needs to be in place.

The capital market of Bangladesh suffers from inadequate number of professional portfolio managers. Increasing the number of merchant banks can meet the gap of specialized portfolio managers. Since NBFIs have the experiences of handling portfolio aspects, more NBFIs may be awarded merchant banking license to work as specialized portfolio managers in the capital market. These types of actions will increase institutional investments in the capital market which is necessary for reducing price volatility in the market. On the other hand, the capital market may opt to establish a commodity exchange that will help ensure the stability of prices of essential commodities and reduce retail market price volatility.

Both the stock exchanges adopted internet trading to facilitate market trading and reduce transaction costs of the investors. However, online trading has both merits and demerits. It is important to secure trading information that are done online. Cyber security measures need to be strengthened to uphold investors' confidence on online trading.

An efficient and vibrant regulator is needed to ensure efficiency in the capital market as well as to ensure discipline in the market. A strong regulator can also ensure corporate governance in industries, which is necessary to establish an efficient and investor-friendly capital market. Therefore, capacity building of SEC could be an important policy agenda.

17.7 Conclusions and Policy Recommendations

This chapter analyzes the current state of Bangladesh's capital market highlighting the challenges and opportunities of the market. The analysis suggests that the capital market in Bangladesh faces three main impediments: underdeveloped secondary bond market, lack of portfolio managers and research, and a lack of vibrant regulator. Though the current state of the capital market in Bangladesh generated a considerable market capitalization, the market still needs to be widened and diversified. A well-functioning capital market is essential for fulfilling the long-term financing needs of both public and private sectors. A better capital market is also essential for the financial system for generating capital. To this end, the market needs to be developed further with a secondary bond market, particularly a robust market of fixed income securities for meeting up long-term financing needs of the investors.

As the capital market in Bangladesh has been suffering from a dearth of quality institutional investors, professional portfolio managers, quality research and information, appropriate measures are expected to address these problems. The growth of BO accounts and omnibus accounts over the years indicates the entry of a huge number of individual investors, most of whom have a lack of adequate knowledge about the market. Most of these investors go for investments in highly volatile stocks with an aim to generate quick money. Therefore, speculators take advantage of the herd behavior of these small investors, which often creates tension in the capital market. Though SEC establishes an institute to offer various training and awareness-building programs for the investors, the situation has not changed much yet.

A vibrant and strong regulator is needed to run the capital market more efficiently. The role of the government is important here to give a signal to operate the market in an efficient manner. Proper rules and regulations need to be developed, and existing rules and guidelines are needed to be updated on a regular basis to bring dynamism in the market. The government and regulator need to work closely to increase confidence of the individual investors. Apart from these, the structural weaknesses of the capital market need to be addressed in an efficient manner in order to have a strong capital market in Bangladesh. The role of monetary policy has been discussed in this chapter in the context of 2010 stock crash. A prudent macroeconomic policy, in particular monetary policy has, thus, a crucial role in the growth and development of the capital market. It is also identified that there is a dearth of good researches on various aspects of the capital market in Bangladesh, which deters informed policy making to some extent.

Appendix

Table 17.8 An overview of the capital market of Bangladesh

Time frame	*September 2009*	*January 2017*
	No. in million	*No. in million*
Total number of listed securities	446	560
Total number of companies	284	294
Total number of mutual funds	18	35
Total number of debentures	8	8
Total number of treasury bonds	135	221
Total number of corporate bonds	1	2
	BDT in million	**BDT in million**
Total number of shares, mutual fund certificates and debentures of all listed securities[a]	3323	59,103
Total number of shares of all listed companies	2871	54,144
Total number of certificates of all listed mutual funds	445	4946.79
Total number of debentures of all listed debentures	409	0.49
Total number of all listed gov. T-bonds	3098	5.49
Total number of all listed corporate bonds	3000	5.850148
Total issued capital of all listed securities	463,334	1,146,930
Total issued capital of all companies' shares	145,115	542,666
Total issued capital of all mutual funds	4316	49,468
Total issued debentures	140	354
Total issued govt. T-bonds	310,763	548,592
Total issued capital of corporate bonds	3000	5850
Total market capitalization of all listed securities	1,382,991	3,667,508
Total market capitalization of all companies' shares	1,045,222	3,072,160
Total market capitalization of all mutual funds	23,711	40,161
Total market capitalization of all debentures	576	576
Total market capitalization of all govt. T-bonds	310,763	548,592
Total market capitalization of all corporate bonds	2720	6019
Exchange rate	Tk. 69.06/USD	Tk. 78.87/USD

Source: DSE monthly review

[a]Total no. of shares/share capital/market capital include bonus/right of shares

Table 17.9 Trading operations of DSE and CSE

Panel A: Trading operations of DSE

End of period	*No. of listed securities (including mutual funds and debentures)*	*No. of IPOs*	*Issued capital (BDT in million)*	*Market capitalization (BDT in million)*	*Total turnover (BDT in million)*	*DSE general index*[a]	*DSE broad index (DSEX)*[b]
2003–04	267	14	46055.00	97587.00	19152.10	967.88	–
2004–05	256	2	49532.00	224923.00	53181.10	1971.31	–
2005–06	303	18	85722.60	215421.90	46008.20	1339.53	–
2006–07	325	10	164279.30	475855.40	164671.60	2149.32	–
2007–08	378	13	284379.70	931025.20	543286.00	3000.50	–
2008–09	443	17	457944.00	1241339.00	893789.20	3010.26	–
2009–10	450	23	607262.90	2700744.60	2563498.60	6153.68	–
2010–11	490	19	806839.10	2853892.20	3259152.60	6117.23	–
2011–12	511	15	933629.60	2491612.90	1171451.40	4572.88	–
2012–13	525	15	983589.70	2530246.00	857089.70	–	4104.65
2013–14	536	13	1032076.40	2943202.30	1125398.40	–	4480.52
2014–15	555	16	1091953.50	3247306.30	1123519.50	–	4583.11
2015–16	559	11	1127410.00	3185749.00	1072461.00		4507.58

Notes:

[a]Stopped displaying DSE general index (DGEN) in DSE website from August 01, 2013; The data displayed in this table differs slightly with the one provided by Bangladesh Bank, mainly due to difference in reporting time

[b]DSE introduced new index benchmark DSE broad index (DSEX) on January 28, 2013, as per "DSE Bangladesh Index Methodology", designed and developed by S&P Dow Jones Indices

IPO=Initial Public Offering

Panel B: Trading operation of CSE

End of period	*No. of listed securities (including mutual funds and debentures)*	*No. of IPOs*	*Issued capital (BDT in million)*	*Market capitalization (BDT in million)*	*Total turnover (BDT in million)*	*CSE all shares price index*
2003–04	195	10	41967.60	85312.30	6688.60	1642.78
2004–05	199	3	46978.70	215010.80	17551.30	3597.70
2005–06	213	19	63750.20	195551.70	11439.10	2879.19
2006–07	219	10	82251.70	399268.20	34377.40	5194.76
2007–08	231	14	103140.80	777742.80	80162.10	9050.56
2008–09	246	18	142465.50	974948.20	125182.50	10477.67
2009–10	232	23	206773.90	2241767.80	217112.30	18,116.05
2010–11	220	19	301553.30	2259777.80	321682.30	17,059.53
2011–12	251	15	375274.90	1878171.40	134854.90	13,736.42
2012–13	266	15	423380.90	1919070.30	101985.20	12,738.23
2013–14	276	13	470839.70	2286678.70	102182.70	13,766.23
2014–15	292	20	501306.30	2370421.30	96480.00	14,097.17
2015–16	298	14	566076.00	2496849.00	77471.60	13,623.07

Source: Bangladesh Securities and Exchange Commission (BSEC), Annual Report (various issues)

Table 17.10 Capital market indicators of selected SAARC countries

Name of the capital markets	*Indices name*	*Year*	*Indices*	*Listed companies*	*Market cap in US$ Bn*	*Turnover in US$ Bn*	*PE ratio*	*Dividend yield percent*	*Percent of GDP*
Colombo Stock	CSE Milanka	2008	1631.34	235	4.29	1.02	5.32	4.72	13.25
Exchange		2015	3625.69	294	20.80	1.79	17.90	2.18	25.81
Dhaka Stock	DSE GEN	2008	2795.34	276	15.14	9.68	18.42	2.48	17.00
Exchange		2015	4583.11	326	40.08	1.16	15.23	3.67	18.38
Karachi	KSE 100	2008	5865.01	652	23.50	0.35	–	–	16.45
		2015	31,709	554	66.07	27.11	–	–	24.42
Bombay Stock	SENSEX	2008	9647.31	4921	647.20	309.18	13.77	1.78	54.99
Exchange		2015	26117.54	7357	1516.22	772.00	18.73	1.29	72.12

Source: DSE website, World Bank, CEIC data, DSE monthly review—December 2015

Note: SENSEX=Stock Exchange Sensitive Index

References

Bangladesh Economic Review. (various issues). Finance Division, Ministry of Finance, Dhaka, Government of the People's Republic of Bangladesh.

Bank, B. *Economic trends (various issues)*. Dhaka: Statistics Department, BB.

BSEC (various issues). *Annual Report*. Bangladesh Securities and Exchange Commission.

Dhaka Stock Exchange Ltd. *Monthly review (various issues)*.

Garretsen, H., Lensink, R., & Sterken, E. (2004). Growth, financial development, societal norms and legal institutions. *Journal of International Financial Markets Institutions and Money, 14*(2), 165–183.

Hossain, M. (2005). Can Japan avert any future banking crisis? *Applied Economics Letters, 12*(7), 425–429 (Taylor & Francis, UK).

Hossain, M. (2011). Market crash and the role of Bangladesh Bank. *The Daily Star, Dhaka*.

Hossain, M., & Rafiq, F. (2012). Global commodity price volatility and domestic inflation: Impact on the performance of the financial sector in Bangladesh. In Mujeri & Mahmud (Eds.), *Adjusting to global economic volatility: The case of south Asia (Chapter 6) 2014*. New Delhi: Academic Foundation.

Masuduzzaman, M., Rahman, M. H., & Ahammed, S. (2013). *Integration of financial market and its implication of stock market development in Bangladesh: An evaluation*. Working paper series: WP 1304. Retrieved from https://www.bb.org.bd/pub/research/workingpaper/wp1304.pdf

Mia, A. H., Qamruzzaman, M., & Ara, L. A. (2014). Stock market development and economic growth of Bangladesh-A causal analysis. *Bangladesh Journal of MIS, 6*(2), 62–74.

Mohtadi, H., & Agarwal, S. (2001). *Stock market development and economic growth: Evidence from developing countries*. Online Available at: http://www.uwm.edu/mohadi/PA-4-01.pdf

Mujeri, M. K., & Hossain, M. (2011). Macroeconomic framework and financial sector development. In M. K. Mujeri & S. Islam (Eds.), *Macroeconomic issues: Background papers for the sixth five year plan* (Vol. 1). Bangladesh Institute of Development Studies and the General Economics Division, Ministry of Planning, the Government of Bangladesh.

Mujeri, M. K., & Rahman, M. H. (2009). *Financing long term investments in Bangladesh: Capital market development issues* (No. id: 2060). eSocialsciences.

Rahman, H., Islam, E., Hossain, S., & Naser, M. S. (2016). *Is the capital market of Bangladesh efficient?* Working paper series: WP 1614. Retrieved from https://www.bb.org.bd/pub/research/workingpaper/wp1614.pdf

Sarbabidya, S., & Saha, T. (2018). Factors affecting investment decisions: A study on Bangladesh stock market. *Journal of Accounting, 8*(2), 1–19.

Shah, S. A. M. (2016). *Capital market development in Bangladesh: A sector reform perspective*. ADB South Asia Working Paper Series.

Index[1]

[1] Note: Page numbers followed by 'n' refer to notes.

M. Hossain (ed.), *Bangladesh's Macroeconomic Policy*,
https://doi.org/10.1007/978-981-15-1244-5

M

The manufacturer's authorised representative in the EU is Springer Nature Customer Service Centre GmbH, Europaplatz 3, 69115 Heidelberg, Germany. If you have any concerns regarding our products, please contact ProductSafety@springernature.com

Printed and bound by CPI Group (UK) Ltd, Croydon, CR0 4YY
30/09/2026
02225442-0018